DEMOCRACY, DEVELOPMENT AND TRIBES IN INDIA

DEMOCRACY, DEVELOPMENT AND TRIBES IN INDIA

(In Two Volumes)
Volume-I

Ramdas Rupavath

GYAN

ISBN : 978-81-212-1248-9 (Set)

ISBN : 978-81-212-1298-4 (Vol. I)

Price : Set (₹ 2000) Price : Volume I (₹ 1000)

First Published, 2015

Published by

Gyan Publishing House
23, Main Ansari Road, Darya Ganj
New Delhi-110002
Ph. : 23242060, 23261060
Fax : 011-23285914
E-mail: books@gyanbooks.com
Website : www.gyanbooks.com

Laser Typesetting : Abhishek Mandal, Delhi
Printed at : G. Print Process, Delhi

Cataloging in Publication Data—DK
Courtesy: D.K. Agencies (P) Ltd. <docinfo@dkagencies.com>

Democracy, development and tribes in India / Ramdas Rupavath.
pages cm
Includes bibliographical references and index.
ISBN 9788121212489

1. India—Scheduled tribes—Economic conditions—Congresses. 2. India—Scheduled tribes—Social conditions—Congresses. 3. India—Scheduled tribes—Education—Congresses. 4. India—Scheduled tribes—Government policy—India—Congresses. 5. Rural development— India—Congresses. I. Rupavath, Ramdas, editor. II. University of Hyderabad. Department of Political Science.organizer.

DDC 305.800954 23

Dedicated to

Christoph

Von Furer – Haimendorf

Contents

Acknowledgements

I would express my gratitude to ICSSR, New Delhi and University of Hyderabad for their co-operation in particular for their wholehearted and continued support to endeavour. I would thank the Dean, and Faculty of School of Social Sciences. I want to offer special thanks to the Faculty and Head, Department of Political Science and non-teaching staff of the Departments for co-operation during the seminar. This volume is a product of a two-day national seminar. This was organised by the Department of Political Science, University of Hyderabad.

I would express my gratitude to the participants of the seminar for their co-operation and submission of the full paper within the stipulated time without which this book should not have taken a shape. The presence of key participants like Prof. Ramakrishana Ramaswamy, Vice-Chancellor, University of Hyderabad, Prof. G. Hargopal, Shri Gaddar (Prajayuddanouka), Prof. Kunhaman, Prof. E. Haribabu and Prof. Sudhir Jacob George, Prof. Shantha Sinha, Prof. Virginius Xaxa, Prof. Prithviram Mudiam, Prof. Manjari Katju, Prof. Sudhakar Rao, Dr. Nchginpao Kipgen, Dr George Tharakan, Prof Sudhakar Reddy, Dr B. Nagarjuna and their academic deliberations has provoked a new academic thrust in the area of Tribal Development in the globalised world.

I want to give special thank to my wife Miss R. Jayasri and daughters Sai Srinidhi and Gayathree Ram, brothers and sisters for their moral encouragement for the publication of this book.

I would like to thank to the research scholars of the Department of Political Science namely, Tapan Kumar Bihari, M. Ramulu and K. John Bosco Sote for their managerial skill in organising this seminar. With this also, I express my sincere thanks to the students and research scholars, school of social sciences for their co-operation during the seminar.

Finally, I put my gratitude to the team at Gyan Publishing House, New Delhi for the valuable suggestions on the structure of the book and help in its production.

I hope this book would be a substantial contribution to Tribal studies in India, even more, help chart a more meaningful developmental path for Tribals in India.

Ramdas Rupavath

Foreword

The book on 'Democracy, Development and Resistance' is a collection of papers presented at national seminar. The thematic issues dealt with in the book are both of theoretical and policy relevance especially in a country like India because of its rootedness in the structure of diversity. No wonder, the issue of democracy has been subject of serious deliberation and discussion both at academic and non-academic forum and at regular intervals. However, more often than not they are deliberated at the macro level, that is, national and state context and that too without any reference to diversity that marks India. Even when it is done it is limited to electoral behaviour and politics.

India is marked by enormous diversity. However, this diversity is primarily couched in respect of five major categories. These are language, religion, caste, tribe, rural-urban. Needless to say, each category is enormously diverse and the diversity within each needs to be confronted in engagement with issue such as democracy. The book examines aspects of working of democracy in respect of tribes in India.

Tribes constitute over eight per cent of the total population of the country. Though numerically small, they are enormously diverse and scattered over the length and breadth of the country. Even within a given geographical territory, they are marked by much diversity. Hence, attempt to situate tribal communities in relation to democracy is interesting and fascinating, more so, since they are in every state except a few in North-east India located in a structure of political, economic, Social and cultural domination by the larger non-tribal community. One of the most critical features of democracy is to challenge the dimension of domination at work.

Tribes have been challenging the subjugation in which they have come to be placed since the colonial rule. The fruits of democracy have escaped the tribal communities in post-colonial India too. This is most evident in economic, social and cultural sphere. Hence, there is increasing assertion and articulation among them in different forms. Those assertions and articulation are integral part of democratic participation since these are modes of expression in which tribes like to determine their own lives. The book attempts to capture those different forms in varying contexts. The issue of government projects and displacement, the question of land alienation from tribes to non-tribes, the aspects of livelihood, education, socio-cultural life, ecology and environment, women and children provide those critical settings. Those interested in understanding tribal issues at grassroots levels will find the book handy and useful.

Prof. Virginius Xaxa
Deputy Director
Tata Institute of Social Sciences,
Guwahati Campus

Introduction and Overview

Indian democracy has been intensively analysed, debated and criticised for a long time. However, democracy is not only just elections and government formation; it is more about values, habits of thoughts and practices. Democracy need not only be election, but also can be replaced with social justice. Through democratic methods, existing unequal social, economic and political injustice can be removed. The tribals are the most affected people in such democratic set up with developmental approach. The new tribal politics will be based on two things: the resource politics of the Adivasis and the survival politics of the informal sector.

Though the Indian constitution takes an unambiguous position against adivasi resources, it continues in different forms. Over the years, the centre of gravity of the Indian polity and economy has shifted to the intermediate class groups that has been widely recognised. Within the class hierarchy, the economic high point is the polarisation between the rich non-tribals and the tribals who are largely landalienated and displaced. Political parties at the centre and the state drastically changed the emergence of powerful non-tribal leaders that have drastically changed the very mosaic of Indian federal polity. It is in this process that we have strong states and a weak centre today. Thus, regional parties are playing an important role in the Indian political process.

The state has shifted its orientation from welfare state to market oriented state due to liberalisation. However, the process of liberalisation has created inequality in the society with the concentration of fruits of growth in few rich classes. The opportunity is becoming unequal. While poverty seldom poses a threat to the system, inequality in a milieu of rising democratic and human rights consciousness can potentially become a grave danger.

After India became independent, our political leaders recognised the importance of the participation of the masses. Earlier, leaders of the Indian state were drawn or belonged to the rich-western educated feudal backgrounds. This did not herald a true democratic state. The scenario began to change only with the political mobilisation of the Dalits, within the parliamentary framework. Democracy means rule by the people, rather than the rule of only the rich and powerful; postulating equality in economic, social and political spheres. In other words, only an egalitarian society can be truly democratic. For that, the precondition is to have equal access to the means of production, not only for expansion of the productive forces but also for enabling and ensuring the fruit on the creative potential of every individual. The growth brought about by a few dynamic and enterprising individuals must be expanded into one brought about by all persons in society. If high growth is the creation of a few, growth will be higher if all realise their creative potential. This calls for a new vision as well as a new strategy of development which can herald democracy from below, organically evolving as a natural and spontaneous process. Political inclusion and economic exclusion are the order of the day. The Panchyati Raj, PESA Act or the Forest Rights Act is not reassuring in this regard. The resources viz land, water, forest, cattle, credit and market are controlled by the few rich non-tribal families creating a new kind of development. According to Foucault, disbursed poor is difficult to tackle. Dr. B. R. Ambedkar remarked that without economic democracy, social and political democracy cannot be realised. He also warned that unless the latter two democracies are brought about soon, the victims of the system would ignore the constitution which the Constituent Assembly had laboriously built. Of course, the system permits individual inclusion even as its functioning is resulting in group exclusion, a phenomenon conspicuously happening, particularly in the case of a social constituency where a person represents. Parliamentary democracy is falling apart at the seams. Competitive politics uneasily coexist with a competitive economy predicated on an unbroken scaffolding of a caste based, hierarchical social and economic order. The transition from state capitalism of the planning era to the market capitalisation of the liberalisation era has only rendered the matrix of opportunities skewed and reinforced the old prejudices.

The knowledge production (media) are controlled by the non-tribal rich upper class elites who sit in judgment about the quality and efficiency of the adivasis and other subalterns. The nominal presence of few persons belonging to these social groups in the academics, too, lacks the power to influence policy and the structure of knowledge. They remain silent till they are safe and so long as they are safe, they do not raise and debate social issues and corruption which is part of our structure. The tribal society and sub-plan budgets are taken away by the non –tribal bureaucrats. Without tackling inequality, corruption continues to thrive in an unequal system. Though the question of equality accepted at the launch of planning commission, declaring the attainment of growth with social justice and egalitarian society, the present scenario is characterised by the verbal fetishism created through the globalised use of words such as tribal empowerment, sustainable development etc. However, words like equality, liberty, and justice find a meager place in the academics and media discourses. Behind these verbal usages, very harmful policies and programmes are introduced and any resistance against these policies, the state uses its forces to suppress the movements. The NGOs and Acts primarily playing the role of depoliticising the tribes, are abetting the policy makers. What is beneficial to a few is presented as beneficial to all. The poor tribes, ignorant and illiterate, whose immediate concern is the next meal, are seldom concerned about policies and programmes which are in reality have no way concern for them. Rather than compete, more profit and capital accumulation, state supports primitive accumulation and private appropriation of public resources happens at large. In Andhra Pradesh or Telengana state, the land alienated tribals agitating for *Jungle* (Forest), *Jamin* (land), *Jaal* (Water) are put in jail. The land alienated tribes are the traditional indigenous people who are denied land rights and displaced and still do not have even the right to agitate. The land struggle in frontier agency and nonfrontier agency results in hostility over the displacement issue and the state force resorts to beating and killing of woman and children. The state has inhuman attitudes towards tribals in India, which violates the very human rights of the tribes in this extant bourgeois democratic milieu. Thus, it becomes deficient in envisioning the upper caste and its top leadership structure in the understanding of the socio-economic reality of India.

The most paradoxical thing is that everybody talk about equality, liberty and fraternity, but in practice most are afraid of democracy. What is available to people is the freedom to agree, not to disagree. These inhuman conditions are the decisions taken by few who are rich and powerful in controlling the disadvantaged people. In fact the legislators are elected by the people funded by the rich, hence, corruption becomes the basic bane to inequality posing a grave threat to tribal sustainability and security. Safe and secure orders are needed to put in place so that the rights of the tribal people are safeguarded to the fullest.

This book aims to place India's democracy, development in the tribal context. This volume is basically focused in the understanding of contemporary tribal societies which require basic appreciation of the historical processes that have been determining the course of successive changes in economic, socio-cultural, ideological and political life of the tribals. Indian states and governments are talking about models of federalism in a large and multinational society, ensuring the rights of ethnic and religious groups in a true pluralistic society, and striving for social justice in a society marked by social hierarchies for a long time. However, the democratic experiment has not been without significant challenges, namely that of ensuring inclusive development. Economic equality, social justice, cultural pluralism, human rights, dignity and security are all important aspects of development which have been consolidated and expanded through the existing structure of participatory democracy. But this has not always been an easy task.

During the last couple of decades, Indian tribes have also witnessed transformation in their culture, with the proliferation of special plan and policies for the welfare of the tribal people. Despite the development, crisis in governance, migration, displacement, and exploitation are rampant. The impact of globalisation on Indian economy is percolating down and their effects are being felt by the tribal people who are displaced from their habitation, ultimately resulting to resistance and ethnic conflict. Introduction of tribal communities to development through state policies needs to be considered from different angles. It is in this context that a state policy is required to be inclusive and comprehensive enough to safeguard tribal interests. To address the issue of situating tribal communities to developmental perspective in a democratic atmosphere provides both opportunities and challenges.

The majority of the articles are mainly empirical essays which seek to answer this linked question at ground level. The majority process of development in the tribal context with democratic process has been highlighted. Some theoretical works like threat to secularism, politics of development, voice of tribals in contemporary democracy are also discussed.

The first aspect which is most sensitive and thought provoking is: **Democracy, Development and Resistance.** On this aspect, it tries to highlight the concerns, concepts and issues related to democracy, development and resistance in regard to the tribals and with relevant case studies. The section talks about how development has come to be a bad omen for the displaced tribals. With displacement, several tribes were uprooted with the onslaught of development. We talk about the case study of Indira Sagar Project in Andhra Pradesh with special emphasis on development projects, displacement and tribal livelihood issues. The livelihoods of the tribals were severely affected as argued by developmental projects and the resultant displacement overdrive. It gives a valuable insight into the risks, rights, alternatives, policy and practices followed by Development-Induced Displacement and Rehabilitation and Resettlement of Indigenous Communities in India. One paper draws perspective from census survey in studying mining and displacement in South Odisha. This section touches various tribal states of India and focuses on how in the name of development, tribal land alienation has been done and who are getting benefits out of this.

The second aspect is **Issues of Governance**. This section talks about issues, concerns and themes related to governance. PESA, tribal development and idea of the commons and related issues are discussed. The struggles and politics of the exclusion in understanding de-notified tribes in India are examined. Democracy and development as in Fifth Scheduled areas are debated.

The issues of **Tribal Voice in Contemporary Democracy** have been highlighted in the 3rd aspect. In the era of globalisation, seldom the voice of the tribals is suppressed and marginalised. So in this regard, we start by looking at the case of Scheduled tribes in North Coastal Andhra Pradesh, whose voices and struggles have been excluded and marginalised. The paper contests the inclusive development. Next paper attempts to question where democracy in India lies and looks at its withering away and its effects on tribal resistance.

The theme, **Livelihood Issues and Concerns,** contains many primary work and highlights various lacunas in the institutions, policies etc. An empirical study on Chenchus of Andhra Pradesh was looking to draw our attention to their livelihood security through land distribution. Next paper talks about migration from village to city in Bangalore and how it affects livelihood, creates displacement and calls for rehabilitation. Another paper deals incisively with the trends in cropping pattern and its impact on the tribal households in the scheduled areas taking the case study of three scheduled area villages in the West Godavari district of Andhra Pradesh.

The next theme of the volume is **Socio-cultural Issues of Tribals**. The first paper looks at the struggles of adivasi towards habitation and how it has been affected by the forces of globalisation and accumulation. Another paper examines the storage practices of tribal community of Warangal district of Andhra Pradesh. There is also a paper that draws a critique on Yerukula reformation in Andhra Pradesh.

In **Public Policy and Tribal Development** theme, it discusses on the arena of tribal development and public policy interventions. The first paper talks in general sense the adivasis from the public policy perspective in India. The next paper evaluates the implementation of MGNREGA and its effects on tribals taking the case study of Nupada district in Odisha. There is a presentation on the embedded identity and politics that is played out in ST reservation in Assam. In the last paper of this svolume, ST as the beneficiary of BPL in Mayurbhanj District, Odisha is examined.

The section of **Social Movement, Ethnic Issues and Conflict** discusses the role of social movements, ethnic issues and conflicts There is a deep seated conflict between tribals and the forest department in scheduled areas. This is brought out by a case study of recently declared Kawal Tiger Reserve in Adilalabad district, Andhra Pradesh. Similarly, tribal-caste conflict is brought out in another paper taking the case study of Kandhamal district, Odisha. Another vital paper is the analysis of the Gujjar agitation of tribal status in Rajasthan that examines contentions, agitations, resistance and state interventions therewith. There is another case study on Niyamgiri Movement in Odisha that examines tribal development and resistance that followed. Another paper takes the case study of Manipur that discusses Meitiei's resistance and the response of the State. The failure of Indian secularism is brought out through the politics of SC and ST conflict in Kandhamal. The Contemporary issues of democracy, development and tribal resistance are widely discussed in another paper. The role of tribal women in MGNREGA is also discussed in the study of Barwani Block of Madhya Pradesh. The policies and challenges of scheduled tribes in Jammu and Kashmir in literacy and educational level are also presented. Then, the tribal education policy of Karnataka is up for review by looking at its attainment and challenges ahead.

In this section, **Tribal Ecology and Environmental Issues**, a paper is presented on environmental approaches to tribal development. The environmental aspect is significant, given the harmony that exists between tribal and nature.

In the section, **Issues of the Tribal Women and Children,** various issues like gender inequalities and development issues are examined in the study of the Toda and Niligiri Hills from an anthropological perspective. The Lamabada community is the next case study that examines the status of girl child in the South Telengana region in Andhra Pradesh.

The section, **Politics of Development,** discusses the concept of development and its effect on tribals in AP is examined and discussed. The role of NYKS on tribal youth development is discussed through the case study of Koraput district, Odisha. Approaches to development are examined and the role of civil society organisation in tribal development is discussed. The myth of development and tribals in Odisha is examined in a macro view.

In **Development, Displacement and Resistance** section, the question of human rights is raised through the study of Posco project in Odisha in the context of development and displacement. The land alienation of tribals in Andhra Pradesh and tribal land alienation in general sense is examined and debated. The case study of Gadchiroliapotential zone of development induced displacement is looked into.

The last section on **Education Status of Scheduled Tribes** talks about the need for empowerment of tribals. The paper on the impact of multilingual education in the education of tribal children stresses the nature of multilingual character and its usage for tribals. A case study of Lanbadi tribe in AP is examined to understand the educational status of scheduled tribes. Another paper talks about the need to bring about awareness of human rights among tribals and non tribals secondary students. This comparative study calls for empowering and enhancing the rights of tribals. Lastly, the achievement and challenges of secondary education of scheduled tribes in Manipur is discussed.

All the articles present an overview of a range of real problem that not only touch the lives of Indian people but also raises significant issues for thinking about democracy and development in the tribal context in India. The world has changed a great deal since 1950, so as India. The country is now carving out a niche in global marketplace thus far dominated by developing countries. Major question, however, remains regarding the accommodation of tribals in democratic system and distributing the share of growth among them. Thus, the basic objective of the book is to contribute in some small way to these continuing debates.

List of Contributors

Sajal Nag is Professor, Dept of History, Assam University, Silchar.

Kandipalli Ramakrishnarao is Lecturer; Govt. D.I.E.T, Bheemunipatnam, Visakhapatnam (Dist), A.P.

M. Ramulu is research scholar, Department of Political Science, School of Social Sciences, University of Hyderabad.

M. Gopinath Reddy is Professor, Centre for Economic and Social Studies, (CESS), Begumpet, Hyderabad–16.

Prajna Paramita Mishra is Assistant Professor, School of Economics, University of Hyderabad.

Salu D' Souza, Senior Research Fellow, Centre for Study of Diaspora, Central University of Gujarat, Gujarat.

Neelmani Jaysawal is Asst. Professor, Department of Social Work, Visva-Bharati, Shantiniketan, West Bengal.

P. Shailaja, Research Scholar, Department of Public Administration, OU, Nizamabad, A.P.

Pranay Kumar Parida is Asst. Professor, GADVASU, Ludhiana.

Ms Smita Raut is Research Fellow, MS Swaminathan Foundation, Koraput, Odisha.

Nupur Tiwari is Assistant Professor, Indian Institute of Public Administration, IIPA, New Delhi.

Prachi Madhumita Mohanty is Research Scholar, P.G. Dept. of Social Science, Fakir Mohan University, Balasore, Odisha.

Prof. Shyam Sundar Acharya is Professor, P.G. Dept. of Social Science, Fakir Mohan University, Balasore, Odisha.

R. Arunjyothi is Krishi Vigyan Kendra, Mamnoor, Warangal, A.P.

Ch. Sowmya is Krishi Vigyan Kendra, Mamnoor, Warangal, A.P.

D. Sreenivas is Krishi Vigyan Kendra, Mamnoor, Warangal, A.P.

Ram Babu Mallavarpu, UGC Post Doctoral Fellow, Centre for Regional Studies, School of Social Sciences, University of Hyderabad.

Ramchandra Jena is Lecturer in Political Science, Gopalpur College, (Berhampur University), Ganjam, Odisha.

Ramesh Kumar is research scholar, Department of Political Science, School of Social Sciences, University of Hyderabad.

Rohit Jain is Associate Professor, School of Rural Development, TISS, Tuljapur Sravya Katta, Osamnia University, Telengana.

Dambarudhar Garada, research scholar, Department of Sociology, School of Social Sciences, University of Hyderabad.

V. Rajunayak, Assistant Professor, Dept of Commonwealth Literacy Studies, EFLU, Hyderabad.

Tapan Kumar Bihari is research scholar, Department of Political Science, School of Social Sciences, University of Hyderabad.

Shivesh is Research Scholar, Dept. of Economics, BHU.

Syed Muhammad Sajjad Kabir is Assistant Professor, Department of Psychology, University of Chittagong, Chittagong-4331, Bangladesh.

Dr Nazmunnessa Mahtab is Professor, Department of Women and Gender Studies, University of Dhaka, Dhaka-1000, Bangladesh.

Dr K. Vidyasagar Reddy is Associate Prof., Dept of Political Science, Mizoram University, Aizawl.

Ganesh Digal, research scholar, Department of Sociology, School of Social Sciences, University of Hyderabad.

Harsha S is Assistant Professor, Department of Political Science, Assam University, Silchar.

1

Fear of Uprising: Post Colonial State, Natural Calamity and the Politics of Development

Sajal Nag

In the beginning of 2001 the elders of the Mizo tribe of Mizoram State (India) forecasted that a famine was likely to strike the State by the year 2007. It would be a rat-famine resulted by the reproductive flowering of the Bamboo plants that carpet the hills of the region. True to the prediction there were reports of beginning of bamboo flowering by the middle of the year. Reporters went to the jungles and splashed photographs of bamboo plants with their flowers. There were also reports that there was a visible increase in the jungle rat population. As the news spread, there was a massive discussion among various circles in north-east India about the impending famine resulting from bamboo-flowering in Mizoram and the consequent increase in the rodent population who feed on human food. It indeed appeared that the famine was likely to occur in 2007. A similar phenomenon occurred in 1959 which had sparked a twenty year long insurgency which ended only in 1986 after a traumatic experience for both the people of Mizoram as well as the Indian state. Truly, the bamboo flowering and the consequent rat-famine sparked off the twenty years long bloody secessionist insurgency in the Mizoram. The tribal elders of Mizoram had warned the State Government of Assam about an impending catastrophe in the form of bamboo flowering and consequent rat famine. But the Assamese statesmen dismissed the prediction as tribal superstition and ignored the warning. But true to the prediction the bamboo plants blossomed all over the hill ranges leading to the increase in the rat population. The State Government was caught unaware and before they could take action scores of lives was lost in starvation. The famine was over in time but the antipathy shown by the

Post-colonial State to its peripheral citizens remained. The Mizos demanded secession from India on the ground that they would not like to be part of State, which did not come to their rescue in times of dire need. The movement graduated to organised insurgency, which the Indian State found difficult to tackle for a long time before the Mizos negotiated for amicable settlement. Fearing a repeat of such development both the state government and the central government were not leaving anything to chance and doing everything possible to pre-empt the event.

The flowering of bamboo is a natural reproductive function. There is nothing unique about it as like all other living organisms this plant too flowers to produce the seeds from which the next generation of bamboo plants are born. What is unique is that unlike most other living organisms, the bamboo plants flower only once in its lifetime after which it dies. The other peculiarity of such flowering is the entire forest of bamboo plants flower at the same time, which is the reason that such event is called 'gregarious flowering.' Subsequently it dies at the same time too. The recorded event of such bamboo flowering stretch back as far as ninth century AD when a particular variety of Bamboo (*Phyllostachys Bambusoides*) flowered in Japan. In fact Plantologist, Dai Kai Zhi used the words '*bamboo flowering*' for the first time in his Manual of Bamboo. Bamboos are arborescent grasses belonging to the family of *Poaceae* and are grouped under the subfamily *Bambusoideae.* Out of the 110 general and 1110-1140 species of bamboos in the world, India according to the latest reports accounts for 18 general and 128 species of bamboos. North-east India has extensive bamboo vegetation covering an area of 3.05 million ha. Out of this the state of Mizoram accounts for highest forest cover with bamboos. It has nine general and 20 species. The reproductive cycle of the Bamboos also vary from species to species Based on the flowering cycle they are classified into three types: (1) annual or continuous flowering (species which flower every year and do not die), (2) Gregarious or periodic flowering when the whole clump flower in an extensive area and die after seed setting. The flowering may continue for to two or three years in an area or in the same clump, (3) Sporadic or irregular flowering which occurs in isolated clumps in one or to two in an area or in parts of one clump. Thus flowering periodicity of bamboos varies from three to one hundred and twenty years.

Flowering Habits – Priority Species

	Species	*Period between flowerings in years*
1.	Bambusa Balcooa	35-45
2.	B bamboo	45-48
3.	B.blumeana	45-100
4.	B.polymorpha	35-60
5.	B.texilis	Regularly found in flower, not fatal

6.	B.tulda	30-60
7.	B.vulgaris	rarely found in flower
8.	Cepha;pstacjuum pergracile	Sporadic
9.	Dendrocalamys asper	Not known
10.	D.giganteus	40-65
11.	D.latiflorus	Sporadic
12.	D.strictus	40-65
13.	Gigantochloa apus	50-60
14.	G. Levis	Sporadic, Not fatal
15.	G. pseudoarundinacea	50-60
16.	Guadua angustifolia	Not known
17.	Melacanna baccifera	35-26, 48,60
18.	Ochlandra travancorica	7 (and 23)
19.	Phyllostachys pubescens	67 and Sporadic
20.	P.bamusoides	60 (and 120)
21.	Thyrsostachys siamensis	35-50

One of the most unusual flowering phenomena occurs in many bamboos. All plants of a species flower at about the same time at lengthy intervals as mentioned above. It is not really flowering. Scientifically it is called '*synchronic masting*.' These terms are used by the Scientists to describe the '*synchronised production or seeds at long intervals by a population of plants*'. *Masting* is the accurate term but *flowering* was the word coined by the colonial authorities, which gained acceptance in common vocabulary. For the colonials the flowering of bamboo was a miraculous event recorded again and again but without seeking an explanation. Among them were Baker, Blanford, Blatter, Bradley, Brandis and Bourdillon and in later times Father Santapu and Chatterjee. It was only in 1967 that the first synoptic survey was available. It was by Daniel Janzen. Janzen regretted that the natural flowering of bamboo was being reduced into a unique event as natural bamboo forests were being denuded across the world. During flowering individual aerial stems sometimes live for much less time than their species cycles and flower only at the end of the cycle when an inborn signal initiates the formation of inflorescences. Fruit development in a few species has also been reported. The size and shape of bamboo fruits vary according to the species. The morphology of fruit was dependent on its character for identification of bamboos. Researches have furnished an account of bamboo fruits belonging to 17 general and 22 species. Although bamboo fruit are generally known as *Caryopsis*, based on morphology, researchers classified them into three types:

1. *Caryopsis*: The *pericarp* as membranous, thin, soft and adheres to the seed coat. The fruit has an apparent ventral suture, which is nearly as long as the whole fruit. An articulate navel is located at the fruit base.

2. *Glans*: have hard, smooth, *crustacous pericarp,* separated from the seed coat. The fruit has no ventral sutra and navel.

3. *Bacca*: has thick fleshy *pericarp* separated from the seed coat. It indicated that the morphology of starch grains can also be used as a distinguishing character for identification.

In certain parts of China, contiguous parts of Myanmar with India, Japan and South Africa, this phenomenon was known to occur. In Japan, the *Moso* species of bamboo bloomed, in the sixty-seventh years in 1997 after a sprout. The bloom of *Moso* for the second time was actually checked in the Kamigamo Experimental Forest Station in July 1997. In Japan, there was a reported outbreak of Smith's red-backed mole subsequent to the flowering of *Sasa Ishizichiana* at Mount Tsurngi-shikoku in 1954-55. In Southern China there was mass flowering of thorny bamboos in 1994, which coincided with severe floods, bring immense suffering to the people. In fact the instance of bamboo flowering in China was brought to notice of the Plant Scientists in the 1980's by Zoologists who were attracted by the plight of the Giant Pandas during the flowering of bamboo plants. It was then observed that there were many instances of mass flowering bamboos causing a complete loss of livelihood to local growers and predecessors. Their trust in the reliability of the resource base is shattered and in many instances the people move away permanently from bamboo as their source of income. The Blue Mountain of Jamaica has one of the best-recorded instances of *supra annual* flowering anywhere. Around the same time such flowering was reported from Trinidad and Tobago as well. In South America too there was a reference of a bamboo bloom with correspondent increase in rodents in the second half of 1800s. Here a peak in rainfall accompanied bamboo flowering. Similarly, research done by Taylor Green of the Pest Infestation Control Laboratory, United Kingdom indicated that in East Africa, an excessive rodent population followed heavy rainfall late in the season the next year. This was because the late rainfall helped weeds and grasses to grow and survive longer than usual thereby providing protection to the rodents from predators, mainly birds and partly because these weeds and grasses also provided additional food to the rodents. In Mizoram too, the 1977 bamboo flowering was accompanied by heavier rainfall. In Thailand in the 1980's due to 'Gregarious Blooming' even the newly planted bamboos flowered and died. It is called '*gregarious bamboo flowering*' because the bamboo clumps flower all at the same time in complete synchrony but once in its lifetime. In the Balaghat district of the Central Provinces in 1869, the *Kattang bamboo (Bambusa Arundinacae)* flowered and coincidentally there was a famine but no suggestion was made that there was any interrelation between the two occurrences. The Indian states of Maharashtra and Uttaranchal also reported the flowering of bamboo but no famine or rat proliferation had been reported. There are other areas of India's northeast where these species of bamboo plants exists, the phenomenon occurs too. Only the famine did not take place, as the affected area was basically not human habitats. But "*nowhere does the outbreak reach the proportion that it does in Mizoram*".

The correlation of bamboo flowering with famine is interesting. Famines are simply food shortage. The shortage could be due to natural or artificial causes. Among the natural causes, shortage caused by infestation of vermin has been listed as one. But such famines were 'minor and localised'. Rats have been also listed as one of the vermin who through depredation cause food shortage. Rats eat almost anything that humans eat causing the most serious damage is to the seeds of grain both before and after harvesting. Grain stored on farms is often not only eaten by rats but also rendered unsuitable for human consumption by being mixed with rat dropping. With population explosion among the rats the destruction of foodstuff also increases. Therefore as far as foodstuffs of human beings are concerned the rats have been identified as a major destroyer.

The gregarious flowering of bamboo may over saturate the food supply of *frugivors* and assure bamboo production. "When the bamboo flowers it is the signal for a feast. Everyone loves the bamboo. Its fruits look like a yellowish-green pear with a tender, white kernel inside. Sometimes the flowering is in clumps, sometime the masting takes place over 95000 square miles...Animals love it. Birds migrate en masse. Janzen reports of a guinea fowl he found which had over 400 seeds in his stomach. Rats, pigs and chicken ravage the area and eat till hunger pangs become a distant fantasy. It is gluttony on an enormous scale. Rabelais would have the right word for it not botanists. No Pied Piper could play a carnival song such as this. There have been reports of as many as 40-60 million rats migrating to a masting. All they do is eat and eat and reproduce. Nothing grows at this time for these rat populations remain in the area for two years. Rice and even root crops like yams and arum growing in the area are devastated. Often villagers have to abandon their homes. As the rats, pigs and birds eat their reproductive cycles shorten. It is a factory-farmers dream as litter follows litter. For chickens, the pigs of the bird world- increased food consumption can lower the time of sexual maturation by fifty days. What is feast to nature, becomes a famine to man as rats, birds and pigs multiply." The 1977 *Thingtam* famine in Mizoram was a living testimony to this occurrence. "Subsequent to the flowering of bamboos rats multiplied in thousands. They moved from village to village from *jhum* plot to *jhum*, in groups of thousands. Often in a matter of hour's whole acres of standing crop, mainly rice would be destroyed. Though efforts were made at baiting and fumigation, traps were laid and pits dug around the *jhums* the effect was marginal. The number of rats was so overwhelming that often pits would get filled in by the bodies of the front-line rats while those following behind would walk over the bodies and enter the fields." This phenomenon however seriously affects the normal balance of nature. Animals' dependent on bamboo vegetative growth such as the Giant Panda and Mountain Gorilla loses a favoured food source entirely after a flowering episode. A glut of bamboo fruit may also incite an explosion of population of rodents that eat the fruits. For example, the flowering of *Muli* or

Terak bamboo (*me locanna bambusoides*) in its native habitat around the Bay of Bengal in cycles of mostly 30-35 years leads to disaster. The accumulation of avocado sized fruits promotes a rapid increase in rodent population, which lead to the loss of human food supplies and epidemic of rodent carrying disease. A research at the Dehradun Institute of Forest Research (India) on the connection between bamboo and rats found that the fruit contained:

1.	Starch (on zero moisture basis)	50.240 per cent
2.	Protein	11.556 per cent
3.	Fat	0.231 per cent
4.	Ash	3.030 per cent
5.	Moisture	9.400 per cent
6.	Others	26.493 per cent

It stated that the rats feed on bamboo seeds which are rich in enzymes like *deamidase, amylase* and *amygdalins*. These trigger an overdose of oestrogen, enhancing fertility of the rodents enabling them to multiply at very rapid scale. According to a research of Dr A K Ghose, a Zoologist based on North Eastern Hill University, Shillong (India), the fruits high protein of nearly 12 per cent and very high starch content of about 50 per cent besides vitamin A which helps augment the fertility of rodents. No clear causal link between the flowering bamboos and the increase in rats has been established, though various theories exist. According to one theory as bamboo seed contain a high concentration of protein – nearly11 per cent – perhaps by eating them the cannibalistic urges of the male rats toward the young is deadened. Also high intake of protein might strengthen the rats thus lowering the rate of infant mortality. It is also conjectured that some hormonal change took place in the rats due to the excessive protein that the bamboo fruit contained enabling the female rats to produce a litter much earlier in age than in normal circumstances. Even in normal circumstances, however, the rats are prolific breeders. Although larger types reproduce once a year, others produce several litters during a single season. Some have only one to two young at a time while others have large numbers. Most rodents are polygamous and mate for the duration of a single breeding season and few like Beavers have permanent mates. The rather high rate of breeding is intensified by the fact that in many of the smaller rodents, sexual maturity is reached at an early age within a month of its birth normally earlier in the females than in the males. The females breed when less than a year old. The house mouse reproduce through out the year with an average of 5.5 litters and 31 young per female per year in building houses and 10.2 and 57 young per year on farms in the United States. Wild Norway rats are able to breed at three to four months and can produce up to seven litters a year containing six to 22 young. Of the species commonly found in Mizoram (*Rarrusnitider* or the Himalyan rat and *Rattus Miviventer mentosu* being two of the main ones), the gestation period is said to be of 20 to 22 days. Considering one female rat can give a litter of 6-12 young ones and that the mother can attain immediate *post-partum* pregnancy, the rate of reproduction can be high. Further, rats can breed throughout the year and the maturity period of as young one is about 60-70 days. If one combines all this, then one family of rats –producing an average litter of eight every month and half of its litter (the female) each again producing eight from their date of maturity- can produce thousands of rats in one year. Obviously, therefore if reproduction was allowed to go unchecked and if there were no other balancing factors in the ecology rats would soon rule the eco-system. Therefore the reports that rodents produce prolifically after consuming the bamboo fruits were not untrue. However, the answer to the riddle lies not in any one factor but in a complicated combination of factors which until discovered will remain an enigma. The tribal elders from ancient times had understood the connection between the increase in rat population and the consumption of bamboo fruits and the resultant famines, which have been subsequently confirmed by the findings of modern science. But until recently most scientists discounted even the tribal belief that famine follow the flowering of bamboo. The other curious phenomenon that occurs is the appearance of White mice at the end of the flowering session. The Arunachali tribes believe that when the white mice appear it signals the end of the flowering session as well as the famine. Strangely the migration of white mice has been recorded in film. It is a mystery where from they come and why at the end of the flowering session. Similarly the increase in rat population obviously results in the increase in snakes. This can be seen as migration of snake population due to increase in food supply in the form of rats- a favourite food item of the snakes. But during 2002-07 famine in Arunachal Pradesh of India, appearance of certain rare varieties of snake was observed and filmed. These were the glass snake (a rare variety of reptile lizard which shed its legs and like other lizards still drop its tail when attacked) and a variety of Pit Viper locally known and feared as '*barta.*' It is found in its very primitive form with huge fangs. Both these snakes species are a source of fear to the local villagers as large number of people die of their bites.

Famine in 2007

In the year 2002 there was a sudden spurt of interest in the Bamboo-flowering phenomenon in Mizoram. The reason of such alround 'interest' is the prediction by the Mizo elders that the next *Mautam* is likely to strike soon. According to the Mizo predictions based on the fifty-years cycle of bamboo flowering, the next famine is likely to break out in 2007. True to the predictions as early as 2000 the high bamboo plants started to bloom into mauve, yellow and crimson coloured flowers in the southern areas of the state conveying an ominous omen of impending doom. The alarm bells had started ringing among all sections of the Mizos as they were reminded of the grim days of the late fifties when over 5000 people perished in hunger as the hungry rats devoured their staple crops. As the Government of Mizoram declared in 2003 that 34 vegetation cites had been sighted where bamboo was found to be flowering, the tribal, now Christians were flocking to Churches to offer special prayers to ward off famine they fear could strike the region anytime. Despite change of faith the Mizos go by their traditional belief that when bamboo flowers death and destruction will follow. The Chief Minister of Mizoram Zoramthanga himself supported the act saying "*It is not a myth or superstitious belief to think that bamboo flowering signals famine. It is a stark reality and we have experienced the witnessed an outbreak of famine in the past under similar circumstances.*" Following the flowering of these plants in parts of Tripura State, which are contiguous to Mizoram, there has been large-scale evacuation as the environment created panic among the people there. It is a common belief among the poverty-stricken tribal population in the interior region of the state that bamboo flowering brought famine, epidemic and starvation. This fear coupled with superstition has resulted in hundreds of tribal families leaving their hamlets. The beginning of flowering has coincided with the advent of viral fever and gastroenteritis epidemic spreading the panic. Similar panic and desertion had been reported from the Nagas, Kukis and Zo tribes of Ukhrul, Tamenglong and Chrachandpur Districts of Manipur State where the bamboo plants flowered with corresponding increase in rat population in mid 2004. Manipur had witnessed the phenomenon in 1954-55, where there was a great rat-famine in Mizoram. Confirming the fear of the people, experts stated that besides a fair chance of famine, *Plague* and *Leptospirosis* might also be a major threat to the people in this region. According to this report what makes the situation worse is the fact that besides eating up agricultural produce the rodents also carry almost 200 types of *pathogens*, which pose a grave threat to human beings.[1] The Governments in those areas were activating their machinery to tackle the menace. In addition there was a threat of agrarian crisis too. Modern science has testified that as the bamboo dies following flowering there is huge erosion in soil. The soil, which was previously bound together by bamboo roots, erodes away which affect the agricultural productivity. Their oral history has it that the previous occupants of their tract had migrated due to this scourge. Historically, the Mizo tribes too were migrating to the hills of Manipur or Plains of Assam only to be rid of this evil event. It cost them hugely in terms of demography. Every Famine would carry away a large number of lives with it. For a tribe poor in its demographic resources, it was a horrifying experience.

The Print-media was quick to pick up the issue. The Telegraph (Calcutta) reported, "*Mizoram Apprehends Rat-Triggered Famine*" (18 March 2001). In July it had a headline "*Mizoram Devises Two-Pronged Strategy to Combat Famine*" (6 July 2001). *The Shillong Times* reported *Mizoram Government to Purchase Rat-Tails*: *A Unique Measure to Check Famine* (15 June 2001). *The North East Sun* had a cover story entitled "Catastrophic Famine to Strike Northeast" (1-14 July 2002). The *Eastern Panorama* (March 2002) as well as *North East Frontier* Magazine ran similar cover stories. The predicted bamboo flowering, consequent rat famine and Mizoram as the land where this unique phenomenon would occur in 2007 brought it worldwide attention. According to The National Geographic News the phenomenon was intriguing as it was interesting:

> "Some species of bamboo flower only every 40-50 years. In an intriguing chain of events, these periods of flowering sometimes lead to the destruction of the basic crops and widespread famine in areas of India where bamboo grows heavily. The last famine of this nature occurred in 1961 through 1965 in the hilly state of Mizoram in eastern India, an area of 21,000 square kilometres with a population of more than 7,00,000. There are hundreds of species of bamboo in the world. Some flower every year, some at regular intervals. But a small percentage flowers in synchrony, over hundreds of square kilometres every few decades. Researchers are not sure how it happens. Science has not been able to explain how the same message is passed among bamboo clumps separated by hundreds of kilometres to flower at the same time… (Perhaps) the rhizomes of the bamboo have some kind of memory trait that make the plants grow in synchronisation, then burst into bloom all at the same time.
>
> After the massive flowering, the bamboo clumps die in a kind of suicide by over production… when bamboo plants flower, they produce a large volume of seeds, which are source of food many predators, especially rats. As masses of flowering bamboo produce this natural bounty, rats are attracted to the area. Fortified by the protein rich seeds, they multiply rapidly. But the supply of bamboo seeds is limited. When it is exhausted, armies of the marauding rodents turn their attention to standing crops, devouring acres of rice, potatoes and sweet potatoes within a few days. As a result, local peasant, who are fully dependent on agriculture for their subsistence are subjected to famine.
>
> The phenomenon mainly occurs in Mizoram (India), which is heavily covered with two species of bamboo. The impact can be so devastating that local folklore is full of tales of this natural cyclical event".

The British Broadcasting Corporation (BBC) in its world news edition as well as South Asia edition reported, "The Indian State of Mizoram is preparing itself for a mass flowering of bamboo – which has the potential to devastate the area. The bamboo only flowers once every fifty years. When it last did so, in the 1950's the abundance of seeds led to plague of rats – which in turn led to widespread famine and thousands of deaths in the region. The bamboo is produced from an underground stem. Shortly after flowering – which it does in waves – it dies. Indian bamboo expert Professor M.P. Ranjan told BBC World Service's Outlook programme that the wave of flowering is expected again in the next two years and potential disaster looms… Dr Ranjan's fellow expert Dr. Eric Bo said "this is going to happen, it is an act of God or whatever your belief. They are going to flower and they are going to die and we know approximately when that is going to happen." The International Forest

Conservation Portal recorded that, "The bamboo forests in India's northeast flower every few decades and folklore is rife with tales of devastating impact of this natural cyclical event." Then quoting an Agricultural Scientist is said, "Why bamboo clumps flower remains a mystery but it is believed to be caused by a characteristic that makes them grow in unison, then bloom. The flowering of bamboo produces huge seeds that attract predators, mostly rats. Strengthened by protein rich seeds the rodents multiply quickly. When the seeds are exhausted armies of rats chomp their way through rice and potato crops and granaries causing famine."

The International Electronic Magazine on Environment, Energy and Sustainable Development, Terra Green also reported,

"The northeastern part of India is gearing up to protect itself from the possible famine triggered by a huge surge in rat population, the result of the flowering of bamboo plantations that began this month and is expected to peak in 2007....Science has no explanation till date about the manner in which the message to flower at the same time is passed among bamboo clumps that are separated hundred of kilometres apart. It is speculated that the rhizomes of bamboo have some kind of 'memory' trait that makes them grow in synchronisation and then burst into bloom at the same time. After massive flowering the bamboo clumps die, a sort of suicide due to over production. In previous years the simultaneous production of seeds by millions of bamboo plants caused a surge in the number of seed-eating rodents, fortified by the protein rich seeds multiplying rapidly. But the supply of bamboo seed is limited. When exhausted, armies of these marauding rodents turn their attention to nearby paddy and potato fields in search of food with devastating effects on these crops."

The website of the International Human Flower Project posted a report for the surfers saying, "When Charles Baudelaire imagined Flowers of Evil, he likely never heard of Mautak bamboo. People in Northeastern India's state of Mizoram refer to Melocanna baccifera as mautam or famine. The Indian peasants and officials are struggling to prevent the next flower fed disaster by harvesting the plant now and distributing poison and rattraps in the region. The flowers produce millions of protein rich seeds that are devoured by rats causing an explosion in the rodent population. When the bamboo seed supply is exhausted, the rats move on to the next available food source–the Mizoram peasents' meagre stores of rice and cereals."

A similar report prepared by Peter Foster, was published in The Daily Telegraph of London which described it as a "Strange Story'. Another website published a rare photograph of the bamboo fruit describing it as 'Disaster Fruit.' It reported, "Most of the bamboo species flower after the end of a long number of years of vegetative growth. The flowering is synchronous over vast tracks of landscape and this phenomenon is called gregarious flowering, which is flowed by death of bamboo clumps. But such peculiar behaviour of the bamboo sometimes create problems for ecology besides human beings. The gregarious flowering of bamboo results in production of large quantities of seeds which in turn, supports population explosion in rats. However, quantity of seeds available for rat diminishes soon after the germination of seeds following rains. The resultant short supply of bamboo seeds on the one hand and a large population of rats on the other lead to a phase when the rodents head towards farmlands in adjoining areas, causing widespread loos to crops. Such a chain of events has the potential to cause a famine. The last gregarious famine with a cycle of 48 years, of muli bamboo occurred in 1959 and the next is expected to start next year and reaching its peak in 2007."

The mass of material available in the Internet on the subject is indicative of the growing curiosity on the subject. It is also noticeable that there is hardly any reading material from the Indian Science fraternity on the issue. Amusingly, most of the material on the phenomenon related to Mizoram, as available in the internet are unacknowledged borrowing from this author's widely read article published in the *Economic and Political Weekly* (March 24-31, 2001) including its printing errors indicating the lack of serious scientifically research reading material. For the Department of Science and Technology, Government of India, Centre for Science and Environment, New Delhi, and Centre for Environmental Education, the phenomenon is still mysterious. Prof. B. Hari Gopal of the Department of Science and Technology, Government of India and Prof. H.Y. Mohan Rao of the University of Delhi were among the first to initiate scientific enquiry into it.

In one of its findings entitled "Bamboo Famine in Mizoram" the Centre for Science and Environment, New Delhi, stated that the state of Mizoram has about 16 species of bamboos, but the most abundant are *Melocanna bamboosoides* and *Bambusa Tulda*. "Whenever each of the two common varieties of bamboo flowers there is an accompanying increase in the rat population which in turn leads to famine. The rats attack standing crops. This result is an acute famine".[2] The invasion of rats was confirmed by S. Barkakaty, the first Indian Superintendent and also the Deputy Commissioner of the then Mizo Hills district of Assam (1949-53) who had occasion to actually see one of the famines (1952-59) reported about the attack of the rats:

> "They come in thousands and spread themselves to cover so wide an area that they eat up the entire paddy of a jhum overnight. When mautam year approaches, the cultivators take every possible preventive measure in their simple way by setting up traps around the jhum and keeping watch day and night to frighten away or kill rats. But these efforts are not sufficient for saving the crop. During such a famine (therefore) people have to depend for their sustenance and survival on wild roots, jungle fruit and anything that is edible. As a result of under nourishment various epidemics break out causing heavy loss of life".

The Chief Minister of Mizoram, Zoramthanga, allaying the fear of the repetition of the devastation of 1957 famine stated, "The biggest difference between then and now is that we are no longer under Assam. We are free to follow our policies. To tackle the phenomenon we have chalked out a multi pronged strategy that focuses on utilisation and generation of more species… the government will not only prevent a repeat of the tragedy four decades back but actually pave the way for a bamboo revolution in the State."[3] The State Government evolved its own contingency plan to avert a famine. It set up a high level "Mizoram State Rodent Control Committee" with the Chief Minister as its chairman. The committee initiated a mass campaign for killing rats in fields and houses to pre-empt their proliferation. It even offered Re 1/- for the tail of every dead rat. In the first 18 months nearly 80,000 rats were killed in the state. Two expert 'Rodent Killers' John Bourne and Valerie Grassmen – bio-sceintist from Canada who has successfully eliminated rodents and pests destroying farms in their country also visited Mizoram in November 2002, on the invitation of the Government.[4] They held wide range discussion with the local experts and submitted report recommending the annihilation of rats using poison, traps and holes dug in the ground. The poison could preferably *bezinc phosphide* and *bromadiolone* and should be scattered in areas away from human habitation before tilling for *jhum* starts.

The Central Government did not to lag behind. It sent Senior Plant Physiologist Professor Mohan Rao from New Delhi to help control the situation who recommended the farmers plant crops that the rats did not eat such as banana, ginger and turmeric instead of the traditional items during the period when vast fields of bamboo were expected to flower. The Government of India financed a number of seminars and workshops. The recommendations of which were placed before the Planning Commission. The Union Ministry of Environment and Forests had roped in experts including International Bamboo and Rattan Network and the United Nations Industrial Development Organisation (UNIDO) for hectic consultation on how to handle this natural growth cycle of the humble bamboo plant which would have a direct bearing on the socio-economic well being and a long term ecological impact. The facts that after flowering, the entire bamboo forest die and rot was a more serious concern. Having dry rotting mass of bamboo corpses covering about 18000 hectares of the region with about 25 million tons of bamboo was a ghastly prospect. More so, because a thriving economy revolves around bamboo. The pulp and paper industry, construction, cottage industry, handloom, food, fuel, fodder and medicine annually consume about 22 million bamboos. If left un-harvested this would amount to a loss of around Rs.12000 million. This will seriously undermine the production of paper industries of the region, as bamboo constitutes their major raw material. Bamboo rotting over hundreds of acres and growth of rat population would has a devastating effect on the *jhum* cultivation which is mainstay of the rural people of the region. Women who make the majority of the rural work force and contribute more to holding up the rural economy would be particularly be vulnerable. Their major source of money income – such as *jhum* field produce, the vegetable from the wild and the bamboo shoots which they gather and sell in town markets-would disappear at least for a crucial period of time seriously affecting family budget. Again, water, which already a scarce resource in most of the hill region of northeast India would become scarcer. This was the experience of past years of calamity. Experts testified that during the bamboo flowering in Mizoram there was a sharp increase in temperature flowed by a spell of dry arid weather, which had direct fallout on the health of the people. Not only that women and children who have to spend hours to fetch water will be forced to spend even more time carrying out the task.

The impending event provided an opportunity to the scientific community as well to study the phenomenon and evolve a strategy to pre-empt the catastrophe. The Jorhat Rain Forest Research Institute organised a workshop in April 2002 which was attended by the officials of various north-eastern states, organisations like International Network for Bamboos and Rattan (INBAR, Beizing), Gramland and Fodder Research Institute (Jhansi), Forest Survey of India (Dehradun), Institute of Wood Science and Technology (Bangalore), Himalayan Forest Research Institute, State Forest Research Institute (Itanagar), Kerala Forest Research Institute (Peechi), United Nations Industrial Development Organisation (UNIDO) and so on. The workshop recommended that Mizoram should go for early harvesting of bamboos before they flowered and attracted rodents.

The idea of harvesting the entire bamboo population has appealed to the Chief Minister of Mizoram, Zoramthanga. Mizoram harvested about forty per cent of India's 81 million tonnes of bamboo. Now with a one time harvesting the head of State wanted to "reverse the flowering phenomenon into an economic opportunity." He felt it could bring a "green gold revolution through bamboo." He proposed setting up an incense factory with machines imported from China or Thailand besides making paper and other handicraft items from bamboos. Professor M P Ranjan, head of the Center for Bamboo Initiatives at the National Institute of Design at Ahmedabad who was part of the coalition of Botanist, Engineers, Architects and Civil Servants trying to counter the catastrophe which he compared to be of the "*same magnitude as a flood or an earthquake*" was also equally enthusiastic about the prospect of harvesting this 'wonder grass' for an industrial purpose.

The Ministry of Environment and Forests put a damper on the proposal stating that about 26 million tonnes of bamboo spread over more than 10 million hectares was going to be affected by the imminent flowering. Only 10 per cent of these bamboos grows in accessible areas and can be retrieved for industrial use. Another major problem in this enthusiasm seemed to be the requirement of a massive storage facility to cope with the glut of such harvested bamboos. Without proper storage the bamboo were likely to quickly rot. India's Ministry of Environment and Forests set up two committees to recommend ways to limit crop losses. One suggested that bamboo was extracted before it flowers and that mixed vegetation was planted immediately after flowering to stop soil erosion. The Second recommended improving harvesting and storage facilities for extracted bamboo and removing export restrictions to find additional outlets for harvested bamboo.

In a separate proposal the Centre for Indian Bamboo Resource and Technology (CIBART) forwarded a pilot project with the Ministry of Rural Development and Manipur State Government, which involved creating a '*buffer zone*'- in which bamboo would be completely removed to deter rats from around bamboo growing villages in the State's Tamenglong District. Plant Scientist Indira Khurana of the CIBART recommended that bamboo seed could be collected from the areas in which it has already flowered and immediately planted in the buffer zone. This would limit the number of seeds available to rats and would also reduce the time during which bamboo would not be available to local communities.

Some Non-Governmental Organisations and individual environmental activists were horrified with the idea of *en masse* harvesting of bamboo plants to prevent it from flowering and resulting in famine conditions. One activist stated, "the first cause for alarm is not the threat of gregarious flowering which is a normal phenomenon but that a United Nations organisation is ringing alarm bells while the Central Government is again getting caught in the UN's hysteria. The Government of India seems to have forgotten that the United Nations Food and Agriculture Organisation (UNFAO) was basically responsible for both the death of the bamboo forests and the destruction of the forest ecosystem in the entire bamboo region of the southern and central India from 1960 onwards. The northeastern region was mercifully spared, as UNFAO had not entered that region.... The second alarming fact is the central government's threat to harvest the bamboos before they flower. If an important species is clear-felled before it flowers and its rhizomes having reached the end of the physiological are exhausted, it would mean a death, a criminal murder of a species."[5] The basic content of the activist was that flowering of bamboo is a normal reproductive activity like any other organic body. The function of a flower is to produce seed to perpetuate its species. This is true of bamboo too except that each species of the bamboo tends to flower gregariously over vast stretches of areas, but only at the end of its vegetative growth which varies from one to 120 years for different species. It implied that while any one species is flowering gregariously all other species is bamboo in that region would continue to live and vegetatively reproduce their culms. Mizoram has other species that would not flower in 2007. Thus while one species flower and die others would continue to live nullifying the fear of the people about the shortage of bamboos. Again, though the fear of invasion of rodents is real there is no reason it could not be effectively tackled. Like bamboo seed, rats also devour bamboo, wheat and rice seeds profusely. If rodents could be prevented from entering the ripe grain fields and storehouse they could be from the ripening seeds of the bamboo too. The activist also refuted the idea the bamboo flowering portend famine. On the contrary, it is the famine, which often is the result of a serial drought results in gregarious flowering of bamboo across the species. It is a defence mechanism – a simple survival strategy of the species to seed, reproduce and perpetuate itself. Bamboo is a grass, rigid and woody with lignin but essentially cellulose, carbohydrate with a large water component. Good rainfall or running water is essential for its growth. Water is both an agent of nutrient distribution in nature and a significant medium of biological activity in plants. Repeated failure of monsoon rings the death knell for bamboo.[6]

Another professional forester from the Indian Forest Service reported that a bamboo species (*Dendrocalamus Structus*) flowered gregariously in Maharashtra in the year 1983-84 and also in Madhya Pradesh and Andhra Pradesh in the following years. He asserted that misconceptions about a natural phenomenon like bamboo flowering are perpetuated by vested interests. "Bamboo flowering is a natural phenomenon. It is preceded by increase in rodent population - a nature's way of controlling profuse seeding. Bamboo seeds are eaten by rats, cattle as well as people. It is quite nutritious and even some believe that bamboo seed is also invigorating and has aphrodisiac qualities." He felt that under such a situation to consider the harvest of bamboo prior to flowering is neither silviculturally sound nor ecologically desirable not is it economically welcome. It will entail wiping out of a precious natural resource altogether from the site as there will be no seeding and regeneration…the idea to harvest bamboos prior to flowering needs to be nipped in the bud. Everything has its time and nature has its own time-table. We have already interfered in nature's way too much."[7] The same sentiment was echoed by another concerned individual, "*More pressing than the US walking out of Kyoto Protocol and Russia following suit is the need to take stock of the impending anthropogenic mess that we are about to create on the subject of bamboo.*"[8]

Confirming the medicinal and aphrodisiac qualities of bamboo seeds another retired bureaucrat appealed to appropriate the bamboo flowering opportunity for meaningful scientific research. "*When the (last flowering of Muli bamboo took place, the villagers collected the seeds which are pear shaped just like William pear - about the same size. They cooked and fried the seed and consumed with rice. After some time it was noticed that the incidence of pregnancy increased among many of the married women. Assuming that consuming the seed had somehow increased the fertility of these women folk, I collected a fair quantity of seeds and send to the company along with my observations and requested them to have the seeds analysed but it appeared nothing had been done. The company however requested me to send more seeds but as it was practically the end of flowering I could collect a few kilograms only. It has been said that the rat population increased due to abundance of food, it may however be the other way round as in man. Therefore if proper research/analysis is conducted the properties of the seed would be discovered which could then be a boon for childless couples.*

The flowering of *muli* bamboo occurs once in every fifty years. One opportunity had been lost during the last flowering but it has now again presented itself and time should not be wasted for (starting) research/analysis of the seed by medical professionals and pharmaceutical firms."[9]

Famine and Post Colonial State

As can be seen the imminent bamboo flowering has activated a huge range of people, groups and Governments. While the to-be-affected people are petrified by the prospect and are praying to survive the impending horror, the Governments, State machinery and Scientists are gearing up to tackle the calamity and mitigate the imagined hardships. This is to be compared against the pre-colonial situation when the Mizo tribe tackled this calamity, which was a part of their life and history, on their own. How and why did they become dependent on external agencies to fight their battle or was it the project of these agencies to create such dependence. It is intriguing because while the rest of the world is taking extreme interest in mitigating this calamity hardly any one is keen to gather the tribal knowledge about the phenomenon and their history of coping with it which could be recorded to provide a meaningful insight in tackling the problem. Interestingly such interest in a famine that was to come six or seven years later was truly unprecedented if one considered the usual slow or no reaction of the Indian State towards the sufferings of the people. The reasons were not far to seek. The 1959 famine in Mizoram and the apathy of the Indian State towards the misery of the Mizo people had given rise to the Mizo National Front which organised and led a twenty-year long violent secessionist movement which the Government of India a difficult time to counter. Now that the insurgency was over, the Government of India did not want to take another chance with this imminent famine. It indicated a 'politics'. In other words, the entire 'interest' shown in pre-empting a famine was tactical, politically motivated – not really a genuine concern of a state for its citizens.

The indications were ominous and the Mizoram Government, traumatised and wise by past experiences has already pressed the emergency button. The administration has started preparations on a war footing to combat the calamity. It has set up a high level State Rodent Control Committee with Chief Minister Zoramthanga himself as the Chairman and C. Rokhuma as his deputy in the committee.

The committee, as a first step, started a campaign amongst people for mass killing of rats in the paddy fields and houses to pre-empt their proliferation. It decided to offer an incentive of Rupee one for the tail of every killed rat. In one year and half nearly 80,000 rats were killed. The Union Agriculture Ministry has also sent a team of rodent control experts, headed by senior plant physiologist Mohan Rao from New Delhi and Hyderabad to help the local administration. The state administration too sought the expert advice from specialists in the field from the North-Eastern Hill University, Shillong, the Indian Council of Agricultural Research, Shillong and the Zoological Survey of India, Regional Office, Shillong. The government devised a two-pronged strategy to fight the impending menace. One, the control of the rat population and two, to store adequate food grains to meet any contingency resulting from the destruction of crops by the rats. This was to be complemented by a massive supply network developed for uninterrupted distribution of food grains to the needy.

The experts from the Government of India recommended that during the bamboo flowering period the Mizo farmers should cultivate items which the rats do not eat, e.g., maize which will prevent a famine. Another expert recommended that there should be early harvesting of bamboo plants before the plants start to rot. This would prevent the crisis.

Politics of Philanthropy

As per their predictions after the last famine in 1977, they were anticipating one more in 2007. True to their anticipation, the six feet high bamboo plants have already started to bloom with mauve, yellow and crimson coloured flowers all over the southern Mizo Hills. This time, it seemed, the calamity was likely to spread to newer areas like Arunachal Pradesh and Manipur. Hundreds of acres of paddy fields in at least 50 villages of upper Subansiri district of Arunachal Pradesh bordering China had been devastated by teeming rats in just about a fortnight. The villagers watched this devastation helplessly as they had never seen so many rats at one time. They were now seeking divine intervention from *Donyi - Polo,* the Sun-Moon God of the indigenous faith and were holding regular prayers to prevent the imminent famine (reported in *The Shillong Times,* 1 September 2003, p. 3).

Similarly the villagers in the Tamenglong districts of Manipur were already facing acute food shortage due to the destruction of the standing crops by the invading rodent population. A total of 62 villages have been affected by the menace. The agriculture department of the state had provided 485 kgs of Bromodialon (Rat poison) till August 2003 without much impact on the rodents. The attack of the Rats was expected to continue for the next few years as the Centre Head already declared the period 2002-07 as the period of Bamboo Flowering and if the present situation continued the district would face a famine situation very soon. (Reported in *Shillong Times*, September 12, 2003)

By January 2008 the famine travelled to other parts of Manipur. In the district of Churachandpur which was adjacent to Mizoram most of the year's crop was destroyed by the rodents.[10] In the Parbung village the farmers could hurriedly harvest only about 10 bags of rice where as in normal times they would harvest 35-40 bags from their jhums. A survey conducted by the All Tribal Students Association, Manipur found that though several parts of Churchandpur have been affected by Mautam, Parbung subdivision with 48 villages was the worst hit. The farmers lost about 80 per cent of their annual foodgrain production. Villagers estimated that Purbung alone could face a shortage of 10,000 quintals of rice in 2008. The government had already been providing 700 quintals of rice per month to Purbung. But due to faulty public distribution system it had not reached many people. It was aggravated by the interference of the underground outfits operating in the area. Rebels had been demanding a certain percentage from the monthly quota of rice.[11] The center also released a huge amount of money to tackle the rodent menace but the funds hardly reached the people of Purbung. To facilitate famine mitigation a new NGO was formed by the name MAUTAM (Matuam Affected Areas Upliftment for Tripura, Assam and Mizoram). It organised a task force under the leadership of John L Pudaite, which will deliver the supplies of rice to the affected people. But poor accessibility still poses a grave problem. Some areas like Sartuinek village in Churachandpur district is inaccessible by road even in 2008. Getting there includes two days long boat ride in upstream Barak and a day long track. The residents of the village which has about 87 families walk five hours to and fro for a sackful of rice provided the MAUTAM task force. The local informants state that there is a backlog of about 64,600 quintals of rice to be given to the Churachandpur district.[12] Besides infrastructural problem there is administrative problem too. Although Mizoram state has declared mautam to be a calamity, Manipur government has not because it affects only parts adjacent to Mizoram. Hence it does not recognise it as a calamity. It therefore was averse to providing relief to the affected zones. Other than siphoning off the central relief material by the underground outfits some rice meant for villagers, easily recognisable by their wrapping, find their way into the open markets of neighbouring Agartala and Silchar. It was the Prime Ministers Office which had to intervene in famine mitigation in Manipur. Following a PMO directive the district administrated planned to use the NREGS (National Rural Employment Guarantee Scheme) to bring relief.[13] Accordingly employment and income was guaranteed to the famine affected people to generate purchasing power among the poor. Reports were collected about the extent of crop damage from Tipaimukh, Henglep, Thanlon, Singnat and Vangai. Using the first fund installment of Rupees Seven Crore, an average of 10-20 days of employment per household was generated in the district. That was tried to be increase to 18-25 days. A toal of 33,000 job cards had been issued in the district till mid January 2008. Under NREGS a household earn Rs. 81 per day. The scheme guaranteed 100 days of work per year and was implemented in Churachandpur sub-division for past four months. Besides the government established grain banks in several villages and the food and civil supplies department was requested to provide additional supply. A village to village survey was conducted to ascertain the damage and requirement. However after an independent five day survey, the Manipur Hill Journalists Union expressed the fear that the benefits of the scheme may not reach the affected villages in time. The report further said that the scarcity of food grains had indeed wrecked the economy of the jhum dependent tribal communities. In the 40 villages a whopping 99 per cent had claimed to be on the threshold of mautam. The Zomi Economic Planning and Development Agency – an NGO fighting the impending famine has been meeting government officials and staging protests since 2005. But it is unhappy that the response of the Manipur government had been very poor. No grain bank had actually been set up as promised. Compared to the state of Mizoram, Manipur's preparedness was pathetic. With poor connectivity, poverty and the disadvantage of living in the interior, forested areas the hill districts of Manipur seem to be in danger of being left alone to fight the famine alone.

In neighbouring Mizoram, the hot spot of famine, the situation was equally grave. One third of the annual harvest of 1,25,000 tonnes per year was destroyed by the rodents. About 72.5 per cent of the farmer population in the state living in 659 villages have been affected by mautam. The rats ate up 38247.1 tonnes of paddy so far. The rats did not spare even vegetables. They devoured fields of pumpkin, chilli, papaya, tomato, cabbage and squash forcing farmers to press the panic button. Vegetable growers in Kolasib, Mamit, Thingdawl and Sherdhip had lost their year's harvest to the menace.[14] The government was undecided about compensating vegetable growers. In the village of Kawnpuii, 100 kilometers away from capital Aizawl, not a single paddy stalk had been harvested. These were devastated by the rodents. The 300 odd families in the village brave hunger and starvation together. They depended on the killing of the army of rats through setting of rat-traps and receive Rs. 2 for every tail of the dead rats as per the government scheme. The night long vigil in the paddy field to trap rats yield some money to purchase rice since their harvest was destroyed in the fields itself. The state government ran food for work scheme for 10 days in the entire year effectively raising the household income up to a mere Rs. 1000. The state government also tried to address the issue through BAFFACOS (Bamboo Flowering and Famine Combat Scheme) in which there were improved methods to kill rats and a food for work scheme where an individual could earn up to Rs. 100 a day. The Chief Minister Zoramthanga wrote to the Prime Minister about the requirement of at least 10,000 metric tones of rice per month.[15] The government of Mizoram was willing to buy it even at the APL (above poverty line) rates. A granary named Joseph's granary for people in need of food during mautam had been set up by Lalbaikdiki, the wife of Chief Seceretary H Houzel as a private initiative. It initially had 7000 kgs of unhusked rice in its store. Meanwhile the state government decided to double the wages for such work and also increase rice quote from two kgs to three kgs per week per adult to mitigate the impact of the famine. The state also sent an SOS to the center to rush at least 10,000 metric tonnes of food grains, particularly rice, staple food of Mizos every month. The State Civil Supplies minister stated that the Center had agreed to supplied around 5000 tonnes of food grains a month in its first phase. The Centre had also promised that the monthly food indents would be further hiked phase wise to meet the acute food crisis. The food stocks will be sent to the railway terminus here and dispatched to Aizawl by truck via National Highway 54. The other supply route would be via Silchar-Lumding metre gauge hill section to Bairabi Mizoram's lone rail head on the Assam-Mizoram border. The Food Corporation of India had already carried 5000 tonnes of rice via this route. The state government would spend about Rs 2.5 crore every month for the transportation of food stock to the villages and ration shops in the urban belts including capital Aizawl.

But the concentration of relief on the urban works had created its own adversaries. On 19th April 2007 there was a violent demonstration by the farmers of the state protesting against the alleged government squandering of money sanctioned by the Centre (channeled through BAFFACOS) to combat the catastrophe of bamboo flowering and impending famine which turned violent. As a result 29 farmers and a police man was injured in the ensuing encounter. It was unprecedented in the history of Mizoram. Mizoram neither had any distinctive class called farmer as everyone was one, nor they had ever politically activated themselves. In a historical move the farmers across the state formed an umbrella organisation called *Zoram Kuthnathawktu Pawl* (Mizoram Farmers Association) and led a protest against the squandering of money sanctioned by the Centre for famine affected farmers. They were severely critical of the Government's policy of introducing turmeric and ginger in place of paddy as the latter crop was bound to fail during the bamboo flowering years. It warned the Government to immediately "stop its corrupt practices or else face violent consequence." ("Farmers unrest in Mizoram" in *North East Sun*, May 15, 2007, p. 10). The *Zoram Kuthnathawktu Pawl* has been the product of the politics around the prospective famine of 2007. The bamboo flowering and the consequent rat invasion had started as early as 2002. Since then the agriculturists were severely affected in Mizoram. But the Government was busy in formulating ridiculous policies like mass killing of rats and premature felling of bamboo vegetation. The government even proposed that the farmers produce turmeric and ginger (which are not eaten by rats) in place of paddy. The government promised to provide financial assistance to this endeavour and buy up the products at higher rates. But the turmeric seeds turned out to be of poor quality and that too was distributed selectively allegedly only to the ruling party supporters. The turmeric harvest was poor and the ginger harvest was refused to be bought back by the government. Hence instead of the promised Rupees ten per kilogram, ginger had been disposed off to private traders for Rupees three to five per kilogram. The farmers were suffering from bamboo flowering related crisis from 2002 to 2007 while the state government was proposing schemes after schemes as mentioned in the introductory chapter. Eventually the poverty stricken desperate farmers formed their umbrella organisation at Saitual village in 2006 and within a year more than 300 branches of it were formed across the state to protest the government's failure against famine mitigation.

The interest shown by the Central Government in the imminent Rat-famine demonstrates the insecurity of the Indian state vis-à-vis its constituents in the northeast. The region is already plagued by secessionism, insurgency, autonomy movement, and ethnic conflicts each of which challenged the Indian state. It earnestly wants to prevent another challenge from Mizoram, which since the Mizo accord (1986) remained peaceful. While it shows, on the one hand, the Indian state learned lessons from the past experience and wants to prevent a recurrence of the Mizo challenge, which sparked off from the 1959 famine. On the other hand, it also shows total lack of concern of the Indian state towards its constituents in northeast. It goes to ridiculous extent to prevent the famine fearing that a 1959 like situation does not arise. But 1959 and 2007 are two different era, nor Mizos are the same. The State of Mizoram is a Special Category State which receives 90 per cent its finances from the Centre. The people of Mizo Hills are hardly dependent on agricultural output. It does not produce even 50 per cent of its food requirement and is totally depended on the supply by the Government of India. As can be seen from the tables below.

Rice Production of Mizoram

Table 1.1 : The Area Under Rice Production

Year	*Total area (ha)*		*Percentage share of jhums*	
	Jhums	*Valleys*	*Rice area*	*Rice per capita output (Kgs)*
1980-81	55264	6923	89	63
1981-82	55858	7220	89	74
1982-83	52484	7195	88	81
1983-84	41281	6390	87	71
1984-85	43378	7486	84	75
1985-86	45920	9092	83	85
1986-87	38893	9452	80	72
1987-88	37803	10661	78	72
1988-89	36616	12772	74	62
1989-90	38349	14640	72	59
1990-91	36716	14607	72	55
1991-92	39175	16464	70	54
1992-93	43858	17439	72	58

Source : Directorate of Agriculture, Government of Mizoram, Aizawl.

Table 1.2 : Total Rice Production and Per Capita Availability

Year	*Area ha*	*Output MT*	*Per capita output (kg)*	*Deficit (Percentage)*
1974-75	47500	28490	76	58
1775-76	49201	31164	80	56
1976-77	73000	28462	70	62
1977-78	68000	16310	39	79
1978-79	64100	21000	48	74
1979-80	63200	20440	45	76
1980-81	62187	59633	126	31
1981-82	63078	30000	61	67
1982-83	59679	45953	90	51
1983-84	47671	36713	70	62
1984-85	50864	40894	75	59
1985-86	55012	64780	115	37
1986-87	48344	86745	118	36
1987-88	48464	49227	82	55
1988-89	49388	53000	85	54
1989-90	52989	59236	92	50
1990-91	51323	63794	96	48
1991-92	55639	70974	103	44
1992-93	61297	83954	118	36

Source : Area and production from Directorate of Agriculture.

N.B. Population extrapolated from census data; per capita requirement assumed as 183 kg/year

Table 1.3 : Gross Cropped Area, 1911-91

Year	*GCA (ha)*	*Percentage to total area*
1911	38228	1.81
1921	35352	1.68
1931	31652	1.50
1941	30912	1.47
1951	57893	2.75
1961	50518	2.40
1971	84626	4.01
1980	86125	4.09
1991	97540	4.63

Source : 1911-61 District Census Handbook, 1961; 1971: *Mizoram District Gazetteers*, TRI, 1989, 1980, 1991: Directorate of Agriculture, GoM; 1981 data not available.

Rice Production of Mizoram

Table 1.4 : The Area Under Rice Production

Year	*Total area (ha)*		*Percentage share of jhums*	
	Jhums	*Valleys*	*Rice area*	*Rice output (kgs)*
1980-81	55264	6923	89	63
1981-82	55858	7220	89	74
1982-83	52484	7195	88	81
1983-84	41281	6390	87	71
1984-85	43378	7486	84	75
1985-86	45920	9092	83	85
1986-87	38893	9452	80	72
1987-88	37803	10661	78	72
1988-89	36616	12772	74	62
1989-90	38349	14640	72	59
1990-91	36716	14607	72	55
1991-92	39175	16464	70	54
1992-92	43858	17439	72	58

Source: Directorate of Agriculture, Government of Mizoram, Aizawl.

Table 1.5: Total Rice Production and Per Capita Availability

Year	*Area ha*	*Output MT*	*Per capita output (kg)*	*Deficit (Percentage)*
1974-75	47500	28490	76	58
1775-76	49201	31164	80	56
1976-77	73000	28462	70	62
1977-78	68000	16310	39	79
1978-79	64100	21000	48	74
1979-80	63200	20440	45	76
1980-81	62187	59633	126	31
1981-82	63078	30000	61	67
1982-83	59679	45953	90	51
1983-84	47671	36713	70	62
1984-85	50864	40894	75	59
1985-86	55012	64780	115	37
1986-87	48344	86745	118	36
1987-88	48464	49227	82	55
1988-89	49388	53000	85	54
1989-90	52989	59236	92	50
1990-91	51323	63794	96	48
1991-92	55639	70974	103	44
1992-93	61297	83954	118	36

Source: Area and production from Directorate of Agriculture, Government of Mizoram, Aizawl.

N.B. Population extrapolated from census data; per capita requirement assumed as 183 kg/year.

Table 1.6 : Gross Cropped Area, 1911-91

Year	*GCA (ha)*	*Percentage in total area*
1911	38228	1.81
1921	35352	1.68
1931	31652	1.50
1941	30912	1.47
1951	57893	2.75
1961	50518	2.40
1971	84626	4.01
1980	86125	4.09
1991	97540	4.63

Source: 1911-61, District Census Handbook, 1961; 1971: *Mizoram District Gazetteers,* TRI, 1989;1980,1991: Directorate of Agriculture, GoM; 1981 data not available.

Table 1.7 : Select Features of Urban Centres in Mizoram

Urban centre	*Population (1991)*	*Percentage to main workers*		*Background*
		Govt.	*Business*	
Aizawl	155240	48	36	Ex-Dist. HQ market, Capital
Lunglei	34609	44	15	Dist. HQ, market
Champhai	20809	19	12	SD. HQ, WRC, ex-GC
Serchhip	13688	20	10	Block HQ, ex-GC
Saiha	13669	44	17	Dist. HQ
Kolasib	13482	27	17	SD. HQ, ex-GC
Saitual	8402	13	10	Ex-GC
Khawzawl	7104	15	7	Block HQ, ex-GC
Vairengte	5607	23	13	Market, ex-GC
Hnahthial	5548	25	9	Block HQ, ex-GC
N. Kawnpui	5290	13	9	Ex-GC
Thenzawl	4502	12	12	Ex-GC
Darlawn	3609	19	9	Block HQ, ex-GC
Mamit	3546	17	8	SD. HQ, ex-GC
Sairang	3527	19	17	Market, ex-GC
Zawlnuam	3455	22	11	Block HQ, ex-GC
Tlabung	3409	41	15	SD, HQ, ex-GC
N.Vanlaiphai	2804	23	6	WRC, ex-GC
Bairabi	2421	12	6	Rail head, ex-GC
Biate	2325	16	3	
Khawhai	2102	7	2	Ex-GC
Lengpui	1808	11	6	Model Jhumia resettlement colony, ex-GC

Source: Primary Census Abstract, 1991.

Dist. – District, HQ-Headquarters, SD-Sub-division, WRC-Wet rice cultivation, GC- Grouping centre

Table 1.8 : Distribution of Total Main Workers by Occupation, 1991

Category	*Persons*	*Male*	*Female*
Cultivators	178101	94877	83223
Agricultural labourers	9527	6181	3346
Livestock, forestry, fishing, hunting, and allied activities	3317	1904	1413
Mining and quarrying	631	604	27
Manufacturing, processing, serving, and repairs in household industry	2958	1997	961
Manufacturing, processing, servicing, and repairs in other than household industry	4606	3844	762
Construction	7158	6923	235
Trade and commerce	15078	6285	8793
Transport, storage, and communication	3304	3257	47
Other services	65637	52138	13499
Total	**290317**	**178011**	**112306**

Source : Census of India 1991, series 17, Final Population Total, Mizoram.

As can be seen from the above data that the State of Mizoram is perpetually food deficit. It is evident that neither Mizoram produces its entire food requirement nor any great part of Mizo population is entirely dependent on agriculture for their sustenance. With 90 per cent of its land rocky and mountainous and the standard agricultural practise being slash and burn it is incapable of supporting its exploding population.Therefore if 'famine' is the academic version of food shortage, the state of Mizoram is in a perpetual state of famine. One has only to examine the extent of its dependence on the centre for food supply to understand it. In fact food shortage and dependence on outside agencies like the state apparatus is a colonial legacy in Mizoram. Like any tribal economy the Mizos too produced bare minimum. The slash and burn cultivation in the rocky slopes of the mountains did not permit any surplus production. The deficit was substantiated by hunting, trade with the plains and even plunders. But the colonial state has succeeded in paralysing even that subsistence producing by discouraging slash and burn agriculture, hunting, raid and plunder as it considered these features of 'savagery.' After the initial period direct trade with the plainsmen was totally halted as the administration did not want tribesmen to come down to the plains. Professional traders from the plains were given the monopoly to trade. A number of the Mizos were employment in administrative and ecclesiastical structures which became a symbol of status and social mobility. There was soon a tendency to give up agricultural pursuits search for white collar employment. The man power short tribal economy was sure to feel the pinch. The cumulative result was disastrous. The Mizo tribal were totally dependent on the colonial apparatus for its food security as well as crisis mitigation which the colonial state did effectively. What is intriguing that such food insecurity has transcended the colonial times and remained a reality even in post-colonial times. The problem lay in the fact that both the post-Independence Mizoram state government as well as the Centre has failed to convincingly allay the fear of the Mizos that such an eventuality is unlikely and even if the predicted famine of 2007 were to become a reality, the Government of India is perfectly capable of feeding the tiny Six lakh Mizo population. The euphoria of an imminent famine also betrays the lack of time and space in the Indian think tank. Instead of trying to attempt an all round development of the people, it is concentrating on preventing famine which is anyway unlikely. This new 'concern' of the Indian state for the Mizo people is therefore another 'politics' to check prospective fissiparous tendency concerning round a famine that might never come. Even if it does come the Government of India is perfectly capable of feeding six lakh people for a short period from its reserves. The hilly state of Mizoram is now dotted with Food Corporation of India stores right into the interiors. There is a well developed network of road and communication system along with air connectivity. Hence supply of food grains to the affected people would not pose much of a problem. The fear of a repetition of a famine-connected uprising in 2007 also betrays the lack of time and space in the Indian think tank. Instead of trying to attempt an alround development of the people, it is concentrating on preventing a famine which is anyway unlikely. This new 'concern' of the Indian state for the Mizo people is therefore another 'politics' to check prospective fissiparous tendency round a famine that might never come. More shocking is the policy of doling out monetary sanctions to the state government for tackling a possible famine. It has encouraged intense competition to share the booty and bred corruption. In a recent academic gathering held in capital Aizawl (April 19-20, 2007), a University Professor requested a BBC correspondence, present in the Seminar, to kindly investigate and expose the embezzlement of funds sanctioned for famine mitigation in public interest. Indeed there are widespread discontent and allegation about the mis-utilisation of funds and its diversion to the cadres of the ruling party. The farmers have been vociferous protesters. The alienation was not confined just to the farmers alone. During the author's field study trips in Mizoram he sensed widespread discontent. Almost all sections of the population were unhappy with the way a prospective famine was being politicised and its funds were being misused. It was alleged that the ruling party was utilising the central funds in favouring and strengthening its cadres. It was also displeased that the central government is only sanctioning funds without constituting any mechanism to monitor its utilisation. Indeed, there is a simmering opposition over the issue of squandering funds meant for famine relief across all sections of the Mizo population. If these are any indications, the much publicised famine mitigation programmes of the present Mizo National Front Government might actually be its nemesis. One famine (1957) created the Mizo National Front, will the other (2007) cause its exit remains to be seen.

2

Impact of Multilingual Education on the Education of Tribal Children in Andhra Pradesh

Kandipalli Ramakrishnarao

Abstract

Multilingual Education refers to "first-language-first" education that is, schooling which begins in the mother tongue of the child and gradually moving to languages of wider.

Key Words: Multilingual Education; Tribal Education; Elementary Education in Tribal areas.

In India the indigenous people are referred to as Adivasis, Tribal people or the Scheduled Tribes (STs). The Scheduled Tribes (STs) constitute 8.6 per cent of the population of India. The Adivasi/Tribal/Scheduled Tribe (ST) child stands at the center of an educational irony. From the mainstream perspective of education, he/she is the most deprived child in the formal system of education. The all India drop-out rate for STs was 52.6 per cent for Classes I–VIII. There are 623 tribal communities in India speak 218 languages out of which 159 are exclusive to them (Singh 2002). Most of the tribal languages do not have a script and are written in the script of either the dominant regional language or another major language. The *Sixth All India Educational Survey* of the National Council of Educational Research and Training (NCERT 1999) shows that, out of 41 languages used in schools (grades 1–10) as languages of teaching or the Medium of Instruction (MoI) and as school subjects, only 13 are tribal languages. Further, only three to four of these 13 tribal languages are used regularly as medium of instruction (MoI). Less than one per cent of the tribal children have any real opportunity for education in the medium of their mother tongues. Exclusion of tribal languages in school education is problematic since a very large number of classrooms throughout the country have a sizeable proportion of tribal children. It is also quite striking that the tribal mother tongues are denied a place in formal school education in practice, despite constitutional and other policy related provisions which mandate education in mother tongues particularly for the linguistic minorities. According to the NCF-2005 children's mother tongues including tribal languages are the best medium of education at elementary level. Right to Education (RTE) Act 2009 also recommends that the medium of instructions shall as far as practicable be in the child's mother tongue. When children's mother tongues are left out of classrooms, the disadvantages that accrue to them and the resultant damage to their chances of success in schools and in life are irreversible. Classroom achievement and severe learning difficulties faced by tribal children. The problems of non-comprehension, poor academic performance in primary schools among schedule tribe children if they were taught in a language which is different from their mother tongue. The problems in tribal children's early education lead to large scale push out and cumulative failure throughout all levels of education which, in effect, push the tribal population to the lowest level of educational attainment in India. Therefore, Sarva Siksha Abhiyan (SSA) has introduced an innovative tribal education programme in Andhra Pradesh and Orissa called the Multi Lingual Education (MLE) which focusses on teaching in the mother tongue for the Primary classes to improve the quality education at elementary level in tribal areas.

Multilingual Education

Multilingual Education refers to "first-language-first" education that is, schooling which begins in the mother tongue and transitions to additional languages. Most of the MLE programmes are situated in developing countries where speakers of minority languages are tend to be disadvantaged in the mainstream education system. Research shows that children whose early education is in the language of their home tend to do better in the later years of their education. Multilingual Education is a transition programme, starting from language of child and gradually moving to languages of wider communication. Curriculum is based on local culture, using local knowledge, customs and resources through which child can develop common concepts in all areas of learning. Mother Tongue (MT) based Multilingual Education (MLE) programmes enable learners to begin their education in the language they know best. As they use their own language for learning, they are introduced to the new (official) language and begin learning to communicate in that language. At the same time, teachers help the learners develop their academic vocabulary in the new language so they can understand and talk in that language. In the MLE programmes, learners continue to develop their ability to communicate and to learn in both languages throughout Elementary Education. A widespread understanding of MLE programmes (UNESCO, 2003, 2005) suggests that instruction takes place in the following stages:

- **Stage I** - learning takes place entirely in the child's home language.
- **Stage II** - building fluency in the mother tongue. Introduction of oral L2.
- **Stage III** - building oral fluency in L2. Introduction of literacy in L2.
- **Stage IV** - using both L1 and L2 for lifelong learning.

The most Important Features of this Process are that:

- Education begins with what the learners already know, building on the language and culture, knowledge and experience that they bring with them when they start school;
- Learners gradually gain confidence in using the new (official) language, before it becomes the only language for teaching academic subjects; and
- Learners achieve grade level competence in each subject because teachers use their home language, along with the official school.

Multilingual Education in Andhra Pradesh

- The Rajeev Vidya Mission (RVM/SSA) Andhra Pradesh has started Mother Tongue (MT) based education, i.e., Multilingual Education (MLE) in tribal areas to enhance the quality of elementary education provided to the schedule tribe children. There are 35 tribal groups in Andhra Pradesh. Before Multilingual Education (MLE) was implemented in the state, same textbooks, written in Telugu script were used across districts. In 2003, a pilot project was started in eight tribal languages by the Tribal Welfare Department. Text books were developed in eight tribal languages— *Banjara, Gondi, Kolami, Konda, Kuvi, Koya Adivasi Oriya and Savara*—and the programme is being implemented in 2248 tribal Primary Schools across the State. Under this programme it is planned that the children will be taught in the mother tongue as the medium of instruction using the language primers with a gradual shift to Telugu/English medium of instruction. 20-30 schools for each language in seven districts were identified by ITDA for the purpose. Education and Tribal Welfare departments worked out plans with Linguists and Educationists for primary schooling in Tribal languages and in 2004, the Multilingual Education (MLE) programme was finally started. All the textbooks have been developed in Telugu script with mother tongue language and teachers appointed preferably from local communities in these schools are imparted special training in Multilingual Education (MLE).
- ***Current Status:*** Currently Multilingual Education (MLE) is being implemented in the state in seven districts and from grade I to grade V. The first grade V batch joined in 2009 till 2008, the programme was being implemented only in 220 schools; however the numbers of schools are reported to have been up scaled to 2248 from the academic year 2010.

• ***Languages:*** Eight tribal languages in which Multilingual Education (MLE) is being implemented are——Banjara, Rajkoya (Gondi), Kolavar (Kolami), Konda, Koya, Kuvi Adivasi Oriya and Sora (Savara).

• ***Districts:*** Srikakulam, Vizianagaram, Vishakhapatnam, Khammam, Warangal, Adilabad, and Kurnool.

• ***Number of Schools:*** 220 – pilot schools; 2248 – current number of MLE schools.

Curriculum Development: The curriculum is based on local culture, using local knowledge, custom and resources through which child can develop common concepts in all areas of learning. For the initial stage of curriculum development, studies were conducted on culture, habits, dialect and values of Tribal people concerned after extensive field visits by experts; Core teams along with local tribal teachers community elders knowledge keepers; NGOs Anthropologists, Educationalists took part in development of curriculum.

Curriculum planning in the MLE Method:

• **Class I** - Child learns in the mother tongue and the curriculum subjects are the tribal language and math.

• **Class II** - Child learns in the mother tongue and the curriculum subjects are the tribal language and math as well as Telugu (second language) orally.

• **Class III** - Language, math, environmental studies in mother tongue and Telugu introduced as second language.

• **Class IV** - Mother tongue and second language as medium of instruction (bilingual textbooks) and introducing oral third language, English.

• **Class V** - Mother tongue and second language as medium of instruction (bilingual textbooks) and reading and writing of third language (English).

• **Class VI**—Transition to second language (Telugu) as medium of instruction in all the curricular subjects.

Need for the Present Study

Multilingual Education is being implemented in 2248 schools an in eight tribal languages in Andhra Pradesh. The investigator had made a small scale research study to know the effectiveness of Multilingual Education in the tribal area of Visakhapatnam district. Visakhapatnam district has the third largest ST population in the state which accounts for 11.1 per cent of the total ST population of the state and 14.55 per cent of the total population of the district. The Multilingual Education is being implemented in *Konda, Kuvi, Adivasi Oriya* Languages in 326 elementary schools in eleven mandals in the tribal area of Visakhapatnam district. This study may provide a report on MLE i.e., problems issues and useful suggestions for more effective implementation of Multilingual Education in tribal Areas.

Statement of the Problem

"*A study on the Impact of Multilingual Education on the Education of Tribal Children.*"

Objectives

1. To study the impact of Multilingual Education on the Education of Tribal children.
2. To study the Utilisation MLE textbooks and other instructional material in tribal languages supplied to the schools.
3. To study the Enrollment, Attendance, and Achievement levels of the students in schools where Multilingual Education is provided.
4. To study perceptions of Teachers, Parents and Students towards the implementation of Multilingual Education in the tribal areas.
5. To study the problems in implementing Multilingual Education in tribal areas.

Hypotheses

1. Multilingual Education had an impact on the Education of the children of tribal areas.
2. There is effective utilisation of Multilingual Education text books in tribal languages where MLE is provided.
3. Enrollment and Attendance are improved in the schools where Multilingual Education is provided.
4. Achievement levels are improved in the schools where Multilingual Education is provided.
5. There is effective class room transaction and the students understand better in schools where Multilingual Education is provided.
6. There is an active involvement of teachers in effective implementation Multilingual Education in schools.
7. The students have the positive perception towards the implementation of Multilingual Education.
8. The parents and community members have the positive perception towards the implementation of Multilingual Education.

Sampling

The researcher selected six mandals out of eleven mandals of tribal area of Visakhapatnam district. Four mandals for each language, i.e., Konda, Kuvi, Adivasi Oriya and three schools from each mandal were selected for the study. Thus 12 schools were selected for each language and total 36 schools were selected through simple random sampling technique. The teachers from all the 36 schools were covered for the collection of data purpose. Totally 54 teachers considered as respondents for this study. Again a few parents and two students from each school were interviewed to know their opinions towards Multilingual Education.

Tool Description

This study was designed a quantitative survey through data collection, data from schools, teachers, students, and parents through observation, questionnaire and interview schedules. For this purpose the researcher designed and developed the following tools.

- *School Observation Schedule:* An observation schedule containing part-A general information regarding particulars of the school and part–B comprises questions to collect the data to assess the implementation of Multilingual Education.
- *Questionnaire for teachers:* It comprises the questions having three point Likert scale to find out the perceptions of teachers towards the implementation of Multilingual Education.
- *Interview schedule for parents:* The tool is used to assess the opinions of parents towards the implementation of Multilingual Education.
- *Interview schedule for students:* This tool is used to assess the opinions of students studying in schools where Multilingual Education is provided.
- *Achievement –Test:* To assess the achievement levels of the students in Multilingual Education the marks in the school registers were taken into consideration. The marks secured by students studying class-2 and class-3 in Baseline test and Half yearly exams in Language; Mathematics and Environmental Sciences were taken. Baseline test and half yearly marks were considered as pre-achievement test and post-achievement test marks.

Data Collection

The investigator collected the information from the selected elementary schools in tribal area of Visakhapatnam district. The school observation schedule was administered to collect the general information regarding the school and to find out the activities in implementation of Multilingual Education in the sampled schools. Through the Questionnaire the investigator collected the data from the teachers working in schools where Multilingual Education is provided. Interview schedule was used to collect the opinions of the parents and students. To assess the academic achievement of the students the Baseline test and Half-yearly marks of the students in Language Mathematics and Environmental Sciences were taken into consideration for comparison. The data collected through the observation schedule questionnaire and interview schedules was used for analytical purposes.

Analysis of Data

To know the implementation of Multilingual Education in the tribal area of Visakhapatnam district the data collected through the observation schedule questionnaire and interview schedules and documentary evidence was computed and analysed in averages and percentages.

Delimitations of the Study

Although the Multilingual Education programme is being implemented in eight tribal languages in Andhra Pradesh the present study was limited to know the implementation of Multilingual Education in the selected elementary schools of tribal area of Visakhapatnam district only. The study is also limited to collect the data from teachers, parents, students of tribal area schools where Multilingual Education is provided.

Major Findings of the Study

(I) Implementation of MLE in Schools

- It is observed that all the children in all schools have been supplied Multilingual Education text books. They are being utilised by the teachers and students for effective teaching learning process in the class rooms.
- Modules and reference books in Multilingual Education are available in 72 per cent of schools. Children Literature in Multilingual Education is available in 81 per cent of schools. It is found in schools that they are being utilised for effective implementation of Multilingual Education.
- It is observed that in schools there is implementation of preparatory activities for class1 and 2 in Multilingual Education and the children are sitting in groups and separate activities are being conducted for A, B, C Group children. Activities for remedial teaching are also being conducted for the backward students (B, C grade students) in Multilingual Education.
- It is found that all schools (100 per cent) are evaluating the progress of the students regularly in Multilingual Education. (i.e., conduct of tests etc.). It is found that in 81 per cent of schools children's work, e.g., notebooks, assignments etc is corrected regularly in Multilingual Education.
- In 61 per cent of schools there is improvement in enrollment by implementing Multilingual Education. It is observed that in 75 per cent of schools there is improvement in attendance and in 89 per cent of schools the School Grade is improved (when compared with previous school grading) by implementing Multilingual Education.
- It is found that schools are getting support and guidance from the school complex in Multilingual Education. It is observed that 72 per cent of schools by the M.E.O/M.R.Ps and 47 per cent schools by the Bhasha-coordinator and 19 per cent of schools visited by the DIET lecturers, RVM officers, D.R.Ps on implementation of Multilingual Education.
- It is found that schools are conducting SMC meetings regularly and there are discussions on Multilingual Education and schools have community involvement in Multilingual Education.

(II) Perceptions of the Teachers towards MLE

- Majority of the teachers (74 per cent) perceived that utilisation of multilingual text books is very effective in schools. It indicates multilingual text books are being utilised very effectively in classrooms for teaching learning process. It is perceived by the teachers that utilisation of modules and reference books in Multilingual Education are very effective.

• It is responded by 80 per cent of teachers' that pupils' participation in teaching learning process in Multilingual Education is very effective and 65 per cent of teachers' perceived that impact of Multilingual Education on students' understanding the lessons is effective. It is responded by 63 per cent of teachers that Multilingual Education helps the teachers maintaining discipline and class room management.

• It is perceived by 72 per cent of teachers that the progress of the students are being evaluated regularly in Multilingual Education. It reveals that evaluating the progress of the students in Multilingual Education (conduct of tests, correction of children's work, assignments etc.) is done regularly in all schools.

• It is responded by 67 per cent of teachers' that utilisation of children literature in Multilingual Education is very effective. It reveals that children literature Multilingual Education is utilised well in all schools by the teachers.

• It is expressed by 69 per cent of teachers that enrollment is improved by implementing Multilingual Education in schools and 76 per cent of teachers' perceived that Multilingual Education has an impact on attendance of the students and impact on improving school grade. It reveals that Multilingual Education has great impact on Enrollment Attendance and achievement levels of the students in the tribal area.

• It is perceived by 74 per cent of teachers' that academic guidance and support from Bhasha coordinator regarding implementation of Multilingual Education is very effective. It reveals Bhasha Coordinators giving good guidance and support for the teachers regarding the implementation of Multilingual Education is effective.

• It is responded by 61 per cent of teachers' responded that there is community and parents support in implementation of Multilingual Education in schools is very effective.

(III) Achievement Levels of the Students in MLE

• The achievement levels of the pupils studying class-2 and class-3 in Language; Mathematics; and EVS have been raised by implementing Multilingual Education. The average marks secured by the students in all subjects in half-yearly exams (Post-achievement test) are higher than the baseline test marks (Pre-achievement test).The achievement levels of the girls are higher than the boys in all subjects. When the achievements in Language and Mathematics are compared students achieved better in language than Mathematics. This reveals that Multilingual Education had impact on improving the academic achievement of the students studying at elementary level in the tribal area of Visakhapatnam district.

(IV) Opinions of the Parents towards MLE

• All the parents 100 per cent expressed their interest towards the implementation of Multilingual Education in tribal area of Visakhapatnam district.

• Majority of the parents (92 per cent) expressed that their children are interested in implementation of Multilingual Education in schools and 73 per cent of the parents told that their children are attending the school regularly because of the implementation of Multilingual Education.

• Majority of the parents 89 per cent expressed that their children had reported that they could understand the lessons better in Multilingual Education and 82 per cent of the parents told that their children studying well at home because of the implementation of Multilingual Education in schools.

• It is expressed by 76 per cent of the parents that Multilingual Education text books are good and useful for their children and 58 per cent of the parents expressed that the content in Multilingual Education text books should be more related to their tribal culture.

• It is expressed by 64 per cent of the parents that multilingual education helps their children understand the lessons better and it also helps to preserve their language and culture. And 78 per cent expressed that the teachers who know their language should be appointed in schools or the teachers may be given training in that particular language. Then only they could teach better to their students.

Opinions of the Students towards MLE

• All the students 100 per cent expressed their interest towards the implementation of Multilingual Education in their schools.

• All the students 100 per cent expressed that they would like to use Multilingual Education text books supplied to them in schools.

• It is expressed by 94 per cent of the students that they could understand the lessons better in Multilingual Education.

• It is reported by 58 per cent of the students that they have been using the children literature supplied to them in tribal languages.

Educational Implications

The present Study has great educational significance in Multilingual Education and Tribal Education. It may facilitate the policy makers. Educational administrators, Curriculum developers, Text book writers and Resource persons by providing information on what is happening at the gross root level, i.e., implementation of Multilingual Education in tribal languages in tribal area. This research study brings the following facts into lime light.

• The Multilingual education had great impact on the Elementary Education in the Tribal areas.

• The teachers need more orientation in implementation of Multilingual Education in tribal areas.

• More Resource material to be prepared and supplied to the schools on Multilingual Education for effective implementation.

• Text books should be more enriched with Local Tribal culture.

• The school complex/MRC/PMRC/DIET should act as Resource centers for academic support and guidance to the teachers in Multilingual Education.

Suggestions for Further Research

The study had given very important and useful findings on the impact of Multilingual Education on the education of tribal children. The results had given some avenues for further study relevant to the field concerned. Hence the suggestions for further research are as follows.

• A similar study can be undertaken on implementation of Multilingual Education on other tribal languages.

• A study can be conducted on the Utilisation of Multilingual Text books.

• Some studies can be undertaken on the Classroom process in Multilingual Education.

• It is also suggested to conduct a separate study the impact of Multilingual Education on achievement levels of the tribal students.

Conclusion

Multilingual Education has a great significance in developing quality Elementary Education in the tribal areas. The present study concerned with investigating the facts and effectiveness of Multilingual Education in the tribal area of Visakhapatnam district. The analysis and interpretation of data collected enabled the investigator to arrive at the following conclusions. It is observed that Multilingual Education text books in tribal languages are being utilised by the teachers and students for effective teaching learning process in the class rooms. The teachers, parents and students have positive perceptions towards the implementation of Multilingual Education. The Enrollment Attendance and Achievement levels of the tribal students have been improved due to the implementation of Multilingual Education.

References

Dhaatri Resource Centre for Women and Children (2011) *A Report on the Status of Primary Education of Adivasi Children in Andhra Pradesh and Orissa in the Context of the Right to Education Act 2009.* Secuderabad A.P. India.

MHRD (2011), *Working Group Report on Elementary Education for the 12th five year plan,* Department of School Education and Literacy MHRD Govt. of India , New Delhi.

Mohanty, A.K. (1990), "*Psychological consequences of mother tongue maintenance and multilingualism in India.*" In D. P. Pattanayak (Ed.), *Multilingualism in India* (pp. 54-66). Clevedon: *Multilingual Matters.*

NCERT (2005*), National Curriculum Frame work -2005 Position papers* NCERT Aurobindo Marg, New Delhi.

NCERT (2009), *Multilingual Education in Orissa,* NCERT, New Delhi.

NMRC (2009), *Andhra Pradesh- MLE Status Report* National Multilingual Resource Centre (NMRC) JNU, New Delhi.

NMRC (2010), *Resources for Multilingual Education in India* National Multilingual Resource Centre (NMRC) JNU, New Delhi.

Sujatha, K.(1999), *Education of Indian Schedule Tribes: A study of community schools in the district of Visakhapatnam* I.I.E.P. UNESCO Paris.

UNESCO (2003), *Education in a Multilingual World.* Paris, UNESCO.

UNESCO (2007), *Advocacy kit for promoting multilingual education: Including the excluded.* Bangkok, UNESCO Asia and the Pacific Regional Bureau for Education.

UNESCO (2011), *Multilingual education in Nepal: A Report,* UNESCO Paris.

World Bank, (2005). *In their Own Language: Education for All.* New York: World Bank.

http://ssa.ap.nic.in

www.nmrc-jnu.org

http://unesdoc.unesco.org

3

Status of Women and Girl Child in Lambada Community: A Study of South Telangana Region of Andhra Pradesh

M. Ramulu

Introduction

India is a country where several communities have been living right from the beginning of Indus civilisation. The earlier texts like Puranas, Vedas, Mahabhartam, Itihasas and some mythological stories have mentioned that the Indian society has been divided into four communities. They are forward castes, Other Backward Castes, Scheduled Castes and Scheduled Tribes. The first three communities have been living within the society. And the fourth community that is tribes has been put aside to the mainstream activities. They have been living in isolated areas. Since their birth, they continue to live in the forests and sustaining through the years. Therefore, they are being called as Adivasis and also Atavikas. They slowly and steadily began to enter into limelight activities. Further, some remarkable developments have also taken place. Finally, the Constitution of India recognised them and included in one of the schedules of the constitution (Vth schedule) stating that they should be provided reservations in all the fields where they fit. At present, they are called as scheduled tribes.

Surprisingly, India is one of the countries which have the large number of tribal population in the world. According to John K Thomas, there are 573 tribes living across the country including all states and union territories.[1] Orissa is the state which has the largest number of tribes, as many as 62 tribal communities comparing with any other Indian State.[2]

Andhra Pradesh is also having quite a good number of tribal populations. According to Andhra Pradesh Tribal Culture Research and Training Institute survey, there are 35 scheduled tribes spreading all over the districts of Andhra Pradesh. Out of these 35 scheduled tribes 12 tribal groups have been categorised as primitive tribal groups. According to 2001 census report, the total number of tribal population in Andhra Pradesh is 50.24 lakhs. They constitute 6.59 per cent of the total population.[3]

The Lambadas

Among the 35 tribes of Andhra Pradesh, the Lambada community is perhaps one community which has the large number of population. The available literature mentioned that their complexion is very good and multi talented tribe inhabiting whole Andhra Pradesh except in East Godavari, Vishakapatnam, Vijayanagaram and Srikakulam. They have their own culture, ethnic identity. They generally prefer to live in special settlements of their own called thandas (Hamlet). The Costal and Rayalaseema region Lambadas are included in Scheduled Tribes list in 1956.[4] But the Telangana region Lambadas incorporated in Scheduled Tribes list in 1977.[5]

According to Shamala Devi Rathod, the word Lambada is synonym of Lambadi, Banjara, and Sugali.[6] She opined that the name of Lambada is probably derived from the Sanskrit word '*Lavan*' which means salt. Earlier, the Lambadas are traditionally engaged in salt business. The word *Lavan* slowly evolved into Lambada. Another synonym of Lambadas is Banjara. The Banjara Seva Sangh Report (1967) suggested that Banjara term derived from Sanskrit word *Vanijyam* meaning trade. 'Vanachara' means wanders in the forest, which denotes their nomadic nature. In the course of the time, the word Vanachara might have changed into Banjara. One Lambada old man expressed his view that they are called Lambadas because they are very tall. The word has been derived from the word 'lamba' which means tall. Lambada signifies the tallness of the person. Another synonym is '*Sugalis*' which means people taking care of cows. The explanation of Sugalis is fresh air breathers.

According to Cheenya Naik and Gona Naik Lambadas are the successors of Prithviraj Chauhan who fought against Mohammad Ghori.[7] After Prithviraj Chauhan was defeated them, they hided themselves in the forests, and changed their dress and language to protect themselves from Mohammed Ghori's army and started wandering in the forests as Vanacharis. It is a belief that the word Banjara taken its origin from Vanacharis. They settled as traders in various places of Rajasthan. Afterwards, they migrated to southern states and settled in different states under different communities. In Karnataka, Himachal Pradesh and Delhi they categorised as scheduled castes. In Maharashtra, Rajasthan, Punjab, Madhya Pradesh, they are listed in backward community. In Orissa, Bihar and Andhra Pradesh, they are categorised as scheduled tribes.

Even though Banjaras settled in various places, they maintain same language that is Banjara Language. Ghorbholi is their traditional language. Men wears dhoti, upper garment and bright colour turbans and women wears 'langa' richly embroidered with mirrors and several folds. This varies from state to state. The Lambada tribe is divided in to five 'pharatries'[8]: 1. Bhukya, 2. Vadthiya, 3. Chowhan, 4. Pamar and 5. Banoth. These pharatries are further divided into number of groups called pada or jath clan in their language. Bhukya pharatry consists of 27 clans, Vadthiya-52, Chowhan-6, Pamar-12, and Banoth -13. All these Lambadas are experts in cattle breeding. They settled in modern times on land and became good agriculturists. From ancient period to modern age, they are living in the villages and they settled in their own settlements called 'thandas'. Those who settled well migrated to the neighbouring cities. We should not forget that 90 per cent of the Lambadas are still living in thandas as agriculturists and agriculture labourers in very critical conditions.[9]

Status of Women

Lambada Women

Social Status

Today's societies are constantly aiming for the high and dignified objectives. Males and females are important players in the growth process. However, in many societies, there is always a question mark regarding the social status of women. In such a scenario, education can play a decisive role in enhancing their status since it increases their awareness and opens up more employment opportunities for them. Therefore, the present study critically examined some of the related social issues like education, decision making, gender inequality, housing conditions and association with social groups such as DWACRA and other communitarian groups.

Women in Decision-making

Social scientists are very fond of speaking at length on the need for treating women with consideration and respect and giving heed to their opinions. What is the ground reality in the area under survey? The responses in this regard are presented in the Table 3.1 below.

Table 3.1 : Role of Women in Decision-making

Response	*Frequency*	*Percentage*
Women	07	11.4
Collectively	25	41.0
Men	29	47.6
Total	**61**	**100**

It can be seen that the largest number of respondents (47.6 per cent) stated that decisions are taken by men alone. Significantly, 41.0 per cent of the respondents said that decisions are taken collectively. A relatively small number of respondents (11.4 per cent) averred that they are independent in taking decisions in their family matters. A few respondents mentioned that their husbands welcome suggestions from them; but in most cases, the final decision is the prerogative of males. So, we could see that Lambada women generally have a lesser say in decision making.

Gender Discrimination

Gender discrimination has become a major problem in India. Even in the so-called advanced and developed societies, we hear of social evils like dowry, physical assault, abusiveness, male domination, etc. Does a similar situation exist in the Lambada community as well?

Table 3.2 : Whether there is Gender Discrimination in the Community

Response	*Frequency*	*Percentage*
Yes	47	77
No	11	18
No comment	3	4.9
Total	**61**	**100**

It is disquieting to note that majority of the respondents (77 per cent) stated that they have been subjected to gender discrimination. According to them, during childhood, a female is under the control of her father or brother. After her marriage, she is dominated by her husband or head of the family, and in her old age, she is under the control of her sons. A very noticeable fact that emerged is that 18 per cent of the respondents said that they were not under the control of men. Also, 4.9 per cent respondents had no comment on this issue. Hence, it can be concluded that majority of Lambada women are under the control of men.

Domestic Violence

In Lambada community, women work hard at home and even outside the home. Their hard work is generally not recognised. Such situations can, at times, lead to marital discord. Disputes often take place due to misunderstandings. In such a case, there is a strong possibility of the wife being physically manhandled. Let us see what our respondents had to say on this issue.

Table 3.3 : Incidence of Domestic Violence

Response	*Frequency*	*Percentage*
Yes	40	65.6
No	10	16.4
No comment	11	18
Total	**61**	**100**

It is rather unfortunate that a very large number of respondents (65.6 per cent) reported that they were beaten up by their husbands on various pretexts, while 16.4 per cent of them said that their husbands did not beat them. The remaining 18 per cent did not have any comments on this issue. Either they were too shy or afraid to tell the truth. However, the fact remains that majority of the women are physically assaulted.

Economic Status

Economical conditions are important indicators of the socio-economic condition of a family or a community. Economic conditions depend on several sub factors. Let us examine some of the indicators in respect of the Lambadas, particularly, the women.

Land Ownership

Land is often seen as a major determinant of prosperity of an individual or a family. As already mentioned, the Lambadas migrated to other areas from North India and initially settled here as traders. They began to engage themselves in various occupation before settling in agriculture. It took several years to transform in to this field. In the process of evolution, the contribution of Lambada woman cannot be ignored. But, even as the Lambadas consolidated their position, they started subjecting their women to discrimination. They were seldom given an equal share in the land.

Table 3.4 : Land Ownership Pattern

Response	*Frequency*	*Percentage*
Yes, in the name of HOF	12	19.6
Yes, in the name of husband	22	36.1
Yes, in the name of children	00	-----
Yes, in the name of R & HOF	04	6.6
No land property (landless people)	23	37.7
Total	**61**	**100**

It can be seen from the above Table that the largest proportion (37.7 per cent) do not own any landed property. Obviously, they work as labourers on lands owned by others. The next significant number of respondents (36.1 per cent) said that the land is in the name of their husbands. This is followed by those who said that the ownership vests with the head of the household (19.6 per cent). No respondent said that the land is held in the name of the children or herself. It, thus, emerges that women and the children in the study area and the community do not have land ownership rights. During personal interaction, it came to light that even among those owning land, most are small land owners, having less than three acres and very few persons own 10-20 acres of land.

Income Level of Respondents

Family income is of great consequence to any individual. It can determine the quality of life that he and his family enjoy.

Table 3.5 : Income Sources of the Respondents

Main Income Source	*Frequency*	*Percentage*
Agriculture	9	14.8
Labour	26	42.6
Self-employment	4	6.6
Job	1	1.6
Agriculture and labour	16	26.2
Agriculture and business	3	4.9
Agriculture and job	2	3.3
Total	**16**	**100**

The above Table speaks about the income sources of the respondents. It can be seen that labour is the major source of the majority (42.6 per cent). This is followed by agriculture and labour (26.2 per cent), self-employment (6.6 per cent) and agriculture and business (4.9 per cent). The number of those in service (government or private) is very insignificant.

Cattle Property

The study also focused on the cattle property of the selected households. Apart from own land and agriculture, cattle are important sources of income in the Lambada community. Hence, this is being considered one of the important features to calculate the economic status of the respondents. These Lambadas owns large number of cattle in their respective houses. Feeding cattle has become part of their day to day life and also hereditary since the ages. The study came to know the importance of cattle after visiting the field. The following table exposes the respondent's cattle property of each individual family.

Table 3.6 : Cattle Wealth of the Respondents

Response	*Frequency*	*Percentage*
Yes	40	65.6
No	21	34.4
Total	**61**	**100**

The table brings out that the larger number of respondents (65.6 per cent) own cattle, which helps to increase the income level of the family. Even those who do not own land, depends on the cattle to strengthen their economic status. In this cattle rearing job, women and dropout girl children are largely engaged.

Table 3.7 : Ownership Pattern Regarding Cattle

Response	*Frequency*	*Percentage*
No cattle	21	34.4
Only bullocks	09	14.8
Only cows	14	23.0
Only goats	04	6.6
Only buffalos	02	3.3
Only sheep	03	4.9
Bullocks, cows and buffalos	05	8.2
All above animals	03	4.9
Total	**61**	**100**

As seen from the above Table, 34.4 per cent of the respondents do not own cattle. Of those who do own cattle, the largest two numbers are in respect of: only cows (23.0 per cent), and only bullocks (14.4 per cent). A noticeable number of respondents (8.2 per cent) reported owning bullocks, cows and buffalos and 6.6 per cent stated that they owned only goats. During personal interaction with the respondents, it was found that children are being withdrawn from schools so that they could tend to the cattle. Another interesting fact that emerged is that since many families have fewer number of children, Lambadas are tending to maintain fewer heads of cattle.

Savings and Debts

Both are important determinants of the degree of prosperity of a household. In many cases, it is lack of sufficient savings that drives a person to fall into the debt trap. This is more so when he is faced with an unavoidable financial commitment. Such persons are easy prey for loan sharks who advance loans at very cruel rates of interest.

Savings

These are generally conditioned by two factors—the income level and the expenditure of the individual and his household. When the income and extent of savings can cater for the expenditure—normal and for meeting obligatory (festivals, marriage of daughters) and unforeseen (like illness in the family)—there may not be any need to go in for loans. During the course of interaction with the respondents, it was seen that 95.08 per cent respondents stated that they have no capacity to save the money for meeting any future needs, like education of their children.

Debts

Due to the gap between income and expenditure, men tend to fall into the debt trap. The sources of loans may be banks, moneylenders, or relatives.

Table 3.8 : Sources of Loan for the Respondents

Response and source of loan	*Frequency*	*Percentage*
Yes, from Bank	18	29.5
Yes, from moneylenders	30	49.2
Yes, from others/relatives	06	9.8
No debts	07	11.5
Total	**61**	**100**

A rather unhappy situation that has emerged is that close to 50 per cent of the respondents have taken loans from money lenders. On the positive side is the fact that 11.5 per cent of the respondents reporting that they are not indebted to anybody. Despite the normal perception that banks do not readily advance loans to the poor sections of society, 29.5 per cent of the respondents said that they had taken loans from banks. The rest seven (11.5 per cent) reported that they are indebted to their relatives as well as to known persons. Some reported whenever they require money immediately, they approach government agencies like banks, since they find it difficult to get money from their relatives. Many of the respondents are landless or small landholders, who may not always be able to furnish the necessary collaterals for obtaining bank loans. Hence, they perforce have to depend on moneylenders, often by paying heavy rates of interest to them.

Housing Condition

Housing is one of the basic necessities of every human being. It provides shelter and protects people from the good and bad weather conditions. The following Table depicts the housing conditions of the respondents.

Table 3.9 : Housing Conditions of the Respondents

Types of House	*Frequency*	*Percentage*
Pakka	47	77
Kacha	11	18
RCC Roof	3	4.9
Total	**61**	**100**

Before analysing the figures that emerged, it would be appropriate to get an understanding of the different types of dwelling units. A *pakka* house is one that can withstand extreme weather conditions like heavy rains or strong winds. A *kacha* house is one that is just better than a hut.

An encouraging fact that can be seen from the above Table is that the majority (77 per cent) of the respondents are residing in *pakka* houses, even though these may be a bit cramped. At least these keep them safe from the extremes of weather. The next largest number of respondents (18 per cent) are residing in *kacha* houses. It emerges that, at least in this area, the Lambadas have been very prudent.

Membership of Self-Help Groups (SHGs)

Self-Help Groups are envisaged to give the members a sense of identity and open up income generating avenues for them. Governments are also motivating the rural women to seek membership of self-help groups. What is the response of Lambada women towards SHGs?

Table 3.10 : Whether a Member of any Self-Help Group

Response	*Frequency*	*Percentage*
Yes	47	77.0
No	14	23.0
Total	**61**	**100**

A positive fact that can be seen is that the majority (77 per cent) of the respondents are members of SHGs. This shows that in this community, women are aware of initiatives established for their welfare and are positively reacting to these. Unfortunately, not all of them could tell the name of their self help group. They mentioned that they were facing problems like difficulty in getting loans from the banks. Some of them do not know anything because they are illiterate. Henceforth, they are unable to motivate others to join their group. Hence, it is can be surmised that the majority members of self help groups (SHGs) are lacking proper guidance. They know nothing about the schemes that are designed for their benefit.

Educational Background

Education can be an important indicator of a person's socio-economic status. The below table illustrates the educational backdrop of the respondents.

Table 3.11 : Educational Background of the Respondents

Educational level	*Frequency*	*Percentage*
Illiterate	49	80.3
Primary	5	8.2
Secondary	2	3.3
Higher	5	8.2
Total	**61**	**100**

It can be seen that the largest proportion (80.3 per cent) of the respondents are illiterates. The second spot is shared by those with education upto primary and higher educational levels (8.2 per cent each). This clearly brings out the fact that majority of the respondents do not have an adequate educational background, which may be impacting the degree of importance given to them in their community.

Health Condition of Lambada Women

Health is one of the important indicators of an individual, especially in the case of women. However, it is seen that in a lot of cases, adequate attention is not being paid to the health of women. The Lambada women are not an exception to this state of negligance. Let us now see some of the factors that can impact the health status of women in the study area.

Marriage

Marriage is highly important occasion in any family. Marriages in rural areas often take place at an early age. These early marriages tend to have an adverse effect on the health of women. Early marriages can lead to early pregnancy with the consequent ill health associated with that. Let us first see the responses regarding the age of marriage of females in the study area.

Table 3.12 : Age of Marriage

Age	*Frequency*	*Percentage*
12-14 years	2	3.3
14-18 years	52	85.2
18 years above	7	11.5
Total	**61**	**100**

It can be seen that the most 'favoured' age spans are 14 to 18 years (85.2 per cent) and above 18 years (11.5 per cent). The instances of child marriage are relatively insignificant (only 3.3 per cent). The large incidence of teenage marriages appears to be primary reason for the poor health of Lambada women. Although there is a law regarding the minimum marriageable age of females, the law is being flouted in this community. There appears to be more concern about their daughters' marriage rather than the policies. The early marriage is also leading to ill-health of the newly born infants.

Health Services

There are many health conditions, which can be treated only by qualified medical personnel. If these conditions are left unattended, there is always the risk of complication arising later on. Women can have some specific medical issues (like pregnancy) which need to be properly monitored. What is the availability of medical services in relatively remote places, like our study area?

The following Table makes interesting reading. Majority of the respondents (88.5 per cent) said that proper medical service were not available in their Thandas. During personal interaction, many of the respondents said that they have to depend medical services available in the nearest towns. This issue needs to be addressed on priority. As regards awareness about pre-natal care, child immunisation and feeding practices, the larger number of respondents (57.4 per cent) replied in the affirmative. However, many of them do not know the chronological order of immunisation in pre-delivery and post-delivery

Table 3.13 : Availability of Medical Services

Objectives	*Percentage of Yes*	*Percentage of No*	*Total and Percentage*
Are proper medical services available in your Thanda?	7 11.5	54 88.5	61 (100)
Are you aware of pre-natal care, child immunisation, and feeding practices?	35 57.4	26 42.6	61 (100)
Is the hospital a safe place for delivery?	11 18.1	50 81.9	61 (100)
Is the home safer for delivery than a hospital?	50 81.9	11 18.1	61 (100)
Are you aware that first Breast feed is very essential for the new born baby?	15 24.5	46 75.5	61 (100)
Have any cases of women/child deaths occurred in your family in the past five years, due to illness?	16 26.2	45 73.8	61 (100)
Are you affected with any gynecological problems in the past five years?	30 49.1	31 50.9	61 (100)
Are you aware of primary treatment for normal diseases?	44 72.1	17 27.9	61 (100)
Do you know the effects of fluoride infected water?	54 88.6	7 11.4	61 (100)
Do you have proper drinking water facilities in your Thanda?	52 85.3	9 14.7	61 (100)

period. The noticeable number of negative responses (42.6 per cent) is certainly a cause of disquiet which needs to be addressed on priority. As regards the place considered safe for deliveries, the opinions in favour of the home and hospital were equally divided. The study found some of women were attracted by the state government welfare schemes like '*Janani suraksha yojana*' and went to hospitals to give birth to children. However, some household still continue to repose faith in the traditional delivery process.

A very positive fact that emerged is that the majority (75.5 per cent) of the respondents said that they were aware about the importance of breast feeding for new born infants. As regards deaths of women and children due to illness during the last five years, 73.8 per cent reported in the negative. More than 50 per cent of the respondents reported that they did not suffer from any gynecological problems during the last five years. However, this type of response should not be taken at face value since some of the respondents may have given this reply out of ignorance.

A significantly large number of respondents (72.1 per cent) respondents stated that they were aware about the primary treatment for normal diseases like fever, cold, etc. However, the treatment here should be taken as the traditional forest-based not - and not the scientific one. As regards the effects of consuming fluoride infected water, 88.6 per cent of the respondents were aware of the negative consequences. To the query regarding availability of proper drinking water facilities, 85.2 per cent of the respondents said that they have drinking water facilities of Krishna River. But the supply is limited since water is released only for a couple of hours. Those who do not have access to drinking water facilities, have to go far to fetch the drinking water.

It can thus be seen that the health condition of Lambada women is very low because of some unhealthy practices. They don't get proper guidelines from the voluntary organisations and the governmental organisations like CHW (Community Health Worker), and ICDS (Integrated Child Development Scheme) members, etc.

Discrimination against the Girl Children

Parents Attitudes towards Girl Child

The married women feel so happy when she is pregnant. She gets respected by all her neighbours. However, once the gender of the child is known, the attitude of the parents can come to the fore. How did the respondents react to thc query on this issue?

Table 3.14 : Attitude Towards the New Born Girl Child

Response	*Frequency*	*Percentage*
Satisfactory	27	44.3
Dissatisfactory	34	55.7
Total	**61**	**100**

Not surprisingly, the largest number of respondents (55.7 per cent) expressed dissatisfaction over the presence of girl children in the family. However, a still noticeable number (44.3 per cent) were satisfied. At the time of pregnancy itself, speculation starts whether it would be a boy or a girl. Unfortunately, if a woman delivers a girl child, this will be the beginning stage for a kind of family problems. Finally, this is resulting in breaking the marriage bonds. This kind of blind belief seems to be deeply rooted in the Lambada community. Why this kind of practice occurred in Lambada community? The study found that this kind of shift taken place because nowadays, the tribal people are considering the girl child as a burden to the family.

Is Girl Child Burden to Parents?

The girl child in such societies is indeed placed in an unenviable position. On one side, she can be treated as an unpaid labourer for performing all types of domestic chores like cooking food, washing clothes and looking after her younger siblings. On top of that, she may be required to assist her parents in their income generating activities. On the other side, is the 'obligation' to pay bride price for her marriage at a subsequent stage. It may not be totally wrong to term the girl child in such communities as a 'necessary evil'. Let us see the attitude of the respondents towards the girl child.

Table 3.15 : Is the Girl Child a Burden to the Family?

Response	*Frequency*	*Percentage*
Yes	38	62.3
No	22	36.1
No comment	01	1.6
Total	**61**	**100**

Not surprisingly, the majority (62.3 per cent) considered the girl child as a burden to the family. However, there was still a noticeable number (36.1 per cent) who did not think so. The respondents cited a number of reasons for considering the girl child as burden to the family. The reasons for such a perception will be discussed in the paragraph below.

Reasons for Perceiving the Girl Child as a Burden

Academics and decision-makers may love to make long speeches on the need to empower women but there is still a huge gap between preaching and actual practice. If this is the case with the so-called developed societies, what are the perceptions regarding girl children in relatively under-developed communities. What are the possible reasons for giving the girl children such a 'poor deal'?

Table 3.16 : Reasons for Considering the Girl Child a Burden

Sr. No.	*Reason*	*Frequency*	*Percentage*
1.	Dowry	24	39.3
2.	More restrictions and expensive	27	44.3
3.	Both Serials 1 and 2 above	10	16.4
	Total	**61**	**100**

The primary reason cited by most respondents (44.3 per cent) was that extra care needs to be taken regarding the health, safety (including the need to protect them from possible molestation) and upbringing of girl children. The next larger category of respondents (39.3 per cent) cited the obligation of having to pay dowry at a later stage. The rest of the respondents mentioned both reasons.

PART-C

Girl Children Selling Cases

This part of the study deals with some of the girl child selling cases that the author came across during his field work. Initially, there was reluctance to discuss the issue and it needed a lot of persuasion before the persons concerned agreed to open up. According to some individuals, this is a recent practice. Altogether, the author heard about 20 cases in three villages of Devarakonda mandal in Nalgonda district, but he could gather meaningful information about only nine of these. These cases are discussed below. These will give an idea of the compulsions and circumstances that are forcing parents to choose such an option.

Case 1

Jarpula Lalitha is a 30 years old divorcee woman from Jarpula thanda and a resident of Mudigonda village in Devarakonda mandal, Nalgonda district of Andhra Pradesh. At the age of 14 years, she was married off to Dasuru a resident of Dubba thanda. Dasuru is an illiterate. He is a landless and daily wage labourer. After four years of their marriage, she was blessed with a female child. This is where the disputes began in their happy relationship. Despite family disputes, they both continued to live together. After two years, she gave birth to a male child. Dasuru has the habit of drinking alcohol and arrack. Whatever money is being earned by him will be spent on drinking. He never bothered about his family and children. He would come home after drinking, and start scolding and harassing his wife and physically assault her and the children. On several occasions, Lalitha went to her parents' home as she couldn't bear the torture. Her parents used to convince her and send her back. With the assurance given by the Naik, the head of the thanda, she decided to stay with him. Her husband continued to behave in the same manner. Rather he increased his bad behaviour with his wife. She was also beaten up by him without any fault. One day, as usually, he came with his routine drinking attitude, and started quarreling with her and beat her up. He picked up an axe and attempted to murder her. Fortunately, she escaped and decided to go to her parents along with children. Her parents have already reached old age. They are not in a position to help her and her children. But they have given a separate plot for her to stay. She built a hut on her own and is living with her children in Jarpula Thanda. Couple of months later, a panchayat was held under the headship of both the Thanda Naiks. In that meeting, her husband strongly refused to accept them as his wife and children. She too decided not to stay with him. At last, in the presence of both Naiks, they agreed to go for divorce. Their marriage has been broken up. The judges did not assure any kind of financial support from her husband. With the verdict given by the Naiks, she has to take care of her children as her husband did not want them as his children. She took the complete responsibility of her children. She is not supported either by her parents or anybody else. As the days are passing, she is finding it difficult to raise her children. She curses herself for having such a miserable life. Having such critical situations, she decided to sell her children. With the help of one of her well wishers, she sold her two children (Bujji four years and Suresh two years) to a person who is living in Hyderabad, for Rs 500. She is now leading a happier life.

To the query whether she was in touch with her children, she replied that she did not know their present whereabouts. However, she did express regret for committing such a mistake. She sometimes, feels lonely at her home.

Case 2

Jarpula Salibai, aged 35 years and wife of Vasram Naik, hails from Jarpula Thanda. The couple are residents of Mudigonda village in Devarakonda Mandal, Nalgonda district of Andhra Pradesh. Both husband and wife are illiterate and daily agricultural labourers. They have a son (Neelya Naik 13 years) and two daughters (Jyoti eight years and other one yet to be named). Vasram Naik is a tuberculosis patient. He has been suffering from this disease for a long time. His mother (75 years) is also staying with him. Salibai is the only working women in their family. Due to several problems at home, she insisted that her son be withdrawn from school and inducted as a worker. In this critical situation, her husband's health deteriorated and doctors advised him to get operated. Since the operation would be quite expensive, she decided to sell her unnamed daughter (approximately eight months). She found a broker named Shivram. She finally sold her daughter for Rs 8,000 to a man is living in Dilsukhnagar, Hyderabad the money acquired by her is now being spent on her husband. He is now feeling better and living happy life. At the moment, they are living in a small hut. When asked whether she feel bad for committing such big mistake, she defended herself by saying dowry has become inevitable in their community. Therefore, she took this step. She is now optimistic about her daughter's future that she might be living happily somewhere. Initially, she refused to share about the incident. She discussed the issue with the author only after getting an assurance that the matter would not be revealed to anyone. She did not want to speak about it because of the fear of the police. Even, her husband expressed the same feelings. They have the mindset that several people have come but none of them helped them.

Case 3

Nenavath Nari, a 40 years old woman, is the wife of Dharma from Achamma Kunta Thanda and has been living in Mudigonda. She has a son (Bhaskar 20 years) and four daughters (Bhagya 18 years recently married, Sharada 14 years, Uma 11years, and an unnamed baby five months). After her first male child, she continuously gave birth to four daughters. They awaited one more delivery but, that failed due to some health reasons. They got disgusted with the girl child in the last delivery. They decided to give away one of their daughters. One woman (Jooli) approached them and introduced herself as one of the members of mission compound of Devarakonda town. She convinced them to give away one of their daughters. She introduced them to another woman from Hyderabad as one who was childless and was keen to adopt a child. Finally the matter as adoption of their younger child was settled and a gift of Rs 500 was given to the family. Nenavath Nari cited reasons like providing insufficient food to her daughter, inability to educate her children, etc., for agreeing to this 'transaction'. Later, the family came to know that they were cheated by Joolie.

Nari does not know to whom the child was actually sold. Both husband and wife made efforts to meet Jooli, but used to escape whenever she saw them.

Case 4

Amgoth Laxmi is a 30 years old and wife of Hanumanthu from Amgoth Sitya Naik Thanda of Mudigonda in Devarakonda mandal. They too are uneducated and landless labourers. They have five daughters (Mounika ten years, Layala eight years, Anitha six years, Pavani four years, Soni 1 month old). Since she wanted male child, she was not ready for tubectomy operation. But, she gave birth to five girls one after another. Her husband was unhappy and began to torture her. He was also blaming her for not producing a single male child. So, she decided to do something as she was harassed by her husband every day. She took a decision to give away her fifth child. Her husband has a very good friend in Adilabad who is a rich man and had no children. She spoke to him and took a decision to give her child. The man happily agreed after listening to her situation. She placed all of her five daughters in front of him. He made sure that he would visit her once again. He came after a week as he promised to her. Finally, he wished to take her fifth child named Soni who is by then one month old. He took Soni along with him. This is how she gave away one of the five children. This incident has taken place in the year of 2004. But, she refused to reveal his name. All this happened because of her husband's wrong behaviour in the family.

Case 5

Mudavath Maroni (30 years) is the wife of Pratap, from Janyanaik Thanda. She is a resident of Kondamalle Pally village of Devarakonda mandal. She has two sons (Prakash twelve years, Chandar ten years) and one daughter (Neelima seven years). In fact, she has two daughters. But, she sold out her second daughter due to several family problems. That's why she is now claiming, I have only one daughter. She actually sold her second daughter but, she managed to convince everyone that she passed away. She sold her daughter to one voluntary organisation known as Mission Compound which is located very close to their Thanda in Devarakonda. Initially, she refused to discuss the matter with the author. Finally, with great reluctance, she agreed to speak about what all happened. In this case too, adverse circumstances drove the family to take such a step.

Case 6

Nenavath Neela is a 30 years old woman living with her husband Bojya Naik in the hamlet of Kevla thanda of Konda Mallepally in Devarakonda Mandal. She has one son (Sudhir 15 years) and five daughters (Vijaya 13 years, Surekha 13 years, Kamala nine years, Vani seven years and Priya two years). As in the earlier cases, she too initially declined to speak about the matter. It needed a lot of patience and persistence to get her to reveal what all happened. She has a very good family friend, Shankar. He once brought a rich man named Krishna a doctor by profession from Hyderabad. He was not having any children. Shankar played a very crucial role in resolving their family problems. After some discussion, both husband and wife decided to give away their fifth child named Priya to Krishna. After that, their daughter was taken to Hyderabad. Unfortunately, few days later, Shankar, who settled the matter, passed away. With this, their communication link with their daughter got broken. Now, they do not know where their daughter is. But, they are hopeful that she is happy somewhere.

To the query whether their financial woes have now eased, the couple replied that they are still facing financial problems. Their income level is very low. Agriculture is the only source through which they earn money and sustain themselves.

Case 7

Ramavath Sakri is the wife of Basha and a resident of Ramavath Thanda in Gottimukkakla of Devarakonda mandal. She has three sons (Ramesh fifteen years, Narsing twelve years and Naresh nine years) and one daughter (Bharati seven years). Actually, she had another daughter, whom she gave for adoption.

When the author contacted Ramavath Sakri and her husband on this issue, they initially denied giving up their girl child to others. It was only after some persuasion that the couple agreed to discuss this matter after taking a promise that this would not be reported to the police. She confessed that they found it difficult to bring up all their children and started looking for some solution to this problem. They both met one of their relatives who had been living in Hyderabad for years together. They also came to know that this person did not have children and was willing to adopt the second daughter of Basha and Sakri. They gave away their second daughter in adoption. She is now going to school in Hyderabad and living happily with her new parents. Basha and Sakri now and then go to Hyderabad and visit her.

Case 8

Nenavath Suvali, a 30 years old woman, is the wife of Balaram from Jal Thanda and a resident of Mudigonda village in Devarakonda Mandal. They belong to a poor and landless family. They have four daughters (Revati ten years, Renuka eight years, Kasthuri six years, and Rupa one year) and one son (Rajesh two years). They mostly depend on manual work for their sustenance. They were always in deep depression since they were unable to provide a better life to their children. This feeling of helplessness probably goaded them to give away their last child named Rupa to someone. Therefore, they consulted one of the brokers called Ramulu from Chandampet and conveyed their decision. The broker agreed to show a better life to their daughter and motivated them to go ahead. They sold their daughter to a man who came from Hyderabad. Unfortunately, the matter was reported to the police, who, along with ICDS (Integrated Child Development Scheme) officials, enquired into the matter. This couple explained the difficulties that they had been facing right from their marriage. Apparently the police was not convinced and filed a case against them and the broker. They were put behind bars for about three days for interrogation. However, they were released soon. Even the child, who was sold out to a Hyderabadi, is now with her parents and is now going to school. They are bit upset over the matter. Balaram also warned me not to write anything bad about them. He defended himself by stating that they thought of giving a better life to at least one daughter. But, "unfortunately, she is with us now. We are still struggling to get better life," he lamented.

Case 9

Nenavath Kamli is the wife of Chandu, living in Kunkudu Chettu Thanda. They have four daughters (Pramila twelve years, Geetha nine years, Sumalatha six years, and Saritha four years) and one son Baburam (three years). Before Saritha was born, her parents decided to give away their third daughter Sumalatha to someone. The broker was helpful in settling the matter. He brought a party from Hyderabad and helped to sell their third daughter Sumalatha for Rs 2500. Fifteen days later, an Anganwadi worker (Rani) and resident of Nagula Pally village informed the police. The police arrested the parents, broker and the persons who purchased the daughter. However, due to the intervention of the police, Sumalatha was brought back. She is now six years old and staying with her grandmother who is now 65 years. Sumalatha's parents, along with their elder daughter, Pramila, have since migrated to Nagar Kurnool. The other daughters have also been placed at their grandmother's place. Occasionally, Kamli and Chandu send money to the grandmother for the upkeep of the children.

Summing Up

The author came across during the course of his field work. All these cases mostly occurred in the period 2002 to 2006. There may be many more such cases, which have not come to light. The reasons for giving up the girl children include: the perceived financial burden in bringing up a girl child, or the desire to ensure a better quality of life (which the parents cannot provide) to such children. Suffice to say, the socio-economic conditions are forcing many Lambada parents to sell or give away their children.

Conclusion

Ours is a hypocritical society we say one thing. We do something other. We profess morality. We preach values. We give sermons on character. We honour our womenfolk. We place them on a lofty platform. We recite scriptures in their honour. We sing in praise of Sita, Savitri and Damayanti. But we are hollow within. We have given equal rights to our women in our constitution. We talk of women liberation movement. But it is a sad reality that our women are slaves as they were ages ago. It is pleasant to talk about women liberation but no one gives them real freedom.

India is a male dominated society. Boys are preferred to daughters. Men are superior to women. Man governs unquestioned. The son is always honoured. But why? He will bring us a rich dowry. He will earn for his parents. He will give shelter to his aged parents. He will light the pyre at the time of cremation. He will carry on his father's generation.What an illustrious achievement! It is a fact universally acknowledged in India that sons are as sincere as daughters. It is also true that sons barring exception send out their aged parents when the later are unable to work, sons inherit their father's wealth.

Daughters are a curse. Parents have to arrange large dowry for them. Daughters are treated as liabilities. It is true to some extent. We have to check the menace of dowry. Girls should reject dowry-hunters. They should organise themselves and fight man injustice against women. They should fight against cruel social inequalities heaped on them. They should women be molested, raped and humiliated in public? Why should not they raise their voice against such injustices?

Women live in eternal slavery. A sister has to depend upon his brother. A daughter has to seek her father's permission for taking up a job. A wife has to move with her husband's and her in-laws permission. A mother dependent on her sons and husband. A widow can't move without her son. Thus we have convinced our women that they are essentially was creatures and they need male support for their living.

Women and girl children have to be given economic independence to their self-respect because Freedom without economic freedom is meaningless. Their educational status has to be improved, the gaps between their economical status and cultural changes has to fill.

References

1. Thomas K. John, *Human Rights of Tribals,*(New Delhi: Isha Book, 2005), Vol.1, p. 55.

2. *Ibid.*

3. Andhra Pradesh Tribal Welfare Department, *New Initiatives in Development of Scheduled Tribes,* (Hyderabad, TCRTI, 2005), p. 2.

4. Andhra Pradesh Girijan Sangam, *Savaneer*, (Hyderabad: Andhra Pradesh Girijan Sangam, 2004), p. 2.

5. *Ibid.*

6. Shamala Devi Rathod, *Class and Caste differences among the Lambadas in Andhra Pradesh*, (Social Scientist, Vol.12, No.134, July 1984), p. 49.

7. Cheenya Naik, B., *Banjara Charitra; Samskruthi-pragati,* (Ananthpur; Hathiram Bavaji Publications,1998), p. 8.

8. Andhra Pradesh Tribal Welfare Department, *Lambadas,* (Hyderabad: TCRTI, May 2002), p. 1.

9. Andhra Pradesh Girijan Sangam Savaneer, 2004.

4

Mining and Displacement in South Odisha: Perspectives from a Census Survey

M. Gopinath Reddy and *Prajna Paramita Mishra*

Introduction

Odisha is endowed with varieties of mineral resources and occupies an important position in India's mineral map. Among all the minerals, Bauxite is a prominent one. The state accounts for 51 per cent of Indian bauxite reserves followed by Andhra Pradesh (21 per cent). According to the Indian Bureau of Mines (2005), India has 2,926 Million Tons (MT) of bauxite resources and these include 524 MT of reserves. [1]

However, according to the production data of 2009-10, India produced 13,95,2002 tons of bauxite. Odisha is the highest producer of bauxite (35 per cent) followed by Gujarat (19 per cent), Maharashtra (14 per cent), Chhattisgarh (12 per cent) and Jharkhand (12 per cent).[2] Bauxite mining is yet to start in the state of Andhra Pradesh. Deposits of bauxite ore are mined and refined into alumina–one of the feed stocks for aluminium metal. At the refinery, alumina is extracted from the bauxite ore; and at the smelter, aluminium is extracted from its oxide alumina.

Aluminium is used in every aspect of our day to day life. They are used in tetra pack, saucepans, foil wraps, laptops, cars etc., (Padel and Das, 2010). In India, aluminium consumption is increasing from less than one kilo per person per year to 15-30 kg per year (Padel and Das, 2010).[3] Over the years there is a growing demand for aluminium as it is used in various aspects of modern life. It is known as a 'green metal' as it is believed to be easily recycled and reduces fuel consumption of car by making them lighter. However, a very small portion of that is actually recycled (Padel and Das, 2010).

As developed countries do not want to keep polluting business in their own countries, developing country like India is new destination. Besides, due

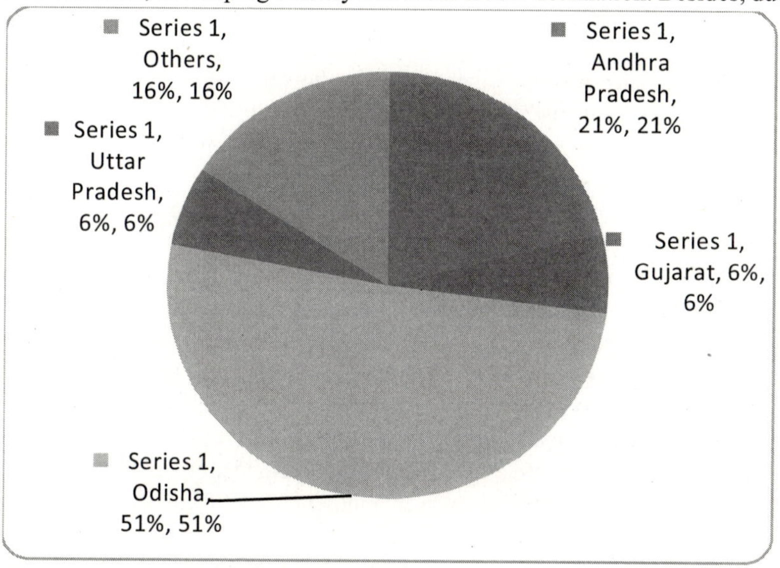

Fig. Bauxite Reserves in India

to costly freights and the emergence of Singapore as a metal futures market, India has become the location of aluminium smelting. In 2009-10, India produced about 14 MT of bauxite from 200 mines. National Aluminium Company (NALCO), a public sector enterprise, alone produced about 35 per cent of this. Odisha accounted for the maximum production.

Out of the ten bauxite deposits in Odisha, mining leases have been granted to two deposits. Panchapatmali deposit in Koraput district is under the operation of NALCO, a Government of India Undertaking since 1986. Maliparbat deposit in the same district has been granted to Hindusthan Aluminium Company (HINDALCO). The present study concentrates on former. Koraput is a district in south Odisha known for rich mineral deposits and high concentration of tribal. The state has a very low literacy rate of 36.20 per cent. In 2006, the ministry of panchayati raj named Koraput as one of the most backward district of India. Naxal activities have spread out to this district and now it is a part of red corridor.[4] Contrary to its poverty, the district is known for its indigenous varieties of rice and hosts many major industries of Odisha.

After getting approval from the government the next step is land acquisition and displacement. Here we study the displacement scenario of Nalco, the leading public sector enterprise of India. This article has been organised as follows. Section one is an introduction to the study. Section two brings out the past picture of Nalco. Section three is on study area. Section four presents our result and finally section five concludes the study.

Bauxite Mining in South Odisha: A Look at Past

In the early 80's it was clear that the bauxite deposits of South Odisha will be exploited with the help of a Western transnational and Andhra deposits with the help of a Soviet aided project. Nalco was set up for exploiting the vast bauxite deposits of south Odisha. It was involved with a French aluminium international (Srinivasan, Vyasulu, Rajagopalan, 1981). There was a public debate on this huge public investment and papers in the leading journal Economic and Political Weekly raised number of questions about the ongoing debate (Srinivasan, Vyasulu, Rajagopalan, 1981; Subrahmanyam, 1982).

Researchers mention that the financial viability and foreign exchange earnings of the project depend on world alumina prices. There are also questions on the interest rate on the Eurocurrency loan (Srinivasan, Vyasulu, Rajagopalan 1981). Babani and Srinivasan (1981) again supported the former authors arguing that world alumina prices have never arrived at 15 per cent of aluminium price. This was going against NALCO assumptions. Subrahmanyam (1982) further supported the argument. There are also questions on why this plant is taken up when resources are lacking to finance projects and programmes covered by the sixth plan (EPW, 1982). However, another reviewed works of EPW (1986) argued it as a major development in the aluminium industry during the 6th plan.

Stanley (1996) gives a clear account of displacement, compensation and rehabilitation in the NALCO Bauxite Mine and Plant at Damanjodi. According to him, 597 villages in 254 villages are displaced, out of which 42.55 per cent are tribal (Table). Out of the total acquired land of 10,058.76 crores, 69.52 per cent had gone for the construction of plant followed by township.

Table 4.1 : Displacement Scenario of Nalco

Affected Villages	*26*	
Affected Families	Tribal	254 (42.55)
	Dalit	56 (9.38)
	Others	287 (48.07)
	Total	597 (100)
Land acquired (acres)	Mines	427.30 (4.25)
	Township	2,638.96 (26.24)
	Plant	6,992.50 (69.52)
	Total	10,058.76 (100)

Source: Stanley (1996).

Stanley (1996) has also given a picture of compensation package given by Nalco. Out of the displaced families 74 per cent are rehabilitated and 59 per cent have received job in compensation. Compensation per acre of land is Rs 2000 and compensation for tree is Rs 100. However, there is no compensation for Common Property Resource (CPR).

Table 4.2 : Compensation Scenario of Nalco

Families Displaced	597
Families Rehabilitated	441 (73.87)
Job Received	352 (58.96)
Compensation per one acre of land (Rs)	2000
Compensation for Tree	100
Compensation for CPR	No

Source: Stanley (1996).

Samal (1996) has taken another study in the same year, which covers the Nalco Anugul sector (smelter). There he has mentioned that Nalco rehabilitation and resettlement policy is regarded as one of the best in India. According to Khatua and Stanley (2006) Nalco paid compensation for patta land alone. There was no compensation for CPR or government and village land. However, they are a good source of earning for the landless villagers. All these studies encourage meeting the displaced people and seeing their situations nearly after three decades. With this background the objective of our study is to compare those displaced situations in the pre-mining and post-mining period.

Study Area and Sample Selection

Our study concentrates on Koraput district of Odisha because this district produces more than 98 per cent of bauxite. Bauxite mines in the Panchpatmali hills of Koraput district is taken because it is the largest single deposit in the world. The National Aluminium Company (NALCO) was established in 1981 to produce aluminium from this rich bauxite deposits. It is Asia's largest integrated aluminium complex. Called as the pride of Odisha, by the Government of Odisha, the company started its operation in 1981. NALCO declared a net profit of 608 crore, the highest on record for the first quarter of 2006, and won Government of India's Indira Priyadarshini Vrikshamitra award for its contribution to wasteland development (Goodland, 2007). It has three operations in Odisha (Stanley, 1996):

(a) Bauxite mining in the Panchpatmali hills of Koraput district with deposits of 112.8 million tons;

(b) Alumina refinery complex in Damanjodi, Koraput district, 11 km from the mines. It has an installed capacity of eight lakh tonnes of alumina annually;

(c) Smelter plant at Anugul district. 4.25 lak tonnes are transported here. The plant has a captive power plant with a capacity of 55.5 MW as against its actual need of 32 MW.

Our study concentrates on the first two areas. It also includes villages near the ash and red mud pond areas. NALCO has divided the surrounding areas into two zones: core zones (area falls within a radius of 5 km either from the plant or the refinery) and buffer zones (area falls within a radius of 6 to 15 km

Table 4.3 : Demographic Features of Affected Villages

Study Zone	*Village*	*Panchayat*	*Block*	*Households Category*				
				SC	*ST*	*OBC*	*OC*	*Total*
Mining Core	Kapsiput	Bhifaarguda	Lakhimpur	1	141	0	0	142
Mining Buffer	Khardiguda	Littiguda	Koraput	0	79	0	0	79
	Putraghati			26	95	79	1	201
Refinery Core	Analabadi	Matalput	Koraput	68	267	144	128	607
	Ambogam	Littiguda		2	131	0	0	133
Refinery Buffer	Mujanga	Mujanga	Dasamanthapur	143	93	0	23	259
	Marchimal	Matalput	Koraput	21	0	15	41	77
ARMP Core Zone	Goudaguda	Charangul	Semiliguda	0	0	0	73	73
	Kharaguda	Podampur	Koraput	4	2	14	13	33
	Champapodar	Mujanga	Dasamanthapur	11	1	9	64	85
ARMP Buffer Zone	Charangaguda	Podampur	Koraput	30	42	0	0	72

either from the plant or the refinery). This has been decided by NALCO in view of the severity of pollution effects. The present study is part of a major research project titled "Bauxite mining in Koraput Region of Odisha: A Socio-Economic Impact Analysis". The main objective of this project is to assess the socio-economic and environmental challenges of bauxite mining. To find out the sample households a census survey is undertaken to understand the extent of displacement, which is a major social issues. The project paper is based on the result of that census survey.

Villages are selected from each zone. There are 12 villages from three blocks surrounded by the refinery and nearly 40 villages from four Gram Panchayat surrounded by the mines. We visited eleven villages and did a census survey to understand the extent of displacement. We interviewed all household heads of these hamlets and villages. Finally we collected information from 1483 households. A demographic feature of the villages is given in table.

In the mining core zone, Kapsiput is our sample village. It has 142 households out of which 141 households belong to the scheduled tribe category. In the mining buffer zone Khardiguda and Putraghati are two sample villages. Khardiguda has 79 households and all belong to the scheduled tribe. Putraghati has 201 households with mixed population.

In Refinery core zone, Analabadi has 607 households. This is a rehabilitation colony consisting of eleven displaced hamlets of the refinery. It also has a mixed population. Second village Ambogam in the refinery core zone consists of 133 households, mostly tribal. This village is almost located in the refinery premises (1.2 km). This village was supposed to be displaced but NALCO delayed the process and later on stopped. These villagers are the victim of all immediate environmental impact. In Refinery buffer zone, village Mujanga has 259 households, dominated by scheduled caste and scheduled tribe population. Marchimal is another village in this area with 77 households with a mixed population but no tribal.

In the Ash and Red mud Pond (ARMP) core zone, Goudaguda is a village with 73 households. All the households belong to *Gouda* caste, whose main occupation is taken as livestock rearing. Both Kharaguda and Champapodar in this area are displaced villages. Now they are resettled in one place but they are different villages. Kharaguda has 33 households with a mixed population and Champapadar has 85 households, dominated by other caste. In the ARMP buffer zone Charangaguda is a village with 72 households, dominated by scheduled caste and scheduled tribe population. Most of them have lost land because of the railway track of NALCO. The next section shows the displacement scenario of these affected villages.

Results and Discussions

The compensation package of Nalco was taken as one of the best compensation package. For the fully affected households, means those who lost home and homestead, Nalco offered them a new house at rehabilitation colony, one job to one person, health card, free education at Nalco school and monetary compensation for tangible losses. They are Rs 500 to Rs 15000 for home and homestead, Rs 2500 to Rs 5000 for wetland, Rs 1500 to Rs 2500 for dry land and Rs 100 for trees. For the partially affected households, those who have not lost home and homestead but other tangible assets, compensation money is same. They also got priority for the contract and wage labour works in the Nalco refinery and mining.

In the mining core zone, 51 per cent of households have lost their agricultural land. For this none of the households have received compensation. These villagers were practicing *podu* on top of the hills and hill slopes.

Table 4.4 : Displacement and Compensation Scenario

Study Zone	*Total HHs*	*Affected HHs*	*Assets lost*		*Compensation Received*	
			Land	*House*	*Land*	*House*
Mining Core	142	72 (50.70)	72	0	0	NA
Mining Buffer	280	138 (49.29)	138	0	136	NA
Refinery Core	740	383 (51.76)	141	361	129	344
Refinery Buffer	336	34 (10.12)	34	0	28	NA
ARMP Core	191	128 (67.02)	86	103	85	103
ARMP Buffer	72	38(52.78)	38	0	36	NA

Source: Field Survey (2011).

After getting the permission to mine that area, NALCO evicted these villagers from cultivating those patches of land. As these displaced households do not have *patta* for their agricultural lands they have not received any compensation for that. In the mining buffer zone 49 per cent of households have lost their agricultural land. These villagers have loss land because of the rehabilitation colony, conveyor belt and another road which connects the mining to the refinery site. Here almost all the households have received compensation and only two households have not received because of unclear document. The compensation package is Rs 1000 to 1500 per acre for dry land and Rs 2500 to 5000 per acre for wet land.

In the Refinery core zone 52 per cent of the households are affected by the refinery. Out of the affected households, 37 per cent (141 households) have lost their agricultural land. Out of that 129 households have received compensation and for others it is still pending. The compensation package is same. On the other hand 94 per cent of the affected households (361 households) have lost their home and homestead area. Out of that 344 households have received compensation. For this they have received Rs 500 to Rs 5000 according to classification like hut, semi-pucca, pucca etc. These households are also settled in the rehabilitation colony and one job (per house) in NALCO. In the Refinery buffer zone only 10 per cent of the total households are affected. They have lost their agricultural land for refinery and a part of red mud pond. Out of 34 households, 28 households have received compensation and for others it is pending.

In the ARMP core zone 67 per cent of the households are affected. Out of all the affected households 67 per cent of the households have lost their agricultural land. All households have received compensation except one. In this area 80 per cent of the households have lost their home and homestead area. Here compensation package is same. In the ARMP buffer zone 53 per cent of the households are affected. Out of the affected 38 households have lost their agricultural land and 36 households are compensated. The next section compares household main occupation in the pre and post-displacement scenario.

As a part of compensation packages, NALCO has provided job to those households who have lost their home and homestead area. Therefore, it is interesting to study how the household main occupation has changed in the post-displacement scenario. Here households head may be a different person in the pre and post-displacement scenario but we have compared the main occupation of the same households.

Table 4.5 : Household Main Occupation: Pre and Post-displacement

Study Zone	*Total HHs*	*Affected HHs*	*Assets lost*		*Compensation Received*	
			Land	*House*	*Land*	*House*
Mining Core	142	72 (50.70)	72	0	0	NA
Mining Buffer	280	138 (49.29)	138	0	136	NA
Refinery Core	740	383 (51.76)	141	361	129	344
Refinery Buffer	336	34 (10.12)	34	0	28	NA
ARMP Core	191	128 (67.02)	86	103	85	103
ARMP Buffer	72	38(52.78)	38	0	36	NA

Source: Field Survey (2011).

In the mining core zone, all households main occupation was farming in the pre-displacement period (Table). However, in the post-displacement period 36 per cent are engaged in NALCO as contract or wage employee. They are not permanent employee of NALCO. NALCO has given the contract works to contractors. These contractors will recruit the contract and wage labour. They do not have job security and they received weekly payment. The work category has been divided into four categories are; High Skilled Works, Skilled Works, Semi Skilled Works and Un-skilled Works. According to work category the wage rates are: High Skilled Worker— Rs 330 per day, Skilled Worker—Rs 280 per day, Semi Skilled Worker — Rs 220 per day, Un-skilled Worker— Rs 190 per day. In the mining buffer zone, farmers dominated the main occupation (82 per cent) in the pre-displacement period followed by wage labourers. However, this per cent has reduced in the post-displacement period and now NALCO contract and wage labourers are the main category.

Table 4.6 : Household Main Occupation: Pre and Post-displacement

Main Occupation	*Mining Core Zone*		*Mining Buffer Zone*	
	Pre	*Post*	*Pre*	*Post*
Farmers	118 (100)	75 (63.6)	193 (81.8)	78 (33.1)
Wage Labours	0	0	43 (18.2)	
Others	0	0	0	9 (3.8)
NALCO Contract/Wage Employee	NA	43 (36.4)	NA	149 (63.1)
Total	**118 (100)**	**118 (100)**	**236 (100)**	**236 (100)**

Source: Field Survey (2011).

In the Refinery core zone farmers dominated the main occupation in the pre-displacement period (94.5 per cent). However, in the post-displacement period majority are NALCO permanent employees. As many households have lost their homestead area in this zone, they have received this job in their compensation package. This is followed by wage labourers and NALCO contract employee. In the refinery buffer zone, in the pre-displacement period both farming and wage labour has a major role. However, in the post-displacement phase wage labour has outweighed farming. As the extent of displacement is very less here so workers employed in NALCO.

In the ARMP core zone also situation is same in the pre-displacement period. The main occupation is dominated by farming. However, in the post scenario it is wage labour and NALCO employee. Here also as the households have lost their homestead land they have permanent employment in NALCO. In the ARMP buffer zone, main occupation was dominated by farmers and wage labourers. However, in the post-displacement period it is dominated by

Table 4.7 : Household Main Occupation: Pre and Post-displacement

Main Occupation	*Refinery Core Zone*		*Refinery Buffer Zone*	
	Pre	*Post*	*Pre*	*Post*
Farmers	665 (94.5)	71 (10.1)	165 (54.8)	100 (33.2)
Wage Labours	27 (3.8)	207 (29.4)	132 (43.9)	172 (57.1)
Others	12 (1.7)	33 (4.7)	4 (1.3)	19 (6.3)
NALCO Contract/Wage Employee	NA	98 (13.8)	NA	10 (3.3)
NALCO Employee	NA	295 (41.9)	NA	0
Total	**704 (100)**	**704 (100)**	**301 (100)**	**301 (100)**

Source: Field Survey (2011).

wage labour. Because of water problem and other environmental impact farming is not a profitable occupation now. As the contractors are exploiting the NALCO contract employees these people prefer to work as wage labourer than contract employee.

In the tribal and hilly habitations CPRs play an important role in the subsistence of the livelihoods of the poor and the marginalised. In particular, these regions, unlike in the plain areas, CPRs access and availably to the village communities in terms of basic needs, such grazing pastures, ponds, streams, forests for minor forest produce play important role for their livelihoods. The access to them is usually free and unrestricted.

Interaction with affected households in these areas revealed that Nalco does not offer any access to their health facilities in terms of issuing health cards and making available medicines and other facilities. The attitude of Nalco, a profit making public sector undertaking towards this section of affected people was found totally inadequate and unsatisfactory. Permanent employment opportunities available to them were also very limited in the plant. Whatever employment was offered is only contractual that too through contractors, not directly by the company. It was also told during the survey that once employed person got married, left the house, the others, especially the elderly become totally dependent without any sources of regular income. Land to land compensation was eminently possible during early eighties, but this option was not followed. It was pity that the affected households became addicted to certain social evils as a result of cash compensation.

Many women from mining surrounding areas are working in mining as cleaners; cement works masonry cleaning and helpers. They are getting employment through the contractors not NALCO. The wage rates are Rs 90 to 120. The women are saying no adequate transport facilities are provided to reach mining site. It was observed that, people from surrounding villages are working in refinery, and they engaged in both technical and non-technical sections. People working in technical sections are technicians, fitters, electricians, and non-technical people working as maintenance workers, daily wage workers in boiling section, and other works.

It was found that transport is the major problem from refinery to refinery surrounding villages. It is observed that men, are using bicycle or motor cycle for their transport and women trek long distances by walk. It is very difficult because they have to walk 9 to 10 kms on Kutcha road to reach refinery and time takes more than one hour. They are saying that due to transport problem they are not able to reach home proper time and have no time to spend with their children at home. They are expecting NALCO to provides transport facility to reach refinery and on time.

Besides the problems enlisted above, there are certain environmental and ecological problems observed in the field. Dust emanating from the conveyor belt carrying bauxite is affecting the agricultural lands and hence their productivity. There is no mechanism to compensate such losses. Natural resources like ponds and streams were adversely damaged due to mining and conveyor belt hence the water sources are totally diminished. It was observed during the survey that some of the problems identified in Goudaguda village. Leakage in caustic soda and septic water pipeline led to septic water flows into the agriculture fields hence fertility is affected and the crop production has been decreased. The canal water is contaminated due to caustic mud and septic water. The village elders said that in 1995 due to contaminated water affected by caustic mud and septic water few livestock were dead. Villagers fought against Nalco and received compensation. Villagers are facing health problems like skin problems, TB and other health problems.

When it comes to other infrastructural facilities, most of the villages are facing water problems. They depend on well and hand pumps for both drinking and domestic usage. For agriculture they depend on stream, ponds and rainfall. Nalco gets water from the Kerandi River which is eight km far away from the refinery. The pipeline is connected to carry water from the river. Due to water pipeline some of the villages have lost their agriculture lands. It was told during the survey that people request to access water from the pipeline was denied by Nalco, though there is huge water wastage due to leakages.

Interactions with associations like Peripheral Development Committee, LDP Welfare Association, LAP Association shows that due to Nalco many people have lost their agriculture lands and houses but Nalco provided job opportunity to few people only and rest of them are not yet benefited. There was no proper guideline for job recruitment. After job recruitment, Nalco has conducted Minimum Literacy Programme to the displaced people. The programme duration was nine months, at that time some of the displaced people who got jobs have died due to health problems and there have spouses applied for their husband's job but Nalco has not offered any job to them. Still these people have been trying to get their jobs with help of the associations.

In the year 1984-85, Nalco started Peripheral Development Programme. The area which is 10 kms from Refinery and Mining consider as a Peripheral Area. Under this programme, Nalco has promised to provide all the facilities like health, education, roads, drinking water and infrastructure development (School building etc.) but did not provide any service to the Peripheral Area. Above Associations presidents said that as for their knowledge the Peripheral Development Funds have been diverted in to other areas. All association members demand that Nalco has to provide jobs to all affected people, and to provide services to notified Peripheral Area. Local priority should be given for the contract works and contract jobs. Health Card access to all the displaced people are needed to be given to all the people irrespective of whether they are directly or indirectly affected.

Conclusion

Nalco, a profit-making public sector called 'the pride of Odisha' cannot really be characterised as such from the perspective of affected population. The data shows very clearly that the most vulnerable sections, viz., scheduled tribes and scheduled castes who have lost lands, houses and other assets could not able to get back their livelihood status as a result of cash compensation policy. The fact that land scarcity was not there in 80's as is felt now, Nalco should have adopted land to land policy. As a result of this approach, we could see from the data that the above sections were reduced from farmers to casual labourers and became helpless. Even the job allocation was confined to one member of the family reducing others to mere dependents. The other infrastructural facilities promised by Nalco were not adequately provided and there are still loose ends in the whole approach. On the whole the resettlement and rehabilitation measures by Nalco are found to be piecemeal and ad hoc. The company with its huge profit base could have done much better to these much marginalised people.

Acknowledgement

This paper is part of a project titled "Bauxite Mining in Koraput Region of Odisha: A Socio-Economic Impact Analysis", funded by the Jamshedji Tata Trust, Mumbai. The authors acknowledge this support. Field work was carried out with the help of M.S. Swaminathan Research Foundation (MSSRF), Jeypore, Odisha. We are thankful to Mr. S.V. Ramana and his team for this support.

Notes

1. The British Geological Society defined mineral resources as natural concentration of minerals, which are or may become of potential economic interest due to their inherent properties. On the other hand mineral reserves are that part of a mineral resource, which has been fully evaluated, commercially viable and has a valid planning permission for extraction. http://www.bgs.ac.uk/planning4minerals/Resources_5.htm

2. http://www.indiastat.com/table/minesandminerals/23/bauxite/19204/617982/data.aspx

3. Padel and Das (2010), described their book Out of this Earth as an anthropology of the aluminium industry. It described vividly the aluminium industry of Odisha, India and the World.

4. http://en.wikipedia.org/wiki/Koraput_district

References

Babani, A. 1981. Orissa Aluminium Complex. Economic and Political Weekly. 16(52): 2113.

Economic and Political Weekly. 1986. Shortage to Surplus? Reviewed Work. 21(41): 1771.

Economic and Political Weekly. 1982. Erosion of Sixth Plan. Reviewed Work. 17(6): 173-174.

Indian Bureau of Mines (2005): Indian Mineral Yearbooks. Indian Bureau of Mines.

Khatua, S. and W. Stanley. 2006. Ecological Debt: A Case Study from Odisha, India, in A.K. Peralta eds (2006) Ecological Debt: The Peoples of the South are the Creditors. Cases from Ecuador, Mozambique, Brazil and India. World Council of Churches. Troika Press: Quezon City, Philippines.

Padel, F. and S. Das. 2010. Out of this Earth. East India Adivasi and the Aluminium Cartel. Orient Balckswan Private Limited: Hyderabad.

Samal K.C. 1996. NALCO-induced transformation: Linkage Effects, displacement, Rehabilitation and Environmental Pollution. Working Paper No. 28, Nabakrushna Choudhury Centre for Development Studies, Bhubaneswar, Odisha.

Srinivasan K.,V. Vyasulu and S. Rajagopalan. 1981. The Odisha Aluminium Complex: Points toward a Debate. Economic and Political Weekly. 16(49):2005-2014.

Stanley W. 1996. Machkund, Upper Kolab and NALCO Projects in Koraput District, Odisha. Economic and Political Weekly. 31(24): 1533-38.

Subrahmanyam, K.V. 1982. Odisha Aluminium Complex. Economic and Political Weekly. 17(5):168-172.

5

Livelihood in Bangalore: Migration from Villages to City–Displacement and Rehabilitation

Salu D'Souza

Introduction

Bangalore city is considered to be the fastest growing city in terms of population, industrialisation and commerce but without the required infrastructure such as electricity, garbage disposal and water supply. The authorities are now giving some serious thought. Rapid Public Transport System, flyovers for fast movement of vehicles and metro rail are being taken up by entrusting such projects involving huge sums to the private agencies. City Transport System too is being augmented with additional fleet of buses and inducting private operators to operate in the city. Telecommunication systems have considerably been improved. Large numbers of people are being persuaded to go in for group housing projects instead of individual houses. All this will certainly make Bangalore a beautiful city and make more and more entrepreneurs to come to this wonderful city to start their business and industrial ventures in and around Bangalore.

People from various places across India come to Bangalore on daily basis. Many are unskilled labourers who somehow find odd jobs during day time and happy to find shelter in the night. From various parts of Karnataka people move from their native places, migrate to Bangalore in search of their livelihood. There are many tribes in Karnataka. The older generation of tribal people did not venture out of their hamlets very often but the present generation of people in various tribes have fallen prey to agents and moved out from their comfort zones only to enter big cities like Bangalore. It is surprising to see that many tribal people sell their goods in various parts of Bangalore.

Tribal Population in Karnataka

There are many tribes across India and their population is large. While dealing with various tribes in India, Ram Ahuja mentions, "The tribal population of India, according to the 1991 census, was 67.76 million. This was almost equalled to the population of the United Kingdom. The tribals formed 8.08 per cent of the country's total population (The Hindustan Times, 11 July, 1995). The number of people belonging to Scheduled Tribes grew much faster during 1981-91 than other people in the country put together. While overall growth of population during the decade was 23.79 per cent, it was 25.67 per cent in the case of STs. The highest rate of growth of STs was in Kerala, followed by Gujarat and Rajasthan. But the proportion of STs in the total population has sharply declined in 12 states, has gone up in 12 states." (Ram Ahuja page 160). This shows that there are considerable number of people inhabit in various tribes that are spread out across India.

The people who belong to various tribes share some homogenous features. Ram Ahuja, in his book, *Social Problems in India*, speaks, "Some of the important features of the tribals are: most of them live in isolated terrains, the main source of their livelihood are agriculture and gathering of forest produce, they do not cultivate for profit, they still largely rely on barter system, they spend a greater part of their earnings social and religious ceremonies, and a large number of them are illiterate and are victimised by unscrupulous forest contractors and money lenders". This has shown that tribal population is much safer in the forests, which is their traditional dwelling place than in towns and cities. But the present generations of tribal people have defied all the norms and are found in towns and cities.

Karnataka has various tribes mostly found in Western Ghats, coastal regions and near the reserve forest. These tribal people have been living in their hamlets for many years. They cultivate in the small lands that they hold and gather forest produce for the additional income. In Karnataka, various successive governments tried their best to evacuate the tribes from the forest areas especially from notified areas of reserve forests but met with severe resistance from concerned tribes.

The Malaikudi Tribes in Karnataka

K.S. Singh has done research on various tribes that inhabit in various parts of India. In his voluminous book, '*The Scheduled Tribes*' which is published by OUP, he mentions about the Malaikudi Tribe, "They inhabit the Sahyadri hill ranges in the Dakshina Kannada and Chikmagalure districts of Karnataka and the Kasargod in Kerala." (K.S. Singh, p. 727). The Malaikudi people who reside in various parts of coastal region, especially from Belthangady taluk exhibit Mangalorean culture and tribal people from Chickmagalure follow Malnad culture. Singh further says, "The term, *malaikudi* has been derived from the words *malai,* meaning hill and *kudi*, meaning top. The term Malayekandi has the word *kandi* in it, which signifies either hill dwellers or children of the hills. The Tulu speaking people of the area call them Malettaya, which also has a similar meaning. The Malaikudi speak a dialect of the Dravidian language, Tulu at home. Tulu and Kannada are spoken by them for inter-group communication. The script they use is Kannada. The population of Malaikudi in Karnataka is 6967 (1981) census. Out of their total population, only 98 persons are returned from urban areas. The Malaikudi claim that they have the right to collect cardamom which grows wild, a right which was granted to them by the Pandavas of the Mahabharata." (K.S. Singh, p. 727)

The government does not find reason to believe in their traditional affairs but justifies the policies that are taken in order to maintain reserve forests that have become the habitat of endangered animals and bring rain to the vast coffee estates and other agriculture related work. Many hydro-electricity projects require huge quantity of water that need to come from various dams and reservoirs, the catchment areas are in these forests. How far the action of the government is justified in issuing evacuation notice is anybody's guess.

If we see Malaikudi tribes, it is interesting to know that there are caste divisions among them. As K.S. Singh observes, "The Malaikudi are divided into two subtribes, namely, Ooru Male and Nalu Male. Among the Ooru Male, there are 18 exogamous clans. The Nalu Male is divided into three house names which are reckoned in the male line. These two sub tribes do not usually intermarry. Monogamy is the usual form of marriage. The men and women of this community are allowed to divorce and remarry. Both nuclear and extended families are found among them, but the extended ones are on the decline. The women perform significant roles in agriculture operations and other economic activities; in the social, religious and ritual spheres, they also carry out domestic chores." (K.S. Singh, p. 728). Their family life is influenced by the globalisation. Many of the Malaikudi members bring the village produce and the forest produce to Bangalore city to sell at good price especially during the time of Hindu festivals like Sankranthi, Ugadi, Ganesh Chaturthi and Deepavali.

The members are self-sufficient in daily foodstuffs but have to work more in order to fetch money. Singh, while touching upon their economic activities opines, "The Malaikudi were hunters and gatherers in the past. Some of the Ooru Male now own land and are engaged in cultivation. Others work as agricultural and plantation labourers. A few families among the Nalu Male group have received land from the government and have raised small coffee plantations. The collection of forest produce is another source of income for them. Some families augment their income by making baskets and mats of bamboo." (K. S. Singh, p. 728). They take wild animals' meat, herbs and honey to the nearest towns and sometime to Bangalore to sell.

Among the Malaikudi people, some are influenced by local culture, travel all the way to Bangalore to work. Women folk are even employed as house servants in the households' of middle class families in cities. K.S. Singh further observes, “The population figures for those returned as Malaikudi shows that 45.21 per cent of their total population are workers. Of them, 41.49 per cent are cultivators, 25.26 per cent are agricultural labourers, 16.86 per cent are engaged in livestock, forestry, plantations, etc.” (K.S. Singh, p. 729). Since the route that leads from Mangalore to Bangalore is always busy, people of Mangalore and Bangalore need more trusted workers in different field. Hence, they employ these tribal men for odd works and women as housemaids. Some even go to hosiery factories that are found in large numbers in cities like Bangalore.

They have unique religious beliefs. To quote from K.S. Singh, “They follow Hinduism and believe in spirits (Bhuta). The 1981 census shows 100 per cent of the Malaikudi as followers of Hinduism. Manjunatha of Dharmasthala and Subrahmanya of Kukke are popular deities among them. Vishnu Sankramana, Nagarapanchami, Kadiruhabba and Dipavali are the few festivals observed by them. Folk songs are sung and male participate in the traditional folk dance.” (K.S. Singh, p. 729). No one has guts to question their belief in Bhuta. It is a unique worship, even the Christian missionaries could not make any head ways in their quest to ‘save souls’.

The regional bond between the Malaikudi tribal people and the local population is very cordial. The Malaikudi accept cooked food and water from the Bunt, Billava, Vokkaliga and Brahman and interdine with the Gowdalu. The Malaikudi serve the landowning Bunt, Vokkaliga and other communities as wage labourers. They share sources of water and crematoria with their neighbours, visit the same temples and take part in the village festivals called Bhuta Kola. A few among them hold white collar jobs and some work as teachers. The literacy rate among them has been on the increase over the past few decades. Their attitude is favourable towards modern medicine but health centers are not easily accessible from their settlements. They have accepted family welfare programmes.

The welfare schemes of government, better purchasing power due to globalisation, modernisation of villages due to Gulf boom among Mangaloreans, have gradually changed the life style of Malaikudi people. K.S. Singh observes that, “Drinking water supply, mass media and communication facilities are gradually reaching the people, though the amenities are not always adequate. The community is covered by the Integrated Tribal Development Programme. Co-operative societies have been established to purchase forest produce like honey collected by them. Firewood is their fuel resource. Those who cultivate land use chemical fertilisers and pesticides. Child Welfare Schemes and the public distribution system have found favour with them. Their attitude towards savings is favourable.” (K.S. Singh, p. 730). Few of them have even travelled to Gulf countries as labourers.

Impact of Displacement and Tardy Rehabilitation Programmes

Many of the tribal people who belong to different tribes from different parts of Karnataka have a taste for city and town life. It has its own history of reaching these people from their inner-most hamlets in forests to high-rise building in towns and cities like Bangalore. These people in 1980s and 1990s were secluded in remote forests areas. Gradually when their population started to grow and the awareness from government agencies particularly from the Census and Health department reached these tribal people, the changes started to take place. Their children attended the local schools in the beginning and later went to small towns for their high school studies. Many went to cities like Mangalore, Mysore and Bangalore for the higher education. This necessitated few tribal families of Malaikudi to shift their bases to these towns and cities that include Bangalore.

Government too requested the tribal people to move from forest areas to few designated places. Some tribes obliged and some did not. Maliakudi tribal people of Dakshina Kannada district particularly from Belthangady Taluk resisted the move of their shifting. Time and again, the new policies of government keep the tribal people on the guard. Many have joined few NGOs to protect their rights. The impact of displacement is not only psychological but also keeps them always in a fear psychosis condition in towns and cities. Many have to conform to the city life style and their freedom is curtailed. These people were used to wear few clothes on their bodies now in towns and cities need to be always wear decent attire that brings financial burden to their families. Rehabilitation programmes from the government side in many occasions is one time settlement and there is no follow up procedure. This makes them vulnerable in case if they meet any tragedy while in cities.

Problems Faced by the Tribal People in the Western Ghats

Every successive government brings out its own policies and rules. Tribal people are not left out from these new policies. Ram Ahuja in his book *Social Problems in India* speaks of how exploitation of tribal population takes place in the name of 'modernisation,' and 'civilisation': "For ages, tribals were considered a primitive segment of Indian society. They lived in forest and hills without having more than a causal contact with the so-called civilised and advanced neighbours. There being no population pressures, there was no attempt to penetrate their areas and impose alien values and beliefs on the tribals. But when the British consolidated their position in the country, their colonial aspirations and administrative needs necessitated to 'open up' the entire country through an effective communication system. The British introduced the system of land ownership and revenue. Annual tax was trebled which was beyond the paying capacity of tribal cultivators. Under the increasing pressure of population, many outsiders also started settling in tribal regions. With their money power, they offered credit facilities at the door step. Initially, it provided relief to tribals but gradually the system became exploitative. Newly established courts of law helped the exploiters. This economic, and later social and cultural exploitation aroused the tribal leaders to mobilise the tribals and start agitations. With the increasing feelings of deprivation, mass agitations, struggles and movements also increased. In short, the causes of tribal unrest may be described as economic, social and political." (Ram Ahuja, pp. 161-162). This sends a wrong signal to all the tribes, hence, they become hostile towards government and their representatives. Does this make them to lose their confidence in democracy and the values that attached towards democratic set up in a democratic country like India?

The tribes in Karnataka face the following problems. They possess small and uneconomical land holdings. Among them, the literacy rate is very low. Their land in good portion is transferred legally to non-tribals. Tribal Development Programmes have not helped them much. They depend on money lenders since banking facilities are not developed in their areas. The unemployed and the underemployed want help in finding secondary sources of earning by developing animal husbandry, poultry farming, handloom weaving and the handicrafts sector. If any government aid comes in their way, it comes with various strings attached to that. In various hilly areas, there is communication problem.

While speaking of their problems, Ram Ahuja observes, "All this depicts the frustrations of the tribals. When the law does not help them, the government remains callous, and the police fail to protect them, and also harass them, they take up arms against the exploiters." (Ram Ahuja, p. 166)

Conclusion

It is true that the major towns and cities in Karnataka, over the years have seen development and steady migrant population. Bangalore being the capital city of Karnataka gets its lion's share in migrant population. How does the city cope up with this migrant population? The few tribal families who shifted their base from their traditional hamlets in the forest to Bangalore are faced with rehabilitation issues and stress of displacement always haunts them. Though there is crime against scheduled tribes, when we search for statistics, it is not alarming in Karnataka while compared to other states especially North East of India. Malaikudi tribe is so assimilated in local culture; it is sometime difficult to distinguish them from the local population in Mangalore and its surrounding area.

While speaking about these tribes, Ram Ahuja opines, "The British had superimposed their own administrative patterns in tribal areas and deprived the tribals of their traditional methods of interacting with people. The tribals have no written laws but the sanction of the community has a force which none dares to violate." (p. 166) The effective check from the government agency is missing. NGOs have unearthed many shocking practices. Ahuja further says, "The bonded labour in tribal areas was prohibited under the constitution. In practice, however, it continues to exist in one form or the other in tribal areas of most of the states." (p. 167). Not everything is disappointing. Over the years, various governments have heard their cries. Ram Ahuja identifies that, "The amount allocated for the tribal sub-plans has been increasing from the 5th five year plan (1974-79) onwards." (p. 167). This is a good trend and it should be continued in the future. He continues to point out that, "The 20-point programme too focused attention on the development of scheduled tribes, including assisting and training of the tribals but also in the formulation of tribal sub-plans." (p. 168). It is observed that modernisation and civilisation damages the culture and tradition. Some time, in order to facilitate changes certain sacrifice/ compromise need to be made from both sides, government/NGO and the tribal population.

The city of Bangalore that has become a favourite place for many migrant workers and few tribal families from Karnataka. The city helps this migrant population to search for their livelihood. How far these migrant people try to assimilate into local culture and make best use from the available resources need to be observed.

References

Ananthakrishna Iyer, L.K., *The Mysore Tribes and Castes* (Mysore: The Mysore University, 1930), Vol. III, pp. 186-187.

Ethnographic Study of Scheduled Tribes: Malekudiya and Yerava, Census of India 1981, Karnataka, Series 9, Paper 5, (Delhi: Controller of Publications, 1984).

Krishna Kumar, (1983), *Educational Experience of Scheduled Castes and Tribes*, Economic and Political Weekly, 18 (36-37), September 3, 1983.

K.S. Singh (1994), *The Scheduled Tribes*, Oxford University Press, New Delhi.

Ram Ahuja (1997), *Social Problems in India*, Rawat Publications, Jaipur.

6

Livelihood Issues: Land Alienation, Displacement, Rehabilitation and Migration

Neelmani Jaysawal

Introduction

Development is a process of expanding the real freedoms that people enjoy. In other words, it is the process of expanding human freedoms which means individual capacities to avoid some deprivations like starvation, under-nourishment, morbidity and mortality (Sen, Amartya, 1999). Therefore, development may not usher in unless an individual's deprivation is removed. Poverty, unemployment, forced displacement and alienation from land reduce the capabilities of individuals to enjoy freedom. But current socio-economic scenario is witnessing displacement and alienation as foundation stone for development. Several developmental projects involve the introduction of direct control by a developer over land which was owned previously by a subaltern individual or group. All these displacement is not only in its physical form but in socio-cultural sphere also. According to the report of World Commission on Dams (WCD), it refers to not only loss of livelihood and means of production but their favourable socio-cultural milieu also (Stanley, Jason). The displacement caused by Dams in India is as high as other developmental projects-caused. Taneja and Thakkar point out that estimates on displacement in India from dam projects alone range from 21 million to 40 million (*ibid*). The Narmada Sardar Sarovar Dam Project in India, which is set to displace 127,000 people, has perhaps been the most widely researched and discussed project involving forced resettlement in history (*ibid*). Due to emergence of New Economic Policy in 1991, the process of forced displacement and land alienation got its speed in India. The areas ranging from tribal hamlets to urban slums lacked the support of government. The inclination of the state towards market forces undermined any pro-people development policy. The forced displacement and land alienation adversely affects children and women in addition to men. They lose their livelihood, ongoing education, existing healthcare facilities and nutrition. The reason is unanticipated migration and involuntary resettlement of people after their displacement and alienation. Therefore, displacement and land alienation may not be explained until its outcome like people's migration and involuntary resettlement is explored explicitly. Jean Dreze says that displacement has been a history of failures (*Report of the workshop held at the India International Centre on September 12 and 13, 2002 organised by the Institute of Development Studies*). The total lack of transparency, the blockage of information from project authority to the displaced community has led to failed Resettlement and Rehabilitation (*ibid*). In his view, displacement should be made voluntary and resettlement policy should ensure augmenting people's views before being resettled. Therefore, it is imperative to define displacement, land alienation, migration and rehabilitation policies:

Meaning of Land Alienation, Displacement, Migration and Rehabilitation

There has been various interpretations of land alienation, displacement, migration and rehabilitation by academicians and courts. According to New York State Court, the land alienation is determined to be conveyance, sale or lease of municipal parks, recreational facilities to another public or private entity such as an adjoining property owner, a developer, or a school district, which results in the facility no longer being used for public park and recreation purposes (*A Handbook on the Alienation and Conversion of Municipal Parkland in New York*).

The Punjab Alienation of Land Act, 1900 states that Permanent Alienation includes sales, exchanges, gifts, wills and grants of occupancy rights.

In terms of land displacement, several authors have given their opinion. According to Pablo Bose, 'displacement may be defined as the forcing of communities and individuals out of their homes, often also their homelands, for the purpose of economic development' (Dhru, Kelly A., 2010).

World Bank states that displaced persons are defined as persons who lose land or right to use land or who lose access to legally designated parks and protected areas resulting in adverse impacts on the livelihood (Involuntary Resettlement Sourcebook, World Bank, 2004).

Similarly, the term 'migration' has been defined by John Hopkins Bloomberg School of Public Health. It says that migration is a geographic movement of people across a specified boundary for the purpose of establishing a new permanent or semi-permanent residence.

International Organisation for Migration (IOM) states, "migration is a process of moving, either across an international border, or within a State.

Encompassing any kind of movement of people, whatever its length, composition and causes; it includes refugees, displaced persons, uprooted people, and economic migrants" (*The phenomenon of migration: Its significance or meaning in human societies throughout history; International Federation of Red Cross and Red Crescent societies*). IOM states that there are about one billion migrants around the world. This number includes 214 million international migrants and 740 million internally displaced persons (IDPs) (*ibid*). Therefore, migration is caused by displacement of people from their land. It forces people to go to new places and start their livelihood afresh.

So, it is also very crucial for us to know about rehabilitation and resettlement of masses. It is an instrument for reducing agony of displaced persons. Through voluntary rehabilitation, an individual may get his grievances redressed caused by land alienation and displacement.

The World Bank states that Resettlement covers all economic, social losses resulting from land taking and restriction of access together with consequent compensatory and remedial measures. It further says that Resettlement includes (a) acquisition of land and physical structure on land (b) physical relocation (c) economic rehabilitation of displaced people to improve income and living standard (Involuntary Resettlement Sourcebook, World Bank, 2004).

The terminology 'Rehabilitation' has also been defined in the similar manner. It has been defined that Rehabilitation is the process of removing or reducing as far as possible the factors that limit the activity and participation of a person with disability so that he can attain and maintain the highest possible level of independence and quality of life: physically, mentally, socially and vocationally (Nairobi 1st Review Conference, 2004).

In the words of Dinah Shelton, "Rehabilitation is the process of restoring the individual's full health and reputation after the trauma of a serious attack on one's physical or mental integrity. It seeks to achieve maximum physical and psychological fitness by addressing the individual, family, local community and the society as a whole" (Villalba, Clara Sandoval, 2009).

In this way, the interpretation of meaning of displacement, alienation, migration and rehabilitation by various authors and institutions reflects diversity of opinion on these issues. It facilitates a space for debate on whether Rehabilitation and Resettlement (R&R) is reducing agony of displacement, alienation or just a mere patchwork of the state. The forced migration which is the outcome of involuntary displacement, is putting obstacles in the stability of livelihood. People are not able to resettle as per their will which leads to regional economic imbalance. In addition to it, they are also prone to several illegal activities due to adverse socio-economic milieu at rehabilitated site.

Therefore, it is very essential to examine the impact of land alienation, displacement and migration on livelihood of people from both micro and macro-points of view.

Impact of Land Alienation, Displacement and Migration on Livelihood

Development-induced land alienation and displacement has affected the livelihood of people in a very adverse manner. Displacement due to development, conservation, disasters or conflict, often leads to tremendous alienation from common property resources (CPRs) such as forests, land, fodder or water (Fernandes, Walter). Displacement in India, is mostly forced and caused by push factors. In Orissa, 30.2 per cent of the one million hectares acquired between 1951 and 1995 comprised forests and about 28 per cent comprised other CPRs (*ibid*). Again in Goa, 50 per cent of the 52000 hectares acquired between 1965 and 1995 comprises of CPRs (*ibid*). This alienation is not only in the form of forest areas but even river, marine lives also. The tribal people have been deprived of Non-Timber Forest Produce (NTFP) which is a major source of their livelihood. The collective ownership over resources has been transformed into individual ownership. In this way, the land alienation, displacement and forced migration has grievously affected the livelihood pattern. It has penetrated not only in tribal affairs but in women affairs also. Women being contributor to livelihood in rural areas have been forced to migrate to urban areas in need of alternative employment. Therefore, it is very essential to know its impact on livelihood in detail.

Internalising Inequality

Due to continuous displacement and alienation, people lose their stable livelihood. Most of these victims belong to either tribal community and dalit or down-trodden community. Once they lose their job at their indigenous areas, they start migrating to urban areas. But nature of employment in urban areas sometimes does not fit into category of these people due to irrelevance of their skill. The highly mechanised industries and services require technologically efficient workforce. In such a situation, the migrant workers feel difficulty in competing and thus develop a sense of inferiority among them. There is developed a huge gap between skilled workforce and these semi-skilled workforce. It further, widens inequality between dalit, tribal communities and general upper-caste communities. Such internalisation also takes place when young *adivasi* girls become domestic helpers in middle-class homes (Fernandes, Walter). The employer, conditioned by the caste mentality of 'untouchables' doing menial work, often sees them as 'low castes' (*ibid*). Over time, they themselves internalise a caste mentality and develop a low self-image of their own community. In other words, inequality gets developed inside society in such a way that even rehabilitation process becomes flawed in nature.

Transformation from Collective to Individual Ownership

Another important outcome of this phenomenon is individual ownership of land and end of protection of livelihood. The rules of the state are not immune from market forces. For example, in the Fifth Schedule as well as in the non-scheduled tribal areas, the alienation of tribal individual land to non-tribals is banned. The law in the Fifth Schedule areas is based on the concept of individual ownership whereas the ethos of most subaltern communities is geared towards community assets (Fernandes, Walter). The political and administrative system is controlled by powerful outsiders who manipulate the land records in their own favour (*ibid*). As a result, according to the official count, 753,435 (48 per cent) of a total of 1,848,000 acres of land in the tribal districts of Andhra Pradesh are in non-tribal hands (*ibid*).

Displacement in this case thus results in changes of land use and the transfer of power. Although the community traditionally owns this resource, the State grants loans and subsidies only to individual *patta* holders (*ibid*). With individual *patta*s becoming the norm, power is transferred to the man, and from him to his son (*ibid*). The tribal community lose collective ownership over land and privilege goes to hereditary owners. Therefore, it results into paucity of access of livelihood to common masses.

Dismantling of Production System

The forced displacement has caused reduction in productivity in agricultural, small-scale industries. Due to disruption of trade and market links, people do not get adequate price for their product which leads to disinterest of people in furthering productivity. Furthermore, farmers and small investors deviate from their production resulting into unemployment and poverty. In the words of Michael Cernea, it is a 'spiral of impoverishments'. Cernea also points out that trade links between producers and their customer base are interrupted and local labour markets are disrupted (Kothari, Smitu, 1996). In addition, there is a loss of complex social relationships which provided avenues of representation, mediation and conflict resolution (*ibid*). While some of the land losers have become farmers with smaller land holdings, many have become landless (Rawat, Vidya Bhushan, Mamidi Bharath Bhushan and Sujatha Surepally, 2010). The conversion of farmland for non-farm uses has also reduced farm labour opportunities for the people who had no non-farm skills (*ibid*).

Loss of Livestock

Livestock keeps an important position in livelihood. Livestock holding by households has various purposes. It can be a source of food, providing dairy products or meat. It is also used as means of payment. The fast reduction of livestock is also one of the major impacts of displacement and land alienation over livelihood. The loss of lands by hundreds of farmers has made it difficult to continue keeping livestock as there was shortage of fodder, a loss of suitable places for cattle sheds, and loss of purpose to keep draft animals (*ibid*). Apart from shortage of land and space, land displacement has pressurised family members of farmers or agricultural labourers to seek job outside the village. It results into unwillingness of these people to keep livestock and maintain it.

Hence, there has been witnessed reduction in cow, goat and sheep rearing which is supposed to be backbone of rural livelihood.

Increase in Deforestation

Alienation of land and displacement has affected trees also. Trees are called important means of livelihood. They are utilised not only for food, commercial purpose but for fodder and organic manure also. The consequent land alienation is felling trees indiscriminately. Most of these trees have been lost in the areas of scheduled caste and scheduled tribe population. On the one hand, these communities are not allowed to collect forest produce, but on the other hand large-scale deforestation has occurred because of various developmental projects and extension of cultivation by reclamation of land (Rupavath, Ramdas, 2009).

Worsening Condition of Food Security

Food security has been one of the major indicators for assessing the outcome of land alienation. Household food security has been drastically altered in post-displacement period. The landless people are forced to buy most of their food articles from the market which requires cash money. Therefore, most of displaced families have got debt-ridden. The increasing cost of food and reduction in agricultural productivity due to land displacement has ushered in food insecurity in the household. For example, in African countries land-use regulations and planning frameworks, inherited from the colonial era, have been ideological tools for maintaining the unequal distribution of land and inequitable security of tenure. Most of the best agricultural land is used for the production of export, with little of the produce finding its way onto the local market. This relation of land and food security has been explained by Maxwell and Wiebe also who stress that reduction or lack of access of land leads directly to a reduction in income and access to food (A Report on Land Tenure Systems and their impact on Food Security and Sustainable Development in Africa, 2004). Maxwell and Wiebe (1998) argue that access to resources is an essential determinant of access to food; food security is a function of food availability, access and utilisation (*ibid*). It has been conceptualised as following figure:

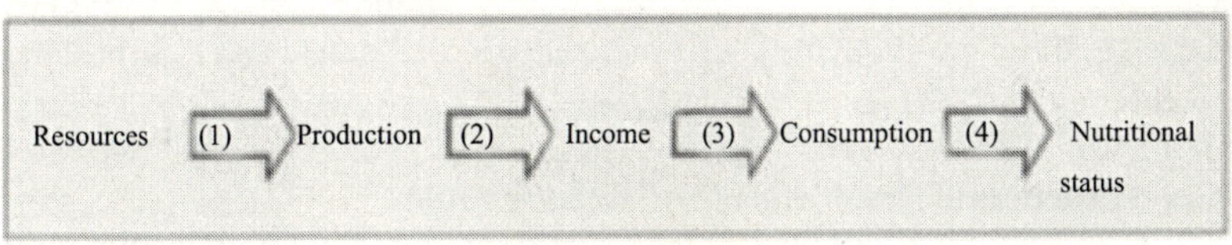

Fig. 6.1: Conventional Conceptual Links Between Land and Food.

Source: A Report on Land Tenure Systems and their impact on Food Security and Sustainable Development in Africa, published by Economic Commission for Africa in December, 2004.

Diminishing Irrigation Facilities

Land alienation and displacement has resulted into paucity of proper irrigation facilities also. Due to immediate alienation of land from their farmers, tube wells and bore wells were also separated. The poor farmer had to depend upon natural rain for irrigation on rest of the land. The huge cost in re-establishing tube wells discouraged farmers to cultivate land and they finally left the agricultural activity.

Reduction in Human Capital due to Ill Health

Existing studies show that migrants are often vulnerable to health risks at their destination, where they may lack access to proper care (Siddiqui, Tasneem, 2012). A large number of the reported illnesses are "mild" chronic disorders such as migraines, sleeplessness, chest and body pains, that may be psychosomatic and stress-related (Rawat, Vidya Bhushan, Mamidi Bharath Bhushan and Sujatha Surepally, 2010). All of the reported illnesses can be a major drain on the affected families because they drain a portion of scarce earnings into health care while also reducing their ability to work and earn a living (*ibid*). In this way, it leads to never-ending cycling process of poverty. The loss of human capital due to frequent illness causes a large proportion of migrant population lose stable source of their livelihood. Therefore, migration increases the risk for loss of livelihood on these above cited grounds.

Having glimpse of above-mentioned agony of land alienation, displacement and migration on livelihood of people, it comes to our mind that there is an urgent need for pro-people rehabilitation. The displacement is widening gap between the resourceful and the resourceless. Even the resettlement and rehabilitation of masses are not in accordance with affected people. The notion of informed consent is all flawed when it comes to resettlement and rehabilitation of aggrieved masses. The land in tribal areas is utilised for developmental activities like promotion of Special Economic Zone (SEZ) but the aggrieved people are not able to get proper resettlement. Although some of project affected persons are resettled physically yet, the lack of favourable socio-economic milieu leave them deserted and impoverished. The absence of basic infrastructure at rehabilitated sites reverses the meaning of rehabilitation. Therefore, this paper has tried to focus on some of pre-requisite good practices of resettlement and rehabilitation which, if applied, may reduce trauma of the displaced people. Lets' see those pre-requisite good practices of Resettlement and Rehabilitation (R & R):

Good Practices of Resettlement and Rehabilitation

For resettlement to be a development experience, the process will not only have to deal with the complexities and risks of resettlement itself but also effectively engage with the whole range of political and institutional factors of those risks, i.e., the power element inherent in the experience of displacement

(WCD Thematic Review, 2000). As envisaged from already discussed challenges, resettlement is driven by force. The social and environmental cost has been abandoned in the wake of development. The estimation of social and environmental impacts and their costs has often been a bone of contention between project proponents and the people who are to be negatively affected. The process is compounded by the complex nature of the problems of quantifying and accounting for social and environmental costs (*ibid*).

Therefore, there have been exemplified some essential good practices for R&R which ensure reversal of situation faced by the displaced people.

Community Managed Resettlement

Community managed resettlement is one of good practices of R&R around the world. It does not mean a mere community participation but community control and its ownership of resettlement programme. Communities more often than not know what they need and can make best use of opportunities that will allow them to satisfy their needs. Given the space and support to articulate their needs and expand their options, communities are capable of making the most efficient and cost-effective choices among resettlement strategies and options (*ibid*). The more the resettlement programme is community and collective centred, the greater the chances of it succeeding. One of the examples in this affair may be quoted from hydroelectric project of ELETROSUL, a publicly owned power generation utility of Southern Brazil. In response to the 1979 announcement of ELETROSUL plans to build a series of dams in the Uruguay river basin in the States of Santa Catarina and Rio Grande do Sul, the communities that were to be affected responded by beginning a process of political organisation, facilitated by rural unions, church activists and sections of the academic community, to protect their interests. They organised themselves into the Comissão Regional dos Atingidos por Barragens (CRAB). (*ibid*). The community (through CRAB) sought to play a more active role in the process. This included the identification, purchase, and preparation of land, construction of houses, farm buildings and community buildings and access roads.

Public Hearings and Reviews

Public hearings and reviews are widely used strategies in certain countries to enable people to participate in decision-making process. The public hearing provides a scope for open discussion over various institutional, social, environmental aspects of any developmental project. The public hearing brings transparency. Independent Reviews are most effective when they are conducted by organisations/people who enjoy a relatively high degree of credibility from all stakeholders and when the methodology of the review is participatory and transparent (*ibid*). The World Bank too has resorted to this, most notably in the case of the Sardar Sarovar project in India, which ultimately led to its withdrawal from the project.

Social Impact Assessment

The assessment of any project from environmental and social points of view brings estimation of effect of project on aggrieved persons. It is imperative that there should be a detailed assessment of socio-economic conditions of the people who may be negatively affected. Again, the adoption of a comprehensive plan to mitigate these impacts and analysing extent of displacement, loss of livelihood is an important indicator of successful resettlement and rehabilitation programme.

Enabling People to be Beneficiaries

Interestingly the idea is an old one, stretching in India as far back as 1902. When plans were drawn up for the Nira Canal System in western India, a detailed exchange of holdings in the command was worked out that could allow for the displaced to be resettled in the area (India Report, 1999). Allotting land in the command areas is the most definitive way of sharing the benefits of the project with the displaced persons. Several irrigation projects in India, particularly in Maharashtra and Madhya Pradesh, attempted to gain land in the command area for rehabilitation using various land reform measures (Land Ceiling Act, Maharashtra Resettlement Act 1976, Madhya Pradesh Resettlement Policy 1986). This approach seeks to emphasise the point that the negatively affected people are actually investees and as they have contributed a factor of production, namely the land for storing the waters/building the canals etc., they are entitled to a share in the returns on the investment.

Defining Eligibility for Benefits of Resettlement and Development Programme for Negatively Affected Persons:

The inclusion of eligibility criteria has potential to benefit the actual displaced person. It is able to address the widespread impact of the diverse aspects of a developmental project upstream and downstream along with its host communities and negatively affected people. The World Bank has defined certain criteria over which the displaced persons may be identified and entitled for actual benefit. It states that persons who do not have formal legal rights to land and other assets, should be provided such claims through a process identified under R&R policy. If such persons have uninterrupted possession of the land for at least one year prior to the commencement of the census, they are entitled to resettlement assistance (WCD Thematic Review, 2000). Considering the benefits of the resettlement programme, special attention must be paid to women-headed households as well as single adult women and widows (*ibid*).

Allotment of Land Acquired by Government from the Project Benefited Area to Schedule Tribe Project Affected Farmers (PAFs), who become Small, or Marginal Farmers or Landless after Acquisition, in lieu of Acquired Land from them: Government shall acquire land within the project benefited area, as per guidelines issued by the Government from time to time such that no person should become small or marginal farmer or landless due to such acquisition. It will alot such land to Scheduled Tribe PAFs (who become small or marginal farmers or landless due to acquisition of their land for the project), if such PAFs so desire, in lieu of lands acquired from them.

Allotment of House Site/Payment of Ex-gratia

The Resettlement and Rehabilitation Policy of Andhra Pradesh has made some provisions in its 6th chapter regarding benefits of R&R as following:

(a) Any Project Displaced Family (PDF) holding upto an area of five Cents of village site and whose site has been acquired shall be allotted house site of an extent of 202 square meters (five Cents) of land in rural areas or 75 square meters of land in Urban areas in the Resettlement zone besides payment of compensation for the structures if any therein;

(b) In case if any Project Displaced Family (PDF) holds village site of more than five Cents, such holder shall be allotted village house site of an extent of 202 Square Meters (five cents) of land in rural areas or 75 Square Meters of land in Urban areas in the Resettlement zone and also be paid ex-gratia for the site in excess of five Cents (for example, if a family holds village site of 20 Cents in Project Affected Zone and have two major sons, residing with such person in case, they take three house sites of five Cents each in Resettlement zone, they will get ex-gratia for the balance of five Cents (20 Cents – 3x5 cents = 15 cents); and

(c) The ex-gratia payable as above shall be on par with the package deal payable in case of acquisition of private /patta lands".

Incorporation of Opportunities for Women' Participation

Good resettlement practices are premised on consultation with women before any resettlement. Therefore, there are conducted various activities like Focus Group Discussion (FGD), baseline surveys in order to get opinion of women. The issues related to design of replacement housing, access to educational and healthcare services, availability of fuel and water and income-generating activities are discussed with women group. As women contribute financially to the household economy through both formal and informal economic activities, their opinion is very crucial before resettling their habitat.

After perusal of above-mentioned good practices of this R&R programme, it comes to our mind that there are certain parameters over which trauma of displacement may be minimised. The consequences of involuntary resettlement can be mitigated through carefully adopted consultation strategies. In this regard, the World Bank has taken initiative through several operational directives like baseline surveys, compensation, inclusion of indigenous people in resettlement policy-making, impact assessment, etc.

Conclusion

The issue of livelihood keeps a very crucial position in determining effect of displacement, alienation and migration. As already envisaged, current development paradigm has brought a spiralling effect of land displacement on livelihood. The initiation of various developmental projects, dams, economic zones have deprived indigenous people of their own stable source of income. On one hand, it has provided employment opportunities and lured poor people to migrate, on the other, it has snatched their land and productivity. The ill-effect of development has engulfed even health of poor and backward classes. They are not able to produce a healthy human capital and thus, get sucked in huge debt. In this case, it is need of hour to review our rehabilitation policy and enable it to redress these grievances of displaced people. There is a need to evolve institutions to protect and strengthen the rights of individuals. It has felt the need to redefine the voluntary and involuntary resettlement. The rehabilitation programme should not be mere eyewash. It must involve certain practices or parameters which may compensate adequately for loss of livelihood. Apart from it, the programme of resettlement and rehabilitation needs to have gender perspective regarding its impact. As women are backbone of most of our household economy around the globe, the analysis of post-resettlement effect on their livelihood also gives a view whether R&R activities are pro-development or not. There must be some safeguards to facilitate women full access and enjoyment of all project related compensation. There should not be any displacement until clear and full rehabilitation of individuals is done. In this way, the above-cited good practices of Resettlement and Rehabilitation (R&R) have attempted to showcase certain solution for coming out of agony of displacement, migration and alienation from homeland.

References

Asil, Mohammed, 2000; Why Displaced Persons Reject Project Resettlement Colonies, EPW, Vol. 35, No. 24 (June 10-16, 2000), pp. 2005-2008, excerpted from http://www.jstor.org/stable/4409382 (accessed on 06-07-2013).

Bartolome, L.J., de Wet, C., Mander, H., Nagraj, V.K. 2000; Displacement, Resettlement, Rehabilitation, Reparation, and Development, WCD Thematic Review I.3, excerpted fromhttp://siteresources.worldbank.org/INTINVRES/Resources/DisplaceResettleRehabilitationReparationDevFinal13main.pdf (accessed on 22-06-2013).

Burra, Sunder, 1999; Resettlement and Rehabilitation of the Urban Poor- The Story of Kanjur Marg, working paper no. 99, excerpted from www.ucl.ac.uk/.../pdf.../SPARC_Burra_story_of_Kanjur_Marg.pdf (accessed on 20-06-2013).

Cernea, Michael, M, 1999; Why Economic Analysis is essential to Resettlement- A Sociologist's view, Economic and Political Weekly, Vol. 34, no. 31, excerpted from http://www.jstor.org/stable/4408255 (accessed on 27-06-2013).

Dhru, Kelly A, 2010; Acquisition of land for 'development' projects in India: The Road Ahead, published by Research Foundation for Governance, India, excerpted from www.rfgindia.org/publications/LandAcquisition.pdf (accessed on 27-06-2013).

Eggenberger, Simon, 2011; Effects of labour migration on Rural Livelihoods in Tajikistan, January' 2011 excerpted from www.nccr-central-asia.org/MSC_THESIS_EGGENBERGERs.pdf (accessed on 27-06-2013).

Fernandes, Walter; India's Forced Displacement Policy and Practice, Is compensation upto its functions, excerpted from http://onlineministries.creighton.edu/CollaborativeMinistry/NESRC/Walter/chp-7.pdf (accessed on 23-06-2013).

Goswami, Uddipana, 2007; Internal Displacement, Migration and Policy in Northeastern India, Eastwest Center Washington Working paper, excerpted from www.eastwestcenter.org/download/3253/32180/EWCWwp008.pdf (accessed on 27-06-2013).

Involuntary Resettlement Sourcebook, Planning and Implementation in Development Projects, World Bank Report, excerpted from http://www4.worldbank.org/afr/ssatp/Resources/HTML/GenderRG/Source per cent20 per cent20documents per cent5CTool per cent20Kits per cent20& per cent20Guides per cent5CDesigning%20Projects/TLPRO10%20invol%20resettlementsourcebookWB.pdf (accessed on 20-06-2013).

Kothari, Smilu, 1996; Whose Nation? The Displaced as Victims of Development, EPW, Vol. 31, No. 24, (June 15, 1996), pp. 1476-1485 excerpted from http://www.jstor.org/stable/4404269(accessed on 06-07-2013).

Land Tenure Systems and their Impacts on Food Security and Sustainable Development in Africa, published by Economic Commission for Africa, December, 2004, excerpted from http://www.uncsd2012.org/content/documents/land_ tenure_systems%20and%20their%20impacts%20on%20Food%20Security% 20and% 20 Sustainable%20Development%20in%20Africa.pdf (accessed on 27-06-2013).

Levitt, Joanna, 2007; The Need for New Approaches to Involuntary Resettlement: Lessons from Cambodia's Highway One Case, excerpted from www.accountability project. org/downloads/Lessons%20from%20HW1.doc ý(accessed on 20-06-2013).

Modi, Renu, 2009; Resettlement and Rehabilitation in Urban Centres, Economic and Political Weekly, February 7, 2009, excerpted from http://www.indiaenviron mentportal. org.in/files/Resettlement%20and%20Rehabilitation.pdf (accessed on 20-06-2013).

Palit, Amitendu, 2012; The Land Acquisition, Resettlement and Rehabilitation Bill, 2011: Providing Solutions or Raising Questions, Journal of Emerging Knowledge on Emerging Markets, Vol. 4, excerpted from http://digitalcommons.kennesaw.edu/cgi/viewcontent.cgi? article=1092&context =jekem (accessed on 23-06-2013).

Rao, C.H. Hanumantha, 2009; Inclusive Growth-Recent Experience and Challenges Ahead, Economic and Political Weekly, Vol. 44, No. 13, excerpted from http://www.jstor.org/stable/40278655 (accessed on 27-06-2013).

Rawat, Vidya Bhushan, Mamidi Bharath Bhushan and Sujatha Surepally, 2010; The Impact of Special Economic Zones in India: A Case Study of Polepally SEZ, Social Development Foundation, New Delhi excerpted from www.iss.nl/fileadmin/ASSETS/iss/Documents/.../85_Rawat_et_al.pdf (accessed on 27-06-2013).

Rupavath, Ramdas, 2009; Tribal Land Alienation and Political Movements: Socio-Economic Patterns from South India, Cambridge Scholars Publishing, UK excerpted from www.c-s-p.org/flyers/978-1-4438-1110-1-sample.pdf (accessed on 06-07-2013).

Sah, D.C. 1995; Development and Displacement-National Rehabilitation Policy, Economic and Political Weekly, Vol. 30, No. 48, excerpted from http://www.jstor.org/stable/4403505 (accessed on 27-06-2013).

Stanley, Jason; Development-induced Displacement and Resettlement, excerpted from http://www.forcedmigration.org/research-resources/expert-guides/development-induced-displacement-and-resettlement/fmo022.pdf (accessed on 22-06-2013).

Sen, Amartya, 2006; Development as Freedom, Oxford University Press, New Delhi.

Sethi, Manpreet; Land Reform in India-Issues and Challenges, excerpted from http://www.foodfirst.org/files/bookstore/pdf/promisedland/4.pdf (accessed on 24-06-2013).

Siddiqui, Tasneem, 2012; Impact of Migration on Poverty and Development, working paper-2, University of Sussex, UK excerpted from http://r4d.dfid.gov.uk/Output/191250/Default.aspx (accessed on 27-06-2013).

The phenomenon of migration: Its significance or meaning in human societies throughout history; published by International Federation of Red Cross and Red Crescent societies excerpted from http://www.ifrc.org/PageFiles/89397/the%20 phenomenon%20of%20migration_TYPEFI_final_En.pdf (accessed on 27-06-2013).

Thukral, Enakshi Ganguly, 1996; Development, Displacement and Rehabilitation: Localing Gender, EPW, Vol. 31, No. 24, June 15, 1996, pp. 1500-1503 excerpted from http://www.jstor.org/stable/4404272 (accessed on 06-07-2013).

Villalba, Clara Sandoval, 2009; Rehabilitation as a Form of Reparation under International Law, The Redress Trust, excerpted from http://www.redress.org/downloads/publications/The%20right%20to%20rehabilitation.pdf (accessed on 22-06-2013).

Wehrwein, G.S. 1937; An Appraisal of Resettlement, Journal of Farm Economics, Vol. 19, No. 1, excerpted from http://www.jstor.org/stable/1230868 (accessed on 27-6-2013).

7

Approaches to Tribal Development

P. Shailaja

Introduction

In India nearly 70 per cent of the population resides in the rural areas. According to 1991 census, 67.76 per cent of persons belong to Scheduled Tribe (ST) in different States and Union Territories excluding Assam, Jammu and Kashmir. This constitute 8.08 per cent of the total population. The percentage of Scheduled Tribe population has marginally increased from 7. 83 per cent in 1981 to 7.95 per cent in 1991. The Scheduled Tribe population has increased by 25.67 per cent during the decade of 1981-1991. The growth rate is high in comparison to the total population of the country (23.79 per cent). Tribal groups or Adivasis are considered to be the earliest inhabitants of India. The government instead recognises most Adivasis under the Constitutional term "Scheduled Tribes" derived from a schedule in the Constitution Order of 1950. While the Order declared 212 tribes located in 14 states as Adivasis, the Government of India today identifies 533 tribes. To many therefore, any aggregate analysis of Adivasis is meaningless because it cannot capture the uniqueness that defines tribal groups.

The relatively slower decline in poverty among Adivasis means that they are increasingly concentrated in the poorest declines. Comprising about eight per cent of India's population, Adivasis accounted for a fourth of the population living in the poorest wealth decline in 2005.

Rights Accorded to Scheduled Tribes by Government Laws

- Constitution – special provisions restrict entry and ownership of land and immovable resources in Adivasi areas by non-Adivasis and outsiders;

• Scheduled Area Land Transfer Regulation Act of 1959 – transfer of land or immovable property from tribal to non-tribal in scheduled area is null and void.

Objectives of the Study

1. To know the status of the Tribes as per with other communities.
2. To study the programmes and policies initiated for tribes.
3. To access the development of the tribes.

Methodology

A detail study was taken up to access the development of the Schedule Tribes their problems and development measures taken up by the government.

Primary and Secondary data collection methodology is used for the present study.

Development

Development is usually conceived as an aspect of change that is desirable, broadly predicted or planned and administered, or at least influenced, by governmental action. Thus, the concept of development consists of (a) an aspect of change; (b) a plan or prediction; and (c) involvement of the government for the achievement of that planned or predicted goal. The term "development" is also used for the process of allowing and encouraging people to meet their own aspirations. It, therefore, must relate to transforming the entire society enmeshing together its economic, social, political and administrative aspects on alround balanced upward change (Basu A.R., 1985).

Constitutional Provisions

The Constitution of India initiated the tribal welfare programmes by incorporating important provisions. These provisions not only put an end to the policy of indifference which had been followed during the pre-independence period, but also gave testimony to tribal welfare programmes, making them a constitutional obligation for the future governments of the country.

1. Statutory recognition of tribal communities.
2. Creation of scheduled areas for the thorough development of the tribals.
3. Special representations in the parliament, in the legislative assemblies and local bodies.
4. Special privileges in the form of reservation of a certain percentage of posts in government services and seats in educational institutions.
5. Recognition of the right to use local language for administration and other purposes and to profess one's faith.

Article 275 (1) of the constitution provides for grant-in-aid from the Union to the States for promoting the welfare of the Scheduled Tribes or for raising the level of administration of the Scheduled Areas. The constitution also provides for the appointment of a commission for Scheduled Tribe's for safeguarding their interests. Thus, tribal development in the true sense and in the present context of India is in fact a post-independence concept and draws the spirit from the Constitution itself.

Regional Concentration of Tribal Communities in India

Table 7.1 : Scheduled Tribe Population and Decadal Change by Residence: 2011

Scheduled Tribe Population 2011			*Decadal Change 2001-2011*			
Total	*Rural*	*Urban*	*Total*	*Rural*	*Urban*	
(1)	(2)	(3)	(4)	(5)	(6)	(7)
INDIA	104,281,034	93,819,162	10,461,872	23.7	21.3	49.7

North-eastern Region: In the mountain valleys and other areas of north-eastern India, covering the States and Union Territories like Arunachal Pradesh, Assam, Manipur, Meghalaya, Mizoram, Nagaland and Tripura live tribes like the Abor, Garo, Khasi, Kuki, Mismi, Naga, etc., who mostly belong to Mongolian racial stock.

Himalayan Region: In the sub-Himalayan regions covering parts of North-Bengal, Uttar Pradesh and Himachal Pradesh live tribes like Lepcha, Rabha, etc., mostly belonging to Mongolian racial group.

Central India Region: In the older hills and Chotanagpur Plateau, along the dividing lines between peninsular India and the Indo-Gangetic basin, live many tribal communities like the Bhumij, Gond, Ho, Oraon, Munda, Santal, etc., covering the States of Bihar, Orissa, Madhya Pradesh and West Bengal and mostly belonging to Proto-Australoid racial stock.

Western India Region: Covering the States like Rajasthan, Maharashtra, Gujarat, Goa, Dadra and Nagar Haveli live a number of tribal communities the most important of them being the Bhil racially belonging to the Proto-Australoid group.

Southern India Region: Covering the States of Karnataka, Andhra Pradesh, Tamil Nadu and Kerala, in the Nilgiri Hills and converging lines of the Ghats live the Chenchu, Irula, Kadar, Kota, Kurumba, Toda, etc., having Negrito, Caucasoid, Proto-Australoid or mixed physical features.

Island Region: Covering Andaman, Nicobar and Lakshadweep Islands live a number of small tribes like the Andamanese, Onge, Sentinelese, etc.

Table 7.2 : Scheduled Tribe Population by Sex and Residence: Census 2011

Male			*Female*			
Total	*Rural*	*Urban*	*Total*	*Rural*	*Urban*	
(1)	*(2)*	*(3)*	*(4)*	*(5)*	*(6)*	*(7)*
India	5,24,09,823	4,71,26,341	52,83,482	5,18,71,211	4,66,92,821	51,78,390

Traditional tribal communities are mainly characterised by:

• A distinct culture, which is community oriented and valuing the power of nature. They believe no one should take advantage of another's weakness.

• Relative geographical isolation and thus experiencing political, economic and social discrimination. The mainstream ruling elite treats the homeland of the tribal communities in India as their internal colony.

• Dependence for their survival mainly on natural resources and being spiritually linked to their lands.

• No centralised political institutions and are organised at the level of the community making decisions on a consensus basis.

• A differing worldview, consisting of a custodial and non-materialistic attitude to land and natural resources.

An Overview of Problems Faced by Adivasis (Tribes) in Andhra Pradesh

Andhra Pradesh (AP) is one of the relatively larger states in India. It accounts for 8.4 per cent of India's total geographical area and 7.1 per cent of population, and ranks fourth geographically and fifth—population-wise among Indian states. The density of population at 308 per square km in the State is lower than the 382 per square km at all-India level. The Scheduled Castes and Scheduled Tribes account for 16.2 per cent and 6.6 per cent of the total population in the state respectively. Religious Minorities account for about one-tenth of the state population. Rural population in the State is predominantly agricultural with more than three-fourths of its workforce being engaged directly in the agriculture sector.

ST population is more than 50 per cent and between 25 per cent to 50 per cent as per Census 2011.

State	*Name*	*Total Population*	*ST Population*	*Percentage of ST*
(1)	*(2)*	*(3)*	*(4)*	*(5)*
01	Andhra Pradesh	84580777	5918073	7.0

Land Alienation

The Adivasi people in the state have historically been vulnerable to largescale exploitation from non-Adivasis from the plains and due to severe neglect from the government. Inspite of the existence of constitutional safeguards and reservations, the apathy of the state government has led to vast areas of land in the agency (tribal) areas being transferred to non-Adivasis or non-tribals. Especially this is prevalent in the foothills where the majority population is adivasi, yet the areas have been excluded from Scheduled Areas, implying that the tribals do not enjoy the legal protections enjoyed by those in the hills.

Forest Issues

The next serious problem is the complexity of issues related to forest lands and the tribals' access to these resources. Ambiguities over revenue-forest boundaries have given opportunities for both departments to victimise the tribals on false cases.

Development Projects in the Region

Non-forest activities like setting up of industries, mining projects, construction of big reservoir and other 'development' projects led to large scale and multiple displacement of tribal population who were forced to migrate. They face constant harassment for being 'criminals' and are forcefully evicted from lands occupied by them. Their rights and access to forest resources are curtailed by government and local communities who were the earlier settlers.

Development Neglect

The performance of the government in the agency areas in the last five decades has a humiliating record whether in providing basic amenities and infrastructure, education, medical services, or in extending support and linkages to agriculture, forest produce, irrigation and other activities. This has ensured that tribals remained illiterate, indebted, susceptible to endemic diseases and neither capable to protecting their traditional institutions nor being able to compete with the mainstream.

The Emerging Macro Policies

The natural wealth of the tribal areas in A.P. is under new forms of threat with the liberalisation policies of the state government. Forest resources, minerals and the natural beauty are projected as the major vehicles of commodification of the region by relaxing the stringent constitutional safeguards related to tribal lands. The government has invited industries to set up tourism projects and holiday resorts, mining projects, develop infrastructure for film industries and forestry/medicinal plantation projects.

Tribal Education: Status and Issues Related to Women and Children

Tribal education in Andhra Pradesh has been a slow process of integration into formal mainstream education. It is replete with problems of lack of understanding of tribal culture, inaccessibility and dispersed nature of tribal habitations, multi-lingual barriers and thrusting of Telugu as the medium of education in tribal schools, socio-cultural disparities between tribes and between tribals and outsiders, poverty and most of all, neglect of development needs and basic amenities for either tribals or non-tribals posted as teachers in these areas and non-allocation of resources for tribal education. Even after more than 50 years of independence, education has not reached the tribal regions largely due to lack of political will in making the tribal communities a priority for development.

Status of Literacy, Enrollment and Dropout among Scheduled Tribes in A.P.

Out of a population of 41 lakhs, the literacy rate among ST men, as of 1991 Census, is a mere 25 per cent and that of women is 8.6 per cent (after a highly imaginative interpretation of the term literate). Official figures for dropout rate at the primary level of education among STs and SCs is between 73 per cent and 82 per cent. While the enrollment of tribal children in primary schools is 4,57,748 students, those who reach high school level in the entire state are about 10,000. While the total number of tribal habitations in A.P. are close to ten thousand, those covered by primary schools are only 6138 leaving atleast a third of the tribal hamlets inaccessible to even basic literacy opportunities.

Dropout rate among tribal children is highest in the primary level itself (66 per cent). From a total population of 20,56,664 ST women, there are just 21 women with post graduate degree! The enrollment of ST girls (1993-94) from the primary level to Class XII is 2,32,486 which is only 36.71 per cent. There are just 6,595 who have reached middle level of school and 28,541 at the primary level - in the entire state! The dropout rate among ST girls is 89.20 per cent most of which is in the primary level itself. In districts like Visakhapatnam where there is a high concentration of Primitive Tribal Groups like the Khonds, Gadabas, Porjas the female literacy levels are much lower (7.83 per cent) than the state average.

Lack of Facilities

Following are some of the observations that need consideration:

- One of the major problems in tribal education is that of language. Most of the tribal languages and dialects are in the most rudimentary stage and there is hardly any written literature. Most of the states impart education to tribal and non-tribal children alike through the medium of the regional language, which makes the education uninteresting and also hurts sentiments for his own language.
- Nature of habitat: Most of the tribal villages are scattered. This entails long travels to attend schools. Unless the school is situated very close to their villages and its site approved by the local people the result shall not be encouraging.
- School building also plays an important role in the growth of education among the tribal folk. Due to mismanagement, bungling and sometimes financial constraints, the building is seldom suitable to run an educational institution.
- Number of teachers: Most of the primary schools run in tribal areas are "single teacher-managed whose presence in the school is more an exception than a rule".

Approaches for the Tribes in Andhra Pradesh

India is a democratic country, where we can find various religions, caste, language and culture. It is a secular state where everyone have the right to follow their own language and religion. We can find drastic change in the developments in the country since the period of Independence in all fields.

The term "development" involves all aspects of human activity, education and health. Till now various committees and commissions were laid for taking policies and programmes for the development of the Schedule Tribes in India, In India, the Rural Development Department and Department of Schedule Tribes is concerned with the development approaches for the tribes as per the constitution of India. The following are the approaches for the development of the Schedule Tribes in India.

Scheme of Development of Primitive Tribal Groups (PTGs)

Based on pre-agricultural level of technology, low level of literacy, declining or stagnant populations, 75 tribal communities in 17 States and one Union Territory of Andaman and Nicobar Island, have been identified and categorised as Primitive Tribal Groups (PTGs). Considering the vulnerability of these groups, a Central Sector Scheme was introduced in the year 1998-99 for the alround development of PTGs. The scheme is very flexible, and covers housing, infrastructure development, education, health, land distribution/development, agriculture development, cattle development, social security, insurance, etc. During 2007-08, comprehensive long term "Conservation-cum-Development (CCD) Plans" for PTGs have been formulated for Eleventh Plan period through baseline surveys conducted by respective State Governments/Union Territory. These Plans envisage a synergy between efforts of State Governments and non-governmental organisations.

Tribal Research Institutes

Fourteen Tribal Research Institutes (TRIs) have been set up by Andhra Pradesh, Assam, Bihar, Gujarat, Kerala, Madhya Pradesh, Maharashtra, Orissa, Rajasthan, Tamil Nadu, West Bengal, Uttar Pradesh, Manipur and Tripura. These Institutes are engaged in providing planning inputs to the State Governments, conducting research and evaluation studies, collection of data, codification of customary law and conduct of training, seminars and workshops. Some of these Institutes are also having museums exhibiting tribal artifacts.

Girls/Boys Hostels for STs

Girls hostels scheme was started in Third Five-Year Plan with the aim of providing residential facilities to tribal girls in pursuit of education. Central assistance of 50 per cent cost of construction to the States, cent per cent to the Union Territories is provided under the scheme. During 1999-2000, funds were released to the States/UTs for construction of 29 Girls' Hostels and 11 Girls Hostels during 2000-2001. Boys hostels scheme was started in 1989-90 under the same pattern as the Girls' Hostels. During 2000-2001, funds were released for construction of 15 boys' hostels.

Ashram Schools in TSP Area

This Centrally-sponsored scheme was started in 1990-91 to provide Central assistance to the States and Union Territories on 50 per cent and 100 per cent basis, respectively. During 1999-2000 were released for construction of 36 Ashram schools.

Vocational Training Centres in Tribal Areas

The scheme aims at upgrading the skills of the tribal youths in various traditional/modern vocation depending upon their educational qualification, present economic trends and the market potential, which would enable them to gain suitable employment or enable them to become self-employed. The scheme provides 100 per cent grant, and is implemented through State Governments, UT Administration and NGOs. The scheme prescribes fixed financial norms. No construction cost is provided.

Strengthening Education among Scheduled Tribe Girls in Low Literacy District

It is a gender scheme of the Ministry. The scheme aims to bridge the gap in literacy levels between the general female population and tribal women, through facilitating 100 per cent enrolment of tribal girls in the identified Districts or Blocks, more particularly in Naxal affected areas and in areas inhabited by Primitive Tribal Groups (PTGs), and reducing drop-outs at the elementary level by creating the required ambience for education. The scheme recognises the fact that improvement of the literacy rate of tribal girls is essential to enable them to participate effectively in and benefit from, socio-economic development.

The scheme covers 54 identified districts in 12 States and one Union Territory where the ST population is 25 per cent or more, and ST female literacy rate is below 35 per cent or its fractions, as per 2001 census. In addition, any other tribal block in a district, other than aforesaid 54 identified districts, which has scheduled tribal populations 25 per cent or above, and tribal female literacy rate below 35 per cent or its fractions, as per 2001 census, are also covered. The scheme also covers PTG areas and gives priority to areas affected by Naxalism. The scheme is implemented by non-governmental organisations (NGOs) and autonomous societies of the State Governments/Union Territory.

Tribal Co-operative Marketing Development Federation of India Limited

The Tribal Cooperative Marketing Development Federation of India Limited (TRIFED) was set up by the Government of India in 1987, with the prime objective of providing marketing assistance and remunerative prices to ST communities for their minor forest produce and surplus agricultural produce and to wean them away from exploitative private traders and middlemen. The federation is a National level Co-operative apex body functioning under the Multi-State Co-operative Societies Act, 1984. The authorised share capital of TRIFED is Rs 100 crore and the paid up capital is Rs 99.98 The Government of India's contribution is Rs 99.75 crore and the balance of Rs 0.23 crore has been contributed by other shareholders.

Coaching for Scheduled Tribes

The scheduled tribe candidates coming from deprived families and disadvantaged environment find it difficult to compete with those coming from a socially and economically advantageous background. To promote a more level playing field and give ST candidates a better chance to succeed in competitive examinations, the Ministry of Tribal Affairs supports a scheme for coaching for disadvantaged ST candidates in quality coaching institutions to enable them to successfully compete in examinations for jobs/admission to professional courses.

The scheme supports free coaching to scheduled tribe students for various competitive examinations viz. Civil Services/State Civil Services/Other Exams conducted by UPSC like CDS, NDA, etc./professional courses like Medical, Engg., Business Administration/Banking/Staff Selection Commission/Railway Recruitment Boards/insurance companies, etc. The financial norms of the scheme have been revised during 2007-08. The scheme covers coaching fees, monthly stipend @ Rs 1000 per ST student per month and boarding/lodging charges for outstation students @ Rs 2000 per ST student per month for the period of coaching.

Grant-in-Aid to Voluntary Organisations Working for Welfare of Scheduled Tribes

The prime objective of the scheme is to enhance the reach of welfare schemes of Government and fill the gaps in service deficient tribal areas, in the sectors such as education, health, drinking water, agro-horticultural productivity, social security net etc., through the efforts of voluntary organisations (VOs)/non-governmental organisations (NGOs) and to provide an environment for socio-economic upliftment and overall development of the Scheduled Tribes (STs). Any other innovative activity having direct impact on the socio-economic development or livelihood generation of STs may also be considered through voluntary efforts.

Under this scheme 90 per cent grant is provided by the ministry and 10 per cent cost is required to be borne by the non-governmental organisations from their own resources, except in Scheduled Areas where the Government bears100 per cent cost. The scheme provides a list of categories of projects viz. residential school, non-residential schools, ten or more bedded hospitals, mobile dispensaries, computer training centers, etc., which could be covered under the scheme, and also prescribes fixed financial norms. The scheme does not provide any construction cost.

Post-matric Scholarship for ST Students

The objective of the scheme is to provide financial assistance to students belonging to Scheduled Tribes pursuing Post-Matriculation recognised courses in recognised institutions. The scheme covers professional, technical as well as non-professional and non-technical courses at various levels and the scheme also includes correspondence courses including distance and continuing education. The scheme is implemented by the State Government and UT Administrations, which receive 100 per cent Central Assistance over and above the committed liability which is required to be borne by them from their own budgetary provisions. The committed liability is equal to the expenditure reached in the last year of the Plan period. Accordingly, the expenditure incurred in the last year of the Xth plan Period, i.e., 2006-2007, has become the committed liability of State/UTs, which is required to be borne by them during each year of the 11th Five Year Plan period. The requirement of committed liability of North Eastern State has been dispensed with from 1997-98. The Scheme is in operation since 1944-45.

Rajiv Gandhi National Fellowship Scheme (RGNF)

This Scheme was introduced in the year 2005-06. Under the Scheme, fellowship is provided to ST students for pursuing higher studies such as M.Phil. and Ph.D. The maximum duration of a fellowship is five years. Every year 667 fellowships are to be provided to ST students. The scheme is being implemented by University Grant Commission (UGC) on behalf of the Ministry of Tribal Affairs. Any ST student who has passed post-graduation from a UGC recognised University can apply under the scheme.

National Overseas Scholarship Scheme for ST

The Scheme provides financial assistance to meritorious students belonging to STs for pursuing higher studies abroad in specified fields of Master level courses, Ph.D. and Post-doctoral research programmes, in the field of Engineering, Technology and Science. The selected candidates are given cost of tuition and other educational fees charged by the foreign university etc., maintenance and other grants along with travel expenses. In addition passage grants are also available to candidates belonging to ST who are in receipt of merit scholarship for postgraduate studies, research or training abroad (excluding attending seminars, workshops, conferences) from a foreign government/organisation or under any other scheme where cost of passage is not provided. Scheme of NOS has been revised in 2007-08 as Plan scheme. Fifteen awards would be sanctioned to ST students per year.

Conclusion

The Government should seriously involve in the development of the tribes existing all over in India. In spite of globalisation and information technology boom existing in the present trends in India. We can find that the tribes in the remote areas are still fighting for their rights. The role and responsibility the government must be involved from the grassroot level for the development of the tribes.The following are the suggestions for the development of the tribes in India.

- Primary Education standards for the ST students must be increased by taking steps by eradicating Dropouts at this level.
- Special attention must be drawn towards the education of the girl belonging to ST community.
- Tribal life must be protected on the hilly and forest areas and protect their rights.
- Defend and strengthen the development framework and priorities of the Tribals, themselves to ensure that their access and control over their natural resources are secured.
- Gather more national and international support so that the gains will not be lost.
- More welfare programmes must be initiated especially for the tribes in the tribal areas.
- Their rights must be protected.

8

Contextualising the Tribal Problem in the Background of PESA: Experience from Odisha

Pranay Kumar Parida and Smita Raut

Abstract

This paper tries to examine the applicability of PESA in reality with specific reference to Orissa, as Orissa is also a tribal dominated state and the undercurrent of strong left wing extremism is visible at this point of time. The authors are trying to find out the reasons for non implementation as well as consequences out of it. At the end of the day, this paper will try to provide some possible way of addressing the urgent needs of tribal's with specific reference to the particular part of the world. The post-73rd amendment scenario is giving us a complex picture regarding the devolution of powers to the grass root level. To find out the gap between theory and practice, in other words between legislation and follow up action, this paper would try to find out the existing status and modalities for proper implementation. As it is found that some states like Kerala, West Bengal, and Karnataka are pioneer in terms of not only legislation but also implementation. Gujarat is known as the birth place of Mahatma Gandhi, who strongly supported Gram Swaraj. As a matter of fact Panchayat plays a great role in the field of rural development, whatever is the level of development in a state. But what about the Panchayats in tribal belt particularly in naxal affected areas? Is PESA is sufficient address it?

Key Words: (Inclusive Growth, Development Paradigm, Marginalised Sections of Society, Tribes Problems in India, PESA, Extremist Movements, Gram Swaraj, And Self-Sustained Development Models).

Introduction

With the onslaught of globalisation process, the whole governance system is undergoing metamorphic change in contemporary time. When we talk about growth, what about 'inclusive growth'? What about 'growth with social justice'? These issues are being examined minutely in the social discourse today. However the inclusion of the marginalised, i.e., dalits, tribals, aboriginal inhabitants in a particular society along with the people in the periphery of development system, due to the structural inequality in our society, has always been marginalised till date. What about the voice of the subalterns? Is it getting reflected in the policy dimensions of our country?

The enactment of PESA by Government of India seems as if a mile stone in this context, despite of having lacunas in the act itself. There is question regarding its implementability. There is lack of consensus among the states regarding the modalities of power transfer to the tribes. The fundamental issue in this background is, let the tribal people decide their governance issues by themselves, having certain independent and autonomous power to them. This is within the broad provision of the Indian Constitution. The notion of 'Gram Sabha' in the backdrop of PESA gives enormous power to the villagers/hamlet inhabitants in the PESA implemented area to decide everything, which is going to affect them, including mining, establishment of industries, royalty collection apart from general duties and responsibilities bestowed upon a panchayat. Are the Panchayts are equipped enough to handle these issues by themselves?

A Brief Historical Reference

A microscopic look into the history of 'governance system' in India will give us a synoptic picture, the way governance was carried out in different regime in different way. Though it has followed a trajectory path, the movement is not always smooth. However, in many of the regimes tried to provide some space to the citizens—more particularly, the original inhabitants certain share in the administrative system as well as its outcome. The system prevailing in the Vedic period was based on the principle of decentralisation and participation in decision making. '*Sabha*' and '*Samiti*' were the popular institutions through which the masses had a direct say in village affairs and had direct control over "Gramini". The village was a self-dependent unit. It generated its own resources, had its own functionaries and its own functional domain.

Despite the emergence of new Institutions like Zagirdari, Panchayats system continued to be quite vibrant and living during Mughal era. But with the Britishers in India and their changed Revenue system, the self-sufficient village reduced to the position of dependent unit. Indigenous system of local government was replaced by the Centralised system resulting in failure on the part of Britishers to understand the role of culture and ecology and more so, over indigenous socio-economic system of Indian villages. British India ignored the principle of decentralisation, accountability, people's participation and tried to establish a local government system based on the centralisation. The British Government lacked the will to empower the Indian People. Hence, they tried to follow the principle of delegation rather than devolution and decentralisation. Gandhi, the ardent supporter of Rama Rajya and Gram Swaraj, had full faith on the Village and Panchayat system of ancient India. In Independent India, he visualised a federal system based on the Village as a Unit of Governance. He held the view that if the Village perishes India will perish too. He strongly advocated that village sufficiency would also lead to the decentralisation of the political power.

In the 73rd constitutional amendment, the Schedule Areas were excluded from the provisions of the Act, as per the Constitution of India, the special provisions for Scheduled areas. However, according to Article 243M(4)(2), the Parliament may by law extend the provisions of Panchayat to the Schedule Areas, subject to exceptions and modifications as may be specified in such law. It was done so to avoid conflict between the traditional institutions and statutory Panchayat. Considering the growing of discontentment among the tribals across the tribal community, the Union Government constituted a Committee headed by Dilip Singh Bhuria in June, 1994 who submitted its report in January, 1994 recommending the adoption of three-tier system in the fifth Schedule Areas. So a Bill was passed in the Parliament on 24th December, 1995 giving rise to new Act namely, Provision of Panchayats (Extended to Schedule Areas) Act (PESA), 1996 (Act No. 40). The rationale behind the Act is to bring at par the tribal population to the general population of Rural Community. The Act ensures that tribal people will be empowered to manage their affairs according to their own culture within the purview of the Act.

The Case Study of Orissa

Orissa has substantial population of tribal's, which not only makes lot of contribution to the political, economic and cultural developments of the state but also the neighbouring states as Orissa touches the boundaries of other tribal dominated states like, Jharkhand, Chhattisgarh, Madhya Pradesh even parts of Bengal. Since the time of Britishers and before them tribal communities have played a significant role in the socio-political-economic history of the region and nation.

The provision of (Extension to the Scheduled Areas) Act, 1996 came into force on the 24th December, 1996. Orissa Gram Panchayat Act, 1964, Orissa Panchayat Samiti Act, 1959 and Orissa Zilla Parishad Act, 1991 have adopted the provisions of the PESA Act. It covers seven districts i.e., Mayurbhanj, Sundargarh, Koraput, Malkangiri, Rayagada, Nawarangpur and Kandhamal in full and Keonjhar, Gajapati, Kalahandi, Balasore, Sambalpur and Ganjam in part spread over 1966 Gram Panchayats in 118 Blocks in full and three Blocks in part. Accordingly 24734 Wards out of 87542 Wards, 1966 office of Sarpanch out of 6234, 1965 office of Panchayat Samiti Member out of 6233 and 256 Members of Zilla Parishad out of 854 come under the Schedule Area. Elections to these offices were conducted as per the provisions of the PESA Act.

It gives us the impression that the State of Orissa had complied, though not fully, with the provisions of the Central PESA Act while modifying its PRI Acts. Mandatory provision in the Central Act ensuring tribal communities: control over natural resources, granting licenses for minor minerals and their exploitation and acquisition of land by government for development projects which proposed to be enforced through Gram Sabhas have not been complied with. Currently the Panchayat Rules of Orissa government confirms the reservation of seats for STs in scheduled area on the proportion of their population. All the posts of chairpersons of the PIRs at all levels are reserved for STs.

The SC and ST development department has made suitable amendments in its existing acts/rules and regulations within the parameter of PESA Act. The Orissa Scheduled Areas Transfer of Immovable Property (by Scheduled Tribes) Regulation of 1956 has been amended by Regulation of 2002 (regulation I of 2002), which has come into effect from 4.9.2002. The Orissa (Scheduled Areas Money-Lenders' Regulations, 1967 (Regulation and of 1968) is in operation since 15th November 1968 with a view to regulating and monitoring money lending activities in the scheduled areas of the state.

Even though certain departments have devolved some powers to PRIs and some of them have brought amendments to the existing rules. But many of them have not amended the department rules. Hence sometime, there are clashes between panchayat acts and department acts. That has led to a situation of more confusion and chaos. As a matter of fact "Activity Mapping" process which was to be carried out by the respective states to follow the 73rd amendment in true letter and spirit that has not been taken place in an appropriate manner. However in this background the following issues are pertinent to be discussed as far as Panchayat in tribal areas are concerned.

Minor Forest Products

Panchayati Raj Department Resolution No. 8131 dt. 26.5.2000 has given the necessary powers to Gram Sabhas based on the Forest and Env. Dept. Resolution No. 5503 dt. 31.03.2000. The Orissa government (Minor Forest Admn. Rules, 2002) has come in to force w.e.f. 15.11.2002 Ownership and Management of 68 MFPs has been entrusted to GPs/Gram Sabha.

Enforcement of Prohibition and Sale of Intoxicant

Revenue and Excise Department vide their Letter No. 22977/R dt. 22.04.1999 by amending the Bihar and Orissa Excise Act 1915 provides that no such licence of exclusive privilege shall be granted except with the prior approval of the concerned Gram Panchayat with the concurrence of the Gram Sasan the G.P. is to give permission within 30 days.

Money Lending

The SC and ST development department has already taken up for amendment of the "Orissa (Scheduled Areas) Moneylenders' Regulation, 1967" to empower the GP for control over money lending and issue of license in Schedule Areas. They have also provided that if any Panchayat gives any false information then the Sarpanch or the concerned officials shall be punishable under the provisions of law. It is under the consideration of Law Department.

Minor Minerals

The Mines and Minerals (Development and Regulation) Act of 1957 (67 of 1957) has been amended on 31.08.04 wherein no perspective licence or minning/quarry lease or its renewal or auction of source shall be granted without recommendation of the concerned GP.

Transfer of Tribal Land

The Orissa Schedule Areas Transfer of Immoveable Properties (by STs) Regulation 1956 has been amended by Regulation 1 of 2002, which has come in to effect from 4.9.2002.

Control of Village Markets

Although Panchyati Raj Department has amended its act transferring the power to Gram Panchayat but the matter has not been finalised. However, the Village Panchayat has been empowered to collect the local fees/ taxes from the village market.

A Brief Analysis of the Act in Terms of Implementability

The passing of the conformity Acts by the respective States is not only a pre-requisite but rather the States have to formulate the rules and regulations to give effect to that. It is a fact that State laws have been amended more as routine than the real application of the spirit of the Act. The detailed analysis of PESA in Orissa is limited to meager cosmetic change in the Panchayat Act without much devolution of powers to the Panchayats in Scheduled Areas or to the tribal's to live through life in their way with their traditional dignity. It has created a vacuum in the governance process, which led to reasonable amount of confusion.

Implementation of the law has been severely hampered by the reluctance of most State governments to make laws and rules that conform to the spirit of the law. What is perceived as weak kneed political will has led to bureaucratic creativity in minimalistic interpretations of the law. Bureaucratic subversion of the letter and spirit of the law has been most visible in interpretation of that provision of PESA by which panchayats at appropriate levels and the gram sabha have been vested with the ownership of minor forest produce (MFP).

It is argued that the power of gram sabha can extend only to forest located within the revenue boundaries of a village. This one provision, if accepted, would nullify the law, because reserved forest in most States is not located within a revenue boundary of a village. The spirit of the law is clearly to extend ownership to the gram sabha of MFP from forests located in vicinity of the village of traditional access. Similarly, the interpretation of the concept of "ownership" of minor forest products (MFP) by gram sabha. The common view is that ownership does not provide gram sabha the right to take any decisions related to stewardship, management or sustainable harvesting of MFPs. Contrary to a whole body of empirical evidence from the national and international experience of JFM and community control of forests, it is claimed that the exercise of "ownership" of MFPs by gram sabha in this sense would inevitably lead to a destruction of forest. Therefore, "ownership" as provided for in PESA, is reinterpreted to mean the right to net revenues from MFP, after retaining administrative expenses of the forest department.

PESA Act – Few Challenges

It is argued by many scholars that PESA is very ambitious in nature, in terms of its implementation. Even some went to the extent of declaring it as a "*mini constitution with the Constitution of India*". It might pose great challenge while implanting in letter and spirit. For example, ownership over the natural resources. It is a fact that the size of the operational holding in the tribal land is eroding due to the State led acquisition and marketisation process. The sale of tribal lands to the non-tribal in the Scheduled Areas is prohibited. But the transfer continues to take place and have become more perceptible in the posed liberalisation period. The PESA provisions are intended to intrinsically protect the resources of the tribal communities and empower them to act against the forcible acquisition. But today, the acquisition of individual's and community's resources for industry in violation of these provisions is leading to conflicts in several PESA areas. This is creating conflicts leading to loss of livelihood and resource and more so over the way of life. As regards to the acquiring the mineral resources for industries, the stakes are similarly loaded against the functioning of PESA Act. If *Samata Judgment (Supreme Court, 1997)* could have been honoured by both Union and State Governments, a model of sustainable mining which was respectful of the tribal community living in mineral rich areas would have avoided many of the current conflicts witnessed on the ground.

The Recognition of Forest Rights Act, 2006 (FRA) was a result of the polity responding to protected struggles by tribal communities and movements to assert rights over the forest land they were traditionally dependent on. The Act turned the Government colonial policy on its head which it established the rights of the State over the forest over traditional rights of the community. However, continuing bureaucratic control, resistant attitude of Forest Department officials to give ownership to the communities and inadequate efforts on awareness have lead to slow implementation of the Act. It is evident from this that there is still poor recognition of various rights favouring the tribal's clearly violating the letter and spirit of PESA as well as FRA.

However to undermine the legitimacy of tribal's for the land reclamation and forest rights or against the takeover of resources or displacement still persists. In other words, tribal community's effort for self-determination and self-governance are to be respected. Though PESA guaranteed in letter and spirit, but at the ground level, there is inadequate attempt for democratic dialogue to resolve the conflict. There is adequate acknowledgement that across the PESA areas, people increasingly wanted more democratic spaces that allow them the life with dignity. But the current alienation is a manifestation of mis-governance and a lasting solution also lie in an honest implementation of PESA and putting people aspirations at the centre of public policies in schedule five areas.

Conclusion

As most of the tribal belt of the country is undergoing a radical left wing armed struggle, which is also partly reflection of mis-governance in that part of the world, it is argued that if PESA has been honestly implemented, then it would have been possible to address the misgovernance to certain extent. As a matter of fact this act may not bring the solution to the whole problem. However it could have addressed the genuine grievances of the people within parameters of the constitution of India, particularly in tribal areas. The effective control over the natural resources and management of minor forest produces in true spirit of PESA will definitely lead to economic development of PESA areas. The agrarian crisis and distress migrations could have solved by genuinely implementing the provisions of PESA. The migration as resulted from forced economic development renders impossible participation in village decision-making and is to the severe detriment of the inclusive and participatory governance envisaged by PESA.

References

1. Dhebar, U.N.: "Dhebar Commission Report".
2. Ghurye, G.S.: "The Scheduled Tribes", Popular Book Depot, Mumbai, 1959.
3. Majumdar, D.N.: "Affairs of a Tribe", Universal Publishers, Lucknow, 1953.
4. Sachidanad: "Culture and Change in Tribal Bihar", Bookland Limited, Calcutta, 1964.
5. Elwin, Verrier: "Nagaland", Research Department, Advisor's Secretariat, Shillong, 1961.
6. Srinivas, M.N.: "Social Change in Modern India", Allied Publishers, Bombay, 1961.
7. Srivastava, S.K.: "The Tharus- A Study of Culture Dynamics", Agra University Press, Agra, 1958.

8. Tandon, J.S.: "The Report of Rourkela Industrial Complex" (MSS).

9. Rao, V.K.R.V: "Social Change and Tribal Society", Journal of Social Research, Vol. IX, No. 2, September 1966.

10. Vidyarthi, L.P.: "Ghaghra—A Village of Chotanagpur", Manager Publications, New Delhi, 1966.

11. Supreme Court Judgment on Samta Case.

12. Evolution of Panchayati Raj in India (2010) Dr Mridula Sharda.

13. Energising Rural Development through 'Panchayats', Bibek Debroy and P. D. Kaushik.

14. Annual Report of Panchayati Raj Department, Govt. of Orissa, 2009-10.

15. Status of Panchayats Report, (SOPR-2009)-2010, IRMA, Anand, India.

16. Status of Panchayats Report, (SOPR-2010)-2011, IRMA, Anand, India.

17. Ajaya Dandekar and Chitrangada, "The Problems of Governance in Tribal India", unpublished Research Report of IRMA, Anand, Gujarat, 2010.

18. Padhi, Arvind, "Challenges to PESA in Orissa", unpublished report of Department of Panchayati Raj, Government of Orissa, 2010.

19. Sharma, B.D., "Tribal Problems in India", Sahayaog Pustak Bhandar, New Delhi, 2006.

9

Rural Decentralisation, People's Participation and Inclusive Growth

Nupur Tiwari

Rapacious Growth and Disparity

The Indian Economy is one of the fastest growing economies of the World and there are signs that it is emerging as the major economic power. However, India represents a paradox where, on the one hand, the GDP growth rate has been rising to 7-8 per cent in the last four years, rural-urban divide, regional divide and rich-poor divide has become glaring. While the world and its financial hubs applaud the country's impressive annual GDP growth, other indicators such as poverty reduction, employment growth, health and education are less encouraging. The latest UNDP Human Development Report 2009 highlights the very large gaps in well-being and life chances that continue to divide our increasingly interconnected world and the HDI for India is 0.612, which gives the country a rank of 134th out of 182 countries. According to the Report of the National Commission for Enterprises in the Unorganised sectors, August 2007 on "Conditions of work and promotion of livelihood in the unorganised sector," the stark fact is that 836 million people in India live on less than Rs 20 a day; yet we have the second richest billionaires in the world in dollars and we have the fourth largest number of billionaires on the planet. The state of food insecurity in the world report of the FAO of the United Nations shows us that in less than five years leading to the turn of the century, India added more newly hungry millions than the rest of the world taken together. Hunger grew at a time when it declined in Ethiopia.

Long before planning commission endorsed the HCR approach, Amartya Sen, after examining the theoretical and practical problems of conceptualisation and measuring poverty, held that the head count measure is "quite unacceptable as an indicator of poverty". Family getting less than two meals a day is probably the most important criterion of poverty. We in India have more than 300 million people still living in deep poverty at less than a dollar a day, while another 350 million live on less than two dollars a day. Nearly two-third of the population is still dependant on agriculture activities and, about 67 per cent of the total crop land is rain fed, hence subject of the vagaries of climate.

In Bihar, Orissa, M.P. where poverty is acute, growth is not located neither in sectors like Agriculture, where labour is concentrated. Despite impressive advances in human and economic development, regional and inter-state disparities are increasing and natural calamities such as floods, earthquakes, and droughts reverse the development process to a great extent and worsen the situation of the disadvantaged and vulnerable groups. Among the states, the North-Eastern and the Central regions, which have large tribal populations, are lagging behind. Among sectors, agriculture has fallen behind industry and the service sector. Although some of the poorest states are rich in natural and forest resources, the predominantly tribal population is unable to take advantage of this. Religious minorities, large sections of Scheduled Castes (SC) and Scheduled Tribal (ST) groups, and women still do not have access to many job opportunities and human development. The informal sector has emerged as the largest job creator, characterised by low wages and income insecurity while wage growth is concentrated only at the top end. India's educational inequality is one of the worst in the world.

India stands at a crucial juncture in its quest for inclusive growth that will bring prosperity across the spectrum. Large amounts of public funds are spent to address these issues but their implementation and the quality of services delivered leave much to be desired. It is well-recognised that the programmes to solve these problems are not performing well. They are too centralised, fragmented in concept as in implementation, insufficiently responsive to varying local needs or accountable to ensure efficient service delivery. The existing mechanism for the delivery of services is not effective, efficient or economical. If on the other hand we use participatory governance, even a small reduction in administrative cost and local accountability would result in huge increase in proportion of outlay reaching the beneficiary.

Governance Reform: Inclusive Governance

Local self-government (LGs) provides the essential means of reconciling accelerated growth with inclusive growth, through inclusive governance as the means of empowering the disadvantaged and enabling them to overcome their poverty. These institutions are the Panchayats, Municipalities, Autonomous District and Regional Councils and other similar arrangements. However, we are a long way away from such robust construction of our local government institutional mechanism. Functions devolved upon LGs are imprecise and overlap with State activities, expenditure responsibilities are either unfunded or restrictively constructed through the assignment of tied funds and staff is inadequate, poorly trained and owe greater allegiance to the State rather than to the LGs themselves. Efforts to vest adequate powers and responsibilities on these institutions continue to be beset by several hurdles. The constitutional provisions have not been an effective trigger for the Panchayats to function as institutions of local self-government, particularly because of weak administrative action for effective transfer of 3 Fs (Functions, Funds and Functionaries).

Efforts at effective devolution are often slowed down, stopped or reversed by several vested interests that have a stake in the current system. The existing mechanism of implementation of the delivery of services is neither effective, efficient and economical. Operation and maintenance of assets and services is even a bigger issue. It is well recognised that the programmes to solve these problems are not performing well. They are too centralised, fragmented in concept as in implementation, insufficiently responsive to varying local needs or accountable to ensure efficient service delivery.

It is the effective empowerment of the disadvantaged through the effective devolution of Functions, Finances and Functionaries to representative institutions of local self-government such as Panchayats (where part IX of the Constitution applies) and Village Councils, Village Development Boards and similar such institutions elsewhere, on the principle of subsidiarity, which states that anything which can be done at a lower level should be done at that level and no higher level, that will pave the way to the effective implementation of other measures of inclusive growth.

That this should be so is an anomaly considering that the Constitution amendments have so firmly rooted Panchayati Raj in our system of governance that 3.2 million elected representatives, including 1.2 million women and well over 22 per cent SC/ST (their estimated share in the rural population), are serving in the local bodies of our vibrantly democratic society at the grassroots. This anomaly is caused by:

(i) Inadequate effective devolution of functions, finances and functions by State legislatures/governments to the Panchayati Raj Institutions; and

(ii) Inadequate provisions for planning and implementation by PRIs in the guidelines issued by Central Ministries for Centrally Sponsored and Central Sector schemes that directly impinge on inclusive growth.

Planning and Implementation at the Panchayat Level

The 11th Five Year Plan states that "In order to achieve the best outcome in terms of balanced development with convergence of resources and enforcement of inter-sectoral priorities it is necessary to shift to integrated planning at the grassroots level leading to the preparation of District Plans" (Para 10.15 in Chapter X on "Governance"). In fact the Eleventh Plan further seeks to substantially empower and use PRIs as the 'primary means of delivery of the essential services that are critical to inclusive growth' (para 1.147) and in order to further empower Panchayats in this direction it further emphasises several steps such as the creation of Panchayat sector window in States and in the central budget, activity mapping, and IT enabling of Panchayats. There is a strong case for strengthening PRIs to bring about the desired results through effective integrated planning and implementation of the various Schemes.

The Central Government undertakes large fiscal transfer to the states in the functional domain of the Panchayats, mainly through Centrally Sponsored Schemes (CSSs) and Additional Central Assistance (ACAs). CSSs are formulated by concerned Ministries and Departments and implemented through counterpart State level departments and para-statal bodies identified for the purpose. The Planning Commission has prepared a list of the CSSs under implementation. For the first year of the Eleventh Plan (2007-08), Planning Commission has indicated that there are 99 schemes operated by 27 central ministries and departments with a total outlay of around Rs 81,620 crore. Seven Ministries/Departments account for 87 per cent of the allocation for CSSs, across 15 schemes) and it can apply sufficient influence through this on the devolution of 3Fs to the Panchayats.[1] This message of strengthening the Panchayats should be specifically provided in the guidelines of every schemes and their respective guidelines could be substantially modified to provide centrality to elected rural local bodies with a view to enhancing coverage and outreach.

The shortcomings that are manifest in the CSS approach as currently seen are rigid conditionalties, no consistent approach to institutional structures, obsession with financial performance, ineffective monitoring of outcomes, administrative overload on departments lead to inefficiency in processing requests for funding and delayed and lumpy releases and lack of consistency in fund transfer systems, leading to lack of transparency in releases.

Even the most perfunctory evaluation and assessment studies on CSSs have shown that for the most part, State departments implement their CSSs through vertical structures, with little attempt at sustainable horizontal integration. The task of initially articulating infirmities and gaps prior to preliminary planning for any given CSS is usually done by functionaries of State departments. Any infirmities and gaps identified are consolidated by State Departments through their vertical structures. There is often mismatch between the felt needs of the local population and plans evolved by State departments. This would eventually reflect in poor ownership of CSSs at the ground level, and even poorer outcomes and impacts.

Effective implementation of CSSs demands participation by users and beneficiaries in fine-tuning scheme guidelines to local situations and requirements. It also generally involves close coordination with related departments and agencies. The present mechanism of implementation of schemes and delivery of services is not economical or efficient. Further, the much needed convergence of related schemes and resources is possible only through the mechanism of constitutionally mandated District Planning and the District Planning Committee. The guidelines of Planning Commission of 25.8.06 which states that, "The DPC will consolidate the two streams-the Panchayat Plans and the Urban Plans, integrate them with the departmental plans for the district and prepare the Draft Five year plan and Annual Plan would go a long way in this direction".

Clearly, any direct and upfront involvement of PRIs in the planning, implementation and oversight of CSSs, being so far run through departmental structures, does impact outputs and outcomes in a positive manner. The committees which are functioning within the overall framework of PRIs are open to the examination and consideration of the Gram Sabha. Besides, as the elected members are accountable to the electorate that they represent, every Committee which is responsible for planning and implementation at the grassroots level should function within the PRI system and then only they can be accountable.

Every activity assigned to a specific level of Panchayat needs to be supported with appropriate authority over functionaries and powers to handle funds/finances. The fund flow for the scheme may be described clearly. This may cover the following points: exact flow of funds from level to level, (the lesser the levels the better), time limits at each level for the transfer of funds to the next level, how IT would be used for electronic tagging and tracking of funds transferred to Panchayats from higher level of governments, including rapid bank transfer of funds, tracking fund transfers to, and expenditures of the Panchayats.

The most important issue and the area of concern is how to ensure the CSSs and ACA relating to functions in the realm of PRIs are actually implemented by them. It is vital to incentivise states to first formulate and then implement action plans that involve bringing Panchayats to the centre stage of CSSs related to service delivery. A participatory approach in designing CSS may be pursued. The broad activities that pertain to the involvement of PRIs can be identification of beneficiaries; enumeration of the target group using household registers of Village Panchayats; verification of data collected from other sources against data available with PRIs; PRIs/Gram Sabhas as nodal agencies for building data bases and constant revision for maintaining updated database; determination of optimal sites for construction through PRIs etc.

Some examples of devolution under CSSs can be taken for instance in National Rural Employment Guarantee Act (Rs 1 lakh crore) Panchayats at all levels are principal authorities for planning and implementation. At least 50 per cent of works in terms of value is to be undertaken at Gram Panchayat level. In National Rural Health Mission (Rs 90 thousand crores) Accredited Social health Activist (ASHA) is to be appointed for each village by Panchayat. Panchayat are to prepare village health plan. The District Health Mission is headed by District Panchayat. There is also a provision of capacity building for Panchayat members in health and public health. In Sarva Shiksha Abhiyan (Rs 70 thousand crores) and Mid-day Meals Programme there is in principle agreement on organic linkage between village level committees and Panchayats. Village Education Committees is to be Standing sub-Committees of Gram Panchayats. Under the Integrated Child Development Scheme (Rs 54 thousand crores) a Joint group is formed between MoPR and Ministry of Women and Child Development to work out details.

In order to ensure that the vast resources that GOI is making available to the CSSs would be correctly used, the responsibility of recognising the beneficiaries must be allocated to PRIs. PRIs are the most suitably placed institutions to specify listings of school dropouts, the aged, elderly, destitute, and handicapped, the marginalised and the weaker sections within their respective jurisdictions. Village Panchayats are mandated to maintain household registers. This mechanism is an ideal basis for determining beneficiary lists for most CSSs. However, these registers are ignored by the line departments as they prepare their own list using the staff of line departments who have little knowledge of ground levels as compared to the elected representatives of PRIs and their office beariers overlook these registers and prepare their own listing of beneficiaries by using staff of line departments who may not have wide enough coverage or as complete knowledge about the ground level as elected representatives and office bearers of PRIs and Gram Sabhas.

Data banks should be built upon PRIs in respect of all CSSs implemented within their jurisdiction by concerned departments. Line departments should, in the interest of more effective and targeted implementation of CSSs, forward all relevant information pertaining to demography of the district/ block/ village, data collected and maintained by ANMs and CDPOs, and any additional information to PRIs on a regular basis. Setting up such data banks with inter and intra level connectivity should be made a component of CSSs.

Benchmark data on which many CSSs are based tends to be unreliable as many departments which prepare the beneficiary lists do not have adequate staff so they revert back to other functionaries, who do not reside in villages and are not trained to collect the datas. These defects can be remedied if PRIs and their staff, as well as Gram Sabhas are treated as the nodal agencies for building up accurate data bases and constantly updating these, to ensure that CSSs are implemented with appropriate coverage and outreach. Selection of projects must be done by PRIs wherever micro level solutions are sought. In the post project mode, CSSs should also provide for operations, future maintenance and management to be carried on through PRIs.

Departments should require PRIs to undertake responsibility for functions relating to monitoring and vigilance under CSSs. PRIs can keep daily track of the attendance of teachers, anganwadi workers and ASHA, extension staff, and so on. Vigilance committees should be chaired by the PRI head. School inspectors could also get very good feedback about issues surrounding quality of teaching, student response, etc., if they interact with PRIs and even occasionally with Gram Sabhas.

The gap in information and knowledge in respect of CSS schemes between departments and PRIs can be bridged if scheme guidelines provide for regular and mandatory reporting by implementing officers to concerned PRIs in writing as well as in the form of presentations. Departments with limited field staff could find it strenuous to report to Gram Sabhas, but they can send progress reports to block or district level local bodies.

Departments can get better results if some key programme interventions are done by PRI staff or under their supervision. Medical examination in schools and immunisation can be done under PRI supervision. PRI staff could be used to run midday meal programmes. Where construction is involved, like drinking water projects and schools, PRIs could take up the work. In the animal husbandry sector, PRIs can earn revenue from water bodies owned by them if they stock them with fish and subsequently issue licenses for fishing.

Often Parallel Bodies (PBs) are created for quick implementation and greater accountability. However, there is little evidence to show that such PBs are free of the evils that are supposed to bedevil PRIs, such as politics, sharing of spoils, corruption and elite capture. In addition, there are issues of 'Missions' bypassing mainstream programme continuity beyond the life of CSSs/ACAs, subsequent operation and maintenance and continued accountability. In fact such bodies compete for political space and usurp the legitimate space of PRIs (though, for the lifetime of the scheme only) and mock at the PRIs through superior resource endowments and visible patronage systems. Several of the arguments quoted by proponents of parallel bodies, such as protection of funds from diversion have now weakened because such protection is easily achieved even through PRIs.

If necessary, the professional component of these PBs could be retained as Cell or Units within the PRIs, carrying out their professional roles including management of funds. Even in the case of schemes that have already been approved and that have a parastatal built into the same, the nodal Ministry may draw up a time-bound action plan that will clearly phase out such bodies or subsume them into sub-committees of the Panchayats.

It is important to leverage the Centrally Sponsored Schemes to demarcate the tasks, responsibilities and activities that lie within the domain of local governments (rural and urban). This will encourage and motivate state governments to systematically engage in appropriate devolution of functions, finances and functionaries. If each CSS clarifies what lies within the domain of local government, and if this is supported with appropriate devolution of the three Fs, there will be significantly less infirmity in the outcomes and impacts of the CSS. More significantly, CSSs will then serve to further strengthen (for their own implementation and oversight) the third tier of elected local bodies with reference to the 73rd and 74th Constitutional amendments.

Delivery of Essential Social Services through Panchayati Raj

The Eleventh Five Year Plan asserts that 'it is absolutely critical for the inclusiveness of our growth process that these large numbers of elected representatives in our Panchayati Raj Institutions are fully involved in planning, implementing and supervising the delivery of essential public services.' (para 1.147). The Eleventh Plan also notes "The delivery of essential social services at the grassroots level is also poor and this is a major causative factor in unequal development. Much higher levels of human development can be achieved within the given structure of the economy, if only service delivery is improved." (para 1.6) The Plan document asserts that States can no longer delay or sidestep the devolution of functions, funds and functionaries to Panchayats and has identified activity mapping, the creation of a Panchayat sector window in both State and Central budgets and effective utilisation of their taxation powers by Panchayats as key steps in this regard. (Paras 10.20 to 10.29)

The existing delivery system for government promoted growth consists of the 'district administration', a small group of official and political personalities to whom the State turns to for information, advice and action. Hybridising the official system with local government administration only provides scope for patronage and non-accountable behaviour. In the absence of proper recording of works undertaken under different programmes, and independent audit of their real content and performance, achievements claimed by official reports are hardly credible. Local self-government provides the essential means of reconciling accelerated growth with inclusive growth, through inclusive governance as the means of empowering the disadvantaged and enabling them to overcome their poverty. These institutions are the Panchayats, Municipalities, Autonomous District and Regional Councils and other similar arrangements.

What is therefore required is that Panchayati Raj be brought centre-stage as the principal governance reform to reinforce economic reform and for delivery of essential social services at grassroots level. However, several initiatives are required to be taken to make the local governments really effective in service delivery. These include:

- ensuring participatory local level planning by the Panchayati Raj Institutions to identify needs, levels of delivery and the enhancements desired by the people in each sector;
- assigning clearly demarcated roles to the PRIs through activity mapping; confining centrally sponsored and State schemes to a small number of important programmes to achieve declared national and State goals and also providing adequate space for the PRIs to participate in these schemes;

• undertaking a well-structured process of administrative and fiscal devolution that matches the resource availability at each level of the Panchayats with functions assigned to it;

• providing capacity to the Panchayati Raj Institutions in the widest sense of the term to perform their responsibilities efficiently; and

• putting in place systems of accountability by duly empowering the Gram Sabha, so that citizens, the ultimate recipients of services, are enabled to hold the PRIs accountable for any inadequacies in service delivery.

Inclusive Growth through Inclusive Governance

We can conclude that the present pattern of growth has the potential of widening the inequality. Such unequal opportunity structure weakens the positive role of growth in reducing poverty and making growth inclusive. If this inequality increases further, social displacement will result and it will be a major obstruction to higher growth. To achieve inclusive growth, it is crucial that the poor are integrated with the dynamic sectors of growth.We cannot overlook the fact that being closest to the people, the Panchayats and their elected representatives have the feel of the pulse, the sufferings of the people and local conditions. The effectiveness of providing services through local bodies cannot be overemphasised as they know their real requirements, and are familiar with every nook and corner of the village and, above all, they are answerable to the people. The Panchayati Raj Institutions are eminently suited for service delivery as they can ensure equity and/or equitability in the provision of services (in view of their nearness to the people), inclusiveness (in view of the assured representation available to all sections of the society in the Panchayati Raj Institutions), accessibility, transparency, local participation, accountability and sustainability of services.

The involvement of Panchayats ensures greater transparency in working and fund utilisation than in execution carried out by central or state agency, many a times. Panchayats should be given powers to decide on technology, cost, location, infrastructure and beneficiary selection; and since they have a role in rural housing, primary health-care, water and sanitation in many states, should be given these functions by the coordinating authority. Adequate resources should be provided to PRIs to build up their capacities and sensitisation and training of PRI members on related areas will have to be promoted and capacity for the same should be institutionalised in the existing institutional framework in the states.

In a mature and responsible administrative system where power is in the hands of the people and their democratically elected local government institutions, relief operations, day-to-day running of civic services, providing medical assistance, etc., could best be done by the local government. Gram Sabhas can play a very meaningful role in selecting the beneficiaries, prioritising the beneficiaries to ensure gender and equity concerns and also in deciding the appropriate rehabilitation or reconstruction programme that is needed for the communities.

Moving from a model of central provision to that of decentralisation to local governments introduces a new relationship between national and local policy-makers, while altering several existing relationships such as that between the citizens, elected politicians and the local bureaucracy. Such inclusive governance, besides ensuring political empowerment, through enabling people to control their own destiny, would also yield significant inclusive growths. Social empowerment through inclusive governance would help safeguard social, ethnic and cultural values of people, which in turn would lead to building trust of their governments in tribal communities. Active participation of people in the political processes and in grassroots planning will bring about the desired transformation of the region by establishing peace and setting in motion the wheels of progress towards prosperity.When grassroots planning processes strikes deep roots, economic empowerment is both strong and sustainable.

Note

Report of the Committee to review modifications to be made in the existing guidelines of Centrally Sponsored Schemes on identifying a domain for the Panchayati Raj Institutions 13th August 2007.

References

(April 2008), *Fifteenth Anniversary Charter on Panchayati Raj.*

Ministry of Panchayati Raj. (December 2004), *Compendium of resolutions of the Seven Round Tables of Ministers in-charge of Panchayati Raj.*

MoPR (December 2004), *Report of the Task force of officials in -charge of Panchayati Raj in States to examine the Centrally Sponsored Schemes.*

MoPR (November 2006), *The State of Panchayats Report; 2006-07.*

MoPR, IRMA (April 2008), *The State of Panchayats Report 2007-08, An Independent Assessment.*

MoPR (March 2006), *Report of the Expert Group on Grassroots level planning.*

MoPR (August 2007), *Report of the Expert Committee on Grassroots level planning in areas not covered by Parts IX and IXA of the Constitution.*

MoPR, Planning Commission. (November 2008), *Report of the Empowered sub-Committee of NDC on Financial and Administrative Strengthening of PRIs.*

MoRD (August 2001), *Report of the Task Force on Devolution of Powers and Functions upon Panchayati Raj Institutions.*

MoPR, Planning Commission. (January 2009) *Manual on District Planning.*

Planning Commission. (August 2007), *Report of the Committee to review modifications to be made in the existing guidelines of Centrally Sponsored Schemes on identifying a domain for the Panchayati Raj Institutions.*

PC-MoPR (2006), *Report of the Working Group on Democratic Decentralisation and PRIs. New Delhi, Planning Commission - Ministry of Panchayati Raj.*

Planning Commission, *Eleventh Five year Plan, Ch-10 (Decentralisation and Strengthening of PRIs.*

Rao, M.G. and U.A. Vasanth Rao (2008), *Expanding the Resource Base of Panchayats: Augmenting Own Revenues,* Economic and Political Weekly, January.

Second-ARC (2007), *Local Governance: An inspiring journey into the future. New Delhi, Second Administrative Reforms Commission, Govt of India.*

S.M. Vijayanand and T.R. Raghunandan (August 2004) *Note of Parallel Bodies.*

10

STs as the Beneficiaries of PDS in the Mayurbhanj District of Odisha

Prachi Madhumita Mohanty

Introduction

Non-traditional security threats have now assumed enormous importance. Contemporary challenges like environmental degradation, poverty and extremism differ from traditional military ones. The state-centric traditional security issue which determined the crucial paradigm during the cold war era is being challenged these days. Traditionally, national security is defined in terms of the ability of a state to protect its interests from external threats. Those interests are broadly defined as territorial integrity, sovereignty and independence of the nation. Human security is a people-centred notion of security, which is threatened by non-traditional challenges in the present time. This includes economic, food, health, environmental, personal, community and political security. Thus traditional security paradigm does not include within its ambit rapidly increasing non-traditional threats to security like, struggle for resources of energy and depletion of other resources, food shortages, infectious diseases, cross-border environmental degradation, forced migration, international terrorism, insurgency, ascendancy of non-state actors in drugs, arms, money laundering and financial crime organisation. (Anthony, 2007) High economic growth has not lessened the depth of food insecurity and malnutrition. All growth is not development, neither is it equal distribution to cater to the minimum needs of common people. This is because; in a country like India the contradiction of poverty in the midst of plenty is prevalent. Poverty is deepest among members of scheduled castes and tribes in the rural areas. A major cause of poverty among India's rural people, both individuals and communities, is lack of access to productive assets and financial resources. High levels of illiteracy, inadequate healthcare and extremely limited access to social services are common among rural people. Microenterprise development, which could generate income and enable poor people to improve their living conditions, has only recently become a focus of the government.

An Odisha Human Development Report says that one of the most significant factors in food insecurity is unequal access to the Public Distribution System (PDS), and its limited utilisation by the poor. No doubt the PDS scheme is meant to cater to the needs of those who are socially excluded. Social exclusion has to be seen as an institutionalised form of inequality, the failure of a society to extend to all sections of its population, the economic resources and social recognition which they need in order to participate fully and meaningfully in the collective life of the community. Both from social and market perspective, discourse on exclusion and inclusion of tribal people are of great relevance in present situation. Because, it is said that exclusion and poverty are mostly interrelated. Conventional poverty indicators reveal that there is a strong correlation between being indigenous or tribal and being extremely poor. Tribal people are more likely to have lower income, unhealthy physical living conditions, especially scarcity of food which is primary need of human beings. Less access to health care, education, and a range of other services, still less to labour, land and capital markets and returns to work as well as weaker political representation make their life miserable. The poverty and social exclusion experienced by tribal people are largely due to discrimination at social and institutional level during colonial and post-independent era. The disadvantaged people feel that they are alienated from mainstream society and isolated from major societal process which produce or distribute social resources. The present paper tries to highlight the abject poverty in which the tribals languish in comparison with other social groups of Mayurbhanj district.

Food Insecurity and the Disadvantaged Sections

Deprived people are disproportionately impacted by the non-traditional challenges such as food insecurity. The scarcity of food is a major problem for unprivileged section. Their vulnerability to multiple adversities means that people require specific attention in order to benefit from development on their own terms. Food insecurity is the limited or uncertain availability or access to nutritionally adequate, culturally appropriate and safe foods. Food insecurity may result in inadequate dietary intakes, overweight or obesity and the development of chronic disease. Food insecurity may result in significant health burdens among the population, and this may be concentrated in socio-economically disadvantaged suburbs. (Nolan et al., 2006) Food insecurity is associated with lower household income, poorer general health and depression. It is prevalent more in urbanised disadvantaged areas. Low-income households are at high risk of experiencing food insecurity. Moreover it can be shown that the government's initiatives of dealing with food insecurity reflect its failure to grasp the realities of exclusion faced by the marginalised or disadvantaged sections of society.

STs as a Special Category of Disadvantaged Section

Tribal communities residing in hilly terrains of Mayurbhanj are physically excluded, as they lack in connectivity and other infrastructural support. As a result, the poor in general and ST and SC people in particular lack access to growth centres and service centres. Though extensive forest resources are an important source of sustenance to a majority of rural poor especially tribals these are highly degraded and lack desired financial and managerial inputs. Optimal exploitation of its vast natural resources has not been possible for lack of heavy investment in infrastructural development. The State Government's capacity to develop infrastructure is very weak and limited. (Bairathi, 1991) The scheduled tribe population continues to have nearly double the incidence of poverty compared to the non-tribals of Mayurbhanj district of Odisha. The incidence of poverty is more. The tribals of the district become the victims of the profit oriented and tactful middleman who purchase the agricultural product and minor forest produce collected by the tribals at a very low rate. Development brought more purchasing power to the tribals to which the non-tribal neighbours and traders take advantage by applying their tactics and manage to siphon away the development benefits occurring to the innocent tribals. The tribals of Mayurbhanj district of Odisha confront some major problems like poverty, illiteracy, unemployment, alienation, displacement, malnutrition, disease, etc. The Central Govt. and State Govt. are putting sincere efforts to uplift the economic condition of the tribal's by implementing different anti-poverty schemes. Despite the fact, the tribal people in the district remain backward socially and economically. (Satpathy, 2011)

PDS Scheme

The Public Distribution System (PDS) evolved as a system of management of scarcity and for distribution of food grains at affordable prices. Over the years, PDS has become an important tool of Government's policy for management of food security. PDS is supplemental in nature and is not intended to make available the entire requirement of any of the commodities distributed under it to a household or a section of the society. Public Distribution System is an attempt to improve availability of food to population living in most vulnerable areas (remote, tribal and drought-prone regions). In an attempt to limit the mounting cost of food subsidy and at the same time ensure that people below poverty line do get subsidised food grains the targeted public distribution system providing food grains at subsidised cost to only the people below poverty line was initiated.

Major commodities distributed under the scheme include staple food grains, such as wheat, rice, sugar, and kerosene, through a network of Public distribution shops, also known as Ration Shops established in several states across the country. Both the central and state governments shared the responsibility of regulating the PDS. While the central government is responsible for procurement, storage, transportation, and bulk allocation of food grains, state governments hold the responsibility for distributing the same to the consumers through the established network of Fair Price Shops (FPSs). State governments have also operational responsibilities including allocation and identification of families below poverty line, issue of ration cards, supervision and monitoring the functioning of FPSs. Under PDS scheme, each family below the poverty line is eligible for 35 kg of rice or wheat every month, while a household above the poverty line is entitled to 15 kg of food grain on a monthly basis. Under Antyodaya Anna Yojana (AAY) the poorest of the poor families in the State are supplied with 35 kg of rice per family per month at Rs 3 per kg since September, 2011. It reveals 91 per cent of respondents are getting benefits from Antyodaya Anna Yojana and the rest are not availing this benefit as they belong to APL group. It is observed in the study that all BPL families under study are getting subsidised rice as per government norms.

Methodology

The present study was conducted in the remote and tribal dominated four blocks of Mayurbhanj in the northern region of Odisha. This data collection was undertaken during March-June of 2013. Initially the required census data relating to the village were perused. Subsequently, the quantitative data were collected from interviewing the members of the household under PDS scheme with a structured interview schedule (n=100). The qualitative data were collected through observation and case studies. Also, data was collected from the key informants which include: members of the BPL, AAY, AY, APL household through formal and informal discussions.

Profile of Mayurbhanj

Mayurbhanj is a tribal dominated district situated in the northern part of the state of Odisha. According to 2011 census, the district covers an area of 10418 sq. kms which constitutes 6.69 per cent of the state territory. The total population was 26.34 lakhs that constituted 6.28 per cent of the state's total population. Density of population in the district is 242 per sq. km. of area as against 316 at the state level. It is rural based district where the rural population constitutes 87 per cent as against state average of 72 per cent. Mayurbhanj is said to be a land of tribals. Out of 62 tribal communities of Odisha, 45 communities are found in Mayurbhanj alone. Among the major tribes Santal, Ho, Bhumija, Bhuiyan, Bathudi, Kolho, Munda, Gond, Kharia and Lodha are important. As per 2011 census, Mayurbhanj district has a total population of 26,33,956 number of which rural population is 23,67,756 and urban population is 2,66,200. Out of total population 13,88,459 belong to ST and 2, 13,835 belong to SC communities and rest belong to other communities. The percentage of ST and SC to total population of the district is 56.6 per cent and 7.68 per cent respectively. The sex ratio shows a total of 1005 females per 1000 males. The tribal education in Mayurbhanj at present faces obstacles due to a number of factors like poverty, tribal eco-system, language and distance, etc. (Agarwal, 2011).

Analysis of Data

Socio-Economic Profile of STs Comparison With Other Groups

Table 10.1 : Percentage of Population in Four Blocks in terms of Different Social Groups (2011 census)

Name of the Block	*Percentage of Category of Social Groups*		
	SCs	*STs*	*Others*
Udala	5.70	73.08	21.22
Kaptipada	4.29	66.67	29.03
Gopabandhu Nagar	11.95	54.71	33.34
Baripada	3.29	73.65	22.43

In the above table it is clear that the STs are the numerically dominant social group in all the four blocks under study. However the size of the tribal population varies from one block to the other. In each of the four blocks STs constitute more than 50 per cent of the total population. In Baripada block there is maximum concentration of ST population. The block having the minimum concentration of ST population is G.B. Nagar. However the minimum is also more than 50 per cent. This finding is obvious in view of the fact that Mayurbhanj is the tribal dominated district.

Table 10.2 : Representative Sample of the Universe

Types of Social Groups	*Name of the block*				*Total*
	Udala	*Kaptipada*	*G.B. Nagar*	*Baripada*	
STs	22	13	10	23	68
SCs	2	1	2	1	6
Others	6	6	8	6	26

The table showing the sample data is quite representative of the universe under study. In the table the members of the ST category are numerically superior. In each of the two blocks 30 cases have been undertaken for study. Since there are more tribals in these two blocks. In each of the other two blocks having less number of tribal population 20 cases have been taken up in each block. Baripada block is found to have maximum number of members belonging to the ST category. In other words, 23 Schedule Tribe respondents have been chosen in the samples taken in Baripada block. However the minimum number of tribal respondents in G.B. Nagar block is 10. Thus the number of ST respondents varies from 10 to 23 and at the cost of repetition it can be pointed out that the sample size has been fixed in proportion to the size of the tribal population in the blocks under study.

Table 10.3: Types of Card Holders in Different Blocks

Name of the Block	*Percentage of Types of Card Holder*					
	BPL	*AY*	*AAY*	*APL*	*Without Any Card*	*Total*
Udala	10 (33.33)	3 (10)	5 (16.66)	4 (13.33)	8 (26.66)	30
Kaptipada	7 (35)	1 (5)	4 (20)	2 (10)	6 (30)	20
G.B. Nagar	7 (35)	1 (5)	3 (15)	3 (15)	6 (30)	20
Baripada	9 (30)	2 (6.66)	5 (16.66)	4 (13.33)	10 (33.33)	30
Total	**33**	**7**	**17**	**13**	**30**	**100**

This table displays different types of card holders namely viz, APL, BPL, AAY, AY. Given the poverty of the people in such a backward district it is quite natural that in all the blocks under the study the BPL card holders outnumber the APL card holders. The number of villagers having no card in all the blocks is quite substantial. The position of the villagers who do not have any card is precarious. It has been found out during interview that none of the APL card holders has been given any card. They are given products only. A lot of complain comes to light regarding the issue of card.

Table 10.4: Educational Status of the Respondents

Types of Social Groups	*Percentage of Educational Status*				
	Illiterate	*Up to class V*	*Up to Class X*	*Up to Graduate*	*Above Graduation*
STs	31 (45.58)	21 (30.88)	11 (16.17)	3 (4.41)	2 (2.94)
SCs	3 (50)	2 (33.33)	1 (16.66)	0	0
Others	3 (11.53)	5 (19.23)	4 (15.38)	9 (34.61%)	5 (19.23)
Total	**37**	**28**	**16**	**12**	**7**

In the above table it is found out that there are maximum numbers of illiterates among the STs across the blocks. Only a few among them is found to be possessing qualification up to graduation. The number of literates and highly qualified persons that is above graduation is found to be more among the higher social category. However the educational position of SCs is no better than that of the STs.

As a corollary of lack of education it is found out that in the above table many a person (36.66 per cent) in the ST category do not have the knowledge

Table 10.5: Reason of not having the Card

Grounds of not having card	*Percentage of Types of Social Category*		
	STs	*SCs*	*Others*
Lack of knowledge of how to get it	11(36.66)	4(13.33)	2(6.66)
No liaison with middleman	6(20)	2(6.66)	4(13.33)
No need of card			1(3.33)

of how to obtain card. The Position of SC is slightly better because 13.33 per cent don't have the knowledge of how to obtain card. The members of other category however are in a better position. Only a small percentage of the respondents attribute its non-possession of cards to lack of liaison with the middle men.

Table 10.6: Awareness as Consumer about the Product

Types of Social Category	*Percentage of Awareness about Quantity and Rate*	
	Affirmative	*Negative*
STs	12(17.64)	56(82.35)
SCs	4(66.66)	2(33.33)
Others	23(88.46)	3(11.53)

So far as the awareness as consumer among the respondents is concerned it is observed that the STs lag far behind the members of other category. 82.35 per cent of STs are found to be lacking in awareness. The position of SCs is found to be better in this respect than the STs. The members of other category are found to be more aware as consumers. This may be due to the fact that the members of other category are better educated than the two disadvantaged sections as has been found in the table 1.4.

Table 10.7: Awareness about Rules Regulating Ration Card

Types of Social Category	*Percentage of Awareness about Rules*	
	Yes	*No*
SCs	2(33.33)	4(66.66)
STs	11(16.17)	57(83.82)
Others	18(69.23)	8(30.76)

So far as the awareness about the rules regulating the issue of cards is concerned the members of the Scheduled Tribe who know the rules are also found to be very small in number. The position however changes in case of members of other category i.e., those who belong to higher social categories determined on the basis of caste. The position of the SCs whose number is very small in comparison with that of the ST is better as has been found out in the table. It is worth noting that awareness about the rules and regulation are technical in nature and only qualified and alert persons can be more acquainted with the administrative rules and regulations. The STs of all the blocks are found to be lacking in that.

Perception of the Respondents

There is no denying the fact that the tribals who are prominent among socially excluded section in Mayurbhanj are benefited by the PDS scheme. Yet they have many complain regarding the issue of cards. They frankly admit that since most of them are illiterate, they feel that the cost of procuring the card is very heavy and exacting. Some of them have lost their cards. Even if they get electricity connection by citing the number which they remember they do not get the products on ration. Regarding the products they find that they do not get the commodities of quantity which they are supposed to get. The distributor tries to befool them by saying that since they are giving products to the non-card holder, they give the card holders less quantity. Some time they also take the alibi they are getting less from the supply office. The distributors are close to well connected persons like MLA and other officials. Thus there is the allegation of hobnobbing among them. It is interesting to learn that the MLA of Udala, one of the blocks under study enjoys BPL card. Thus the perception of the respondents especially the tribal ones is not healthy regarding the officials associated with the PDS. They look upon the owners of fair price shop will disdain.

Governmental Measures and Critical Estimate

The public distribution system (PDS) is in a woeful condition. The 1997 BPL lost its validity in 2002 and the last BPL survey was undertaken in the state in 2002. But the 2002 BPL list has not been published yet. Although the rules stipulate that the BPL survey has to be conducted every five years, the 2007 survey has not been carried out so far. Another setback to the poverty amelioration programme in the region has been the erroneous identification of the poor, with corruption playing a big role in the faulty distribution of BPL cards. People who are above the poverty line (APL) such as government schoolteachers, owners of big houses, middle class traders, big farmers, and contractors have obtained BPL cards through manipulation. No one has doubted the utility of PDS being the need for supply of food grains to the poor of the country at affordable rates. Procurement and distribution of food grains is a huge and gigantic task but then the whole system is degraded by corruption. There are more leakages and maladministration and benefits to the poor are low. Inefficiency and corruption has made PDS weak at several levels. The system lacks in transparency, accountability, monitoring and enforcement. Survey is not being conducted regularly and properly, with the result that people Above Poverty Line (APL) have been issued, Below Poverty Line (BPL) cards and those eligible for BPL cards have been ignored. Bogus cards are in abundance. Immediate measures are required to stop the diversion of food grains. Delivery systems under the PDS have to be improved so that the real beneficiary gets its due entitlement at fixed price, fixed quantity, fixed time and wholesome quality. Innovative methods are required to improve the system.

The whole system has to be totally revamped and modern technology would appear to be the only answer.

Conclusion

In the conclusion it can be pointed out that the PDS scheme is no doubt ameliorative of the poverty prevalent among the tribals who constitute the most prominent section among the socially excluded groups of population. But the present study exposes the loophole in the scheme. It points out the inefficiency and rampant corruption involved in the implementation of the scheme. The government officials and the owners of fair price shops allegedly indulge in corruption. They violate the rules and deprive the intended beneficiaries of their due many a time. The poor tribals have to depend on the whims of the distributor. The lack of education, illiteracy also further complicates the problem. The victims do not get organised and most of the time they are unaware about the rate and quantity of product. They are even unaware about the rules and regulation relating to the obtaining of cards.

In view of the findings one can suggest that education and awareness of the targeted group is very much essential for the proper implementation of the PDS scheme. The tribal respondents also have expressed the desire to be more aware and they expect of the distributors to make them aware about the PDS scheme. We can conclude finally by saying that awareness on the part of the targeted groups and transparency on the part of the officials in highly essential for the effective implementation of the PDS scheme.

References

M. Caballero-Anthony. Non-Traditional Security and Multilateralism in Asia: Reshaping the Contours of Regional Security Architecture? The Policy Analysis Brief, the Stanley Foundation, Muscatine, IA, June 2007.

Nolan M, Williams M, Rikard-Bell G, Mohsin M., Food Insecurity in three Socially Disadvantaged Localities in Sydney, Australia, Health Promot J Austr. Dec 2006, www.ncbi.nlm.nih.gov

Agarwal, A.N., Indian Economy-Problems of Development and Planning, Wishwa Prakashan, 2011.

Bairathi Shashi, Tribal Culture, Economy and Health, Rawat Publications, 1991.

Satpathy, Asit Ranjan, Poverty and Socio-Economic Development of Tribal's Communities in Mayurbhanj District of Odisha, Econspeak Volume 1, Issue 3, Sri Krishna International Research and Educational Consortium, 2011, http://www.skirec.com.

11

Development and Tribal Resistance: A Study of Niyamgiri Movement in Odisha

Shyam Sundar Acharya

Abstract

The social movement has a conflictual core. The Niyamgiri movement has brought to the fore the clash of interest between the Vedanta company on the one hand and the survival instinct of the Dongria and Kutia Kondh on the other. The tribals have been supported by the environmentalists, civil society organisations and even leaders of some political party. It has caught the global imagination. A debate has ensued between the different paradigms of development. The apex court of India has brought of late, the Gram Sabhas of the adjoining villages of the Niyamgiri hills in to the centre stage. They have been asked to decide the fate of bauxite mining in Niyamgiri hills. Amid the controversy between the central government and the state govt. regarding the number of villages in which Gram Sabhas are to be held, some Gram Sabhas have started giving vent to their resistance against the swamping of their cultural identity, religious feeling and snatching away of their means of livelihood.

Keywords: Conflict, Dongria Kondh, Gram Sabha, Kutia Kondh, Movement, Niyam Raja, Resistance.

Introduction

In India the rural and tribal areas are selected for launching of development projects and much vaunted or proudly talked about industrialisation, due to their rich natural resources. The resultant displacement of the inhabitants of the area brings about the uprooting and disruption of social, economic and moral webs of life spun over generations. The majority of those displaced are the tribals who have been exercising control over and dependent on the common property resources including the land on which they live. As a corollary to displacement, they are deprived not only of their homeland but also of the access to the common property resources on the basis of which they used to eke out their livelihood. In many cases, the problems of displacement, environmental degradation, loss of livelihood and the cultural identity are interwoven and enmeshed in the much boasted about process of industrialisation. The Niyamgiri movement of Odisha is one such case.

The structure of the paper on "Development and Tribal Resistance: A Study of Niyamgiri Movement in Odisha" is as follows. A brief outline of the methodology on which this piece research work is based will be given at the outset. Then a theoretical presentation of the social movement will be made. It will include the definition and distinguishing features of the social movement. Then a profile of Niyamgiri hills along with Dongria Kondh and Kutia Kondh will be provided, followed by enumeration of the factors leading to the launching of the movement. Next the course of the movement will be dealt with. There will be a portrayal of the tribal resistance and the attitude of the governmental and non-governmental organisations. Next the tussle between the central government and the state government in the wake of the ruling of the Supreme Court to obtain the decision of the Gram Sabhas relating to the bauxite mining will be taken up. The paper will end with a conclusion.

Methodology

The study is based on secondary sources. The paper writer has utilised the Internet and library sources. In addition newspapers, both national and local dailies, journals, books have been of immense help in tracing the factors leading to the movement and its tortuous course. The 73rd Amendment Act, the Panchayats Extension to Schedule Areas Act (PESA), The Forest Right Act, etc., have been perused to assess the legality/illegality of the operations carried on in Niyamgiri. The recorded interview of the leaders and people mostly tribals associated with the movement in the form of DVD has been made use of in this research work.

Social Movement Definition

It is difficult to give a precise definition of the term 'social movement' which will be acceptable to the scholars of all disciplines or even to ones belonging to the same discipline. Before venturing to define a social movement, one has to make an analysis of the social process. Social process may be characterised as consisting of inter related social activities, interactions and events entangled with ideology on the one hand and related to social and cultural changes on the other. Then a social movement can be defined as an organised effort on the part of section of the population involving collective mobilisation based on ideology to bring about either partial or total change in the social system. (Rao, 1978)

Features

A social movement involves collective action as distinct from individual action. But only when the collective action is somewhat sustained as distinguished from sporadic occurrence, does it assume the shape of a movement. The sustained collective action must evince a minimal degree of organisation ranging from a loose, informal or partial level of organisation to the highly institutionalised and bureaucratised movement. (Shah G, 2002) A social movement has three other important features. Those are ideology, orientation to change and leadership. Though social movements develop a positive programme action, they also give vent to dissatisfaction, dissent and protest against existing conditions. They, in other words have a conflictual core. They offer a positive programme of action to remedy the situation. The commitment of a social movement to change and the *raison d'etre* of its organisation are founded upon conscious volition, normative commitment to the movement's aims or beliefs and active participation on the part of the followers or members. It is the conscious volition of individuals acting collectively that promotes the embodiment of ideologies in social movements. Leadership which initiates or emerges in the course of the growth of the movement plays a crucial role in articulating ideology and objectives developing strategies and programmes and sustaining the enthusiasm of the participants. (Shah G. 2002)

Movement and Violent Collective Outburst

The forms of collective action such as riot, rebellion and revolution involve violent collective outbursts. A riot is an outbreak of temporary but violent mass disorder. It is characterised by suddenness and for its fire and fury against the target group. It dies out in a short period but leaves behind a trail of death and destruction. Riots and crowd are relatively unstructured. While revolution signifies the revolt of all sections of society and their participation in the total dismantling of the state, rebellion is more frequently confined to the efforts on the part of a portion of a state to throw off the authority. (Sehuman, 1948)

Social movement may or may not be mobilisation against the authority and may or may not involve armed uprising and the use of violence. Riot, rebellion and revolution on the other hand do, involve the use of violence. Another point worth noting is that while revolution stands for the overhauling of the economic, social and political order, social movements generally mobilise the participants to realise specific goals and objectives. One needs to recognise that movements emerge in an open society characterised by democratic tradition. But revolutionary society snuffs out democracy, robs people of their freedom, gags the channels of free communication and ultimately closes in upon itself as a closed regimented society, abolishing all possibility of the emergence of social movements. Revolution thus marks the end of social movement. (Singh R, 2001) It is corroborated by Touraine, 'Every revolutionary creation of a new order is led to destroy the social movement it is based on Saturn ate his children, revolutions eat their fathers'. (Touraine, 1985)

Niyamgiri Hills: A Profile

Niyamgiri Hills which have hit the frontlines of the newspapers and around which social movement has intensified to catch the attention of the people not only at home but also abroad are located in the state of Odisha. The hills range over 250 Kilometers across the districts of Rayagada, Kalahandi and Koraput in Odisha. The hill ranges lie between 9° 26′ to 19° 43′ N latitude and 83° 18′ to 83° 28′ E longitude. A total of 721,323 ha of land including 672,018 ha of forest land and 49,305 ha of non-forest land harbours high altitude flora and fauna with Himalayan and Nilgiri varieties. It is the habitat of many endangered species and is protected under section 18 of the Indian Wildlife Act. This area was also proposed as a wildlife sanctuary by the Indian Ministry of Environment and Forests (MOEF) in 1989. Vamsadhara and Nagavali two major rivers originate from Niyamgiri Hills and most of them flow perennially.

Bauxite Deposits

Bauxite deposits are situated on the upper portion of hills as 'caps'. By nature they are porous and permeable, which makes them good retainers of ground water up to 30 per cent of volume. This water manifests itself in the form of perennial streams where the Bauxite Layers meet the underlying impermeable layers of laterite located at great heights they act as glaciers in Himalayas feeding the rivers with water during the lean season.

Tribals of Niyamgiri

Niyamgiri Hills are better known to the anthropologists as the country of Dongria Kondhs. There are two tribal groups such as Dongria Kondh and Kutia Kondh noted by the Government of India as 'Primitive Tribal Groups' and thus eligible for special protection. (TOI, 2010) The Kondhs are believed to be from the Proto-Australoid ethnic group. While the Kutia Kondh inhabit in the foothills, the Dongria Kondhs live in the upper reaches of the Niyamgiri hills and call themselves Jharania meaning those who live by the Jharana (streams) conned to Niyamagiri hill tracts. Hundreds of perennial streams flow from Niyamgiri hill and there are hundreds of Dongria villages by the streams. The Dongrias are looked upon as the protectors of these streams, hills and jungles by the people of the nearby plains the Dongoris have derived their name from '*Dongar*' meaning agricultural land on hill slopes. The Dongars are created through shifting cultivation. The Dongrias have crafted an agro-forestry system that uses mountain slopes and streams to great advantage they are self sufficient to the extent that only four households out of 50 supplement income with wage labour. (Manecksha F, 2010) They have adequate knowledge about the rich biodiversity of their land, they cultivate millet, beans and fruit expertly on small land holdings and make use of the rare orchid species and other plants to deal with ailments ranging from fractures and arthritis to stomach disorders.

Cultural Identity

The world view of the Dongrias is polytheistic animism and they associate the mountain, earth (dharini) and forests with various deities. They have a god or deity for everything and anything. The mountain is particularly sacred and is represented by triangle in all their cultural iconography like decorations on the walls of their houses or the clothes they wear.

The Dongrias lead a secluded but sustainable life drawing all sustenance from the Niyamgiri for them. Niyamgiri is Niyam Raja, lord of the laws and they worship nature as the sole provider and sustainer of life. They regard Niyamraja as the first king and consider him to be their eternal spiritual sovereign. The entire territory inhabited by the Dongrias is treated as the kingdom of Niyamgiri. Niyamgiri hill is in other words the abode of Niyamraja. The Dongrias think that the name Niyamraja is related to his role as lawmaker as directed by dharma devata. He is viewed as benevolent in most cases, but gets angry when the jungle laws established by him are violated. He is perceived as punishing those who undertake mass hunting in the forest or clear forest patches without appeasing him. The Dongrias look upon Niyamraja as the much deity and without worshiping him they do not think it possible to worship other Gods and Goddesses. The beliefs of the Dongria Kondh are conducive to the protection of the hills, forests and the ecosystem. There is a close link between the cultural identity of the tribals of Niyamgiri and nature.

Backdrop of the Movement

Niyamgiri hills are much talked about these days because of the movement that kicked off against the bauxite mining in Niyamgiri by a British company, Vedanta Resources. On 5th October, 2004 an official agreement was signed between the Odisha Mining Corporation (OMC) and Sterlite Industries, a subsidiary of Vedanta Resources for the purpose of mining of bauxite resources at the foot of the Niyamgiri mountains near the town of Lanjigarh. On 22nd September, 2004 Company had already been granted the Ministry of Environment and Forest's clearance for the construction of the refinery independently of the mining project. That was produced by the company on the basis of wrongful information to the effect that the refinery would not require forest land. However the investigative report of the CEC (Central Empowered Committee) shows that on 16th August, 2004 Vedanta had applied for reallocation of forest land to the forest department at the MOEF. It is worth noting that the CEC is a panel of experts created by the Indian Supreme Court in 2002. It was asked to consider and make recommendation about Vedanta Alumina refinery and bauxite mine planned in and around the Niyamgiri hills. Vedanta went ahead with the construction of the refinery. In Feb 2005, the MOEF's Forest Department issued a so called show cause notice to the company for having cleared and levelled woodland in violation of the Forest Conservation Act.

On 23rd May, 2005, the Ministry ordered the construction work at the refinery to stop Vedanta then pleaded that the refinery could be built, without using forest land and the MOEF's imposition therefore, was not irrevocable. The company then withdrew the application regarding use of forest land. The Ministry also accepted that on the recommendation of Orissa state authorities. The ministry revoked the stop order given to the company.

In its report to the Supreme Court, the CEC however recommended that the environmental clearance for the refinery project be revoked and the mining operation at Niyamgiri banned. The Supreme Court did not pronounce on the CEC recommendation, but referred the case to the MOEF for further analysis. The MOEF engaged the Wildlife Institute of India (WII) to verify the expected impact of the mining project on the biodiversity of the Niyamgiri Hills. The report was to be produced in the court on 13th October, 2006 with the Ministry's recommendation to the Supreme Court, but during the session the MOEF requested a postponement. The CEC prepared a new report on Vedanta commissioned by the Supreme Court and submitted in January 2007, in which the conclusion of its previous report are confirmed and partially reinforced. (Heffa Schucking, 2012)

Hornet's nest was stirred by the Supreme Court ruling that the concerned Gramsabhas would decide the fate of the mining operations in Niyamgiri. But before coming to that controversy between the centre and the state government of Odisha one needs to examine the factors leading to the launching of the movement which epitomised the clash of civilisation and marked a watershed in debating different paradigms of development.

Different Paradigms of Development

The Dongria's vision of what constitutes prosperity is in sharp variance with the picture of development offered by the state and company. "How can development come if the mountain is gone? How can we live if the wind is polluted?" asked Kumti Majhi, a local leader of Kendobuddi. (Maneckesha, 2010)

The villagers of Rengopali, Kendubuddi, Jaganathpur, Bandhagudda, Kinari and several others surrounding the plant were initially tempted by promise of jobs and prosperity to them, since they hail from one of Odisha's poorest districts. But as the refinery began operations, using bauxite brought from Korba, villagers discovered that their health, right to water and livelihood were being severely jeopardised. The waters of Bansadhara river and stream got polluted. No care was taken to deal with fly ash and red mud (alkaline mud) by products of an alumina refinery. Bauxite being a gift of nature is not just meant for aluminium processing but also the site and source for perennial stream. Aluminium the final product of bauxite, is increasingly being used in high consumption and luxurious life styles, but comes at the cost of the tribal's life line.

Development and Displacement

Dongria Kondh and other tribal communities opposed the bauxite mining project in Niyamgiri hills since its inception. They opposed it to avoid any kind of displacement and ruination of their hill god 'Niyamgiri'. (Mohapatra, 2012) The lands of the Kutia Kondh and Dalit households have been acquired by the Vedanta aluminium refinery in Rengopali and Bandhagudda villages. They are left only with their homestead land. Most of the land for the factory was illegally acquired; including some reserved forest which the company still claims was never there. Twelve villages were bulldozed, but the company only partially rehabilitated 100 of the families who live in Niyamgiri Vedanta Nagar, a shoddy housing colony right beside the belching plant and some un-housed tribals live in shanty towns around the plant. (Pokharel, 2011) Thus deprived of their agricultural land and livelihood but forced to live in close proximity to the refinery, these villagers live an abject existence. The dreams of jobs and prosperity too went sour with nothing but daily wages for labour being offered.

Environmental Hazard

Bauxite mining probably destroys more surface area than mines of other materials. It is not only land extensive, but also noisy and dusty. The disposal of alkaline, otherwise known as 'red mud' has great environmental hazard. Escape of caustic soda, used to extract alumina from raw bauxite, in to the ground water is quite likely which will increase sodium concentration in the well water etc., and high sodium is undesirable in potable water since it leads to hypertension. There are the risks of the spread of diseases in to the community with the arrival of a non-local work force. Concerns are expressed about the spread of sexually transmitted diseases to the Dongria Kondhs. The mental health of the Dongria, their identity as a people would be devastated by this mine. When indigenous communities suffer from such blows there are certain common outcomes like depression, community fragmentation, suicide, etc. There is no reason to be sanguine that such traumatic experiences would be avoided by the Dongria. The real health problem faced by the local people is no less daunting than the likely outcome stated above when the plant became operative, emission of toxic elements in to air and water by the refinery is polluting the water and air. The springs and fountains that have been an integral part of the tribals have gone toxic causing skin, kidney and cardiac ailments to the tribals. Not only adult members, even small babies are suffering from bronchial asthma, lungs problems, scabies and other skin ailments caused due to the pollution of air and contamination of water. Many have succumbed to various water borne diseases.

People's Movement

The factors cited above triggered a people's movement. Resistance against the company by the villagers most of whom were Kutia Kondhs took place in the form of a battle cry to reclaim their natural resources "*Jameen, jal, jungle hamara hai*" (the land, waters and jungles belong to us). To the Dongria Kondh in the words of their leader Lado Sikaka, 'Niyamgiri is not a pile of money, that mountain is our life'. The Dongria Kondh and other tribes inhabitating the Niyamgiri forests have been resisting the threat of mining of bauxite in their sacred mountain since 1997 when Odisha mining corporation entered into an MOU with Sterilite Industries Ltd. (Shiva Vandana, 2012) The resistance gained in momentum when Vedanta revealed the second part of its operations- to start mining for bauxite over 700 hectares of the Niyamgiri hills. The Niyamgiri Suraksha Samiti was formed in April 2004 with the participation of over 1000 tribals.

The Niyamgiri movement is a democratic people's struggle in which is a democratic people's struggle in which Odisha's tribals were backed by urban youth, intellectuals, political parties and NGOs both at the national and international level.

Political Support

Political leaders began expressing their displeasure with the state's industrial policy. Bhakta Charan Das, the then congress MP of Kalahandi confessed at a public meeting that he had been misled into believing that Vedanta would bring about development. He announced his opposition to the mining. Rahul Gandhi even claimed himself to be a real 'Sipahi' for the Adivasis. Another protest movement called Green Kalahandi was born. Several voluntary bodies, lawyers, activists; CPIML workers swelled the ranks of the Green Kalahandi movement.

Repressive Measures

The protestors' resistance was sought to be countered by violence unleashed by the goons at the behest of the company. The police restored to gross violation of human rights and followed intimidatory tactics like mass arrests and lodging false case against protestors. Cases were lodged against Sadananda Naik of Jaganathpur after he dared demand compensation for a man who lost his life by coming under the wheels of Vedanta vehicle.

The dramatic turning point of the movement came in 2004 when police imprisoned 14 activists including two women. The youth of Kalahandi including those in the town protested vociferously and the Kalahandi Sachetan Nagarik Manch was constituted. The movement thus became more vigorous and turned out to be a democratic people's struggle in which everyone came together to a common platform to oppose Vedanta. Vedanta Group alleged that the NGOs like Survival International and Action Aid instigated locals to go to hilltops and set up houses where the company has proposed to mine bauxite. No one deny that these NGOs helped in projecting the movement and the cause of the marginalised sections at the international level.

International Level Impact

The movement caused ripples which reached the shores of Britain. The Church of England withdrew its holding in Vedanta on the grounds that the company had been insensitive to the needs of the locals.

According to a release issued by the Survival International, Naveen Patnaik was invited to address a seminar at the Institute of Development Studies (IDS) near Brighton on 'progress that has been made in human development in Odisha'. He, however, pulled out on learning that several human rights organisations including Survival International and Amnesty International as well as students from IDS planned to attend the lecture and quiz him about his record. The release quoted the Survival's director Stephen Cory as stating 'there has been an alarming state wide abuse of tribal peoples' rights during Naveen's rule. Families trying to defend their lands from industrial projects have met police bullets, batons and brutality. The tribal peoples of Odisha have learnt that their leader places the profit of the industrialists' over and above their rights. (*Times of India*, 2012)

Pallisabha at the Centre Stage

Of late, the Niyamgiri movement has taken a new turn with the Supreme Court's April 18 order to hold Gram Sabha in 12 hill slope villages of Rayagada and Kalahandi districts to decide the fate of Vedanta's mining plan in Niyamgiri hills. Fresh row has erupted over the matter. Union tribal affairs minister in a letter to the Governor of Odisha raised objections to limiting Gram Sabhas to 12 villagers noting that the Dongria Kondh's spiritual and emotional bonding to Niyamgiri is not limited to these 12 villages.

Moreover, Niyamgiri Suraksha Samiti (NSS) spearheading mining campaign in Niyamgiri and Panchayat representatives of the locality announced that they were preparing for holding Gram Sabhas in 112 villages. The NSS leader and member of primitive Dongria Kondh Lado Sikaka said the tribals have already made preparation for the meeting at the villages. The NSS convener Kumuti Majhi reiterated the Samiti's resolve to oppose mining in the hills. "We pray Niyam Raja. Any mining activity will affect our religious faith". Majhi said and added 'Niyamgiri is not only for humans. It is also for animals and bird living there'. (Times of India, 2013) Inspite of the controversy between the centre and the states on the issue of the number of villages where Gram Sabhas will be held the state government went ahead with its proposal after it got the nod from the Law Department and Advocate General. The Ministry of Tribal Affairs had written to the chief secretary that the state govt. could not arbitrarily determine the list of villages where rights of forest dwellers are guaranteed under the Forest Rights Act or where cultural and religious rights are likely to be affected. (TOI, 2013) In the first phase of Pali Sabha meeting held on 18th July the Dongoria Kondhs have already communicated their resolve not to allow mining operation in Niyamgiri hills.

Conclusion

Social movements do develop in a democracy. Democracy in other words, allows space for these. It is quite natural that the Niyamgiri movement sprouted because of the conflict between the corporate interests on the one hand and the urge for survival of tribals on the other. The tribal resistance sharpened because of their fear of their cultural identity, religious feeling being swamped and means of livelihood snatched away. The promise of jobs to the tribals in the factory soon proved to be elusive and illusory. The democratic struggle started by the tribals soon came to be backed by intellectuals, political parties, NGOs, both national and international. The leadership remained undaunted despite the repression let loose by the state government machinery and the goons of the company. The conflictual core of the social movement became focussed. The environmentalists also joined the struggle and protested against the destruction of the ecosystem of the Niyamgiri hills, the possible drying up of the perennial streams which are the life line of the tribals who live by their side and depend on these for their sustenance.

The combined resistance of the cross section of the population and different organisations with the Dongria Kondh and the Kutia Kondh at the center bore fruit. Even the political authority of Odisha had to withdraw from addressing in an organisation in Britain on 'Human Development in Odisha', thanks to the organised effort of International NGOs.

At the critical juncture of the movement the Supreme Court has brought the Gramsabha/Pallisabha in the villages to the centre stage. In the midst of the controversy raging between the Central Government and the state govt regarding the number of villages to hold Gram Sabha, determine the fate to mining some Gramsabhas/Pallisabhas have already given vent to their voice against the forces of modernisation and so called developmental process. The researcher can end this piece of writing on an optimistic note that there are indications that all the vested interests unmindful of the genuine desire, human rights of the tribal people are going to be defeated and hopefully the perennial streams of the hills will continue to flow and sustain and nourish the lives of the tribals and their common property resources will be intact. One may be sanguine to finally conclude that the objectives with which the movement started are going to be realised and the strategies adopted are going to pay off.

References

Rao, M.S.A., 1978, Conceptual Problems in the Study of Social Movements in India, Vol. 1, Manohar, Delhi, p. 2.

Shah, Ghanshyam (Ed.), 2002 Social Movements and the State, Sage Publications, New Delhi, p. 16.

Ibid. p. 17.

Schuman, Fredrik L, 1948. Insurrection, In R. Edwin and A. Seligman (Eds) Encyclopaedia of Social Science, Vol. VII-VIII, Macmillan, New York, pp. 116-18.

Singh, Rajendra, 2001, Social Movement, Old and New, A Post Modernist Critique, Sage Publications, New Delhi, p. 37.

Touraine, Alac, 1985. An Introduction to the Study of Social Movements, Social Research, Vol. 52, No. 4, pp. 749-87.

Times of India, 5th Sept. 2010, Bhubaneswar, p. 2.

Manecksha, F., 5th Sept. 2009, Jameen, Jal, Jungle Hamara Hai, ToI, Bhubaneswar, p. 2.

Heffa, Schucking, Sept. 2012, Report, 'Bauxite Mine Niyamgiri Hills India' www.Bauxite Mining Niyamgiri Hills Environment. PDF. Co.

Mohapatra, Basudev, May 10, 2012, "In the Name of Development: Right and Livelihood Source of Tribals Sacrifice for Vedanta Aluminium", Www.Hotnhit News.Com

Pokharel, Krishna, 18th May 2011 'Red Mud Spill And People's Resistance at Niyamgiri: A first Hand Report From The Struggle', Www.Odishalocals Fear Red Mud Spill, Wall Street Journal PDF.

Shiva, Vandana, 2012, 'Report on Policy Dialogue : Niyamgiri, A Test Case For The Defence of Our Forest and Tribals, www.Navdaya.Orgnews.

Times of India, 25th May, 2012, Bhubaneswar.

Times of India, 10th July, 2013, Bhubaneswar.

12

Traditional Storage Practices Adopted by the Tribal Community of Warangal District, Andhra Pradesh

R. Arunjyothi, Ch. Sowmya, D. Sreenivas

Abstract

Protection of stored agricultural products against insect attack is essential for safe and steady supply of high quality grains. Indigenous practices of grain storage are advantageous as they indulge in little or no cost and are readily available. The study was carried out with an objective to document the traditional storage practices adopted by the farmers of tribal communities of Warangal District of Andhra Pradesh state. Data collection was done through direct interview method with the farmers maintaining the storage structures. This paper highlights the scenario of the crops cultivated since five decades by the tribal community and identifies the indigenous grain storage practice adopted and the constraints encountered in practicing the traditional method.

Keywords: Traditional Storage Practice, Paddy Storage, Gummie, Constraints encountered in Storage, Time Series Analysis, Gender Sensitive.

Introduction

Post harvest, the produce is stored for a long period before consumption for future use. In storage, insects, mites, micro-organism, birds, rodents and environmental factors like moisture cause significant losses. Proper storage of food grains is necessary to prevent spoilage, to increase keeping quality and for monetary reasons. The practice of following traditional method for storage of various household items dates back to the very earliest periods of known history. Certain practices are unique to a given culture of a society and vary between countries, regions, villages and even communities based on their habitat and the crops cultivated. Tribal communities have accumulated knowledge of household practices over generations by observation, experimentation and by handling age old people's experiences and wisdom. Many of the indigenous practices adopted by them find their credibility even in the modern era. According to Nagnur Shoba *et al* (2006), the logic behind use of the traditional fool proof storage system to protect stored produce from insect infestation for considerably longer periods was the user friendly material used for storage structure and its association with scientific reasoning. Keeping this in view an exploratory study is conducted to know the traditional grain storage practices adopted and the extent of modifications taken place in the past five decades in the tribal communities of Andhra Pradesh.

Methodology

Warangal District of Andhra Pradesh has eleven tribal scheduled mandals as identified by the Integrated Tribal Development Agency (ITDA). The study was conducted in two tribal communities concentrated mandals viz. Jafergadh and Narsampet during 2012. Through stratified random sampling method three tandas from each Mandal and from each tanda 10 houses (altogether 60 houses) were selected for the purpose of the study. The tribal communities were selected by appraisal of several indicators namely rainfall, overall agricultural development and cropping intensity in consultation with the officers of these respective Mandals. Focus group discussion was conducted to know the various crops grown since five decades and time series analysis was done. The key informants in the group included progressive farmers belonging to small, marginal and big farmer categories, aged farmers, farm women and farm labourers, and retired employees including teachers and other executive employees of that area. Snowball technique was adopted in identifying the indigenous grain storage structures in the selected communities. Description about the practices that are prevalent and the constraints encountered in practicing the traditional method was gathered.

Results and Discussion

Time series analysis of crops cultivated over five decades is presented in Table 1.

Time series analysis through focus group discussion revealed that during 1960 and 1990 the major crop cultivation in the tribal communities included cereals, pulses, millets and vegetables. Jowar and Ragi, were the major crops as they were the staple food of that time. It was also revealed that inter cropping was practiced. During 1980s paddy was introduced in little portions on experimental basis in these communities. It is interesting to know that so grown rice was served as meal only for school going boys in the family. With the advent of green revolution in 1960s and its spread till 1990s, the focus has shifted towards cultivation of paddy in large scale resulting in gradual reduction

Table 12.1 : Major Crops Cultivated in the Tribal Areas during 1960-2010

Duration	*Cereals Pulses and Millets*	*Vegetables and Fruits*
1960-1970	Jowar, Maize, Bajra, Greengram, Fox Tail Millet and (Korralu), Horse Gram, Seasam, Cow Pea, Bengal gram, Black gram, Green Gram, Groundnut and Sunflower. Jowar was the local staple diet.	Gourds, Drumstick leaves, Tamarind leaves and other locally grown fruit bearing plants. Melons, Berries, Mangos were prime fruits.
1970-1980	Jowar, Bajra, Greengram, Maize, Bobbarlu, Fox Tail Millet (Korralu), Ragi and oil seeds like Sunflower and Ground Nut.	Pumpkins, Drumsticks, Local leafy vegetables like Bacchala and Gongura. Fruits include Gauva, Custard Apple, Berries, Lemon, Mangoes.
1980-1990	Paddy cultivation increased at a substantial rate in place of Jowar. Bajra, Maize, Fox tail millet, Greengram, Redgram. Jowar and other millets usage decreased and spices were introduced.	Pumpkins, Drumsticks, Brinjal, Potato and locally available leafy vegetables.
1990-2000	High yield varieties like B.P.T-5204 and Tella Hamsa variety was cultivated in large scale in the community. Jowar, Bajra, Redgram and Blackgram cultivation decreased radically.	Tomato, Potato, Cabbage, Spinach, Amaranthas Peas, Coriander, Guava, Papayas, Mangoes and Banana.
2000-2010	Pulses and millet cultivation radically decreased. Rice, Maize and cash crops like Cotton were cultivated.	Brinjal, Tomato, Methi, Pudina, Amaranthis, Gongura, Coriander and Spinach.

in the cultivation of other cereals, millets and pulses. Jowar and Ragi cultivation was radically reduced by 2010 and they were replaced by rice which became the staple food of the population. Presently, maize, cotton and paddy have become the preferable crops irrespective of the land holding of the farmer. With regard to vegetables and fruits cultivation, till 1990s indigenously grown brinjal, pumpkins, drumsticks and leafy vegetables like bacchala, gongura were grown while among fruits guava, custard apple, berries, and mangoes were in cultivation. During mid 1990s new vegetable varieties were introduced including cabbage, cauliflower, tomatoes varieties, beans, spinach, and coriander. Banana and papaya were included among fruits.

One of the main reasons attributed for the shift towards paddy cultivation was changes in cropping pattern and this shift towards paddy is due to high yield varieties which are fertilizer responsive and also declaration of minimum support price by government. This scenario has gradually lead most of the farmers to abstain from storing other commodities except paddy which might be due to the fact that paddy is in demand as cash crop and it being the staple food.

This analysis reveals that the tribal areas are influenced by the policies and market demands, thereby cultivation of pulses, cereals and millets has undergone a radical change in the past five decades.

Grain Storage Practice

Focus group discussion revealed that most of the farmers had given up traditional method of grain storage primarily because of the continuance it demands and secondly, accessibility of the grains at marginal rates. Mushrooming of the seed supply firms is also reported as a reason in withdrawal of the traditional practices by farmers. Very few progressive farmers who were in the elderly age group of more than 55 year age were found maintaining the traditional storage structures called Gummie to store paddy. The primary reason attributed by the practicing farmers in storage of the grains is for seed purpose. The other reasons included the availability of helping hands and knowledge of the elderly people at home and to meet the requirements of special occasions like marriages of the children.

Gummie

Gummie meaning a hidden place in local language (Telugu) is a chief grain storage structure exclusively designed to suit storage needs of an individual household for short term. Normally, it is used to store larger quantity of the same commodity. The grains or seed material is stored in these Gummies are kept safe away from wide range of pests for nearly six months. The better viability and quality of the seeds in this storage may be due to the fact that the method adopted is user friendly and is associated with scientific reasoning.

Gummie is a barrel like structure made from seasoned Palmyra splits (Borassus Fablellifer L which are closely intertwined as a canopy to form a cylindrical structure with an opening at the top. It is mainly used to store paddy (Orizya sativa) for future use. It is an indoor storage structure erected in a dry place in the home. The size of the gummy is determined by the farmers based on his need. The normal size of the Gummie is 1.7 mt height, 1.5 m width in circumference, capacity of about 400 kg. Once the structure is woven, the exterior is plastered with a thin layer of clay and fortified with cow dung. It is then placed over a foundation of stones or on the ground and allowed to dry. Nowadays the interior of the structure is lime washed. When the structure is fully dried the grains to be stored are deposited in leaving 6 cm space at the top to be filled with hay or dried paddy grass. The structures are then covered with intricately woven mats made up of dried leaves of Palmyra or wooden planks. The whole structure along with the wooden planks is plastered over with clay and cow dung and is allowed to dry.

The clay and cow dung coating on the structure acts as impervious coating which will prevent even small insect pests. The hay/husk used in the top cover has insect deterrent action which prevents insects setting down on the structure which was in agreement with the report of Solomon Kiruba (2009). Nowadays plastic sheets are used at the bottom layer and as well at the top layer as a cover to prevent the penetration of any moisture into the storage. Processing of grains pre-storage is also one of the important activity followed. To be stored grains are first thoroughly sun dried in the month of March and April to make them pest free. Stones, malformed, broken, undersized and diseased seeds, weed seeds, chaff and other rubbish are removed from the dried grains and only graded ones are stored. Singh and Sharma (2003) reported that UV in solar radiation had sterilising effect of on grains when sun dried. These findings are in coherence with present study.

Another advantage of the Gummie is that, once made the same structure can be reused for storage for about five years while only roof replacement is required. The material used in its make is locally available, cost effective and eco friendly. As these structures are woven by the professional basket weavers of the same community tending and mending of the structure whenever required would not be a problem.

Constraints in Traditional Storage Method

Respondents have reported about few major constraints in traditional storage practices which are note worthy. Primarily constraint reported was about the space occupied by the storage structure. As the structure need to be placed free from moisture and protected from rodents it is generally placed in middle of the dwelling rooms rather than to the corner of the house. In order to stores about five tons of paddy a minimum of about 10x10 square feet room is required for free movement during loading and unloading. Second problem reported was about the maintenance of the storage structure. Generally the storage structures are erected on the mud floors. Since it is made of biodegradable material, it needs regular upkeep. To keep the pests at bay, the floor of the room where Gummies are erected are to be frequently plastered with cow dung at least once in a week or fortnight and it is considered exclusively a women's job; thereby an extra household activity for women. Moreover after every six months the grains are to be taken out and subjected to sun drying and again stored in Gummies after the structures are once again coated with clay and cow dung in the inner and outer sides and dried. Sarangi and Singh (2009) have also reported that lack of proper care and regular upkeep of the structures attract the rodents which not only contaminate the product but spoil and make it unfit for human consumption. Another constraint reported was about the unloading of the grains from the structure. As the structure has only one wide opening at the top and need to be thoroughly plastered after every use, farmer generally take out about 40-50 kg paddy at a time because, taking in small quantities as and when required involves laborious process. Moreover, unloading activity requires at least two people, preferably men as it requires a person to mount on the structure and take out the grain. Thereby the storage structure lacks gender sensitivity.

Conclusion

The study reveals that crop cultivation in tribal areas in the past five decades has undergone a radical change influenced by the policies and market demands. Majority of the farmers are interested in cultivating only paddy, maize and cotton while completely neglecting the cultivation of pulses and millets. Hence there is a need for the policy-makers to rethink in bringing out balanced crop cultivation. The survey also reveals that very few elderly farmers who are well acquainted with the process of maintaining the traditional storage method only are storing the grains for the seed purpose. Young generation is indifferent towards traditional storage method because of it being laborious and exigent to handle. To overcome the constraints in the traditional storage practices a slightly modified system with separate outlet and inlet, drudgery free and gender sensitive storage structures to suit present day storage needs is required. Though chemical methods of management of pests in storing grains are highly successful, they leave behind the toxic residues. But traditional grain storage methods are worth stimulating since they are eco friendly and are proven to impart high shelf life to the commodity stored, and are highly effective in preventing infects infestation.

References

Solomon K, Sathiadas S M and Samaragdi P (2006). Prospects of traditional seed storage strategies against insect infestation adopted by two ethnic communities of Tamil Nadu, South Peninsular India., Bulletin of Insectology, 59(2), 129-134.

Sarangi S.K., Singh R., Singh K.A. (2009) Indigenous method of rat proof grain storage by Adi tribes of Arunachal Pradesh. Indian Journal of Traditional Knowledge, 8(2), 230-233.

Nagnur Shoba, Channal Geeta and Channamma N (2006) Indigenous grain storage structures and method of storage. Indian Journal of Traditional Knowledge, 5 (1), 114-117.

Singh S and Sharma G (2003) Pulse beetle management through solar energy in stored green gram seeds. Seed Research, 31(1), 84-89.

Karthikeyan C, Veeraragavathatham D, Karpagam D and Ayisha Firdouse (2009). Traditional storage practices. Indian Journal of Traditional Knowledge, 8 (4), 564-568.

13

Development-Induced Displacement and Resettlement of Indigenous Communities in India: Policy and Practice

Ram Babu Mallavarpu

Abstract

The paper attempts to analyse the critical problems of development-induced displacement, human and environmental consequences and inadequacies in rehabilitation and resettlement (R&R) policy and its practice for the welfare of the project displaced/affected indigenous communities, and also to ensure their livelihood opportunities because of large scale development projects in India with special reference to Andhra Pradesh. This study is based on anthropological approach and stresses on the need to rethink the present model of development with the least displacement or no displacement alternative models.

Keywords: Displacement, Rehabilitation, Resettlement, Policy, Practice and India.

Introduction

The tribal population of the country according to 2001 Census was about 84.3 million, constituting about 8.2 per cent of the total Indian population. The total tribal population in AP according to 2001 Census is about 42 lakhs, which accounts for 6.31 per cent of the State's total population. The economy of some of the tribals in forest area has been primarily *konda-podu* (sweden) cultivation. More than 90 per cent of the tribals exclusively depend upon land even today (Rao 1993).

India is the third largest in dam building in the World and it now has over 3,600 large dams and over 700 more under construction. India's development policies and strategies have focused attention on indispensability of irrigation as important input for agriculture. Large-Scale Irrigation Projects are important for higher agriculture growth, besides establishment of Industries and Power Projects. India gave tremendous encouragement to the large river valley projects or large multipurpose dams. The dominant ethos was 'big is the best' and the conviction is that large multipurpose projects are the panacea to all the problems of poverty and underdevelopment.

For this purpose irrigation and other infrastructure projects most often acquire people's lands and also cause displacement. Furthermore, the Government is authorised by the Land Acquisition Act (LAA) of 1894 introduced by the British Government and this has been continued with some amendments in 1967 and 1984. This Act facilitates the Governments to acquire the people's land, by compulsion for both the public and private purposes (Swamy Maheswara, 1996; Upadhyay, Sanjay, Ram, Bhavani, 1998).

Despite of several protective laws, the appropriate governments have been acquiring the tribal lands for establishing various development projects in scheduled areas as these areas are endowed with rich minerals and other natural resources. Even though, there are well defined guidelines, procedures and norms for providing proper Resettlement and Rehabilitation (R&R) measures for the welfare of Project Affected Persons (PAPs), they have not been practiced in right spirit. Absence of rehabilitation Act at national level and violation of protective laws, regulations, legislations, and court orders causing deprivation PAPs, especially the tribals and weaker sections (Ram Babu 2006 and 2008).

In case of Andhra Pradesh, *jalayagnam*, a massive irrigation expansion programme has been taken up by the Government with a vision to bring all-round development in its backward regions. This has already displaced as many as 1,02,795 households belong to 516 (313 fully and 203 partly) displaced villages (as per the progress report of the GoAP on R&R of irrigation projects as on 31-05-2009). The irrigation projects like Polavaram initiated under *jalaygagam* in the region caused to large scale displacement of various tribal and weaker communities in scheduled areas. So far, several R&R programmes have been initiated for the welfare of tribal PAPs. Because of displacement and inadequate measures of R&R, the tribal communities in these villages have been voicing for the better R&R package and occurrence of PAPs movements for their rights in different parts of the project affected regions is its testimony.

However, large developmental projects most often disturb the habitat of the ST communities, and destroy their traditional ways of life and emotional attachment with land, water and forest on which they depend for livelihood. Developmental projects so far implemented in India, since independence have led to displacement of various tribal societies, commercial exploitation at the hands of outsiders, and degradation of forests and other natural resources causing losses to ecological and sustainable environments. Earlier studies have proved these facts and also highlighted various inadequacies in implementation of R&R packages.

In most of the cases, they do not have awareness on the benefits and burdens of such large projects, and other issues related to displacement and resettlement. The scope of the proposed study is to know the impact of R&R programmes initiated for the welfare of tribal PAPs of Polavaram irrigation project in the West Godavari, East Godavari and Khammam districts with special emphasis on prevailing R&R policy and its implications.

Eastern Ghats and Inhabitant ST Communities: Geographical Setting

The Eastern Ghats is a discontinuous range of hills along the East-coast of India, located between 10º05′ and 22º30′ Northern latitude, and 76º23′ and 86º50′ Eastern longitudes in North East to South West strike. It covers a total area of 75,000 sq km with an average width of 220 km to the North and 100 km to the South (Pullaiah, Sandhya and Karuppusamy, 2011).

It is distributed in four States of Odisha, AP, Tamil Nadu and Karnataka. Its Odisha region covers 18 districts of Mayurbhanj, Keonjhar, Balasore, Jajpur, Angul, Dhenkanal, Cuttack, Khurda, Nayagarh, Phulbani, Boudh, Kalahandi, Gajapati, Ganjam, Rayagada, Nabarangpur, Koraput and Malkanagiri. In AP, it is located in 15 districts of Srikakulam, Visakhapatnam, East Godavari, West Godavari, Khammam, Mahaboobnagar, Nalgonda, Guntur, Krishna, Kurnool, Prakasham, Nellore, Cuddapah, Anantapur and Chitoor. It covers nine districts of Vellore, Erode, Salem, Namakkal, Dharmpuri, Tiruvanamalai, Tiruchirapalli, Pudukkaottai and Villupuram of Tamil Nadu. In Karnataka it falls in the Chamrajnagar and Kolar districts (Pullaiah, Sandhya and Karuppusamy, 2011).

The tribal communities which have been living in the Northern part of Eastern Ghats in Orissa are 62. The important groups among them are Kandho, Gond, Santal, Saura, Kolha, Shabar, Munda, Paroja, Bhutada, Bhuiyan, Kissan, Oraon, Bhumiya, Bhadadi, Kharia, Binjhal, Mirdhas and Juang. The tribal communities in Eastern Ghats of Tamil Nadu are of three groups such as Sholaga, Uraly and Malayali. The total number of inhabitant tribal communities in the Eastern Ghats region of AP is 35. They are Andh, Bagata, Bhill, Chenchu, Dhulia, Gadabas, Gond, Goudu, Hill Reddi, Jatapus, Konda Kamara, Kattunayakan, Kolam, Konda Dora, Konda Kapu, Konda Reddi, Kondh, Kotiya, Koya, Kulic, Mali, Manne Dora, Nooka Dora, Naikpod, Nayak, Pradhan, Porja, Reddi Dora, Rona, Savara, Thoti and Valmiki (Thurston 1909; Singh 1992-1998). It represents the geological past of Deccan plateau and displays a rich variety of flora and fauna and other natural resources. It is the home to large number of Asiatic elephants in the World as well as large animals, i.e., Nilgiri Tahr, Leopards, Gaurs, Sambar and Tigers. Its costal area provides fishing opportunities to the local communities. Like Western Ghats, Eastern Ghats is also ecologically important for the sustenance of the natural environment of the country (Pullaiah, Sandhya and Karuppusamy, 2011).

Scheduled Areas and Legal Framework

The total extent of the Scheduled areas of AP consists of 31,485.34 sq km covered by 6,734 Tribal Sub-Plan (TSP) villages and 5,936 Scheduled villages. Most of the tribal areas are located in Khammam, Visakhapatnam, Vijayanagaram and Srikakulam. All these Scheduled areas, as well as the TSP areas are covered by 10 Integrated Tribal Development Agencies (ITDAs). The total geographical coverage of all ITDAs in AP is more than 1,75,668 sq km (Kumari 2004). The Constitution of India recognises tribals as the most vulnerable communities and provides many means of protection to them. The Vth and VIth Schedules of the Constitution aim to prevent acquisition, holding or disposal of the land in the Scheduled areas by non-tribals.

It attempts to ensure that the tribals remain in possession of their land for livelihood, economic empowerment, social status and dignity. Furthering the support, several State Legislations and Regulations have been passed to protect tribal land from alienation. The Andhra Pradesh Scheduled Areas Land Transfer Regulation (APSALTR), 1959 (as amended in 1970) is applicable when land is to be acquired in the Scheduled areas. According to the Panchayatraj Extension to Scheduled Areas Act (PESA), 1996 the *grama-sabha* clearance along with full information disclosure is required prior to establishment of any development project (Babu 2006). As per the Scheduled Tribes and other Forest Dwellers Recognition of Forest Rights Act (STs&FDs RoFRA), 2007 the tribals have several provisions for obtaining *pattas* for their *podu* (agricultural) lands (in the forests) and also to claim for the Community Rights (CRs) over the CPRs and NRs.

Development Projects and National Interest

It is of importance to note that most of the projects are located in the backward area of the tribal communities, as the forest and mountainous tracts, which are the traditional habitats of them, endowed with rich mineral resources, and abandoned flora and fauna. Most of the rivers originate and drain through several tribal regions. The resources available in the tribal areas are perceived as the property of the Nation by the policy makers and never viewed as the source of livelihood for tribal communities. The large scale development projects displace the tribal communities either through the submergence/acquisition or change in user-ship of their land / property for project sites in the name of the National interest (Babu 2007).

Land Acquisition and Public Purpose

The Land Acquisition Act (LAA), 1894 (still continues with some amendments in 1967 and 1984) facilitates the appropriate Governments to acquire the people's land by compulsion for both the public and the private purposes (Swamy 1996). This Act helps the State as a weapon for immediate land acquisition in the name of public purpose. Further, the Act did not define the term 'public'. In most of the cases, the Government officials have been paying the compensation to oustees after prolonged time, where as they acquire the land with one notification and with in no time, but the LAA did not say anything on the nature of compensation payable to oustees and time period for payment of compensation (Upadhyay, Sanjay, Ram and Bhavani 1998).

The land acquisition in Scheduled areas is not possible, as there are number of protective Laws, Legislations, Regulations, Court Orders and Judgments, Government Orders (GOs), etc., which prohibit the land transfer in Scheduled areas. Despite of all these protective Laws made by the Governments for the welfare of tribals, the appropriate agencies of the Governments have been acquiring the tribal lands in the name of public purpose and National interest in contravention to all the Constitutional provisions. It indicates that all these Laws which were made for the protection of tribals have been manipulated, where the legal access to tribal lands and resources is denied (Babu 2006).

Livelihoods vs. Paps: Ecological, Socio-cultural and Economic Perspectives

The ecological balance in tribal areas is primarily maintained through cultural practices in the form of taboos or prohibitions or norms, which define the nature and extent of exploitation within the communities. Any imbalance in this relation either by changes in nature or culture because of displacement due to development projects acts as man-made catastrophe and leads to destruction of livelihood patterns which was the very basis for survival of communities (Rao 2007). The ecosystem from the tribals' point of view is the relationship they have as individuals and as community with the NRs around them. This includes the use of NRs for livelihood and the various values, beliefs, practices and cultural norms which regulate the use of these.

These systems were evolved not only to ensure a continuous supply of livelihood requirements but also to reinforce the continuation of a relationship between the individual, the community and nature. The tribals looked upon themselves as an integral part of nature. It is imperative here to critically examine this relationship because there has been a continuous shift in the individual-community-nature relationship with the progress of civilisation and an increasing alienation from nature. Such a shift in relationship must be dealt with great concern and viewed as a part of the process of development (Mahesawri 2006, Biksham and Krishna 2007).

The tribals in the region mainly cultivate pulses and vegetables as well as maize, jowar, cotton, chilly and tobacco. They collect more than 100 varieties of Non-Timber Forest Produces (NTFPs)/Minor Forest Produces (MFPs) and 250 other medicinal products from the nearby forests which are thick, dry and deciduous wood lands of *Tectona terminalia* series. Most of these products, i.e., nuts and fruits are used for household purpose and also for sale at the weekly market fairs (shandis) and as well as at the ration shops, established by the Girijana Co-operative Corporation (GCC).

The NTFPs/MFPs generally collected by the tribal communities in the region include tene (Honey), usiri (*Emblica officinalis*), ippa (*Bassia latifolia*), chintha (*Tamarindus Indica*), vepa (*Azadirachta indica*) tapsi (*Sterculia urenus*), musti (Strychnos nuxvomica), tangedu (*Cassia auriculata*), rela (*Cassia fistula*), veduru (*Bambusa arundinacea/Dendrocalamus strictus*), ganuga (*Pongamia pinnata*), beedi (*Diospyros melanoxylon*), etc., which are available in different seasons. The coffee, silver oak, cashew, eucalyptus, rubber, mulberry, etc., plantations have been growing by extending to nearby forest land. This may also leads to major threats to livelihoods of tribals, forest flora and wildlife in future (Babu 2006).

The tribal societies, which have been still in the hunting, gathering and slash-and-burn stages, have a much closer relationship with nature and its management (Roy Burman 1995, Fernandes, Menon and Viegas 1998). In the wake of development and modernisation, there has been a near total disintegration of the tribal ecosystem. This has led to the breakdown of the tribal community and their culture with the overwhelming majority of individuals within the tribal society being unable to cope with a society which has nearly become de-linked from nature. The tribals understood and interacted with nature in a manner, which according to many environmentalists, is unique and a key to the future management and relationship with nature. It is also important to analyse the reasons and processes involved in integrating the tribal community into the mainstream and the accompanying changes in the man-community-environment relationship (Carr-Harris, Menon and Gupta 1994). According to the reports of ITDAs and other the available field data, most of the tribals work as labourer in their fields which have been cultivated by the non-tribal farmers on lease. The fertile lands, possessed by the tribals earlier, have been already alienated by the non-tribal settlers with several illegal methods. Apart from agriculture and NTFPs/ MFPs collection, they also rear cattle, sheep, pigs, goats, hen, etc. for their agriculture and commercial purposes. As the tribals are illiterates, and due to their simplicity, they are unable to cope up with the market operations, from time to time. Consequently the gullible tribals have been exploited by the traders and non-tribals in most of the cases. Most often they are forced to take loans from traders and money lenders, and remain indebted (Babu 2006).

Even though they are in transition, they may not bypass their cultural practices and knowledge systems in view of thier deep-rooted value orientations and livelihood concerns. Most of them have been living in extreme poverty even without basic amenities, i.e., healthcare, drinking water and education. Poverty, hunger, malnutrition and impoverishment are the important evils which have been facing by the most of the tribal communities since long time.

Threats of land alienation, indebtedness, displacement and inadequate resettlement measures are the major problems, which have been haunting these tribal groups. Paradoxically no proper protection is extended to the tribal communities for the loss of their lands to the single most important source of their expropriation, namely, the State itself (Babu 2006).

Displacement and R&R Policies

Displacement is not only the physical eviction from a dwelling, but appropriation of productive lands and other assets to make possible an alternative use (Cernia 2000). The affected people as who stand to lose as a consequence of project include all or part of their physical and non-physical assets, including communities, homes, productive lands, resources such as forests, range lands, fishing areas, important cultural sites, commercial properties, tenancy, income earning opportunities, and socio-cultural networks and other activities. However, unlike displacement from natural calamities, which are beyond human control, displacement due to man-made catastrophe such as dams and mines is not inevitable in view of many risks.

While such adverse social impacts are generally unavoidable in the broader perspective of the National interest and public purpose in real sense, there is great need to minimise such adverse affects and for providing alternative sites for resettlements through provision of housing, infrastructure related to education, road, drinking water, electricity, hospital, etc. and also extending suitable remunerative economic rehabilitation support, thus enabling the adversely affected people to regain their former levels of living standards. According to the Asian Development Bank (ADB), 1998 the rehabilitation refers to incomes, livelihoods, and social systems of the displaced to at least the level of their pre-project status and this requires careful planning and implementation of the R&R management plan.

The National Policy on Rehabilitation and Resettlement (NPRR), 2003 was issued by the Ministry of Rural Development (MoRD) on 17/02/ 2004, and the State policy was issued by the Government of AP (GoAP) on 08/04/2005. The GoI has approved the National Rehabilitation Policy (NRP), 2006 on 11/10/2007 to replace the NPRR, 2003. A close study of various provisions of these policies, however, does not stand for the same. These policies provide no safeguard against double/triple displacement, which occurred in the past due to poor planning in resettlement process and project assessment, especially in the dam related submergence and displacement (Babu 2006). However, due to the people's movements all over the country against SEZs, the GoI has also promised to bring the broad Land Acquisition, Rehabilitation and Resettlement (LARR) Bill 2011 to formulate the LARR Act. But in reality, this has not been finalised so far by the GoI (Patrik 2009, Ramachandraiah and Srinivasan 2011).

Conclusion

Need of the hour is to address problems of the displaced victims with better remunerative/comprehensive economic policy measures in other words

LARR Act in order to overcome the defects existed in the present R&R policies, and also to protect the human rights of the vulnerable communities to integrate them as equal partners in the whole developmental process which assume greater importance for the wellbeing of the displaced in view of the onslaught of national and international capital in the age of so-called liberalisation, privatisation and globalisation.

14

Politics of Inclusion and Exclusion of Tribals in the Local Governance in Odisha: Issues and Concerns

Ramchandra Jena

Panchayati Raj system has influenced the village life extensively as one of the most important units of democratic decentralisation. Decentralisation of powers is nothing but transfer of powers from one tier of governance to another and, in same way, from one segment of population to another. Power moves from the dominant to the oppressed, men to women, caste Hindus to Dalits, upper castes to lower castes and bureaucrats to people's representatives. Power will not move on its own. It has to be made move. So, a driving force is needed. The task is not so easy as may be envisaged, particularly in an extremely unequal society like India.[1]

All most all states have enacted their Panchayat laws in order to confirm with the spirit and content of the 73rd Constitutional amendments. Accordingly the new laws, elections have been conducted. Reservations have been provided to the excluded and marginalised groups specially for SCs and STs. With these developments an impression has been created that the whole representative democracy has been transformed into a participatory democracy and the hitherto excluded have been included in governance and administration through the device of reservation of seats in local bodies.[2] However, there are still several problems when we examine the issues of substantive inclusion of the marginalised in the functioning of these elected bodies and in what they are able to achieve for their constituents in terms of promoting Good Governance. The forces of patriarchy and caste are the two socially powerful forces that deter women and Dalit participation respectively. Bringing such marginalised groups into the political sphere requires addressing the issues of dominance and exclusion both at the level of institutional structures and processes as well as at the larger social setting which the marginalised groups inhabit. Secondly, Panchayats are engaged with service delivery diverting all their attention to the provisioning of developmental goods and services such as water, electricity, housing, education, sometimes at the cost of promoting social justice. Thirdly, the rapid economic growth agenda of the state, particularly under neo-liberalism and globalisation has unraveled a new set of questions on role and mandate of Panchayats relating to the governance of commons on which people's survival is dependent. Even the tribal regions which fall under Panchayat Extension to Scheduled Areas Act (PESA) both the government and the industry have collaborated to negotiate directly with people without engaging Panchayats. PESA Act 1996 extends Panchayats to the tribal areas of eight States of India namely, Andhra Pradesh, Bihar, Gujarat, Himachal Pradesh, Maharashtra, Madhya Pradesh, Odisha and Rajasthan with the intention to enable tribal society to assume control over their own destiny to preserve and conserve their traditional rights over natural resources.[3] However, most states have been indifferent to the Act as well as corresponding transfer of powers to the tribal population (to access and utilise natural resources for consumption and livelihood).

Thus 'Inclusion of the marginalised groups in local governance' has been a serious problem in our civil society. 'Inclusion' in this context means the inclusion of the marginalised and unprevilaged tribals in local governance.[4] However, 'inclusion' cannot be understood, without having any reference to 'exclusion'. Exclusion needs to be countered to promote inclusion. Since exclusion and inclusion are inter-related, new insights on inclusion through sincerely analysis requires on both: causes, consequences and means of exclusion as also the ways in which marginalised groups work towards their inclusion. Tribals have suffered social and economic marginalisation for a long time and therefore are considered for affirmative action. Particularly in the rural setting, the socio-economic hierarchies are inter-related. Hence, the groups who occupy low position in social hierarchy such as Dalit, and tribal also invariably occupy low position in economic hierarchy.[5]

While the focus on exclusion - inclusion has largely centered on how they take place within local governance institutions, an important area needing further solution relates exclusion of Panchayat institutions in situations of political conflict or economic contestation. More study needs to address this field to generate insights on what happens to inclusion when local governance institutions themselves get excluded from the processes of development and governance.[6]

From the above discussions it is clear that there are two aspects that have significant implication for inclusion of the marginalised:

First, the Larger Macro Political and Economic Context in which Local Governments Operates

How local governments can or cannot promote inclusion in the contexts of (a) violent conflicts and political unrest, and (b) neo-liberal economic growth, globalisation and commoditisation of commons such as land, water and forests.

(a) ***Violent conflicts and political unrest:*** We have a stable democracy in India and India is the largest democratic country in world. Despite this political conflicts have aggravated in specific regional contexts. Two types of conflicts have raised in the recent times—the armed conflict in the North Eastern region which has taken the shape of separatist movements; and conflicts between the state and the Maoist groups (popularly known as Naxalites) in Chhatisgarh, Jharkhand, Odisha and Andhra Pradesh, West Bengal where the Maoist groups claiming to be *messiahs* of the poor have launched violent assault against the government. It is imperative to explore how political contexts as described above affect the functioning of local governments and implications of this for the resource poor communities and those considered being most vulnerable to unrest such as poor and women.[7]

(b) Neo-liberal Economic Growth, Globalisation and Commoditisation of Commons such as Land, Water and Forests

In the present scenario of neo-liberalism and globalisation we are witnessing economic conflicts between those whose resources are threatened by rapid economic growth and those who are actively pursuing these have intensified immensely. In pursuing economic growth Panchayats as local decision-making institutions are either bypassed or co-opted by the economically powerful forces in executing their agenda. In many parts of India people are protesting against the establishment of special economic zones whose resources are to be loosed on which their survival depends. For examples, people of Singur and Nandigram in West Bengal and Kalinga Nagar in Odisha are protesting against the establishment of the Special Economic Zones.[8] Similarly in tribal areas of Odisha mining operations by multinationals have faced opposition from local people. In other parts of India, it is not entirely unknown for financial incentives in the short run inducing a peaceful cooperation of the Panchayats in the neo-liberal agenda of the state but in the long run carrying with the possibility of the communities loosing control over their natural resources.

Secondly, the Local Micro Social Contexts in which the Local Governments Function

How inclusion takes place in the contexts of social and economic inequalities in which Dalit, tribal and women lives. Within the micro sphere there are three critical problems:

(a) Manipulation of Structures and Process Underlying the Functioning of Local Governments: The Constitution Amendment Acts and the confirmatory acts passed by the State Governments have created opportunities for inclusion of the marginalised through affirmative action. There is a clear and unequivocal conceptualisation of the local governments as inclusive of those who have been in the periphery of society and have largely been isolated from the decision-making process. In practice however, when Panchayats interact with the local socio-economic structures the possibility exists for the power structures to get mirrored within the governance institutions. The marginalised groups who occupy weak positions in social and economic hierarchy can find themselves weak even within the local governments. While the representation of the weaker sections is officially sought through affirmative action, in the actual practices that take place within the institutions, they are subjected to multiple types of discrimination and exclusion. In many instances the actual decision is taken before hand without giving consideration to the opinion of the marginalised members, or their voices could be rendered silent through verbal abuse and other symbolic practices (e.g., making them sit on the floor while others sit in chairs) Hence, we find women getting excluded in a predominantly male space; and low castes and poor getting excluded when the locally dominant caste and economically powerful groups occupy the positions of power in Panchayat institutions. In the sphere of local governance, there are many spaces that are significant for exclusion to be played out right from the stage of calling of elections to the holding of the Gram Sabhas.[9]

(b) Mobilisation for Inclusion: In many cases Panchayats are manipulated to keep the effort to counter such exclusion. Marginalised groups nowadays are questioning their exclusion and mobilised towards inclusion. Efforts are underway in recent times to address the 'power and politics' played out in the spheres of local governance. Such mobilisations in recent times are visible in several ways. These include:

(i) Forming collectives by discriminated groups such as federations of women elected representatives (ii) Alignment with political parties (iii) Occupying alternate (and sometimes competing) spaces available for local development such as water users group, village education committees, self help groups /micro-finance groups etc.[10]

(c) Violence against the Marginalised to Prevent their Inclusion: Violence against the marginalised by locally powerful groups to prevent their inclusion is the extreme form of exclusion. Such type of violence are often happens to women and Dalits. In this regard, patriarchy and caste are the two most dominant socio-cultural forces that determine positions of tribals and Dalits in social hierarchy.[11] Violence in the sphere of local governance can manifest as physical, verbal (e.g., abusive language), and even symbolic (e.g., spreading rumours). Women have often faced such violence both within their homes and outside for entering local governance. Dalits have faced violence from high castes. Violence creates fear among the victims and the groups they belong so that they do not dare challenging the power structures within local governance.[12]

In reality many State Governments have reluctantly fulfilled the formalities to satisfy the Constitutional requirements. Beyond that, they have not looked at the spirit of the Constitutional Amendments. Hence, the inclusion of marginalised groups could not take a concrete shape as envisaged in the Constitutional Amendments. Still it is in a budding stage. It will take time to institutionalise the marginalised groups in the fold of decentralised democratic process. Further, marginalised groups have not been mobilised to participate in the process of development and governance.[13]

Participation cannot be imposed on the marginalised from above; it should be voluntary and based on good will to participate. Here by participation we mean direct involvement of people and not indirect involvement through their representatives. An equitable sharing of the benefits of development by marginalised groups is possible only when there is equitable participation by them in the process of development.[14] By doing so, marginalised groups can influence the decisions at the higher levels through their joint efforts and common voice. This may be termed as "bottom up approach to integrated rural development." The process can be accelerated only when the marginalised groups become conscious on their rights and privileges and build up strength to achieve justice for themselves in the sharing of benefits of development.[15]

Marginalised groups' participation or involvement can better be understood as:

(a) participation in decision-making; (b) participation in implementation of development programmes and projects; (c) participation in monitoring and evaluation of development programmes and projects, and (d) participation in sharing the benefits of development.[16]

Direct participation of the marginalised groups in decision-making is possible only at the village level. Even at the village level, discussion regarding community development projects such as drinking water, social construction etc, is confined in the hands of small caucus of so called village elites. These schemes must be discussed freely in the open assemblies in the presence of all the villagers so that marginalised groups have some say in the decision-making and execution of these schemes. More specifically, most of SC/ST and women representatives were facing the problem of non-cooperation from the official and upper castes/dominant sections of their Grama Panchayats. These problems have not only been obstructing developmental works but also not enabling elected representatives to participate in the Panchayats. These problems are not confined to Odisha only but exists everywhere in different degree of intensity. However, experiences gained so far also show that the affirmative action for women and marginalised group in local governments has resulted in social identities and political awareness among them and created an urge to become a part of mainstream political, economic, and social life. After initial clashes between higher castes and lower castes, there are no indications of social cohesion at local levels. The political space given to marginalised sections has to some extent dealt a blow to the asymmetrical social structure and given greater space for their participation and involvement in decision-making at the local level.

Conclusion

The whole exercise of inclusion of marginalised is equivalent to that of transfer of power from the British to the Indians. The task of doing such an exercise is not so easy as it has to be carried out internally within our society. It requires a movement of the masses. For mobilising the masses for the new task, the leaders are to be trained. Different stakeholders are to be prepared perceptively. Without support of the civil society organisations, the full potentials of the decentralisation of powers can not be harnessed and hence preparing the civil society is the need of the hour. In order to make participation of marginalised groups effective, efficient and successful there is a need of vital change in traditional, social attitude. There is also need for positive attitudinal change and mental make-up of the dominant folk in favour of women participation. They should be given appropriate training to improve their knowledge base and capacity level relating to their rights, responsibilities and duties in the functioning of Panchayat bodies. They should be made acquainted with the procedures of Panchayati Raj rules, regulations and financial management. There is also need for launching more and more awareness campaigning in favour of women empowerment. Mass media, NGOs, Political Parties, Self Help Group's (SHGs), Mahila Mandals have a significant role to play in this context.

References

1. G. Palanithurai, Critical Interventions on the critical issues by the civil societies, South Asian Politics, New Delhi, August 2008, p. 20.

2. Parida K. Jayant, Women in Panchayati Raj Institutions-A Case Study in Orissa, Women in Politics (ed.), Dasarathi Bhuyan, Discovery Publication, New Delhi, 2008.

3. G. Palanithurai, New Panchayati Raj System: Status and Prospects, Kaniska Publishers, New Delhi, 1996, p. 21.

4. Amrit Patel, Role of PRIs in implementing rural employment guarantee scheme, Kurukhetra, August 2006, p. 27.

5. Dr Mahipal, Panchayati Raj and Bharat Nirman, Kurukshetra, October 2006, p. 65.

6. Yatindra Singh Sisodia, Peoples' Participation in Grama Sabha, Kurukshetra, May 2006, p. 35.

7. Mahi Pal, Panchayati Raj and Development, Yojana, August 2004, p. 51.

8. Kempe R. Hope, 'Rural Development and Social Change', Rural Development Digest, Vol. 3, January 1980, No. 1, Hyderabad, p. 5.

9. Government of India, Planning Commission, Third Year Plan, 1961-65, New Delhi, 1961, pp. 338-39.

10. S.N. Rath, Development of the Welfare State in Orissa, S Chand and Co, New Delhi, 1977, p. 201.

11. Ghurye G S Caste and Class in India, Popular Publication, Bombay, 1950.

12. Srinivas M N, Religion and Society among the Coorgs of South India, Asia Publishing House, Bombay, 1952.

13. Bailey F G, Politics and Social Change in Orissa, Oxford University Press, Bombay, 1959.

14. Kuppuswamy B, Social Change in India, Bikash Publishing House, Ghaziabad, 1979.

15. Panchayati Raj and Weaker Sections, U. Gurumurthy, Ashis Publication House, New Delhi, p. 9.

16. Ramesh K. Arora (Editor), People's Participation in Development Process, the HCM State Institutive of Public Administration, Jaipur, 1979, p. XXX.

15

Contentious Agitations and State Intervention: An Analysis of Gujjar Agitation for Tribal Status in Rajasthan

Ramesh Kumar

Abstract

The fact that adaptation of development planning has improved living conditions of millions of people across the country is inadequate to exempt the ways and processes of development from an enquiry while dealing with the dynamics of development and democracy in post-colonial India. This is partly because of the fact that even after a six decade long experiment the country is still grappling with some central questions concerning human welfare such as the challenges of inclusive development. Recently, these challenges were highlighted by Gujjar agitation for tribal status in Rajasthan. The main demand behind the agitation is to ensure various benefits of the public policy of affirmative action which has been designed for the development of various tribes of India. By analysing the factors responsible for the agitation and consequent resistance this paper attempts to view this agitation as a sign not only of the changing dynamics of the politics of tribal development but also of growing discontentment among various sections of society with the ways and processes of development in India.

Introduction

Gujjar agitation in Rajasthan is one among many recently surfacing contentious voices of discontentment in various parts of India which are directly related to issues concerning state and public policy. Discontentment ranging from team Anna Hazare to Aam Admi Party (Common Man Party) to anti-rape protesters and, from Jats in Haryana to Gujjars in Rajasthan to Madigas in Andhra Pradesh is an indicator of changing nature and role of state and public policy in people's life. Issues of corruption, discrimination, exclusion, exploitation etc. have come to be the main agendas of these people's demands for a strong Lokpal Bill, strict laws to prevent sexual misconduct, reshaping of reservation policy and so on. Who are these people, public, civil society, tribals, citizens, common man, Indians? What is the nature and scope of these agitations, identity politics or social movements? How has state responded to these agitations? These are some questions which scholars have long been debating. The nature and scope of debates surrounding these questions are very broad and complex; investigation of such a broad and complex issue requires enough space and time which is beyond the aim and scope of this paper.

The aim of this paper is to analyse Gujjar agitation for tribal status in Rajasthan within the broad framework of social movement.[1] By analysing the factors responsible for the agitation, this paper attempts to view this agitation as a sign not only of the changing dynamics of the politics of tribal development but also of growing discontentment among already marginalised sections with the ways and processes of development in India.

The paper is divided into three sections: the first section deals with conceptual aspects of social movements; the second discusses Gujjar Agitation; and, the third is a brief narration of state response to Gujjar agitation. The paper ends with a concluding note on the problem of classifying Gujjar agitation under the existing categories of social movements.

(I) Concept

Social Movements

One of the necessary features of a social movement is an essentially sustained collective mobilisation for bringing about either partial or total change in the existing system of relationships, values and norms in the light of an ideology through either formal or informal organisation. Such type of collective mobilisation is directly related to the nature of leadership and organisation.[2] According to Ghanshyam Shah, leadership and organisation along with objectives, ideology, and programmes are interdependent components of social movements which influence each other.[3] It is so because, as M.S.A. Rao argues, leadership plays crucial role in formulating ideology; and ideology in turn remains central in directing the course of a social movement.

Leadership in its various forms helps not only in shaping organisational aspects such as structures of federal and local associations but also plays a significant role in evolving different levels of commitment to ideology of a social movement. Ideology engages leadership in establishing identity of a group in relation to other groups. This involves recognition of the presence of opposition reference groups, for relative deprivation by its very definition indicates an unequal relationship among various groups. The situational perception of each other's relative status determines the intensity of relative deprivation which decides the nature and direction of a social movement.[4]

Relative deprivation is one of the criteria which are generally followed in explaining a social movement's emergence; other two important criteria are strain and revitalisation which have been dealt with extensively by scholars such as Neil. J. Smelser and A.F.C Wallace.[5] The concept of relative deprivation has been developed and utilised in studying social mobility and social conflict by scholars such as R.K. Merton, W.C. Runciman, Marx, T.R. Gurr, D.F. Aberlé, etc. Merton developed the concept of relative deprivation in relation to reference group theory.[6] Runciman developed this concept further in relation to reference group and problems of inequality and social justice.[7]

According to MSA Rao, the criterion of collectively expressed multidimensional relative deprivation is preferable as it is very helpful in explaining change-orientation of movements. Crucial from this angle relative deprivation, however, is a necessary yet insufficient condition for the emergence of a social movement. A situational perception of relative deprivation caused by the presence of conflict along with an efficient leadership provides the required strain which is one more necessary condition. However, not all social movements are caused by these two criteria only. For example, a reform movement aimed at satisfactory betterment of a section of society is not the necessary consequence of relative deprivation and strain only; in such cases the criteria of revitalisation is utilised.[8]

Ideology, locus, and consequence are popular criterion of classifying social movements. Movements such as linguistic, religious, sectarian, caste, peasant, worker, tribal, ethnic, feministic and student are treated as movements based on locus. Whereas those based on protest, revitalisation and millenarian ideology are considered as ideology based movement. Movements which are oriented at reform, transformation, and revolution fall within the criterion of consequence.[9]

Despite a general agreement on some core characteristics of social movements, scholars differ when it comes to the context of social movements. For instance, it is argued by post-colonial scholars that what may be new for most European and American countries need not necessarily be same for most Asian countries. It is so because the term 'new' is closely identified, in the popular literature on social movements in the American and European countries, with the terms post-industrial and post-modern. Clearly, the meaning of these terms cannot be applied in totality to the realities of most Asian countries. Being the survivor of colonial states, industrial and technological empowerment is still an important objective for these countries. More important, in countries like India village society is not identical to the so called post-peasant societies of most American and European countries.

The fact that there is a contextual difference between what constitutes old and new movements in most American and European countries and most Asian countries has been suggested by recent literature on social movements. Seen from this perspective, issues and challenges before contemporary developing societies are viewed as something new though these might be taken as part of old social movements in developed countries.[10] In developing countries, now the challenges of poverty eradication and democratic decentralisation etc. are fast becoming agendas of newly emerging trends such as identity, sustainable development, and participatory democracy. Doubtless, there has been a shift in the nature and scope of collective mobilisation at local, national and global level during the last six decades. In a post-colonial country like India, for the last two and half decades, one aspect of this shift has been an increasing emphasis on alternative modes of development.

Under the umbrella of new social movements in India, there has been an increase in the literature on dalit movements, tribal movements, women movements, environmental movements, etc. Recent agitations of Jats in Haryana and Gujjars in Rajasthan regarding reshaping of reservation policy; anti-corruption movement of Anna Hazare et al; and, anti-rape protests etc. are viewed by many much as yet another addition to the category of new social movements in India. It remains to be examined in what way these trends of mass mobilisation can be understood as parts of new social movements.

Social Movements in India: Social mobilisation has found expression in many parts of India.[11] However, themes such as identity, development, and participatory democracy can be identified as recently emerging themes in the studies concerning collective mobilisation of people in India. As a newly emerging trend, the idea of identity involves social justice that finds scope mainly in mobilisation based on caste, class, dalit, and women issues. On the other hand, the theme of sustainable development includes issues concerning alternative modes of development.

The ideas of caste and class as a symbol of political identity are recurrent themes in many studies on collective mobilisation concerning social transformation in India. Caste, instead of withering away, has survived pre-colonial, colonial times and is continuing in post-colonial times. Caste still exists at the horizon of tradition and modernity; it has not been replaced by a more democratic framework of social organisation.[12] However, it has survived after losing its ascriptive meaning and in its new form it has become functional in horizontal and differential mobilisation.[13] Nevertheless, caste-based mobilisation ranging from regional to national level points to its functional role in recruitment of political leadership and increase in awareness of masses.[14]

Caste as a factor in increasing political awareness of masses has accelerated the idea of caste associations. Further, significance of caste as a factor in social justice has influenced *dalit* mobilisation in India. Caste has therefore remained a central concept in old social movements.[15] Nonetheless, as stated earlier, caste has re-emerged as a part of new social movements while surviving the politics of development. Moreover, development too has been reconceptualised and in its contemporary form it is identified with the ideas of inclusive development. Those who are deeply involved with the process of empowerment, they are emphasising alternative techniques of development which are treated now as a part of new social movements in India.

The idea that centralised ways of development are not suitable for the countries of the South have motivated scholars such as Ponna Wignaraja and others to categorise alternative modes of sustainable development as part of new social movements.[16] Now the meaning of sustainable development has been extended to ecological and cultural dimensions also. The rise of ecological movements in India in recent decades as a reaction to non-sustainable projects of development points to a new thinking on sustainable development which is seen by scholars such as Harsh Sethi as new responses to the problem of sharing natural renewable resources.[17]

Regarding, cultural dimension of development, writers such as Ramashrey Roy holds the view that movements like Swadhyaya have inspired new thinking of sustainable development which goes beyond economic condition, and in this form such movements offer a concept of self help where conventional meaning of social service and elitism becomes irrelevant.[18] Whether the movements like Swadhyaya are capable of removing elite bias in cultural dimension of sustainable development will depend on the level of awareness about participatory democracy and humane thinking for fellow human beings. However, a country like India is still far from such awareness.

One of the most important constituents of social movements in India has been tribal movements. While reviewing literature on tribal movements in India, Ghanshyam Shah has highlighted the fact that the nature of tribal movements depends upon various factors which differ from region to region in India. For example, unlike the tribals of North-East Frontier, the tribals of eastern and Central India have close interaction with caste Hindus; therefore, they do not demand political status outside the Indian Union.[19] He has highlighted the fact that in post-Independent India, leadership has come from educated tribal elites. Regarding, participants of tribal movements, he highlights findings of K.S. Singh on tribal movements who concludes that the organising character of tribal unrest emerges only among large homogeneous, land owning communities whose economic base is relatively strong.[20, 21]

The preceding discussion suggests that no single factor can be attributed to the rise and decline of social movements. It also becomes clear that there exist not a single study fully devoted to the analysis of contemporary Gujjars' social, political, and economic status in Rajasthan. Therefore, it is yet to be established whether Gujjar agitation can be treated as a social movement. If yes, under what category of social movements, tribal movement, backward class movement, dalit movement? Keeping this introductory engagement with social movements in view, it is now apt to turn to Gujjar agitation in Rajasthan.

(II) The Issue

Gujjars in Rajasthan: The question concerning origin of Gujjars remains disputed—there exist different stories about Gujjars' origin and historical past.[22, 23] However, as of now Gujjars are treated by many as predominantly rural, pastoral and agriculturist community who are a part of the caste system which does not face much exclusion and discrimination in society. In the four Varna-based hierarchical social order, Gujjars are placed above the category of ex-untouchables and below the dominant castes in Rajasthan such as Brahmins, Rajputs, etc. The population of Gujjars in Rajasthan is estimated to be around 60-65 lakhs which constitutes 7-8 per cent of Rajasthan's population.[24] Gujjars are found mainly in Dausa, Sawai Madhopur, Karauli and Bharatpur districts of Rajasthan. In order to understand Gujjars' place in socio-economic and political order of society in Rajasthan, one needs to take into account the prevailing socio-economic and political aspects of pre-colonial and colonial Rajasthan.

Feudal Rajasthan: In pre-colonial and colonial Rajasthan, Gujjars were a part of hierarchically organised feudal socio-economic and political society where Rajputs used to enjoy highest power and status in Rajasthan. According to K.L. Sharma, "Rajasthan represented a sort of *feudalism* which did not exist in British India".[25] Sharma suggests that feudalism in Rajasthan was a "mode of polity, administration and social relations", it was a "social formation as well as a mode of production" wherein caste and class were inseparable; and in practice, caste was relatively less rigid system compared to other states. For instance, though Rajputs were ranked after the Brahmins and above the Vaishyas in principle, yet they rarely behaved as a *dwij* (twice born) caste compared to the Brahmins and the Vaishyas.

Sharma finds an almost "non-existent commensal distinction between the Rajputs and the agricultural castes like Jats, Ahirs, Gujars, Malis and Meenas". Despite being ranked below the Brahmins and the Vaishyas in terms of ritual hierarchy, Rajputs were powerful rulers and used to enjoy highest status and power in the state. The Brahmins had to acknowledge Rajputs' superior status, and only in response to this the Rajputs used to acknowledge Brahmin's superior ritual status. Hence, feudal mode of social relations was superior to caste hierarchy in Rajasthan. This fact, according to Sharma, makes Rajasthan a different case in understanding caste and class in India.[26]

The above discussion on feudal mode of social relations is instructive to understanding Gujjars' place in such a society. One can say that ritual hierarchy was dependent upon political power and economic status. It follows then that mobilisation for ritual superiority would hardly find much scope in such a social formation. Could this be one of the reasons that Rajasthan witnessed less number of social movements aimed at upward social mobility compared to other parts of India? The question remains to be examined thoroughly; however, the investigation of such an important question is beyond the scope of this paper. Nevertheless, the above discussion on social formation in a feudal society is helpful in understanding the changing political context in Rajasthan after 1947.

Post-1947 Rajasthan: At the time of Independence, Rajasthan consisted of 19 Princely States, two chieftains and a British administered province of Ajmer-Merwara besides a few pockets and territories outside its main boundaries. The feudal social formation got a definite setback when India was declared an independent country in 1947.[27] The formation of Rajasthan as a state of India was undertaken during the time period between 1947 and 1956. The final stage of merging various parts of Rajasthan into the Union of India was completed in November 1956, under the State Reorganisation Act 1956.[28] At present, Rajasthan is the largest state of India in terms of geographical area.

Mobilisation of Gujjars: As far as Gujjars' status in post-1947 Rajasthan is concerned, until 2004, unlike many other socio-economically backward classes they were not listed in the Scheduled Castes (SCs)/Scheduled Tribes (STs)/ Other Backward Classes (OBCs). Partly as a result of which, Gujjars were outnumbered in state controlled jobs by Jats and Meenas. [29]

A sense of being left out in the process of state initiated and controlled beneficiary schemes motivated some Gujjar leaders to organise Gujjars on the issue of representation in state controlled jobs. One of Gujjars' earliest attempts in this direction was rejected by the state government of Rajasthan after finding that the Gujjars did not fulfill the conditions set by the Dhebar Commission in 1960 for being included in the ST list.[30] Next attempt was in 1976 when Gujjars "presented to the then Union Home Minister Brahmanand Reddy the memo demanding their inclusion in the ST list".[31]

However, no result came out until 1994 when the then Chief Minister of Rajasthan Bhairon Singh Shekhawat recommended the centre on the basis of the State OBC Commissions' recommendations earlier in the year that Gujjars be included as OBCs.

The issue of Scheduled Tribe Status reemerged during the year 2003 when the then Chief Minister of Rajasthan Vasundhara Raje, during electoral campaign, assured Gujjars about their inclusion in the ST list if her party comes into power. In the same year, the then Prime Minister Atal Bihari Vajpayee assured "the Jat Mahasabha for their inclusion in the OBC list against the recommendations of the OBC commission and they were notified in the list of the OBCs in 2004 before the parliamentary elections. The Gurjars never opposed this move of the inclusion of Jats in OBC".[32]

But with the inclusion of Jats in the list of OBCs in the same year, Gujjar felt deprived and ignored. Since then, Gujjars in Rajasthan have become skeptical of their ability to compete with Jats—who are able to extract maximum of the benefits offered by opportunities in the political and educational sectors, and therefore have been persistently demanding Scheduled Tribe status—as a replacement of current Other Backward Class status.[33]

(III) Agitation for Tribal Status

The demand for ST status started gaining ground since 2000. So far, three major protests during the time period of 2006-2012 remain important events of Gujjar agitation.

1st Agitation—2006-2007: In September 2006, for the first time Gujjar protested violently at Hindaun. The agitation was intensified with the formation of Gurjar Arakshan Sangharsh Samiti under the leadership of Kirori Singh Bhainsla, a retired Colonel of the Indian Army.[34] Bhainsla wants Gujjars to become "part of the national mainstream through education and political participation" and that is why he treats the demand for reservation as just the means and not an end. [35] With this motive, Bhainsla started mobilising Gujjars on the issue of ST status by conducting a door-to-door awareness campaign in order to make them understand their relative backwardness.

On May 29, 2007, Bhainsla led a series of violent protests at Patoli where 26 protesters died. Gujjars preserved dead bodies of fellow protesters, who were killed in police firing around Patoli village, using salt and ice for the duration of the entire period of agitation. The main targets of protestors were the Jaipur-Delhi, Jaipur-Agra and the Mumbai-Delhi transport routes. The protest also involved Gujjar-Meena clashes in various parts of Rajasthan. The state government was compelled to call the army in order to control the situation in almost 11 districts affected by Gujjar-Meena clashes. In the first week of June 2007, the state government had to impose the National Security Act. After a series of negotiation, the agitation was withdrawn following a compromise between the Gujjar leaders and the then Chief Minister Vasundhara Raje.

2nd Agitation—2008: However, the agitation was resumed in 2008 after the denial of ST status by the Chopra Committee. This time, the agitation continued for almost a month (23rd of May to 17th June 2008). The epicenter of this agitation was Pilupura in Bharatpur.[36]

Once again the agitation was called off after the Vasundhara Raje led government agreed to give five per cent reservation to Gujjars under special category. However, the issue remained controversial in the wake of legal complexities of special category reservation. The state high court of Rajasthan stayed the reservation and sought clarification from the government regarding the legality of five per cent reservation beyond 50 per cent. Gujjars found them caught in the trap of law and politics of reservation; it triggered yet another agitation in 2010 under the leadership of Bhainsla.

3rd Agitation—2010: The peaceful agitation was to start at Pushkar near Ajmer from 26 March.[37, 38] However, it was postponed after governments' invitation for talk. But nothing could be worked out even after a series of talks with government till 31 March. Gujjars started thinking of their agitation once again; this time, instead of starting at Pushkar, the agitation was launched from Gudla village, 400 km from Jaipur with hundreds of Gujjars led by Bhainsla on April 11.[39] This time the demand of five per cent special category reservation was made the sole basis of negotiation. After 2010, the agitation did not involve any large scale protest; however, since then, there have been many *mahapadav* (sit-ins) by Gujjars under the leadership of Bhainsla who is still trying to get ST status for Gujjars.

Lately, in June 2012, around 3000 Gujjars came out with a surprise *mahapadav* (indefinite mass protest) under the leadership of Kirori Singh Bhainsla in Chhan village in Khandar tehsil of Sawai Madhopur district. This time it was based on a twelve point demand which included appointment of the chairperson of the OBC commission in the state, appointment of a chairperson to the Dev Narayan Board, withdrawal of criminal cases lodged against Gujjars during the previous agitations, release of pensions and compensations for those killed and injured in the earlier agitations and construction of schools and hostels for the community's students, etc.[40]

As of now, Gujjar agitation has become a major political issue for both Gujjars and political parties in the state of Rajasthan. Gujjar leaders are still demanding separate reservation within the category of Scheduled Tribes.[41] Gujjars have started thinking of entering into politics with the motive to join the third political front emerging against the Congress and the BJP ahead of the assembly elections.[42]

Rationale behind the Demand for Tribal Status: Gujjars have tried to offer the rationale for their demand of tribal status in accordance with the criteria adopted by the Government of India for verifying any group's claim as tribals. These criteria include: (1) Primitive Traits (2) Distinctive Culture (3) Geographical Isolation (4) Shyness of Contact (5) Backwardness.

Gujjars' argument is that they should be treated as a tribe because of their primitive traits such as living in forest areas; using indigenous ways of curing diseases such as magic and witchcraft etc; practicing animal sacrifices; indigenous ways of dispute resolution; and, motifs of using trees and animals to tattoo men and women's bodies. Regarding distinctive culture, Gujjars claim that they worship deities such as Dev Narayan which differs from Hindu's worship; they observe yearly homage to the dead in the form of "*shraddha*". They live in Kabilas (groups or hordes) and have pastoral and forest based economy, primitive agricultural tools, indigenous techniques of irrigation, distinct language (namely, Gojri) and folk songs (such as Rasiya, Kanhiya, etc.,), pastoral dress pattern, etc. They are almost identical to Meenas who are included in the list of STs. Gujjars argue that their habitations geographically isolate them from the urban areas which they rarely visit; Gujjar women are very shy, cover themselves with veils and remain away from urban life. Gujjars are non-vegetarian, drink alcohol and do not marry outside; they give death feasts, practice junior levirate, Nata, etc. There is a prevalence of child marriage, polyandry, bride price etc. among them. Politically their representation is limited—very few in govt jobs. Their economy is based on cattle breeding; many Gujjars are nomads and landless labourers and so on.[43]

(IV) State Response

During the years 2007 to 2012, the successive state governments of Rajasthan and Gujjar leadership tried to negotiate reservation criteria. A series of meetings and committees dominated the politics of Gujjars' demand for S.T. status. So far, three committees have reported to state government regarding the need for special package for the welfare of Gujjars. The main issues dealt with by these committees are as follows:

The Justice Jasraj Chopra Committee: The Committee, constituted on 13th June, 2007, visited about 147 villages and surveyed the life of Gujjars in 400 another habitations. The Committee prepared its report and submitted it in six months; it was considered a first of its kind report covered in around 100 pages. It recommended a special financial package in order to improve Gujjars' living conditions; however, it rejected Gujjars' demand for ST status.

The Ramdas Agrawal Committee: In March 2008, the government appointed yet another Committee constituted by four members under the chairmanship of Ramdas Agrawal (a sitting Member of Parliament from Bharatiya Janata Party). The Committee submitted its report in May 2008 by recommending "a geographic-specific Rs 282 crore special package" for 9-10 lakh Gujjars living in the districts of Alwar, Sawai Madhopur, Karauli, Dholpur and Jhalawar districts of Rajasthan.[44]

The I.S. Israni Committee: Constituted by an interim order of the High Court to defuse law and order situation arising out of Gujjars' agitations in the State, the committee recommended the government to grant quota and special backward class status to the community. It endorsed the recommendations of Justice Chopra Committee, which had recommended five per cent reservation for Gujjars in 2007. Apart from recommending the government to engage specialised lawyers for contesting the court cases in favour of Gujjars, the committee also recommended that Gujjars' other demands such as financial assistance to students, scholarships, compassionate appointments, withdrawal of cases pending against them should be taken up in accordance with law.[45]

Against the backdrop of recommendations of various committees, though the state government has assured five per cent reservation under a new category called Special Backward Classes, Gujjar leaders are not satisfied with this provision as this category includes some other classes such as Gadoliya Luhar, Banjara, Raika etc.[46] The Rajasthan Gujjar Arakshan Sangharsh Samiti accused ruling party for politicising their demand for ST by converting their status from OBCs to SBCs (Special Backward Classes). The issue of SBCs, according to Gujjar leaders has become a legal issue and this is nothing but a strategic step of the ruling parties to pacify their other supporters such as Meenas, Rajputs and Jats, etc.

Conclusion

Apart from elements of old social movements, Gujjar agitation includes some new elements such as a warlike strategy of mass protests and aggressive reaction to state response, participation of women, etc. Factors such as leadership, an explicit expression of relative deprivation etc. have played prominent role in the agitation. It was one of the very few occasions of mass protests when the state had resorted to call in the army, though it was not used during the agitation. It emerges from the discussion on that leadership has played the most important role in the main Gujjar protests of 2007, 2008, and 2010.

It was the organising capability of Bhainsla that could sustain long protests during the three and half years' agitation. Apart from this, except Bhainsla's failed attempt to win a parliamentary seat of Tonk from Sawai Madhopur in Rajasthan on behalf of BJP, the leadership did not provide any scope to political parties for politicising the agitation. On all other occasions, Gujjar leadership strongly opposed all the ruling and opposition parties for their failure in ensuring constitutional safeguards in the form of ST status; Gujjars went on to call their elected members back from the state assembly also.

From the criterion of relative deprivation, Gujjars' claim rests upon their situational self-perception of relative deprivation—mostly that of economic and political deprivation, and unique cultural identity and social practices with reference to other groups such as Meenas and Jats, etc. Ideologically, caste factor has come to dominate the agenda of Gujjar agitation. The agitation included mass protests which involved women's participation and aggressive reactions to state response with the motive of fight for right. It would not be an exaggeration to say that this agitation is a sign not only of the changing dynamics of the politics of backwardness and tribal development through reservation policies but also of growing discontentment in various sections of society with the ways and processes of development in India.

But such a conclusion then opens up questions which direct our attention to the relationship between state, public policy and growing discontentment in various sections of society. At the same time, it will be a premature conclusion to classify Gujjar agitation under any single category of social movements in India. The agitation is still going on and therefore it is very difficult to determine its nature and scope. Nonetheless, it is clear that the nature and scope of discontentment expressed through Gujjar agitation is something new which needs to be foregrounded. Whether Gujjar agitation is a sign of changing patterns of middle class politics or a form of civil society unrest or a form of 'tribal' resistance to state mediated market policies or an assertive voice from the marginalised section in Rajasthan needs to be explored and examined more extensively.

Notes

1. This paper is based on the data obtained from library archives and print and electronic media about Gujjars and their agitation in Rajasthan.
2. M.S.A. Rao, *Social Movements in India*, Vol. One, Manohar Publications: New Delhi, 1979, pp.1-2, 7.

3. Ghanshyam Shah, *Social Movements in India: A Review of Literature*, Sage Publications: New Delhi, 1990, p.18.

4. M.S.A. Rao, *ibid,* pp. 7-10.

5. The concepts of strain and revitalisation have been extensively discussed by Neil. J. Smelser in his *Theory of Collective Behaviour,* New York: The Free Press, 1962; and by A.F.C. Wallace in his "Revitalisation Movements", American Anthropologist, New Series, Vol. 58, No. 2 (Apr., 1956), pp. 264-281.

6. R.K. Merton and Alice S. Rossi, "Contribution to the Theory of Reference Group Behaviour", in *Social Theory and Social Structure*, The Free Press: New York, 1968, pp. 287-338.

7. W.G. Runciman, *Relative Deprivation and Social Justice,* University of California Press: Berkeley, 1966.

8. M.S.A. Rao, *Social Movements in India*, *ibid*., pp. 4-6.

9. *Ibid.,* pp. 3, 11-13.

10. There has been a tendency, which is increasingly becoming popular, among scholars to classify social movements under the categories of the 'Old' and the 'New'. The distinction is made generally on the basis of the changing nature and scope of social movements. Accordingly, the movements covered under the category 'old' are concerned with peasant mobilisation related to agrarian issues, tribal movements, workers' movements etc. Whereas 'New' issues of environment, women, dalit, caste and conversion, human rights etc. are treated as part of new social movements.

11. For example anti-brahmin movements in Maharashtra, self-respect movement in Tamil Nadu, non Brahmin movements in Karnataka, Sri Narayan Dharma Paripalana Movement in Kerala etc. are some of the movements aimed at bringing about change in the condition of socially deprived sections of Indian society.

12. Rajni Kothari, *Caste in Indian Politics,* Orient Longman Private Limited, Hyderabad, 1970.

13. Lloyd I. Rudolph Susanne Hoeber Rudolph, *Modernity of Tradition: Political Development in India,* Orient Longman Private Limited, Hyderabad, 1967.

14. See Ghanshyam Shah, Caste Association and Political Process in Gujarat, Popular Prakashan: Bombay, 1975; M.S.A. Rao, Social Movements and Social Transformation: A Study of Two Backward Classes Movement in India, Manohar Publications: New Delhi, 1987.

15. See Gail Omvedt, Dalit and the Democratic Revolution: Dr. Ambedkar and the Dalit Movement in Colonial India, Sage Publication: New Delhi, 1994.

16. See Ponna Wignaraja (ed.) New Social Movements in the South: Empowering the People, Vistaar Publications: New Delhi, 1993; Ponna Wignaraja and Susil Sirivandan, Pro-Poor Growth and Governance in South Asia: Decentralisation and Participatory Development, Sage Publications: New Delhi, 2004; Ponna Wignaraja and Susil Sirivandan (eds), Readings in Pro-Poor

Planning through Social Mobilisation in South Asia, The Strategic Option for Poverty Eradication, Vol. 1, Vikas: New Delhi, 1998; Ponna Wignaraja, Susil Sirivandan and Akmal Hussain (eds), Economic Democracy through Pro-Poor Growth, Sage Publications: New Delhi, 2009; Ponna Wignaraja, Akmal Hussain, Harsh Sethi, and Ganeshan Wignaraja, Participatory Development: Learning from South Asia, United Nations University Press, 1991; G.V.S. De Silva *et al*, Towards a Theory of Rural Development, Progressive Publications, 1988.

17. Harsh Sethi, "Survival and Democracy: Ecological Struggles in India", in Ponna Wignaraja (ed.), *New Social Movements in the South: Empowering the People*, *ibid.*, pp. 122-148.

18. Ramashrey Roy, "Swadhyaya: Values and Message", in Ponna Wignaraja (ed.), *New Social Movements in the South: Empowering the People*, *ibid.*, pp.183-194.

19. Ghanshyam Shah, *Social Movements in India: A Review of the Literature,* New Delhi: Sage Publications, 1990, p. 95.

20. See, K.S. Singh, "Tribal Autonomy Movements Chhotanagpur" in *Tribal Movements in India,* Vol. II, Edited by K.S. Singh, Delhi: Manohar.

21. *Ibid.*, 96.

22. This paper does not cover the history of Gujjars as a ruling class in pre-colonial and colonial Rajasthan.

23. For example, colonial writers' reference to Gujjars, See John Beames *History, Folklore and Culture of the Races of North Western Provinces of India,* Vol.1, Delhi: Sumit Publications, 1978 (First Indian reprint), pp. 99-102; rev. M.A. Sherring, *Hindu Tribes and Castes,* Delhi: Cosmo Publications, 1974 (First Published in India), pp. 235-237; R.V. Russell, *The Tribes and Castes of the Central Provinces of India*, Vol. III, Delhi: Cosmo Publications, 1975.

24. (First Published in India), pp.166-171. For Indian writers' reference to Gujjars, See G.S.Ghurye, *Caste and Race in India,* Bombay: Popular Prakashan, 1969, pp. 31-33, 109, 127.

25. Javaid Rahi, "Gujjars of Rajasthan and S.T. Status", Countercurrents.org, www.countercurrents.org/rahi 060608.htm, June 2008.

26. K. L. Sharma, "Feudalism Caste and Class in Rajasthan" in *Caste and Class in India* (Ed), New Delhi: Rawat Publications, p. 210.

27. *Ibid.*, pp. 211, 217.

28. For more on decline of feudal order in Rajasthan see K. L. Kamal, "Politics of Declining Feudal Order" in *State Politics in India*, edited by Iqbal Narain, Meerut: Meenakashi Prakashan, pp. 299-322.

29. Present Rajasthan came into being as a result of seven stages of merging process during 1947-1956. The first stage was that of forming the Matsya union in March 1948. It consisted of Alwar, Bharatpur, Dhaulpur and Karauli. Next, Banswara, Bundi, Dungarpur, Jhalawar, Kishangarh, Kota, Pratapgarh, Shahpura and Tonk joined the Indian union and formed a part of Rajasthan in March 1948. In April 1948 Udaipur joined the state and with

this the merger of south and southeastern states was almost completed. Next was the merging of the kingdoms of Bikaner, Jodhpur, Jaisalmer and Jaipur in March 1949; with this, Jaipur became state capital. Later in 1949, the United States of Matsya, comprising the former kingdoms of Bharatpur, Alwar, Karauli and Dholpur, was incorporated into Rajasthan. On January 26, 1950, 18 states of united Rajasthan merged with Sirohi to join the state leaving Abu and Dilwara to remain a part of Greater Bombay and now Gujarat. In November 1956 under the State Re-organisation Act, 1956 the erstwhile part 'C' State of Ajmer, Abu Road Taluka, former part of princely State Sirohi (which were merged in former Bombay), State and Sunel Tappa region of the former Madhya Bharat merged with Rajasthan and Sirohi sub district of Jhalawar was transferred to Madhya Pradesh.

30. This paper does not cover the history of Gujjar mobilisation since Independence; such an exercise deserves space much larger than this paper. Suffice is to say here that Gujjars in the politics of post-1947 Rajasthan did not have powerful voice. Gujjar leadership at national and state level remained almost nil for over six decades; the only exception is that of Congress leader Rajesh Pilot. He held ministerial post in the Union Cabinet and was close to Rajiv Gandhi. His son Sachin Pilot is following his footsteps and is currently a Congress leader, he too has held ministerial post in the Union Cabinet.

31. *Hindustan Times*, 1st June 2007.

32. Kavita Srivastava, "State Violence and Caste Confrontation in Rajasthan", kafila.org/2008/06/11/kavita-srivastavas-report-on-last-years-gujjar-confrontation-in-rajasthan/ 11th June 2008.

33. *Ibid*.

34. In recent years, especially during the first decade of this century, political activities of Gujjars in Rajasthan and Jats in Haryana remained central in the politics of caste-based reservation policy in northern India. In the states of both Rajasthan and Haryana events and activities ranging from blocking of roads and railway tracks to negotiation meetings with chief ministers to *dharnas* to *bandh* etc. got extensive media coverage [For example see, "Flip side of the Jat agitation in Haryana", *India Today,* 8th March 2012; "Gujjars unhappy over Rajasthan's Quota Decision", *The Hindu*, November 29-30, 2012]. On the other hand, Jats of Haryana have been agitating for inclusion in the Other Backward Classes as they claim that it is unfair to include them in the General Category [While the Jats in Rajasthan (except in Bharatpur and Dhaulpur Districts) are included in the Central List of OBCs, the Jats of Haryana do not figure in the list]. However, the genesis of Jat agitation for inclusion in Other Backward Class list is ambiguous and complex, and it is paradoxical to their socio-economic and political status in Haryana. It may be noted that both the states of Rajasthan and Haryana differ in their performance regarding development and participatory democracy. Haryana has reached almost at the peak of development in terms of economic prosperity. In terms of per capita income

Haryana ranks second among Indian states whereas Rajasthan is still far from being a well to do state. Per capita income of Haryana at Current Prices was Rs 94680 in the year 2010-11; Haryana is next only to Goa which ranks first among Indian states with the highest Per Capita Income Rs 168572 at Current Prices in the year 2010-11. Per capita income of Rajasthan at Current Prices was only Rs. 39967 in the year 2010-11. Further, both the states have population belonging to Gujjars and Jats and, both the castes differ in their socio-economic profile in these states. While Jats are influential in both the states Gujjars lack such influence in Rajasthan and Haryana. Yet, the main issue behind the agitations is the policy of affirmative action. Given, it remains, therefore, a puzzle as to why the two socially, economically, and politically varied sections of society from the two socially, economically, and politically varied states are demanding reservations? Nonetheless, demands for reshaping of reservation policy is not restricted northern India only; the struggle of Madigas in Andhra Pradesh represents one of such demands.

35. Kirori Singh Bhainsla is from Karouli district in Rajasthan, one among Gujjar strongholds in Rajasthan. He did his schooling in a village and graduated from the Maharaja's College in Jaipur. He joined the Army as a sepoy and became a Colonel before retirement in 1991. He witnessed the 1965 and 1971 wars.

36. *Outlook*, February 06, 2011.

37. The reason for selecting the site of protest has been explained in a newspaper report in the following way: "Unlike last year, the protest site was chosen with care this year. As many as 84 Gujjar-dominated villages surround the protest site, which ensures that there is no dearth of food, water and other resources for the protesters. In fact the sit-in protest site has the ambience of a traditional festival. Every two hours the protesters rush to check the arrival of the latest *pakwaan*. The lunch of *puris* and *sabzi* makes way for the freshly packed *halwa*. Mounds of wasted food can be seen lying at the site and there is no shortage of *chaach rabri*. Water, stored in mobile tanks, is brought from the nearby villages. Women in the villages are busy cooking throughout the day and the food is sent to the protesters in locally fabricated vehicles called *jugaad", The Tribune,* June 22, 2008.

38. Pushkar is a place of religious importance for Gujjars.

39. *Outlook,* March 19, 2010.

40. *Ibid.*, April 11, 2010.

41. *The Times of India,* June 8, 2012.

42. *The Hindu,* Nov 29, 2012.

43. *Ibid,* July 4, 2013.

44. Javaid Rahi, "Gujjars of Rajasthan and S.T. Status", Countercurrents.org, www.countercurrents.org/rahi 060608.htm, June 2008.

45. *The Hindu,* May 18, 2008.

46. *Ibid.*, May 3, 2010.

References

Beames, John. *History, Folk-lore and Culture of the Races of North Western Provinces of India*, Vol.1, Delhi: Sumit Publications, 1978, pp. 99-102.

Ghurye, G.S. *Caste and Race in India*, Bombay: Popular Prakashan, 1969, pp. 31-33, 109, 127.

G.V.S. De Silva *et al*, *Towards a Theory of Rural Development*, Progressive Publications, 1988 .

Hindustan Times. 1st June, 2007.

India Today. 8th March 2012.

Kamal, KL. "Politics of Declining Feudal Order" in *State Politics in India,* edited by Iqbal Narain, Meerut: Meenakshi Prakashan, pp. 299-322.

Kothari, Rajni. *Caste in Indian Politics*, Orient Longman Private Limited: Hyderabad, 1970.

Merton, R.K. and Alice S. Rossi, "Contribution to the Theory of Reference Group Behaviour", in *Social Theory and Social Structure*, The Free Press: New York, 1968, pp. 287-338.

Omvedt, Gail. *Dalit and the Democratic Revolution: Dr Ambedkar and the Dalit Movement in Colonial India*, Sage Publication: New Delhi, 1994.

Outlook. 19th March 2010, 11th April 2010, 6th Feb 2011.

Rahi, Javaid. "Gujjars of Rajasthan and S.T. Status", Countercurrents.org, www.countercurr ents.org/rahi060608.htm, June 2008.

Rao, M.S.A. *Social Movements and Social Transformation: A Study of Two Backward Classes Movement in India*, Manohar Publications: New Delhi, 1987.

__________ *Social Movements in India,* Vol. One, Manohar Publications: New Delhi, 1979, pp.1-2, 7-10.

Rev. M.A. Sherring, *Hindu Tribes and Castes*, Delhi: Cosmo Publications, 1974, pp. 235-237.

Roy, Ramashrey. "Swadhyaya: Values and Message", in Ponna Wignaraja (ed.), *New Social Movements in the South: Empowering the People*, *ibid*, pp.183-194.

Rudolph, Lloyd I. and Susanne Hoeber Rudolph, *Modernity of Tradition: Political Development in India,* Orient Longman Private Limited: Hyderabad, 1967.

Russell, R.V. *The Tribes and Castes of the Central Provinces of India*, Vol.III, Delhi: Cosmo Publications, 1975, pp.166-174 .

Runciman, W.G. *Relative Deprivation and Social Justice*, University of California Press: Berkeley, 1966.

Shah, Ghanshyam. *Social Movements in India: A Review of Literature*, Sage Publications: New Delhi, 1990, pp. 4-6, 18, 3, 11-13, 95-96.

______________ Caste Association and Political Process in Gujarat, Popular Prakashan: Bombay, 1975.

Sharma, K. L. "Feudalism Caste and Class in Rajasthan" in *Caste and Class in India,* edited by K. L. Sharma, New Delhi: Rawat Publications, pp. 210, 211, 217.

Sethi, Harsh. "Survival and Democracy: Ecological Struggles in India", in Ponna Wignaraja (ed.), *New Social Movements in the South: Empowering the People*, *ibid*, pp. 122-148.

Singh, K.S. "Tribal Autonomy Movements Chhotanagpur" in *Tribal Movements in India*, Vol. II, Edited by K.S. Singh, Delhi: Manohar.

Smelser, Neil. J. *Theory of Collective Behaviour*, New York: The Free Press, 1962.

Srivastava, Kavita. "State Violence and Caste Confrontation in Rajasthan", Kafila.org, Kafila. org/2008/06/11/kavita-srivastavas-report-on-last-years-gujjar-confrontation-in-raj asthan/11th June 2008.

The Hindu. 18th May 2008, 29-30th November 2012.

The Times of India. 8th June 2012, 28th Nov 2012, 19th July 2013.

The Tribune. 22nd June 2008.

Wallace, A.F.C in his "Revitalisation Movements", *American Anthropologist*, New Series, Vol. 58, No. 2 (April, 1956), pp. 264-281.

Wignaraja, Ponna Susil Sirivandan and Akmal Hussain (Eds), *Economic Democracy through Pro-Poor Growth*, Sage Publications: New Delhi, 2009.

Ponna Wignaraja, Akmal Hussain, Harsh Sethi, and Wignaraja, Ganeshan. *Participatory Development: Learning from South Asia,* United Nations University Press, 1991.

Wignaraja, Ponna (ed.) *New Social Movements in the South: Empowering the People*, Vistaar Publications: New Delhi, 1993.

Wignaraja, Ponna and Susil Sirivandan, *Pro-Poor Growth and Governance in South Asia: Decentralisation and Participatory Development*, Sage Publications: New Delhi, 2004.

Wignaraja, Ponna and Susil Sirivandan (Eds), *Readings in Pro-Poor Planning through Social Mobilisation in South Asia, The Strategic Option for Poverty Eradication*, Vol. No. 1, Vikas: New Delhi, 1998.

16

Globalisation, Accumulation by Dispossession and the Adivasi Struggle for Right to Habitat

Rohit Jain

Introduction

Before independence and post-independence the Adivasi dominated regions of India especially the states of Jharkhand (earlier South Bihar), Orissa, Chhatisgarh, Madhya Pradesh and Andhra Pradesh have witnessed violent conflicts over resource control and use. The situation has worsened in the nineties after the advent of New Economic Policies. The new policies not only accentuated the conflict but opened up new areas and regions for exploitation by the multinational companies adversely affecting lands and habitats of lakhs of Adivasi communities. The process which David Harvey calls 'Accumulation by Dispossession'.

This process has not gone unchallenged by Adivasi communities and today in many parts of the country, bitter struggle goes on with the State and the Multinational Companies regarding the course of Development in the Tribal regions. The Adivasis systematically have been dispossessed through colonial legislations from their habitats – land, water forests. After independence the post colonial state has continued with colonial legislations like the Land Acquisition Act of 1894, the Forest Act of 1927 which are completely out of sync with the basic tenets the Indian Constitution. One estimation says that more than five lakh Adivasis have been displaced and dispossessed from their habitats.

The struggle of the Adivasis is now no longer confined to fight for their piece of land or a small plot of forest but for their lost habitats, because that only will ensure their life with dignity. The post colonial state after the policies of liberalisation have facilitated multinational companies to start operations in the rich mineral habitats of the Adivasis resulting in fierce struggles like the Vedanta Struggle, the Utkal Alumina Struggle, the Kalinganagar Struggle, etc. In this struggle the people are aided by the spaces created by the progressive legislations like the PESA and the Forest Rights Act 2006 which go beyond the notion of land and instead talk about reclaiming the lost habitats. The recent SC judgment on Vedanta to hold gramsabhas to determine their rights is one such example. These acts also hit at the whole process of 'Accumulation by Dispossession' or what Marx called 'Primitive Accumulation.'

The Adivasi struggle against this process of 'Accumulation by Dispossession' can only go forward by redefining and re-strategising their struggle in the form of 'Right to Habitats' and redefine development. Only then the Adivasis can protect their lands, forests and water in the era of Globalisation and Financial Capitalism.

This paper is broadly divided into three sections – The Existing conflict in some of the Adivasi regions, the role and the status of legislations like PESA and the Forest Rights Act and the recent struggles for 'Right to Habitat' and forest governance which are now emerging using the spaces opened up by the above legislations.

(i) The Existing Conflict

II- A. Displacement and Dispossession

The existing conflict in many parts of India, especially in the eastern regions of India is not new. Conflict in the colonial period has spilled over after Independence and has got intensified in the post liberalisation period. Major conflict has been over control, utilisation and displacement from livelihood resources. The State has been one of the major usurpers of resources from the people leaving large sections of populations dispossessed and marginalised forcing them to the margins of existence. The appropriation of resources and resultant dispossession from their livelihood resources and habitat has been through a process which David Harvey calls 'Accumulation by Dispossession'. According to Harvey these processes include:

"... commodification and privatisation of land and the forceful expulsion of peasant populations; the conversion of various forms of property rights (common, collective, state, etc) into exclusive private property rights; the suppression of rights to the commons; the commodification of labour power and the suppression of alternative (indigenous) forms of production and consumption; colonial, neo-colonial, and imperial processes of appropriation of assets (including natural resources); the monetisation of exchange and taxation, particularly of land; ..."

Different regions in the country and especially tribal regions in the states of Jharkhand, Odisha, Chhatisgarh, Madhya Pradesh, Maharashtra, West

Bengal and Telangana region of Andhra Pradesh are witnessing this process of 'Accumulation by Dispossession' where natural resources like land, forest and water are being appropriated for development and infrastructure projects, mining and industrial estates. As a result, Development induced refugees have increased exponentially. Felix Padel[1] in his article quotes that 'An estimated 60 million people have been displaced by industries and dams in India since 1950, about half of these Adivasis and a quarter Dalits, three million in Orissa alone.' Nandini Sundar[2] in her article in EPW tells us that "The two major projects post independence, the Dandakaranya resettlement project and the Balladilla iron ore mines which started exporting to Japan in 1966, provided neither land nor employment to the locals. Instead the rivers Sankini and Dankini ran red with effluent. In the 1960's under the leadership of the ex-Raja, Pravir Chandra Bhanj Deo, people protested asking for land, access to forests and cheaper rice."

The situation has not much changed since the opening of Balladilla mines. Protests against displacement and dispossession have grown all over these states. Struggle against Koel Karo dam, Netraghat firing range, Posco, Vedanta, Utkal Alumina, Kalinganagar are pointers of what is going on in different parts of the country. Land Alienation has contributed to growing unrest among the marginalised. The State has played a major role in alienation of resources from the tribals and the marginalised contributing to the escalating conflict. Different reports by the government point out how dispossession of Tribals have taken place over a period of time and how it still continues.

The Frontline Report FDI vs Tribes[3] describes the situation in Chhattisgarh as follows:

"The mineral rich areas of the State lie in the dense forest that has been the home to its tribal population for centuries. Around 90,000 ha is already under mining for major minerals and coal. The top most mining districts in the State are Korba, Surguja, Raigarh and Durg with mostly employment intensive public sector mining. But ever since the Central Government relaxed its use to allow 100 per cent FDI in mining in 2006, thousands of tribal in the mineral rich northern and southern Chhattisgarh had to leave their forest homes where they had lived for years."

II-B. Role of the State in Conflict in Tribal Areas

The Draft Report by the Committee on State Agrarian Relations and Unfinished Task of Land Reforms Study dwells on different forms of Tribal Land Alienation. The report[4] states that 'The data gathered from the village studies and from the records of the various governments all point out to the inescapable conclusion that alienation of tribal land continues unabated and alienation of land has actually accelerated in areas where irrigation and modernisation of agriculture are making rapid strides and roadways, industrialisation and urbanisation is enveloping larger areas in the towns and cities.'

The above report lists four forms of tribal land alienation. "They are:

1. **State sponsored tribal land alienation through:**

(a) Acquisition for highways, mining, industries, cities, special economic zones in the absence of a strong 'land for land' rehabilitation provision and stringent implementation will only add to the numbers of tribals alienated from their lands.

(b) Co-lateral land alienation due to pollution, erosion and land damage in the zone of influence.

2. **State connived land alienation**

This takes place with the knowledge and direct or indirect participation of revenue functionaries and officials at various levels.

(a) Defective surveys and settlements and no-recording of possession

(b) Irregular or inaccurate enjoyment surveys.

(c) Permissions granted for purchase of tribal land

(d) Inefficacious implementation of restoration legislation

3. **State acquiesced land alienation**

Land alienated by non-tribals through numerous routes with the active connivance of the local revenue functionaries and the passive connivance of the higher revenue authorities. Some of these are:

(a) Informal, Unrecorded or Disguised Tenancies.

(b) Benami purchases.

(c) Gift by tribals

(d) Long Term Leases, Power of Attorneys, Usufructory Agreements

(e) Manipulation of records and boundaries and loopholes in land laws.

4. **State Negation of Tribal Rights to Land and Land-based Resources**

(a) Unlawful declaration of 'deemed reserved forests without fulfilling the requirementsof forest survey and settlement is a reality in a very large proportion of the forests in the country. In Madhya Pradesh and Chattishgarh, 82 per cent of the total forest area falls in the category of deemed forests where neither rights have not been recorded nor entitlements recognised. The ancestral homelands of an overwhelming majority of the tribal people in the states of AP, MP, Chattishgarh, Gujarat, Orissa and Rajasthan have been transferred to these 'deemed reserve forests'. Over 20 thousand kilometers of the forest tracts in Andhra Pradesh are disputed. The livelihoods of hundreds of thousands of tribal people are caught in the dispute. Similar is the case of over a million land holders in MP and Maharashtra who are trapped in the Orange Areas dispute.

(b) Improper or Incomplete Survey and Settlement procedures has been examined earlier, but it will suffice to say that these two processes have been used to allow either the state or non-tribals to become legitimate holders of tribal lands. The settlement proceedings in Santhal Parganas and in Orissa prove this point.

(c) Continuation of 'loopholes' in legislations.

(d) Non-rectification of colonial legacies particularly the use of the colonial rule of 'res nullius' is rampant in the settlement process in Orissa and the acquisition of common property resources of tribal communities across the nation particularly in the mining tracts of Jharkhand, Orissa and Chattishgarh."

The Report further points out to the failure of the State to protect the interests of the Tribals in the states having Vth Schedule areas. The Report[5] says "the Fifth Schedule Dispensation in the nine states, which have a significant presence of tribal people ...... this dispensation conferred enormous powers on the head of the executive, but these have not been used efficaciously even in the past six decades. The second is the presence of minerals in all the states under the fifth schedule dispensation. Earlier the temples of modern India reduced millions of tribal people to ecological refugees, now the minerals seen as the building blocks of modern India put the tribal people at risk of losing their land through acquisition and further disruption of their societies and economies."

Nandini Sundar[6] further emphasises this point when she states that,

"In the 1990s especially the formation of Chhatisgarh, there has been a concerted emphasis on industrialisation taking advantage of the region's rich mineral deposits. Despite a token gesture to tribal entrepreneurship what is quickly emerging is that the process depends on how easily Adivasis can be forced into parting with their land."

Starting with the Steel plant at Nagarnar, followed by acquisition of land for the Tata Steel plant and Essar Steel plant at Lohandiguda Dhurli and Bhansi. All rules have been violated by the powers that want to acquire the land at any cost. These projects involve large scale forest diversion and displacement. Opposition to these projects and other similar projects is being quelled by brute force.

The State in the process of appropriating resources have gone to extreme lengths by pitching tribals one against another. Salwa Judum in Chhattisgarh sponsored by the State is one such example. Salwa Judum has played a major role in assisting the state and industries to get the land cleared in the Bastar region from the incumbents i.e., the Adivasis the rightful owners of the land. Nandini Sundar[7] informs us about the real intent of Salwa Judum :

"The Following 'orientation' programme for Salwa Judum activists and SPO's observed by ACHR in Konta camp is revealing. According to Achla (Konta SDPO telling the villagers): "You leave your forests and shift to the road sides. You will be adequately compensated by the industrialists and commercial concerns, who are ready to take your land and develop it. You will get employment and other provisions. But if you stay back in the forest, Naxalites will kill you". At a minimum, no one would dispute that "sanitising" the area of Maoists and ensuring "peace" is necessary to lure investors."

The above version is also corroborated by The Draft Report by the Committee on State Agrarian Relations and Unfinished Task of Land Reforms which terms the whole process as 'The Biggest Grab of Tribal Lands after Columbus'. The Report[8] describes the ground situation as follows:

"A civil war like situation has gripped the southern districts of Bastar, Dantewara and Bijapur in Chattishgarh. The contestants are the armed squads of tribal men and women of the erstwhile Peoples War Group now known as the Communist Party of India (Maoist) on the one side and the armed tribal fighters of the Salva Judum created and encouraged by the government and supported with the firepower and organisation of the central police forces. This open declared war will go down as the biggest land grab ever, if it plays out as per the script. The drama being scripted by Tata Steel and Essar Steel who wanted seven villages or thereabouts, each to mine the richest lode of iron ore available in India......... The Salva Judum was headed and peopled by the Murias, some of them erstwhile cadre and local leaders of the Communist Party of India (Maoist). Behind them are the traders, contractors and miners waiting for a successful result of their strategy. The first financiers of the Salva Judum were Tata and the Essar in the quest for 'peace". The first onslaught of the Salva Judum was on Muria villagers who still owed allegiance to the Communist Party of India (Maoist). It turned out to be an open war between brothers. 640 villages as per official statistics were laid bare, burnt to the ground and emptied with the force of the gun and the blessings of the state. 350,000 tribals, half the total population of Dantewada district are displaced, their womenfolk raped, their daughters killed, and their youth maimed. Those who could not escape into the jungle were herded together into refugee camps run and managed by the Salva Judum. Others continue to hide in the forest or have migrated to the nearby tribal tracts in Maharashtra, Andhra Pradesh and Orissa. 640 villages are empty. Villages sitting on tons of iron ore are effectively de-peopled and available for the highest bidder. The latest information that is being circulated is that both Essar Steel and Tata Steel are willing to take over the empty landscape and manage the mines."

The large scale appropriation of resources by the State, resultant dispossession of marginalised sections especially Tribals aided by colonial and post colonial laws and security a security set up has resulted in a 'Civil War' like situation in many parts of the country. Many tribal regions in the country are dotted by the presence of paramilitary forces in combat with their own citizens. Undeclared war zones exist in different parts of the country. This has given rise to tribal militancy in many of the states. Felix Padel[9] examining the causes of Tribal Militancy gives Atrocities committed with impunity by security forces/Salwa Judum as one of the main causes. He also gives other causes

- System of Endemic exploitation which tribal communities face, which gets further compounded by acquisition of tribal lands by mining companies and corporate and brutal suppression of non-violent movements against displacement.
- Increasing land alienation, displacement and dispossession.
- Failure of the Judicial system to deal with injustice and atrocities committed by security forces and SalwaJudum personnel.

- Polarisation into two sides who believe in war
- Operation Green Hunt – the war against Maoists is itself the main cause of tribal militancy. As Felix Padel puts it "Terror tactics by the security forces are a main cause spread of tribal militancy, alongside repression of genuine, non-violent movements against enforced displacement."

The process of 'Accumulation by Dispossession' by the State and the security set up has rendered civil society institutions, panchayati raj institutions especially Gram Sabhas infructuous in many regions of the country. This brings us to the whole question of what relation does the State have with its subjects and resources i.e., people and resources it is supposed to govern? Is it 'War on its own people' as many have commented.War for what purpose and whose benefit? If it is 'War' then where will it lead us? History is witness to the fact that wherever State has neglected its subjects, the results are disastrous. We stand at the cross roads where the whole issue of governance needs to be reexamined from the viewpoint of democratising political space and giving people a chance to govern their own institutions and resources effectively.

II. Movement for Democratising Political Space and Restructuring of Relationship

III-A. Struggle against the Land Acquisition Act

Different ongoing struggles have continuously resulted in experiments and movements for restructuring of the relationship between the people and the postcolonial state. Post-independence we inherited a state with colonial laws and a new Constitution resolving to secure for all its citizen Justice, Liberty, Equality and Fraternity. Decision by the State to carry on Governance of the Post-colonial Indian State through the colonial administrative structure and colonial laws meant that for majority of the poor and the marginalised, realities of life did not change. Even after Independence, the Governance and administration remained colonial in nature. Soon after a few years of independence many people's movements came up challenging the eminent domain of the State to dispossess them.

The major struggles have been against the 1894 Land Acquisition Act and the 1927 Forest Act, both of which have been instrumental in alienating people especially the Adivasis and the marginalised from their habitat and resources. Based on the concept of Eminent Domain, it made State the owners of all the resources with people finding no place to participate and determine their future. The major question which the people started asking was for whose interest the post colonial state was trying to advance. This question became more pertinent after the post liberalisation period when neo-liberal policies on land, water and forest conservation gained ground and massive dispossession of the Adivasis and the marginalised started taking place on an unprecedented scale.

The State used the colonial law Land Acquisition Act of 1894 to dispossess people from their lands. The acquired lands in most cases after the post liberalisation period was for the industries. Biggest land grab has been orchestrated by using this law. The CAG report[10] on the Land Acquisition Process in Odisha reveals the true picture. The recent Performance Audit of 'Acquisition and allotment of land' covering six districts of the Orissa State was conducted by CAG during March to September 2011 specifically looking at issues of public purpose and invoking of the emergency provisions at the time of land acquisition. The findings of the report are not only shocking but reconfirms the intent of the State to advance the interest of the corporate. Some of the main findings of the above report are:

- "The performance audit revealed that area under cultivation in the State reduced by 1.17 lakh ha during 2005- 10 while land put to non-agricultural use increased by 2.99 lakh ha in the State during the same period. The Revenue and the Disaster Management Department allotted 50276.887 acres of land including 33355.127 acres (66.34 per cent) of acquired private land to 107 promoters/ companies for setting up of industries in 16 districts.
- Scrutiny of 'public purpose' for projects (promoters/companies/PPP) for which land was acquired in 6 districts in Orissa reveals that there is enough doubt regarding fulfillment of the 'public purpose' as defined in the LA Act, as in none of the cases cost of compensation was even partially borne by the government.
- The Department misused the emergency provision under Section 17 (4) in 85 LA cases involving acquisition of 4967.08 acres of private land between July 2002 to March 2011, depriving the likely land-losers of the opportunity to be heard. None of the conditions prescribed in executive instructions of September, 1985 for invoking the emergency provisions were fulfilled in all these cases. Further the land was not even put to use even after one year three months to six year three months from the date of publication of notification under section 4(1) against the stipulated time period of six months.
- Fixing of market value of land on lower side by LAOs/Special LAQs tended to help the land buyers, most often industries at the cost of land losers, largely farmers. Under assessment of compensation by Rs 224.29 crores was noticed in 35 LA cases for acquisition of 4003.481 acres of land for 10 entrepreneurs/industries and IDCO due to erroneous fixation of market value of land. There was under-assessment of additional compensation by Rs 9.76 crores in 18 LA cases in test checked districts."

The performance audit Land Acquisition process in Orissa by CAG confirms what is already known to the people. One can safely assume that the similar picture exists in other states. Most vociferous protests by people have been against the LAQ Act. This is the reason that PESA Act took this aspect into consideration and inserted a clause Section 4 (i) where the Gram Sabha or the Panchayats at the appropriate level had to be consulted before acquiring land in the Scheduled areas for development projects. As per the SC Judgment in Supreme Court Advocates-on-Record Association (SCAORA) Vs Union of

India declared that the word 'consultation'occurring in Article 124(3) of the Constitution should be read to mean concurrence. Though this was referring to appointment of judges, but the word consultation acquired a different meaning. This spirit has been completely violated in actual implementation of PESA. Classic example was that of setting up of the steel factory at Nagarnar (Chhattisgarh). Gram Sabha passed a resolution against setting up of the factory. On the gun point the concerned officials tore the resolution and got the Gram Sabha to pass a new resolution and forced the people to sign it.

III-B. PESA, Forest Rights Act and the New Legal Paradigm

This brings us to a completely new aspect that partial change in restructuring of relationship between the state and the people will not work. It will require changes in the administrative set up to implement the new laws like PESA or the Forest Rights Act 2006 as these laws envisaged to decolonise the administrative machinery. These acts laid down a new blueprint of governance which goes beyond the imagination of the bureaucracy with a colonial mindset. That is why we find no implementation of PESA and partial implementation of the Forest Rights Act, 2006.

Reading of the Chapter on 'PESA, Left Wing Extremism and Governance: Concerns and Challenges in India's Tribal Districts' makes interesting reading. The following section gives us the essence of PESA[11]:

"In 1996, the Parliament passed the Panchayats (Extension to Scheduled Areas) Act or PESA, with the political class acknowledging the dire need to protect the rights and resources of the communities in Schedule V areas, by recognising and upholding their right to self-governance.The law, according to Dileep Singh Bhuria, the Chairman of the committee that worked on it, could 'mark the beginning of a new era in the history of tribal people...'

How was this act a departure? PESA recognised the gram sabha (a habitation was the natural unit of the community, and its adult members constitute the gram sabha, as against the elected gram panchayat) to be pre-eminent. The gram sabha was recognised as being competent to act on a range of powers, including:

- the power to prevent alienation of land in the Scheduled areas and to take appropriate action to restore any unlawfully alienated land of a Scheduled Tribe
- the ownership of minor forest produce
- the power to enforce prohibition, or to regulate or restrict the sale and consumption of any intoxicant
- the power to exercise control over money lending to the Scheduled Tribes
- the power to exercise control over institutions and functionaries in all social sectors
- the power to control local plans, and resources for such plans including tribal sub-plans

- the power of prior recommendation in granting prospecting license or mining leases for minor minerals as well as for grant of concessions for the exploitation of minor minerals by auction

- the right to be consulted on matters of land acquisition

- the power to issue utilisation certificates for government works undertaken in their village"

PESA envisaged a complete new relationship based on self governance where people were considered competent to take decisions. According to Pradip Prabhu[12] "PESA moved from development delivery to empowerment; from implementation to planning; from circumscribed involvement to conscious participation.

On the whole issue of land alienation and land acquisition process the PESA Chapter[13] tells us the following:

"The power envisaged for the gram sabha in respect of 'prevention of land alienation as also restoration of illegally alienated land' is unequivocal. However suitable provisions in the Panchayati Raj Acts or the relevant land regulations have not been made. The only exception is to that is the state of Madhya Pradesh and now Chhattisgarh. A clear and categorical provision has been added in the Madhya Pradesh Land Revenue Code after the enactment of PESA, which empowers the gram sabha to restore the unlawfully alienated lands to the tribal landowners. A unique feature of this law is that in case the gram sabha is unable to restore such lands it has been empowered to direct the sub-divisional officer in this regard who shall restore the possession within three months.

This radical provision has remained virtually unimplemented for the simple reason that no rules have been framed in this regard. Further, to ensure actual devolution, a state's pre-existing laws had to be amended in line with the provisions of PESA. In all the states barring Madhya Pradesh and Chhattisgarh, land acquisition acts have not been amended in line with the provisions of PESA.

The process of consultation before acquisition of land, as envisaged under section 4(i) of PESA, has not been formalised in most of the states. The state of Madhya Pradesh (including Chhattisgarh), however, has made elaborate rules in the year 2000 about consultation with concerned gram sabhas before acquisition of land. These rules envisage 'consultation with gramsabha before issuing notification under Section Four of the Land Acquisition Act.' A detailed procedure has been prescribed so that consultation is transparent and informed. The objective is to enable the people to come to a rational decision based on facts. The collector and are presentative of company are mandated under rule 3(vi) to attend the final meeting of the gram sabha before it formally adopts a resolution for or against the acquisition.

Thus, theoretically there is a paradigm shift in a crucial aspect of governance concerning acquisition of land in favour of the people. The proceedings in the open assembly of the gram sabha precede the proceeding in the court of the collector. The collector is expected to satisfy the people in the natural familiar setting of the gram sabha, where the people feel empowered, before he starts the formal process of land acquisition.

It is, however, a matter of deep regret that these rules are not being followed in their true spirit.There are cases where the formal resolutions of gram sabha expressing dissent have been destroyed and substituted by forged documents. What is worse, no action has been taken by the state against concerned officials even after the facts got established. The message is clear andominous.

There is collusion in these deals at numerous levels. Even in these two states, which have done the most extensive work among the PESA states on their legislations, the gram sabhas are only given the power of consultation and not consent, thus diluting the principle of self-governance. Further the gram sabhas are being convened at a level much larger than a habitation. The progressive edge of PESA gets diluted further as the term consultation is not defined properly nor have state governments outlined the ways of recognising a negative response from the community towards acquisition".

PESA radically restructures governance in Schedule V areas, but lack of political will and promote interests have prevented the State governments to make the necessary changes in law to align it with PESA. Wherever they have been done, they have not been followed. But one fact cannot be denied that PESA has created a political space for people in Schedule V areas to struggle against the anti-people policies of the government. On the issue of land alienation and land acquisition, PESA clearly provides space to negotiate with the officials.

Along with PESA, another act Forest Rights Act, 2006 created space to take back the forests and land which was there and had got alienated because of the colonial laws. The Forest Rights Act not only challenged the colonial paradigm of displacing people from their resources but carved out a legal framework which was in consonance with the basic principles of the Indian Constitution – a grassroot democracy which provides the citizens the right to control, manage and conserve their livelihood resources.

The key feature of the Act is that it does not create rights prospectively. Prof. Pradip Prabhu[14] states this as follows:

'This law is not focused on a future event but on a past event, locked in the silence of history, whose key is intergenerational memory and the spoken word of the forest subalterns ...... Rights Act does not create rights prospectively, it creates a new inclusive frame or recognition of rights that already exist in rem but were not recognised de jure, due to the operation of the alien colonial legality of res nullius and eminent domain. Hence, the law calls upon the administration to rectify the errors of 'exclusion' of colonial and postcolonial forest expansion, recognise pre-existing rights and record them in its present juridical frame.'

Thus the Act has set in motion a process where Forest Dwellers started claiming the resources which was already theirs but their ancestors had lost due to exclusionary legal regime and secondly the forest bureaucracy were to assist the people in recognition of their rights in the present legal regime. A far cry from their role as masters of the forests to helping people manage their livelihood resources.

In a nutshell the Forest Rights Act 2006 gives the forest dwellers the Rights to:

- Forest land for habitation and self-cultivation
- Minor forest produce
- Fish and other products of water bodies
- Grazing
- Seasonal resource access of nomadic or pastoralist communities
- Protect, regenerate, conserve, and manage community forest resources
- Intellectual property and traditional knowledge relating to biodiversity
- Traditional and customary rights such as right of way, collection of soil for household purposes, and access to religious sites.

In addition many groups have used other provisions in the Forest Rights Act to

- For Conversion of forest villages into revenue villages,
- Struggle for rights of communities displaced due to state development interventions,
- For creation of development facilities in the forest villages such as schools, health centers, roads, electricity, and irrigation.

III. Struggle for Implementation

The provision of the right to protect, conserve, regenerate, and manage community forest resources under Section 3(1)(i) of the Forest Rights Act has created a scope for the legal recognition of these traditional community conservation initiatives in forest land (including wetlands and mangroves). Many community conservation groups have already claimed and obtained legal rights over their community forests since implementation of the Forest Rights Act began. Prior to the Forest Rights Act, the customary rights of the PVTG (Particularly Vulnerable Tribal Communities) communities over these territories had not been recognised by the government. The communities with customary territorial rights are now using Section (3)(1)(e) of the Act, which provides for communal tenure rights for the PTGs over their habitats.

Unlike PESA, Forest Rights Act, 2006 is being implemented in many states but with differential success rates. Major opposition has come from the Forest Department who do not want to part away with their powers. Community Forest Rights is one such area. Interestingly Community Forest rights claims are being rejected in many areas but in areas where Maoists are active, community forest rights claims have been granted to the communities.

But with NAC getting involved and pressure from ground is forcing the state to grant community forest rights where people have put their claims.

PESA and the Forest Rights Act have created spaces for people movements for 'Commoning of Enclosures' and strengthened the struggle against the process of 'Accumulation by Dispossession'. In recent times the people's struggle against Vedanta project in Orissa to save the Niyamgiri Hills – habitat of the Dongaria Kondhs and the SC judgments to hold Gram Sabhas to determine their religious rights in the area provide a glimpse of the empowering nature of the Act. 12 gram sabhas are to be held. The four gram sabhas have already declared their rights and rejected the Vedanta project. The hearing in the rest of the gram sabha will be soon done in the near future.

PVTG's in different parts of the country are filing claims to reclaim their traditional habitats under section (3)(1)(e) of the Forest Rights Act, 2006. This has not only created problems for the state as many habitats have been encroached by the state by giving mining leases to mining companies. This has prompted the Orissa Government to seek clarification from the Central Government regarding the application of the above clause.

Many villages in the tribal regions have started using the provisions under the Forest Rights Act to assert their rights to use and sell Minor Forest Produce from Forest and Wildlife protected areas. With the forest department unwilling to let go their revenue from Minor Forest Produce, intense struggle is going on. Mendha Lekha and Marda village in Gadchiroli District of Maharashtra won community rights to manage their forest resources. These rights included to collect and sell Tendu leaves used for Beedi making and Bamboo. Based on this example other 60 villages filed their claims of which only 8 were recognised with riders.[15]

The State continues to find ways to bypass to dilute the provisions of the Forest Rights Act. Recently the Central Government has tried to dilute the Forest Rights Act to allow greenfield project in Forest Areas especially infrastructure projects like highways passing through forest areas. The proposed dilution is to limit the role of Gramsabhas in whose jurisdiction the proposed infrastructure is being planned.

The struggle to empower people's institutions and the move by the neoliberal state to continue dilute and disempower the institutions is going to run parallelly. PESA and Forest Rights Act, 2006 have laid down the foundation for a new governance in Schedule V areas and Forest regions. Though the process is slow as it involves radical change in bureaucratic mindset and functioning, it can be delayed but not stopped. PESA rules are now being made by different states though reluctantly.

Along with PESA, Forest Rights Act, 2006 has created an aspiration among the people to take control over their resources and a correspondingly increased conflict. Both the Acts have provided a much needed space for the people to renegotiate its relationship and reduce the conflict.

References

1. Padel Felix 2010: Mining and Movements - Causes of Tribal Militancy in Social Action Vol. 60 July – September, 2010. New Delhi.

2. Sundar Nandini: Maoism and Salwa Judum in Economic Political Weekly, Vol. 41, No. 29 (July, 22-28, 2006). Mumbai.

3. Mahaprashasta, Ajoy Ashirwad 2010: FDI vs Tribes in Frontline July 3-16, 2010.

4. Ministry of Rural Development, Govt of India Draft Report Vol. 1, 2009.

5. Ministry of Rural Development, Govt of India Draft Report Vol. 1, 2009.

6. Sundar Nandini: Maoism and Salwa Judum in Economic Political Weekly, Vol. 41, No. 29 (July, 22-28, 2006). Mumbai.

7. Sundar Nandini: Maoism and Salwa Judum in Economic Political Weekly, Vol. 41, No. 29 (July, 22-28, 2006). Mumbai.

8. Ministry of Rural Development, Govt of India Draft Report Vol. 1, 2009.

9. Padel Felix 2010: Mining and Movements - Causes of Tribal Militancy in Social Action Vol. 60 July – September, 2010, New Delhi.

10. CAG Audit Report (civil) for the year ended 31 March, 2011. Government of India.

11. Dandekar Ajay and Choudhry Chitrangada: PESA, Left –wing Extremism and Governance: Concerns and Challenges in India's Tribal Districts. Commissioned by Ministry of Panchayati Raj, Govt of India, New Delhi.

12. Prabhu Pradip 2004: PESA and the Illusions of Tribal Self-governance in Combat Law, Vol. 2, No. 5. New Delhi.

13. Dandekar Ajay and Choudhry Chitrangada: PESA, Left–wing Extremism and Governance: Concerns and Challenges in India's Tribal Districts. Commissioned by Ministry of Panchayati Raj, Govt of India, New Delhi.

14. Prabhu Pradip 2010: Inclusion in Law and Exclusion in Praxis: The Scheduled Tribes and Other Traditional Forest Dwellers (Recognition of Forest Rights) Act 2006 Vol. 6, Socio-Legal Review 2010.

15. Mahapatra Richard and others, 2010: How Government is subverting Forest Right Act in CSE WEBNET 12/10/2010.

17

Democracy, Development and Tribal Resistance: Contemporary Issues

Sravya Katta

I have no land, no money. My house is on stake and the interest on loan taken from the money lender is increasing. Every year the green carpet is turning into industrial sector, rivers our source are polluted. My children are following me to produce a meal for our family. No safety for my girl and women are dying due to no healthcare. I have no voice and no power. What should I do?

A Tribe is group of people who have a common culture, language and way of living. They are a dialect, different from other tribal groups with territorial affiliation. It's a social group with restrictive social contacts, legal and political relations. Tribes are the most vulnerable group in society who keep separate from rest of Indian society in order to conserve and preserve their ethnic identity. Often, their contact with outsiders was through exploitation by moneylenders, landlords, merchants.They have a different morality, a religion, a different belief. Even the way they live, food habits, instruments used for occupation, dressing up and it's a different world for them. Tribal's from different sects have their own world view. They exhibit their own economy of design which is lacking in modern society. Religion is of great importance for them, they follow their ancestors and stick to their culture. They develop among themselves for better way of living. The techniques what they use is basically natural without any touch of technology.

Are they satisfied within this small group having their own way of living? As the globe rotates faster, faster the scenario changes. That enough means Adivasi, i.e., original people are satisfied with is not sufficient. The value added system has penetrated into them making a specific entity called nomadic philosophy. The essence of tribe is their culture which they want to protect. This has to be carried for generations in remembrance of the sect. Lately, the languages used by these sects are decreasing as the sects are vanishing. The languages are unwritten and not recorded. The touch of technology for health care, education, occupation shall protect them. But, they are scared to be exposed to the world. Tribes locate themselves near river for their primary occupation food. The green pastures and the silent whispers are turning to concrete, engine sounds- a threat to the land they live in.

Development has different connotation is different context. It means a step further for a change, progress. The understanding of this term shall not be same in different minds. Development in 1950s meant a change to the basic needs focusing till the boundaries of families. After a decade or so the term meant for agriculture, occupation. Later, it was for the sustainable development, equity, etc. Few decades back development was meant nothing but was in practice unknowingly as it was not understood. Development is a continuous process with no end. It is a multidimensional process involving reorganisation and reorientation of the system. UNESCO's concept of development is based on realisation that communities define themselves in terms of cultural identities and development cannot be effective unless it is centered around that image. For this it is important to understand the concept of tribe and tribal development. Tribal development can be classified into isolation, integration and assimilation approach. It was felt that the contract with rest of India and mainly the non-tribal's would expose them to virtually unlimited exploitation. They need their own economic space and letting them grow in their self-created developmental paradigm.

During the British rule, tribal policy was of isolation, making differences between the tribal society and the civilisation. It was a non-interference zone for stretch of decades. British's wanted to keep tribes away from contact with others. They wanted to leave tribes untouched and took deliberate measures to keep them away. But this policy couldn't last for long. This approach towards them made the sect move closer and stronger. Integration Assimilation approach was to make them connect to the neighbouring non-tribal's which took place in different parts of the country. Tribes started to accept the Hindu culture. This change of choice, became the main criticism that they are moving away from their norms and culture. Integration approach consists of two types for development: protective and promotional measures. Planners choose this way due to the past experimental approaches. With Independence, the policy shifted and provisions were made for them by the government to protect the interest of tribal's from getting exploited.

Since liberalisation, there has been an increase in the GDP growth and crossed the mark of seven per cent. Annual employment growth has remained the same. The approach towards socio-cultural has changed. Infant morality rates has been controlled. Increase in concentration towards the health-care and safety measures has been concentrated into. Education indicators are discouraging. Though few steps has been taken to educate their children, the quality of education was lacking. Students drop-out ratio only increased. Girl education was low, girls were prone to early marriages and early motherhood due to which their health deteriorated. There was no control of child birth which added feathers to the exceeding population.

After Independence, the initiative by the government of introducing Five Year Plan has marked a significance role of tribals. Every plan made include a provision for upliftment of tribals. The scheme have ranged from infrastructure building to empowerment, solitary area development to integrated area development. Plans which were made not only concentrated towards a main issue but supported the tribes in minute issues also. Each aspect for development was read, discussed and accepted. Different approaches were used for execution. There were changes made to the outdated approaches which did not bring any outcome. What was left to see was whether these measures taken were accepted by the sects and did any good to them. Reason the development was at snails speed. Programmes and protection available to the tribes reached few. Those who couldn't avail these facilities offered by the government remained at the same position. Yet the government has guaranteed benefits in a way of schemes and provisions to decrease the gap in development between tribes and others.

Pandit Jawarlal Nehru came laid down fundamental principles[1]. These principles are that the tribal should develop along the lines of their genus and we should avoid imposing anything on them, they should be encouraged by their traditional culture. Tribal people rights in land forest should be respected. An outsider should be appointed at the beginning of the administration and development work, once settled we should train and build a team of their own people and avoid outsiders. We should not overwhelm them with multiplicity of schemes, rather work through and not in rivalry to support their institutions.

Constitution of India initiated tribal welfare programmes by incorporating important provisions. These provisions gave testimony to tribal welfare programmes, making them constitutional obligation for the future governments of the country. Special representations in the parliament, assemblies, local bodies, privileges in the form of reservation in governmental services and reservation in the education institutions has been provided. These reservations in educational sector has not restricted few institutions but reservation has been made in reputed institutions also. Certain benefits has been provided and reserved for the tribes to make them comfortable and profess one's faith. According to the Fifth Schedule, Union executive is given the power of giving direction to the states in matters relating to the administration of scheduled area. Sixth Schedule designated tribal areas in Assam and Meghalaya where autonomous district councils and regional councils have been constituted with powers to make laws for management of land, forests, cultivation and appointment of a commission for schedule tribe for safeguarding their interest.

The constitution mandates the outlays from the consolidated fund to state for promoting welfare of schedule tribes under Article 275(1) of Constitution of India. Constitution also provides for the appointment of a commission for safeguarding the interest of scheduled tribes. Some of the committees were formed by the government of India under chairmanship of politicians/ government officials. Under the chairmanship of U.N. Dhebar, schedules areas and scheduled tribes commission was formed and observed that the problem is not to disturb the harmony of tribal life but to work for their advancement by not imposing anything upon the tribals.

Article 15(4), 46, 224, 339 speak of special provisions meant for the administration and control of scheduled areas and tribals for their welfare and protection for promoting the welfare of the scheduled tribes and for raising the level of administration to state level.

This provisions were made for uplift and for the welfare of the tribal. Development of the tribes as a social responsibility of the President and the Governor in the state are responsible to administer these aspects. Both the Union and State has come forward to promote laws. Making of the law for schedule tribes is one part and importantly the execution of these laws is another part. Difficulty level raises dealing with the execution part as the access to the tribes is less. Most of them are unaware of the laws and their rights. They fall prey to the money lenders and non-tribals around their area as they are the source of communication for them. The gap of communication should be eliminated by forming committees who concentrate on particular selected committees rather than dealing with all the tribal sects. These committees shall study the group and provide them their needs. This can be an easy way to build up the comfort zone. Strategies should be made for development in terms with the geographic and demographic conditions. These strategies shall be according to the conditions of the sects. It is always better to deal these groups separately rather than grouping them together.

In 1954 community development projects were taken up. Government made special economic development projects. In the recent past, lot of commissions and committees were appointed to solve the issues and remove imbalances. It was not only to remove the difficulties faced and to provide them with opportunity but not to disturb their existing cultural way of living. So far some of the commissions and committees formed:

1. The Social Welfare Team of the Committee on plan projects 1959.
2. The Verrier Elwin Committee on Tribal Development.
3. The Committee on Tribal Economy in Forest Areas -1967.
4. The Schedules Areas and Scheduled Tribal Commission (Dhebar Committee 1961).
5. The Special working Group on Co-operatives for Backward Classes - 1961 (Shri M.D. Bhargava as its Chairman).
6. The Task Force on Development of Tribal Areas -1972.
7. The Dube Committee -1972.
8. The Study Team on Co-operative Structure in Tribal Development Project Areas -1976.

9. The Study Group on Relief of Indebtedness Land, Alienation and Restoration in Development Agency Area -1973 (Shri P.S. Appu as its Chairman)

10. The team of Marketing, Credit and Co-operation in Tribal Areas -1978 (Shri K.S. Bawa Committee).

11. The Working Group on Development of Scheduled Tribes during the 7th Five Years Plans (1985- 90).

12. The Dhebar Commission.

The first five year plan was a start-up and did not play any specific role towards the development. It was an introduction to educational schemes, welfare scheme. Multi-purpose Tribal Projects in selected tribal area was introduced by the administration system after the first five year plan. The second five year plan had concrete developmental schemes recognising socio-economic conditions. The third five year plan not only concentrated on improving the conditions in the tribal areas, Verrier Elevin Committee implemented Tribal Development Block system involving the people with the aid of Panchayat institutions. Fourth five year plan envisaged extension of these blocks from 10 to 15 years. About 75 crores were utilised for the development programmes. A number of different schemes were introduced in the fourth five year plan like land colonisation schemes, farming schemes where the societies were introduced and concessions/benefits were given to them. Fourth five year plan was not a bit hit as actual planning was not done at the grass root level. A new strategy was evolved in the fifth five year plan. In view of weakness of the earlier plan this plan made the foundation for sub plan for the areas of tribal concentration. The attention was towards area development, family oriented programmes. It was noticed that few areas outside the tribal sub plan strategy was left out. A target of 50 per cent was adopted for the first time. This plan was achieved to a large extent. Seventh five year plan concentrated on area cum family development. They conducted family oriented programmes for eradication of poverty in tribal areas.

National Schedule Tribes Financial and Development Corporation has been set up in the tenth five year plan. This is an apex institution for financing economically to the projects for Scheduled Tribes. This institution has been set up to provide financial assistance at reasonable rates and provides grants for skill development. Certain limitations have been attached by providing backwards class in the Scheduled Tribes more opportunities compared to others. This step could fill up the gaps. Monitoring the utilisation of funds, level of grants-in-aid to states, providing financial assistance to NGOs, scholarships for pursuing post-matriculation courses and establishment of educational institutions concentrating on women empowerment was the highlights of tenth five year plan.

Special employment programmes, enhanced outlay for the rural development were strategies of the eighth five year plan. The target was to increase the income levels of both the underemployed and employed poor.

Short term objective was to provide temporary jobs to individual so that there is a contributor to each house. Sectorial development programmes were organised to generate larger and more sustainable employment.

Ninth plan objective was to correct historical inequalities and increase the economic growth. It concentrated on the health care by providing basic necessities, clean food and water. Priority to agriculture was given to ensure that the tribes have enough sources for themselves.

The Eleventh plan brought in a new vision, from the first year plan it was building basic foundation, controlling the system, providing amenities, agriculture aspects. But, this plan has brought in a new trend concentrating on infrastructure, schemes for highways, mass irrigation, providing with new houses.

These plans allowed the individual to express and realise own conceptualisation of development. Gross Domestic Product growth rate has been increased. Target for most plans was achieved otherwise it reached near to the target. These plans did not restrict itself to certain levels it went on from providing basic amenities till construction of infrastructure and laying of highways. The industrial growth was remarkable by achieving higher returns than the target.

Context of tribal rights and claims were to preserve the culture of tribal's with the right to socio-economic development. We need give due care to the preservation of the liberties and identities. Their identity is utmost important next to culture, every group has a story of exploitation and loss of status to tell. These developments shall only be add on, not to change the nature and gist of their culture and habitat. We are aiming at providing the best choices to tribes rather than turning rural land to urban land. The Sachar report finds minorities face challenges relating to three inter-related issues: Identity, Security and Equity.

Nehru proposed an approach for tribal poverty which was to penetrate infrastructure, provide state finance, etc. According to Elwin's philosophy he said that we are not concentrating on the upliftment but to restore to them the liberties of their own countryside. Tribal's need facilities, security and education not the modern comforts and technology.

Panchsheel which is five principles which remain avantgarde of tribal development theory:

(a) People should be allowed to develop on the lines of their own genius and nothing should be imposed on them

(b) Their rights on land and forest should be respected

(c) Induction of too many outsiders should be avoided

(d) Work for the tribal's should be done through their own administration

(e) Results should be judged by the quality of outcome but not the amount of money spent on.

Development should be done involving tribal in both planning and implementation. Concentration should be on the empowerment and identity with culture specific and based on the need. Development and administration of tribal areas is accepted as the responsibility of the central government even though they are parts of the concerned states.

The initiative for development to raise the standard of living was started in 1951. This was achieved in the form of National Extension Schemes. Integrated Area Development Programme (IADP) and Integrated Tribal Development Projects (ITDP) started functioning after Tribal Development Block (TDB) and Tribal Integrated Development Project (TIDP) which started in 1972 failed in practice. NES followed Community Development Project (CDP).

Even after all these schemes made, few people felt that the tribal development has not receive desired concentrated attention. The four phrases, providing immediate relief, resource mobilisation and social service, education and growth, basic need and eliminating poverty was not administered properly even though many provisions were made in support. The scenario changed in 1960's, NGO's such as Aga Khan Rural Support Programme (AKRSP) and Navinchandra Mafatlal Sadguru Water and Development Foundation was formed involving citizen group to provide the means to livelihood.

Review of Existing Programmes

Under Integrated Rural Development Programme (IRDP) tribes are divided into categories. People earning below Rupees 4800 are identified and given assistance for employment which in turn raise the poverty line. Suitable changes was introduces in seventh five year plan after assessing the sixth five year plan. It was assumed that people earning more than Rs. 4800 to 6400 would be able to raise the poverty line in the process of growth. To understand the earning standards of each family, data was collected by independent research institutions for entire country. The motto was to provide at least one bread earner in each family to satisfy the basic needs. The purpose was to make the number of households to cross the poverty line but this turned out to be relatively small.

Under Training of Rural Youth for Self Employment (TRYSEM), the plan concentrated on developing the rural youth by giving them assistance for employment. It provided technical skills and to upgrade the traditional skills. From the time this system came into force, the graph was always straight up. During 1990-91 number of youth who got employed was 70 per cent. The policy to provide employment was similar to IRDP.

Under Development of Women and Children in Rural Areas (DWCRA), this was an exclusive scheme to provide economic activities for women. This programme identified the activities which could generate sustained income. Operationalising it played inadequate because of lack of cohesion among women.

In 1989, wage-employment programme called the Jawahar Rozgar Yojana (JRY) was merged into National Rural Employment Programme (NREP) and the

Rural Landless Employment Guarantee Programme (RLEGP). These were centrally finances programmes limited to landless. JRY was launched with total allocation of Rupees 2600 crores. They wanted to generate additional employment which would benefit the poor or to contribute to create rural infrastructure. Contribution came up from the Centre and the State. These amount was allocated for different purposes. Out of the total State's allocation, six per cent was allocated for housing under the Indira Awaas Yojana (IAY) which is allotted to the scheduled castes and scheduled tribes and freed bonded labour. Some part went for the Million Well Scheme (MWS) to provide wells free of cost to poor. Where such wells are not feasible, it was utilised for minor irrigation activities. Development programmes were planned and implemented at district level called District Rural Development Agency (DRDA).

State level schemes, concentrated in particular areas to resolve the problems with no time delay. It is an added advantage as it becomes difficult for the Centre to administer each corner. Some of the popular ones are Maharashtra Employment Guarantee Scheme (EGS), Special Employment Programme in Gujarat, Drought Prone Area Programme concentrating on utilisation of land using techniques and for productive methods for dryland agriculture.

The apex problem is from the non-tribal's on issues related to land. Many Acts has been enacted to provide rights including schedule caste and schedule tribes. Some of the Acts are Land Grabbing Act, Land Encroachment Act, Land Acquisition Act, Forest Rights Act 2006, SC/ST (Prevention of Atrocities) Act, 1989, etc. Land reforms policy concentrated on abolition of intermediaries as they were acquiring lands at a lower cost from the tribes by selling at a higher rate. Legislature made provision to abolish transfer of land from tribal and non-tribal. Tribe's main asset is their land; their livelihood towards agriculture has to be protected. Tenancy reforms, redistribution of surplus ceiling land, consolidation of holdings was practiced. For a better administration, recording of such transfers and the purpose of such transfer should be recorded from time to time. This will also help us to determine the ownership of such particular transfer. It will provide tribes for a better documentation of such transfer, not by mere words. During early fifties, Zamindars exploited scheduled tribes. There was retaining of self-cultivation lands. Due to which the production stopped aiming no source of income for the tribes. Zamindar felt this was a best step to grab lands as tribes found it difficult to repay the loan with no source of income.

Panchayati Raj Institutions are inexistence in almost all the states in mode of election. Seventh five year plan was to increase such institutions in the country. There were increase in total of gram panchayat, panchayati samities and zila parishads. The representatives belonged to the village. The main objective was to make these institutions strong, reflecting the felt needs of the people. Constitution Amendment Bill (Constitution 72nd Amendment Bill, 1991) was introduced in Parliament in 1991 to revitalise the panchayats, to provide

Gram sabha to each village with direct elections. Reservations of seats were allotted to schedule tribes. Grants to panchayats are provided from the consolidated fund of the state.

Under Minimum Needs Programme, there were eight components which were termed to be the basic elements for rural development like elementary education, rural health, roads, supply of water and electricity, providing houses, supplement of required nutrition. These supplements were provided as per the inter-state variations. Similarly certain funds should be given to the states to allocate for street lighting, distribution of clean water in schools, bio-gas, social forestry, community centers, etc.

Integrated Rural Energy Programme (IREP), despite the quality of life in the rural area continues to be much below the desired levels. A major constraint in rural areas in the non-availability of energy which leaves hole in production needs. This programme understands the pattern of energy consumption at the micro level and through it plans to supply energy. Supplement is as per the state level requirement, utilisation and consumption in household sectors, small scale industries, etc.

As it is a two-fold process, this achievement should come up from the tribes also. Compulsory training should be provided to the student once they complete their education. This would help them to draw a path or adjust to the situations when working in the outer sector other than scheduled areas. Similarly, training-cum-production centers should be available. For women empowerment, loans with no interest at initial stages should be provided. Development in cottage and small scale industries can provide good opportunity for employment. Special multi-purpose tribal projects should be established in the selected areas. Involvement of NGO's to support such projects should be welcomed. To make farming more economic and profitable, corporate farming societies should provide them with new techniques and improved methods to cultivate. A proper understanding of market axis, selling and distribution, storage, fixation of prices should be taught.

The programmes themselves need not be changed but the manner of its implementation shall be mended. Rather than applying such schemes or programmes involving various groups in tribes. It can be divided or sub-divided into groups. Certain projects and schemes would be selected for implementation depending upon the nature of the groups. Strategy would consists of creating the right environment for success rather change the present practice. Firstly, the policy has to be made them administered. Changes should be brought down from time to time suiting the scenario and nature of the region. Not every policy is clean without blemishes. Success will be achieved when such blemishes are observed and removed before any damage is caused. Prerequisite for success is a balance between tribal's felt needs and real needs. It's a two way learning process, in which the tribal's are educated by the development agent and vice versa. It is not only the duty of the government to make policies and follow a path to the development, each one of us contribution towards the development would play a vital role.

Improvement or Impairment: Impact of Displacement on Tribal Communities

Development projects have led to large scale displacement of the tribal population in the country having overwhelmingly disastrous impact. Displacement has been particularly disruptive of tribal livelihoods and cultures, abruptly terminating their access to the common property resources. Tribal people constitute about 50 per cent of those displaced by big dams and industrialisation and they are also the group most negatively affected by displacement because their culture and identity is rooted in the soil. The Land Acquisition Act, 1894 (as amended in 1984), the only legal instrument available in the country to address the issue of development-induced displacement deprives tribal of compensation and rehabilitation benefits as they do not possess any legal documents to prove their ownership right on the land they occupy and earn their livelihood even if for centuries together. Coming from politically marginalised and disadvantaged strata of society, these groups often end up neglected and impoverished. In this paper, I seek to examine how development-induced displacement impacts tribal population and how the resettlement planning and policies can reinforce the disparities that already exist in society.

Swept off the Land: An Introduction

Like becoming a refugee, being forcibly ousted from one's land and habitat by a dam, reservoir or highway is not only immediately disruptive and painful, it is also fraught with serious long-term risks of becoming poorer than before displacement, more vulnerable economically, and disintegrated socially.[1]

In India, national development has been largely equated with economic growth and surplus. Large, centralised industries, irrigation projects have been symbols of such development, which through the process of industrialisation promised to set India on the path of modernisation and development. One of the inevitable outcomes of this has been massive 'displacement'. While development projects offer increased opportunities for some, they also impose costs borne by most marginalised members[2]. Large-scale development projects result in massive displacement of population. Globally, it is estimated that approximately 10 million people are displaced each year as a result of development activities (Cernea 1999). Development-induced displacement in India has brought severe economic, social and environmental problems to the displaced people making it a matter of crucial concern. A review of existing literature on development-induced displacement reveals that there is a vast amount of literature available on development and its benefits but there is a striking paucity of data on the problems created by it especially displacement, resettlement and rehabilitation. There is also a conspicuous lack of any national policy regarding these issues.

Displacement is not a recent phenomenon. A great amount of dislocation of life had taken place even in the pre-independence era but the actual dislocation they caused was minimal as the land was in abundance. Displacement became a significant problem during the colonial period and got intensified after independence. And with the onset of globalisation, it has assumed larger proportions making it a serious concern of national significance (Murickan 2003). It is an irony that there are no reliable official statistics of the numbers of people displaced by large projects since Independence. Many researchers place their estimates between 10 and 25 million. In an influential 1989 study, Fernandes, Das and Rao provide an estimate of some 21 million displaced persons. Scholar and administrator, Dr. N.C. Saxena places his estimate of persons displaced by big projects since 1947 at nearly double this figure — 50 million. This is also the figure quoted by celebrity writer Arundhati Roy in an essay 'The Greater Common Good: The Human Cost of Big Dams'. It is worth quoting her persuasive reasoning:

"According to a detailed study of 54 Large Dams done by the Indian Institute of Public Administration, the average number of people displaced by a Large Dam is 44,182. Admittedly 54 Dams out of 3,300 is not a big enough sample. But… it's all we have… let's err on the side of abundant caution and take an average of just 10,000 people per Large Dam. 33 million… That's what it works out to…What about those that have been displaced by the thousands of other Development Projects? Fifty million people…I feel like someone who's just stumbled on a mass grave". (Roy 1999)

Development projects like dams, mines, thermal power plants, industries, roads, railways, ports, national parks, tourist resorts and the like necessitates the acquisition of private and community resources, deprives the family of the common property resources (CPRs) and forces people to move out of their home affecting their very life sustenance. In order to conceal the trauma displacement causes to the affected people, policy-makers and international financial institutions use the term '*involuntary relocation*', though in reality, it is nothing but 'forced eviction'. The UN clearly identifies 'forced eviction' as 'gross violation of human rights'. The policy makers even claim that the displaced persons are beneficiaries of the compensation and rehabilitation package. It is ironical that ones who suffer the most from the project are called beneficiaries.

The policy-makers justify displacement by arguing that "some people will have to suffer if the Nation has to prosper". Nehru, India's first Prime Minister, while laying the foundation-stone for India's first major river valley project, the Hirakud Dam in Orissa in 1948, said to the tens of thousands facing the grim prospect of displacement: 'If you have to suffer, you should do so in the interest of the country' (Roy 1999). The same sentiments were echoed 36 years later by Prime Minister Indira Gandhi in a letter to one of India's most respected social workers, Baba Amte. She wrote 'I am most unhappy that development projects displace tribal people from their habitat, especially as project authorities do not always take care to properly rehabilitate the affected population. But sometimes there is no alternative and we have to go ahead in the larger interest…' (Kothari 1996)

Displacement and the Tribes

"Some people will have to suffer if the Nation has to prosper"[3]

Studies have shown that it is invariably the weaker sections like the Tribals who are sacrificed again and again at the 'altar of development'. For example, in India, Tribal people account for 40-50 per cent of communities affected by development—induced displacement, though they constitute only 8 per cent of the country's population.[4] Fernandes and Paranjpye[5] rightly point out.

Though involuntary displacement occurs at a point of time, it sets in motion a series of inevitable events, which often constitute several years of psychological trauma due to the disruption in the established pattern of life of the people displaced. Production systems are dismantled, close-knit kinship groups get scattered, long established relationships are disrupted, traditional sources of employment are lost, market links broken and customs related to child care, food security, intra-community credit transfers etc., get dissolved. The obvious result of such sudden changes is impoverishment, both economic and social. The psychological trauma is profound, because people find themselves landless, jobless, without food and access to community resources.

Tribals are socially, economically and politically the weakest and the most deprived communities in India. Independent India promised to give equal opportunity to all her citizens by providing special protection to the weak. But it is unfortunate that poor, marginalised communities have been further impoverished in the process of 'national development'. They have been uprooted from their ancestral land, often forced to migrate to urban slums in search of employment or become landless labourers. In an unequal society like India, dams or hydroelectric projects serve as yet another instrument of dominant classes for appropriating the two most important natural resources – water and land – from less powerful communities like tribals or *adivasis*. Besides, in many cases, like for example, Surya dam in western Maharashtra, dams have been built in the name of tribal, deprived classes and eventually serve the important cities like Mumbai (Singh 1998).

Tribal people have almost never shared the benefits of the projects which have displaced them, be it irrigation or electricity. For instance, Machkunda dam in Orissa generates 720 MW of electricity annually but families displaced by the dam live in darkness (Sainath 1996). Singh (1998) states, "…displacement caused by large dams has actually resulted in transfer of resources from the weaker sections of the society to the more privileged …large dams do little to alleviate the existing social inequalities, on the contrary, they further aggravate the already skewed social structure in favour of socially, economically and politically powerful". On similar lines, John Rawls opine that an unsuccessful resettlement scheme not only failed to benefit the affected persons, but also created new inequalities by depriving them not only of income and wealth, but also of social goods in two other categories – liberty and opportunity and the social bases of respect.[6]

Tribal economy is largely self-sufficient, based on nature and is sustained and nurtured by their close proximity to forest, river and mountains. These are the resource rich areas which consequently are most likely to be dammed or mined. Many tribal belts have been identified as "development sites" ideally suited for building large multi-purpose river valley projects like mines, thermal power stations or paper factories. As pointed out by Fernandes (1991), comparatively smaller proportion of dams built immediately after independence were located in tribal areas, but the trend changed in 1970s. Once the resources in more accessible areas were exhausted, in the later phase more and more dams were planned in tribal areas, naturally displacing a large number of tribal people.

As has been mentioned earlier, the tribal/*adivasis* are predominantly located in forest areas rich in biodiversity. As these areas are culturally and ecologically sensitive areas, the Constitution of India has provided safeguards and legislation to protect both the people and the country's natural resources. The most important provision is the Fifth Schedule of the Indian Constitution, which has demarcated certain predominantly tribal areas as Fifth Schedule areas. Under this Schedule, the main legal protection for the STs is that no land or immovable property of the tribal people in the Scheduled Areas can be transferred to persons other than tribals (Mehta 2009). These scheduled areas and their tribal inhabitants are confronted by two kinds of land alienation situations. The first takes place due to the fraudulent occupation of tribal lands by non-tribal traders, money-lenders and landlords. The second threat concerns the transfer of tribal lands in the form of leases or sale to industries and commercial enterprises with the active support of the State. Some examples of such lease transfers that have taken place comes from Andhra Pradesh which includes paper industries like ITC Bhadrachalam, Birla Periclase in Visakhapatnam district for mining, Orient Cements in Adilabad district for cement plants.

Tribal people have common property resources (CPRs) which are shared by the community members; development projects abruptly terminate access to these common resources as no thought is given to the role of common property resources in their lives. Displacement deprives them of these communal customary rights to their territories. The resettlement literature is full of case studies of how development projects ignore the customary rights of the tribal people and treat them as illegal occupants of government land. Hence, the most important serious consequence of development-induced displacement has been for the tribal people, the dispossession of land, both agricultural and homestead, along with the loss of their traditional occupation. The tribals are deprived of compensation and rehabilitation benefits as per the Land Acquisition Act, 1894 (as amended in 1984) because they do not possess any legal documents to prove their ownership right on their land they occupy and earn their livelihood even if for centuries together. Coming from politically marginalised and disadvantaged strata of society, these groups often end up neglected and impoverished. In India, the Adivasi or tribal people, although only representing eight per cent of the total population, make up 40-50 per cent of the displaced.

Another sad consequence of displacement is multiple displacements which have been documented in number of studies across the country. Multiple displacements of people are the successive displacement of the same families from one place to another following execution of development projects in those areas. The displaced people of Rihand dam, Hirakud dam and Hindustan Aeronautics Limited (HAL) are some of the examples in the country. In the early 1960s, the displaced people of Rihand dam had to face displacement from their new place of habitation for the second time in 1970s because of the coal mining projects, and again for the third in mid-1980s due to the setting up of a number of industries. In each time of their displacement, they were progressively pauperised (Thukral, 1996). Similarly, the displaced people of Hirakud dam, who were resettled in the mid-1950s in the upper catchments areas of the reservoir, faced displacement for the second time in 1980s due to the Ib Thermal power project that came up there and again in 1980-1990s due to the Ib valley coal mining projects. The displaced people of HAL, who were relocated in the early 1970s, were evicted for the second time in 1980s due to the execution of Upper Kolab dam project. They apprehended further displacement due to the establishment of Naval armament depot and agricultural farm coming up in the area.

Resettlement and Rehabilitation Policy in Practice

What makes the problem of displacement graver is the fact that there is no national legislation or policy on Resettlement and Rehabilitation (R&R) so far for the development-induced displaced people in the country though the displacement of people from their land and livelihood has been a part of India's history even before the advent of British. Sadly, the use of land has always been defined by the needs of dominant groups, and displacement of other subservient groups has often been justified and rational since times immemorial.

The Land Acquisition Act, 1894, amended in 1984 is the only legal instrument available in the country to address the issue of development-induced displacement that places no legal obligation on either the project authorities or the state, beyond a limited conception of adequate 'compensation' thereby showing that government has made too weak an effort to minimise the extent and trauma of displacement and to comprehensively resettle the displaced.

The people have been left to fend for themselves in a world about which they know nothing. Even when development is planned, its impact on the people is ignored, the consideration is strictly in economic terms, which lack genuine concern for social consequences and does not take into account the infringement of rights. As a result, there has been much greater displacement after independence resulting in further impoverishment of the already poor. Surprisingly, the country does not have a rehabilitation policy or law though millions have been deprived of their livelihood and there has been an enormous increase in the number of displaced persons (DP) and other project affected persons (PAP). Hence, it is obvious that decision-making about 'development' is not exclusively, or even primarily, technical or managerial in nature, but essentially political, reflecting power to impose costs on some groups and to benefit others.

Land Acquisition policy is about the question of resources, ownership and development. It is not only about land but everything attached to the land, water, forest, coal, minerals etc. which gets acquired in the name of public purpose and development causing immense pain to millions of tribals, farmers and workers and those dependent on these. Various draft policies have been under preparation by the Government of India since the mid-1980s, but none ultimately saw the light of day. The draft National Policy, Packages and Guidelines for Resettlement and Rehabilitation, 1998 (NRR 1998) was prepared and widely debated by the Government of India, including with people's movements, though it is reportedly still stalled at the level of the cabinet. The draft NRR 1998 is still used as a benchmark, because it constitutes the most comprehensive official draft policy so far, and its preparation involved wide consultations including with people's movements and social scientists. But it is important to bear in mind that it has not received official sanction so far, and the prospect of this happening in the near future remains uncertain, even remote. The NRR 1998 considered by the Government of India, states as its initial objectives:

To minimise displacement and to prevent state-induced impoverishment of people on account of compulsory acquisition of land for the State, semi-government or private interests, leading to loss of livelihood and shelter, and to search for non-displacing or least displacing alternatives to people displacing projects. (NRR 1998)

There is a much awaited new 'land acquisition, resettlement and rehabilitation bill' which has been under discussion for more than six years now and has been renamed as "Right to fair Compensation, Resettlement, Rehabilitation and Transparency in Land Acquisition Bill, 2012" with a claim to better reflect government's commitment towards securing a legal guarantee for the rights of project affected and ensuring greater transparency in the land acquisition process. It is also claimed that the Bill will ensure, in concert with local institutions of self government and Gram Sabhas, a humane, participative, informed, consultative and transparent process for land acquisition.

In principle, this Bill is the government's effort at addressing the problems in the 1894 Land Acquisition Act, which is not only completely outdated, but has only promoted forcible land acquisition across the country. Land acquisition in India continues to take place without any resettlement and rehabilitation, drastically affecting not only people who lose their land, but also those who lose their livelihood. It is the first time that a land acquisition bill specifically talks about the resettlement and rehabilitation of the project affected persons, and also a first to acquire land for private corporations. Unfortunately, the Ministry of Rural Development (MoRD) is not agreeable to many of these reasonable proposals. It is feared that the government not act as the property dealer for private corporations. Public purpose itself is defined by the MoRD in a manner worse than in the British Act. This Bill is considered pro-corporate and pro-investors.

Since the World Bank has funded a significant proportion of mega-dams in India, and therefore has considerable influence on official policy, it is important to throw light on the relevant clauses of the 1998 World Bank policy. The first overall objective of the World Bank's policy on involuntary resettlement is stated to be that, 'Involuntary resettlement should be avoided, where feasible, or minimised, exploring all viable alternative project designs'. It lays down that in financing projects, the Bank should satisfy itself that the borrower has explored all viable alternative project designs to avoid the need for involuntary resettlement and, when it cannot be avoided, to minimise the scale and impacts of resettlement (for example, it is pointed out that realignment of roads or reduction in dam height may reduce resettlement needs). (World Bank 1998)

It is possible to state this principle even more categorically, that forced relocation must be avoided, except in very exceptional circumstances. In such cases, all necessary measures must be taken to minimise the scale and impact of displacement.

In 1990, the World Bank developed guidelines to protect those displaced by development projects. The basic principle of the World Bank's Involuntary Resettlement Policy is that the displaced should enjoy some of the benefits of the project and their standards of living be improved or at least not degraded. The Asian Development Bank formally adopted an involuntary resettlement policy in 1994. Like the World Bank policy on which it was modelled, it seeks to avoid involuntary resettlement, if possible, to minimise displacement where it is unavoidable, and ensure that the displaced people receive adequate assistance to restore their living conditions to at least the pre-project levels. A review mechanism (called the Accountability Mechanism) was also created in 1995 to address concerns of persons affected by ADP-assisted projects. In a 1997 resolution, the Sub-Commission on Prevention of Discrimination and Protection of Minorities affirmed "the right of persons to be protected from forcible displacement and to remain in peace in their homes, on their own lands and in their own countries".

The NRR 1998 states as its goal the endeavour 'to minimise the trauma of displacement on account of compulsory acquisition of land', and to establish statutory minimum standards for packages and benefits to ensure that displaced persons are better off as the result of the project. The Bank policy states that, 'where displacement is unavoidable, resettlement programmes should be conceived and executed as development programmes, providing sufficient investment resources to give the persons displaced by the project the opportunity to share in project benefits'.

It also mandates that the affected people should be 'offered opportunities to participate in planning and implementing resettlement programmes'; and that 'displaced persons should be assisted in their efforts to improve their former production levels, income earning capacity and living standards, or at least to restore the production levels, income earning capacity and living standards they would have achieved in the without-project case'. (World Bank 1998).

The advantage of this formulation is that rehabilitation is not merely reduced to a set of palliative measures for welfare and relief; it is an integral component of the development project ensuring that all affected persons actually benefit, and are not pauperised by it.

But the World Bank is not taking any proactive steps to check what the ground reality is. Hence, the need of the hour is that the Banks should not lend its financial and institutional support to projects that result in involuntary impoverishment of communities that are deemed to be 'in the way' of development projects. The World Bank must undertake a shift in emphasis and start according priority to those who are not traditionally privileged. The Bank should take a different approach and be more responsive to the needs, concerns and priorities of the poor and disenfranchised communities that are affected by development. In addition, the Bank must take responsibility for the impacts of policy failures to date.

Theoretical Models of Displacement and Resettlement

There are many theoretical models that seek to define the precise contours of the responsibility of the state, and what constitutes 'just rehabilitation'. The two most influential theoretical models (which have not been developed specifically in the context of India but are widely applicable) are those of Scudder and Cernea. Scudder states that the goal of dam-induced resettlement should be that both the resettled and host populations become project beneficiaries. This means that,

'The income and living standards of the large majority must improve to the extent that such improvement is obvious both to themselves and to external evaluators' (Scudder 2005). To achieve this objective, he suggests reliance on his four-stage model. 'Briefly, the four stages are characterised by planning; efforts by the re-settlers to cope and to adapt following removal; economic development and community formation within resettlement areas; and handing over and incorporation'. According to him, the responsibility for successful resettlement is not a one-shot affair—'at minimum, it should be implemented as a two-generation process' (Scudder 2005). However, this model had limited application as it was developed initially to analyse voluntary displacement, and was not intended to apply to those resettlement operations that failed to complete the last two stages.

World Bank sociologist Michael Cernea developed the highly influential Impoverishment Risks and Reconstruction Model (IRR) of rehabilitation. He believes that 'targeted measures – economic, technical, legal and cultural — must be undertaken to orient from the outset the planning of resettlement towards the reconstruction of livelihood, so as to prevent impoverishment'. When the state takes up a project entailing displacement, 'the people who will be displaced are subjected to huge risks, typically without their knowledge, participation or consent' (Cernea 1997). Cernea in his 'impoverishment risk reconstruction' (IRR) model, contended that *'all forced displacements are prone to major socio-economic risks, but not fatally condemned to succumb to them'*. Cernea argued that although there is a high possibility of potential impoverishment, such transformation is avoidable. He outlined three core components of the relocation process, namely 'risk, impoverishment, and reconstruction' and argued that a reconstruction process that takes measures to deal with 'risks' could defy 'impoverishment'. He has outlined eight impoverishment risks—landlessness, joblessness, homelessness, marginalisation, food insecurity, increased morbidity, loss of access to common property resources and community disarticulation (Cernea 1997).

Cernea's hypothesis is that the state can reverse the risks by the following reconstructive actions:

- from landlessness to land-based resettlement;
- from joblessness to re-employment;
- from food insecurity to safe nutrition;
- from homelessness to house reconstruction;
- from increased morbidity to better health-care;
- from social disarticulation, marginalisation and deprivation of common assets, to community
- Reconstruction and social inclusion.

Against this background, Cernea defines clearly the role of the state for rehabilitation, "The state assumes a responsibility when it forces people to relocate and it has a responsibility for not leaving them impoverished. For the state, the recovery of re-settlers' livelihoods is first a matter of political will and financial resources. Resource allocation is a political matter, not just an economic one. My simple argument holds that, because government agencies employ the weight of the state and the force of the law to impose expropriation and displacement, it is incumbent upon the same government to also enable those displaced to get back on their feet and benefit from the development for the sake of which they are displaced". (Cernea 1999)

Therefore, what these development models require are precise policy guidelines and legal and institutional mechanisms required to secure the goals of just rehabilitation such as sustainable livelihoods and an equitable sharing of project benefits.

Development and Displacement—the Road Ahead

Historically all development projects have caused displacement and displacement has been a saga of marginalisation, yet, given the growing needs of modern society, all projects cannot be stopped. What is required is to consider the larger implications of displacement while assessing the viability- social, environment and economic, of a project as a pre-emptive measure to tackle the problems. Though cost-benefit analysis is undertaken presently too, but the credibility of the methods adopted is questionable as the authorities fail to evaluate the social and environmental costs. The "public" who is going to be affected is never consulted before finalising the projects and the oft-mentioned formula of 'people's participation', which has become part of almost every project document, has become a travesty of people's lives. The condition of all projects, completed or those in pipeline, have been same from Bhakra Nangal on Sutluj to Indira Sagar on Godavari.

The road from displacement to resettlement and eventually rehabilitation is a long one. Thus, the complexities and difficulties of involuntary resettlement will still be experienced. Every major programme that necessitates resettlement must therefore explore all options to avoid displacement, if possible, or reduce the number of people affected.

Development dilemmas do have solutions. The need of the hour is to find them. Development is necessary and inevitable but its social costs are not inevitable. Hence, the social costs should be reduced purposively and mitigated systematically and if it cannot be eliminated fully, they should be carried by the society and not just the victimised group.

Bibliography

Burman, B.K. (1993) *'Tribal Population : Interface of Historical Ecology'* In Mrinal Miri (ed.) '*Continuity and Change in Tribal Society*' Indian Institute of Advanced Study, Shimla, pp. 175-216.

Cernea, M.M. (1997) *'The Risks and Reconstruction Model for Resettling Displaced Populations'*, World Development, Vol. 25, No. 10.

——————— (1999) *'Why Economic Analysis is Essential to Resettlement: A Sociologist's View'* in Michael M. Cernea (ed.) (1999) 'The Economic of Involuntary Resettlement: Questions and Challenges'. World Bank, Washington D.C.

——————— (2000) *'Risks, Safeguards and Reconstruction: A Model for Population Displacement and Resettlement'* in Risks and Reconstruction: Experiences of Resettlers and Refugees. The World Bank, Washington D.C.

Colson, E (1971), *"The Social Consequences of Resettlement: The Impact of the Kariba Resettlement Upon the Gwembe Tonga"*, Manchester University Press, Manchester.

D'Souza, B and Dakshayani Madangopal (2010), *"Marginal Zones Development-induced Displacement in Mumbai"* BFC Publishing House, Bangalore.

Fernandes, W. (1991). '*Power and Powerlessness: Development and displacement of tribals'*, Social Action, Vol. 41, pp. 243-270.

Fernandes and Vijay Paranjpye (eds.) (1997) '*Rehabilitation Policy and Law in India: A Right to Livelihood'*, Indian Social Institute, New Delhi.

Kothari, Smithu (1996) '*Whose Nation? The Displaced as Victims of Development'*, Economic and Political Weekly, Vol. 31, No. 24. June 15, pp. 1476-85.

Mehta, Lyla (ed.) (2009) *'Displaced by Development: confronting Marginalisation and Gender Injustice'*, Sage Publications, New Delhi.

Mishra, Om Prakash (ed.) (2004) *'Forced Migration in the South Asian Region: Displacement, Human Rights and Conflict Resolution'*, Manak Publications, Delhi.

Murickan, Jose (2003) '*Development-Induced Displacement: Case of Kerala'*, Rawat Publications, Jaipur.

Oxfam (1997) '*Safeguarding Standards in Resettlement: Oxfam's Recommendations on the Proposed Revision to the World Bank's Policy on Involuntary Resettlement'*, Oxfam UK/I Policy Department.

Padel, F; Das, Samarendra (2008) *'Orissa's Highland Clearances: the Reality Gap in R&R'*, Social Change, Vol. 38, No. 4.

Parasuraman, S (1999) '*Development Dilemma: Displacement in India*', Macmillan Press, London.

Parasuraman, S. (1993) *'Impact of Displacement by Development Projects on Women in India*', ISS Working Paper Series No. 159, Institute of Social Studies, The Hague.

Reddy, I U B (1993) *'Displacement and Rehabilitation'*, Mittal Publications, New Delhi.

Roy, Arundhati (1999) '*The Greater Common Good: The Human Costs of Big Dams*'. *Frontline*, June 4.

Sainath, P. (1996). *'Everybody loves a good drought'*. Penguin Books, New Delhi.

Scudder, T (2005) '*The Future of Large Dams: Dealing with Social, Environmental and Political Costs'*. Earthscan, London.

Singh, S. (1997). *'Taming the waters. The political economy of large dams in India'*. Oxford University Press, Delhi.

Thukral, E. G. (1992) *'Big Dams, Displaced Peoples: Rivers of Sorrow, Rivers of Joy'*, Sage Publications, New Delhi.

Thukral, E.G. (1996) *'Development, Displacement and Rehabilitation: Locating Gender'*, Economic and Political Weekly, Vol. 31, No. 24, Mumbai, June 15.

Verma, Manish Kumar (2004) *'Development, Displacement and Resettlement'*, Rawat Publications, Jaipur.

Web References

http://www.adb.org/Documents/Policies/Involuntary_Resettlement/involuntary_resettlement.pdf accessed on April 9 2010

http://www.worldbank.org/resettlement accessed on April 9 2010

http://daccessdds.un.org/doc/UNDOC/GEN/G97/129/72/PDF/G9712972.pdf?OpenElement accessed on april 12 2010

http://www.dams.org/kbase/thematic/tr11.htm, accessed 10 April, 2010

References

1. Cernea, M (1996), 'Bridging the Research Divide: Studying Development Oustees'. In D'Souza, B and Dakshayani Madangopal (2010), 'Marginal Zones Development-induced Displacement in Mumbai' BFC, Bangalore.

2. D'Souza, B and Dakshayani Madangopal (2010), 'Marginal Zones Development induced Displacement in Mumbai' BFC, Bangalore.

3. Words of Jawahar Lal Nehru, In Roy, Arundhati (1999) 'The Greater Common Good: The Human Costs of Big Dams'. Frontline, June 4.

4. D'Souza, B and Dakshayani Madangopal (2010), 'Marginal Zones Development induced Displacement in Mumbai' BFC, Bangalore.

5. Fernandes and Vijay Paranjpye (eds.) (1997) 'Rehabilitation Policy and Law in India: A Right to Livelihood', Indian Social Institute, New Delhi. In Murickan, Jose (2003) 'Development-Induced Displacement: Case of Kerala', Rawat Publications, Jaipur.

6. Drydyk, J (1999), "Development-induced Displacement and John Rawls' General Conception of Justice", Ethical Studies, Dept of Philosophy, Carleton University. In D'Souza, B and Dakshayani Madangopal (2010), "Marginal Zones Development-induced Displacement in Mumbai" BFC, Bangalore.

18

Democratic Decentralisation and Participation in the Context of Local Governance in the Fifth Scheduled Areas

Dambarudhar Garada

Abstract

The new development paradigm that has emerged since mid-1980s, as a modification to the second phase of post-colonial development debate, which has placed a high value to local governance and community participation in delivering development. This new paradigm, while on the one hand emphasise issues of inclusion, participation, and devolution of decision-making, on the other has created scope for structural reforms that provide an appropriate institutional framework to reduce the imposition of state institutions. What has emerged in the process is that of decentralisation, which tries to fulfill the institutional void at the local level to ensure inclusion, participation, local service delivery and better developmental outcomes. The increasing insistence on inclusion and community participation for delivering developmental services in late 1980s– partly owing to the inherent inadequacies of the central state to deliver such services – has made it clear that democracy, despite its promises of devolution of power and accountable government, does not by itself benefit the poor, the under-privileged, and disadvantaged sections of society, which have long faced social, economic and political exclusion. It also became apparently clear that community participation at local level for provisioning of developmental services could not be achieved in an otherwise democratic set up, in the absence of proper institutional mechanisms to practice it. In its attempts for democratisation, the Indian state enacted the 73rd Constitutional

Amendment Act in 1993, making provisions for devolution of power to the local levels, and gave a constitutional status to the Panchayats. Further, in its commitment to introduce the process of decentralisation reforms in the tribal regions of the country, Government of India in December 1997 enacted the 'The Provisions of the Panchayats (Extension to Scheduled Areas) Act' (PESA Act), which paved the way for inclusion and self-governance in the nine states that come under the 5th Schedule of the Indian Constitution. Thus, Decentralised governance is an essential pre-requisite for inclusive governance, which enhance the people to participate more directly in the governance process. In a democratic state decentralisation is believed to strengthen the governance by engaging people in decision-making process. With this backdrop, the study has been made an attempt to examine the functioning of Gram Sabha and political participation of the tribal people in the democratic local governance in the Scheduled Areas in Orissa context.

Key words: Decentralisation, Governance, Participation, Representation.

Introduction

One of the most recent trends in the field of democratic development is inclusion the hitherto excluded group through increasing local participation in decision-making in the course of democratic decentralisation. The development approaches of 1990s were emphasised on macro-economic growth as the only means to successful development. Later the focus shifted to a more people-centered development with emphasis laid upon the involvement of people in their own development. Because the idea of development is to facilitate benefit to the people those who are not on the receiving end of the benefits. So in this regard democracy works as the agency through which the development can be possible. The idea of development is possible through democracy only when more participation from the local level will come about. Therefore increasing local participation in decision-making through decentralisation will enhance transparency, accountability and the effectiveness of development (Bryld 2001).

Despite the development initiative of 1990s to inclusion and community participation in delivering developmental services has repeatedly failed due to the inherent inadequacies of the central state to deliver such services. Conversely, the introduction of devolution of power does not benefit the under-privileged, and disadvantaged sections of society, which have long faced social, economical and political exclusion. The objectives of Decentralisation in the democratic set up could not be achieved due to the failure of proper institutional mechanism. The incapability of democracy to take the poor and marginalised section of people along with the development process and ensure participation often originates because of the very nature of liberal representative democracy, which has so far emphasised on procedural aspects instead of a substantive aspect of democracy. Procedural aspects like periodic elections, electing representatives have always gained priority in liberal democracy in contrast to substantive aspects such as citizen participation in collective decision making. The neglect of substantive aspects like participatory decision-making in liberal democracy has paved the way for further reforming the existing democracy, which Castaneda (1994) termeds as '*democratisation of democracy*'. In the due course of the '*Democratisation of Institutions*' with progressive inclusion of the hitherto excluded sections of society through decentralisation reforms, therefore, has emerged as the new governance paradigm to address the drawbacks of liberal representative democracy, provide with a platform to realise community participation for providing developmental services; and tackling the persisting problems of exclusion, poverty and powerlessness.

Acknowledging the importance of the Participation and Representation, the study was attempted to explore the extent of participation and representation of the scheduled tribe in the local self-governance in the Scheduled Areas of Orissa as enshrined in the PESA (Panchayat Extension to Scheduled Areas).

The empirical data for the study was conducted in two Panchayat of Rayagada district in Orissa. The selected Panchayat for the study is reserved for ST (Scheduled Tribe) and headed by male and female. The two Panchayat was selected on the basis of purposive sampling, as both the Panchayat fall under the PESA Act. Each Panchayat consist 11 elected representatives including the President of the Panchayat that account 22 elected representatives. All the 22 elected representatives were taken as the respondents for the purpose of the study. Both the two Panchayat are heavily tribal concentrated at the rate of 60 and 93 per cent respectively. Both primary and secondary sources will be used to elicit relevant data for the study. The secondary sources will include: Books, journals, relevant literature and other academic document in the concerned area scanning various government documents and Panchayat official records. A combination of, interview, focused group discussion and case study method was used for the proposed study. The primary data from the field was collected with the help of a structured and a semi-structured interview schedule. The structured schedule was used to interview the elected members of the chosen Gram Panchayats. In order to elicit information relating to the socio-economic, political and decision-making profiles of the respondents.

This paper has been organised into five sections, following this introduction, which posed the background for the paper and discussed the objectives and methodology of research. The second section deals with the theoretical approaches to the proposed study. The third sections engage in a conceptual discussion of participation, representation and decentralisation. The fourth sections deal with the Indian context of decentralisation. The last section critically engages in the practice of decentralisation with empirical evidence.

Theoretical Approach

Democracy process is a necessary and proper vehicle for achieving the social justice. Democratic politics entails a rule of law, promotion of civil and political liberty. The practice of thin democracy sidelined the marginalised section of people from the very process of inclusion democracy. Because the people's representative take vague stands on certain issues and thus recipient of the benefit of inclusionary democracy have a little relation to the policy process until the next election (Young 2000). Conversely our democracy contains 'structural inequalities 'such as inequality of wealth, social and economic power, and access to knowledge, status etc.; and this socio-economic inequality produced political inequality. The structural socio-economic inequality thus often operates to exclude or marginalised the voice of the people in the democratic process. This thin democratic practice prompted the questions of inclusion which comes from basic political right, from opportunity to participate and equal citizenship in politics. Therefore the political mobilisation within formal democratic institutions is usually the only realistic options for disadvantaged people and their allies to improve social relations and institutions. Robert Dahl (1989) argues that historically there have been two transformations of democracy. These transformations have brought about different models of democratic governance and different interpretations of the concept of democracy. By the first transformation Dahl refers to the emergence of the classical model of democracy in Greek city-states, most notably in Athens, that took place during the fifth century BC. The classical Athenian democracy was based on citizens' direct participation in decision-making in popular assemblies, and the selection of certain public officials by a lot. Until the 19th century, the Athenian model epitomised the way in which the concept of the democracy was interpreted. The second transformation refers to the emergence of modern representative democracy in nation states in the late 18th and in the 19th century. The modern interpretation of democracy evolved especially during the 19th century. The central feature of this conception is the popular election of the representatives who make political decisions on behalf of the represented.

In order to understand the importance of representation in the modern form of representative democracy it is necessary to distinguish the differences between the Athenian model of direct democracy and the modern representative democracy. First, the classical model of direct democracy was very much concentrated in the small city-state, whereas the modern democracy concentrated in large geographical areas. In this context it is virtually problem to direct participation by the citizen in the decision-making process. Secondly, in the classical model citizenship was not defined exclusively. Some segments of the population were not included in the political process as they were not having the political equality. But in modern democracy citizenship has defined absolutely, where inclusion is the preface and all the citizen has equal rights and opportunity to participate in the democratic governance process what Robert Dahl (1989) referred as '*equal worth of individual*'.

Yet again representation in the discourse of contemporary democracy has been challenged by an alternative politics from '*politics of ideas*' to '*politics of presence'* (Phillips 1995). The politics of 'ideas' in the liberal democracy is merely a difference. The difference in terms of policies, preferences, ideas share and represent by the representative on behalf of the represented. In this context the politics of presence have the solid existence in the contemporary politics and has shifted and demands for equal representation, political equality and political inclusion of groups that have come to see themselves as marginalised or excluded.

The contrast within the Athenian model of direct democracy and liberal representative democracy, 'deliberative democracy' has taken place as the alternative means to promote the just equal society in many developed countries. It would be wrong to assume that the deliberative democrats reject the ideas of Representative or participatory democracy rather they insist deliberative democracy as the alternative means through which citizen can hold their representatives accountable. The deliberative democrats argue that greater participation not only gives more citizens the chance to enjoy the benefits of taking part in deliberation, it also can help develop the virtues of citizenship, encourage citizens to consider political issues in a more public spirited mode.

Deliberative democracy affirms the need to justify decisions made by the citizen and their representatives. In a deliberative democracy it is expected either from the representative or any other authority to justify the laws they would impose on one another. Therefore in a democratic setup the representative gives reasons for their action and respond the reasons that citizen give in return. Citizen response in the sense that whether the ideas imposed on them by the representative has any influence on them or not. Thompson and Gutmann (2004) termed this relationship as the '*reason-giving'* process. Therefore, in the democratic process of governance citizen should not be treated as merely as an object, or as passive subjects to be ruled but as an autonomous agent who take part in the governance of their own society with active participation. This reason giving action of the representative produces a justifiable decision and the value of mutual respect.

In other words Deliberative democracy focuses on the communicative processes of opinion and will-formation that precede voting. Accountability replaces consent as the conceptual core of legitimacy. A legitimate political order is one that could be justified to all those living under its laws. Thus, accountability is primarily understood in terms of "*giving an account*" of something that is, publicly articulating, explaining, and most importantly justifying public policy. Although theorists of deliberative democracy vary as to how critical they are of existing representative institutions, deliberative democracy is not usually thought of as an alternative to representative democracy. It is rather an expansion of representative democracy (Chambers 2003). In addition to that the idea of representation may also be justified from the normative perspective of the theory of deliberative democracy. The basic normative idea of deliberative democracy is that political decisions should be based on public discussions among autonomous, equal and rational citizens.

Conceptual Framework of the Study

Representation

The paradox of contemporary democracy is constituted by the disjuncture between democracy and representation. This division has been propelled to the forefront of the political agenda by the incapacity of the representatives to represent the popular will (Chandhoke 2009). This disjuncture between the two crucial concepts becomes a focal point of the current discourse of democracy on the concept of political representation. Political presence or empowerment through representation is crucial in liberal democratic set up, principally because of three important reasons. First, most societies are large, heterogeneous and complex which does not permit to direct participation. Second, demands, perspective and interest are plural due to the diverse nature of societies as well as conflicting. Third, the highly complex nature of modern legislation and administration, which demand expertise and deal multifarious issues, disallow direct control over policy. Therefore interest needs to be present by an agent who mediates between the two basic protagonists of the democratic text, the citizen and the state. For these reasons the representatives are the key player in the democratic system (Chadhoke 2009). Thus the concept of representation has taken place the context of power relation among the representative and the represented. Consequently representation is a relation between two people where the representative plays the key role in a democratic set up withholding authority to perform the various actions of represented. Apart from the normative postulation of representation the 'politics of voice' however pose problems for the concept of representation. Are representatives capable of advocating the interest of that section of the constituency to which they do not belong? Can, for example, a male representative puts forth the interest of women? Is it possible for him to understand women life experience before or as he represents their needs and interest? Can an upper class or caste representative do justice to the interest of lower class or caste? Because it has been alleged that representatives bodies failed to mirror the plurality of a given society and fall short of representing the interest of the marginalised section of society (Young 2000). Thereby the concept 'representation' becomes a stubborn problem because it would seem hardly anyone can represent anyone else.

Further Anna Phillips has also argued that those representatives who are able to share the social characteristics of their disadvantage constituency are better advocates of their interest. Such agents are able to understand better the problems that bedevil particular categories of society (Philips 1995). Further, Helena Catt (1999) distinguishes two types of representation, i.e., delegation and trustee. The role of delegates is to act on behalf of represented. Trustee refers the role of representatives as to make 'good' and 'wise' decision for everyone. The central argument of Catts' representative democracy is the idea of people's power; because they choose the representatives and those representatives are regularly accountable to the voters for the decision that they make for the collective. Representatives are meant to make decisions for population, either as delegates with instruction or as trustees relied upon to.

Apart from above conceptual work of different political scientist, Mansbridge works hold an important insight for contemporary discussion of democratic representation. Mansbridge (2003) in her article '*Rethinking Representation*', Mansbridge identified four forms of representation in modern democracies: Promissory, Anticipatory, Gyroscopic and Surrogacy representation. Promissory representation is a form of representation in which representative are to be evaluated by the promises they make to constituency during the election campaign. In the promissory representation the representative bound to follow the instruction and work for the interest of the represented. In Anticipatory representation representative focus on what they think their constituents will reward in the next election and not on what they promised during their election campaign of the previous election. Thus, anticipatory representation challenges those who understand accountability as primarily a retrospective activity. In gyroscopic representation, representatives 'look within' to derive from their own experience conception of interest and principles to serve as a basis for their action. Finally, surrogate representation occurs when a legislator represents constituents outside of their district, where the representatives and the constituents do not have any electoral relationships. Each of these different forms generates a different normative criterion by which representatives should be assessed.

Corresponding to the above theoretical literature the concept of political representation seems to be as an advocacy on behalf of the underrepresented. In the deliberative democracy advocacy play the key role to deliver the justice in favour of the marginalised section of society. Representation in deliberative democracy emphasises on opinion and consent formation.

Participation

Participation has been an old associate of developmental discourse. Its meaning kept changing along with the meaning of development. As development changes from service delivery to mean of empowerment and then to governance, so did participation from effective and efficient ways of delivery of development to ownership of development through active engagement and paying for developmental benefits to finally rights to engage and demand accountability. It can be clearly differentiated the shift of the meaning of participation from the developmental discourse to the active engagement by the citizen in the process of governance and democracy (Cornwall 2000).

By the late 90s, perhaps somewhat in a dialectical response to the growing neutrality of the way that the term participation was being used by powerful development actors, where it began to see the re-emergence in development discourse of participation as a 'right' of citizens rather than 'opportunity' given to 'beneficiaries' and a renewed emphasis on the inclusion of the marginalised in development process (Gaventa 2002). In this sense the idea of participation as a 'rights' also invokes a move from participation of 'beneficiaries' or 'stakeholders' to the more political idea of participation of 'citizen', who themselves bear both rights and responsibilities.

Thus the participation debate begins to enter the governance field and begins to link the participatory development, participatory democracy and participatory governance agenda (Gaventa and Valderrama 1999; Gaventa 2002). Thus the central ideas of participation is to give citizen meaningful role in local government decision that affect them, while accountability means that people will be able to hold local government responsible for how it is affecting them. Together these two processes are what constitute the heart of the 'democratic' component of the democratic local governance (Blair 2000). Political participation in a democracy has a wider implication, which ranges from popular participation in electing representatives to the actual participation of representatives in the process of governance. Earlier the emphasis was on political participation while giving citizens a right to vote disregarded their capabilities in contributing effectively in designing public policy, and regarded that 'it was up to the experts, the professionals, politicians and managers to ensure that citizens' needs are well served' (Richardson 1983). But the idea of participation has been changing over the period of time from 1970s onwards with a new meaning, which distinguished this newly established concept of 'community participation' from that of 'political participation', which includes voting, political parties and lobbying (Cornwall and Gaventa 2000).

With the current preoccupation of most developing countries with policies of decentralisation and democratisation, and more so with the introduction of affirmative action in the last decade, the meaning, nature and scope of public participation has increased considerably. This third wave of participation is posed differently from its first and second waves, where participation was conceptualised as only casting votes in elections and involvement of citizens in policy implementation formed somewhere else (Cornwall and Gaventa 2000). Participation in the 1990s, with the emphasis of reservation policies at the levels of local government, has become both a right in itself and a means for ensuring effective governance, since the twin aims of decentralisation, i.e., deepening democracy and good governance can be achieved by active participation of the people. Participation as is understood today in the context of democratic local government is different from its meaning in the 1970s when the concept meant only involving citizens as users of state-delivered beneficiary programmes. As a political concept as well as a process, participation has now a dynamic implication with the recent policies of devolution, where the people are not only expected to voice their opinions in elections, but also enjoy the power to participate in the actual decision-making process. With greater recognition of civil society and increasing emphasis on good governance, the concept of participation, in democratic local governance, has shifted from 'beneficiary participation in state-delivered programmes to an understanding of participation as a means of holding the state accountable through new forms of governance' (Cornwall and Gaventa 2000).

Defining Decentralisation

One of the most recent trends in the field of democratic development is increasing local participation in decision-making through decentralisation. The democratic politics which intend to be the inclusionary democracy where one of the important components is to increase the scope for citizen participation, maximising the accountability and transparency are seen to be falling short of fulfilling the principles of parliamentary democracy in practice. On account of its many failures, the centralised state everywhere has lost a great deal of legitimacy, and decentralisation is widely believed to promise a range of benefits. It is often suggested as a way of reducing the role of the state in general, by fragmenting central authority and introducing more intergovernmental competition and checks and balances. It is viewed as a way to make government more responsive and efficient (Bardhan 2002). Decentralisation is very much important in the context of local governance because in the democratic country like India the local politicians may have more incentive to use local information than national or provincial politicians, since the local elected members are answerable to the local electorate while the national or state level elected members have wider constituencies, where the local issues may get diluted. Another important rationale for adopting decentralised governance is that when the policy bargaining take place, under decentralisation, locally elected representatives select public goods which is locally suitable for the constituents whereas in the centralised system, policy choices are determined by a legislature consisting of elected representatives from each district, so that conflicts of interest between citizens of different jurisdictions play out in the legislature (Besley and Coate 2000). Another important argument for the adaptation of decentralised governance is that the central states agencies lack the 'time and place knowledge' to implement policies and programmes that reflect people's 'real' needs and preferences (Ostrom et al., 1993: 51). Without any prior knowledge of the local needs the elected representatives formulate policies and programmes for the represented which is either not relevant or become failure due to the administrative apathy. So it is conceivable to entrust the power and control over the governance structure and assign more devolution power to the local authorities and communities.

Decentralisation is a political and economic process that implies fundamentally, a redistribution of power and resources. In this context, Rondinelli (1981) defines decentralisation as the transfer of authority to plan, make decisions and manage public functions from the national level to any individual organisation or agency at the sub-national level. This definition of decentralisation restricts itself to territorial decentralisation, and excludes the question of transfer of authority from central to peripheral organisations. Democratic decentralisation, however, implies more than the downward delegation of authority. Fundamentally, it entails a system of governance in which citizens possess the right to hold the local public officials to account through the use of elections, grievance meetings and other democratic means (Johnson 2003). Hence, the underlying case for democratic decentralisation is an assertion that a more decentralised state apparatus will be more exposed and therefore more responsive to local needs and aspirations (Crook and Sverrisson 2001). This, it is argued, will produce systems of governance that are more effective and accountable to local people (Crook and Manor 1998, Manor 1999).

Democratic Decentralisation in Indian Context

Democracy in India has been instrumental in enabling people to vote every few years and elect their representatives. At various levels, this has brought in political functionaries who have been instrumental in, or have claimed to be instrumental in, providing benefits to their constituents. Representation has largely been related to the benefits that accrue to the constituents, and constituents often relate to their representatives as potential beneficiaries of some form of personal advantage (Inbunnathan 2001). After independence efforts were made to create and strengthen the institutions of local self-governance but all in vain as the issues of people's participation at grass roots level were not taken into serious considerations. Despite the plethora of schemes and massive investment in the rural sector, the rural scenario remained underdevelopment with no infrastructures and basic amnesties (Sisodia 2002).

The disappointment of the first and second wave of development paradigm during the colonised India has pushed up a new development paradigm that has emerged since mid 1980s. The new de-colonised development paradigm as an alteration to the second phase of post colonial development debate has given an important place to local governance and community participation in the heart democracy in delivering development. This new development emphasises on issues of inclusion, participation, and devolution of decision making, and also created scope for structural reforms that provide an appropriate institutional framework to reduce the imposition of state institutions (Veltmeyer 1997). The outcome of the power centralisation and excessive imposition of state institution is decentralisation, which tries to accomplish the institutional barrier at the local level to ensure inclusion, participation, local service delivery and better developmental outcomes.

The increasing persistence on inclusion and community participation for delivering developmental services after six decade of independence – partly owing to the inherent inadequacies of the central state to deliver such services – has made it clear that democracy, despite its promises of devolution of power and accountable government, does not by itself benefit the poor, the under-privileged, and disadvantaged sections of society, which have long faced social, economic and political exclusion. It also became apparently clear that community participation at local level for provisioning of developmental services could not be achieved in an otherwise democratic set up, in the absence of proper institutional mechanisms to practice it. Recognising the need for greater democratisation and progressive inclusion, many governments carried out political reforms ensuring decentralisation to promote empowerment and inclusion. In its attempts for democratisation, the Indian state enacted the 73rd Constitutional Amendment Act in 1993, making provisions for devolution of power to the local levels, and gave a constitutional status to the Panchayats. The new decentralisation efforts were coupled with inclusive policies of reservation of seats for weaker sections such as Scheduled Castes, Scheduled Tribes and women. The institution of Panchayat Raj after the 73rd Amendment Act in it's rejuvenating form seek to achieve the objectives of democratic decentralisation to accelerate socio-economic development and usher in equity and social justice. This change in Indian political system is the result of a growing conviction that the big government cannot achieve growth and development in a society without the people's direct participation and initiative. This opened a new chapter in the history of democratic decentralisation in India, which gave an opportunity to the hitherto excluded categories to raise their voice, and in turn, include themselves in making of decisions that affect their lives. Further, in its commitment to introduce the process of decentralisation reforms in the tribal regions of the country, Government of India in December 1997 enacted the 'The Provisions of the Panchayats (Extension to Scheduled Areas) Act' (PESA Act), which paved the way for inclusion and self governance in the nine states that come under the 5th Schedule of the Indian Constitution.

The concentration of PESA (Panchayat Extension to Scheduled Areas) Act has shifted from development delivery to empowerment; from implementation to planning; from limited involvement to conscious participation (Prabhu 2004). The notion has been changing as regard to the involvement of tribal people in the local-self governance and their level of participation increasing. Because the underlying spirit of the Extension Act is on devolution rather than delegation of powers and authority to Gram Sabha and Panchayats that is the adoption of decentralised participatory democracy in the form of Gram Sabha rather than representative decentralised democracy in the form of Panchayati Raj institutions (Pal 2000). Thus PESA envisaged a radical shift in the balance of power from the state machinery and from economic and political elites, to the community. Despite the seminal legislation the experience of PESA has been tragically affected, because at the end it is the state government who execute all plans and policy. In contrast to the devolution of power to the local governance is debatable in the sense that even though the local governance made any provisions which affects the locality, again the execution power rested on the state government.

Practice of Decentralisation

Representation of the Scheduled Tribe in Local Governance

The local governance in India has been designed in the way that there is an important role for the local people to participate in the functioning of local governance. To participate in the process of local governance, Gram Sabha is the institution where direct democracy is, in principle, possible, with local people being involved developmental activities. However, the direct role of the people has some limitation, and in general, the execution of any policy and plan and functioning of the Panchayats largely depend on the bureaucracy and the elected representatives. In this context the role of the representative is to act as an agent to materialise these needs of people. The study shows that due to too much of external forces the elected representative does not function properly as they becomes the dummy on the hand of elite and some other political forces. It is observed that the representative works under the direction of elite and influential people. The inherent logic of such practice is that during the election the so called elite within the tribal group and non-tribal select the candidates those who are subservient to them. During the election they manage to buy the vote of common people in favour of their preferred candidates in which the election expenditure incurred by this section of people. That forced to the elected representative to work on behalf of the non-tribal and elite within the tribal group. Another factor was observed in the rural politics that the politics in local self-governance has undergone a massive transformation from the political party point of view. The political party also playing key role from controlling representatives to manage the Panchayat affairs. Political parties also in the similar fashion manage get candidate within the party to contest in the election and after getting elected the representative has to follow the party guidelines. In the sense that to whom benefit should be given, to who accommodate or excluded from the beneficiary programme is decided by the party functionaries in the Panchayat/ village level. Putting the view of Pitkins (1967) concept of representation which means acting in the interest of represented in a manner responsive to them has two specific dimensions, one is 'interest' and the second is 'responsiveness'. In the context of the practice of decentralisation in the scheduled areas it seems the representative represent the interest of the few sections of people and responsible towards the few on account of their activities. Hence it can be argued that representatives are not only a dummy/puppet in the hands of the few but also represent the voice of the few rather represent the constituents who voted them to represent their voice in the local governance.

Second, communication/interaction is important in the representative democracy in which the representative represents the voice of represented in the forum of local governance. Until and unless well communication between the representative and represented the problem of the localities cannot be sorted out. Interaction ensures that representatives are aware of what the people want, and development, therefore, would be more focused on the interests of the constituencies. But this principle is far away from the practice. From the field it was observed that the interaction between the representative and the citizen hardly take place. Once the representative is getting elected they never appear in the public domain or their respective constituencies. Most of the representative cited the reason they disappear from the public domain or their constituency is that as they do not meet the expectation of people with regard to the developmental activities of the constituency. Interestingly it was found that they vanish from the public domain due the cause of interrelation between the politicisation of Panchayat affairs and power. Politicisations in terms of the intervention of the political party in day to day function of the local governance. The political parties disrupt the Panchayat proceedings if the decisions of the local governance do not swing in favour of them or if the local functionaries do not get any share out of the decisions. Then they politicise the whole activities of Panchayat on the basis of party politics. On the other hand devolution of power to the Panchayat is not sufficient to meet the expectation of people. Because Panchayat alone cannot take decision to execute the plan and programme, for that the consent has to get from the Panchayat Samities (Block). Conversely, the elected representative has not such power to execute the developmental programme of their own. Again they need to contact the higher authority for implementing such programmes who always puppets in the hand of the few dominant sections of people. This structure of power relation among them does not permit the representatives to bargain benefits for their respective constituency, which always keep them out of track from the public sphere or from constituencies.

At the same time a considerable amount of representatives of the Panchayats indicated that they had not been interested in politics when they contested in the Panchayat elections. Compulsions of various kinds swayed these persons to contest. For instance, most women file their candidature for election in local governance not out of their own will. They were more or less compelled to contest by male members of their families, political worker, and some dominant group of the village, which led to *de facto* representation by their husband and the political functionaries of village level. The *de facto* representation creates a gap between representatives and the represented. In such a case compulsion representation they may lose interest in carrying out their functions as representatives. These activities of the representatives question the normative appeal of the ideas of representation from the 'politics of ideas' to 'politics of presence' and the very nature of representative democracy within the sphere of local governance.

Attendance in Gram Sabha/Panchayat Meetings

Participation of representative in the local governance was assessed by examining the following factors such as: attendance in Gram Panchayat meetings, participation in decision making in various developmental activities, participation in selection of beneficiaries, attendance in Gram Sabha, etc. An attempt has been made to know about the number of Panchayat meetings held in a year and their participation. The representative of the two Panchayat viewed different opinions regarding the Panchayat meeting. Out of the total respondents only a small proportion does not attend the Panchayat meeting. Even though they are not attending Panchayat meeting regularly, however, the Panchayat record shows their regular attendance at the Panchayat meeting. Further it was found that during the Panchayat meeting even the quorum procedure is not followed. It was found during the interaction of their non-participation in the meeting that due to lack of information is the major cause stated by the respondents. Other causes they revealed that as most of the elected representatives are from agricultural labour and non-agriculture background, so they cannot afford to lose a single day. Further the representatives stated the reason to not lose a single day is that; first, though they attend the Panchayat meeting the incentive providing to them per meeting is not enough to meet the expenses of the day. Secondly, in the Panchayat meeting the representative has got nothing to do, because the officials need their physical presence. Moreover the officials inform the representative only for namesake. Here it can be said that the tribal economy is playing important role which usually do not permit them to participate. Both the agriculture and non-agriculture labourer need to go out from village for searching livelihood option for everyday.

Participation in Sitting Agenda

One of the primary tasks of the Panchayat is to conduct the monthly meetings with regard to identify the specific problems of the localities and sort out it with collective decisions. The agenda of the Panchayat meetings includes; identifying beneficiaries of the proposed developmental programme, initiative new development programmes, identifying location and awarding contracts. The study shows that the elected representatives merely raised the problem of their respective constituencies. Only the Sarpancha was found to be comparatively vocal from among the total representatives. During the interaction it was found that the Sarpancha participate and decide the agenda not by his own choice rather instruction given by the local influential people. Though the representative comes to participate they hardly raised their voice. Their participation is only passive in nature. They never got the opportunity to speak out their constituent's problem; it is only the Sarpancha and some other influential people who dominate the proceedings. Low attendance at Panchayat meetings and limited capacity to raise issues often came in the way of discussing the problems of Panchayat, and in turn in the process of decision-making. Simply sitting and listening to the proceedings of the meetings and nodding their heads have and nodding their heads has been the form of participation for most of the representatives.

Participation in Developmental Activities and Decision Making

Participation is vital in the representative democracy, where the representatives mediate between the institutions and people. To examine this aspect various activities has taken into account. Participation of the representatives in those activities found to be very low. Most of the respondents cited that they do not take part in any developmental programme due to the monopoly of Panchayat officials. The officials never respond their demand and citing the reason that there is no fund sanction for the particular activities. Whenever the representative puts their demand before the Sarpancha and Panchayat officials they divert the main issues try to manipulate other unnecessary things. As a result the representatives do not show interest to participate in developmental activities. The representatives feel that if there is no response at all their opinion then it is meaningless to participate in the decision-making process. On the other hand they are not getting information of regarding the meetings and venue which clearly spell out the communication gap between the local representative and Panchayat officials. Moreover the attitude of Panchayat officials and Sarpancha is questionable. It was found that the attitude of Panchayat officials and Sarpancha is not helpful. They co-operate those representatives who work under their direction and settle out their constituent's problem. They consider the views of the respondents if he/she is somehow influential and affiliated with a political party. These are the factors which forced the representative for their non-participation in the developmental activities.

Gender and Participation

It is found that the attendance at Panchayat meetings of women representative is pathetic. In both the Panchayat not even a single woman has attended the meeting except the women Sarpancha. During the interview they cited several reasons for absence in meetings. All of them said that languages and venues are the barrier for them to attend at the meeting. It was found during the investigation that the venue of the meeting is shifting time to time as per the officials and other influential people's convenience. This move of venue sometimes creates confusion and impediment among the women representative to attend the Panchayat meeting at the cost of their family and household work. Language is another factor in their absence in the Panchayat meetings. The majority of the women representative of the two Panchayat is not fluent in state language which poses the problem in their participation. As the Panchayat officials are from non-tribal background, which is the reason that they feel shy in front of them to speak. In addition to that the agenda and resolution are being written in the state prescribed language which they do not understand. As a reason they do not speak up anything with regard to the proceedings of the meeting. It is also observed that due to the presence of their in-laws usually they do not come forward to attend the meetings. Thirdly, household work is another factor of their absences in the meeting as they have to look after the family. On the other hand economy of the tribal household also expect from the women. Women in the tribal societies look after the economic activities and other household work during the absence of their family head. These are the major factor contribute to keep aside the representative from local self-governance.

Concluding Remarks

The above analysis of representation and participation in the two Gram Panchayat of Orissa described in a somewhat unenthusiastic manner reveals that devolution of power after the commencement of the 73rd Amendment Act and further the PESA act could not help the scheduled tribe representatives to perform as better representatives in their constituency. The findings however contrast with conception of Sen's (1999) definition of democracy as '*public discussion*'. The study shows that intuitional bias restricts the elected representatives and the public to access in the public domain which is the reason for the failure of public discussion. The local self-governance is lagging behind Sen's approach to people who are most affected by a decision should make the decision, where only few takes decisions on behalf of the majority. The practice of decentralisation in the local self-governance in the Scheduled areas has three major problems, namely, *reciprocity, publicity, and accountability.* This is why the purpose of deliberative democracy has not been achieved. Reciprocity prescribes that before making any proposals the representative should offer justification and consultation to their constituencies. But the ground realities are something different which need to be addressed. The study shows that there is no fair deal between the representative and their constituents. The idea of publicity in the context of local governance is to provide the information to the constituents but the study shows that the representatives do not provide the information regarding the future course of action. Even they do not disclose the venue of the meeting for which some of the representatives failing to participate in the important meetings. The third problem in the scheduled areas is accountability, where the elected representatives are not accountable of their functions. Most of the representatives do not hold any face to face interaction. Apart from the above issues, the study reveals the fact that limited participation of the scheduled tribe representative in Panchayat activities impeded the process of representation. The negligible participation of the scheduled tribe representative is blocking the way towards making inclusion in Panchayat of Orissa. The absence of active participation of the scheduled tribe representative through the decentralisation is an important factor for the failure of the local-self governance. Besides their backwardness in terms of education, information, awareness, etc. failed to identify their interests, despite having structural arrangements to pursue those interests.

References

Bardhan, P., 2002. Decentralisation of governance and development. *Journal of Economic Perspectives,* 16 (4), 185-205.

Besley, Timothy and Stephen, C., 2000. *Centralised versus decentralised provision of local Public goods: A Political Economy Analysis*, Unpublished Paper, London School of Economics.

Blair, H., 2000. Participation and accountability at the periphery: Democratic local governance in six countries. *World Development*, 28 (1), 21-39.

Catt, H., 1999, *Democracy in practice*. London: Routledge.

Castaneda, J. G. (1994): *Utopia Unarmed: The Latin American Left after the Cold War,* New York: Vintage Books.

Chambers, S., 2003. Deliberative democratic theory. *Annual Review of Political Science,* 6, 307-326.

Chandhoke, N., 2009. Participation, representation and democracy in contemporary India. *American Behavioural Scientist*, 52 (6), 807-825, Sage Publication.

Cornwall, A., 2000. Bridging the gap? 'Good governance', citizenship and rights. SIDA studies, 2, 60-68.

Cornwall, A. and J., Gaventa, 2000. From users and choosers to makers and shapers: repositioning participation in social policy. *IDS Bulletin*, 31 (4), 50–62.

Crook, Richard, C. and Manor, J., 1998. *Democracy and decentralisation in South Asia and West Africa*. Cambridge: Cambridge University Press.

Crook, R. and A. S. Sverrisson (2001): '*Decentralisation and Poverty Alleviation in Developing Countries: A Comparative Analysis or, is West Bengal Unique*?', *IDS Working Paper 130,* Institute for Development Studies, Sussex.

Dahl, R.A., 1989. *Democracy and its critics*. London: Yale University Press.

Dryzek, S., 2000. *Deliberative democracy and beyond.* Oxford: Oxford University Press.

Gaventa, J., 2002. Exploring citizenship, participation and accountability, in making rights real: Exploring citizenship, participation and accountability, IDS bulletin, 33 (2), 1-11.

Gaventa, J and Valderrama, C., 1999. Participation, citizenship and local governance. Background Paper, Conference: Strengthening Participation in Local governance, Brighton: institute of Development Studies.

Gutmann, A. and Thompson, D., 2004. *Why deliberative democracy*? Princeton: Princeton University Press.

I, Anand, 2001. Representation and accountability in local government: The panchayats of Karnataka. Working Paper, 96, Bangalore: ISEC.

Johnson, C., 2003. Decentralisation in India: poverty, politics and Panchayati raj. Working Paper 199, London: Overseas Development Institute.

Litvack, J. J, Ahmad and Bird, R., 1998. Rethinking decentralisation in developing countries. *Sector Studies Series,* Washington, D.C.: The World Bank.

Luckham, R., Goetz, A.M. and Kaldor, M., 2000. Democratic institutions and politics in contexts of inequality, poverty, and conflict: A conceptual framework. *IDS Working Paper*, 104, Brighton: Institute of Development Studies.

Manor, J., 1999. The political economy of democratic decentralisation. *Development Series,* Washington DC: World Bank.

Mansbridge, J., 2003. Rethinking representation. *American Political Science Review*, 97 (4), 515-28.

Ostrom, L., Schroeder and Wynne, S., 1993. *Institutional incentives and sustainable development: Infrastructure policies in perspective*. Oxford University Press.

Phillips, A., (1995): *The politics of presence*, New York: Clarendon.

Prabhu, P., 2004. PESA and the illusions of tribal self-governance. *Combat Law*, 2 (5).

Rondinelli, Dennis, 1981. "Government Decentralisation in Comparative Perspective: Theory and Practice in Developing Countries." *International Review of Administrative Science.*

Rondinelli, D. and Cheema, G.S., 1984. Decentralisation in developing countries: A review of recent experiences. *World Bank Staff Working Papers*, 581, Washington, D. C.

Young, I. M., 2000, *Inclusion and Democracy*. Oxford: Oxford University Press.

Veltmeyer, Henry, 1997. 'Latin America in the New World Order', *Canadian Journal of Sociology*, 22 (2): 207 – 29.

19

Concept of Development: Development and its Effects on Adivasis in Andhra Pradesh

V. Rajunayak

In this paper, I begin with a brief discussion on the concept of development and how the other scholars viewed the concept of development in a critical perspective. The main focuss of this paper is to look at developmental projects such as dams and coalmines which effect the Adivasi life in Telangana region. I will discuss the developmental implications on Adivasis and How the concept of development displaces the Adivasis from their habitations.

Introduction

I begin with a short poem "Displacement" by Vadtya Pantulu Naik published in *The Hindu Literary Review* on July 7, 2013. In his poem Naik laments the plight of the Banjara women:

For years now…
Without getting down where she is headed
Displaced from where she is seated
She is continuing to board the bus,
Giving way to others and getting down! (*The Hindu,* 2013)

This poem has been written on the Banjara Hills, a posh locality in Hyderabad now and Telangana in state. It is a metaphor of the development, amidst the disparities and inequalities.

Development is not purely an economic phenomenon, but rather a multi-dimensional process involving reorganisation and reorientation of entire economic and social system of nation and its people. Thus, development is process of improving the quality of all human lives raising peoples' living levels, i.e., incomes and consumption, medical services, and education through relevant growth process. In his book *State, Society, and Tribes: Issues in Post-Colonial India,* Virginius Xaxa states that:

Rapid advances have been made at the cost of natural resources. The greater the development, the greater the destruction of the natural resources. Increasing realisation of the danger of unchecked ecological and environmental damage has prompted a renewed interest in the conservation of environment and even its regeneration (101).

H.W. Arndt was first the thinker who advances this illuminating idea. In exploring the semantic history of the term "development", he states that the publication of the British Development Act of 1929 brought a radical change in the perception of development. Further, in Meier's view, development is an idea that is used to arrive at policy prescriptions and their implementations, but the idea itself is devoid of any materiality. Discourse analysis, on the other hand, tries to grasp the idea of development as inseparable from the actions it produces, their modalities, and the apparatuses it calls into play. It is the material effectiveness of the idea of development that the concept of discourse tries to capture (82). It is in this context that the discourse analysis understands development as practice, and statements on development as events. Graham Huggan and Helen Tiffin raise several fundamental questions such as:

What is development? How should it be defined and measured, and whose interests does it serve...these questions are complex, all the more so in that the word 'development' is taxed with considerable semantic difficulties of its own. Development is generally recognised to be a strategically ambiguous term, adapted to the different needs of those who use it, and shot through with self-congratulation and condescension, based as it all too West (27).

Ferguson dissects the experience of the development in Lesotho and brings to visibility how the World Bank sponsored developmental interventions, have in effect constructed the very reality of rural Lesotho as "primitive, underdeveloped and backward". In a collections of essays edited by Wolfgang Sacham (1992), critical theorists of development have sought to unsettle the conceptual foundations of the dominant developmental thinking by tracing out the archaeology of basic concepts such as, to name a few, poverty, need, resources and environment. These are the basic things a state looks for to select an area, which has the above said characteristics to make it possible for development at act as an elaborate mechanism of control. Thus the state was produced as the "other" of the "modern and advanced" societies of the country, as "traditional and backward", as the space of underdevelopment inhabited by the Adivasis characterised solely in terms of deficiency, absence, and lack. This identity of being "underdeveloped and backward" was inscribed on the Adivasis and how they related to the immediate environment, in which they lived, was completely ruled out. The best example is coalmines and dams in

Telangana region. Here development does nothing but strives to transform the "traditional" into the "modern." It is very difficult to locate the fundamental shift from the earlier notion of "development as a systemic transition" to one of "development as improvement".

The earlier claim was that development necessarily means a process of capital accumulation through industrialisation accompanied by disintegration of pre-capitalist premodern economic organisations and social institutions, busting of the bonds of caste, creed, and race, and their replacement by capitalist/ modern economic, cultural, and social institutions. In the early 1970s, this view of development as an all-encompassing, macro level transformation yielded place to a different notion of development that aimed at meeting the needs of the poor. Thus, the needs defined in terms of nutrition, shelter, health, and education....in direct ways that are not necessarily mediated by a programme of overall "transformation" of the traditional order and "improvement of the conditions of the poor" as the developmental goal. In other words, development as capitalist transformation through accumulation was to a large extent supplanted by an approach that emphasises the possibility of uplifting the conditions of the poor by "ensuring and improving" the conditions of existence of their familiar ways of life and activities they have been traditionally engaged in.

Development is usually conceived as an aspect of change that is desirable, broadly predicted or planned and administered, or at least influenced, by governmental action. Hence, development is not merely an economic phenomenon; it is rather a societal phenomenon encompassing all aspects of human life. A number of studies on development of Adivasi communities have been carried out by researchers from various disciplines. The problems of Adivasi development have long baffled the policy-makers, administrators and social scientists in India, and the debate on the meaning, character and direction of their socio-economic transformation continues. Earlier studies carried out by Anthropologists and other Social Scientists among various Adivasi communities have constantly raised various problems of Adivasi due to the idea of development and offered suggestions for bringing better results. Based on various committees' reports and studies on Adivasi development, efforts have been subsequently made to improve the Adivasi situation by providing various kinds of provisions and schemes.

However, unfortunately, the Adivasi have not been able to derive sufficient benefit from this process of planned development. It is a fact that Adivasi's development problem in the country cannot be considered in customary senseas. It varies from one region to another. Each year, thousands of Adivasis across the country are forcibly relocated and resettled away from their homes, lands and livelihoods due to large-scale development projects such consumption of as dams, reservoirs, power plants, roads, plantations, urban renewal, oil, and mining projects.

Development is one of the primary causes of forced migration in the Telangana regions today. Figures on the number of people forcibly uprooted from their homes and communities are incomplete and are careful approximations at best. They do, however, give us a clear indicator of the magnitude of the problem. Experts estimate that over 250 villages have been displaced by the construction of the Polavaram dam. According to the recent study published in Economic and Political Weekly by M Bharath Bhushan, Palla Trinadh Rao, and E. Revathi discuss the idea of displacement as fallows:

Large scale displacement in this very tribal region, submerging 276 villages in AP alone as per official figures, poses serious threat to the ethnic, linguistic and cultural identity of the Koya tribe. Displacement of the scheduled tribes under Polavaram dam is a violation of human rights and is without consent and consultation of the tribal population.

The number of Adivasis are forcibly displaced each year is also increasing. The impact of a project is rarely limited to Adivasis within the identified project area. The construction of a dam or a mine, for example, typically does not displace only those people and communities located on lands used for the project. People living downstream from a dam may suffer the loss of fisheries needed to sustain themselves. An entire community may suffer health impacts due to pollution from a mine. Both circumstances commonly force people to move, and both are examples of development on the other hand forceful displacement. People forcibly uprooted by development are typically displaced within the borders of their own Thandas, Gudam and Villages. This distinguishes them from refugees, who are legally defined as having fled across Khamam and Warangal border to escape danger or a fear of persecution. And the persecution happens when the Adivasis fight against the development. Because the Adivasis are internally displaced people, they are not protected by the instruments of law. There is no internal body specifically charged with protecting the rights of internally displaced people or to address their needs. In fact, it is often much more difficult for outsider to reach people who are internally displaced.

Impact of Developmental Project on Adivasis

The people who bear the brunt of the personal, social and environmental costs of projects rarely share the benefits. On the contrary, displacement commonly leads to the impoverishment of those who are forced to move, which create new poverty in project, especially in coal mine areas. A multi-year study of development-induced displacement concluded that impoverishment and disempowerment have been the rule rather than the exception with respect to resettled people around the world. Due to this displacement Adivasis of Andhra Pradesh particularly from Polavaram are rendered as landlessness, homelessness. As a result adivasis had a bad effect on their livelihood which further leads to a sense of insecurity. Thus, it increases in morbidity, stress and psychological trauma; a displacement leads to economic marginalisation often accompanied by social and cultural marginalisation, and a profound social disintegration.

People displaced by development are prone to suffer from life-threatening diseases, epidemics, and loss of physical and mental health. Yet the Adivasis commonly have less access to hospitals and health clinics. Families often lose access to educational facilities as well, resulting in lost or delayed educational opportunities for children. Existing patterns of leadership, social organisation, and subsistence are dismantled. Kinship ties and other informal networks that provide mutual support are dispersed or unaccessible precisely when the need for them is the greatest. Coming from politically marginalised and disadvantaged strata of society, these groups often are neglected and at the receiving end.

In Andhra Pradesh, the Adivasi, although only representing seven per cent of the total population, out of that 40-50 per cent are displaced. Particularly, in Telangana, Adivasis are displaced by constructions dam and open crust mines, subsequently they find it hard to depend on rivers, land for their livelihood. In the most of the cases have reportedly been inadequately compensated. Though, development and displacement are nonetheless relevant and applicable to situations of displacement caused by development projects. Given a choice of constructing or not constructing the Polavaram dam and the digging of coal mines, the Adivasis are against. But the fundamental question is whether or not they have a choice in the decision: a large majority of them feel that there is no choice and that their concens have not been addressed at all so far by the state machinery is concerned. Nelson Madela writes a poem on apartheid community which resonates the similar story:

What I am talking about is not a piece of bone touching a piece of metal,
Or even the overlapping of one culture and another,
What I am talking about is the brutal clash between what is indigenous and good,
And what is foreign and bad.

We cannot allow these foreigners who do not care for our culture to take over our nation. I predict that, one day, the forces of African society will achieve a momentous victory over the interloper. For too long we have succumbed to the false gods of white man. But we shall emerge and cast off these foreign notions (12).

Mandela's words precisely are applicable in Indian context here. The policies of development never care or try to understand the cultures of Adivasis. They are displaced by giving false promises. The attachment with forest and land that provides them livelihood is neglected on the name of development. In his book *Lo (K) cal Knowledge: Perceptions on Dalit, Tribal and Folk Literature*. Anand Mahanand argues the 'development' what it means to a Adivasi he brings this argument from *Mother Forest*. C.K. Janu says that: "No one knows the forest like we do. The forest is mother to us. More than a mother because she never abandons us (20)." From her narrative it is evident that Adivasis are more depended on the forest products. The state wants the resources like water and forest to develop the individual multinational companies by neglecting the Adivasis voices. Janu's concept of development is different from what the state and civil society thinks. She says that the tribal people do not need the kind of development conceptualised by the state and civil society. It is for their profit. In her own words: "All development projects emphasise profits for civil society. That is why they build shining roads to colonies that do not even have a bicycle. They are made for the bank vans that come to recover loans (50)" she argues that that developmentality should take into consideration the environmental factor and Adivasis interests. However, in his article "A Separate Telangana Promises and Prospects of the people" Ramdas says that:

> Looking at the stark reality, the social scientists and both state and central governments have to question themselves as to whether the reservations and Acts made for the welfare of the tribal people are truly being implemented. By looking at these hamlets, we can understand the success of the tribal welfare and development programmes. The tribal people are suffering even without their basic needs being fulfilled, and tribal girls are being sold like commodities....Is it not necessary for the members of the tribal community to be conscious of their pitiful conditions and raise their voice to fight for their own rights (120).

However, it clear that the myth of the development that it claims to heal. It is clear that the development I agree with the point which Ramdas is making to bring the tribal development issues. They are very serious and important issues to address in the present context. On the name of the development tribal areas are became vulnerable. However, as a result of the vicious cycle initiated by industrial clear felling and displacement for development projects, there has been a transition to destructive dependence on natural resource. As we all know tribes in India, though at different stages of development, still live primarily off the land and forests. The accelerated development of the Adivasi areas of the Telangana region of unplanned development is a major factor which is effecting the Adivasis very badly. In his book *Tribal Land Alienation and Political Movements: Socio Economic Patterns from South India.* Ramdas says that:

> Since Independence many development schemes and protective measures have been attempted by the central and state governments for the tribal areas of Andhra Pradesh. However, the conditions of the majority of the tribals have deteriorated. While exploitation and backwardness are found in many communities and social groups in India, it has resulted in social alienation among tribes (12).

As Ramdas says it is not only land alienation but also 'development' of these Adivasis areas has been achieved at the very high cost of progressively worsely deteriorating economic conditions of Adivasi life and environmental conditions of ordinary future citizens of the country. I would rather say that the third world is littered with failed development models. So called "development" requires careful scrutiny with an open eye to its possible improvement and to the viability of its replication. I end my article with a note of hope that their voice will be heard soon and such a task should not be impossible as more and more students from these communities are now entering the academia. I assume this study will yield novel insights into the issue of development and displacement in the guise of 'development', particularly in relation to the *Projects and Open Crust Coal Mines* in Telangana. Thus, one needs to actively engage the question of "How should it be defined and measured, and whose interests does it serve?" I hope this work will help in rejuvenating Adivasi life epitomise an honest portrayal of thoughts and emotions, besides giving new directions and vistas to the scholarly discourse already in place.

References

Anand Mahanand. *Lo (K) cal Knowledge: Perceptions on Dalit, Tribal and Folk Literature.* Authorspress, New Delhi, 2013.

C.K. Janu. *The Mother Forest: The Unfinished Story of C.K. Janu.* Trans. N. Ravi Shankar. Kali for Women, Delhi, 2004.

Graham Huggan and Helen Tiffin. *Post-colonial Ecocriticism: Literature, Animals, Environment.* Routledge Taylor & Francis Group, London and New York, 2010.

K. Damodar Rao. "*The Hindu*" Literary Review, July 7, 2013.

Kalyan Sanyal. *Rethinking Capitalist Development: Primitive Accumulation, Governmentality and Post-colonial Capitalism.* Routledge Tayalor & Francis Group, New Delhi, 2007.

M S Prabhakara. "Nelson Mandela (1918-2013) Some Recollections and Reflections" Vol. XLVIII, No. 51, Economic and Political Weekly, December 21, 2013, p. 13.

Rupavath, Ramdas. "A Separate Telangana Promises and Prospects of the People" Economic and Political Weekly, July 20, 2013, Vol. xlviii, No. 29.

.....*Tribal Land Alienation and Political Movements: Socio Economic Patterns from South India.* Cambridge Sholars Publishing, Newcastel upon Tyne, NE62XX, UK, 2009.

Virginius Xaxa. *State, Society, and Tribes: Issues in Post-Colonial India.* Pearson Longman, New Delhi, 2008.

20

Impact of Mahatma Gandhi National Rural Employment Guarantee Act on Socio-economic Conditions of Tribals: A Case Study of Nuapada District of Odisha

Tapan Kumar Bihari

Abstract

From the independence, planners have focussed special attention towards the development of the indigenous people of the land. So, the Central and State governments have launched various schemes for the Tribals for their socio-economic development and tried to bring them into the mainstream. But various reports narrate the unchanged socio-economic condition or unsatisfactory change. Still now also the benefit of development has not touched them. Tragic story of migration, poverty, hunger, malnutrition and starvation death have been found after the sixty five years of independence.

There have been several institutional measures since independence developed at the initiative of the centre, state and voluntary organisations in bring the benefits of the growth to the ground level of the society specially to the tribal. There is a rhetoric that the poverty alleviation programme initiated at the center provides for the poorest of the poor. This is not so the case at the grassroot level as there are several institutional constraints like lack of special provisions under MGNREGA in addressing the needs of Tribals. MGNREGA is designed as a safety net to reduce migration by rural poor households in the lean period through a hundred days of guaranteed unskilled manual labour provided when demanded at minimum wage on works focused on water conservation, land development and drought proofing.

This paper attempts to address the cause behind the gap between the rhetoric of development for the tribal and the reality of benefits doled out to the tribal poor in the context of MGNREGA.

"Unemployment is a cause of poverty, diversity and a way towards the destruction of a country's prosperity and generation of employment is a focal objective to eradicate poverty, utilisation of potentials of large part of human resources in rural areas to build an unique all round developed welfare India."

In the above context MGNREGA is considered as a "Silver Bullet" for eradicating rural poverty and unemployment, by way of generating demand for productive labour force in villages.

Introduction

Rural poverty and unemployment in India have grown in an unprecedented manner during the last few decades. There is a growing incidence of illiteracy, blind faith, hungry people, mal-nourished children, anaemic pregnant women, farmer suicides, starvation deaths, migration resulting from inadequate employment, poverty, and the failure of subsistence production during droughts. In order to make solution of these problems and to provide livelihood security to rural unemployed, Government of India (GOI) enacted the National Rural Employment Guarantee Act (NREGA) in 2005. It is the biggest poverty alleviation programme in the world which is started with an initial outlay of Rs 11,300 crore in year 2006-07 and now it is Rs 40,000 crore (2010-11). This Act is now called as Mahatma Gandhi NREGA. The Act provides a legal guarantee for 100 days of employment in every financial year to adult members of any rural household will to do public work related unskilled manual work at the statutory minimum wage. Thus it is a universal programme. This minimum wage varies from state to state, in some states it is Rs 80 whereas in other it is Rs 125 or Rs 120. According to the Act the minimum wage cannot be less than Rs 60. The 100 days of work figure was estimated because the agricultural season is only supposed to last roughly around 250 days and unskilled workers have no alternative source of income in the remaining parts of the year.

History of MGNREGA

NREGA has come after almost 56 years of experience of other rural employment programmes, which include both Centrally Sponsored Schemes and those launched by State Govt. These comprise the National Rural Employment Programme (NREP) 1980-89; Rural Landless Employment Guarantee Programme (RLEGP) 1983-89; Jawahar Rojgar Yojana (JRY) 1989-1990; Employment Assurance Scheme (EAS)1993-99; Jawahar Gram Samridhi Yojana (JGSY) 1999-2002; Sampoorna Grameen Rojgar Yojana (SGRY) from 2000; National Food For Work Programme (NFFWP) from 2004 were national rural employment schemes. Among these, the SGRY and NFFWP have been merged with NREGA in 2005.

Time-line of MGNREGA

The following Table 20.1 shows the time line of MGNREGA whereby the scheme got its modifications during the years of its running.

Table 20.1: The Time Line of MGNREGA

Aug 2005	*Feb 2006*	*Apr 2007*	*Apr 2008*	*Oct 2008*	*16 Feb 2009*	*Oct 2009*
NREGA legalised	Came into force in 200 districts	130 more districts included	Universalisation of the scheme	Wage transaction through banks/post offices	MOU with the postal dept.	Name changed to MGNREGA

Source: www.nrega.nic.in

As the Table 20.1 depicts, when the Act got first introduced in 200 most backward districts of the country in Feb 2006, it was proposed to extend to the remaining districts only after five years, after seeing the popularity of the Act. But in the next year itself the Act was extended further to 130 more districts and within months after that the Act got universalised by bringing the entire country under its horizon with the exception of districts that have a hundred per cent urban population and got soon named after Mahatma Gandhi (in Oct 2nd, 2009) to make the Act more reachable to the masses and thus it became Mahatma Gandhi National Rural Employment Guarantee Act (MGNREGA). In the context of Odisha all the tribal-dominated districts were covered from the very beginning.

Significance of MGNREGA

MGNREGA actually aims to achieve the objective as enunciated in the Article: 41 of the Indian Constitution—"giving citizens the right to work". The Act is significant due to the following reasons:

- While the earlier wage employment programmes did not provide any guarantee of job, this Act provided guaranteed job. This guarantee for wage employment is now uniformed all over the country like never before.
- It is a development initiative, chipping in with essential public investment for creation of durable assets, without which the growth process can't be possible in the most backward regions of rural India.
- Almost all the previous programmes were allocation based rather than demand based. NREGA, which was launched in 2006, is considered to be unique from this stand point.
- The key element of MGNREGA is the provision of employment by the state to those people who are unable to find alternative employment, which provides a form of social safety net to the rural unemployment people.

• In other wage employment programmes, anyone can be engaged as labour while in MGNREGA only job card holders that apply for employment can be engaged as labourers.

• There is no time frame in other wage employment programmes but in MGNREGA, employment will be given within 15 days of demand, payment also within 15 days of work.

• In other wage employment programme the duration of employment is dependent on duration of work by implementing agency while in MGNREGA, a job card holder applies for maximum 100 days.

The other key attributes of this Act are labour-intensive work, decentralised participatory planning, women's empowerment, work-site facilities and above all transparency and accountability through the provision of social audits and right to information. The use of information technology in this programme is considered to bring about greater transparency through intensive monitoring and faster execution. The payment of wages through bank and post office accounts is other innovative step that is likely to reduce fudging of muster rolls on the part of the implementing agencies since the actual payments are beyond their reach.

Thus MGNREGA is not only a welfare initiative but also a development effort that can take the Indian economy to a new prosperity.

Goals of MGNREGA

Long-term objectives of the Act include:

• Enhancement of livelihood security in rural areas by guaranteeing 100 days of wage employment in a financial year to every registered household.

• Creating productive assets

• Protecting the environment

• Reducing migration

• Empowering rural women and the poor through the provision of a right-based law.

• Fostering social equity.

• To create strong social safety net for the vulnerable groups by providing employment source, when other alternative are inadequate.

Thus MGNREGA has three distinct goals:

• Protective

• Preventive

• Promotive

It protects the rural poor from vulnerabilities by providing them demand based employment. It prevents risk associated with agricultural investment and forced migration of rural poor. It brings prosperity in rural economy via increased consumption demand. Thus MGNREGA can be considered as a growth engine.

Salient Features of MGNREGA

(i) Right Based-framework:

- All adult members of a rural household willing to do unskilled manual work have the right to demand employment.

-The GP after due verification will issue a job card.

-After verification, the GP will issue a job card (contain details of the member) to the household with photograph free of cost within 15 days of application.

(ii) Time Bound Guarantee of Employment:

-Employment will be provided by the GP within 15 days of work application, else unemployment allowance will be paid.

-A household may avail to 100 days of guaranteed employment in a financial year, depending on its need.

(iii) Permissible Works:

-Water conservation; drought proofing (including plantation and afforestation); flood protection; land development; minor irrigation.

(iv) Labour Intensive Works:

-A ratio of 60:40 will be maintained between wage and material.

-Contractors/machinery is not permitted.

Payment of wages:

-Wages will be paid at the wage earners through their bank/post office accounts.

-Payment of wages to be made in every week and in any case not later than a fortnight.

(v) Decentralisation:

- Gram sabha (local community) will recommend works to be taken up.

- Gram panchayats will execute at least 50 per cent of work.

- PRI will have a principal role in planning, monitoring and implementation.

(vi) Work Site Management and Facilities:

-Work should be provided within 5 km radius of the village.

-In case the number of children below the age of six years accompanying the women working at any site is five or more, provisions shall be made to assign one women worker to look after such children. The person assigned for this shall be paid the statutory minimum wage.

-Thus creche, drinking water, first-aid and shade are to be provided on the work sites.

- Timely measurement to be ensured.

(vii) Women Empowerment:

-At least one-third of the workers should be women.

- Equal wages will be provided to both men and women.

(viii) Transparency and Accountability:

-Proactive disclosure of information.

- Social Audit by the Gram Sabha is compulsory.

- Regular monitoring at all levels.

-grievance redressal mechanism is to be set up.

(ix) Funding: 90 per cent borne by Central Goverment and 10 per cent by State Government.

The Implementation Structure of MGNREGA

MGNREGA has a five-tier structure of implementation starting from GP at the bottom to the Central Government at the top.

1. *Gram Panchayat (GP):* GP is the nodal agency at the bottom level that has the authority to select, design and implement 50 per cent of the works. Selection of works, monitoring and supervision are done by the Gram Sabha (village council). GP has the responsibility to register households, issue job cards, receive applications for employment, provide employment and monitor the NREGA works.

2. *Block Panchayat:*The rest 50 per cent may be undertaken either by the block Panchayat or the district Panchayat or both. Block Panchayat monitors and coordinates the plans and works at the block level. Computer updating of MGNREGA works, muster roll entries, etc is done at the block level under the guidance of the MGNREGA programme officer.

3. *District Panchayat:* District Panchayat, in addition to implementing non-mandatory works, coordinates MGNREGA activities at the district level. Besides, it has the responsibility to prepare both the district annual plan and the five-year perspective plan. These two plan documents are the bases which guide the implementation of MGNREGA at the village level. These documents are prepared at the district level in consultation with the GP and Block Panchayats.

4. *State Government:* Next in hierarchy is the state government which acts as a facilitator in the flow of MGNREGA funds and helping in preparation of manpower. It has the responsibility to set up the State Employment Guarantee Council. The latter has the role to advice the government from time to time on MGNREGA implementation in the state. Besides, the council is also entrusted with the responsibility of monitoring and evaluation of the MGNREGA in the state.

5. *Central Government:* At the top of the hierarchy comes the central government. The Ministry of Rural Development, New Delhi is the nodal agency for MGNREGA implementation. It has the responsibility to set up Central Employment Guarantee Council for receiving advice on MGNREGA implementation. It may also undertake independent evaluation and monitoring of the scheme. It has the responsibility to prepare the budget and disburse funds.

1.1. Decentralised Planning and MGNREGA

MGNREGA is a unique Act which recognises the legitimate role of Panchayats in addressing their fundamental duty as expressed in the 73rd Constitutional Amendment of providing "economic development and social justice" in their area. The recognition of PRI as the principal agency of implementation under MGNREGA has opened up enormous opportunities for decentralising development respecting local solutions to local people.

1.2. Review of Related Literature

Sen Roy, Dipjoy and Debabrata Samanta (2009) attempted to measure the outcome of good governance practiced by Gram Panchayats (GPs) of West Medinipur district of West Bengal through the employment generated under MGNREGS. Data regarding different parameters related to core characteristics of good governance such as participation, transparency, accountability, effectiveness and efficiency, equity was taken into consideration in this study. This study mainly gives importance on potential implementation of MNREGA needs adequate efficient governing body and motivation.

As per the Panchayat and Rural Development Dept. Report on the performance of NREGA in 2007-08, the average number of person days created per household in West Bengal was 25; whereas in the study area it is 19 clearly shows under performance. The average participation rate of 19 per cent with maximum of 40 per cent and minimum of five per cent shows a good performance compared to 13.1 per cent state average rate (WB Human Development Report 2004). Average women participation rate (22 per cent) is rightly better than the overall participation rate; showing good equality among genders. Equity which states the equality of men and women in decision-making procedure found statistically significant. Accountability also found significant and shows positive relation with the MGNREGS performance. This represents efficiency and effectiveness of Govt. plays a positive role in successful implementation of MGNREGS. More transparency will tend to increase person days creation. Likewise more participation, i.e., the attendance in Gram Sansad meeting the more average person days will be created. Thus, to conclude it, this study says increasing the performance of governing body (here GPs) can improve the MGNREGS performance, hence helps to reduce the poverty level.

Khan, Amir Ullah and M.R. Salluja (2007) looked at the direct and the indirect effects that the NREGP has on employment generation and poverty reduction in a local. For this, a detailed survey in a poor agricultural village with 400 households, nearly 2500 people, was undertaken to highlight the impact of the NREGP. The survey recorded income and expenditure levels by type of household including large, small and marginal farmers, agricultural labour etc. The survey also recorded production activities undertaken by the inhabitants.

This village study reveals that most people do not access the scheme, as they haven't heard of the programme. They would like a more proactive role of the panchayat in deciding the infrastructure to be constructed. Almost everyone wants more work from the scheme and better facilities at the work place. There is enough evidence of fudging and mismanagement of records.

Indian Institute of Technology, Madras, Chennai (2009), "Evaluation of National Rural Employment Guarentee Act: In Districts: Cuddlore, Dindigul, Kanchipuram, Nagai, Thiruvallar, State: Tamil Nadu": This study generally reveals the impact of MNREGA in the state of Tamil Nadu by taking five districts into account. In each districts four GPs were chosen.

This study shows many positive aspects of the programme. These are mainly:

- Villagers consider NREGA is promising to be a boon for improving rural livelihood.
- Provision of job within the village is very much encouraging to villagers.
- NREGA also ensured gender equality in rural Tamil Nadu.
- The programme employed a very good proportion of scheduled caste and backward caste people.
- Involvement of SHG members improves people's MGNREGS awareness and this is very important for future MGNREGS planning.
- Financial inclusion strategies like bank account opening and rural ATM for MGNREGS beneficiaries at four villagers of Cuddalore block has resulted in multiplier effects of savings, financial safety etc.
- Registrations are open throughout the year.
- Most of the respondents perceived that payment were received within a week.

Dey, Subhasish and Arjun Bedi (2010) studied the functioning of the MGNREGS between February 2006 and July 2009 in Birbhum district, West Bengal. Their study reveals that in order to serve as an effective "employer of last resort", the programme should provide more job days during lean season and wages should be paid in a timely manner. This study shows that, in Birbhum, there is universal awareness about the MGNREGS, job card have been made available to all those who have applied and MGNREGS related information is well maintained and relatively accessible. But there is a long delay in wage payments during the first year of the programme, since then, the payment lag has declined and it is now in the range of 20 days.

Nayak, Narayan, Behera, Bhagirath, and Pulak Mishra (2008) conducted their study in two districts of Orissa mainly Mayurbhanj and Balasore. During the first phase itself, Mayurbhanj was selected along with other 18 backward districts of the state including KBK districts. The next phase, five more districts of Orissa were included under the scheme including Balasore. Mayurbhanj completed three years of NREGA implementation while Balasore has completed two. Both the districts are reported to have achieved certain goals and failed in others.

This study shows that the state as a whole as well as the two sample districts are well in certain physical and financial parameters like provision of employment to those who demand jobs and maintenance of wage and non-wage ratio. However their performance in certain other important parameters like utilisation of funds and creation of demand for jobs is not very encouraging. While the target is to guarantee 100 days of employment to each household, not many households have achieved this target. According to this report well thought out effort is necessary to address these problems of NREGA in the state.

Dreze (2007) looks at the corruption in rural employment programmes in Orissa and how this has continued in a MGNREGS as well. However, he believes that there is tremendous potential of NREGA in the survey areas. Where work was available, it was generally found that workers earned close to (and sometimes more than) the statutory minimum wage of Rs 70 per day, and that wages were paid within 15 days or so. This is an unprecedented opportunity for the rural poor, and there was evident appreciation of it among casual labourers and other disadvantaged sections of the population. There is the hope among workers that NREGA would enable them to avoid long-distance seasonal migration. Further, there is plenty of scope for productive NREGA works in this area, whether it is in the field of water conservation, rural connectivity, regeneration of forest land, or improvement of private agricultural land.

Mathur (2007) thinks that a system of regular and continuous flow of authoritative information is essential. There is room for the government to take up concurrent evaluations, more effective monitoring, time-series studies, and focused reports on critical aspects like minimum wages, muster rolls. To improve implementation, the government needs to solve problems, modify policy directives, and issue operational guidelines for the district, block and village levels. The government must take the lead, be proactive, mobilise institutions and groups, and use the media effectively. MGNREGS involves several lakh government officials, panchayat functionaries, elected representatives, NGOs and community groups. They play a critical role but had little preparation for the challenge. MGNREGS, in fact, is a programme of national importance which has been marginalised. While the ministry of rural development is the nodal ministry at the centre, every relevant department and agency requires being involved.

Mathur (2009) states that in social audit undertaken in Andhra Pradesh, it was found that in certain villages, some people stated that they had not been paid for the work done. When comparisons were made of the payments as per the pass-book with the payment as per the job card, it was discovered that the job card did not contain the inner pages that record the work done by each person; the job card itself was incomplete. Earlier, several officials, Field and Technical Assistants and Mates admitted to irregularities and about Rs 50,000 were returned.

Institute of Applied Manpower Research, Delhi (2009), "All India Report on Evaluation of NREGA, A Survey of Twenty Districts." This study is based on evaluation of the MGNREGS which assess its impact by taking 20 districts from Northern, Western, Southern and North-East region of India and 300 beneficiaries from each districts. This study reveals that in many districts, affixing of photograph on job cards is not followed and in some places the beneficiary paid money for getting it. Job card was not designed to have sufficient space for all the entries in detail. Many households did not get the work within the stipulated 15 days time of demand for work, neither were they paid any unemployment allowance. On the utility of maximum number of days of works, only small fractions of households could utilise more than 35 days of work, remaining still lagging behind. The reason for non-utilisation of maximum permissible 100 days of work is late starting of the scheme. In most of the worksites, excepting crèche, other facilities like shed, drinking water were provided. Due to the income generation through this scheme, the numbers of beneficiaries at the low earning level are reduced to nearly half in size. There is a rise of families who are spending more on food and non-food items.

Significance of the Study

In this context the present paper attempts to understand the implementation procedures of the MGNREGS and its impact on tribal livelihoods in the tribal-dominated panchayat, of Nuapada District of Odisha. Attempts have been made to capture the role of Gram Panchyat to generate sufficient employment opportunities, the procedures of registration, issuances of Job cards and application for employment.

Research Questions

- What extent MGNREGA has helped in sustaining the tribal livelihoods?
- Does MGNREGA become successful in improving the living condition of the poor?
- Does it successful in reducing migration?
- Is it really a livelihood generating programme than wage-earning scheme?
- Are the people really aware about MGNREGA work?
- Is the Act properly implemented as per its rules?

Objective of the Study

The main objectives of the present study are:

- Understanding the implementation procedure of MGNREGA in the study village.
- Understanding the impact of MGNREGA on tribal livelihoods.

Methodology

Purposively Santoshpur Gram Panchayat of Bisra Block in Nuapada District was selected including three hamlets i.e., Jaratoli, Pahadtoli and Militoli. A sample of 150 households including both job card holders and non-job card holders was selected randomly from Santoshpur GP. Here, non-job card holder households are selected for knowing the reasons for their non-participation in the MGNRES activities. Before finalising the study area a pilot visit was made by all the students. A good rapport was established with all villagers to convey about our works. At the initial time of field work each houses were numbered and household information data was collected prior to our questionnaires' data collection. Both quantitative and qualitative information on the details of processes and procedures of MGNREGS implementation and households expenditure and income were gathered by using both open ended and close ended questionnaire and households schedule. Sarapanch, Gram Sathi and Nayab Sarapanch questionnaire were designed to elicit information at the GP level. Excepting investigator's own questionnaires, study was carried out on the basis of personal interviews. Transect walk into the MGNREGS worksites were conducted to have firsthand experience on the MGNREGS works at the community level.

Significance of the Study

The present paper attempts to understand the implementation procedures of MGNREGS and its impact on tribal livelihoods in a tribal dominated panchayat of Nuapada district, Odisha. This paper focuses on the role of GP to generate sufficient employment opportunities, the procedures for registration, issuance of job cards, and application for employment. This would enable us to understand and examine the institutional mechanisms under which the entire programme is being implemented. The problems and prospects of MGNREGA can then be better understood and accordingly, necessary measures can be devised to make the programme realise its set objectives.

Starting from 200 districts, the coverage of NREGA was increased to all the rural districts in the country. However, despite coming out of a countrywide struggle for enactment of MGNREGA, the performance of the NREGA varies a lot across the states.

Findings and Analysis

The major question raises how to implement the Act, which can give justice to the poor for whom the act was designed. To a certain extent, the effective implementation is consequent upon greater awareness and participation of beneficiaries and PRIs, since they have a greater role to play according to the Act. However, technicalities apart, effective implementation of the Act is also conditional on the effort of the state governments in ensuring effective implementation of the Act by doing away with the contractor system, simplifying the implementation design and above all, the political will to ensure its successful implementation.

The State like Odisha came to the notice after the Supreme Court's order for a Central probe into the diversion of funds and non-implementation of rural employment scheme, MGNREGA, in Odisha (Dec 14, 2010). Orissa recorded 21 days in 2006 and eight days in 2007-08 per households. During 2009-10 only

995193 households have been given works out of more than 54 lakh job card holders in the state because only1021008 households demanded work (Dreze, 2010).

As per a leading newspaper in Odisha (The Samaj, 23rd March) while during 2011-12 Odisha government has able to spent 64 per cent of the MGNREGS fund allotted, it is around 94 per cent in Sundargarh. However, while 3,17,201 households in this district have registered under MGNREGS only 2162 households have received work for 100 days and 32,572 households have received less than six days of work. The remaining households never got any work. However, nobody is able to answer what for most of the households did not get any job and other very few days.

The present study which is confined to a Panchayat falls in Sundargarh district of Odisha. The sample used in the present study consists of 150 households including 82 (54.7 per cent) job card holders and 68 (45.3 per cent) non-job card holders of Santoshpur village. An analysis of the primary data collected from these households provides the following findings:

Socio-demographic Profile of the Respondents: The sample households selected for the study cover households from various caste and ethnic communities.

Caste of the Respondents: Caste and ethnicity plays a major role in any kind of development project. The presence of various castes and ethnicity creates a heterogeneity situation, which stands as a hurdle in the process of implementation (Mishra, 2007).

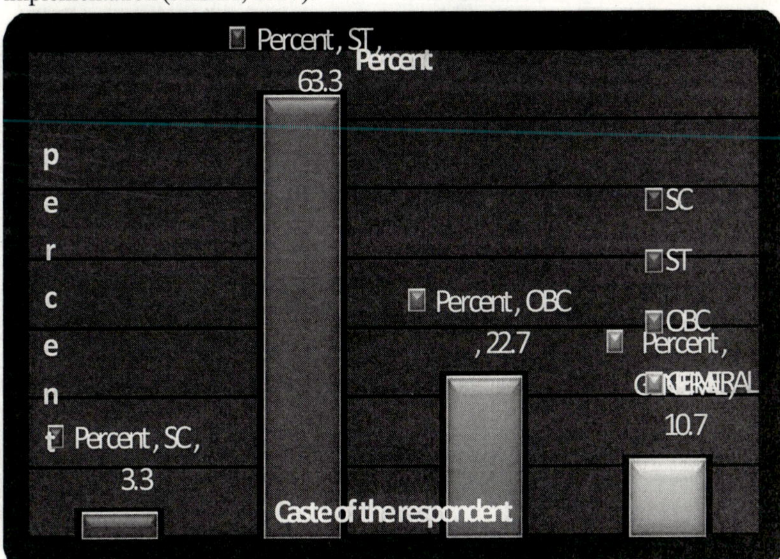

Fig. Caste and Ethnicity of the Respondents.

Source: Primary Data.

The above figure shows that out of 150 households, majority (63.3 per cent) of the households are belonging to ST population. The rest of the households distributed among OBC, SC and General Communities. They are respectively 22.7 per cent, 10.7 per cent and 3.3 per cent. It reflects that the Studied Panchayat is numerically dominated by tribal communities.

Main Source of Income

Almost all the households were depending on forest resources for their income. However, in course of time lots of change has seen. The intervention of various development projects, outsiders have brought a lost to the forest resources. It has disturbed the symbiotic relation between man and nature. The dependence of forest has gone down.

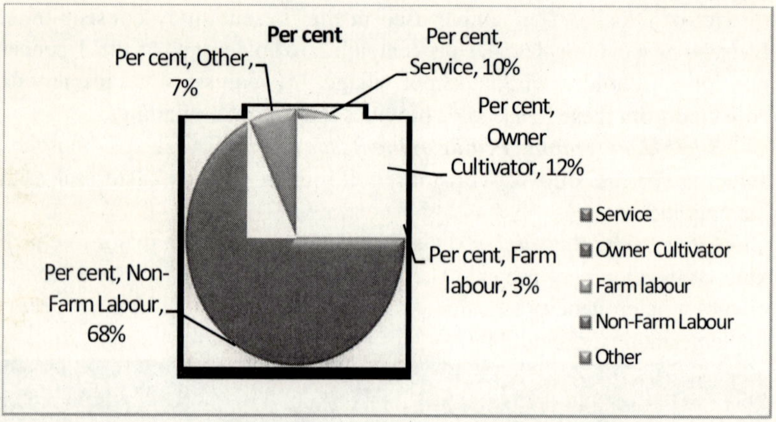

Fig. Religion of the Respondents.

Source: Primary Data.

The majority of populations (68 per cent) in Santoshpur village are involved in non-farm sector having poor economic status and livelihood insecurity. Among the non-farm labourers the number of STs (54.9 per cent) and OBC (29.4 per cent) are more in comparison to other castes.

Distribution of Job Card Holder according to Caste, Religion, Educational Qualification, Landholder and BPL Card Holder.

The implementation of NREGA came with the introduction of Job card to the villagers.

The Table 20.2 shows that among the job-card holders the majority (68.3 per cent) are ST. Out of all job card holders 58.5 per cent are Hindu, 50 per cent illiterate, 42.7 per cent are landless and 64.6 per cent are non-BPL card holders.

Among the non-job card holders, the majority consists of STs (57.4 per cent), illiterate (45.6 per cent) and landless (41.2 per cent). Thus, there is need for improvement, as maximum number of respondents in this village have not

Table 20.2: Distribution of Job Card Holder according to Caste, Religion, Educational Qualification, Landholder and BPL Card Holder

Caste	*SC*	*ST*	*OBC*	*General*		
	2.4%	68.3%	23.2%	6.1%		
Religion	Hindu	Muslim	Christian			
	58.5%	22%	19.8%			
Educational qualification	illiterate	Lower primary	Upper primary	High school	Inter mediate	Graduate
	50%	3.7%	28%	13.4%	4.9%	0%
Land holder	0-1 acre	2-3 acre	4-5 acre	Landless		
	36.6%	17.1%	3.7%	42.7%		
BPL card holder	BPL card holder	Non BPL card holder				
	35.4%	64.6%				

Source: Primary data.

got job card till yet. Among the non-job card holders, many families are belong to the most vulnerable sections like women headed households, senior citizens and poorer sections while the rich, influential people, authorising committee itself getting much benefits on the name of poor and unemployed youths.

Implementation of MGNREGA

Awareness

NREGA is distinctive for its unique vision to redefine avenues of providing employment opportunities to the deprived in rural India. But the possibility and efficient chances of employment largely comes with the better level of awareness as it marks the level of accessibility. This issue of awareness emerges one of the hindrances to the local community. It thus necessitates sufficient awareness amongst the intended beneficiaries regarding provisions like guaranteed days of employment, unemployment allowance, minimum wages, availability of complaint register, etc. However, the situation in this front is not very encouraging in the study areas. As most of the worker respondents are illiterate and belong to the economically poor class, the extent of awareness about NREGA has emerged out to be a major concern in all the hamlets. Around 93 per cent of the villagers are aware about the MGNREGS. Among them the majority are the STs (63.3 per cent) and illiterate (48 per cent). But workers' awareness on how to apply for job cards, awareness about minimum wages and demand for work was reportedly very low. Around seven per cent villagers are not at all aware about MGNREGS. Those who are aware about it out of them only 41 per cent of the respondents are aware of the number of minimum days of employment guaranteed to each household under the scheme. Only 54 per cent households in this panchayat are having job cards.

The procedural and implementation aspects of NREGA have never been free from confronting some basic challenges like general awareness, understanding policy nitty-gritty, sufficient access etc. Having given the socio-economic background of the respondents, the structural issues such as transparency, maintenance of documents and accountability were difficult things to actualise from the workers' point of view. When asked whether beneficiaries knew about the time span of getting employment from the date of the submission of applications under the NREGA, only 20 per cent respondents revealed that they were aware of any such guidelines like to get employment within the 15 days from the date of application for jobs.

Source of Information

Source of information	*Percentage*
Panchayat office	71.3
Media-radio	.7
Neighbour	17
Any other	4.0
NA	7

Source: Primary data.

The major source of information for the villagers regarding MGNREGS is PRIs including Sarpancha, Gram Sathi and GP officials. Around 71.3 per cent of the villagers claimed that they informed about MGNREGS from GP office which indicates that GP officials playing a significant role in spreading information on MGNREGS. However, the GP has not played any major role in proper implementation of this project. It has confined itself mostly in spreading the message about job card.

Provisions for safeguard of transparency and accountability are incorporated into the Act and also in the MGNREGA guidelines. For instance the MGNREGA guidelines require muster rolls to be available in the Panchayat office and also at work sites. This can go a long way to preventing corruption in wage payments, since it makes the muster rolls available for public scrutiny and social audit. But the reality is somewhat else.

Interestingly, a large section of the respondents (40.7 per cent) across panchayat report that they hardly see notifications in advance regarding the MGNREGS meetings. This perhaps indicates that notices are not widely circulated by the panchayat. The place and mode of notification may also cause hindrance. This is so because the notifications are generally put in the government offices and villagers hardly visit these offices. They visit such offices only when they desperately feel to do so. Further, most of the job seekers being illiterate do not have the ability and inclination to read the notification even when it is written in vernacular language. This is likely to restrict not only the job-seekers' participation in the scheme but also incorporation of their needs and views in works.

Mismanagement of Job Cards

Majority of households (84.14 per cent) expressed that they got their job cards without waiting for much time and without unnecessary visits to GP office while 15.86 per cent claimed that they had to run many times to GP office even Block office for getting job cards. Some interesting things were found in the initial days during 2006. It was revealed that few villagers first got employment without card and after working some days, got their job card at the work place. Bribe was also taken from Govt. employees, rich families, by the Sar panch, Gram Sathi and GP secretary in order to give one or two job cards to a single household. Not only that but also there is religion and street biasness and favouritism seen in case of getting job card. Some of the Muslim women claimed that as the Sarpancha is belonging to ST community he has ignored their demand for card in many times. However due to interference of Block Development Officer few of them got the card.

"After complaining through the member of Disha office, BDO came to our village and at last we got our job cards," Said Sabina Khatun (35 years), a woman from Muslim community. She also said, they faced some trouble in getting their payment for which they had to do strike/dharna at BDO office."

As per the MGNREGA guideline, affixing of photographs on job cards is mandatory without any charge. However, not a single job card found with photograph in the field. There is also manipulation of job cards by the panchayat secretary and Gram Sathi for which in most of the job cards, entries were either fake or blank. With respect to average days of employment provided to the households, it is 50 man days according to muster roll, while according to job card entries and labour statement it is 60 and 15 respectively.

Sobha Tanti (40 years), a woman from SC community, had worked for 15 days and was paid for those number of days, but in her job card, 60 days of work mentioned. Likewise (28 years) Baber Ansari, has worked only for 15 days but there was entry of 72 days in his job card. It shows that this system is highly corrupted. No officials are worried about the poor tribal. Regarding the job card updating, no such initiation is being taken by GP.

While large majority of the job card holders reported that they keep the cards in their own custody, few respondents (20 per cent) have reported that their cards are normally kept in the custody of the ward members or sarpanchs or gram sathis. This may largely be due to the ignorance of the job-seekers on custody of the cards. It is also giving an opportunity for officials to manipulate.

Faulty Design of Job Cards

The main purpose of job card was to enable MGNREGA labourers to "verify their own employment and wage details". But there is no such column to mention about "wage paid" in the job card issued in this area, for this it is impossible to verify from the job card, the wages paid to an MGNREGA worker.

Application for Employment

The average number of respondents applied for employment is very low in the study area (23.17 per cent). Those who applied for job are mostly non-tribal beneficiaries and among them not a single person got unemployment allowance. However, this does not necessarily mean that there is low demand for employment in the study area. The poor tribal have not much courage to go to the GP office and claim for job. Still most of them feel that the job they used to get through MGNREGS is nothing but mercy of sarpanch. Even in some cases it was found that those who are really needy of those cards have not received the cards. Whereas few villagers who are working in public sectors have taken job cards and are not at all applying for job. Thus among the job card holders 82.93 per cent of people have worked under MGNREGA while 17.07 per cent haven't worked. During the field work it was observed that these households are giving their cards to other households for getting benefits through them.

Regarding employment, respondents shared that they have not availed complete 100 days in a year. Even in last five years nobody got 100 days of employment. The villagers of Santoshpur gram panchayat worked under MGNREGS for around 15 days in last five years. Only 10 per cent households received around 50 days of works in last five years.

Poor Quality of Works

There is no proper execution of works. Hence, it is a matter of concern that throughout the GP, the approved works are not always publicly displayed. It was revealed by the villagers that there was no Gram Sabha meeting regarding the activities of MGNREGS. Even maximum numbers of people are not aware about Gram Sabha meeting which reflects non-participation of villagers or community in decision making. The villagers used to work in any work assigned by the contractor or Sarapanch. The internal understanding between contractors, Sarapancha and JE used to confine the work in paper only. Site account registers in respect of receipt and issue of materials to the work and Temporary advance register in respect of advance availed for payment of wages had not been maintained, despite their mandated requirement for departmental execution. MNREGA guidelines permit execution of road projects providing all weather connectivity in rural areas. However, during field work it was observed that the road remain kutcha and incomplete and is not able to provide all weather access.

"Although, there is a road nearer to mountain, but it has no value as it is unnecessarily made, incomplete, and kutcha which has already disappeared due to rain water and now it is same as before," said by Baber Ansari (28 years).

Poor Planning and Lack of Co-ordination among Villagers and Official Members

The majority of population said that only road work has been undertaken in their Gram Panchayat which is incomplete due to conflicts among villagers

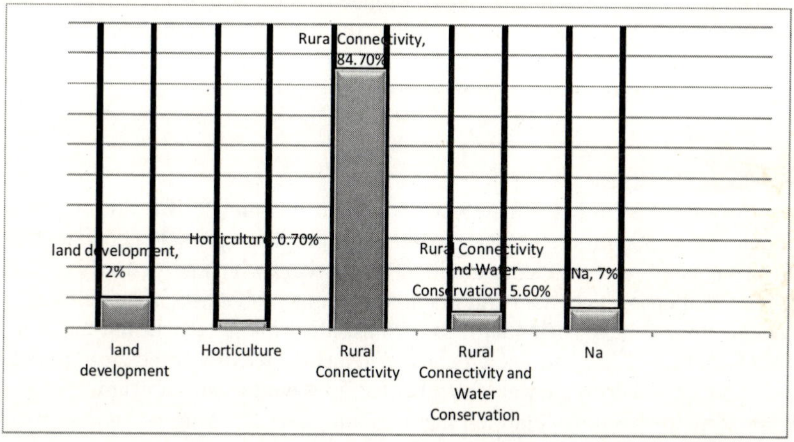

Fig. Types of works undertaken in Santoshpur village under MGNREGA.

as well as between members of panchayat office and forest dept. Though, there was fund around Rs 300000 came for watershed activities in 2010 but it was returned to Block office, as the work stopped before it starts due to above reason.

Payment of Wages

The data from the field reflected that there is huge irregularity in payment of wages. While only 28 per cent of beneficiaries claimed that they received the wages within a month, the rest claimed that there is no certainty in getting wages. But they received it mostly after two months. The contractors were quite conscious while paying the wages. They used to delay in paying wages to those labourers who are illiterate and no voice. It is observed from the field that around 81 per cent of the beneficiaries are not having the minimum wages fixed by the centre. While the MGNREGA guidelines permit equal wages for equal work, it is not happening in reality. As per the views of few villagers widow and old women are receiving lesser wages in comparison to men.

Sumitra Gauda, this woman already crossed 65 years, earned only Rs 30 from MGNREGA work for supplying water to workers. According to her, the Scheme from Govt. is good, but those who are taking in charge of it, are not implementing properly.

Now, MGNREGA has become very organised. The bank accounts are opened in the name of the wage workers. The money is directly transferred to the accounts and there is no one in between. But in the study area, around 46.35 per cent of the beneficiaries have not opened their account either in bank or in post office while 53.65 per cent beneficiaries have account. It may be due to lack of interest or lack of awareness. According to some villagers, if there is regular work and regular payment, we will be interested to open account. Around 67.07 per cent of the beneficiaries have received their wages directly through cash while 32.93 per cent beneficiaries received their wages through account transfer. Reading out of the muster roll at the time of payment is mandatory under the MGNREGA. However, the situation is not very encouraging in this regard. All the respondents have pointed out that the muster roll is not read out.

Worksite Facilities

Any studies on MGNREGS would sound incomplete if it doesn't talk about worksite facilities. A proper working condition is a primary necessity for ensuring safety and efficient condition for workers which particularly in the case of women is much more important. According to MGNREGS guidelines, it is mandatory to have basic facilities such as safe drinking water, first-aid kits, shades, period of rest and also crèche facility. But it was observed during field work that except drinking water no other facilities were arranged near worksite. Even some respondents claimed that in some cases drinking water was also not available. While discussing worksite facilities like shade, some of the respondents claimed that the trees near to worksite were used and treated as shady shelters. Thus manipulation by the local implementing agencies and absence of any monitoring mechanism at the same time resulted in the creation of unsafe and sub-standard working conditions.

Compulsion of Works on Workers

There is also compulsion on worker regarding work i.e., one cannot dig more than half chauka in a day.

No Social Audit Held

The operational guideline detailed the procedure of Social Audit forums to be held by gram sabha on NREGA works six months basis. But in this village Social Audit is never held.

Small Children are Working under MNREGA

As per the MNREGA guidelines, only adult members above 18 years who are interested to do unskilled work at the statutory minimum wage can work under MGNREGA. But in Santoshpur, small children are found to work under it.

Nasima Khatun, her son (16 years) has worked days under MGNREGA and got Rs 300 while the job card is in the name of her husband Samin Ansari.

Names of Dead People are there in the Job Cards

Jekria Tirkey (30 years), whose father is already dead, but the job card is in his name till yet.

Redressal of Grievances

Redressal of grievances is an integral part of the NREG scheme. Majority of the respondents of the field do not know that there is provision for grievance redressal.

Profile of Non-Job Cardholder Households

Around 45 per cent households are the non-job cardholders. This may be due to their lack of interest to work under the MGNREGS as they have greater mobility for alternative money making job opportunities even at a distance place. Among the sample non-job card holder households around 50 per cent households have already applied for job cards. The waiting time after the applications for job cards as reported by the respondents vary between five to 24 months. The reasons for non-issuance of job cards may be due to several factors such as relative socio-political and economic strength of the households in the village, awareness level, close relationship with the PRI functionaries' etc. Those who have not applied for job cards may be due to lack of interest and awareness.

About Gram Sathi

To make the MGNREGS activities more vibrant Government of Odisha lunched the Gram Sathi scheme. In this scheme two persons in each village are recruited in each village to assist the implementation of MGNREGA especially organise cardholders to start a job, write muster rolls, help check measurement, payment of labourers etc. However, Gram Sathi in this panchayat are not trained and aware about the policies.

About Sarpanch

The sarpanch is the most important agent of implementation of the MGNREGS as he/she works at the local level with the help of Gram Sathi and Village Level Workers (VLW). As the GPs are authorised to spend 50 per cent of the NREGA fund, the sarpanch need to play a major role in this regard. They are involved in the planning, designing and implementation of MGNREGS. Awareness of the sarpanch regarding different aspects of the scheme is thus crucial for its successful implementation. The observation from the field reveals that the sarpanch is not much aware about the scheme. Julia Tigga, a tribal lady who is sarpanch in this panchayat is not much active and aware about MGNREGS. Her husband who acts as a contractor is misleading the entire programme. While distributing work and job cards he is taking care of those who voted for him. Even though he is well about some rules and regulations, he is not ready to share it among villagers.

MGNREGA and Tribal Livelihood

MGNREGS is the most significant scheme to uplift the overall quality of life of rural households. One of the major objectives of the scheme is the improvement of the income levels and enhancement of livelihood security in rural areas by guaranteeing 100 days of wage employment in a financial year to every registered household. However, the data from the field reflected that there is little impact of MGNREGA on tribal livelihoods. By comparing the annual income of beneficiaries before MGNREGA and after MGNREGA, it is found that there is increase of 28.52 per cent in income of the beneficiaries. Like that there is increase of 47.42 per cent in expenditure of the beneficiaries. Before the implementation of MGNREGA the villagers were generally spending 64.24 per cent from their income while after the implementation of this scheme they are spending 73.69 per cent of their income.

Annual Households' Expenditure before and after MGNREGA

Table 20.4 : Source-wise Annual Households Expenditure before and after MGNREGA

Source of expenditure	*Percentage of Before MGNREGA*	*Percentage of After MGNREGA*
Food	69.13	59.29
Clothing	7.68	8.28
Health	3.46	3.57
Cooking fuel	0.99	1.24
Education	0.9	1.2
Transport	2.14	2.63
Social/religious function	3.95	4.55
Alcohol	1.91	2.19
Electricity bill	0.96	2.83
Phone bill	0.35	2.55
Agri.Equipments and seeds	2.36	2.31
Household assets	1.38	2.04
Recreation	0.27	0.31
Maintenance of House	4.52	7.01

Source: Primary data.

The above data shows that due to change in income there is also change in expenditure. Generally, the expenditure of villagers were more on food items around 69.13 per cent and less on other non-food items before implementation of MGNREGA. But after the implementation of this scheme the expenditure on food items gradually shifted to non-food items which include both luxury and necessity items. For this the expenditure on food items is gradually decreasing (59.29 per cent) and on non-food items is increasing. This reflects that there is some impact on tribal livelihoods but this impact is considered as very little. This is because no proper and regular work which is the direct result of poor implementation.

On the issue of asset creation nothing much is observed from the field. Except road work no other works are being taken here. Recently, some initiations have been taken by Sarpanch for the SC/ST land development. In all three hamlets including Jaratoli, Militoli and Pahadtoli, people had expressed their disappointments with MGNREGA works. Here, the following diagram shows that maximum numbers of respondents (68 per cent) have the negative opinion on MGNREGA.

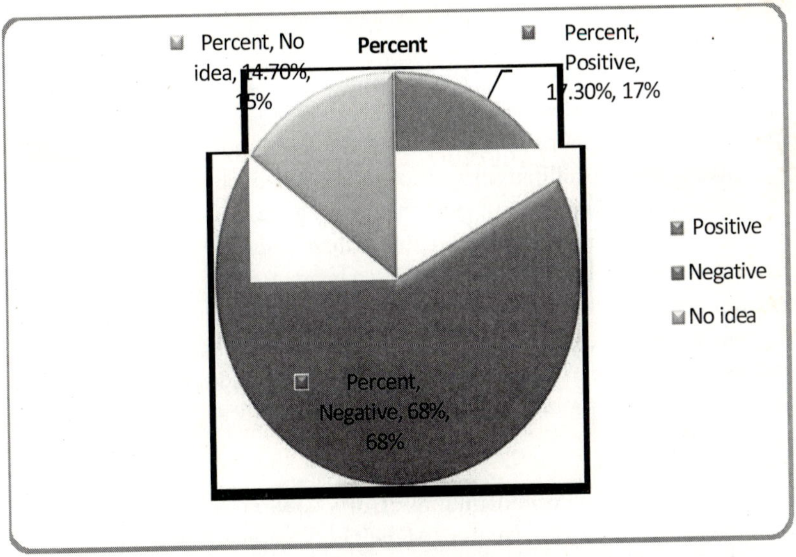

Fig. Positive and negative response on MGNREGA.

According to some villagers, whatever the poor gets from MNREGA work spends only to feed his stomach and also in alcohol for few days, nothing left for saving, clothing, and maintenance of house as well as children's education.

Impact on Migration

By securing livelihood, MGNREGA also mitigates seasonal/distress migration which has been a significant source of employment and income for a large proportion of rural population. But there are two types of risks associated with working under MGNREGS. First, in most of the cases, the wages are paid on piece rate basis and depending on his/her performance; a worker may get even less than the minimum prevailing market wage rate. Second, as per the provisions under the scheme, a household should get minimum 100 days of employment. But, the GP fails to provide 100 days of employment to job seekers. Such limited and irregular supply of works restricts the job-seekers from working under MGNREGS. Regular employment opportunities also motivate many of them to migrate to other states like Gujarat, Maharashtra, Nagpur, Raipur and Tata.

Conclusion

MGNREGA is landmark legislation in the history of social security legislation in India after independence. Enacted after a successful struggle for a comprehensive employment guarantee law, this legislation is a partial victory towards a full-fledged right to employment. Though MGNREGA is a well thought out legislation, a powerful tool in the hands of the common people to get their basic livelihood, but its poor execution, deprives of them of their basic rights. The study reveals that despite numerous problems, MGNREGA is a programme that has begun to make a difference in the lives of women. For example, women have started asserting their voices in the family matters and nature of spending money. Though, awareness still continues to be a stiff challenge, women in study area have become pro-active learners and participants in the schemes. Furthermore, it is popular among the workers, who routinely ask if more work could be made available to them under the MGNERGA, they would like to do. Clearly, there is a massive demand for MGNREGA work, and the administration should respond to it by increasing the scale of employment. Both our executive leader and law maker should take due care that the scheme reaches the people who deserve it. Change should be made at ground levels in the system. Due care should be taken for effective implementation of the scheme.

Suggestions

- There should be continuous efforts towards creating adequate awareness on different provisions of MGNREGS amongst the people.
- Efficient utilisation of resources under the scheme requires bringing in transparency and accountability. Provision for social audit at the panchayat level on a regular basis can play a significant role in this regard.
- The leadership style should be democratic in nature. This will facilitate greater community participation, information sharing, expression of opinion by the rural mass, and development of social networks.
- A great deal of work that needs to be carried out as far as awareness, fair implementation and assurance of accessibility is concerned.

References

1. Baisakh, P. (2007). Has NREGA Reduced Poverty in Orissa? *Odisha diary,* July 23.

2. Dey, S. and Bedi, A. (2010). *'The National Rural Employment Guarantee Scheme,* in Birbhum, *Economic and Political Weekly,* XLV (41). pp. 19-25.

3. Dreze J. (2007). NREGA: Dismantling the contractor raj, *The Hindu*, 20th November.

4. Indian Institute of Technology, Madras, Chennai (2009). Evaluation of National Rural Employment Guarantee Act: In Districts: Cuddlore, Dindigul, Kanchipuram, Nagai, Thiruvalallur: State: Tamil Nadu, May.

5. Jain, S.P. (2001). "Emerging Institutions for Decentralised Rural Development", NIRD Publication, Hyderabad.

6. Karalay, G.N. (2005). "Integrated Approach to Rural Development: Policies, Programmes and Strategies", Concept Publishing Company, New Delhi.

7. Kashyap, C. L. (1989). "Management and Planning of Rural Development in India", Sterling Publishers, New Delhi.

8. Khan, A.U. and Saluja, M.R. (2007). *Impact of MNREGA on Rural Livelihoods*, Paper Presented in 10th Sustainable Development Conference on Sustainable Solutions: A Spotlight on South Asian Research, Islamabad, Pakistan, December 10-12.

9. Mathur, L. (2009). Silent but successful initiative, *The Hindu*. 1st March.

10. Mathur L. (2007). Employment Guarantee: Progress So Far, *Economic and Political Weekly*, Vol. 42, No. 52, pp. 17-20.

11. Mohsin, N. (1985), "Rural Development Through Government Programmes", Mittal Publications, Delhi.

12. Roy, D.S. and Samanta, D. (2010), *Good Governance and Employment Generation through NREGA: A case Study of Gram Panchayat in West Bengal*, Documentation. Prepared for the Conferencc on "Infrastructure, Finance and Governance: Push for Growth, Organised by Ministry of Rural Development, GOI.

13. Shah, M. (2004). National Rural Employment Guarantee Act: A Historic opportunity, *Economic and Political Weekly*, December 11, pp. 5287-5291.

14. http://www.nrega.net

15. http://www.nrega.nic.in/guidelines.htm

16. http://www.righttofoodindia.org

21

Forest Resources–An Ideal Alternative for Tribal Development and Health Care

Shivesh

Abstract

The Indian sub-continent is inhabited by 53 million tribal populations belonging to over 550 tribal communities that come under 227 linguistic groups. They inhibit varied geographic and climatic zones of the country. Their vocation ranges from hunting, gathering, cave dwelling nomadics to societies with settled culture living in complete harmony with nature. Forests have been their dear home and totally submitted themselves to forest settings. Their relationship with the forest was symbolic in nature. They have been utilising the resources without disturbing the delicate balance of the eco-system. Tribals thus mostly remained as stable societies and were unaffected by the social, cultural, material and economic evolutions that were taking place with the so-called civilised societies. But this peaceful co-existence of the tribals has been disturbed in recent years by the interference in their habitats. Traditional communities living close to nature have, over the years acquired unique knowledge about the use of living biological resources. Modernisation, especially industrialisation and urbanisation has endangered the rich heritage of knowledge and expertise of age old wisdom of the traditional communities. A study on the utilisation of local tribals revealed that they hold precious knowledge on the specific use of a large number of agents of wild plant and animal origins, the use of many are hitherto unknown to the outside world. The tribal people are the real custodians of the medicinal plants and thus by using their talents they can be developed as real custodian of Health Care in Indigenous field.

The present paper explains how medicinal the knowledge of medicinal plants can prove to be an ideal alternative for tribal development especially in the area of Health Care.

Introduction

The Indian sub-continent is inhabited by 53 million tribal populations belonging to over 550 tribal communities that come under 227 linguistic groups.

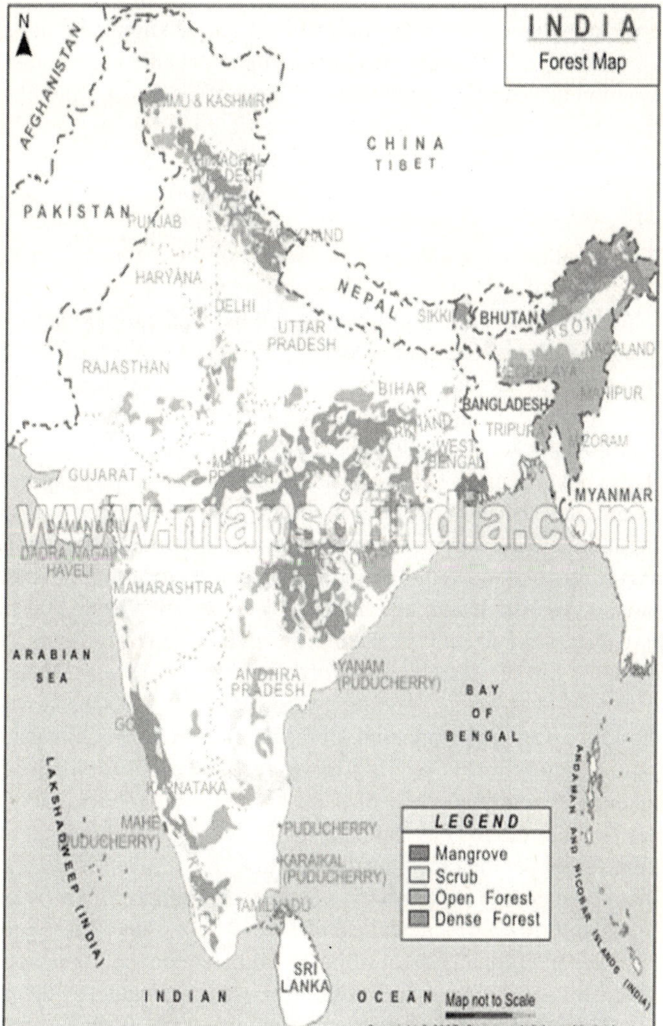

Fig. Showing Forests Density on State-wise in India.

They inhibit varied geographic and climatic zones of the country. Their vocation ranges from hunting, gathering, cave dwelling nomadics to societies with settled culture living incomplete harmony with nature. Forests have been their dear home and totally submitted themselves to forest settings. Their relationship with the forest was symbolic in nature. They have been utilising the resources without disturbing the delicate balance of the eco-system. Tribals thus mostly remained as stable societies and were unaffected by the social, cultural, material and economic evolutions that were taking place with the so called civilised societies. But this peaceful co-existence of the tribals have been disturbed in recent years by the interference in their habitats. Traditional communities living close to nature have, over the years acquired unique knowledge about the use of living biological resources. Modernisation, especially industrialisation and urbanisation has endangered the rich heritage of knowledge and expertise of age old wisdom of the traditional communities. A study on the utilisation of local tribals revealed that they hold precious knowledge on the specific use of a large number of agents of wild plant and animal origins, the use of many are hitherto unknown to the outside world.

The tribal people are the real custodians of the medicinal plants. Out of 45,000 species of wild plants, 7500 species are used for medicinal purposes.

The World Health Organisation (WHO) has been promoting a movement for 'Saving plants for saving lives'. This is because of the growing understanding of the pivotal role medicinal plants play in providing herbal remedies to health maladies. India is the home of several important traditional system of healthcare like Ayurveda.

This system depends heavily on herbal products. Several millions of Indian households have been using through the ages nearly 8000 species of medicinal plants for their healthcare needs. Over one and half million traditional healers use a wide range of medicinal plants for treating ailments of both humans and livestock across the length and breadth of the country. Over 800 medicinal plants pecies are currently in use by the Indian herbal industry. However, barring some 120 species, all others are collected from the wild. This collection often involves destructing harvesting when parts like roots, bark, wood, stem and the whole plant (herb) are used. Unregulated wild harvest, alongside habitat loss and degradation is leading to resource depletion which in turn is endangering the very survival of these species. No wonder, many of these species listed in the red data book of the IUCN and the Botanical Survey of India are valued for their medicinal properties.

The tribal people of Orissa have been in the practice of preserving a rich heritage of information on medicinal plants and their usage. These people have faith in their traditional system of healthcare and generally practice it. They have their own traditional physicians who use these plants as their material medica. They have rich and outstanding traditional knowledge and wisdom regarding material for healing of commonly occurring ailments. They have both the know-how and do-how for preparing the medicine and its administration. Unfortunately, this information is yet to be collected systematically and comprehensively and maintained in databases in a manner they would help in protecting their IPR.

Herbal History and Tradition in Indian Context

The Rigveda, the oldest document of human knowledge mentions the use of medicinal plants in the treatment of man and animals. Ayurveda gives the account of actual beginning of the ancient medical science of India, which according to western scholars was written between 2500 to 600 B.C. Charaka and Susruta wrote around 1000 B.C. Charaka concentrates more on medicine while Susruta deals with surgery in details along with therapeutics. After the invasion of India by the Greeks and Mohemmadans successively, the Indian system of medicine came to decline and no original works were then undertaken. During and after the British rule, there were two opinions, one supporting the rich treasure of knowledge of Indian system of medicine and the other discarding it, calling it an old system based mainly on empiricism considering that this system has survived to such an extent the ravages of time, it cannot be brushed aside as "unscientific". It might be interesting to note that a large percentage, approximately 80 per cent of the population of the world still relies on the old systems in some form or the other, and on the indigenous material medicine for human and animal treatment, due to cultural traditions and low buying capacity. When we combine this economic factor with proven efficacy, our herbal drugs stand out as the better choice for millions. History shows that many of our important pharmacopial drugs were known and were also used in some form or the other possibly long before they were introduced into the western medicine and before their actions were investigated on scientific lines.

Measures to conserve biodiversity have been taken in India since hoary past. Elements of this aspect of traditional wisdom can be gathered through analytical studies of the ethnic societies which are less influenced by the modern civilisation and also by scrutinising the ancient texts written in Sanskrit, Pali, Tamil, etc. The Vishnu samhita is one of such scripture in Sanskrit language. It appears that this work contains some direct instructions in connection with conservation of the bio-diversity.

According to the text of Vishnu samhita, causing any harm to the plant(s)/ animal(s) is a sin. Even purloining of part(s)/ product(s) of any of these living beings is a crime. The sinner/criminal is liable to chastisement in this life and also after death. The punishment are of diverse nature: pecuniary, corporal, expiatory and donation of specific article(s) to Brahmins. In this scripture there are some indirect instructions too, which can be gleaned by analysing the dietary regulations and the use of bio-diversity in different religious rites.

Traditional and folklore medicine bequeathed from generation to generation is rich in domestic recipes for common ailments. Traditional medicine encompasses protection and restoration of health over millennia. The best known examples of traditional medicine, differing in concept and protocol, are well developed systems such as acupuncture and Ayurved a treatments that have been widely used to sustain human health in India.

Developed countries, in recent times, are turning to use of herbal drugs and remedies. About 1400 herbal preparations are used widely, according to a recent survey in member states of European Union. Herbal preparations are popular and are of significance in primary health care in Belgium, France, Germany and the Netherlands.

Such popularity of plant derived products has been traced to their increasing acceptance and use in the cosmetic industries as well as to increase public costs in the daily maintenance of personal health and wellbeing. Examples of such beauty oriented therapeutically are skin tissue generators, antiwrinkling agents and anti-age creams. Also among the poor, cures and drugs derived from plants constitute the main source of health care products.

Despite the increasing use of medicinal plants, their future is being threatened by complacency concerning their conservation. Reserves of herbs and stocks of medicinal plants in developing countries are diminishing several important species are in danger of extinction as a result of growing trade demands for safer and cheaper healthcare products and new plant based theapeutic markets in preference to more expensive targets-specific drugs and biopharmaceuticals. Such concerns have stimulated action in chronicling and conserving medicinal plants.

References

Anderson, Clifford R., *Your guide to health,* Orientalwatchman Publishing House (Pune, 6th sept, 2001) pp. 644-712.

Ambasta, S.P. (Ed.), The useful plants of India, Publications and Information Directorate (CS1R).

Bakhru, H.K., *Herbs that heal*, Orient paperbacks, (New Delhi, 1992).

Chopra, Nayar, Chopra: *Glossary of Indian Medicinal plants*, CSIR, (New Delhi, 1956).

Chiej, Roberto, *The Macdonald Encyclopaedia of Medicinal Plants,* Macdonald and Company Limited, (London, 1988).

Das, Bhagwan, *Fundamentals of Ayurvedic Medicine, Konark Publishers*, (Delhi, 1989).

Dastur, J.F., Medicinal Plants of India and Pakistan, D.B.Taraporewala Sons Pvt. Ltd., (Mumbai, 1988).

Jain, S.K., *Glimpses of Ethnobotany,* National Book Trust of India, A.S. Green Park, (New Delhi,1981), pp. 7-270.

Kar, A. and Choudhary, B.K., *Important mineral content of a few Ayurvedic herbs with a discussion on Medicinal aspects*, Indian drugs. 31(3) -127-130.

Khanna, G., *All about herbal remedies*, Vikal Publishing House, Pvt. Limited (New Delhi, 1994).

Kloss, Jethro: *Back to Eden, life line books*, (California, 1975).

Nadkarni, K.M., *Indian Materia Medica*, 3rd edition, Popular Book Dep., Bombay, 1954.

Nayar, S.L. and Chopra, I.C., *Research in Indigenous Drugs*, In Glossary of Indian Medicinal Plants, CSIR, New Delhi, I-XI.

Nagarjuna, S. *et.al., Cultivation and utilisation of medicinal plants*, CSIR, (Jammu Tawi,1982), pp. 584-604.

Schultes, R.E. The role of Ethnobotanist in the search for the new medicinal plants, 1962, Lioydia 25(4): 257-266.

22

Problems and Prospects of Mainstreaming Gender in the Bangladesh Civil Service

Syed Muhammad Sajjad Kabir

Nazmunnessa Mahtab

Abstract

Gender mainstreaming is a globally accepted strategy for promoting gender equality. The main objective of the study was to examine the government policies and practices of gender mainstreaming in the relevant ministries selected under the study. The selected ministries were: Ministry of Planning and Economic Resources Division (ERD); Ministry of Finance; Ministry of Health; Ministry of Labour and Manpower; Ministry of Women and Children Affairs; and Ministry of Education. Data were collected on a quantitative and qualitative basis based on primary and secondary sources. Findings stated that although the number of women participating in the civil service examination and entering the service had been increasing, they were especially those coming from the urban areas. In effective administration of the quota system had been a major problem in establishing a balanced position in the distributions of positions among women in the civil service. Majority of women, however, were in the lower ranks of the hierarchy, and women were very scarcely seen in higher and mid-level positions. Despite constitutional guarantees and other governmental initiatives to remove gender discrimination from the civil service, women continued to fight against a variety of obstacles to advance their career and achieve success. Positive discrimination (quota) for women was limited to initial recruitment; it had not been extended to include promotion. Unco-operative and negative treatment and attitudes of men and systematic constraints in career building and advancement had implications for women's morale, motivation and performance. Thus it was evident that women in the Bangladesh civil service had to break both the brick wall and the glass ceiling to enter, work and survive in the unfriendly, deplorable environment and advance their career.

Keyword: Bangladesh Civil Service, Gender Mainstreaming, and Women Empowerment.

Introduction

Gender Mainstreaming

Gender mainstreaming is the process of assessing the implications for women and men of all planned action, including legislation, policies or programmes, in all areas and all levels. It is a strategy for making women's as well as men's concerns and experiences an integral dimension of the design, implementation, monitoring and evaluation of policies and programmes in all political, economic and social spheres so that women and men benefit equally and inequality is not perpetuated. Implementing a gender mainstreaming strategy requires organisations to think about gender in all aspects of their work. In Fourth World Conference on Women held in Beijing (1995) convened by the United Nations ratified the Platform for Action as a transformatory global agenda for achieving gender equality and women's empowerment. Gender mainstreaming was identified as a key strategy and it has been an integral part of equal opportunities policy throughout the world. But in the years that followed neither the ideals nor the strategy have been easy to fulfill. After Beijing, although some international and national organisations and government departments took steps to implement gender mainstreaming, this often did not go beyond formally adopting a gender mainstreaming policy. Despite major efforts over the past years for advancing gender equality and equity, women are still under represented in various aspects of life around the world. There are differences from country to country, region to region, because disadvantage is caused by cultural, historical and social factors.

Gender Mainstreaming in Bangladesh

Mainstreaming gender is a strategy that has been strongly emphasised in the Beijing Platform for Action. The Government of Bangladesh has endorsed, without reservations, the Platform for Action (PFA) of the Fourth World Conference on Women recommended that state parties prepare their own national plans of action for the implementation of PFA, within their country by 1996. Accordingly, the Government of Bangladesh with the support by Canadian International Development Agency (CIDA), Danida and UNICEF undertook an elaborate process to develop the National Action Plan, which was completed in June 1998. The PFA was structured into twelve critical areas of concern.

On the basis of these twelve critical areas of concern, in Bangladesh twelve ministries/divisions were selected on a priority basis to address these issues. However, as each critical area of concern involved more than one ministry, a few more ministries were included making a total of fifteen ministries. These ministries/divisions are as follows: Ministry of Women and Children Affairs; Ministry of Agriculture; Ministry of Education; Ministry of Environment and Forest; Ministry of Fisheries and Livestock; Ministry of Health and Family Welfare; Ministry of Home Affairs; Ministry of Industry; Ministry of Information; Ministry of Labour and Manpower; Ministry of Law, Justice and Parliamentary Affairs; Local Government Division; Rural Development and Cooperative Division; Ministry of Social Welfare; and Ministry of Planning and Planning Commission. The implementation and monitoring of the National Action Plan (NAP) became the responsibility of all the ministries and not of any particular ministry or sector. All ministries needed to take an active role in implementing the NAP within their own sphere and coordinate activities with those of other ministries towards the same goal. Furthermore, these line ministries were required to actively participate in promoting a policy of mainstreaming a gender perspective in all of their sectoral programmes with a view to ensuring sustainable development through fulfillment of PFA objectives (MOWCA, 1998).

The study recognises that various policies and measures that have been undertaken by the international agencies and national governments have impacted Bangladeshi women in a non-linear fashion. While governments' sincere commitments and efforts are praiseworthy, women's lives and working conditions over the last few decades call for further investigation on their experiences and impacts of these policy measures and thus open up space to raise questions on the efficacy of these policies to ensure women's advancement and gender equality as well as the role of different implementing agencies. Against this background the present study has been undertaken to assess the effective implementation of the National Action Plan for bringing about women's advancement in Bangladesh, with emphasis on "gender mainstreaming" activities.

Objectives of the Study

The main objective of the study was to examine the government policies and practices of gender mainstreaming in the relevant ministries selected under the study.

The specific objectives were to:

- Present a comprehensive view of the position of women in BCS cadres;
- Examine the government policies and practices relating to increase women's participation in the cadre services;
- Analyse policy towards empowerment of women in Bangladesh;
- Assess the implementation of women and gender related policies in Bangladesh;

• Assess the awareness of the concerned Ministry regarding gender mainstreaming;

• Determine the strategy of the concerned Ministry for effective implementation of gender mainstreaming policies and programmes;

• Identify the process of institutionalisation of gender mainstreaming in all the Ministries working towards women's advancement and at all levels;

• Examine the efficacy of gender mainstreaming as a strategy to ensure gender equality;

• Identify the gaps and challenges in existing policy and processes and suggest alternative vision and agenda for the future;

• Identify the barriers/obstacles, problems behind low representation of women in the BCS.

• Suggest remedies to overcome the problems, to improve the overall situation of women to face the challenges of achieving gender equality and empowerment through the prospects of maintaining gender mainstreaming in all aspects of their life.

Methodology

However, specific focus will be given on the position of women in the *Bangladesh Civil Services*. The study will include six specific Ministries of the Government of Bangladesh. These are: (1) Ministry of Planning and Economic Resources Division (ERD); (2) Ministry of Finance; (3) Ministry of Health; (4) Ministry of Labour and Manpower; (5) Ministry of Women and Children Affairs; and (6) Ministry of Education.

The study was based on the collection of data based on primary and secondary sources. Data was collected on a quantitative and qualitative basis. Quantitative data focused on the number of women entering the Bangladesh Civil Services in the different Cadres. This included—

• Review of previous number of women identifying the rate of increase or decrease of women entering the services;

• Review of relevant literature, official reports and documents, policies and plans of the Government of Bangladesh;

On the other hand qualitative data was based on:

• Meetings and discussions with BCS officers including both females and male using unstructured questionnaire to assess their knowledge and perception about governance issues, women's issues and concerns.

• Intensive interviews, meetings, and discussions with WID Focal Point officials of the respective ministries under study;

• Participatory discussions held to obtain their opinion on several issues relating to their roles and responsibilities, their expectations as women officials, their relationship with their male colleagues.

• Review of Gender Mainstreaming Training Programmes organised by different Ministries under study and also by different agencies conducting training programmes for capacity building of the officials of different Ministries of the government.

• Focus Group Discussion (FGD) was undertaken with officers representing different Ministries, Departments during their training programme on "gender mainstreaming" organised by the Department of Population Sciences, University of Dhaka. A total of 50 (25 in each group) officers were interviewed, their opinion and views taken into consideration regarding their idea of gender mainstreaming and programmes and policies of the government offices or agencies represented by them.

• However, as all the Ministries could not be covered as planned, detailed interviews were taken from individual BCS officers working in different Ministries and posted in different places.

Findings of the Study

The findings are presented in *three* sections: The *first* section is based on the status of women in the Bangladesh Civil Service. The *second* section is based on limited information collected from the following Ministries, such as the Ministry of Planning, the Ministry of Health and Family Planning and the Ministry of Information. The *third* section consists of detailed information collected from individual officers representing different Ministries, and working at both national and field levels.

Women in Bangladesh Civil Service (BCS)

The BCS is a broad based service with all its member cadres as Class 1 Gazetted officers. Recruitment to the cadre services is done through the Public Service Commission (PSC) on the basis of open competition. The higher civil service in Bangladesh (BCS) is horizontally categorised into 29 cadres and vertically into six ranks. Appointment to the BCS is usually at the rank of assistant secretary or its equivalent in some other cadres (such as Magistrate at the Upazila level). After liberation in 1971, Bangladesh civil service was born. In the reform of 1980, there were 14 cadres and 22 sub-cadres. In 1987, this was changed into 30 cadres, but at present the Bangladesh civil service has 29 cadres. Since 1972, women have been participating in the civil service of Bangladesh. However, it was found that the civil service remained under represented by women. Till 1980, there were no women in administration, judicial, postal and communication cadre; only one woman was in the revenue department of finance division, four women were in Foreign Service and six women were in Information department. Prior to 1982, there were very few women in the civil service. Since then an increasing number of women have been appearing in the civil service examination and getting recruited to various cadre services. By 1986, it reached at 1417 (Karim, 2008). Recognising this problem, the Constitution of Bangladesh has made significant provisions to provide equal opportunity for males and females in every sphere of life. In addition the government adopted quotas (reservation of posts) for women in entering the civil service and took many policies not only to increase women's representation in the civil service but to integrate women into the mainstream of development (Mahtab, 2003). The government has made special arrangements to enhance female participation in the civil service, by reserving a 10 per cent employment quota for gazette posts and 15 per centf or non-gazette posts for the females. Data from 1994 to 2002 shows that there were only two Joint Secretaries, eight Deputy Secretaries in the civil service (Mahtab, 2007). Although the Government of Bangladesh has shown a strong commitment to gender equality at policy and strategy level, there has been a failure to consistently translate the commitment into actions. The participation of women in Bangladesh civil service is still very poor. Only 6.44 per cent of women are working in the civil service (Mahtab, 2007). Despite government's initiatives, women's participation in the civil service has not increased dramatically during the last three decades. Table, clearly depicts the views expressed by the women officers.

Table 22.1: Representation of Women at Different Levels of Civil Service

Position	*Total*	*Male*	*Female*
Secretary	52	50	2
Additional Secretary	171	159	12
Joint Secretary	429	395	34
Deputy Secretary	1418	1248	170
Senior Assistant Secretary	1492	1221	271
Assistant Secretary	941	695	246

Source: Ministry of Establishment, June 16, 2010.

Ministry of Planning

The Ministry of Planning is presently involved in the task of preparation of the Sixth Five Year Plan and the concerned officials have realised that including gender issues into the Poverty Reduction Strategy Paper (PRSP), that is "engendering", will lead to equity, efficiency, effectiveness and finally empowerment. Recognising these aspects of gender equality, the Government has adopted several areas of concern as well as potential measures for making further progress towards gender equality targeted till the year 2015. As mentioned by the Ministry of Planning, these include: combating continuing negative sex ratios; eliminating violence against women; reducing high maternal mortality; removing restrictions on women's employment and economic opportunities; ensuring formal equality; supporting quotas and affirmative actions at all levels and in all spheres; creating women friendly institutional environment; and generating sex-disaggregated statistics.

Ministry of Health

Compared to the other Ministries under the study, the Ministry of Health is in a better position with regard to gender issues in Bangladesh. A review of the activities included in the National Action Plan of the Ministry of Health and Family Welfare clearly indicates that this Ministry has achieved progress in relation to the major areas of concentration outlined in the plan. With regard to health issues concerning women the Ministry was involved in the National Action Plan developed by the MOWCA (2003-2007). This was prepared after the completion of the period of the initial National Action Plan of GOB (1997-2002). The plan addressed issues of: Adolescent Girls; HIV/ AIDS; Disabled and Mental Health concerns of women and children under 18; Reproductive Health Problems; Healthcare services for ageing women; Care and Treatment to patients with burns (due to violence and other causes); Adequate measures within the health system to identify and respond to cases of violence/sexual abuse against women; Specific programmes for men aimed at providing complete and accurate information on safe and responsible sexual and reproductive behaviour to support their partners and promote their health during pregnancy, child birth and after child birth; and Nutritional Status of girls and women.

Ministry of Information

The Ministry of Information seems to be in a better position in relation to gender issues. There is greater coordination between the WID Focal Points and the Sub-WID Focal Points and coordination meetings are held regularly between these officers. The officers are receiving training on different issues related to gender. In this regard the different training Institutes have been asked to adopt measures for this purpose. As a result, the participation of women in these training programmes have increased.

Findings based on Interviews, Discussions, Focus Group and Observations

A total of about 110 officers were included in this section. Officers represented different batches and different cadres too. The main focused areas are as follows:

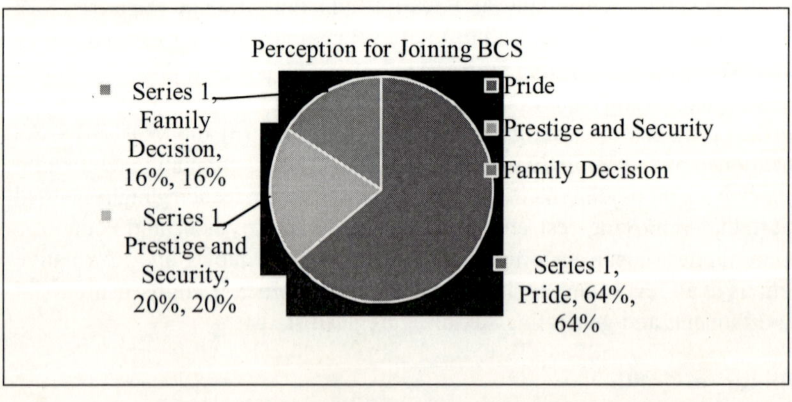

Fig. Opinion and Perception for Joining BCS.

Opinion and Perception for Joining BCS

On the question of the choice of joining BCS, majority of the women officers (64 per cent) expressed their pride in joining the government service; some (20 per cent) referred to the prestige and security of joining government service as opposed to private service; while the rest (16 per cent) mentioned that they joined the service because of family's decision. This finding clearly reveals that today in Bangladesh educated girls especially from the urban areas have the right and freedom to make free choices regarding choice of making a career without family interference or objections.

Merits and Demerits of Working as BCS Officers

Regarding opinion of the women officers as to the merits and demerits of the service 79 per cent of the officers mentioned about the system of the quota through which women could be recruited, while about 21 per cent expressed their dislike about the quota system, because they thought that the system of quota was an additional process of discriminating women from getting their usual share through merit.

Benefits of Service

In comparison to their male counterparts regarding benefits received as BCS officers the women officers responded quite negatively. About 90 per cent responded that they actually receive no benefits regarding participation in training, delegation in foreign visits, representation in different decision making committees; only four per cent mentioned that they seldom have the opportunity of availability of such services. Another important issue covered in the study was that of promotion. In Bangladesh, political affiliation has become an important criterion to determine promotion. Political connections do influence the promotion system in the BCS and anyone with relatives, friends of Ministers or members of Parliament have easy access to go up the ladder. Women being at the lowest rungs of the career ladder are often debarred from this opportunity. In addition, the civil service (bureaucracy) has become highly politicised in the sense that all recruitments, and promotion are made on the basis of politics as to which party they belong to. In this case it is the men who receive all the favour. Women lag far behind men.

Gender Equality

It was rather amazing to know from the male officers (about 65 per cent) that 'gender equality' was fully achieved for women folk of the country. By this they were emphasising on the policies of the government with regard to provision of free education for girls up to Class 12, together with Stipend and Scholarship, whereas boys were not been given any such additional advantages. According to men, the quota system to increase the intake of women in the civil service and other public agencies has been an important starting point towards gender equality in Bangladesh and an additional preference accorded to women officers. Some of the male respondents (35 per cent) presented a completely different view regarding gender equality. According to them there is no need for any issue of gender equality for women when it is clear that both women and men enjoy the same facilities in the services. They were totally refusing that any element of gender equality were required for the women officers. On the other hand women officers (80 per cent) were totally on the denial regarding achievement of gender equality. According to them women were denied their basic human rights of enjoying freedom of expression of their opinion, their participation in the affairs of their departmental issues and even taking part in important decision where they are not even considered.

Working Situation of Women Officers

An attempt was made to interview some women officers to learn more and explore about their opinions with respect to their work, working conditions, likes, dislikes, complaints and attitudes. The working situation of the women officers has been described as the circle starts with (i) negative and unco-operative attitudes of the male officers towards their female colleagues; (ii) inferiority complex of male officers in comparing their wives (mainly a housewife doing household chores) with their female colleagues (happily working in office), thus resulting in frustration and unfriendly attitudes towards the female colleague; (iii) observing the pretty, smart, beautiful female colleague and developing a desire or aspiration to own her; (iv) finding difficult in accepting the dedication, sincerity and efficiency with which the women officers work; (v) jealousy on the part of other women officers who cannot work with equal skill or dedication. It is a very difficult and degrading atmosphere that the women officers have to work and they themselves cannot come out of this

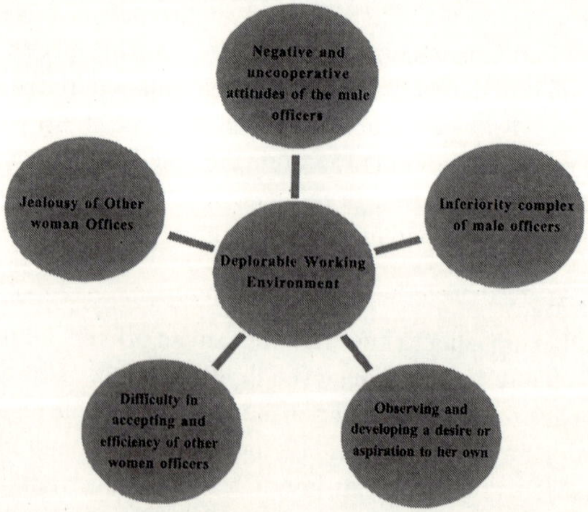

Fig. Vicious Circle of Working Condition of Women Officers.

devastating and suffocating environment and ultimately succumb to the unwanted working environment.

Problems Faced by Women Officers

Whenever a women officer is absent from office without the notifying her superior she is often harassed by her boss and usually hears objectionable remarks which she cannot disclose or share with anyone as it becomes a matter of losing her prestige. On the other hand many male officers are generally and frequently absent from their office premises, often to have tea, smoke or see a friend in other department without informing anyone least his boss. Most of these officers often stay beyond office time to make up for the time spent otherwise and try to demonstrate their dedication and sincerity towards their work thus pleasing or satisfying their superiors. Apart from this, if any woman officer excels in her performance she is usually criticised as trying to please her boss, and her work is never given any recognition. Sometimes when they have to stay in office beyond time they are not entitled to any transport facilities to return home and they may face insecurity in staying so long in office.

Agenda for Gender Policy

Regarding gender policy, both women and men responded that the Constitution of Bangladesh drafted in 1972 guarantees certain rights and privileges to women as fundamental rights. Article 27 of the Constitution states that "All citizens are equal before the law and are entitled to equal protection of the law". Article 28 (1) of the Constitution states that the State shall not discriminate against any citizen on grounds only religion, race, caste, sex or place of birth. According to Article 28(2) "Women shall have equal rights with men in all spheres of the state and of public life". Article 28(3) states that "No citizen shall, on grounds only of religion, race, caste, sex or place of birth, be subjected to any disability, liability restriction or condition with regard to access to any place of public entertainment or resort, or admission to any educational institution". Again Article 29(1) states that "No citizen shall, on ground of ...sex ...be ineligible for, or discriminated against in repent of any employment or office in the service of the Republic". The constitutional guarantees ensure that women of Bangladesh possess full political rights with men.

CEDAW

Bangladesh has ratified the Convention on the Elimination of all forms of Discrimination against Women (CEDAW). In its report adopted at the Session of CEDAW held in the United Nations Headquarters in July 2010, Bangladesh presented the combined Sixth and Seventh Periodic Report where the Committee noted with satisfaction the existence of constitutional guarantee to equality between women and men as well as laws ensuring protection of women in Bangladesh. The government has withdrawn reservations about some provisions of CEDAW, relating to personal rights such as family benefits and guardianship of children. The withdrawn reservations of Bangladesh pertain to Article 13 (a) and Article 16 (1) (b) of the Convention. Article 13 (a) gives women the right to family benefits. Article 16 (1) (b) says "State's parties shall take all appropriate measures to ensure that men and women have the same rights and responsibilities with regard to guardianship, worship, trusteeship and adoption of children.

National Policy for the Advancement of Women

The National Policy for the Advancement of Women, which was declared by then Prime Minister, Sheikh Hasina, on March 8, 1997, has emphasised on engagement of women in all stages of development mainstreaming including the civil service and to establish equal rights. The policy has given special emphasis on women's employment and administrative employment. The main goals of the policy are: establish equality between men and women in all spheres; eliminate all forms of discrimination against women and girls; establish women human rights; develop women as human resource; recognise women's contribution in social and economic spheres; eliminate poverty among women; establish equality between men and women in administration, politics, education, games, sports and all other socio-economic spheres; eliminate all forms of oppression against women and girls; ensure empowerment of women in the fields of politics, administration and the economy; develop appropriate technology for women; ensure adequate health and shelter to women; and create positive images of women in the media.

Problems and Challenges

In identifying the needs assessment of the different ministries under study it was found that the ministries are faced with numerous constraints and limitations that impede the proper and effective implementation of all projects and programmes undertaken by them.

Lack of Understanding of Gender Issues by the Focal Points: During the interview and discussion with officials it was found that they are ignorant of understanding the use of the term. Gender has, not yet been commonly accepted as an analytical construct in development.

Lack of Proper Understanding of Gender Mainstreaming: Since the 1990s the concept of gender mainstreaming has been incorporated in the macro-framework of the country's plan documents. However, during the study it was revealed that there exists a gap between rhetoric and reality. There is still a great lack of understanding of the concept of gender mainstreaming by all concerned with women's issues. As a result of this, WID issue means to relatively improving the status of women rather than establishing gender equality or promoting women's empowerment.

Frequent Transfer and Ineffectiveness of Focal Points: It has also been found that a new officer who may be designated as WID Focal Point may not be able to deal with the issue due to his severe work schedule in this Ministry, thus resulting in the negligence or overlooking of women's issues and concerns.

Overlapping and Duplication of Projects: It has been found that many of the projects undertaken by the different Ministries have overlapping objectives and goals. For example, projects addressing the issue of violence against women are simultaneously been implemented by Ministry of Health and Ministry of Information. This leads to wastage of resources and time.

Lack of Training Skills: Almost all the ministries under study have identified that they do not possess adequate training skills to undertake projects related to diverse issues for women's development. More significantly, some of the officials have mentioned that never got the opportunity to receive any training on gender issues, or other aspects of development.

Inadequate Monitoring of Activities: Some of the ministries have undertaken too many activities at the same time. As a result, these activities are not being properly monitored. If each of the Ministries plan to implement specific programmes/projects within a definite time schedule, it becomes easier for monitoring the activities.

Donor Influence in Project Selection: The availability of donor assistance also influences the selection of WID interventions which is according to donor priorities. Often donor's own priorities do not necessarily meet the needs of the women for whom the project is undertaken.

Institutional Incapacity: The most serious problem faced by the work of its three implementing agencies, i.e., the Department of Women's Affairs, the Bangladesh Jatiyo Mahila Sanstha and the Shishu Academy are lack of committed and dedicated officials to undertake and implement projects for women's development. The field officers of the Department at the district and upazila levels are also constrained by extreme shortage of skilled/efficient personnel and proper logistics which is so crucial for the implementation of development projects at the grassroots level.

Stereotyped Mind-set, Negative and Reluctant Attitude of Males Involved in Women's Development: There is still a negative and rather reluctant attitude among male officers who are involved in the different Ministries in dealing with women's policies/programmes/and projects. They are yet to consider, understand and promote activities in bringing about gender equality in all spheres of life.

Apart from these general problems, individual Ministries under the study indicated some specific problems and needs assessment relating to their concern. These may be summarised as: fund crisis; lack of appropriate training; health services infrastructure and hospital facilities; lack of coordination among the inter ministerial and sectoral components addressing women's development; weak dissemination of gender issues; gender unfriendly work environment; lack of recognition of gender inequalities; and contradictory value systems on gender mainstreaming.

Existing Challenges and Emerging Needs

During the meetings, discussions with relevant officials in different Ministries, organisations, and professionals working with women's development issues and concerns, the challenges and emerging needs were identified.

- Developing gender mainstreaming policies.
- Introducing gender budgeting monitoring.
- Increasing the percentage of women officers and staff.
- Offering more training opportunities to women.
- Including more women in decision-making committees.
- Ensuring commitment for formulating and implementing gender policy.
- Ensuring visibility of engendered commitment and behaviour by the top level officers.
- Institutionalising gender policy and programmes.
- Ensuring allocation of adequate budget for women's programmes / projects.
- Creating a positive mend-set among the policy-makers.
- Improving working relationships between men and women.
- Initiating and improving monitoring and evaluation systems.
- Creating a more gender-friendly working environment to reduce harassment towards women and men in the workplace.
- Developing gender-friendly attitudes within the Ministries.
- Providing more transport facilities for women working late or odd hours.
- Ensuring accountability and transparency at all levels of programmes and activities.
- Establishing effective communication and coordination among the institutions.

Strategic Actions for Addressing Future Challenges

- Developing sustainable institutional commitment for mainstreaming gender.
- Ensure involvement of top management in gender sensitisation programmes.
- Encourage political commitment on the issue of gender mainstreaming from the top-level management.
- Ensure participation of policy makers/planners in gender-related programmes.
- Organise exposure visits for the policy makers and planners in both inside and outside country for exposing them to gender sensitive programmes and activities.
- Develop and implement gender policy with the support of top level management.
- Ensure appropriate allocation of budget and other required measures for implementing gender policy.

• Ensure effective utilisation of allocated resources for the purpose of gender mainstreaming.

• Develop appropriate monitoring indicators for assessing gender mainstreaming.

• Establish gender-friendly norms and practices.

• Ensure that institutional rules, regulations and procedures are gender-sensitive.

• Establish Day Care Centers, assess the needs of the Day Care Centers, and develop an effective mechanism for managing the Centers.

• Create gender facilities in each respective institution, address both practical and strategic gender needs and develop an action plan to address those needs.

• Ensure proper documentation of gender mainstreaming activities.

• Take adequate efforts to ensure proportionate representation of women in various decision-making bodies/committees.

• Undertake research for changes of behaviour and attitude towards gender equality.

• Capacity building of officials and all other functionaries should be undertaken through adequate training both at home and abroad.

• The Ministry of Women and Children Affairs should be more open and transparent with regard to policies addressing women's development in the country.

• Lastly, and a most important strategy is to encourage and strengthen partnerships and cooperation between the Government and NGOs, women's organisations, civil society, academic institutions, to form a common agenda and a common platform in the implementation of the National Action Plan, the Millenium Development Goals, the Poverty Reduction Strategy Paper (PRSP), in order to promote gender equality, development, peace, institutionalise gender mainstreaming, and achieve empowerment of women.

The following recommendations were offered:

1. Recognise that women in Bangladesh have been playing a vital role in the gradual social transformation of the country.
2. Emphasise civil society/human rights issues as a priority in discussions and negotiations with the Government.
3. Increase participation for the women representatives in regional and international workshops and conferences.
4. Expand scholarships and exchange programmes in all fields particularly for women.
5. Invest in more research and advocacy on the correlation between gender equality and political and economic development in Bangladesh.
6. Support more research and awareness raising activities on women's issues.

7. Support the documentation and dissemination of Bangladeshi women's achievement and challenges.

8. Change the mind-set and attitudes of men towards women.

9. Provide adequate and proper logistics support for women and a women friendly environment in the work place.

10. Provide adequate budget for undertaking women's activities.

References

Anne, *M.G. et al.* (1995). *Gender Issues in Bangladesh*, BRIDGE, Report No. 26, Institute of Development Studies, Brighton.

Astrida, N. (2002). *Gender Mainstreaming*: A Handbook, UNDP.

Habib, Z. (2000). *Through the Brick Wall, and the Glass Ceiling: Women in the Civil Service in Bangladesh*, Vol. 7, Number 3, pp. 197-209, Blackwell Publishers Ltd, USA.

Kabir, S.L. (2008). *Towards Gender Equality in the Bangladesh Civil Service, Empowerment*, Vol. 15, pp 41-54, Dhaka.

Karim, R. (2008). *Women in Bangladesh Civil Service: Vulnerability and Challenges*, Full Paper for the 12th World Congress of Rural Sociology, 6-11 July, Goyang, Korea.

Mahtab, N. (2003). *Performance Analysis of the Ministry of Women and Children Affairs in the Light of the Micro Chapter related to Women and Children Affairs of the Fifth Five Year Plan* (1997-2002), PLAGE, Dhaka.

Mahtab, N (2007). *Women in Bangladesh: From Inequality to Empowerment*, A.H. Publishing House, Dhaka.

Momtaz, J. (2007). *Gender Mainstreaming in Bangladesh Civil Service: Prospects and Constraints*, Asian Affairs, Vol. 29, No. 1, pp. 41-72, January-March, Dhaka.

MWCA (GOB) (1998). *National Action Plan for Women's Advancement: Implementation of the Beijing Platform for Action (PFA)*, Dhaka, Bangladesh.

MWCA (GOB) (2004). *Report on the Thematic Group on Women's Advancement and Rights Contribution towards Gendered Poverty Reduction Strategy Paper (PRSP) for Bangladesh*, Bangladesh Secretariat, Dhaka.

MWCA and UNDP (2004). *Report of the Joint Strategic Planning Workshop on Gender Mainstreaming*, Capacity Building for Gender Mainstreaming Project (BGD/97/037, Dhaka.

23

Political Empowerment of the Marginalised Groups in Nagaland: Emerging Alternatives

K. Vidyasagar Reddy

At the outset, this paper is aimed at understanding certain emerging alternatives that were expected to ensure political empowerment of the marginalised communities like the Scheduled Caste Groups (SCG) and others in Nagaland and India in the contemporary times. Since political empowerment is closely connected with other dimensions of development, an attempt is also made to spot main problems that these groups undergo in the state and beyond. For instance, educational and employment opportunities were being disrupted during the course of globalisation. Besides, all such processes seem to be occurred in the backdrop of globalisation; its implications on the state and civil society have also to be examined to the extent of their impact on their political empowerment. In other words, this paper seeks to show up peculiar responses of state and civil society to multiple implications of globalisation thereon.

As part of identifying the major contradictions within the Indian social hierarchy that had some bearing on the plight of SCG, this paper delineates the role of caste in Indian politics in the recent period. Besides, certain emerging alternative both ideological and institutional that could ensure political empowerment of these groups in Nagaland and Northeast India (NEI) have also been put forward. This paper examines the issues of political empowerment of the SCG among others in Nagaland keeping in view of prevailing socio-economic and political setting in the country. Finally, the paper also argues that the Bahujan Samaj had emerged as a tangible alternative socio-political movement so as to change the status quoist political development to begin with, and social transformation thereafter.

Social Hierarchy

Indian society had always been divided not only vertically and horizontally but also otherwise. In the post independent India too, similar trends of heterogeneity and segregation were discernible in the social arena. The root cause of such divisiveness stems from the caste system in the country. A prominent Indian Sociologist GS Ghurye observes, 'Caste in India is a Brahminic child of the Indo-Aryan culture cradled in the land of the Ganga and Yamuna and hence transferred to other parts of the country'.[1] The caste system can be described as an elaborately stratified social hierarchy, distinguishing India's social structure from any other nation. Like 'race' in the US, caste played havoc in India, as both these categories were compared to slavery in the writings of Dr. B.R. Ambedkar.[2] To quote him, 'there is so much similarity between the position of untouchables and the position of the Negroes of America that the study of the latter is not only natural but necessary'.[3]

The history of the caste system is multifaceted and complex. Besides, the caste system is generally related to the occupational pattern of different groups. Caste is the general form of social organisation in the country and it differentiates social groups along upper and lower lines. While the Brahmins enjoy the status of 'upper caste', the Dalits, otherwise described as Scheduled Castes, as 'lower castes' experience social exclusion. More particularly, these groups, who constitute large chunk of the marginalised communities, were denied land, property, assets and even education. Deprived of all human rights, these communities were at the receiving end lifelong. Obviously, they were given no representation in the governance of the nation.

The word 'Dalit' came to light in the 1930s and it was also used by Dr Ambedkar during the same period in his Marathi writings and speeches.[4] Obviously, Dr. Ambedkar had become a symbol of vision for the masses, a vision of freedom from unequal socio-cultural, religious deprivation, economic backwardness and political inequalities. He attacked Brahmanism and Hindu caste hierarchy and also tried to build an egalitarian society based on human values.[5] According to Sukhadeo Thorat and Katherine S. Newman, who provided the theoretical beginning on the discrimination with particular reference to the caste system in their paper.[6] They highlighted the ways in which caste persists as a system of inequality that burdens the Indian economy with inefficiencies in the allocation of labour and other critical resources, reducing the full development of human capital.

In consequence, far from disappearing as the economy modernises, discrimination remains a problem which is not amenable to self-correction, but rather requires interventionist policies to remedy. Either State or society is needed to undertake systematic social project to reform the caste relations in the country. Or else, far from dissolving under the impact of modern economic and political forces, caste had become more firmly entrenched in the life of nation. In the words of Norman D. Palmer 'although caste seems to be dealing in importance as a social factor it is increasing to be in importance as a political factor.[7] Thus, the role of caste in politics has often been referred to as casteism that may be defined as the tendency to mould the life of nation on the basis of caste. In fact, the marginalised communities like the Scheduled Castes, Scheduled Tribes, Backward Classes and Religious Minorities had faced the wrath of social and economic discrimination. Particularly, the Scheduled Caste Groups (SCG) had inherited an adverse predicament in social and economic spheres in Nagaland and elsewhere in India. In fact, since these groups being located in the excluded societies like the Northeast India, they suffered setbacks more than their counterparts elsewhere in India.

Northeast India

Incidentally, the Northeast India had been inhabited for centuries and people lived in communities with their hilly environment. Endowed with valuable natural resources and attractive climatic conditions, the region could have developed at a rapid speed. In fact, socio-cultural development in the region is remarkable. Since the Northeast region has got distinct makeup geographically, socially and culturally, which resembles with and is noticed in the Oriental countries, developmental challenges are numerous. Although NEI states remain economically backward, they are ahead of others culturally and spiritually. The NEI with a population of 45 million and a GDP of $59 billion share a long land border with Myanmar, making it contiguous with Association of South East Asian Nations (ASEAN). The Northeast India witnessed many a hindrance that kept its 'seven sisters' aloof from the mainstream India.

Emerged as a 'gateway' of India to the Southeast Asian countries, the NEI can become very crucial in its socio-economic development. Besides, religious organisations like church, which are quite influential in the NEI, can also be put into place as part of the developmental initiatives in the region. To be more precise, the role of Christianity is very positive and heartening in this region, as the communities that belong to different denominations of church lead a more spiritual and communitarian life in the states like Mizoram and Nagaland. Fellow-feeling among them is spectacular and worth noting. These communities have internalised certain social and moral values in themselves. They seem to have developed an orderly life style in their villages. Thus, community initiatives have always been useful in the case of NEI and its development.

In any case, failed to exploit the natural resources, the region remained backward and underdeveloped for decades together. Owing to peculiar geographic locale of north-east India, it is one of the most disaster-prone and backward regions in the country. Although bordered with five countries and strategically located, the region is underdeveloped. In other words, the region is of great differences and complexities, uneven development, regional deprivation, internal colonialism, cultural oppression and lack of integration are some of the root causes behind the conflicts and insurgencies. Although certain amount of peace prevails in some states of the region, Nagaland seems to be still under the grip of violence of the state and the oldest insurgent group, the National Socialist Council of Nagalim (NSCN-IM).[8] Thus, the region got affected adversely due to the man-made conditions like the policies of regimes at Delhi and elsewhere. While causes for the bad governance in the region were attributed to the so-called insurgency and violent law and order, its effects were faced by the people in the region itself.

Thanks to the British legacy, the Delhi leadership continued to consider the Northeast region as frontier region for long. Failed to respond to the democratic aspirations of the people and communities in the region, the national government made many a mistake in the past. However, with the review of its age-old concerns of security and foreign policy, some regimes had focused their attention on the domestic interests, particularly in the NEI in recent decades. And thus, it conceived some plans so as to do something whereby the region and its people were assimilated into mainstream India. Some piecemeal measures were attempted, but in vain. Certain economic packages and developmental projects were implemented in these states. Yet, expected progress was not achieved. At the political level, periodic elections were being conducted and duly elected regimes had been put in place in the NEI. Still, inter-state and inter-region conflicts continue to take place, at times violently. Similarly, ethnic strife and intra-community conflicts have not been resolved to any satisfactory extent. More than the others, Nagaland and Manipur have been engaged in tackling law and order problems, whereby developmental programmes get distracted. Obviously, of all the marginalised communities, the SCGs have been at the receiving end in the state and outside.

Globalisation Impact

In the present global milieu, one cannot run away from the inexplicable process of globalisation. As any other Third World state, India was also subjected to many a pressure and pull in the International politics. India is changing, more so in the wake of globalisation. Since it is not just a phenomenon, but a process, its multiple effects are hardly comprehended. And, the pace of change varied from time to time, and region to region. Besides, certain social institutions of countryside such as family, caste and tribe relations are under great stress and transformation. Caught in the web of mixed economy, the state was passing through critical phases of development in the initial decades of governance. External agencies like the IMF and World Bank among others were laying the foundations of dependency for development. Once got entrapped into the vicious circle of globalisation, India could no longer get out of it. Thus, India became an active player in this process, in which NEI cannot be an exception.

Globalisation is a process in which the whole world is brought together in one huge supermarket of goods and services.[9] Apparently, this has presented the nation with several challenges to be faced with at home and outside. In the wake of executing the three components of globalisation phase viz., Liberalisation, Privatisation and Globalisation (LPG), Indian government embarked upon the path of openness and development, in almost all directions. As part of this market economy, the state had to explore new trade routes or those that were closed so far for variety of reasons, as in China and Myanmar, for instance. But, the benefits of new policy initiatives have been grabbed by those non-locals, or 'others', who had no stakes in the NEI. In other words, local communities in Nagaland and 'sister states' in the region had been excluded from participating in the 'look east policy' and its implementation.

The dalits and adivasis that desired the state support were adversely affected, as reservation policy became disused. The globalisation process had added fuel to the fire. Already excluded from socio-cultural sphere of power, these communities were getting alienated from economic representation. Left to their fate, they were compelled to fight for the protection of reservation facilities besides seeking their effective implementation in the wake of globalisation and after. Obviously, this process evoked many a protest in various parts of the country. At least upper strata of the society can withstand the pressures of the globalisation to some extent. But, the marginalised cannot face the onslaught of the Multinational Corporations that make decisions with little or no regard for the elected governments at all levels. Thus, more particularly, Dalit issues and caste discrimination could draw the attention of state, civil society and social movements. For, their adverse impact on dalits among other marginalised during the course of globalisation is far reaching.

With the rise of market state, the political state exposed its weakness so glaringly that it could not take on the emerging dalit movements. Specifically, with the emergence of dalit movements like the bahujansamaj in early 1980s, Indian state had been responding in a populist way. At times, the state was demonstrating its capacity to implement the constitutional obligations and thus enacted several provisions. Yet, it failed to enforce its governmental agencies to implement the same in toto. At other times, the state introduced the policies of distracting nature whereby the attention of the marginalised was drawn towards non-developmental issues. Interestingly, while trying to shirk its Constitutional and social obligations, the state was responding in a peculiar way. In fact, the response of the state to such movements smacks of retreat and despondency. In any case, the state was not willing to forgo the support of these communities and thus trying to regain the past support for itself.

At the national level Indian civil society that represents the interests of the upper strata of the country had also failed to respond to the aspirations and needs of the marginalised. In fact, elite and caste Hindu groups were challenging the state and its agencies overtly and covertly when they tried to implement certain constitutional obligations. As part of the bureaucracy and media, these elitist groups were sabotaging the schemes and policies that were aimed at the benefit of the marginalised in the country. Similar trend is discernible at state and local levels. It is dominant castes and communities, numerically or otherwise, which played the role of depraved in the context of public policy implementation that favoured the marginalised.

Emerging Alternatives

Given this political scenario, dalits and the marginalised have been compelled to emerge as socio-political movements at the state and national levels. As state and its governmental agencies exposed their failures in implementing the constitutional obligations, leave alone social ones, their dependence on these institutions cannot safeguard their interests. Civil society organisations and networks that collude with MNCs and International agencies have also played similar role. In the name of religion and community, certain identity movements had also emerged as alternatives to protect the interests of the marginalised in the last two decades. But, none of them offered any solace to the victims of globalisation and privatisation in the country. Instead, some of these networks had manipulated and used the Dalit groups and their leaders for implementation of their hidden agendas.

Again, since the traditional political parties that were under the control of the upper castes had also failed to stand for the welfare of these groups, they were let down. Meanwhile, the leaders and cadres of these communities having realised the significance of their political value in elections and agitations started deserting their traditional political parties. Incidentally, the Congress system that was largely dependent upon the support of marginalised communities had to fall down and pave the way for rise of new parties and groups at local level in some states. Clearly, its reflections are discernible in the rise of coalition politics in the country.

Thus, the marginalised had to construct new social movements under their own leadership, in the name of caste and community identities. Unlike other movements, these dalit movements having claimed Ambedkarite thought as the guiding ideology raised the issues of casteist hierarchy, social inequality, self-respect, political democracy, and thereby social transformation in the country. While some of these movements were confined to local and regional level in a state or two and raising some specific issues and concerns of the Dalits and Adivasis, and of course disinclined to affiliate with any political party, some others were almost different. Thus, these groups realised the futility of alliance with any political party.

Incidentally, couple of their social and political movements like the one of bahujansamaj, organised on a national level, has had long term strategies and goals. Subscribing to the crucial slogan of Dr. BR Ambedkar, 'Political Power is master key', these movements were organised under one political umbrella by Manyasri Kanshiram. Founded as a socio-political reform movement of employees of the backward and minority communities like the SCs, STs, OBCs, and Minorities among others, the BAMCEF worked for more than a decade in the nook and corner of the country. In fact, the new social movement that was led by him was basically aimed at their political empowerment in the country. Unlike earlier movements, that were seeking some benefits and schemes from the governments at the centre and in states, in terms of reservations and subsidies alone, the bahujan samaj movement was aimed at attaining political power for itself. Since bahujansamaj is a majority component of the electorate in India, it sought political power, of course, through constitutional and peaceful means.

Political Empowerment

Thanks to Dr B.R. Ambedkar's efforts through Indian Constitution and otherwise, political regimes at the Centre and in States made some positive efforts at different levels so as to ensure socio-economic justice to these communities in general and SCG in particular. Since all the political regimes since being 'upper caste-dominated' and due to 'manuwadi-mindset' social status quo was preserved. As these regimes were biased against the marginalised and the SCG, constitutional provisions have not been implemented in letter and spirit. Failed to ensure social transformation and economic emancipation, the state maintained a stony silence to the ongoing developments in the field of education, employment and politics. It is only after a couple of decades of independence, that they were expectant to use their Constitutional rights in education and employment. This inclusive policy of the reservations has been the most appropriate strategy that could empower these marginalised communities. Yet, nothing substantial is changed in the life and conditions of the marginalised. Besides, these groups were being targeted and attacked physically and otherwise. Despite enacting numerous law and provisions, the SCG continue to be harassed and victimised on a regular basis.

Viewed in this backdrop, Dr Ambedkar had advocated that if the SCG wanted to fully enjoy the benefits of their legal rights, as enshrined in the Constitution, they would have to connect together all the marginalised groups on the basis of unity and fraternity, bring them on a strong political platform and capture the "Master Key" of political power. To cite a few lines from what Dr Ambedkar said, "Understand our ultimate goal. Our ultimate goal is to become the rulers of this country. Write this goal on the walls of your houses so that you will never forget. Our struggle is not for the few jobs and concessions but we have a larger goal to achieve. That goal is to become the rulers of the land." Thus, Dr Ambedkar declared the political goal of his struggle.[10]

Further, he stressed on the concept of political power when he said, "Politics should be the life-blood of the Scheduled Castes."[11] Since politics of Congress party, the mouthpiece of the dominant castes was detrimental to the interests of marginalised, Dr Ambedkar tried to form a broad-based movement of all the victims of Brahmanism, who came to be described as bahujan samaj, later on.

In other words, political empowerment of the marginalised alone could clinch the issue in their favour. This is the basis for the formation of Bahujan regimes at the Centre and in States. Only such governments could enforce the constitutional and legal rights of the marginalised and provide opportunities to them to move forward in all spheres of life besides enabling them to lead a life of self-respect in the state or elsewhere.

Mansyasri Kanshiram organised the marginalised communities who are numerically majority (around 85 per cent), otherwise known as the bahujansamaj, to take on the minority communities (*Brahmin, Kshatriya* and *Vyshya*) in the political battle. Describing it as a social missionary movement, Kanshiram had converted bahujan samaj into an alternative political movement and thereafter into the Bahujan Samaj Party (BSP) in early 1984. Influenced by the Indian Constitution that assure equality, justice and liberty to all its citizens, the bahujan samaj does not project any other ideology and programme, but seeks to implement the Constitution in toto.

Ever since the Bahujan Samaj Party (BSP was formed, there emerged an alternative path of struggle that promised capturing state power for the dalits and other marginalised communities.[12] Within a decade of its existence, the party became a recognised national party, having its strong base in the state of Uttar Pradesh (UP). By the year 2007, following the death of Kanshiram, Mayawati became the chief minister (fourth time) on the support of her party alone! More than what she achieved as the power centre, Mayawati created confidence among these communities.

Unlike other movements, the bahujan one is unique in the sense that it offers a political alternative to the prevailing socio-cultural (Manuwadi) situation in the country. As against the ideology of caste and casteist discrimination in the country for over several centuries, there emerged a counter ideology in the form of social reform movements in various parts of India. Since the 'Manuvadis' used to promote and strengthen the casteist ideology in the country, those who became victims of caste discrimination had to fight against it. Besides, several saints, social reformers and activists also fought against the castiest practices as they were responsible for the inequality in the society.

Thus, Bahujan Samaj Party (BSP) is a product of the contemporary era of profound ideological uncertainties and political crisis of all established systems. It is the political expression of dalit and low caste communities, standing precariously on the base of partial gains won as result of past movements. In many ways, the BSP appears also as an 'anti-party' rather than a party. Its refusal of 'brand ideology', refusal of 'political alliances', refusal to 'place' itself in the political spectrum its assessment of all parties by the single criterion of their orientation to break the caste hierarchy prove it to be an anti-party entity.

Finally, bahujan samaj as a viable national alternative offered the dalits and marginalised a platform for political empowerment in the country.

As observed by Prof. Sudha Pai the theory and praxis of social justice, which forms the core of the ideology of the BSP, have provided it with a distinct character and identity, different from other political parties. The party believes that the Nehruvian concept of justice, enshrined in the Constitution and promised by the Congress since Independence, has failed to reach the Dalits.[13] Rather, the educational, social and economic hegemony of the upper castes/ classes has ensured that the benefits of post-Independence development, despite the establishment of democratic state, have not been channeled towards them. Thus, their search for proper alternative ends with the rise of bahujan samaj movement that promised them socio-economic emancipation, of course through political empowerment of dalits and the marginalised.

To conclude, due to caste hierarchy in India, marginalised communities have always been at the mercy of state and society. Despite Dr Ambedkar's struggles and works in the form of Indian Constitution thereafter, marginalised have not been benefitted to the extent they were targeted to be. Thus, their social and economic exploitation continued unabated in different forms. The process of globalisation had undermined the Indian state and its responses like the reservations in education and employment. Initial enthusiasm for globalisation as a beneficial set of processes has yielded to an understanding that the phenomenon is largely associated with increasing social inequality 'within' and between communities as well as instability and conflict. Thus, it is time to assess the impact of globalisation on Indian economy and society, as it has not yielded any spectacular outcomes in any state including that of Nagaland.

Not only state and its agencies were against the interests of the SCG, but even the civil society and political parties that pay lip sympathies towards the marginalised hardly take note of their plight. Obviously, adaptation of these diverse groups with the mainstream society is yet not complete. Less said the better about the NEI that continues to be the conflict-ridden area in the country. Long neglect of the region by the successive governments at the centre for variety of reasons compounded the crisis to an extent of violence and insurgency, more so in Nagaland and its borders. In fact, the dalits and adivasis are those who were adversely sandwiched between the state and globalisation, thus they need to fight it out more than before. While there are some dalit alternatives that engaged them in social and cultural movements, none of them changed the course of their progress.

Whereas, with the emergence of bahujan alternative in the form of BSP, the dalits and other marginalised communities seem to have recognised their long term goal of social transformation and economic emancipation. Like other states in the NEI, Nagaland can be considered as an excluded entity in multiple respects. Although marginalised communities in the state had launched persistent struggles for over a half century, their aspirations remain unattended. Since the SCG constitute the same marginalised communities, their struggles cannot be viewed differently. Nor can these be alienated from those of the others in the region. Thus, the SCG can join a broad front of marginalised communities 'within' and 'without' the state of Nagaland, if their political empowerment is to be accomplished once for all. Of those emerging political alternatives today, BSP is an effective one, indeed!

Notes and References

1. Ghurye GS (1979), "*Caste and Race in India*" (Bombay: Popular Prakasan Pvt. Ltd.) p.106.
2. BR Ambedkar, *The Annihilation of Caste*, (Bombay: BR Kadrekar, 1937). p. 38.
3. In his letter to W.E.B. Du Bois that was published in The Papers of W.E.B. Du Bois (Stanford, NC: Microfilming Corporation of America, 1980).
4. John C.B.Webster (1999), "*Who is a Dalit*", In: *Dalits in Modern Indi-vision and Values*, S.M.Michael (ed.), (Vistaar, New Delhi), p. 68.
5. Keer, Dhananjay (1954), "*Dr B.R. Ambedkar Life and Mission*", (Popular Prakashan, Bombay), p. 270.
6. SukhadeoThorat and Katherine S. Newman (2007): "*Caste and Economic Discrimination: Causes, Consequences and Remedies*", Economic and Political Weekly, October 13, 2007.
7. Dubey, S.N.(2008). *Indian Government and Politics*, Laxminarayana Agarwal Publications, New Delhi.
8. In his keynote address to the National Seminar at Mizoram University, Aizawl (November 2007), Sanjoy Hazarika made a reference to the prevailing situation in the NEI. Patnaik JK (ed), Peace and Development in Mizoram: Role of the State and Civil Society, Dept of Political Science, MZU, Aizawl.
9. Glory E. Dharmaraj, '*Globalisation*', in Concepts of Mission (New York: General Board of Global Ministries, United Methodist Church, 1999).
10. In a meeting on 24th September 1944 at Madras. BR Ambedkar, Writings and Speeches (Bombay:Education Dept, Government of Maharashtra, 1979).
11. In the Working Committee meeting of All India Scheduled Castes Federation, on 4th October, 1945.
12. Founded by a scientist at Pune, having resigned and worked as a social activist for two decades, Manyasri Kanshiram in 1984.
13. Sudha Pai (2002): "*Dalit Assertion and the Unfinished Democratic Revolution*" – The Bahujan Samaj.
14. Tribe-Caste Conflict: A Study of Kandhmal Districts of Odisha.
15. Ganesh Digal.
16. Research Scholar, Dept. of Sociology, School of Social Sciences, University of Hyderabad, Hyderabad.
17. Background of the Study Area and the Problem.
18. The socio-cultural life and practices of the Pano deeply related to Kandha. The Pano are speaking both Oriya and Kui language.[1] Those are

speaking Kui language are called Kandha Pano. The Kandha is one of the important tribal groups of Odisha. They had the custom of human sacrifice which was stopped during the British period. In the custom of human sacrifice the Pano has an important role by supplying the human for sacrifice. Sometimes the Pano are offered their own relatives for human sacrifice if they failed to get from the outside. Scholars have classified the Kandhas in three categories are such as *Kutia Kandha, Dongria Kandha* and the *Desia Kandha.* The Kutia Kandhas are found mainly in Kotagarh, Tumudibandha and Belghar area of the Baligurha subdivision. The Dangaria or Malua Kandhas are live in high lands in hilly areas. The Desia or Oriya Kandha lives in the plain areas. The Kandhas have intermingled with the people belong the Hindu community and have adopt the many of their customs, although a large number of them follow some of the rites and rituals of their.

19. The Pano also in Kandhamal, are identifying by in two categories such as Oriya Pano or Sasi Domanga, Kandha Pano or Kui Domanga.[2] In Bailey work he classified such as Baud out caste and Ganjam out caste.[3] The Oriya Pano are influenced by dominant Oriya culture, where as the Kandha Pano/Kui Domanga are influenced by Kandha culture and language. But there is a lineage similarity between Oriya Pano and Kandha Pano/Kui Domanga.

20. There are the linguistic differences among the Pano community in Kandhamal. The Pano are endogamy and practicing the lineage system for selecting their partner for marriage. The Kandha are also endogamy and practice territorial clan system for their marriage and selecting partner. There is no inter-marrying between the Kandha and Pano community. Both the Kandha and Pano from Phulbani, Baliguda, G. Udayagiri and Tumudibandh region are having cultural and linguistic difference and practices different social rituals. The Pano in Kandhmal are regarded as untouchable.

21. The Kandhmal district is one of the backward and tribal dominated districts in the state of Odisha. The majority of the population of the district is Kandha and Pano. In the past the Kandha and Pano were having harmonious relationships with each other. The Pano were playing very imperative role in Kandha's life. The Pano occupies an important position in demographic equation in relation to Kandha in Kandhmal. The socio-cultural life and practices of the Pano is deeply related to Kandha.

22. The present district of Kandhamal is made up of the fragments of Boudh, Phulbani, Ghumsar, Udayagiri and Baliguda. The contemporary history of the Kandhamal district is documented with the arrival of the British in the nineteenth century. The history of Kandhamal depicts that the present subdivision of the Kandhamal district, Baliguda region was under the Madras presidency. Kandhamal, which was originally the part of the Boudh state, experienced a chequered history during the same period.

23. It was thc British rule that fragmented the parts of Kandhamal from Boudh.

In the year 1994 after separation of Boudh from erstwhile Boudh-Kandhamal district, the Kandhamal district in present day has two sub-divisions, Phulbani and Baliguda. The Baliguda sub-division was part of the Ganjam district of the Madras Presidency prior to independence. In Madras Presidency there was a notion of hill tribe which received special protection in the agency area against non-tribal.

24. The Kandha and Pano.

25. The majority of the population of the district is Kandha and Pano. In the anthropological, sociological literature the Kandha are tribe and the Pano are ex-untouchable, outcaste and in modern popular term they are called Dalit. The Kandha are present a picture of unity in diversity. They are classified into different socio-cultural and linguistic groups. They have diverse religious beliefs and social customs. There are also differences in rituals and modes of worship. Amidst these diversities, there is a strong fundamental unity, a feeling of weness and emotional solidarity among the Kandhas. According to the constitutional categories as the Kandha are categories as scheduled tribe and the Pano are categories as scheduled caste. In the past the Kandha and Pano were having harmonious relationships between them.

26. Review of Literature

27. Bailey (1957) in his book *Caste and the Economic Frontier: A village in highland Orissa*, states that there was agitation about the temple entry in Bisipara in 1948, by the Pano people, but that was objected by caste Hindu and tribal and that was leads to a conflict situation between the caste Hindu, tribal and the Pano of the locality. The caste Hindu, and the tribal armed with battle-axes, the traditional weapon of these hills, at all the entrance to the temple and threatened to kill any Pano caste who tried to go inside the temple. After that the Pano have built their own temple to the same deity in a garden in their own street.

28. Mohapatra and Bhattacharyya (1996) in their article *Tribal-Dalit Conflict: Electoral Politics in Phulbani* states that the immediate cause for the Kandha-Pano conflict was the entry of a Pano youth into a Shiva temple in the village of Khudutentuli on January 14, 1994. The Adivasi took an exception to this action and organised their people to purify the temple. The Pano, adopted an aggressive posture which enraged the adivasis. The adivasis retaliated by attacking and damaging the house of the Pano and objected to the cutting down and carrying of bamboo by the Pano. These incidents soon led to full-scale mobilisation of both sides and the first murder took place on February 20, 1994; a Pano youth was killed in the village Linepada. By the end of June, the number of people killed rose to 18, a few hundreds were injured in group clashes and a large number of Pano fled from their villages and took shelter in Phulbani town. Nearly, five thousand Kandhas, mostly from Linepada, Khajuripada, and Phulbani blocks, marched in a rally from Kaladi village, led by a Kandha youth Lambodar Konhar. The main slogan in the rally was, "*wherever*

you find a Pano, kill him; Pano domination will not be tolerated, if it goes on, there will be fire".

29. Kanungo (2008) in his article *Hindutva's Fury against Christians in Orissa* states that the Christian minorities in Orissa, experienced the fury of the worst-ever communal rage-churches were set on fire, Christian institutions, orphanages and hamlets were destroyed, pastors were attacked, one nun was burnt alive and there were reports of the gang rape of another. Fearing this fury, thousands of Christians fled their homes to take shelter in the forest. The violence was not confined to Kandhamal district alone; it shook other districts as well, killing, injuring and terrorising Christians and rendering thousands homeless. In Kandhmal, the Kandha and the caste Hindus find it hard to digest the growing assertion of the Panos, who were once untouchable and at the bottom of the social ladder. The caste Hindu, the Sangh Parivar and the Kandha see the assertive Panos as a threat to their hegemony, hence, the Sangh Parivar in collaboration with the caste Hindu has been mobilising Kandhas as Hindus against the Panos who are dalit Christians by giving it a communal colour.

30. The Conflict.

31. The conflict has become a very common form of social and political struggle among the Kandha and Pano in the Kandhmal. The fundamental question is what the root causes of this conflict? What are the determining factors of this conflict? What the nature of this conflict? How this conflict turns into violence forms?

32. Whether the social differences between the Kandha and Pano consciously identify and such differences are used as a powerful mobilising weapon for socio-economical and political causes. Is it the socio-economical inequality or religious and political factors become a contributing factors of conflict among the Kandha and Pano.

33. The Structure of Kandh-Pano Relationship and Conflict.

34. The inter-dependent relation has become a very common form of social and political conflict among the Kandha and Pano in the Kandhamal. The fundamental question is what the root causes of this conflict? What are the determining factors of this conflict? What the nature of this conflict? How this conflict turns into violence forms? Whether the social differences between the Kandha and Pano consciously identify and such differences are used as a powerful mobilising weapon for socio-economical and political causes. Is it the socio-economical inequality or religious and political factors become a contributing factors of conflict among the Kandha and Pano.

35. Due to the frequent interaction with Kandh and Pano, primarily the Pano are influence by Kandha culture. The culture of Pano in Kandhmal is quasi-tribal in nature. That's why the Pano are neither tribe and nor Hindu. Both the Kandha and Pano have some similarities and differences. The structure of Kandha and Pano relationship in Kandhmal is hierarchical in nature and master-slaves relationships. But the so-called anthropologist and anthropological literature makes the Pano as Hindu. Not only Pano any Dalit

community can be get equality, dignity and justice from Kandha tribe and Hindu.

36. The Kandha are simple, dignified and honest people, but alcoholic in nature. They dislike to doing business don't know the use of market. They don't try to change themselves according to the time. The Kandha are considering the Pano are criminal, exploiter, cheater, unclean and untouchable and use the derogatory and harsh language and treatment to the Pano many times. Many times the Pano are humiliated by the Kandha in village and public places. The Kandha are abusing the Pano saying that Pano should not have the land rights in Kandhmal, they are unwelcome people, now settle here taking our property, marrying our daughter and forcible enter to our temple.

37. This is an undeniable truth that the some Pano are exploiting and cheating the Kandha. But not Pano are exploiter and cheater. Christian Pano are also trying to take scheduled tribe status to get education, employments and other constitutional facilities which are meant for the Kandha. The Kandha are close intimacy with the Pano and they developed a very good relationship in the past. As the owner of the lands, the Kandha are given their lands to not only Pano community but the various caste group. But the Pano were working on their field and home but the other caste for very small money or liquor. Many Sundhi caste people and Karan caste people posses' large area of tribal lands in Kandhamal but the Kandha are silence about that. The Kandha and Pano are lived happily as long as the Pano are depends upon on the Kandhas and working for them but after the independence the situation drastically changes.

38. When the Pano were not working for the Kandha, the Kandha are reclaiming the land which their forefathers sold to the Pano. The entry of the caste Hindu, to the Kandhamal, the Kandha are lost their maximum lands. The Kandha are alleged that Pano are stolen their land but when somebody seek the proofs they are not disclose anythings. Due to their ignorance and alcoholic nature Kandha, the Kandha are sold their lands for drinking liquor and lost their lands to Sundi and Karan caste. The transfer of land to caste Hindu is enormous compare to Pano but not a single Kandha leader saying about all these things.

39. After the independence of the nation, there is a drastic shift in the Kandha-Pano relations. For the first time the educated Pano of Kandhamal are realised the importance of vote and their rights. The educated Pano realise the value of vote and the right to vote is essentially constitutional rights. In the election they decide why to vote and whom to vote. Compare to the Kandha the Pano were more politically active and awareness about the politics. The Pano are transformed themselves from landless, untouchable to educated groups they make themselves to survival in a difficult situation, and when the opportunity comes they grab it, they creates more opportunity for them, although they have faced humiliation and discrimination. But the Kandha are remain uneducated, alcoholic and never try to improve their standard of living.

Because of this today the Pano are visibly educated, have better jobs, have better homes, using neat and clean clothes and send their children for education.

40. In the early days of independence only few Kandha are participate in politics whereas a large number of Pano participate in politics. The Kandhas are generally doing not show their interest in politics up to 1994. They only busy with their traditional agricultural and activities. To maintain the local power there was a race between Kandha and Pano one side and Pano-Caste Hindu other side. Earlier days, the Kandha was naturally powerful but after independence due to the democracy, there was space for Pano to participate in politics and exercising the power. Both the Kandha and caste Hindus started dislikes to the Pano interest and motivation towards politics and education. Earlier days the Pano has no space to share the power but after independence the Pano has also influence the local power structure. The Pano are realising only education and politics can help them to come out from the deep rooted Kandha dominance. The other way the Kandha are unable to cope with the changing scenario and try to dominate Pano in some villages. But later the Kandha realise it is not possible for them to dominate the Pano in traditional way. The changing scenario where the Pano became politically more influential has created a conflicting situation among the Pano and Kandha. Under the security cover of democracy and constitutional safeguards the Pano discards the Hindu religion, existing caste system and untouchability which were rude shock to the Kandha and caste Hindus. The Kandha and caste Hindu consider that the Pano are challenge to their social status and tradition. The Pano community was always looked down by the Kandha and caste Hindus. Some Pano those are in trade and business tried to exploit and cheat the Kandhas. Earlier days the Pano are working for the Kandhas, they served them in various purpose, cattle herding, supplying animal sacrifice, serving at the cremation grounds, working as messenger and beating drums in the festivals and marriage ceremony turn into a different social groups those are more conscious and aware about their rights and dignity. The past relationship and present drastic change among the Pano, led to a tremendous discontent among the Kandha and a hostile relationship emerged and the Kandha and Pano conflict has assumed greater significance. The Pano adopt the aggressive posture in their attitudes. The village level decision-making process, in the politics, in employment, education and petty business the presence of Pano which enraged both the Kandha and caste Hindu community. The Pano are disowned many tribal and village tradition. In some village the Pano youth marry the Kandha and other caste girl. The Kandha are believing that taking the advantage of being a scheduled caste, the Pano are utilise the funds meant for social and economical development of Kandha. The Kandha are suspecting the growing economic and political power of the Pano. The Kandha have always looked at the Panas with a sceptical way. The Kandha has always doubts in their minds

about the Pano. In their mind they believe that only the Pano are exploiter and cheater.

41. Due to the growth of the population, shortage of resources, due to poverty there is competition between the Pano and Kandha for survival. In the past, the Kandha are enjoying their life but due to time change drastically, they are in disadvantage position due to their ignorance, alcoholic, and sex addict nature they are not interest in education. Although, there are lots of Government Schools for tribal people in the Kandhamal but the representation of Kandha student are very less, whereas compares to Kandha the Pano are little ahead in education. Despite their lower social status in views of the Kandha and caste Hindus the Pano are fairly better than Kandha neighbours. Although, maximum number of Pano are poor and landless but still they managed to get little comfortable and prosperous life compare to their Kandha neighbours.

42. The Kandha are very sincere and committed to their religion. They dislike the people those are converted to Christianity. The Christianity, modern education, employment brought a different way of standard of living and consumerism to Kandhamal, where the Kandha are lag behind to the Pano. The Pano are very claver and business minded people. The Christian Pano also uses the false tribal certificate to get government jobs and manipulated. With the modern education, employment and consumerism the Kandha are considerably backward compare to Pano. There are many reasons of cause of conversion to Christianity. The main reason is the discrimination and humiliation faced by the Pano, education, employment and healthcare facilities provided by the highly dedicated missionaries. After getting education and some Kandha and Pano are trying to change themselves and improve their way of behaviour and standard of living. The missionaries also try to change the superstitious customs, practices and teach them about health, hygienic, well dress, importance of life, problem of alcohol, and the importance of education.

43. The missionaries teach the man and woman not consume liquor and alcohols, to cut their nails, to keep clean their house, clothes and their body. The missionaries are requested the man to cut their hair and the women are requested to wear clothes to cover their breasts and entire body. The missionary are requested to send their son and daughter to school and not to tattoo the face of their daughters. The missionaries also teach the problem of premarital sexual relations, extramarital sexual relations and marrying second wife.

44. The missionaries give a new set of code of conduct and morality which leads a discipline and peaceful life. Though the missionaries are tried their best to convert the Kandhas but the Kandha are resisting and only few are converting. But a large number of Pano are converting to Christianity. The converted Christian Pano are considering inferior by the Pano those are in Hindu fold and the Pano those are in Hindu fold consider inferior by the Converted Christian Pano. Same as in the Kandha, the Christian Kandha are considering inferior by the non-Converted Kandha and the Kandha those are

not converting consider inferior by the Converted Christian Kandha. This change is one of the major problematic and conflict situations in the Kandhamal.

45. To counter culturally, politically, and educationally the missionaries the Hindu group such as VHP and RSS playing a major role to attract the Kandha to the Hindu fold. Since 1968 using many method and creates many stories to attract the Kandha into Hindu fold and propagate venom against the Pano and Christian in the areas. The RSS and VHP people are spreading the rumour that Pano are different people they are cow eater, the Hindus are worshipping the cow but the Pano are killing cow, Pano are respecting Christianity which is foreign religion so Pano are not respects our land. The Pano and Christian are enemy of Hindu religion, Bharat Desh and Kandha. The Pano are exploiter, cheater they illegally grabbing the Kandha lands. The Pano are the existential threat to the Kandha society, their women and their future. The Kandha are Hindu they helps the Hindu god Ram to rescue Sita from Ravan. The role of the Sangh Parivar, particularly the Vishwa Hindu Parishad's mission of Hinduisation of Adivasis and aggressive campaign against Christian missionaries in Kandhamal areas is the one of major reason of conflict. The politics of identity and demand of scheduled tribe status by Christian Pano is another major reason of conflict in Kandhamal.

46. Conclusion.

47. Thus, from the above discussion the tribe-caste conflict has many dimensions and the conflict is mainly due to the power relation between the Kandha and Pano in Kandhamal. The tribal are ideologically influence and following the caste Hindu, VHP and RSS agenda and making communal conflict out of any individual issues and painting with communal colour. For the tribal the land, forest, even stone are belongs to the tribal only without their permission the Pano does not have any right and space to use this. The Kandha tribe has no problem with caste Hindu people in Kandhamal because of their ideological inclinations.

48. Notes.

49. 1. Kui is the tribal language spoken by Kandh tribe and Pano people in Kandhamal.

50. 2.The land first belonged to a people called "Kurmo" and Kandha came and drove them out from the hill, now this lands belongs to "Kandha" tribe, in Bailey, F.G.1971. Caste and Economic Frontier's village in Highland, Manchester, Manchester University Press, p. 26.

51. 3. Bailey, F.G.1971, Caste and the Economic Frontier: A Village in Highland Orissa, Manchester, Manchester University Press, p. 9, 211.

52. References.

53. Bailey, F.G. 1957. *Caste and the Economic Frontier: A village in highland Orissa*, Manchester: Manchester University Press.

54. Kanungo, Pralaya. 2008. "*Hindutva's fury against Christians in Orissa*", *EPW.* Vol. 43, No. 37. September 13. pp.16-19.

55. Mohapatra and Bhattachrayya. 1996. Tribal-Dalit Conflict: Electoral Politics in Phulbani, *EPW*, Vol. 31, No. 2/3, January, pp. 160-164.

56. Padel, F.1995. *The Sacrifice of Human Being: British rule and the Konds of Orissa*, New Delhi: Oxford University Press.

57. Pradhan, Promodini and Ranjana Padhi. 2008. 'Fear in Kandhamal', *EPW,* Vol. XlII, No. 44.1st November, pp.11-14.

24

Tribe-Caste Conflict: A Study of Kandhmal Districts of Odisha

Ganesh Digal

Background of the Study Area and the Problem

The socio-cultural life and practices of the Pano deeply related to Kandha. The Pano are speaking both Oriya and Kui language.[1] Those are speaking Kui language are called Kandha Pano. The Kandha is one of the important tribal groups of Odisha. They had the custom of human sacrifice which was stopped during the British period. In the custom of human sacrifice the Pano has an important role by supplying the human for sacrifice. Sometimes the Pano are offered their own relatives for human sacrifice if they failed to get from the outside. Scholars have classified the Kandhas in three categories such as *Kutia Kandha, Dongria Kandha* and the *Desia Kandha.* The Kutia Kandhas are found mainly in Kotagarh, Tumudibandha and Belghar area of the Baligurha subdivision. The Dangaria or Malua Kandhas live in highlands in hilly areas. The Desia or Oriya Kandha lives in the plain areas. The Kandhas have intermingled with the people belong to the Hindu community and have adopt the many of their customs, although a large number of them follow some of the rites and rituals of their own.

The Pano also in Kandhamal, are identifying by in two categories such as Oriya Pano or Sasi Domanga, Kandha Pano or Kui Domanga.[2] In Bailey work he classified such as Baud outcaste and Ganjam outcaste.[3] The Oriya Pano are influenced by dominant Oriya culture, whereas the Kandha Pano/Kui Domanga are influenced by Kandha culture and language. But there is a lineage similarity between Oriya Pano and Kandha Pano/Kui Domanga.

There are the linguistic differences among the Pano community in Kandhamal. The Pano are endogamy and practicing the lineage system for selecting their partner for marriage. The Kandha are also endogamy and practice territorial clan system for their marriage and selecting partner. There is no inter-marrying between the Kandha and Pano community. Both the Kandha and Pano from Phulbani, Baliguda, G.Udayagiri and Tumudibandh region are having cultural and linguistic difference and practices different social rituals. The Pano in Kandhamal are regarded as untouchable.

The Kandhamal district is one of the backward and tribal dominated districts in the state of Odisha. The majority of the population of the district is Kandha and Pano. In the past the Kandha and Pano were having harmonious relationships with each other. The Pano were playing very imperative role in Kandha's life. The Pano occupies an important position in demographic equation in relation to Kandha in Kandhmal. The socio-cultural life and practices of the Pano is deeply related to Kandha.

The present district of Kandhamal is made up of the fragments of Boudh, Phulbani, Ghumsar Udayagiri and Baliguda. The contemporary history of the Kandhamal district is documented with the arrival of the British in the nineteenth century. The history of Kandhamal depicts that the present subdivision of the Kandhamal district, Balliguda region was under the Madras presidency. Kandhamal, which was originally the part of the Boudh state, experienced a chequered history during the same period.

It was the British rule that fragmented the parts of Kandhamal from Boudh.

In the year 1994 after separation of Boudh from erstwhile Boudh-Kandhamal district, the Kandhamal district in present day has two sub-divisions, Phulbani and Baliguda. The Baliguda sub-division was part of the Ganjam district of the Madras Presidency prior to independence. In Madras Presidency there was a notion of hill tribe which received special protection in the agency area against non-tribal.

The Kandha and Pano

The majority of the population of the district is Kandha and Pano. In the anthropological, sociological literature the Kandha are tribe and the Pano are ex-untouchable, outcaste and in modern popular term they are called Dalit. The Kandha are present a picture of unity in diversity. They are classified into different socio-cultural and linguistic groups. They have diverse religious beliefs and social customs. There are also differences in rituals and modes of worship. Amidst these diversities, there is a strong fundamental unity, a feeling of weness and emotional solidarity among the Kandhas. According to the constitutional categorise as the Kandha are categorise as scheduled tribe and the Pano are categories as scheduled caste. In the past the Kandha and Pano were having harmonious relationships between them.

Review of Literature

Bailey (1957) in his book *Caste and the Economic Frontier: A village in highland Orissa*, states that there was agitation about the temple entry in

Bisipara in 1948, by the Pano people, but that was objected by caste Hindu and tribal and that was leads to a conflict situation between the caste Hindu, tribal and the Pano of the locality. The caste Hindu, and the tribal armed with battle-axes, the traditional weapon of these hills, at all the entrance to the temple and threatened to kill any Pano caste who tried to go inside the temple. After that the Pano have built their own temple to the same deity in a garden in their own street.

Mohapatra and Bhattacharyya (1996) in their article *Tribal-Dalit Conflict: Electoral Politics in Phulbani* states that the immediate cause for the Kandha-Pano conflict was the entry of a Pano youth into a Shiva temple in the village of Khudutentuli on January 14, 1994. The Adivasi took an exception to this action and organised their people to purify the temple. The Pano, adopted an aggressive posture which enraged the adivasis. The adivasis retaliated by attacking and damaging the house of the Pano and objected to the cutting down and carrying of bamboo by the Pano. These incidents soon led to full-scale mobilisation of both sides and the first murder took place on February 20, 1994; a Pano youth was killed in the village Linepada. By the end of June, the number of people killed rose to 18, a few hundreds were injured in group clashes and a large number of Pano fled from their villages and took shelter in Phulbani town. Nearly, five thousand Kandhas, mostly from Linepada, Khajuripada, and Phulbani blocks, marched in a rally from Kaladi village, led by a Kandha youth Lambodar Konhar. The main slogan in the rally was, "*wherever you find a Pano, kill him; Pano domination will not be tolerated, if it goes on, there will be fire*".

Kanungo (2008) in his article *Hindutva's Fury against Christians in Orissa* states that the Christian minorities in Orissa, experienced the fury of the worst-ever communal rage-churches were set on fire, Christian institutions, orphanages and hamlets were destroyed, pastors were attacked, one nun was burnt alive and there were reports of the gang rape of another. Fearing this fury, thousands of Christians fled their homes to take shelter in the forest. The violence was not confined to Kandhamal district alone; it shook other districts as well, killing, injuring and terrorising Christians and rendering thousands homeless. In Kandhamal, the Kandha and the caste Hindus find it hard to digest the growing assertion of the Panos, who were once untouchable and at the bottom of the social ladder. The caste Hindu, the Sangh Parivar and the Kandha see the assertive Panos as a threat to their hegemony, hence, the Sangh Parivar in collaboration with the caste Hindu has been mobilising Kandhas as Hindus against the Panos who are dalit Christians by giving it a communal colour.

The Conflict

The conflict has become a very common form of social and political struggle among the Kandha and Pano in the Kandhamal. The fundamental question is what the root causes of this conflict? What are the determining factors of this conflict? What the nature of this conflict? How this conflict turns into violence forms?

Whether the social differences between the Kandha and Pano consciously identify and such differences are used as a powerful mobilising weapon for socio-economical and political causes. Is it the socio-economical inequality or religious and political factors become a contributing factors of conflict among the Kandha and Pano.

The Structure of Kandh-Pano Relationship and Conflict

The interdependent relation has become a very common form of social and political conflict among the Kandha and Pano in the Kandhamal. The fundamental question is what the root causes of this conflict? What are the determining factors of this conflict? What the nature of this conflict? How this conflict turns into violence forms? Whether the social differences between the Kandha and Pano consciously identify and such differences are used as a powerful mobilising weapon for socio-economical and political causes. Is it the socio-economical inequality or religious and political factors become a contributing factors of conflict among the Kandha and Pano.

Due to the frequent interaction with Kandh and Pano, primarily the Pano are influence by Kandha culture. The culture of Pano in Kandhamal is quasi-tribal in nature. That's why the Pano are neither tribe and nor Hindu. Both the Kandha and Pano have some similarities and differences. The structure of Kandha and Pano relationship in Kandhamal is hierarchical in nature and master-slaves relationships. But the so-called anthropologist and anthropological literature makes the Pano as Hindu. Not only Pano any Dalit community can be get equality, dignity and justice from Kandha tribe and Hindu.

The Kandha are simple, dignified and honest people, but alcoholic in nature. They dislike to doing business, don't know the use of market. They don't try to change themselves according to the time. The Kandha are considering the Pano are criminal, exploiter, cheater, unclean and untouchable and use the derogatory and harsh language and treatment to the Pano many times. Many times the Pano are humiliated by the Kandha in village and public places. The Kandha are abusing the Pano saying that Pano should not have the land rights in Kandhamal, they are unwelcome people, now settle here taking our property, marrying our daughter and forcible enter to our temple.

This is an undeniable truth that the some Pano are exploiting and cheating the Kandha. But not Pano are exploiter and cheater. Christian Pano are also trying to take scheduled tribe status to get education, employments and other constitutional facilities which are meant for the Kandha. The Kandha are close intimacy with the Pano and they developed a very good relationship in the past. As the owner of the lands, the Kandha are given their lands to not only Pano community but the various caste group. But the Pano were working on their field and home but the other caste for very small money or liquor.

Many Sundhi caste people and Karan caste people posses' large area of tribal lands in Kandhamal but the Kandha are silence about that. The Kandha and Pano are lived happily as long as the Pano are depends upon the Kandhas and working for them but after the independence the situation drastically changes.

When the Pano were not working for the Kandha, the Kandha are reclaiming the land which their forefathers sold to the Pano. The entry of the caste Hindu, to the Kandhamal, the Kandha are lost their maximum lands. The Kandha are alleged that Pano are stolen their land but when somebody seek the proofs they are not disclose anythings. Due to their ignorance and alcoholic nature Kandha, are sold their lands for drinking liquor and lost their lands to Sundi and Karan caste. The transfer of land to caste Hindu is enormous compare to Pano but not a single Kandha leader saying about all these things.

After the independence of the nation, there is a drastic shift in the Kandha-Pano relations. For the first time the educated Pano of Kandhamal are realised the importance of vote and their rights. The educated Pano realise the value of vote and the right to vote is essentially constitutional rights. In the election they decide why to vote and whom to vote. Compare to the Kandha, the Pano were more politically active and awareness about the politics. The Pano are transformed themselves from landless, untouchable to educated groups they make themselves to survival in a difficult situation, and when the opportunity comes they grab it, they creates more opportunity for them, although they have faced humiliation and discrimination. But the Kandha are remain uneducated, alcoholic and never try to improve their standard of living. Because of this, today the Pano are visibly educated, have better jobs, have better homes, using neat and clean clothes and send their children for education.

In the early days of independence only few Kandha are participated in politics whereas a large number of Pano participate in politics. The Kandhas are generally does not show their interest in politics up to 1994. They only busy with their traditional agriculture and activities. To maintain the local power there was a race between Kandha and Pano one side and Pano-Caste Hindu other side. Earlier days, the Kandha was naturally powerful but after independence due to the democracy, there was space for Pano to participate in politics and exercising the power. Both the Kandha and caste Hindus started to dislike the Pano interest and motivation towards politics and education. Earlier days the Pano has no space to share the power but after independence the Pano has also influence the local power structure. The Pano are realising only education and politics can help them to come out from the deep rooted Kandha dominance. The other way, the Kandha are unable to cope with the changing scenario and try to dominate Pano in some villages. But later the Kandha realise it is not possible for them to dominate the Pano in traditional way. The changing scenario where the Pano became politically more influential has created a conflicting situation among the Pano and Kandha. Under the security cover of democracy and constitutional safeguards the Pano discards the Hindu religion, existing caste system and untouchability which were rude shock to the Kandha and caste Hindus. The Kandha and caste Hindu consider that the Pano are challenge to their social status and tradition. The Pano community was always looked down by the Kandha and caste Hindus. Some Pano those are in trade and business tried to exploit and cheat the Kandhas. Earlier days the Pano are working for the Kandhas, they served them in various purpose, cattle herding, supplying animal sacrifice, serving at the cremation grounds, working as messenger and beating drums in the festivals and marriage ceremony turn into a different social groups those are more conscious and aware about their rights and dignity. The past relationship and present drastic change among the Pano, led to a tremendous discontent among the Kandha and a hostile relationship emerged and the Kandha and Pano conflict has assumed greater significance. The Pano adopt the aggressive posture in their attitudes. The village level decisions-making process, in the politics, in employment, education and petty business the presence of Pano which enraged both the Kandha and caste Hindu community. The Pano are disowned many tribal and village tradition. In some village the Pano youth marry the Kandha and other caste girl. The Kandha are believing that taking the advantage of being a scheduled caste, the Pano are utilise the funds meant for social and economical development of Kandha. The Kandha are suspecting the growing economic and political power of the Pano. The Kandha have always looked at the Panos with a sceptical way. The Kandha has always doubts in their minds about the Pano. In their mind they believe that only the Pano are exploiter and cheater.

Due to the growth of the population, shortage of resources, due to poverty there is competition between the Pano and Kandha for survival. In the past, the Kandha are enjoying their life but due to time change drastically, they are in disadvantage position due to their ignorance, alcoholic, and sex addict nature they are not interested in education. Although, there are lots of Govt Schools for tribal people in the Kandhamal but the representation of Kandha student are very less, whereas compares to Kandha the Pano are little ahead in education. Despite their lower social status in views of the Kandha and caste Hindus the Pano are fairly better than Kandha neighbours. Although, maximum number of Pano are poor and landless but still they managed to get little comfortable and prosperous life compare to their Kandha neighbours.

The Kandha are very sincere and committed to their religion. They dislike the people those are converted to Christianity. The Christianity, modern education, employment brought a different way of standard of living and consumerism to Kandhmal, where the Kandha are lag behind to the Pano. The Pano are very clever and business minded people. The Christian Pano also uses the false tribal certificate to get government jobs. With the modern education, employment and consumerism the Kandha are considerably backward compare to Pano. There are many reasons of conversion to Christianity. The main reason is the discrimination and humiliation faced by the Pano, education, employment and healthcare facilities provided by the highly dedicated missionaries. After getting education, some Kandha and Pano are try change themselves and improve their way of behaviour and standard of living. The missionaries also trying to change the superstitious customs, practices and teach them about health, hygienic, well dress, importance of life, problem of alcohol, and the importance of education.

The missionaries teach the man and woman not to consume liquor and alcohols, to cut their nails, to keep clean their house, clothes and their body. The missionaries are requested the men to cut their hair and the women are requested to wear clothes to cover their breasts and entire body. The missionary are requested to send their sons and daughters to school and not to tattoo the face of their daughters. The missionaries also teach the problem of premarital sexual relations, extramarital sexual relations and marrying second wife.

The missionaries give a new set of code of conduct and morality which leads a discipline and peaceful life. Though the missionaries are tried their best to convert the Kandhas but the Kandha are resisting and only few are converting. But a large number of Pano are converting to Christianity. The converted Christian Pano are considering inferior by the Pano those are in Hindu fold and the Pano those are in Hindu fold consider inferior by the Converted Christian Pano. Same as in the Kandha, the Christian Kandha are considering inferior by the non-Converted Kandha and the Kandha those are not converting consider inferior by the Converted Christian Kandha. This change is one of the major problematic and conflict situations in the Kandhamal.

To counter culturally, politically, and educationally to the missionaries the Hindu group such as VHP and RSS playing a major to role to attract the Kandha to the Hindu fold. Since 1968 using many methods and creates many stories to attract the Kandha into Hindu fold and propagate venom against the Pano and Christian in the areas. The RSS and VHP people are spreading the rumour that Pano are different people they are cow eater, the Hindus are worshipping the Cow but the Pano are killing cow, Pano are respecting Christianity which is foreign religion so Pano are not respects our land. The Pano and Christian are enemy of Hindu religion, Bharat Desh and Kandha. The Pano are exploiter, cheater they illegally grabbing the Kandha lands. The Pano are the existential threat to the Kandha society, their women and their future. The Kandha are Hindu they helps the Hindu god Ram to rescue Sita from Ravan. The role of the Sangh Parivar, particularly the Vishwa Hindu Parishad's mission of Hinduisation of Adivasis and aggressive campaign against Christian missionaries in Kandhamal areas is the one of major reason of conflict. The politics of identity and demand of scheduled tribe status by Christian Pano is another major reason of conflict in Kandhamal.

Conclusion

Thus, from the above discussion the tribe-caste conflict has many dimensions and the conflict is mainly due to the power relation between the Kandha and Pano in Kandhamal. The tribals are ideologically influenced and following the caste Hindu, VHP and RSS agenda and making communal conflict out of any individual issues and painting with communal colour. For the tribal the land, forest, even stone are belongs to the tribal only without their permission the Pano does not have any right and space to use this. The Kandha tribe has no problem with caste Hindu people in Kandhamal because of their ideological inclinations.

Notes

1. Kui is the tribal language spoken by Kandha tribe and Pano people in Kandhamal.
2. The land first belonged to a people called "Kurmo" and Kandha came and drove them out from the hill, now this lands belongs to "Kandha" tribe, in Bailey, F.G 1971.Caste and Economic Frontier's village in Highland, Manchester, Manchester University Press, p. 26.
3. Bailey, F.G 1971, *Caste and the Economic Frontier*: A Village in Highland Orissa, Manchester, Manchester University Press. pp. 9, 211.

References

1. Bailey. F.G. 1957. *Caste and the Economic Frontier: A Village in Highland Orissa*, Manchester: Manchester University Press.
2. Kanungo, Pralaya. 2008. "*Hindutva's fury against Christians in Orissa*", *EPW*. Vol. 43, No. 37. September 13. pp.16-19.
3. Mohapatra and Bhattachrayya. 1996. Tribal-Dalit Conflict: Electoral Politics in Phulbani, *EPW*, Vol. 31, No. 2/3, January. pp. 160-164.
4. Padel, F.1995. *The Sacrifice of Human Being: British rule and the Konds of Orissa*, New Delhi: Oxford University Press.
5. Pradhan, Promodini and Ranjana Padhi. 2008. 'Fear in Kandhmal', *EPW*, Vol .XIII, No. 44, 1st November, pp. 11-14.

25

Movement and Politics of ST Reservation in Assam

Harsha, S.

This article builds on the increasing recognition of the fuzziness of the boundary between institutionalised and non-institutionalised politics, or between social movements, electoral politics and the state. As Jack Goldstone argues, social movements in most of the world have become an essential part of "normal politics." The "actors, fates and organisations" of social movements are often closely intertwined with political parties: they are not simply "challengers" outside the polity, as the traditional image of social movements implied (A. Goldstone, ed. 2003). Such an emphasis on the interconnections between movements and the political sphere builds on the work of Sidney Tarrow, which emphasises the importance of the political context in which movements operate in determining their strategy and ability to achieve their goals (Doug McAdam and Sidney Tarrow 2010).

The social movements that emanated in India after 1970 were commonly described as non-party political formations, reflecting their emergence at a moment of crisis in India's political system. Many of the new social movements raised critiques of prevailing process of development in different regions in India. The ST reservation movement in Assam can be termed as a social movement which is characterised by agitations, threats and appeals by insurgents groups, violence and submission of memorandum.

According to a noted scholar Marc Galanter, the provisions for reservations for Scheduled Tribes are distinct not only in their scope but in their intent, for preservation of their separate integrity rather than complete assimilation is one element in policy towards them. In the case of SC, OBC and the de-notified tribes, it is hoped that the disabilities and disadvantages that separate them from their compatriots will eventually be overcome by the preferential treatment.

That is the aim of the policy is to eliminate their distinctiveness by dispelling all of the differences that set them apart from other Indians. The aim of the Scheduled Tribes policy is more complex- to balance improvement of their condition and a degree of assimilation with preservation of their distinctiveness and a measure of autonomy. Marc Galanter opines that Scheduled Tribes have not demanded reservations. On the contrary developments in Assam state demonstrates that non-STs have been demanding ST status and existing STs are either demanding hill status or their own generic identity.

Status of ST Reservation in India

Table 25.1: State/UT-wise proposals pending for inclusion in, exclusion from and other modifications in the list of Scheduled Tribes of the State/UT

Sl. No.	*Name of the States/UTs*	*No. of proposals for inclusion in/exclusion from/other modification in the list of Scheduled Tribes of the State/UT*
1.	Andhra Pradesh	2
2.	*Assam*	9
3.	Bihar	4
4.	Chhattisgarh	14
5.	Goa	1
6.	Himachal Pradesh	2
7.	Jammu & Kashmir	4
8.	Jharkhand	5
9.	Karnataka	4
10.	Kerala	3
11.	Madhya Pradesh	2
12.	Maharashtra	2
13.	Orissa	167
14.	Rajasthan	1
15.	Tamil Nadu	6
16.	Tripura	1
17.	Uttarakhand	2
18.	Uttar Pradesh	5
19.	West Bengal	7
20.	Pondicherry	1
	Total	**242**

Source: Twenty Third Report of Standing Committee on Social Justice and Empowerment (2011-2012) (Fifteenth Lok Sabha) of Ministry of Tribal Affairs, the Constitution (Scheduled Tribes) order (second amendment) bill, 2011, GOI.

The Table 25.1 shows that Orissa has the highest pending proposals for inclusion in, exclusion from and other modifications in the list of Scheduled Tribes in India followed by Chhattisgarh and Assam respectively.

Although the number of proposals related to Assam are only nine, the state has witnessed a series of agitations, lobbying and politicisation of ST reservations. Hence, a disaggregated analysis of reservation issue in Assam deserves further investigation and the next section takes up this.

Ethnic Groups and ST Reservation in Assam

The tribes of Assam can be broadly classified as hill tribes and plain tribes with a total population of 3,308,570 persons (2001 Census). They constitute 12.4 per cent of the total population of the state. The plain tribes constitute 10.23 per cent of the total population of the state, whereas the hill tribes constitute just 2.18 per cent. They are essentially cultivators, and hence agriculture is the mainstay of their livelihood. Assam is the only state in the country where STs are sub-divided into ST-Hills and ST Plains and this corresponds to their place of residence. ST (hills) relatively enjoys more reservation benefits compared to their plain counterparts because of their remoteness and backwardness in the hills such as Karbi Anglong and NC hills of Assam.

Table 25.2: List of Ethnic Groups Recommended by Assam Government for ST Reservation

1.	Karbis and Dimasas of Plain District
2.	Halam
3.	Tamang
4.	Phakes (Phakeals), Khamyang, Turung and Aiton under Man (Tai) Speaking Tribes
5.	Adivasi (Tea Tribes), Ahom, Matak, Maran and Chutia
6.	Amri Karbi
7.	Change of Nomenclature of "Miri" to "Mising" and inclusion of "Thengal Kachari"
8.	Sarania Kachari
9.	Bodo Kachari

Source: Twenty Third Report of Standing Committee on Social Justice and Empowerment (2011-2012) (Fifteenth Lok Sabha) of Ministry of Tribal Affairs, GOI.

The Table 25.2 presents the total no. of nine ethnic groups recommended by the Assam government for ST status. Having given the overview of ethnic groups and ST reservation in Assam, an attempt has been made below to outline the nature or dimensions of the demand.

Nature of Demand or Movement

The Table 25.3 demonstrates the nature of the demand or movement in Assam and the groups involved in it. The table illustrates that there are three types of demands namely I. Non-ST groups demanding ST status, II. ST Plain groups demanding ST Hill status and III. Thengal Kachari's Dimasa's and Mishing's demanding change in their nomenclature. Having given the nature

Table 25.3

I. Non-ST to ST status
Koch Rajbongshi, Moran, Motak, Chutia, Ahom, Adivasi (Tea Tribes), Halam, Tamang, Phakes (Phakeals), Khamyang, Turung and Aiton under Man (Tai) Speaking Tribes
II. ST (Plain) to ST (Hill)
Bodo Kachari, Amri Karbi
III. Demand for Identity
Thengal Kachari, Dimasas of Plain districts, Mishing.

Source: Author's categorisation based on nature of demand.

of the nature or dimensions of the demand, the next section turns to the role played by different ethnic groups and their organisations.

Table 25.4: Ethnic Groups and their Organisations Demanding ST Status

1. Koch Rajbongshi	All Assam Koch Rajbongshi Sanmilani (AAKRS), Chilarai Sena, All Koch Rajbongshi Student Union (AKRASU)
2. Moran	All Assam Moran Students Union (AAMSU) Asom Moran Sabha (AMS), Sadou Moran Kala Sanskriti Bikas Kendra (SMKSBK), Moran Jatiya Mahila Parishad (MJMP) and Moran Jatiya Karmachari Saikhik Bikas Mancha (MJKSBM)
3. Chutia	All Chutia Caste Conference, Assam (ACCCA) and All Assam Chutia Students Union (AACSU)
4. Ahom	All Tai Ahom Students Union (ATASU),
5. Adivasi (Tea tribes	All Adivasi Students' Association of Assam (AASAA), Assam Tea Tribes Students Association (ATTSA)
6. Thengal Kachari	All Assam Thengal Kachari Organisation, (AATKO)
7. Bodo Kachari	Bodo People's Front (BPF), All Bodo Students Union (ABSU)
8. Dimasa	All Dimasa Student Union (ADSU)

Source: Author's compilation based on a Survey of Organisations.

An attempt has been made in Table 24.4 to illustrate different ethnic groups and their organisation demanding ST status. A brief account of these groups has been given below.

The Koch Rajobngshi community has been known as a rich dynastic group with rich lingo-cultural heritages in the history of Assam. The Koch Rajbongshis have had their own dialects, culture, and way of livelihood. At present political scenario of Assam, they are considered as one of the important contending groups in homeland demands next to the Bodos. They are demanding ST status and the separate state of *Kamptapur* through their organisations like All Assam Koch Rajbongshi Sanmilani (AAKRS) and All

Koch Rajbongshi Student Union (AKRASU). Besides the ST and Kamatapur issues, AKRASU is championing the issue of protection of rights of the Rajbongsis especially those living in BTAD areas.

The Chutia is an ancient ethnic group of Assam that spoke Tibeto-Burman language, but now they are speaking Assamese language. The group has a rich dynastic history centering on *Sadia town* of upper Assam. In due course of history, the Chutias have lost their lingo-cultural identity and socio-economically the Chutias are treated as marginalised. Hence, in order to protect their socio-cultural identity the group has been demanding ST status under sixth schedule of Indian constitution. All Chutia Caste Conference, Assam (ACCCA) and All Assam Chutia Student Union (AACSU) are two main organisational wings along with others that have been spearheading their movement for ST status.

The Ahoms, the largest ethnic group of the state is also demanding constitutional recognition to their socio-economic backwardness under Sixth Schedule of Indian Constitution. They are known as the richest dynastic community in the history of Assam ruling the state for about six hundred years. (Saikia, Y: 2006). They are claiming ST status because of their glorious past. The Ahoms have only one organisation, the ATASU, who is very much vocal in putting forward their demand for ST recognition in the state.

Thengal Kacharis belong to the larger Bodo group and they are demanding recognition as a separate ethnic community and the status of a scheduled tribe independently. It is to be noted here that they are getting this facility at present in the name of Sonowal Kacharis, another ethnic tribe of Assam. The name of the Thengal Kacharis was there in the list of scheduled castes and scheduled tribes of Assam till the year 1976. But then it was secretly removed, without any notification. After this incident, the Thengal Kacharis have not been bestowed ST status as a separate community. The "All Assam Thengal Kachari Organisation, (AATKO)" is the ethnic organisation whose main aim is to unite all the scattered members of the community and to fight unitedly for their rights. The spearheading the demand for ST status, preservation of the culture and tradition are some of its other objectives.

The Bodo Kachari, the largest tribal group of Assam, has been demanding for separate homeland by curving out the territory of Assam. Although Bodo Kachari is a generic term applied to a number of ethnic groups, here the term Bodo Kachari is used to refer only to the Bodo people living in BTAD, Karbi Anglong and Dima Hasao districts of the state. The Bodos have several organisations through which they are spearheading their homeland demands. Amongst the many, the ABSU and Bodo Shahitya Sabha's (BSS) are very active in preserving and development of Bodo identity distinct from the others. On the other hand, the Bodos have some extremist organisations such as the BLT (now returned to mainstream politics) and NDFB who believe in pursuing their politico-economic interests through violent means. Creation of separate

Bodoland encompassing all Bodo inhabitant areas of the state is the main demand of the Bodo extremist organisations.

The Dimasas belong to the Indo-Mongoloid group of people and have similarities with other members of Bodo group such as Garos, Kachari, Mech and Rabhas. The Dimasa peoples are the inhabitants of Dima Hasao Autonomous District Council, Karbi Anglong Autonomous District Council, Cachar District, Nagaon District of Assam and the Dhansiri region of Nagaland State. The All Dimasa Students' Union (ADSU) has been clamouring for the recognition of their community all over the North East India as 'Dimasa' by amending the constitution. (Barman B: 20011)

Adivasi

The Adivasis who inhabit Assam today can broadly be divided into two communities: the tea garden workers; and those who left the tea gardens at the end of their contracts and settled in and around the area after procuring a little land (mostly through government schemes). They are most numerous in Khokrajhar in western/Lower Assam, in Marigaon, Nagaon, Sonitpur and Darrang in Middle Assam, in Golaghat, Jorhat, Sibsagar, Dibrugarh and Tinsukia in eastern/Upper Assam, in North Chachar and Karbi Anglong in southern Assam, and in the Barak Valley.

According to a recent study of the Adivasi problem in Assam, the community is at a critical juncture today in terms of its social, political, cultural and economic identity. The Adivasis' situation, he suggests, is dire, and has been made even more perilous by the recent granting of regional autonomy to territories such as Bodoland, Lalung, Karbi and Mishing.

Against this background of disenfranchisement, some prominent Adivasi organisations such as the All Adivasi Students' Association of Assam (AASAA) and groups active with tea garden workers such as the Assam Tea Tribes Students' Association (ATTSA) are agitating for the granting of ST status to the state's Adivasis. This, they feel, would go a long way towards ameliorating the historically-oppressed condition of the Adivasis in Assam. Indeed it is often the central, if not only, point of many of their campaigns. Sriram Anantha, Narayanan, *(2010) in his paper Scheduled Tribe Status for Adivasis in Assam exposes the arguments put forward by scholars and ethnic groups against granting of ST tag to Adivasi. He rebuts these arguments and makes a fervent appeal in support of ST reservation to Adivasi community in Assam based on logical arguments and his empirical study.*

Regional Politics of Assam and ST Reservation

The regional politics of Assam has had a lasting impact on the Assam government's indecisiveness with regard to ST reservation. In this context, the Karbi Anglong Autonomous Council and Bodoland Autonomous Councils have played an important role.

In Karbi Anglong and NC Hills there is a staunch opposition for granting ST (H) status to Bodo Kachari's. The Karbi's and Dimasa's feel that according ST (H) status to Bodo Kacharis would come in the way of their enjoyment ST (H) reservation benefits. The party politics of these two autonomous councils is also characterised by opposition to granting of ST (H) status to Bodo Kachari's. The CPI (M) party and Autonomous State Demand Committee Party of Karbi Anglong alleged that Congress ruled Karbi Anglong autonomous council indulged in vote-bank politics by favouring ST (H) status to Bodo Kachari's and they went to the extent of gheraoing the office of the Council.

According to noted scholar H. Srikant (2000) militancy in Assam is not a mere law and order problem but a reflection of a deeper malaise affecting the whole society. Neither can it be dubbed as radical politics of the marginalised communities against hegemonising forces.

In Assam militant organisations are also playing an important role in supporting and opposing ST status to certain groups. Militant organisations in Karbi Anglong and Dima Hasao districts are vehemently opposing ST (H) status to Bodo Kachari's. DHD a militant organisation in Dima Hasao district submitted memorandum changing the nomenclature of Dimasa's living in the plain districts of Assam. The Ex-Bodo Liberation Tigers (BLT) cadres want the total implementation of Clause-8 of Bodo accord in which central government had assured that it would sympathetically consider the Bodo's demand of according hill status to Bodo's living in Karbi Anglong and Dima Hasao districts. National Democratic Front of Bodoland (NDFB), a militant organisation active in Bodoland area has opposed ST status to Adivasis's of Assam. A prominent insurgent group United Liberation Front of Assam (ULFA) has wholeheartedly supported ST status to six communities and had urged the Tarun Gogoi led state government to fulfil their demand and insisted him to declare Assam as tribal state.

Role of the State

The attempt has been made in this section, to trace the role of the state and its organisations in responding to the issue of ST reservation.

The Congress Party of the state both in the opposition and as a party in the government has taken a stand on the issue. However, its assertions and promises have been ambivalent in nature. The Congress Chief Minister Tarun Gogoi, who belongs to Tai Ahom community and who supported the ST tag for six communities, has not done anything substantial to fulfil his promises.

The Asom Gano Parishad (AGP) a prominent pan Assamese regional party which came into power in the 1985, capitalised on many regional and pan-asamese issues such as banishing illegal immigrants, and making Assamese language compulsory at the primary level. The politics of AGP sponsored *Assamiyaisation,* encountered opposition from ethnic groups such as Bodos, Karbis and the Dimasas who renewed their assertions for autonomy as well as for separate statehood later. However, the AGP has been non-committal with regard to the issue of ST reservation issue.

Bodo Peoples Front (BPF) another regional political party of Assam was born in 2005 just after the creation of BTAD and fought election in 2006. This party has been representing the sentiments of the Bodos living in the state. Hagrama Mohilary, the ex-BLT leader is the founder president of BPF. This party is mainly concerned about the political solution of the Bodo problem of the state. Since formation, the BPF have got immense support in elections. Leaving aside its espousal of the cause of Bodo Kacharis, BPF has not taken any stand with regard to the issue of ST reservations in the state.

Concluding Observations

Based on the aforementioned analysis, the paper makes following concluding observations.

- Agitation and Movement for ST reservations in Assam reinforces the claims made by scholars such as Goldstone, Tilly and Tarrow with regard to the fuzziness of the boundaries between the movements and the state and its organisations.
- ST reservation movement in Assam is struck between two goals, one that is the autonomy or statehood being demanded by some groups such as Bodos, Koch Rajbonghshi and the demand for ST reservation. Concomitant pursuit of two demands has undermined the impetus of reservation movement.
- The movement and demands put forward by groups such as Dimasa's of plain districts, Thengal Kachari's and Mishing's drives home the point that Tribals are not content with ST reservation benefits, but in addition they want the recognition of their identity.
- In the entire gamut of reservation movement the role of the state becomes prominent. The state government has categorically neither rejected nor endorsed the claims of any of the groups. Even the mere change of nomenclature demanded by Dimasa's of plain districts, Thengal Kachari and Mishing is still hanging fire. Hence, the state is constrained by social forces, regional parties and militant groups in taking a firm stand on this issue.
- Considering the socio-economic backwardness of Adivasis's and their contribution to local society and state, they need to be accorded ST status.
- Collective Action within and between the groups is also one of the impediments for the movements. Although, often the six groups such as Koch Rajbongshi, Moran, Motak, Chutia, Ahom, Adivasi are coming together to fight under a single platform, they are falling apart due to various reasons. For instance, (a) Within the *Mancha* some groups especially the Koch Rajbongshi and the Tea tribes continue their movements separately. (b) The main convenors of the *Janagusthiya Aikya Mancha* have often tried to pursue their party political interests by the name of the *mancha*. (c) Although originally it was a non-political *mancha*, but later on some organisations of it like the ATTSA and

AAMSU's decision to campaign in favour of ruling congress party in the parliamentary as well as legislative elections had increased dissatisfactions within the *mancha.* Hence, some organisations of the *mancha* such as ATASU and AACSU had decided to oppose Congress party in elections.

- Lack effective leadership is also one of the reasons for the movement losing its momentum.

References

Anantha, Narayanan, Sriram. (2010). *Scheduled Tribe Status for Adivasis in Assam, South Asia: Journal of South Asian Studies, 33(2)* pp. 290-303.

Barman, Bidhan. (2011). Assertion of Dimasa Identity: A Case Study of Assam. *IOSR Journal.*

Despande, Ashwini. (2013). *Affirmative Action in India.* New Delhi: University Press.

Fernandez, Walter. (2003). Assam Adivasis: Identity Issues and Liberation, *Vidyajyoti Journal of Theological Reflection.*

Galanter, Marc. (1984). *Competing equalities: Law and the Backward Classes in India.* New York: Oxford University Press.

Goldstone, Jack A. (2003). *States, Parties, and Social Movements;* New York: Cambridge University Press.

Mc Adam, Doug, Sidney Tarrow, Charles Tilly. Ed. (2001). *Dynamics of Contention.* New York: Cambridge University Press.

Migdal, Joel S. (1988). *Strong Societies and Weak States: State-society Relations and State Capabilities in the Third World.* New Jersey: Princeton University Press.

Prabhakara, M.S. (2007). Behind the Adivasi unrest in Assam. *The Hindu,* Monday, Dec 3, 2007.

Ray Raka, Mary Fainsod Katzenstein. (2005). Social Movements in India: Poverty, Power, and Politics, UK: Rowman & Littlefield.

Saikia,Y. (2006). Religion, Nostalgia, and Memory: Making an Ancient and Recent Tai-Ahom Identity in Assam and Thailand. *The Journal of Asian Studies, 65(1),* 33-60.

Shah, G. (2002). *Social movements and the State;* New Delhi: Sage Publications.

Singh K.S. (2010). *The Scheduled Tribes.* New Delhi: Oxford University Press.

Srikant, H. (2000). *Militancy and Identity Politics in Assam. Economic and Political Weekly,* Vol. 35, No. 47, pp. 4117-4119.

Tarrow, Sidney. (1994). *Power in Movement: Social Movements and Contentionus Politics,* New York: Cambridge University Press.

Index

T

DEMOCRACY, GOVERNANCE AND TRIBES IN THE AGE OF GLOBALISED INDIA

Democracy, Governance and Tribes in the Age of Globalised India

(In Two Volumes)
Volume-II

Ramdas Rupavath

GYAN

ISBN : 978-81-212-1248-9 (Set)

ISBN : 978-81-212-1299-1 (Vol. II)

Price : Set (₹ 2000) Price : Volume II (₹ 1000)

First Published, 2015

Published by

Gyan Publishing House
23, Main Ansari Road, Darya Ganj
New Delhi-110002
Ph. : 23242060, 23261060
Fax : 011-23285914
E-mail: books@gyanbooks.com
Website : www.gyanbooks.com

Laser Typesetting: Abhishek Mandal, Delhi
Printed at : G. Print Process, Delhi

Cataloging in Publication Data—DK
Courtesy: D.K. Agencies (P) Ltd. <docinfo@dkagencies.com>

Democracy, governance and tribes in the age of globalised India / Ramdas Rupavath.
pages cm
Includes bibliographical references and index.
ISBN 9788121212489

1. India—Scheduled tribes—Economic conditions—Congresses. 2. India—Scheduled tribes—Social conditions—Congresses. 3. India—Scheduled tribes—Education—Congresses. 4. India—Scheduled tribes—Government policy—Congresses. 5. Rural development—India—Congresses. I. Rupavath, Ramdas, editor. II. University of Hyderabad. Department of Political Science.organizer.

DDC 305.800954 23

In Loving Memory of My Parents

Smt Sony and Shri Jayaram Naik Rupavath

Contents

Acknowledgements

I would express my gratitude to ICSSR, New Delhi and University of Hyderabad for their co-operation in particular for their whole-hearted and continued support to endeavour. I would thank the Dean, and Faculty of School of Social Sciences. I want to offer special thanks to the Faculty and Head, Department of Political Science and non-teaching staff of the Departments for co-operation during the seminar. This book is a product of a two-day national seminar. This was organised by the Department of Political Science, University of Hyderabad.

I would express my gratitude to the participants of the seminar for their co-operation and submission of the full paper within the stipulated time without which this book should not have taken a shape. The presence of key participants like Prof Ramakrishana Ramaswamy, Vice-Chancellor, University of Hyderabad, Prof G. Hargopal, Gaddar (Prajayuddanouka), Prof. Kunhamam, Prof E. Haribabu and Prof Sudhir Jacob George, Prof I. Ramabrahmman, Prof G. Sudharshnam, Prof Shantha Sinha, Prof Virginius Xaxa, Prof Prithviram Mudiam, Prof Manjari Katju, Prof Sudhakar Rao, Dr Nehginpao Kipgen, Dr George Tharakan, Prof Sudhakar Reddy, Dr B. Nagarjuna and their academic deliberations has provoked a new academic thrust in the area of Tribal Development in the globalised world.

I want to give special thanks to my wife R. Jayasri and daughters Sai Srinidhi and Gayathree Ram, brothers and sisters for their moral encouragement.

I want to give special thanks to the research scholars of the Department of Political Science namely, Tapan Kumar Bihari, M. Ramulu and K. John Bosco Sote for their managerial skill in organising this seminar. Also, I express my sincere thanks to the students and research scholars, school of social sciences for their co-operation during the seminar.

Finally, I put my gratitude to the team at Gyan Publishing House, New Delhi for the valuable suggestions on the structure of the book and help in its production.

I hope this book would be a substantial contribution to Tribal Studies in India, even more, help chart a more meaningful developmental path for Tribals in India.

Ramdas Rupavath

Foreword

Indigenous peoples are on the cusp of the crisis in sustainable development. Their communities are concrete examples of sustainable societies, historically evolved in diverse ecosystems. Today, they face the challenges of extinction or survival and renewal in a globalised world. The impact of globalisation is strongest on these populations perhaps more than any other because these communities have no voice and are therefore easily swept aside by the invisible hand of the market and its proponents. Globalisation is not merely a question of marginalisation for indigenous peoples it is a multi-pronged attack on the very foundation of their existence and livelihoods.

The volume 'is a collection of papers presented at national seminar in Department of Political Science of University of Hyderabad. The issues which are dealt in the book are both relevance in theoretically and policy level. This book specially focused on how the marginalised community can be included in the mainstream of society not only sharing the benefits of the globalisation but also in the decision making process. This theme has been a subject of serious deliberation and discussion both at academic and non-academic forum and at regular intervals. However, more often than not they are deliberated at the macro level, that is, national and state context and that too without any reference to diversity that marks India.

Broadly speaking, the contributors of the book has highlighted how the marginalised section of the society, i.e. Adivasis can be achieved their share in the context of globalisation. The book not only evaluated various welfare programmes but also dealt theoretically in the context of tribal's

Ramdas Rupavath the coordinator of the seminar and editor of this volume, worked to make the seminar a success following which he put together this volume and saw it through to press.

The contributors to this book analyse many shortcomings and problems of Indian democracy in the context of globalisation but by and large they conclude both that it is robust and that it can be deepened and extended. It is the right conclusion to each.

Prof.Shantha Sinha
Department of Political Science
University of Hyderabad

Introduction and Overview

Indian democracy has been intensively analysesd, debated and criticised for long time. However democracy is not only just a elections and government formation, it is more about values, habits of thoughts and practices, democracy need not electoral but replacement with social justice. Through democratic method existing unequal social, economic and political justice situation can be removed. The tribals are most affected people in such democratic set up with developmental approach. The new tribal politics will be based on two things the resource politics of the Adivasis and survival politics of the informal sector.

Though Indian Constitution takes an unambiguous position against *adivasis* resources, these continue in a different forms. That over the years the centre of gravity of the Indian polity and economy has shifted to the intermediate class groups has been widely recognised. With in the class hierarchy, the economic high point is the polarisation between rich non-triblas and the triblas who are largely land alienated and displaced. The political parties at the Centre and the State drastically changed emergence of powerful non-tribal leaders who have changed the very mosaic of Indian federal polity. In this process we have today strong states and weak centre. Regional parties are playing important role in the Indian political process.

The State has shifted its orientation from welfare state to market-oriented due to the liberalisation. However, the process of liberalisation has created inequality in the society with the concentration of fruits of growth in little rich class. The opportunity is becoming unequal. while poverty has seldom posed a threat to the system any where, inequality in a milieu of rising democratic and human rights consciousness can potentially become a grave danger.

After India became independence our political leader's recognition of the fact of the participation of the entire people. The leader of the rich ad western educated, feudal back ground was the rulers of the Indian state. This scenario began to change only with the political mobilisation of the *dalits*, of course, within the parliamentary framework. This did not heralds true democracy. Democracy to be people rule, rather than the rule of the rich and powerful;

there must be equality, economic, social and political. In other words, only an egalitarian society can be truly democratic. for that the precondition is equal access to the means of production, not only for expansion of the productive forces, but also for enabling and ensuring the fruiton of the creative potential of every individual. The growth brought about by a few dynamic and enterprising individuals must be expanded into one brought about by all persons in society. If high growth is the creation of a few, growth will be higher if all realise their creative potential. This calls for a new vision as well as a new strategy of development which can herald democracy from below organically evolving as a natural and spontaneous process. Political inclusion and economic exclusion are the order of the day. The panchyat raj or pesa Right Act of Forest Rights act are not reassuring in this regard the resources viz., land, water, forest, cattle, credit and market controlled by the few rich non-tribal families. this has created new kind of development according to Foucault disbursed poer is difficult to tackle. Wthout economic democracy, social, political democracy cannot be realised this was the remark by BR Amedkar and also warned that unless the latter two democracies brought about soon, the victims of the system would throw the Constitution which the constituent Assembly laboriously built. Ofcorse, the system permits individual inclusion even as its functioning is resulting in group exclusion, a phenomenon conspicuously happening particularly in case of the social constituency he was representing parliamentry democracy is bursting at the seams competitive politics uneasily co-exist with a competitive economy prdected on an unbroken scaffolding of a caste-based, hierarchcal social and economic order.the transiton from state capitalism of the planning era to the market capitalism of the liberalisation era has only has rendered the opportunities matrix skewed and reinforced the old prejudices.

The knowledge production, media are controlled by the non-tribal rich upper class elites, who sit in judgment of the quality and efficiency of the *adivasis* and other subalterens. Of course, there is nominal presence of a few persons belonging to these social groupsin the academics, but they lack lack the power to influence policy and structure of knowledge. They remain silent un less until they are safe so long as they they dono raise and debate social issues the corruption which is part of our strutre. The tribal society and sub-plans budgets taken away by the non –tribal bureaucrats. with out tackling inequality corruption and corruption thrives in an unequal system though the the question of equalty accepted at the launch of planning commission with the declaration attaining growth with social justice and to egalitarian society.in fact, the present scenario is characterised by the verbal fetishism created through the globalised use of words such tribal empowerment, sustainable development what not the word equlity, liberty, and justice finds a place in the academies and media discourse.behind verbal usage very harmfull policies and programmes are introduced.any resistnace against these policies the state use the forces to suppress the movements. the NGOs and and Acts primarly playing depolitising the tribals, are abetting the policy makers. what is beneficial to a few is presented as beneficial to all.the poor tribes, ignorant and illiterate, whose immediate concern is the next meal,are seldom concerned about policies and perspectives are no where concerned to them.rather than competition, more profit and capital accumulation,state support primitive accumulation and private appropriation of public resources.In andhrapradesh or Telangana state the land alienated tribals agitating for *Jungle* (Forest) *Jamin* (land) *Jaal* (Water) was put in jail. The land alienated tribes are the traditional indigeneous people who were denied land rights and displaced and do not have even the right to agitate.the land struggle in frontieir agency and non-frontieir agency hostility over the displacement issue when brutal state force beating, killing including children, women. the state using in human attitudes towards tribs in India and violating human rights. it seems, in the extant bourgeois democratic milieu and it is deficient in envisioning, upper caste and its top leadership structure and involute in its understanding of the socio economic reality of India.

The most paradoxical thing is that every body talk about the equality, liberty and fraternity but in practice most are afraid of democracy. what is available to people is the freedom to agree not to disagree. This is the in human condition is decision taken by a few who are rich and powerfull for the people. Infact, the legislators are elected by the people funded by the rich.since inequality that lead to corruption basic bane and gravest threat to tribal sustainable security a no threatening order needs to put in place.

This book aims to place India's democracy, development in the tribal context. This volume is basically to focussing to understand contemporary tribal societies which requires a basic appreciation of the historical processes which have been determined the course of successive changes in economic, socio-cultural, ideological and political life of the tribes. Indian state and governments are talked about as models of federalism in a large and multinational society, ensuring rights of ethnic and religious groups in a truly pluralistic society, and striving for social justice in a society marked by social hierarchies for a long time. However, the democratic experiment has not been without significant challenges, namely that of ensuring inclusive development. Economic equality, social justice, cultural pluralism, human rights, dignity and security are all important aspects of development which have been consolidated and expanded through the existing structure of participatory democracy. But this has not always been an easy task.

During the last couple of decades, Indian tribes have also witnessed transformation in their culture, with the proliferation of special plan and policies for the welfare of the tribal people. Despite the development, crisis in the governance, migration, displacement, and exploitation are rampant. The impact of globalisation of Indian economy is percolating down and their effects are being felt by the tribal people who displaced from their habitation, which ultimately resulting upon resistance and ethnic conflict. Introduction of tribal communities to development through state policies needs to be considered from different angles. It is in this context that a state policy is required to be inclusive and comprehensive enough to safeguard tribal interests. To address the issue of situating tribal communities to developmental perspective in a democratic atmosphere doubted provides both opportunities and challenges

The majority of the articles are a set of mainly empirical essays which seeks to answer this linked question at ground level. The majority process of development in the tribal context with democratic process has been highlighted. Some theoretical work like threat to secularism, politics of development, voice of tribal in contemporary democracy has included.

The first aspect which is most sensitive and thought-provoking was **Democracy, development and Resistance.** On this aspect, it has highlighted concerns, concepts and issues related to democracy, development and resistance in regard to the tribals and with relevant case studies. The session talked about how development has come to be a bad omen for displaced tribals. With displacement, several tribes were uprooted with the onslaught of development. We talked about the case study of Indira Sagar Project in Andhra Pradesh with special emphasis on development projects, displacement and tribal livelihood issues. Livelihoods of tribals were severely affected as argued by projects of development and the resultant displacement overdrive. There was a valuable insight into risks, rights, alternatives, policy and practices followed by Development-Induced Displacement and Rehabilitation and Resettlement of Indigenous Communities in India. There was another paper that drew a perspective from census survey in studying mining and displacement in South Odisha. This session has touched various tribal state of Indian and focussed how in the name of the development trilbal land allenation has been done and who are getting benefit out of this.

The second aspect was **Issues of Governance**. This session talked about issues, concerns and themes related to governance. PESA, Tribal development and idea of commons and related issues were discussed. The struggles and politics of the exclusion in understanding denotified tribes in India were examined. Democracy and Development as in Fifth Scheduled areas was debated.

The issues of **Tribal voice in Contemporary Democracy** have been highlighted in the third aspect. In the era of globalisation, seldom the voice of the tribes are suppressed and marginalised. So in this regard, we started with looking at the case of Scheduled tribes in North Coastal Andhra Pradesh whose voices and struggles have been excluded and marginalised. The paper contests the inclusive development. Next paper attempts to question where democracy in India lies and look at its withering away and its effect on tribal resistance.

This theme, **Livelihood issues and concerns** contains many primary work and highlights various lacunaes in the institutions, policies and etc.. An empirical study on chenchus of Andhra Pradesh was looked to draw our attention to their livelihood security through land distribution. Next paper talked about migration from village to city in Bangalore and how it affects livelihood, creates displacement and calls for rehabilitation. Another paper dealt incisively with the trends in cropping pattern and its impact on the tribal households in the scheduled areas taking the case study of three scheduled areas villages in the West Godavari district of Andhra Pradesh.

The next theme of the seminar was **socio cultural issues of tribals**. There was first a paper that looked at the struggles of *adivasi* towards habitation and how it has been affected by the forces of globalisation and accumulation. Another paper examined at the storage practices of tribal community of Warangal district Andhra Pradesh. There was also a paper that drew a critique on Yerukula reformation in Andhra Pradesh.

In **Public Policy and tribal Development** theme, it has been discussed arena of tribal development and public policy interventions. The first paper talked in general sense the *adivasis* from the public policy perspective in India. The next paper evaluated the implementation of MGNREGA and its effect on tribes taking the case study of Nupada district in Odisha. There was a presentation on the embedded identity and politics that is played out in ST reservation in Asssam. In the last paper of this session, ST as the beneficiaries of BPL in Mayurbhanj district Odisha was examined.

The Session **Social Movement, Ethnic issues and Conflict** discussed the role of social movements, ethnic issues and conflict resulted thereof was discussed. There is a deep-seated conflict between tribes and forest department in scheduled areas. This was bought out by a case study of recently declared kawal tiger reserve in adilalabad district, Andhra Pradesh. Similarly, tribal-caste conflict was bought out in another paper taking the case study of kandhamal district, Odisha. Another vital paper was the analysis of Gujjar agitation for tribal status in Rajasthan that examined contentions, agitations, resistance and state interventions therewith. There was another case study paper of Niyamgiri Movement in Odisha that examined tribal development and resistance that followed. Another paper takes the cast studies of Manipur that discussed Meitiei resistance and response of the State. The failure of Indian Secularism was brought out through the politics of SC and ST conflict in Kandhamal. The Contemporary issues of democracy, development and tribal resistance were widely discussed in another paper. The role of tribal women in MGNRGEA was also discussed in the study of Barwani block of Madhya Pradesh. The policies and challenges of Scheduled Tribes in Jammu and Kashmir at literacy and educational levels were also presented. Then, the tribal education policy of Karnataka was up for review by looking at its attainment and challenges ahead.

In this session, **Tribal ecology and Environmental issues**, a paper was presented on environmental approaches to tribal development. The environmental aspect is significant given the harmony that exists between tribal and nature.

In the session **issues of the tribal women and children** various issues like gender inequalities and development issues was examined with the study of Toda, Niligiri Hills from an anthropological perspective. The Lamabada community was next case study that examined the status of girl child in south Telangana region in Andhra Pradesh.

The session, **Politics of Development** discussed on the concept of Development and its effect on tribes on AP was examined and discussed. The role of NYKS on tribal youth development was discussed through the case study of koraput district, odisha. Approaches to development were examined and the role of civil society organisation in tribal development was discussed. The myth of development and tribals in odisha was examined in a macro-view.

In **Development, Displacement and resistance** session the question of human rights was raised through the study of posco project in odisha in the context of development and displacement. The land alienation of tribals in Andhra Pradesh and tribal land alienation in general sense was examined and debated. The case study of Gadchiroliapotential zone of development induced displacement was looked into.

The last session on **education status of scheduled tribes** talked the need for empowerment of tribals. The paper on the impact of multilingual education in the education of tribal children stressed the nature of multilingual character and its usage for tribals. A case study of Lanbadi tribe in AP was examined to understand the educational status of Scheduled Tribes. Another paper talked about need to bring about awareness of human rights among the tribals and non-tribals secondary students. This comparative study calls for empowering and enhancing the rights of tribals. Lastly, the achievement and challenges of secondary education of Scheduled Tribes in Manipur was discussed.

All the above articles will present an overview of a range real problem that not only touch the lives of Indian people but also raise significant issues for thinking about democracy and development in the tribal context in India. The world has been changing a great deal since 1950, so as India. The country is now carving out a niche in a global market-place dominates thus far by the developing countries. Major questions remains however about the accommodating the tribals in the democracy and distributing the share of growth among them. Thus, basic objective of the book is to contribute in some small way to these continuing debates.

List of Contributors

KM Metry is Professor and Head, Dept of Tribal Studies, Kannada University, Hampi.

Malli. Gandhi is Professor, Regional Institute of Education, NCERT, Mysore.

Ramdas Rupavath is Associate Professor, Department of Political Science, School of Social Sciences, University of Hyderabad, Telengana State.

Jakka Parthasarathy is visiting professor (ICSSR), Dept of Tribal Studies, Kannada University, Hampi-Vidyaranya.

Harsha S is Assistant Professor, Department of Political Science, Assam University, Silchar.

Antibum Ranglong is research Scholar, Department of Political Science, Assam University, Silchar.

Akhaya Kumar Nayak is Lecturer in Pol. Sc. Ragunath Jew College, Cuttack, Odisha.

Bharat Chandra Rout is Research Associate, ICSSR, New Delhi.

Bikku is research scholar, Department of Anthropology, School of Social Sciences, University of Hyderabad.

Chitta Ranjan Mishra is research Scholar, Central University, Gujarat.

Dasarathi Bhuiyan is Lecturer, P.G. Department of Political Science, Berhampur University, Odisha.

Dattatary Bhandalkar is research Scholar, Tata Institute of Social Sciences, Mumbai.

Niharranjan Mishra, Assistant Professor, Department of Humanities and Social Sciences, NIT, Rourkela, Odisha.

Dinabandhu Sahoo, Research Scholar, Department of Humanities and Social Sciences, NIT, Rourkela, Odisha.

C. Rama Mohan Reddy is Lecturer in Political Science, Govt. Degree College, Jammalamadugu Town, YSR, Kadapa.

T. Sasikanth Reddy is Lecturer in English, S.C.N.R Govt. Degree College, Proddatur Town, YSR Dist, A.P.

Johani Xaxa is Reader, PG Department of Political Science, Public Administration, Sambalpur University, Odisha.

Palla Trinadha Rao is Advocate and Researcher, Rajmundry, A.P.

Pradip Kumar Parida is Asst Prof., IIPA, New Delhi.

Satchidananda Misra is Reader in Political Science, Revenshaw University, Odisha.

Satyam Sunkari is Assistant Professor, Council for Social Development (CSD), Hyderabad.

KV Sridevi is Principal, School of Education, Amrita Vishwa Vidyapeetham University, Mysore.

Asha BN is Principal, Somani College of Education, Mysore.

BK Mahakul is Faculty, Department of Political Science, Hidayatulla National Law University, Uparwara, Raipur, Chhattishgarh.

Girija Brahma is research Scholar, Department of Political Science, School of Social Sciences, University of Hyderabad.

Himanshu Sekhar Mishra is research Scholar, JNU, New Delhi.

Janmejay Sahu is research Scholar, Department of Political Science, School of Social Sciences, University of Hyderabad.

Ashok Behera is working in NYKS, Zonal Office, Odisha.

Janmejaya Mishra is with Aga Khan Rural Support Programme (India), Gujarat.

Justin Jos is student in National Law University, Cuttack, Odisha.

KR Rama Mohan is Assistant Director, Centre for Study of Social Exclusion and Inclusive Policy, Andhra University, Visakhapatnam, A.P.

B. Nageswara Rao is Assistant Professor, School of Economics, UOH.

Kapil Sikka is Research Scholar, Dept of Political Science, Jamia Millia Islamia, New Delhi.

Vijender Singh Beniwal is Research Scholar, Dept of Political Science, Jamia Millia Islamia University, New Delhi.

L. Reddeppa is Associate Professor, Council for Social Development (CSD), Hyderabad.

1

Tribal Education of Karnataka: Attainments and Challenges

KM Metry

Introduction

The term tribe has been widely used in sociology and anthropology. The term tribe originates from the Roman word *'tribua'*, meant a political unit and was used to refer to social groups defined by the territory they occupied. Morgan (1877) defined the tribe as a group which possessed social institutions but not political ones. Maine (1861) characterised it as a group in which legal relations were based on the principle of status rather than that of contract. In this sense of a pre-political or pre-contract society, the term passed into general usage as a synonym for a primitive social group. There is another use of the term tribe, linked especially to the history of Indian which has different implications from those other advanced communities. Tribe in the context of post–colonial India has been the subject of considerable debate particularly on their ability to understand the knowledge of literacy or education.

Education, means with a broad range of meaning, embracing both the notion of socialisation or enculturation in general and the specific process of formal education which may also be called 'schooling'. The growth of formal educational institutions is generally linked to specialisation in society and to the development of literacy. Formal education is generally designed predominantly with technical and occupational needs in mind and its purpose is to prepare students to fill available occupational roles, as well as to encourage certain values and attitudes.

In a democratic India, education is a key to the development of disadvantaged and constitutionally not identified social groups.

Education system of the country encompasses formal education which is imparted in and through institutions and follows prescribed and/or recognised curriculum as well as pedagogy under the framework of the policy and rules formulated by the state.

We focus on educational institutions—their role in providing equal educational opportunities, develop skills, questioning mind and lead to improving life chances.

In other words, value addition of educational institutions in developing capabilities of students in general and of the SCs and STs students in particular.

This paper seeks to examine the tribal education and its attainments and challenges in Karnataka state.

Tribal Education in Karnataka

In India, the total number of tribal groups, identified by Government of India, are 461, of which 172 are sub-segments (KS Singh: KM Metry: 2006: 133) many of these groups are as good as discrete categories. The total population of Scheduled Tribes in India stood at 5,16,28,638 (1981 census), 6,77,58,000 (1991 census) and 8,43,26,240 according to 2001 census. Their population constitutes 8.14 per cent of the total general population.

In Karnataka as on 15th August, 2010, fifty tribes have been constitutionally recognised as Scheduled Tribes. The total population of the Scheduled Tribes in Karnataka, as per 2001 census are mentioned in the Table 1.1.

Table 1.1: Scheduled Tribe Population in Karnataka (2001)

Total	*Population*	*Male*	*Female*	*Percentage of literacy rate*
Total	3463986	1756238	1707748	48.27
Rural	2934530	1486073	1448457	45.26
Urban	529456	270165	259291	64.26

The Directorate of Tribal Welfare is implementing several schemes for the progress and development of the STs in the state. The extent of infrastructure facilities like physical space, equipment, teaching aids and teacher-pupil ratio available in the schools are some of the indicators for the quality of education provided in Ashram schools.

Though the Ashram schools are the best means of educating the tribals, the outcome of these in some of the areas is not upto the mark due to various factors.

Further socio-cultural and economic conditions of the tribals may not permit them to succeed even at primary level of education. It is commonly accepted that socio-cultural and economic aspects of the family greatly influence the educability of the children in all societies.

The literacy rate among the STs which was 36.0 per cent in 1991 increased to 46.3 per cent in 2001. The female literacy rate among the STs in 1991 was 23.6 per cent and it increased to 36.6 per cent in 2001.

The literacy rate for rural ST women is 33.3 per cent compared with 56.9 per cent for men. Overall the STs in the state have markedly lower literacy rates than other groups. The fact that they are above the all India average in respect of men and women is of course an indicator that Karnataka has performed better than many other states.

Many schools in tribal areas suffer from high drop out rates. Children either never enroll or attend for the first three to four years of primary school.

For instance the Gross Enrollment Ratio (GER) in 2001 for STs for Classes I-VIII (90.12) was significantly lower than the gross enrollment ratio for all students (98.81) and SCs (104.57). This inequality is heightened even more by the gap between the gross enrollment ratio for South Karnataka (110.62) and North Karnataka (74.21). Gross enrollment ratio for girls (103.64) is also much better in the southern districts than in North Karnataka (70.22).

Scheduled Tribes in South Karnataka more closely approximates the overall GER of other social groups. The northern districts are caught up in a cycle of deprivation. They have the higher levels of ST population and also have poor human development indicators.

Girls are the first to be pulled out of school to work at home and take care of siblings to enable their parents to work. In such cases, families do not find the many incentives offered by the government such as free uniforms, textbooks and even scholarships, an adequate compensation for lost wages. For boys agricultural labour, coolie work and family work is the main reason for dropping out. '*Akshara Dasoha*', the recently introduced mid-day meals programme (*Bissivuta*) for school children showed a more sustained impact on ensuring the enrollment and retention of the tribal children in the schools.

There is a marked disparity in the enrollment of boys (3,209) and girls (1,652) in Tribal Ashram schools in Karnataka. The 2001 Census data reveals that around half of the ST population is in the workforce. Women constitute about 41.7 per cent of the workforce. More than 85 per cent of the working population is in rural areas.

This clearly indicates the highly precarious livelihood conditions of STs in Karnataka bearing the serious consequences on the education of the tribal children. The children joined in the Ashram schools also had serious impact on them with these conditions.

Government Programmes for Ashram School Education in Karnataka

Direction and Administration of Tribal Areas

The Government of Karnataka established the Directorate of Tribal Welfare on 30.8.1994 for the welfare of the STs. The Directorate is implementing several schemes for the progress and development of the STs in the State.

There are 122 Ashram schools benefiting 9,125 ST children run by the Directorate. Primary education from I to IV standard is being given to these students. Besides during 2006-07 the Government set up five new Morarji Desai Residential Schools for the educational benefit of Scheduled Tribe children.

Educational Policy in Tribal Areas of Karnataka

Apart from the general policy relating to the development of the Scheduled Tribes, the Government of Karnataka has not come up with any specific policy decisions relating to the use of Tribal Language in tribal education in the Ashram schools. However, under the *Sarva Shiksha Abhiyan* (District Primary Education Programme) '*Soliga Siddhi*'—a special book for Soliga children of Standard First was published in 1999 and distributed for use in Ashram Shalas with a high concentration of Soliga children. '*Soliga Siddhi*' (SS) was the first and only such specialised textbook for tribals developed at the initiative of Dr H. Sudarshan whose NGO, Vivekananda Girijana Kalyana Kendra (VGKK) has been working for several decades with the Soliga tribe in Chamarajanagar district. The project did not progress as envisaged to cover the other tribal languages as the SS experiment did not generate the expected results.

In Karnataka the general policy of using regional medium at the primary stage of education, which is applicable to the entire State, is also being used in the case of the Ashram Schools. On the other hand, the Government of Karnataka in the field of primary education is implementing or number of schemes and programmes for the tribes. They include the following:

1. Free textbooks, uniforms, school bags and note books are supplied to Scheduled Tribe children from Classes I to IV.
2. Children studying in Government Schools upto V standard with 80 per cent attendance are provided with three kgs of rice per child every month under mid-day meals.
3. 'Keli Kali' (hear and learn) programme especially for the children of Classes I to IV through Akashavani broadcasting.
4. Under the Samudayadatta Shale Programme people themselves are made to involve actively bringing back the dropout children back to school.
5. School Adoption Programme is another novel exercise where in Government Schools, which are in slums or backward areas and not so developed are entrusted to the care benefactors who voluntarily come forward to improve school education.
6. Chinnaraangala a bridge course programme was started during 2001-02 to bring back the drop out and non-enrolled school age children into the mainstream and to have access, retention and achievement.
7. '*Shaishika Samkrina*' is initiated by the Government of Karnataka to provide education for the poor among tribal girls only.
8. '*Nali Kali*' (a process of joyful learning) was launched in October 1995. The curriculum is learnable by the child in a manner with minimum levels

of learning expected to be achieved. The teacher encourages responsibility among children and the learner learns at his/her own pace.

9. '*Chaitanya*', the content-based training programme was launched in 2001 to bring about a gradual transformation of newly-recruited teachers in developing professional competencies and commitments.

10. In order to achieve Universal Elementary Education the *Sarva Shiksha Abhiyan* (SSA) was launched in 2001 covering the whole country. The SSA programme is an attempt to provide an opportunity for improving human capabilities to all children through provision of community owned quality education on a mission mode.

Current Situation of Tribal Education in Karnataka

The tribal education in Karnataka even though is in progress through Ashram schools, it is blistering with a number of problems. They can be identified under five areas namely, economic factors, social factors, administrative factors, cultural factors and school factors. Poverty of parents, lack of parental demand, child labour, lack of Early Childcare Education (ECE) facilities are some of the economic factors which stand in the way of education of the tribal children. Illiteracy of the parents, early marriages, community loyalties and lack of awareness are some of the problems which retard the educational development of the tribal children. Tribal festivals, tribal traditions, value system and problem of language are some of the cultural factors which stand as a hurdle with tribal children's education. There are a large number of school factors and administrative factors which hamper the educational development of the tribal children. To quote some of them are lack of access, incomplete schools, teacher absenteeism, poor quality of teaching, unserviceable curriculum, unsuitable working hours, etc., and lack of co-ordination among different managements, delays in supplies and incentives, weak inspectorate, lack of enrollment campaigns, lack of community control, lack of incentives for better performance are some of the school and administrative factors which are standing in the way of the education of tribal children. The following diagrammatic representation provides the specific problems of ST children in their education.

Factors Affecting the Education of Tribal Child in Ashram Schools

Economic Factors

- Poverty
- Agriculture labour
- Caring cattle
- Lack of parental demand
- Opportunity cost
- Child labour
- Domestic work
- Seasonal work participation

- Migration
- Lack of ECE Facilities

Social Factors

- Lack of awareness
- Community loyalties
- Early marriages
- Lack of community
- Involvement
- Illiteracy of parents
- Sibling care

Administrative Factors

- Lack of co-ordination among different managements
- Delay in supplies incentives
- Weak inspectorate
- Deputation of teachers to other places
- Non-involvement of NGOs
- Lack of enrollment campaigns
- Lack of community control
- Non-residence of teacher
- Lack of teacher quarters
- Lack of incentives for better performance

Cultural Factors

- Value system
- Tribal traditions
- Tribal festivals
- Unattractive textbooks
- Language problem

School Factors

- Lack of access
- Incomplete schools
- Lack of physical facilities
- Disinterested teachers
- Teacher absenteeism
- Poor quality of teaching
- None teaching
- Unattractive classrooms
- Unserviceable curriculum
- Unqualified teachers
- Vacancies of teachers posts
- Punishment by teacher
- Continuous sickness due to malnutrition
- Non-suitability of working hours and holidays
- Absenteeism due to ill-health

- Literacy rate among the ST children
- Enrollment
- Retention
- Dropouts
- Low Attendance of Tribal Children in Schools
- Problem of Absenteeism
- Disparities in the Existing Ashram Schools in Karnataka
- School Education: Access and Participation
- Socio-economic and Cultural Constraints
- Content and Curriculum
- Language and Medium of Instruction in Ashram Schools
- Shortage of Teachers
- Lack of Suitable Teachers
- Attitude of Non-Tribal Teachers Towards Tribal Children
- Lack of Basic Facilities
- Inefficiency in Ashram Schools
- Mismanagement, Nepotism and Corruption in Ashram Schools
- Absence of Central Monitoring Unit

Notes and References

1. Karnataka, *Human Development Report, 2005.*

2. Karnataka, *State Gazetteers.*

3. Midatala Rani, *Problems of Tribal Education in India*, New Delhi, Kanishka Publishers, 2009.

4. Government of Karnataka, Bangalore, Social Welfare Department, *Annual Report 2006-07.*

5. Padma S. Sarangapani, Indira Vijay Simha, Assessment of Utility and Usage of Soliga Siddhi Textbooks Developed for Soliga Tribal Ashram Shalas of Chamarajanagar District, *Project Report*, National Institute of Advanced Studies, Indian Institute of Science Campus, Bangalore, December, 2005.

6. Bibuthi Mishra, "*Re-orienting Tribal Education*", The Hindu, dated 3/8/2004.

7. Newspaper Clippings, *The Hindu, Deccan Herald, Star of Mysore, Kannada Prabha, Prajavani, Mysore Mail, Vijaya Karnataka.*

8. *Annual Report, 2000-2001*, Social Welfare Directorate, Government of Karnataka, Bangalore (Kannada).

9. *Abyudya – Manual of Welfare Programme for the Development of Scheduled Castes and Scheduled Tribes*, Government of Karnataka, Bangalore, 1996 (Kannada).

10. Biligiri, H.S, "*Problems of Tribal Languages in India*", in *Language and Society in India.* Indian Institute of Advanced Study, Simla, Vol. 8, 1969, pp. 245-250.

11. Edgar Turston, *Castes and Tribes of Southern India*, Cosmo Publications, Madras, 1909, Vol. 1 to 7.

12. Gnanasundaram, V, Use of Tribal Languages in Education – Some Issues and Problems (*Seminar Paper*).

13. *Nali-Kali*, District Primary Education Programme, Mysore, ND.

14. *National Policy on Education*, Government of India, New Delhi, 1986.

15. *Neravu-Nirdeeshana*, Information and Publicity Department, Government of Karnataka. 1995 (Kannada).

16. *Perspectives for Education Sector - Policy Paper for VIII Five Year Plan.* Department of Education, Government of Karnataka, 1989.

17. *Report of the Directorate of Tribal Welfare*, Government of Karnataka, Bangalore, ND.

18. *25th Report of the Commission for Linguistic Minorities*, Government of India, New Delhi, 1985.

19. Roy Burman, B.K., "Languages of the Tribal Communities of India and their use in Primary Education" in *Language and Society in India*, Indian Institute of Advanced Study, Simla, Vol. 8, 1969, pp. 251-259.

20. Sudhir Shukla, "*Aliens in Their Own Home*", The Hindu, dated 14th March, 1993.

21. *Social Welfare Department Programmes 1991-92*, Government of Karnataka. Bangalore (Kannada), ND.

22. *Sarvashiksha Abhiyan – Perspective Plan 2002-2010*, Office of the District Project Co-ordinator, DPEP, Mysore, ND.

23. *Tribal Education in India, Publication No. 20*, Tribal Education Unit. Department of Adult Education, NCERT, 1967.

24. *Welfare Programmes for Scheduled Tribes*, Directorate of Social Welfare, Government of Karnataka (Kannada), ND.

25. Midatala Rani, Functioning of Ashram Schools in Karnataka in Budakattu Adhyayana Journal (Hampi: Kannada University, 2012).

26. Census of India 2001in SC Bhatt and Gopal K Bhargava (Editors), *Land and People of Indian States and Union Territories,* Vol. 7, Kalpaz Publications, Delhi, 2006.

2

Salvation Army Boon or Bane? A Critique of Yerukula Reformation in Andhra Pradesh

Malli Gandhi

"As white man's rat has driven away the native rat so the European fly drives away our own, and the clover kills our fern, so will the Maoris disappear before the white man himself".

—A Maori Proverb

Numerous tribes in India were proclaimed "criminal" by the British government were declared as ex-criminal, denotified communities during the year 1952. Even after 63 years of Independence they are living in miserable conditions. They are placed at a disadvantaged position in the present caste-based system. The Government has to consider the anomalies in identifying and characterising the various denotified communities in the country. Their condition is worsening day by day. The present reservation provided by the government is not sufficient to meet the developmental demands of these communities. The aims and objectives of the paper is to discuss the impact of the CT Act on the DNT communities in general and Yerukulas in particular, modernisation of the criminal tribes and the role of the Salvation Army, and the impact of the Indian leaf tobacco company in transforming the Yerukulas as industrial wage workers from itinerant trading communities.

The British imperial government launched many projects to declare certain wandering communities as criminal tribes. The most important project that was launched was introducing the Criminal Tribes Act of 1871, and preparing a detailed demographic profile of Indian population as their subjects.[1]

The forest tribes led a nomadic life. These tribes were engaged in barter trade with the surrounding agricultural communities, exchanging forest produce such as herbs and honey, salt, clothes and grain. Nineteenth century colonial economic policies destroyed the occupations of a number of such communities. The salt policy of the government destroyed the trade of Koravars, Yerukulas, Korchars, Brinjaries and Lambadis.[2] Like Yerukulas and Banjaras many groups were badly affected by the forest policies. Lieutenant Balmer wrote: "The crimes they are addicted to are dacoity and highway robbery. They are the most troublesome of our wanderers".[3]

In the last quarter of the 19th century the British Government launched census operations throughout the country. The colonial administrators did not understand the cultural pluralism of the Indian people and their sense of accommodation and adjustment with different religions and communities. The colonial masters started looking at these communities with the glasses of modernity. Michel Foucault said: The episteme of difference has taken precedence over the episteme of resemblance".[4] The imperial rulers could not understand the meaning of nomadism. They could not understand that nomadism as a way of life for a large number of communities in India and outside. Nomadism was the way of their life. It is their philosophy of their life. They did not like to stick on to one place. They do not want to change the nature and intervene in its practices.[5] Thus many classes of people and communities lived with nature and practised nomadism. Their nomadic way of life was misunderstood by the imperial rulers and administrators. They considered them as uncivilised, uncultured, savage and barbarous. They thought that these nomadic people will pose a threat to the law and order to the society. They were very poor, they lack definite means of production to earn their living. Therefore, the colonial government assumed these communities as thieves and dacoits. Thus, they are dubbed as criminal tribes. David Arnold wrote: "The Criminal Tribes Act of 1871 was used against the wandering groups, nomadic petty traders and pastoralists, gypsy types, hill- and forest-dwelling tribals, in short, against a wide variety of marginals who did not conform to the colonial pattern of settled agricultural and wage labour".[6]

The different laws on the so-called criminal tribes have been influenced by the colonial considerations of political mechanism and economic needs. The colonial administrators believed that maintenance of law and order would be a mere exercise in vacuum unless a better control could be achieved over the indigenous population. It was then imperative that a strong and shifting population could not be conducive to the so-called 'good' government and the colonial notion of 'Pax Britanica'. In order to achieve this, unlike in the West where legislation regulated incidences of crime, in India, interception of crime was attempted. The colonial government here tried to confine would-be-male factors to settlements.[7] Some wandering tribes without any fixed habitat became, dubbed as 'criminal' and were setup in settlements. Mackenzire writes, "these tribes led a vagrant life in jungles, hills and deserts with no fixed abodes. They wandered about with their bag and baggage and pitch their tents on the outskirts of a village or some secluded place".[8] A gypsy way of life necessitated by early trading activities, came to be described as vagrancy or lust for wandering. It was stated that, "if the local government has reason to believe that any tribe, gang or class of persons or any part of a tribe gang or class is addicted to the systematic commission of offences it may declare that such tribe, gang or class or part of the tribe, gang or class as a criminal tribe".[9]

Yerukulas were declared a criminal community under the Criminal Tribes Act, 1991. The salient features of.the Criminal Tribes Act were as follows:

1. Before a community was declared a criminal tribe, 'respectable members' of a village were consulted, who were invariably either headman, or high caste sections or landlords; often these categories overlapped. The notified criminal tribe members had to take the permission of the headman before they could enter or leave a village. There is evidence that these headmen-cum-landlords used the act to extract free labour from the criminal tribe members before they allowed an itinerant community to pass through the village.

2. One of the provisions required the notified criminal tribe members to report to the nearest police station to register their attendance twice a night. These powers were used by the subordinate police for extortions and harassment so widely that it caused some administrative concern.

3. The criminal tribe members were forced to work in mills, factories, mines, quarries and plantations by the police administration as a part of relieving their own vigilance duties, and handing over to the employers extraordinary powers of control under the Criminal Tribe Act. Under this, even ordinary workers could be declared criminal tribes in case their work performance was not satisfactory and in fact in crucial ways this act also effectively replaced the Workmen's Breach of Contract Act, especially on the plantations. As far as this particular use of the Criminal Tribes Act was concerned, any low caste, vulnerable section of the people could be declared a criminal tribe and forced to work in an enterprise; any persons including a manager of an enterprise could be made responsible for their control and any site, including an enterprise could be declared a criminal tribe settlement.

4. A section of those declared criminal could be interned into special settlements set up under one of the provisions of the Criminal Tribes Act.[10]

The Criminal Tribe settlements were managed by several Christian missionaries and philanthropic societies who worked for their moral upliftment and modernisation of the criminal tribes.

The following missionaries may be cited:

1. The Canadian Mission,
2. Arya Samaj,
3. The Servants of India Society,
4. The Salvation Army,
5. The American Baptist Telugu Mission,
6. The Ramakrishna Mission, etc.

The Government found the successful work done by the Missionaries such as Salvation Army.[11] The Salvation Army was the first organisation that stepped into the activities among the Criminal Tribes. Dadabhai Naoroji said, "The Salvation Army's help has been requisitioned from time to time. Whether it is Salvation Army or whether it is any other reforming body. The religious zeal is very often a necessary element in pursuing difficult task of people of this kind and winning them from evil ways".[12]

Criminal Tribe settlements were established in such districts where grave crime was prevalent. In order to provide a settled and modern life the government opened agricultural, industrial, reformative, and voluntary settlements. The earliest nomadic settlement was established by the American Baptist Telugu Mission in 1912 at Kavali (Bitragunta). Sitanagaram settlement was established in 1913. Vedullapalli or Betapudi settlement was established in 1914 by the Salvation Army. The Lingala settlement was established during the year 1917 by the Nizam's government for the welfare and development of the Yerukulas in the erstwhile Madras Presidency-Andhra State.[13]

Stuartpuram or Betapudi settlement was one of the biggest settlements in Madras Presidency. There were about 10,000 Yerukulas lived for several decades from 1911 onwards. The settlement was named after Stuart, the moving force behind settlements in general. He was a senior government official and incharge of the police establishment. The spirit behind these settlements was punitive rather than reformative.[14]

By 1910, several CT settlements were established in Madras Presidency. Many itinerant communities were singled out for settling by the policy. The official directive of the government was "worst characters, especially wandering gangs" must be settled.[15] The Salvation Army was entrusted with the reformatory work of the itinerant communities. The responsibility of the sedentary criminals was taken up by the police. Stuartpuram settlement became the literal 'site' for the British Administration and the Salvation Army to 'experiment in crimino curology'. The Salvation Army was responsible for a number of settlements. It is the main organisation working with the criminal communities in India.[16]

The Salvation Army was identified itself with the imperial aims of England. It was born in 1870s when the British imperialism was in the peak point. It was called itself as the Salvation Army. The Salvation Army encashed on the popular image of romanticised imperialism. It had adopted marches, flags, brass bands and uniforms for its employees. 'General' Booth was their head. Their officers had signed on the 'articles of war'. Their newspaper was called *The War Cry*. They had open air 'bombardments' not prayers or meetings. They do not say that they were going to start work in a new region. First they occupy the new territory and then they declare religious war. In short, the Salvation Army was a shadow imperial body. It had identified with the aims and projects of England. General Booth had envisaged for the English poor what he called the settlements as city colonies and farm colonies. For the Indian 'Criminal' classes he declared them as 'settlements'. The imperial term 'settlement' took a modern meaning. The itinerant communities were to be settled down instead of wandering aimlessly.[17]

Stuartpuram Settlement was meant for the well-behaved people. Those persons who were reformed and non-criminal members were drawn from Sitanagaram were placed in the settlement.[18] When the Government provided land to the Salvation Army in Guntur to set up the settlement there were a number of protests posed in different ways. The local landlords were particularly infuriated. They charged that the CT members escaped at night and committed crime. Thus, this settlement was declared as a 'criminal' settlement. The government increased the police force to watch their movements carefully.[19]

Stuartpuram settlement was initially planned as an agricultural settlement. A total number of 500 acres of sandy land and 1000 acres of swamp land were handed over to the Salvation Army by the government, free of assessment.[20] Due to various reasons the plan of the government was failed. Essentially, the land was of very poor quality, and the implements of the agriculture production were primitive. The Yerukulas were not keen on tilling the land. They were not enthusiastic agriculturists in the beginning. The manager of the settlement once said: The Salvation Army found it very tedious to convert them into good cultivators industrious to work on land they were forced and could not be induced. Through driven like a flock of sheep, the first crop failed . . . No crowbars, no proper spade and no physical strength. So work turned out did not reach the desired length. In the beginning, I had recourse to a stick, I was glad, as it brought the desired result quick.[21]

There was free opposition by the landlords in the area. They objected the very concept of low caste communities being granted land. In addition to their fear, they understood if the paddy land suitably irrigated, was very profitable and valuable for them. It was stated that: "the monied folk of Bapatla had counted . . . on buying the swamp land at cheap rates and rack renting the actual cultivator whenever a crop could be raised".[22] This plan was unwillingly foiled by the administration by parcelling out large tracts of land to the Salvation Army. The protest by the landlords was also in a large measure due to their anxiety about losing the services of Yerukulas as agricultural workers on their own land.[23]

All this opposition took place in the era when landlords were important political allies of the British administration, and on balance, the administration decided not to alienate the landlord/headmen sections any further. Irrigation facilities, plans to make available water from the Krishna river to the settlement – were withheld, and alternative means of supporting the settlement had to be now seriously considered.[24]

The Indian Lead Tobacco Company (ILTD) began its administration with the help of the Salvation Army. The Company invited the Yerukulas as alternative employees. The ILTD had existed in Guntur district since 1908 in order to procure local tobacco. The ILTD started to work as the leaf wing of British American Tobacco Company and Peninsular Company. By 1925, the factory was able to employ half of the total adult population of the settlement. According to government policy, once infrastructure for the settlement had been provided by the government, the settlements were to be self-supporting. But the income from the land was found not enough for the Yerukulas. Therefore, the entire settlement gradually depended on the factory for employment.[25] The Salvation Army had no other means of finding employment for the Yerukulas.

The company's initial contact with the Stuartpuram settlers seems to have been through the mats made by the Yerukula women and children. They made the mats and baskets very fast. The mats and baskets were, infact, an essential part of the manufacturing process at the factory. The Salvation Army was the medium through which the sales took place to the ILTD. Slowly, women came to be employed in the factory as regular wage workers. The men continued to work fruitlessly on the land. The financial situation of the settlement was quite stable for a few years after the women settlers from Stuartpuram began to work in the tobacco factory. The ILTD management, the Salvation Army and the government was very optimistic with regard to the future progress of the Yerukulas.[26]

Stuartpuram became a large settlement in terms of numbers as whole communities – not individuals – were put in at a time. The CT Act was meant to work with the concept of whole communities. Even the Salvation Army said they were embarrassed by what they called "this rain of riches". The Salvation Army officials said: "To others, these criminals may hardly appear in the light of riches, but to us each bears the image and supersubscription of the Divine Mint".[27]

Stuartpuram is the largest settlement. It needed extensive police presence outside to prevent escapes and inside, the Salvation Army took attendance upto five times in a day, including nights.[28] There was strict punctuality and discipline for the adults, males, children and women. The system of fines and corporal punishment to deter disorderly behaviour was imposed. Incidentally, virtually no outsiders were allowed into the settlement for scrutiny, and enquiry committees could enter into the settlements. When the nationalists took up this issue in 1940's seriously this has come down a little bit.[29]

Stuartpuram settlement was primarily an agricultural settlement. The official rationale was that it should become an agricultural colony. Agriculture was the chief profession of the Yerukulas in the settlement. The British Government had the deep anxiety for the reclamation of the waste land, forest and swamp lands. In fact, land reclamation was synonymous with the reclamation of the criminals.[30] Once cultivable, the land could start paying revenue. A large tract of waste land was given to Salvation Army for cultivation by the Yerukulas. This needed some reorganisation of the community's social and cultural priorities.[31]

Drastic modern transformation in the lives of the Yerukulas was followed. Most important modern transformation was the itinerant mode of existence was suddenly replaced by a forced settled life. The Salvation Army divided the community into families, which were now the new operational social and economic unit – each family was given a small piece of land, which it was responsible for cultivating or else punishment was followed.[32] The family was further broken up by removing the children to another part of the settlement. The Salvation Army felt that the 'rising generation' should be kept away from their wicked parents, and brought up in a more wholesome atmosphere. Separate schools and dormitories were established for these children, and they were allowed to meet their parents only on Sundays during Church activities. The two components of the modernisation of the Yerukulas were: (1) moral education and (2) hard work. The Salvation Army concentrated on the Yerukula boys and girls for moral education and on the adult men and women for hard physical work.[33]

The Salvation Army did not normally prepare women for wage work in any of its settlements. Ideally, they were to be trained in feminine virtues and were expected to sew, embroider and cook for their families. In Stuartpuram settlement, a new division of labour within the family was devised and appropriate gender roles were defined. In fact, mat-making, which was a traditional activity of both men and women of the Yerukula community, was now handed over exclusively to women. It was combined with their indoor activities. The Yerukula men now ploughed and tilled the waste land, though it was unsuccessful many times.[34]

There were a number of ways in which the Yerukula women was fashioned and modernised. True women were fashioned out of what the Salvation Army called "thievish raw material".[35] For example, they were taught to pay attention to their appearances. The Salvation Army even held periodic parades of the most neatly dressed women and gave the winners prizes.[36] The women were not allowed to go outside the settlement on a pass if they looked like "so many vagrants".[37] The before and after photographs of the women in the Salvation Army records show the 'after' version with a completely changed Hinduised appearance, complete with neatly tied saris, oiled hair with flowers and vermillion marks on their foreheads.

After more than a decade of such remoulding, something happened. The newly-domesticated women were required to work outside their homes for a wage as the land was found unable to support the families. The government expected the Salvation Army to make the settlements under their care completely self-supporting once the initial infrastructure had been paid for. Due to severe financial crisis the Yerukula women was persuaded or forced in hundreds to go and work in the newly-established tobacco factory near Ramanagaram a few miles away from the settlement.

The Salvation Army systematically inculcated in them an indoor culture of housekeeping and child rearing. The Yerukulas used to walk seven kms everyday and spend 12 hours outside their homes, earning a wage in the ILTD factory. The Salvation Army asked the government to provide crèches for the infants and toddlers in the settlement, so that the young mothers could go as well for the factory work. Thus within a period of 10-12 years, the Yerukula women alone earned as much as 80 per cent of the entire settlement income.

The Yerukula women became the principal earners in their families. The Salvation Army consolidated the new moral code for them. The Salvation Army began to take a more active role in their personal and material life. This was done in order to keep their own control and to make sure that economic independence did not confound gender identities and gender roles.

The Yerukula women used to have the freedom to choose their spouses. The Salvation Army granted permission for marrying the males in the settlement limits only. The Salvation Army officials had always been votaries of proper match-making in the settlements. The Salvation Army became very active on the issue of the marriages of the Yerukula males and females. They wrote to the government wanting "a voice in the choice of spouses" and got it. They were finding to their alarm that bride price, something they had been trying to suppresses as it meant mere selling of females, now rose steeply, sometimes as much as rupees five hundred. The Salvation Army substituted it with dowry, which they gave themselves. It always consisted of saris and vessels for the bride, the true symbols of lost domesticity. Incidentally, in other settlements, the Salvation Army used to insist that the man be able to support his wife before letting them marry. They also forbade completely what they called "desertions" by women of their husbands. Ironically, the women lost their autonomy in material affairs at a time when they were the principal contributors to the family income.

The ILTD company where the women worked supported the Salvation Army on the severe discipline in the settlement, and showed their active role in the affairs of the families of the Yerukula women. In fact, the ILTD management became active on the issue of interfering in the personal issues of the Yerukulas in the settlement. The strict discipline, punctuality, regularity, sincerity, orderly behaviour and a system of harsh punishments – resonated very well with the ILTD factory life. The ILTD management found that these workers were "less trouble some" than others. The Salvation Army insisted on an irrevocable form of marriage worked in the favour of the company. They could not continue to pay a family wage which was much lower than the sum paid to an individual man and woman. By the year 1930, the whole families of the Yerukulas in the Stuartpuram settlement became the employers of the Salvation Army. The men sued to work upto 20 hours a day in different shifts. The Salvation Army had an interest in keeping families together in the settlement. The Yerukula men and women requested the management to intervene and help them in getting their wives to stay with them. The ILDT literally threatened the women with the loss of their jobs in case they divorced their husbands.

Today Stuartpuram of course was officially not called a criminal tribe settlement any more and the Yerukula community was not criminal tribes anymore – after Independence, the CT Act, under which they had been notified by the Colonial administration, had been repealed. Salvation Army now a much depleted organisation both as far as its authority and number of personnel were concerned. However, it is still operating in the settlement with a church, schools, hostels and a few welfare activities.

The entire gamut of modernising the Denotified Communities depends on how best educational facilities are provided to the children of the DNT communities. Education paves a way for them to become a part and parcel of the mainstream of national life. Education helps to channelise their energies into productive purposes. Education is an effective weapon and instrument of social transformation. Education plays a significant role in changing the fortune and life-style of the children of the DNT communities. Their economic plight and environmental influence have direct impact on their education. A detailed study of the schooling facilities presents a grim picture in all DNT colonies today. The children in these schools when examined were highly intelligent, active and alert. Lack of education among them leads to lack of social and political consciousness. Another problem that the Yerukulas are facing today is the inferiority complex that they have suffered since a long time. This is due to their economic backwardness. A stigma is attached to the community. "The stigma of their being 'criminal' strained them more glaringly as people always doubted a person who had spent sometime in a criminal reformatory". In order to modernise the Yerukulas what is urgently required is to remove them from the influence of petty crime, the pernicious influence of the environment of the 'settlement', profitable industrialisation, improvised agricultural facilities, proper and conducive environment, improvised health facilities, banks, free from oppression, stigma, harassment and exploitation.

Notes and References

1. Singh, Birinder Paul, Ex-Criminal Tribes of Punjab, *Economic and Political Weekly,* Vol. XLIII, No. 51, December 20-26, 2008, p. 58.
2. Gandhi, Malli, Development of Denotified Tribes: Policy and Practice, Sarup and Sons, New Delhi, 2006, p. 7.
3. Government of Madras, Madras Criminal Tribes Manual, Criminal Tribes Act VI of 1924, brought upto 31st March 1927, Madras 1928.
4. Singh, Birinder Paul, *op.cit.*, p. 58.
5. *Ibid.*
6. Arnold, David, 'Crime and Crime Control in Madras 1885-1947' in Yang (ed), Crime and Criminality in British India, University of Arizona Press, Tucson.

7. Gandhi, Malli, *op.cit.*, p. 10.

8. Mackenzie, Mildred, E., *The Mud Bank*, Pensilvania, 1894, p. 60.

9. Madras Criminal Tribes Manual, *op.cit.*, p. 18.

10. Radha Krishna, Meena, Colonial Construction of a Criminal Tribe, Yerukulas of Madras Presidency, *Economic and Political Weekly,* July 8-15, 2000, p. 2256.

11. Malli, Gandhi, Denotified Tribes: Dimensions of Change, Kanishka Publishers, New Delhi, 2008.

12. Government of Madras, Home Department, G.O. No. 1675, dt. 2.12.1919.

13. Lalitha, V., The Making of Criminal Tribes, Patterns and Transition, New Era Publications, Madras, 1995.

14. Malli, Gandhi and Lalitha, V., *Tribes Under Stigma: Problem of Identity*, Serials Publishers, New Delhi, 2009.

15. Radha Krishna, Meena, *Dishonoured by History 'Criminal Tribes' and British Colonial Policy*, Orient Longman, Hyderabad, 2001, p. 14.

16. Radha Krishna, Meena, 'The Criminal Tribes Act in Madras Presidency: Implications for Itinerant Communities', *The Indian Economic and Social History Review,* Vol. 26, 3.

17. Radha Krishna, Meena, 'Surveillance and Settlements Under the Criminal Tribes Act in Madras', *The Indian Economic and Social History Review, 29, 2.*

18. Government of Madras, Note showing the progress made in the settlement of Criminal Tribes in the Madras Presidency up to January 1925, Madras, 1927, p. 28.

19. Government of Madras, *Note showing the Progress made in the settlement of Criminal Tribes in the Madras Presidency up to September, 1916*, Madras, 1917, p. 21.

20. Government of Madras, Law (General) Department, G.O. No. 1327, dated 14.2.1925, p. 3.

21. Government of Madras, Law (General) Department, G.O. No. 1714, dated 22.10.1921, p. 4.

22. Government of Madras, Home Judicial Department, G.O. No. 305, dated 7.2.1918, p. 3.

23. Government of Madras, *Note Showing the Progress Made in the Settlement of Criminal Tribes in the Madras Presidency upto September 1916*, Madras 1917, p. 22.

24. Home Judicial Department, G.O. No. 2074, dt. 18.8.1916, p. 5.

25. Government of Madras, Law (General) Department, G.O. No. 3187, dated 14.11.1924, p. 1.

26. Government of Madras, Law (General) Department, G.O. No. 1551, dated 10.7.1927, p. 3.

27. Mackenzie, Mildred, E., The Mud Bank, Pensilvania, 1894, p. 42.

28. Radha Krishna, Meena, 'Surveillance and Settlements under the Criminal Tribes Act in Madras', *The Indian Economic and Social History Review, 29, 2.*

29. Radha Krishna, Meena, Colonial Construction of a 'Criminal' Tribe, Yerukulas of Madras Presidency, Economic and Political Weekly, July 8-15, 2000, p. 2558.

30. Government of Madras, *Judicial Department, G.O. No. 2308, dated September 22, 1916.*

31. Government of Madras, *Note showing the Progress Made in the Settlement of Criminal Tribes in Madras Presidency upto 1925*, Madras 1927.

32. Government of Madras, Home Judicial Department, G.O. No. 1759, dated August 5, 1918.

33. *Ibid.*

34. Government of Madras, *Public Works Labour Department, G.O. No. 1654L, dated July 6, 1928.*

35. Salvation Army, *The War Cry*, London, June 1913.

36. Government of Madras, Judicial Department, G.O. No. 1759, dated August 5, 1918, p. 4.

37. Government of Madras, *Note showing the Progress Made in the Settlement of Criminal Tribes upto 1925*, Madras, 1927, p. 40.

3

Socio-economic Conditions of Tribals and Resulting Social Alienation

Ramdas Rupavath

Since Independence many development schemes and protective measures have been attempted by the Central and State governments for the trial areas of Andhra Pradesh. However, the conditions of majority of the tribals have deteriorated. While exploitation and backwardness are found in many communities and social groups in India, among tribes it has resulted in social alienation. The existence of a distinct culture and life style make the problems of tribals different from those of other deprived groups in India. In this chapter, an attempt has been made to focus upon social alienation in Adilabad district, while specific economic problems such as land alienation have been dealt with in the next chapter.

Tribal Society and Culture

The tribals of this area belong mainly to the Gond tribe. They form a socially dominant section among the rest who belong to the Bhil, Koya, Kolam, etc., tribes and are much fewer in number. Their mother tongue is Gondi, Tribal life among the Gonds exhibits unique symbiosis of man and nature. Their culture being an outcome of living with nature and learning from it. Traditionally Pujaris also called 'Kolams', were a priestly class who performed rituals and were the medicine men and story tellers of the tribe. They enjoyed social prominence together with the tribal chiefs. Tribal spiritual life was rich with creative mythologies and religious stories. Each clan member even today possesses the house deities of the tribe though there is a village priest called the "Devari" and clan priest (Kalotra) and a village seer (Bhaktal). There is no discrimination among the Gonds on the basis of sex. Women traditionally had an important position within the family and society. The Gonds even today have their distinct folk dances and music. However, they celebrate the main "Hindu" festivals of Diwali, Dussehra etc.[1]

Since independence Gond society has been profoundly influenced by the twin process of 'Sanskritisation and modernisation.[2] Due to this the social and economic life of the Gonds has undergone change. For example, change has taken place in the position given to women and the rituals associated with marriage. Gond women traditionally were very independent and took part in both cultivation of land, setting of produce etc. Today, due to cultural contact women are secluded. While earlier marriages were simple affairs, today the custom of dowry has penetrated into tribal life forcing many into the hands of local moneylenders. Non-tribal intrusion has created an unequal social fabrication and mentality.[3] Non-tribals in order to sustain their economic exploitation and hegemony over the tribals have attempted to propagate the Hindu religion as superior to the tribal god who is described as 'evil spirits'. The backwardness of described as an outcome of religious beliefs and practices. This has led to breakdown of the social fabric and adoption of Hindu practices such as pilgrimages to Tirupati. Animist practices such as free worship has been replaced by temple workshop. The establishment of institutionalised religion has made temple surroundings place of commercial activity useful to the non-tribal trading classes. Haimendorf records that the 'Khelaspur Jatara' a tribal festival has been replaced by a temple, which has been used as a platform by politicians during election campaigns. Temple offerings (amounting to Rs 1911 in 1977) have attracted Hindu priests, and have treated disputes within the tribe.[4] A court order however, returned the control of the temple to the tribal population.

The Gonds still practice traditional method of agriculture. They are dependent upon the rains for irrigation. Jowar is the main crop cultivated, but is available for only three months in the year. Rest of the time they survive on forest produce. The dependence of tribals on nature has led to most of them living close to starvation.

Of the 35 lakh tribals population only 6.6 per cent are literate in Adilabad.[5] Table 3.1 shows that very few tribals have managed to even get a few years of schooling. The first attempt to educate the Gonds was made in the 1940's by the Nizam's government.[6] Books were published in the language of the Gonds, however this did not have any impact. In the post-independence period the government of Andhra Pradesh has not taken any keen interest in educating the tribals. The Gonds consider children as a source of income and are reluctant to send them to school.[7] In recent years due to increasing pressure on land and resulting protests the state government has tried to introduce schools and increase literacy and vocational training. In 1989, the Andhra Pradesh government introduced 451 tribal hostels and 12 residential schools.

Table 3.1: Educational Levels of the Scheduled Tribes in Adilabad District, 1981

Total Tribals	*Matriculation*				*Higher Secondary /Intermediate*		*Non-technical Diploma or certification of equal des.*		*Technical Certificates*		*Graduate and above*	
	M	F	M	F	M	F	M	F	M	F	M	F
Gond												
Rajgonds	704	33	422	21	92	3	-	-	19	1	33	1
Naikpod	564	26	152	4	42	-	-	-	11	-	13	1
Sugalis												
Lambardar	10	5	3	-	1	-	-	-	-	-	-	-
Yerukal												
	21	2	3	1	-	-	-	-	-	-	-	-
Kolam												
Manana	1	-	-	-	-	-	-	-	-	-	-	-
Varlu												
Konda doras	-	-	-	-	-	-	-	-	-	-	-	-
Konda	-	-	-	1	-	-	-	-	-	-	-	-
Reddy	84	4	4	16	2	5	-	-	-	-	-	-
Bhil	-	-	-	-	-	-	-	-	-	-	-	-
Koya	1384	70	580	25	134	3	-	-	19	1	46	2
Yenadis												
Total												

However, such facilities have been utilised only by the children of a few rich farmers and according to the Gondwana Sanrakshna Samiti, such schemes do not benefit the tribal population. The first attempt to educate Gonds was made in the 1940s by the Nizam's government.

And are merely to fill the quota of education seats set aside to schedule tribes. Most of the tribal students in the scheme were unable to pass the matriculation examination. Training for provision of skilled or semi skilled jobs would be far more beneficial. For example, after the violent incident in Allampali Taluk where 12 policemen were killed in a land mine explosion the Telugu Desam Government announce that 1000 teachers posts would be reserved for scheduled tribe candidates. However, very few of the trial population had the required certificates and qualifications.[8] Thus lopsided development policies and schemes introduced by the Government policies and schemes introduction by the Government have not been of much use and help only some vested interests.

Changing Local Structures of Powers

In the pre-independence period in Andhra Pradesh there were 37 tribal chiefs some of whom bore the title of Raja '*Mokashi*' or '*Deshmukh*'. They had political power within their jurisdiction and exercised varying degrees of feudal oppression. They were assisted by village headmen in solving tribal problems. In the 1940s these traditional structures of power were removed by the Nizam's government in spite of resistance by the tribals.[9] The Nizam's government succeeded in abolishing the old system and replacing it by a village headman nominated by the Village Panchayat who settled dispute and had judicial authority. Thus before independence itself the old tribal structure had begun to disintegrate.

There was further erosion of local authority after independence with the passage of the Hyderabad Tribal Regulation Act in 1963.[10] Under this the village headman came under the control of the district bureaucracy under the new Panchayat System members are elected each block, who in turn elect the Sarpanch. In some cases it is reported that non-tribals have been able to manipulate the system and become a sarpanch; a position that gives it holder considerable patronage and power. Sarpanch has the power to grant licenses for shops and collect some local taxes.[11] They however have power to settle disputes. Some villages in the blocks have village headman who help the local tribal population to dig wells, plant trees etc.

The erosion of local autonomy has had an impact on the social and economic life of the tribals. Under the traditional tribal structure outsiders had to gain permission from the village headman to reside in the area. Massive demographic increases, after 1951 and the opening up of tribal areas due to the process of modernisation and inclusion of tribal areas in States, propelled non-tribals into tribal territory. In Adilabad this has led to non-tribals from the coastal area establishing factories cement mills, paper factories shops etc. The labour in these factories also consists of non-tribals, hence modernisation has not provided employment to the local tribals. It has led to establishment of liquor shops or increased prostitution. Commercialisation has led to breakdown of the traditional systems of authority within the tribal system.[12]

Table 3.2: Structural of Power at the Gram Taluk and District Levels Established in 1983 by Tribal Leaders

Rai Centres		
Gram Sabha	*Taluk level*	*District level*
1. Napapal: Village headman 2. Sar Pathal: Additional village headman 3. Raipatal : Asst. Village headman 4. Geeta Daralal: Maintaining the records. 5. Gatilal: Accountant 6. Devari: In charge of religious rituals 7. Hawaldar: Messenger.	1. Sri Medial : the President 2. Rai Medial : General Secretary 3. Geeta Medial: Joint Secy. 4. Ghat Medial : Accountant 5. Raipatals: Advisors to Sir medials.	1. Zill mall: President 2. Bpa Mandal: Vi. President 3. Zilla Rai: Gen. Secy. Medial 4. Khaajandhar: Accountant

In 1983 in order to help the tribals and grant them greater autonomy to manage their local affairs the Gondwana Sangrashna Samiti was established by educated tribal leaders.[13] It is a village level council, which solves local problems and helps implement developmental schemes. The various tribal groups in the villages nominate a representative to the Council. It consists of 7 – 14 members. In addition to this tribal leaders have also established developmental or "Rai Centres" patterned on their traditional power structures. These have been set up at the Gram, Taluk, and District levels. These help the tribals settle internal problems. Moreover, any Government schemes to be taken up at village level must obtain the consent of concerned Gram Sabha/village council. Contractors are not allowed, nor the Patel or Patwari, in the village council or Rai Centres. The Village Council can impose fines between Rs 50 to Rs 500. (assault, theft, etc.). They are also managing tribal lands and controlling forest produce.

The Samithi also introduced the grain procurement system. Each tribal agricultural family must donate 60 kgs of grains and Rs 50. Those who are not in a position to donate at one time can give in installments. The Integrated Tribal Development Scheme also contributes an equal quantity of grains and cash as government subsidy. They have set up grain banks, which advance loans for religious ceremonies and marriages at very low interest rates.[14]

Investment by the Government in Tribal Welfare

Table 3.3 gives the per capita and total expenditure by the Government of Andhra Pradesh over the various Plan periods. It is only from the fifth Plan period that there is a sharp rise in the amount invested. Under the Five Year Plan the Government has undertaken Schemes to construct pucca houses and cattle sheds. Integrated Tribal Development Schemes have also been formulated under the Tribal Development Schemes have also been formulated under the Tribal Development Agency.[15] A Girijan Co-operative Corporation was set up under it. It was expected to purchase the timber collected by the tribals and thereby eliminate private timber contractors. Primary Societies affiliated to the co-operative were supposed to supply at proper rates, the daily requirements of the tribals, provide hedit etc. However, the co-operative has been giving very low rates to tribals, for example Rs five-eight per kg. Of gum while private contractors pay Rs 12 per kg. This led to tribals setting their produce to contractors rather than the co-opertive.[16]

Nationalised Banks have entered the area. A study shows that 61 per cent debtors are landless holders. A quarter of the loans advanced by the official and government agencies 67 per cent are used for consumption purposes. The Andhra Pradesh government introduced a drinking water scheme named Jeevandhara" to provide drinking water irrigation facilities.[17] Under it Rs 15000 were given to each selected family in installments to dig wells on their own. According to the government 10,000 wells for agricultural purposes and 11,000 wells for drinking water have been dug. The Integrated Tribal Development agency had also started new loans to tribals for buying bullocks. However, many tribals have alleged that old and useless bullocks were supplied and only after a considerable period of delay.[18] Medical facilities under the ITDA are also very poor.

Table 3.3: Per Capita Expenditure and Total Expenditure during Plan Period in Andhra Pradesh for Schedule Tribes

Plan	*Period*	*Per capita Expenditure in (Rs)*	*Total expenditure Rs in Lakhs*
I	Plan	15.05	118.77
II	Plan	18.89	250.25
III	Plan	13.56	178.77
IV	Plan	59.00	977.77
V	Plan	266.00	4,879.85
VI	Plan	750.47	13,598.00
VII	Plan	1,639.16	30,026.00

Source: Statistical Abstracts of A.P. 1960 and 1983, Bureau of Economics and Statistics. Government of Andhra Pradesh.

Many plans put forward by the government are not relevant to the needs of the tribal areas. Schemes like medium irrigation, small industry, commercial forestry etc. Which often constitute a sizeale portion of the tribal sub-plan are often irrelevant or counter-productive as far as the local tribal economy is concerned.[19]

Control over Forests

There is a symbiotic relationship between tribals and the forest. It has been their home for a long time and provided them with many required resources. The forest conservation and regulation act was passed in 1920.[20] This imposed rules on the tribals, mainly restrictions; on collection of forest produce. This led to conflicts between the tribals and the government. The tribals required wood to build huts and for their ploughshare.

In the post-independence period, forest policy has led to hardship in tribal communities. On the one hand, these communities are not allowed to collect forest produce, but on the other hand large-scale deforestation has occurred because of various developmental projects and extension of cultivation by reclamation of land.[21] Instead of the entire community being consulted about the extraction of forest produce, arrangements are often made between chiefs and contractors bypassing the community, as the forest department was interested mainly in the collection of revenue this alliance was encouraged, leading to destruction of forests. This has also led to increase in wealth of chiefs and their capacity for graft and duplicity.[22]

In the case of Adilabad, notwithstanding various lambadas and regulations to prevent deforestation, a large part of the forests have been, as reported by a fact-finding committee continuously "dereserved" by the Congress Government in 1980 to facilitate private trade. Thus of the 500,000 acres of forest land dereserved in the last years in the state, more than 150,000 acres are from Adilabad. The net result of this policy has been the progressive alienation of the forest from the tribals. Consequently, they have been reduced to the status of daily wage labourers at the mercy of private contractors and forest officials.[23]

Table 3.4 shows the plantation area in Andhra Pradesh in 1983-84.

Table 3.4: Plantation Area up to 1983-84

Species	*Total Areas (in hectares)*	
	Department	*Corporation*
Teak	76,114	---
Eucalyptus	26,271	20.522
Bamboo	28,139	10,138
Cashew	18,949	16,511
Coffee	130	2,438
Red Sander's	1,913	---
Sandal Wood	2,670	---
Silver oak	8,942	---

(Contd.)

(Contd. Table 3.4)

Species	*Total Areas (in hectares)*	
	Department	*Corporation*
Babul	12,415	---
Casurima	13,690	---
Sissoo	1,435	---
Burrara	300	---
Piner	325	---
Other Miscellaneous	55,743	---

Source: A.P. forests at a glance 1983-84 Chief Conservator of Forest A.P. Hyderabad.

Table 3.5: Major Wood-based Industries in Andhra Pradesh

S.No.	*Name of the Company*	*Present installed capacity in T/Yr.*		*Variety*	*Approximate raw material commitment by the forest department in tonnes*
1.	A.P. Paper Mills Rajahmundry East Godavari	Paper	75,000	Bamboo Hardwood	1,10,000 75,000
2.	Sirpur paper mills Kagaz Nagar Adilabad	Do	61,00	Bamboo Hardwood	75,000 45,000
3.	Sree Rayalam Kurnool	Do	42,000	Bamboo Hardwood	45,000 45,000
4.	Badhrachalam Paper Boarder	Do	50,000	Bamboo Hardwood	60,000 74,000
5.	A.P. Rayons Limited Yetura nagaram Warangal	Rayon grade pulp	27,000	Hardwood Eucalyptus	75,000 10,000
6.	Novopars India Limited Patancheru (Ranga Reddy District)	Particle board	20,000	Hardwood	38,000
7.	Hyderabad Plywood Limited	Plywood	0.018 lakhs sq.mts.	Teak teaknon-teak	700 cm. Mts 1,700

Source: A.P. forests at a glance 1983-84, Chief Conservator of Forests A.P. Hyderabad.

It shows that the government of Andhra Pradesh has been concentrated on growing mostly teak, eucalyptus and bamboo, which are needed by the paper industry, and the big timcr markets in urban areas. This shows growing commercialisation of forest areas in the state. Table 3.5 gives the major wood industries in the state and the raw material supplied to them by the forest department. Hence, it is not the tribals the industrial class which is benefiting from the forests. The wood from the forests is largely deployed in urban areas and it is the contractors who are profiting from the same. Left activists have claimed that highly placed politician and bureaucrats are also involved in elicit timber trade.

The process of industrialisation in tribal areas has also resulted in the pauperisation of tribals. Many tribals have become property fewer workers after industries were set up and land were acquired from them with minimal compensation. The construction of roads into the tribal areas has hastened this process. The forest guards also exploit the tribals in Adilabad demanding illegal taxes. Data collected during fieldwork shows that in Adilabad they demand Rs 17 to 40 per plough in additional contribution in grain from each household. Atrocities against the tribal population in general have also increased in recent years. Table 3.6 below gives the atrocities reported against Scheduled Tribes between 1979 and 1983. Many more go unreported.

Table 3.6: Atrocities Reported on Schedule Tribes in 1979-1983

State	*No. of Cases Reported During Years*					
	1979	*1980*	*1981*	*1983*	*1983*	
Andhra Pradesh	13	14	29	31	33	
	Atrocities in 1983					
	Murder	Violence	Rape	Arson	Others	Total
Andhra Pradesh	1	8	9	1	14	33

Source: Report of the Commission for Scheduled Castes and Tribes, Sixth Report, April 1983, Chap V: Government of India, New Delhi, 1984.

Thus, we find that in spite of several protective measures, the economic conditions of the tribals has deteriorated and they are also experiencing social alienation, both of which constitute important causal factors in recent tribal movements. This has been due to extensive exploitation of the rich natural resources of their habitat decline of traditional activities without any viable alternative, and consequent marginalisation and exploitation of cheap labour. This has been accompanied by alienation of agricultural land, which is the subject of the next chapter.

References

1. Von furer-Haimendorf. (1977). *The struggle for survival*, Oxford University Press, Delhi, 1982.
2. M.N. Srinivas, *Social change in Modern India*.
3. Von Furer-Haimendorf. N.I. *Ibid.*

4. *Ibid.,* pp. 117-178.

5. B.D. Sharma: *Tribal Development Concept and Frame*, Prachi Prakashan, New Delhi, 1978.

6. Von Furer-Haimendof N.1.p. 175.

7. Andhra Prabha (Telugu Daily Newspaper) 21st July, 1990.

8. The President of the bond wave. Savrakshan Samiti (GSS) – a local organisation – supplied this information in an interview in Adilabad.

9. Von-Furer Haimendorf m. p. 153.

10. Hyderabad Regulation Act 1963, pp. 159, 163.

11. *Ibid.*

12. Fieldwork in the area was done and member of the GSS were interceived. See chapters IV part II.

13. K. Balagopal, "Adilabad Girijan Portaloo" (Telugu) Srujana, 1981, p. 7.

14. Report of the Commission for Schedule Castes and Schedule Tribes Sixth Report April 1983-March 1984. Government of India, New Delhi, 1984.

15. President of G.S.S.

16. E.P.W. September 24, 1983 p.VII, a report.

17. President of G.S.S.

18. Balagopal, Agrarian Classes and Conflicts pp. 71, 74.

19. "A.P. Forest at a Glance" Adilabad Birijan Porataloo" (Telugu) Srujana, 1981, p. 7.

20. This has been reported by among other (i) J. Breman, of Peasants, Migrants and Pampers: rural Labour Circulation in West Asia, Delhi, O.U.P. 1985. (ii) G. Shah, "Ethnicity and Politics: A Study of Scheduled Tribes in Gujarat" (Mins) Surat: Centre for Social Studies, 1978.

21. Ashok Mitra, "Tribal Habitat", Frontier 9, 1977 pp. 24-26.

22. Frontier, Vol. 13, 42, 1981, pp. 6-11.

23. In an interview with Varavara Rao, noted left-leader and Intellectual on 10-11-1991.

4

Gender Inequality and Development: A Study on the Toda of Nilgiri Hills in Anthropological Perspective

Jakka Parthasarathy

Introduction

In modern anthropology, the term 'gender' has increasingly replaced the term 'sex' in discussions of socially and culturally determined differences in the behaviour, role and status of men and women. Charlotte Seymour Smith (1986:129) has aptly remarked that "more recently gender has been used to refer to the social, cultural and psychological patterning of differences between males and females. The distinction between sex, which is biological phenomenon, and gender, which is a cultural classification, allows for the separation of the biological and cultural aspects of differences between males and females, thus avoiding a biological determinist position". Social inequality is a concomitant of human classification according to differential status, power and prestige. Some authors would reserve the term 'stratification' for inequality or ranking in tribal societies. In the so-called patrilineal societies, the gender inequality is based on criteria such as man and woman, division of labour, distribution of status and personal attributes.

The notion of development, in its broadest sense, includes both economic development and the social and cultural changes which accompany it. Thus economic development is the process of transition from one type of economic system to another, implying both economic growth and socio-cultural change. Recent anthropological studies have presented an increasingly critical attitude towards the concept of development.

This paper seeks to examine the gender inequality and its close bearing on the concept of development among the Toda, a primitive tribal group, inhabiting Nilgiri district of Tamil Nadu.

Method of Study

The study was conducted among the Todas, inhabiting in selected nine Toda settlements, among which three settlements are exposed to town, three are located in inaccessible region and other three are identified amidst or nearby non-tribal neighbourhood community in the respected taluks of Udhagamandalam, Kotagiri and Coonoor in the Nilgiri district of Tamil Nadu state. The author of this article is living on the upper plateau of the Nilgiri district, nearby tribal entitlements, since 1984. The events and occurrences among the Todas were observed and considered now while collecting the data and interpretations for this study. Participant observation and case study techniques were used as tools of methodology. The recent data is cross-checked with the adult Todas and their neighbourers. The secondary data was collected based on the indigenous literature on the Todas and the process of hill development. The gender inequality among the Todas was considered on the basis of a few cultural traits found among them.

Area of Study

On the earth, in this world, Todas are found only on the upper plateau of the Nilgiri hills in Tamil Nadu state of India. The present paper is based on the data collected from nine Toda munds (settlements) located in the Nilgiri district. The Nilgiri district, also called as 'The Nilgiri hills', is one of the smallest districts in Tamil Nadu. The district is a hilly area of 2549.0 sq kms located at the junction on the eastern and western ghats. With an average elevation of 6,500 ft, the Nilgiri district is bounded on the west by Kerala, on the north by Karnataka and on the south-east by Coimbatore district. The Nilgiris are characterised by cool climate and upper plateau is covered with unique 'shola' (montane forests) vegetation. Throughout three principal periods-aboriginal, colonial, national independence, the Nilgiri region has constituted a singularly instructive enclave. The district is divided into six taluks and Ooty (Udhagamandalam) town is the headquarters for the district administration. According to 2001 census, the total population of the Nilgiri district is 7,64 lakh out of which the total Scheduled Tribes population is 28373, constituting 4.32 per cent of the total general population. The tribal communities living in the district, namely, Todas, Kotas, Irulas, Kurumbas, Paniyans and Kattunayakans. These tribes are considered as indigenous groups, whereas, non-tribal Badagas, an agricultural dominant community along with other non-tribal groups are considered as migrant groups. On the Nilgiri plateau, Todas, Kotas and Kurumbas are living on the upper plateau; Irulas are living in the middle zone of the hills; Paniyans and Kattunayakans are living at the foothills of the Nilgiris. The details of the studied sample Toda settlements and their population are mentioned in the Table 4.1.

Table 4.1: Details of the Studied Sample Toda Settlements and their Population

Sl.No.	Name of the Taluk	Name of the Toda mund	No.of House holds	Total Population Male	Female	Total
1.	Udhagamandalam	1. Manjakal mund	27	89	73	162
		2. School mund	16	47	41	88
		3. Tarnad mund	19	49	46	95
2.	Kotagiri	4. Bedukkal mund	12	34	31	65
		5. Nerin mund	9	28	24	52
		6. Pankod mund	11	31	29	60
3.	Coonoor	7. Nirkas mund	16	42	46	88
		8. Timod mund	9	31	26	57
		9. Kabirmund	7	16	18	34

The Toda

Todas are known by several names like Tudas, Tudavans, Toras and Todar. The Government of India identified the Toda people as one of the Primitive Tribal Groups of India. The first government census in 1871 revealed the total Toda population in Nilgiri region as 693 persons. In 1971 census their population was 930 persons, now according to 2001 census, the total population of the Toda was 1560 persons. According to Toda Youth Forum census in 2012, the Toda population is 1648 persons. As compared to the sex ratio for overall population (933 females per 1000 males), the sex ratio among the Toda is 908 females per thousand males. Anthony R Walker (1986: 58-59) adds that, "it is not difficult to discover why the Toda community has never been large and why, until recently, it singularly failed to conform to the general pattern of population increase in India. Traditionally, these people practised female infanticide. After a woman had borne one or two daughters, it seems, subsequent females were suffocated at birth by an older woman. The custom was officially prohibited by Sullivan, Collector of Coimbatore, towards the end of 1819, but the disproportionate sex ratio recorded in every census until 1951 suggests that the practice must have continued with some regularity until at least the turn of the century."

The Toda village or hamlet is called a mund, means a herd or a cattle-pen. It is usually a collection of seven to fifteen half barrel shaped huts with a smaller doorway. A typical Toda mund comprises five to ten dwelling huts, one dairy (temple) hut and one buffalo-pen (shelter) along with one calf shed. Toda people are white (fair) in colour, being tall, strong built and well-shaped. The striking feature of the women is the arrangement of their hair which is dressed in ringlets and flows waving down to the shoulders. The traditional garment of a Toda is known as put-kuli, is of thick white cotton cloth with red and blue strips which is embellished further embroidery by the Toda women, is thrown around the body by men and women, worn in a slightly different manner like ancient Greek toga. Jewellery is worn by both men and women. They are lacto-vegetarians.

The Toda community is divided into two endogamous divisions known as Tarthar and Teivali, which are further divided into fourteen exogamous clans. In the past, the Toda followed the fraternal polyandrous form of marriage, a plural marriage, warrants that the husbands who marry a woman are brothers in relationship among themselves. The life cycle rituals are markedly different from other tribes. During the dead body cremation, they sacrifice buffaloes.

The Toda were purely a pastoral people. The Toda women are experts in embroidery work. The Toda tribal council is not a permanent body but only a group of elderly Toda men selected by common consent for a particular dispute. Their concept of religion is associated with the dairy and sacred buffaloes. Toda divinities are called as 'gods of the mountains'. Anthony Walker (1986: 120) found that, "of all deities, the goddess 'Tokisya' is the most important to the Todas. To her is attributed the division of the sacred buffaloes and dairies between the subcastes and clans. Indeed she is believed to be the creator and supporter of the greater part of the social and ritual institutions of the Toda people". A few Todas have embraced to Christianity. Todas speak their own dialect.

Gender Inequality among the Toda

As mentioned earlier, the major social division of Toda society is into two endogamous groups called Tarthar and Teivali. After birth, Toda male or female belongs to one of the two endogamous groups and also a member of an exogamous patriclan and also an exogamous matrilineal clan.

The most striking feature common to two Toda endogamous divisions is the gender relationships to the sacred dairy temple complex, where, the Toda women are not allowed even to go near by the sacred dairy temple and they allowed only to see the rituals conducted by men only from long distance, at least 200 meters. A woman is incorporated by marriage into her husband's patriclan, while retaining some ties with the clan into which she was born. Since infant marriage is a ritual requirement in this society, this incorporation takes place at a very early age. Socialisation of female girls towards gender inequality took place after infant marriage. Traditionally, three tasks everyday are particularly associated with the Toda women: sweeping the hut, pounding the grain and then winnowing, besides rearing children, cooking and doing embroidery work on the cotton shawl. Women must also fetch water from the domestic water supply, cleanse their household utensils and wash clothes when necessary.

Among the Toda the care of buffaloes falls exclusively in the male domain. Culturally the separation of women from the tasks of the herdsman is absolute. The women are not allowed to milk certain of the buffaloes and not allowed even churning the milk to get butter. The ownership of buffaloes is only by men. The religion of the Todas is a highly ritualised buffalo-cult. They have sacred (temple) and ordinary (domestic) buffaloes. Toda ritual life revolves around the operations of their sacred dairies, which are worshipped by Toda men and dairy male priests by offering buffalo milk. Their women are totally kept away from there rituals. Their women are not, even by mistake, should cross or touch the boundary of the dairy temple. The gender inequality are found among the Todas in their traditional practices like polyandry, social paternity, kinship terms, and marital uncertainties like wife-capture, defloration rites etc.

Development of the Nilgiri Hills and the Changing Toda Society

The Nilgiri district has a little history. Its inhospitable climate and highest mountains never attracted the territory invaders, except the bold Toda people who were pastorals. The marginal invasion of the hills by Hindu kings and Muslim rulers led gradually towards British East India Company. In 1822, the British rulers made the upper plateau of the Nilgiri hills, where Todas live, as India's first hill-station. A military cantonment was established and the British soon built a network of roads linking the hills with the plains of Coimbatore, Mysore and Malabar, thus making the high plateau more accessible to lowlanders. A narrow-gauge mountain rack-railway running from plains Mettupalyam to high hill, Ooty was erected. From 1870 to 1937 the old Madras Presidency administration was migrated to the Nilgiris. The settled British administrators discovered the Nilgiri soils and climate for commercial crops. European fruits, vegetables, tea, eucalyptus etc., were introduced. Most of the local inhabitants took up wage-labour on the plantations and labourers from the lowland plains flocked to the hills. The post Independence Tribal Development Programmes by the Government, the centrally sponsored 'Hill Area Development Programme (HADP) and the quick income generative schemes for tribal communities have changed the scenario of tribal areas. Now let us know briefly about Toda community development during British period and after Indian Independence.

British Period

The British dominated Government and an English Missionary Society have promoted welfare programmes for Toda people. The British administration promoted the Toda in the following areas:

1. *Toda Lands*

Toda patta lands were preserved with legal conditions that Toda grazing lands were to be kept within the community for the sake of the Toda themselves and no Toda shall permit any other person except Toda to cultivate or assist in the cultivation of such lands. The concern of the Government was to prevent the alienation of Toda lands and to preserve the shola forest.

2. *Community Leadership*

British ruler appointed a Toda 'headman' to whom he gave the title of monegar, with a reason that lack of a leader among the tradition-conscious Toda society.

3. *Education*

The notion of educating Toda children was moved fairly early in the British period. A school was set up for Toda children near Pykara region.

4. *Social Welfare*

British Government had demanded the cessation of female infanticide and interfered with traditional Toda social institutions. It constituted a Toda welfare committee in the year 1926 with a Toda Amelioration Scheme with four main objectives:

1. To obtain financial assistance for the Toda so that they might be freed from the clutches of money lenders.
2. To provide for the healthcare of the community.
3. To encourage the Toda to abandon such 'detrimental' Social customs on were believed to be abetting their decline in numbers, namely polyandry, the defloration of prepubescent females and the tolerance of sexual promiscuity, and
4. To encourage the Toda to broaden their economic base from pastorals to one of herding and horticulture (Anthony Walker: 1986: 257).

5. *Health*

The Government ordered a special medical survey of the Todas and survey was conducted in 1927, and found that wide spread incidence of venereal disease. It was also found that nearly 20 per cent of the Toda women are sterile and community is suffering with the low state of bestiality.

6. *Agriculture*

Potato cultivation was encouraged on Toda patta lands.

7. *Christian Convection*

The Basel Mission Society had succeeded to convert a few Todas to Christianity.

Post Indian Independence Period

1. *Toda Land Issues*

Todas demanded the Government to assign permanent and unrestricted rights over all their patta lands. In 1956 the Toda registered, The Nilgiri Thothuvar Munnetram Sangam and med this noniety to demand their land rights. Till today their demand of legal rights on their lands is continuing.

2. *Agriculture*

Todas established themselves as potato farmers and vegetables cultivators, besides grower of fodder crops. They realised the economic advantage to be had from farming their land for themselves.

3. *Animal Husbandry*

Being a traditional breeders of buffaloes, Todas are well-adapted to rear more buffaloes and started selling milk to milk collection centres.

4. *Health, Education and Social Welfare*

Government introduced mobile medical unit in Toda habitat. A special 'Toda ward' was established in Government Hospital. The Servants of India Society started a school and government schools are started admitting Toda children. First time in the year 1985, government officials attention was received on Toda women's welfare and housing. All India Handicrafts Board had encourages Toda women to Traditional Toda embroidery work.

5. *Toda Women Self-help Groups*

Women self-help groups are formed among the Todas and began to work since 2006 with the help of loans provided only to women members. This helped Toda women empowerment in the Nilgiri hills.

Impact of Development on Gender Inequality

The development of the Nilgiri hills and tribal development programmes made dent in creating awareness among the Toda men and women towards modern life and the taste of mainstream life styles. Though men are concentrated on the buffalo economy and agriculture, but women totally accepted the value of education. A Toda woman in 1994 has become a first graduate among the Todas. The women, being expects in embroidery, nowadays they also started embroider other items for sale, such as table cloths, placemats, bedcovers and also cell phone cover, mini bags with their traditional designs of embroidery. Some women also visit neighbouring hamlets and others accompany their husbands to market. Some anthropologists even remarked that 'the tender fingers of women engaged in embroidery work and the strong hands of men that milked the buffaloes have now turned rough due to the handling of digging forks and agricultural implements for cultivation. As mentioned elsewhere (Rivers: 1906; Parthasarathy: 2008) the traditional outlook of the Toda men and rigid following of cultural inequality of gender issues, led the modern Toda women feel social pinch when they were excluded during the rituals of life-cycle ceremonies and the religious practices at sacred dairy temples. Even today most of the Toda women hate the age old practice of wife-capture and other cultural practices. The Toda women today still remember, often, their great grandmother's petition, during the year 1910, to the government to give them means to legalise their marriages and their petition concluded, you have protected our buffaloes, will you not protect us women? (Ling: 1910: 14-15). In the year 2011, a few women tried to give the petition on the same lines to the collector of Nilgiris, who was a woman of IAS cadre. The study concludes that primitive belief system, division of work, Indigenous ethnography, kinship terms, existence of sacred buffaloes, bow and arrow ceremony, social paternity etc., are the major causes for the existence of gender inequality in Toda modern society.

Acknowledgement

The author is thankful to Dr KM Metry, Professor and Head, Department of Tribal Studies, Kannada University, Hampi (Karnataka) for his encouragement to write this paper.

References

1. Ling, Catherine F., 1910, Dawn in Toda Land: A Narrative of Missionary effort on the Nilgiri hills, South India, London, Morgan and Scott.
2. Parthasarathy, Jakka, 2008, The Toda of the Nilgiri District, Tamil Nadu: A Study of a Pastoral Tribe and Development, TRC-HADP, Govt of India, Ooty.
3. Rivers, W.H.R, 1906, The Todas, Macmillan and Co. London.
4. Seymour-Smith Charlotte, 1986, Macmillan Dictionary of Anthropology, Macmillan Reference Books, London.
5. Walker, Anthony 1986, The Toda of South India: A new look, Hindustan Publishing Corporation, Delhi.

5

Tribal Development and Insurgency Movement in Tripura

Harsha S and *Antibum Ranglong*

Abstract

Tribal Development in Tripura could not be studied without insurgency movement. Since partition of India badly affected the tiny state, there was uprising from the tribal section. Insurgency movement started with the objective of liberation and sending back the immigrant. On one side, tribal were represented as having link with Christian missionaries. However, the government, both center and state, takes various measures to counter-balance the political situation. But, tribals in Tripura are still the most backward (socially, culturally and economically), as compared to other north-east tribals. The paper discusses the practical situation.

Key words: Development, Insurgency, Autonomy, Decentralisation.

Introduction

After the merger in the Indian Union on 15th October, 1949, the demographic setting of Tripura was totally changed. Tribal becomes a minority in their own land due to huge influx of Bengalis from neighbouring Bangladesh (former East Pakistan). 'Tripura is the only state in the north-east which has been transformed in the recent past from a predominantly tribal to a predominantly non-tribal state due to the massive influx of Hindu-Bengali migrants from Bangladesh.'[1] Tribals who once live a happy life with forest base resources were alienated in their home land. In fact, much has been discussed by various social scientists on the socio-economic and political history of Tripura.

Tribal development in Tripura has a long history like many other states in North-East India. In the name of tribal development and tribal liberation, different groups of insurgency outfits crop up. There were continuous demands for more power and responsibility to tribals. So, for looking after the interests of the tribal communities of Tripura, the Government of Tripura decided to set up an Autonomous District Council to introduce internal autonomy in tribal compact areas and thereby protecting the socio-economic and cultural interests of the Tribal population in Tripura. Accordingly, the Tripura Tribal Autonomous District Council Bill was unanimously passed by the Tripura Legislative Assembly on March 23, 1979.

Autonomous District Council and Tribal Development

As stated earlier, the Tripura Tribal Areas Autonomous District Council (TTAADC) was established as an independent district council, administering the tribal areas within the State after a series of democratic movements launched by the tribal people of Tripura. Following the 49th amendment of the Constitution of India, TTAADC was brought under the provisions of the Sixth Schedule of the Constitution with effect from 1st April, 1985.

Despite the Council's impressive principles to uplift the indigenous tribals in Tripura, it still remains a topic of criticism. 'Though under the Sixth Schedule, the TTAADC is also the custodian of and entrusted the task of preservation of the society and culture of indigenous people within its territorial jurisdiction, customary laws have not been codified. There is a large gap between the approved budget and the flow of funds from the state government to the Council, which undermines both planning and execution.'[2]

Unlike, District Council in other part of North-East India, TTAADC is unique, as its jurisdiction is not contiguous with revenue district boundaries. It straddles four revenue districts (recently, another four new districts were formed). It is a large body and covers an area of 7132.56 sq. km (67.98 per cent of the geographical area of the state), extending to all four Revenue Districts of the State.[3] Thus, there is constant criticism that no clear role is assigned to the TTAADC, which is a multi-district body, in the decentralised planning process. Moreover, 'the state government releases share of taxes and Plan Grant in installments. Most of the resources of the council are incurred for the payment of salary and allowances of the staff. Little fund is left for utilisation in development programmes.'[4]

As a consequent, demands for more power to the Council are raised from different angle. A delegation of the Congress and Indigenous Nationalist Party of Tripura (INPT) met Union Home Secretary Sambhu Singh on 31st January, 2014.[5] The delegation pressed to table a bill providing for allowing more power to TTAADC. To express their dissatisfaction, the INPT held a five hours long sit-in-demonstration at the Vivekananda Maidan, Agartala, on 15th February, 2014, to seek more power for TTAADC.[6] So, it is suggested that TTADC should be more empowered because development is not possible without more autonomy and financial empowerment.

Education and Tribal Development

Ignorance and illiteracy among the tribals are the basic problems to development in any part of our country. The case is same to Tripura. However, the '*Times of India*' (a reputed national dailies), published on 8th Sept., 2013, sketch out that, 'India's northeastern state of Tripura achieved the first position in literacy with 94.65 per cent, beating Kerala (93.91 per cent), Tripura Chief Minister Manik Sarkar, announced here on Sunday. Sarkar said at a function on the occasion of International Literacy Day that Tripura jumped to first position among the states of the country in literacy from the 12th position in the 2001 census and the fourth position in the 2011 census. Sarkar further said that after Tripura attained 87.75 per cent literacy in the 2011 census, a government survey was conducted by the eight district magistrates in August 2012, which found that only 131,634 people of the state's 3.7 million people, including those aged 50 and above were illiterate.'[7]

It is a matter of pride for the people of Tripura to be on top of the country in literacy. But practical experience shows that tribals in Tripura are still far behind in gaining access to proper education. As per the provision of the Sixth Schedule to the Constitution of India, primary schools were handed to TTAADC. Maximum of the primary schools administered by TTAADC are functioning with staff recruited through Sarva Siksha Abhiyan (SSA). They have little interest in the job with meagre salary. Classes end up within one hour or two.

Besides, the tribal in general preferred English Medium of instruction than Bengali. Thus, maximum of the rural tribals go to expensive private English Medium School for their education. Those parents who could not effort their children to send to such schools ultimately become the victims. It can be said that majority of the educated rural tribals in Tripura, are the product of Private English Medium Schools run by various Christian congregation.

So, it is suggested that the task should not end up in establishing maximum schools in tribal belt. Does it practically function is the point to be noted. If the rural tribals are more in favour of English Medium, the government should take necessary steps, as it has already started. The literacy may reach the climax, but if quality education does not reach the tribals, it will have little impact on tribal development.

Insurgency and Tribal Development

Tripura used to be one of the worst insurgency affected state in North-East India. Unprecedented influx of Bengali refugees created a sense of insecurity among the tribals. Tribals feel that development process among them retarded severely. Feeling of insecurity led to aggressive reaction from the tribals which ultimately create insurgency movement. First organised-armed tribal movement was known as *Sengkrak* (clenched fist) which manifested itself in mid-sixties. This movement was started as a reaction against settling down of non-tribal refugees in the Tribal Reserve Forest Areas. A Sengkrak activist launched a large number of violent attacks but was however, controlled in 1968.

Again, B.K. Hrangkhawl, a young tribal leader of Tripura Upajati Juba Samity (TUJS), a regional party for the tribal, formed an underground organisation styled as Tripura National Volunteers (TNV) on 10th November, 1978 with a design to conduct insurgent activities in collaboration with the Mizo National Front (MNF) of Mizoram. He was arrested in June, 1980 and was imprisoned. On his released from jail, in Dec. 1980, he announced dissolution of TNV. However, on 10th Nov. 1982, TNV was revived again with B.K. Hrangkhawl as its President. But on 12th December 1988 a Tripartite Accord was signed by the Government of India, Government of Tripura and the TNV. B.K. Hrangkhawl and his party surrendered before the government with arms and ammunitions.[8]

After the formal end of TNV insurgency movement, a series of groups came into existence. There were several split and reunion among them. Mention may be made, like Army of Tripura People Liberation Organisation (ATPLO) Tripura Resurrection Army (TRA), Tripura National Liberation Front (TNLF), Tripura Tribal Volunteer Force (TTVF), All Tripura Volunteer Force (ATVF), Tripura Tribal Democratic Force (TTDF), All Tripura Volunteer Association (ATVA), Tripura Tribal Action Committee Force (TTACF), Liberation of Tripura Tribal Force (LTTF), Tripura National Sengkrak Force (TNSF) etc. Most of these groups have ceased to operate and were non-active during their existence.[9]

The last phase of insurgency in Tripura started from1989. It is dominated mainly by two groups, namely, National Liberation Front of Tripura (NLFT) and All Tripura Tiger Force (ATTF). Both the groups are armed with sophisticated weapons, well trained and have links with other North-Eastern insurgent groups. The Government of India has declared both these groups as unlawful, under the Unlawful Activities (Prevention) Act, 1967, on the proposal of the State Government. Whereas, the main objective of the NLFT is to establish an Independent Tripura through an armed struggle, ATTF on the other hand, were expulsion of all foreigners who entered Tripura after 1956, restoration of land to tribal under Tripura Land Revenue and Land Reforms Act, 1960, and removal of names of migrants who entered Tripura after 1956 from electoral roll.

Now, the question is whether insurgency movement in reality helps the tribals in fulfilling their demands and objectives. Ideally speaking, in case of Tripura, establishing and Independent Tripura is a utopia. Besides, removal of all foreigners who entered Tripura after 1956 is simply a vision that cannot be achieved. But, to a certain extent tribal insurgency in Tripura have succeeded in making the government focus its attention on the development of tribal areas and in improving the conditions of the tribals.

Thus, 'in pursuance of looking after the communities of Tripura, the Parliament in 1960 passed, *'The Tripura Land Revenue and Land Reforms Act,'* under Articles 186 of the said Act. It was further amended in 1974 by laying more rigorous conditions in respect of transference of holdings. It laid down that if any tribal community desire to sell his land, the first offer shall have to be made to his co-sharer and failing that, the offer may be made to the adjoining tribal land-holders. In the absence of any such tribal, the offer shall have to be made to any landless Scheduled Tribes living in that area.' Besides, the establishment of TTAADC can also be regarded as a government mechanism to fulfill the aspiration of the tribals. It was in fact, created as a result of continuous demands from all sections of the Tripura tribals. Insurgency movement in this sense has been very beneficial to tribals and gave relief to some of their problems. However, it is not desirable to encourage this sort of movement for any types of demands, since political disorder can be resolve through negotiation and compromise.

Often, causes of existence of insurgency in North-East India are usually made associated with unemployment and lack of exposure among the tribal youth. But, causes can be different with places. Tripura is relatively different with rest of the north-east region. Exploitation and assimilation is so extreme, that the well aware tribal youth would not find alternative, at one point of time, than going for armed struggle. But, the government of Tripura under the rule of Communist Party of India Marxist CPI (M) has considerably counterbalanced the insurgency activities. Jobs, employment and assistance were given to the surrendered insurgent based on their skill and talent. Nevertheless, this might not be the end of insurgency in Tripura. There is a rumour about fresh reorganisation of tribal youth. The government should be aware of all the cause and effect relationship.

Linkages between Insurgency and Christianity

In this connection, it is unfortunate to mention that some writings were available on tribal insurgency in Tripura, which make direct link between religion and insurgency. They claim that the 'Christian Missionaries with the help of underground Mizo evangelical teachers of Baptist Missions exploited this growing unrest and converted some of the boys and girls with a move to politicise their culture and make them indifferent from the mainstream of national life.'[10] 'All the top leaders of insurgency initiated either by Army of Tripura People Liberation Organisation (ATPLO) or Tripura National Volunteers (TNV), in Tripura is committed to Christianity.'[11] They further claim that the 'insurgents ranks included a large number of young boys and girls who had been converted to Christianity, although, they were of Hindu parenthood, by underground Mizo rebels working in Baptist missions as evangelical teachers.'

To disagree with, the fact is that, tribal Hindu tradition is not alike with that of Bengali system, at least in Tripura. The Hindu tradition among the tribals in Tripura is so primitive that, once a person converts to Christianity, he/she got enlightenment (to have knowledge of the surrounding), and becomes aware of the entire practical scenario. Being assimilated, exploited and alienated, one cannot remain a spectator and overlook the ground political situation. So, many young Christian boys used to join the insurgency outfits. But, in case of Tripura, religion is not the criteria for recruitment and in fact, the outfits comprised both the tribal Hindu and Christians. Besides, the Christian Missionary never and ever politicised the situation but rather give sermons to discontinue insurgency movement and go suit with the law of the land.

Conclusion

Tribal development in Tripura has yet to take its shape. Majority of the tribals lived in rural areas. The benefits of development have remained concentrated in the western segment of the State, thus, leaving out huge areas in eastern parts largely inhabited by Scheduled Tribes far behind, in respect of various amenities.

The ignorance of tribals has given advantage to flourish trade and business by non-tribals who hold the reins of economic and political powers in the tribal areas and functioning of the government machinery. Directly or indirectly, they have huge control over the lands and resources of the tribals. Tribals being inseparably bonded to land and forest, face serious problems with non-tribals in regaining their control over their lands.

Non-tribals dominate the government machinery in the tribal areas. They often feel envious about the various welfare programmes designed for tribals, and try to get into an exploitative relationship with the local traders, contractors. This results in few benefits actually reaching the tribals. While tribals revere the natural resources as life sustaining forces, the non-tribal's outlook is of short term commercial exploitation. This disregard for tribal-nature symbiosis is causing not only a threat to tribal survival but is also leading to depletion of resources in the tribal areas.

The government has to recognise that the tribal people have a distinct socio-cultural life and the administration has to understand and respect these systems while designing and implementing development programmes. Programmes should be sympathetic to tribal needs, addressing the real issues and conflicts. It should be emphasised, that the machinery should work without social and political bias toward tribal communities. The state government should also follow a people-friendly and sympathetic development policy with programmes and projects planned in the tribal areas. It should first consider the social and economic progress of the local communities.

In conclusion, it is a fact that, unless decentralisation and empowerment to tribals are engendered, development activities could not be speedy. To address this problem, government of India has enacted Sixth Schedule (establishment of Autonomous District Council) for the tribals in north-east India. Autonomous Council is an important mechanism for empowering the tribals to administer themselves and to preserve their culture and tradition.

So, instead of charging the tribals as troublemaker, lawbreaker and with all sort of insurgency activities, they should be rather empowered with a democratic norm of decentralisation and self-rule.

References

1. Subramaniam, K.S. (2000). Tribal Insurgency and Rural Development in Tripura. *Economic and Political Weekly,* Vol. 35, No. (8/9), pp. 601-602.

2. Report of the Expert Committees, on *'Planning for the Sixth Schedule Areas,'* Sept. 2006, New Delhi: Ministry of Panchayat Raj, Govt. of India, p. 63.

3. An Official Website of TTAADC contains basic link of Council's related information, (http://www.ttaadc.nic.in).

4. Report of the Expert Committees, *ibid.* p. 63.

5. A Statement Published in the Website, http: // www.*tripurainfo.com* , dated: 1st February, 2014.

6. *Ibid.*, Dated: 15th February, 2014.

7. A Statement Published in the *'Times of India,'* Dated: 8th Sept. 2013.

8. Upadhya, R. (2005). Tripura Bleeds: In the Crossfire of Mainstream Political Parties and Virulent Ethnic Conflict. *South Asia Analysis Groups,* 15th Nov. No. 1613.

9. Information obtained from the insurgency section of the website http://www.tripurapolice.nic.in.

10. Tripura Land Revenue and Land Reforms Act, 1960. No. 43, Government of Tripura.

11. Upadhya, R. (2005). *Ibid.* 15th Nov. No. 1613.

12. Bhattacharjee, S.R. (1989). *Tribal Insurgency in Tripura*, New Delhi: Inter India Publication, p. 151.

13. *Ibid.*, p. 152.

6

Voice of Tribals through RTI Act, in Contemporary Democracy: A Case Study of Odisha

Akshaya Kumar Nayak

India is having a largest democracy with a model federal structure and a truly pluralistic society, which promises to provide social justice to the common men since independence. In this era of liberalisation, privatisation and globalisation, India has emphasised on participatory, decentralised and sustainable development for all. At the same time the greatest challenge before India is to provide social justice to the Scheduled Castes and Scheduled Tribes people by ameliorating their socio-economic and educational conditions. Not only the scheduled tribal, scheduled castes and denotified tribes constitute the weakest section of India's population, from the ecological, economic and educational angles. But also, they constitute the matrix of India's poverty. Though the tribals are the sons of the same soil, and the citizens of the same country, but they have been subjected to the worst type of socio-economic and political exploitation, and living away from the modern and civilised society. There are about two hundred million tribal people in the entire globe. According to 1981 census, the scheduled tribe population in the country was 5.16 crore, consisting of 7.76 per cent of total Indian population which means one tribesman for every 13 Indians. There are about 428 scheduled tribe communities in India speaking 106 languages in 19 states and six union territories. About 50 per cent of the tribal population of the country is concentrated in Madhya Pradesh Chhatisgarh, Jharkhand, Bihar and Odisha.

Odisha is regarded as the homeland of Tribals. It has a Tribal population of 81,45,081 (as per 2011 census) accounting 22 per cent of the total population of the state and 9.7 per cent of the total population of the country. Malkanagiri is having highest number of STs—57.4 per cent. Followed by Mayurbhanj—56.6 per cent, Rayagada—55.8 per cent and Nabarangpur—55 per cent. Out of 62 STs in Odisha, '*Khond*' is the most populous followed by *Gond, Santal, Kolha, Munda, Saora, Shabar, Bhottada, Bhumij, Bhuiya, Oraon, Paraja* and *Kissan*.

The tribal people of Odisha live in cloistered, exclusive, remote and inhospitable areas such as hills and forests. Their livelihood is based on primitive agriculture, a low value closed economy with a low level of technology that leads to their poverty. They have low level of literacy and health. But, they developed their own distinctive culture, language and religion, who have a marginal degree of contact with other cultures and people. Most of the STs of Odisha have adopted either Hinduism or Christianity.

But, the Tribals of Odisha are confronted with a number of problems like:

- Food insecurity,
- Low level literacy (poor education),
- Poor health-care facilities and prone to fatal diseases,
- Poor communication facilities,
- Language a stumbling barrier,
- Loss of habitation (Loss of land rights)
- Poor employment opportunities and low-level income
- Displacement and migration due to mines and development projects,
- Growing extremism,
- Lack of awareness,
- Huge distance from modern urban life,
- Poor agricultural and irrigation facility,
- Increasing Ethnic Tension in tribal areas,
- Forcible conversion of religion,
- Exploitation by the rich Non-Tribals,
- Land grabbing by the Non-Tribals,
- Replication of tribal traditional/Indigenous arts and craft design by non-tribal multi-nationals,
- Administrative apathy and carelessness of the administration,
- Corruption among the politician and officials,

Since independence both the Government of India and Government of Odisha have formulated many plans programmes, projects and set up many commissions to uplift the tribals from the bottom of our social fabric.

They are:

1. The Social Welfare Team of the Committee on Plan Projects 1959.
2. The Verrier Elwin Committee on Tribal Development.
3. The Committee on Tribal Economy in Forest Arear–1967.
4. The Scheduled Areas and Scheduled Tribal Commission (Dhebar Committee 1961).
5. The Special Working Group on Co-operative and for Backward Classes 1961.

6. The Task Force on Development of Tribal Areas 1972.
7. The Dube Committee 1972.
8. The Study Team on Co-operative Structure in Tribal Development Project Areas1976.
9. The Study Group on Relief of Indebtedness Land Alienation and Restoration in Development Agency Area 1973.
10. The Team of Marketing, Credit and Co-operation in Tribal Areas 1978.
11. The Working Group on Development of Scheduled Tribes during the 7th Five Year Plan (1985-1990).

On the other hand, the Government of Odisha has created 21 Integrated Tribal Development Agencies (ITDAS), covering 118 Tribal Development Blocks; 46 Modified Area Development Agencies (MADA) in 47 Blocks; Disbursed Tribal Development Agencies (DTDA). Apart from this, there is Departments of ST and SC to monitor the Tribal Development works. The Government of Odisha become the best state in India in distributing Patta both for the individual and community claims in settling land rights of the Tribals under the Forest Rights Act. It has decided to open 1000 hostels for ST boys and girls; to provide pre-matric scholarship; to provide two pairs of school uniforms from class-1 to VIII; Free bi-cycle to ST boys and girls; Free Coaching for ST students of Higher Secondary Level; to provide capacity building training; to set up project management unit (PMU).

But, there is huge gape between the theory and practice. Still the tribals are considered as Tribabls of the remote dark world. In most of the cases the clouds of development passes over them without a little drop of rain. Because the tribals are the illiterate and what they need is 'Awareness' through proper education.

At this juncture the best weapon to protect the Tribal Rights is——'The Right to Information Act (RTI Act) of 2005', which is a milestone in the history of India. By using this Act the poor, and the vulnerable Tribals will understand their rights, and every unit of National and state level developmental plans and projects. They can ask the officials from the Panchayat to the state and the National Government, about the developmental programmes and check exploitation from top to bottom. The voice of Tribals can be raised in Indian democracy by using RTI Act. The best example is the RTI clinics set up in the Kalahandi district of Odisha, which have enabled the poor and the marginalised communities to demand and protect their entitlements. It was possible under the joint venture of UNDP and the ministry of Law and Justice, Government of India.

So, the RTI Act can protect the tribals from the nasty politicians, corrupt officials and the fraud NGOs. It can bring them to the mainstream of modern civilisation with participatory and contemporary democracy.

7

Determinants of Students Dropout in Indian Higher Education

Bharat Chandra Rout

Background

Students in higher education undergo various processes of institutional/ societal and personal interactions when they progress through education. Student behaviour that is related to their retention therefore requires theoretical constructs that encapsulate the multiplicity of institutional, personal/familial and interactional factors emerging from the environment of student participation in higher education. Many national and international studies on student retention are based on the empirical enquiry of problems of student drop-out and attrition—very often looking various possible factors that impact student retention. On the basis of findings they come out with their own theoretical constructs. For instance, Tinto's theory of individual departure [Tinto, 1975, 1987, 1993] in which Tinto has developed a longitudinal interactionist model of student departure which has been widely accepted by the research community on the basis from which to work. Similarly, Rong C. [2008] studies the impact of financial aid on students' decision to dropout from higher education and on the basis of which the author provides an analytical and theoretical framework to study student retention. Probably one of the benchmark work on student departure is done by Durkheim [1951] in his theory of suicide and student departure, in which he argues, the individual persistence in, and drop out from institution of higher education can be viewed as arising out of a longitudinal process of interactions between an individual and with the given attributes, skills, prior educational experiences, dispositions and academic and social systems of the institution [Durkheim, 1951, cited in Tinto, 1987].

Thomas [2002] makes a clear distinction among various conditions that enable students to continue in higher education and absence of which presumably hurdle students to continue and complete a higher education degree. They are academic preparedness [i.e., the extent to which students feel they are ready to study for higher education], academic experiences [i.e. curricula, teaching-learning issues, relationships with staffs and students etc.], institutional expectation and commitment [i.e., the expectation that student had about higher education and the extent to which they thought the institution they were attending would realise their goals], academic and social match [i.e., the extent to which students felt they fitted in at their institution and this included both academic, social and cultural inclusiveness], finance and employment [i.e., this is the way financial issues influence student decision to continue or leave higher education], family support and commitment, university support services etc.

Existing Literature on Student Dropout

Most of the research studies conducted in India on student retention/ dropout have focussed on the contribution/influence of socio-economic factors and institutional/academic factors on student persistent in higher education. Some notable studies are reviewed below.

Socio-economic Characteristics

Several studies have reported a low rate of completion and a high rate of failure in examinations and low standards of achievement have marred the efficiency of the Indian education system. Further studies found that just about 50 per cent out of the total enrolled in a given year get their degree [Singh, 1981; Rawat 1970; UNESCO, 1965]. Singh and Sharma [1981] observed that for every ten students joining in the colleges, not more than five are likely to get their degree. They emphasised that the stagnation and wastage is so prevalent that everyone comes to accept it as a fact of life. In a similar account Rawat [1970] found that any hundred college freshmen entering the first year of college, the likelihood of completing the degree is 41 per cent. Phadke [1980] and Ahuja [1980] study the drop out behaviour of ST college students in rural regional/local colleges. They found the college wastage is strongly associated with tribal culture and life style, the way they have been told about education and more significantly the factors that barrier their mainstreaming.

Kamat and Deshmukh (1963), studied the students of Fergusson College of Poona University and found that more female than male students' dropout and that the number of married students in both the sexes is very small. Studying the socio-economic background of the regular students he found that more than 50 per cent of male students and more than 70 per cent of women students belong to high socio-economic status. In relation to the previous level of education and merit, 66 per cent drop out was among the students who scored less than 50 per cent marks, 42 per cent drop out was among the students who scored between 50 and 55 per cent and 28 per cent dropout among those who scored more than 55 per cent in S.S.C. This study also shows that dropout increases with the advance in age in entry, the type of school from which the student comes. Bean (1979) in his study found that male and female students leave HE for different reasons. One of the important reasons for droppingout was dissatisfaction with the course. Educational quality, as well as usefulness of education for getting a job, was also related to be significant variables. He also found that the opportunity available for transferring to another course college was another important reason.

The findings from the studies by Sewell and Shah [1967], Sharma [1972], Khan and Singh [1978], Reddy [1971], Jackson [1978] and Astin [1964] more or less in a similar account suggest that socio-economic background has tremendous influence on intelligence level, planning for and completion of Higher Education. Reddy (1971) found that children whose fathers were engaged in manual work or had blue collar job were less adjusted than children whose parents were in good business or professions like teaching, medicine and engineering.

Institutional [Academic] and Attitudinal Aspect

First, there are several studies who have revealed that dropout is a phenomenon of and resulting from student institution interactions. They argued that students who dropout from HE are students who have a negative attitude towards their institution, poor attendance and low achievement and faces non-congenial atmosphere in institution [Turkel and Abramson, 1986, Chitnis, 1972]. For instance, Chitnis (1981) studied the dropouts and situation of the SC students in Bombay and found that the negative attitude of the other students towards them and non-conjugal atmosphere at college were the main reasons for them to dropout of HE. Malik (1984) studied the university students attitude towards HE and found that age, sex, rural urban area, parental level of education play important role in influencing the attitude. She found that there is a positive correlation between age and attitude. The first generation learner had a more positive attitude towards HE then the second generation learner. Yet, other researches reveal that lack of personality adjustment, lack of motivation, emotional problem, inconsistencies etc., are reasons for student dropout from HE [Malik 1984; Grace 1957; Edelbrock 1975; Maxwell 1960; Astin 1964; Bayer 1968; McCloy 1980]. Kumar (1980) demonstrated that the students having lower academic performance appear to have more personal problems.

Moreover, social and academic integration of student, prior academic preparedness, minimising social distance, collaborative and inclusive teaching-learning strategies etc., have significant direct effects on classroom participation, meaningful interaction and eventually on the examination grade of students [Smith and Naylor 2001; Donovan 1984; Thomas 2002]. Mathews (1957) and others found that the greatest cause of academic failure was lack of interest including meaninglessness of course of studies. Moreover, Forster [1959], Schonell [1962, 1965] found that students' performance was influenced by their adaptability, maturity, self-discipline, intrinsic motivation, pupil-teacher relationship, motivation by parents, and personal qualities of persistence and toughness. Blanchfield (1971), Bragg (1956) and Yoshino (1964) studied the educational background of dropout and non-dropouts and found that the dropout had relatively low of educational background as compared to the non-dropouts. Maxwell (1960), Astin (1964), Bayer (1968) and Edelbrock (1975) studied the personality characteristics of the dropouts and they were of the view that dropouts were low adjusted, had more personal and emotional problems than the non-dropouts.

Research studies on student dropout that are briefly reviewed above clearly brought out two significant dimensions. First, a good number of studies and their findings agreed upon the fact that socio-economic characteristics of students significantly influence their prospects of continuing/droppingout from higher education. Student age, gender, nativity, socio-religious background, parental education and occupation and family income, etc., have tremendous influence on students' decision to continue/withdraw from studies. Second, several other research studies explored various academic/institutional and attitudinal factors which are strongly associated with student decision to complete higher education.

Our results on student dropout in higher education in India are based on data from one important sources. First, by using 64th round of NSS data [2007-08], we provide an estimate of the factors that are significantly affecting student continuation in higher education at all India level. These data give results for five to 29 years who had enrolled sometime but currently not attending [completed] higher education, and is done for both rural and urban samples separately.

The paper is divided into three sections. Section A specifies the logistic regression models by defining the data sources, variables and their definitions. Section B deals with the estimates and results of the determinants of students who could not complete higher education [estimates from 64th round of NSSO]. The final section of the paper discusses the findings and concludes the paper.

SECTION—A

Specification of the Models: Data, Variable and their Definitions

Studies on student dropout have used various methods of analysis. For example, many studies have done discriminate analysis (Chapman and Hutcheson 1982; Stork and Berger 1978; Terenzini and Pascarella 1977), multiple regression (Aitken 1982; Bean 1980; Kohen Nestel and Karmas 1978; Lunneborg and Lunneborg 1973; Munro 1981; Peng and Fetters 1978; Terenzini and Pascarella, 1978), probit analysis (Rumberger 1983), chi-square analysis (Leob and Duff 1974) and simple tabulations (Naylor and Sanford 1982). However, when the dependent variable is qualitative and dichotomous, for instance in a 'yes' or 'no' format logistic regression is an ideal choice of analysis.

One of the significant objectives of this research is to identify the factors responsible for student dropout in higher education. In this paper, logistic regression models for qualitative dependent variables are run to know the determinants of students' dropout from higher education. Logit analysis can be used to determine which independent variables and interactions are required to describe student dropout behaviour. Logit analysis also enables one to develop predicted probabilities of dropping out for each combination of the independent variables (Ott Mary *et al.* 1984). Qualitative response regression model refers to models in which the response or regress and variable is not quantitative or an interval scale. A logistic model provides the probability or likelihood of happenings (changes) in dependent variable by the influence of independent/explanatory variables. The model gives odds ratio which is explained as the ratio of the probability of success to the probably of failure. In addition to the odds ratio, I shall present the corresponding 'Marginal Effects' in order to assess the magnitude of impact of explanatory variable.

For example,

If, Pi = the probability of a student securing sixty per cent marks in 12th, (probability of success), and 1 – Pi = the probability of not securing sixty per cent in 12th (probability of failure).

Thus, odds ratio in the logit model = (Pi/1–Pi)

A ratio of the probability in favour of securing 60 per cent in grade 12 to the ratio of not securing 60 per cent in grade 12.

Model 1: Determinants of Students who could not Complete Higher Education [NSS 64th Round]

Data Sources, Variables and their Definitions

The data source for logistic model 1 is National Sample Survey's 64th Round 'Participation and Expenditure in Education' survey (July 2007 to June 2008). The survey covers the whole of Indian Union except Ladakh, Kargil, interior villages of Nagaland and villages in Andaman and Nicobar Islands which remain inaccessible throughout the year. By adopting a stratified multi-stage sampling technique the survey covers 12688 First Stage Units (FSUs) for central sample and 13624 FSUs for state sample. FSUs are census villages/wards in the rural sector and blocks in the urban sector as per the 2001 census.

For the purpose of present analysis sample students were identified who have had enrolled sometimes in a degree in higher education but did not complete (some have completed) their degree. For this purpose enrollment in grade 13 and above years of education (enrolment in graduate, post-graduate and above degree) are considered as by that year of education it is ideally considered to be higher education.

Dependent Variable: Whether Completed Higher Education [Yes= 0, No= 1]

Independent Variables: Sex, types of institution last attended, marital status, religious background, social background, hectares of land possessed by household, types of education, reasons for droppingout/discontinuing studies, monthly per capita household consumption expenditure (MPCE), Household type etc. Appendix 1 reports detailed percentage tables of independent variables in relation to the dependent variable.

Table 7.1: Definition of Key Variables used in the Model

Variables	*Definitions*
Sex	Dummy variable that takes the value of one in case of male and zero for female
Types of Institution last attended	A dummy variable that takes the value of one if the students' last attended institution is government and zero
Marital Status: Never married, currently married and widowed/separated/divorced	Each is a dummy variable that takes the value of one for each marital status and zero otherwise.
Religion: Hinduism, Islam and non-Hindu/Islam-'Others'	Each is a dummy variable that takes the value of one for each category of religion and zero otherwise.
Social Category: SC, ST, OBC and non-SC/ST/OBC Others	Each is a dummy variable that takes the value of one for each social category and zero otherwise.
Land possessed by Household (in hectares): < 0.005, 0.005 to 0.01, 0.02 to 0.40, 0.41 to 1.00, 1.01 to 8.00	Each is a dummy variable that takes the value of one for each interval of land possessed and zero otherwise.
Types of Education: General, Professional/technical and Vocational	Each is a dummy variable that takes the value of one for each types of education and zero otherwise.
Reasons for droppingout/discontinuing.	Each reason is a dummy variable that takes the value of one for that particular reason and zero all else
MPCE Quartile: Below 20 per cent, 20-40 per cent, 40-60 per cent, 60-80 per cent, 80-100 per cent	Each of these expenditure quartiles are dummy variables that takes the value of one for each quartile and zero all else
Household Type: *Rural*- self-employed in non-agri., agri. Labour, other labour, self-employed in agri. *Urban*- Self-employed, causal labour, other labour	Each of these household type is dummy variable that takes the value of one if the household belong to that particular type and zero all else.

SECTION-B

Empirical Results

Tables 7.3 and 7.4 present empirical results of two logistic regression models on the basis of coefficients and corresponding marginal effects for both rural and urban India separately. The type of institution last attended (i.e., govt./private) is found to be only significant for the urban sample. The results indicate that a student whose last attended institution is government is more likely to complete higher education *vis-a-vis* a student whose last institution is private in urban India. An additional student whose last attended institution is government has higher probability of completing higher education by 1.7 per cent compared to a student whose last attended institution is private in urban India. Even though many private higher educational institutions in urban places are mushrooming day by day, the role of government in providing mass higher education has well been visualised to provide quality and subsidised education for poor and ensure degree completion. For instance, nearly 71 per cent students whose last attended institution is government are from families with less than Rs 3000 per capita household consumption expenditure in rural areas and the same figure for urban India is 68.5 per cent with per capita household consumption expenditure less than Rs 6000. In addition to the above reasons, high fee structure, strict curriculum and examination patterns, lack of teacher student and peer interactions etc. in private institutions are other reasons responsible for lower completion rate of higher education.

The marital status of the student is significant for the urban sample but insignificant for the rural sample. The probability of not completing higher education for currently married and widowed/divorced is 3.8 per cent and 26.7 per cent respectively higher compared to a student who is not married in urban India. In other words, compared to a student who is not married, the probability of completing a higher education degree is reduced by 3.8 per cent points and 26.7 per cent points respectively, if we add one student from each marital category of 'currently married' and widowed/divorced from urban India into the sample. The findings here are closely associated with the assumptions of existing theories on sociology and gender studies on marriage who in a nutshell claim that due to various commitments connected with marriage (the extent of commitments in case of married, frustration due to loneliness in case of widowed/ separated etc. differ for both newly married and widowed/divorced and therefore the differing coefficients), it is less likely that a married person/couple and divorced/separated would complete higher education compared to an unmarried student enrolled in a degree in higher education.

The religious background of students found significantly influencing the probability of not completing higher education and is only significant for rural India in our analysis. A student from Islamic background has higher probability of not completing higher education compare to a student from Hindu background in rural India. In the case of other religions, the probability of completing a higher education degree is higher compared to a student either from Hinduism or Islam background. While an additional student from Islamic background will add the risk of not completing higher education by 7.2 per cent; an addition of a student from non-Hindu/Islam others religious background will raise the probability of completing higher education by 2.2 per cent and both are in comparison to students from Hinduism background. This finding is therefore validated by the findings of the Sachar committee report [Government of India;

2006] which provides date the various deprivations and under-development of Indian Muslims in social, economic and educational indicators.

The social background of students does influence the probability of completing a higher education degree and the influence is dissimilar in rural and urban India. A scheduled tribe student has advanced the probability of completing higher education compared to a non-SC/ST/OBC others category student in rural India. On the other hand, both SC and OBC students have a lower probability of completing higher education compared to non-SC/ST/OBC others students in rural India. While an additional student from ST group in higher education will increase his/her probability of completion by 1.9 per cent, an addition of each of an SC and OBC student will reduce the probability of completing higher education by 2.3 per cent and 5.3 per cent respectively around three per cent higher probability of not completing for OBC compared to SC students in rural India. The results for ST need to be used cautiously since there are few cases from ST category in our sample of rural India. Moreover, both SC and ST coefficients are not significant for rural sample. In Urban India, on the other hand, the probability of completing higher education is lower among SCs, STs and OBCs compared to non-SC/ST/OBCs other category students and the results are statistically significant for all social groups. In other words, an addition of a ST student will increase the probability of non-completion by 9.2 per cent; nearly three per cent and seven per cent more compare to the probability of non-completion for SC and OBC respectively in urban India. While the probability of not completing higher education is higher for OBCs in rural India, in urban India more number of ST students is less likely to complete higher education compared to all other social groups.

The variable land possessed [in hectares] by the household is significant for both rural and urban samples. In rural India, a student from the household possessing less than 0.005 hectare of land is more likely to discontinue higher education compared to a student coming from the household possessing more than one hectare of land. An additional student in higher education from a household possessing less than 0.005 hectare of land will add the risk of non-completion by 2.6 per cent compared to a student from the household possessing more than one hectare of land keeping all other things constant. In urban India a student from household possessing less quantity of land is more likely to incomplete higher education.

Types of education pursued are found to statistically and significantly influence the probability of completion in higher education in both rural and urban samples. A student pursuing a professional degree course is more likely to complete higher education (marginal effect is by one per cent) compared to a student pursuing a degree in general stream in rural India. On the other hand, the probability of completing higher education for students pursuing vocational higher education is less compared to students pursuing general higher education. The marginal effect in this case indicates that an additional student pursuing vocational higher education will add to the risk of non-completion by 17.8 per cent compared to the addition of a general stream student into the system. Unlike in rural India, the probability of completing higher education for both professional and vocational stream students is high compared to general stream students. The probability of completing a professional degree is 4.9 per cent and completing a vocational degree is 1.3 per cent higher compare to completing a general higher education degree in urban India. Keeping all other things constant, while a professional stream student is more likely to complete his/her degree across rural and urban India, the probability of not completing a vocational degree is only true in urban India.

With regard to the various reasons responsible for students not completing higher education, we found all most all of the reasons are positive and significant in the model in both rural and urban India. Keeping all other things constant, reasons like 'not able to cope with or failure in studies', 'institution is far off', 'student is not interested in studies' and 'mismatch in the timings of educational institution' are significantly contributing to non-completion of higher education in rural areas. An additional student in higher education who is not able to cope with educational environment and frequent failure in studies increases the probability of not completing the degree by 85 per cent compared to financial related reasons that lead to withdrawing from studies. Moreover, the marginal effect of each of the reasons for non-completion indicates that the probability of not completing a degree for students when the institution is far off is 62.2 per cent *vis-a-vis* a student not completing a degree because of financial problems. Further, adding a student who is not interested in studies will increase the probability of dropping out by 55 per cent compared to adding a student who has financial problems to continue with higher education. Apart from the significant effect of the above factors, for a student who helps the household enterprises the probability of not completing higher education is increased by 31.2 per cent. A student whose parent is not interested in his/her education contributes to his/her dropout by 19.2 per cent. Moreover, a student who participates in other economic activity contributes to non-completion by 14.3 per cent and a student who works for regular wage/salary contribute to non-completion by 7.8 per cent all in comparison to a student who has dropped out because of financial difficulties. In summary, the magnitude of impact on a student who finds himself/herself unable to cope with the academic environment and/or experiences in failure of studies is highly positive and significant with regard to incompletion of the degree, followed by a student who finds his/her college/university in a far off place. Following this, a student who encounters timing problems is highly and more likely to discontinue followed by the student who finds little or no interest to study in higher education.

For urban India, the reasons responsible for student non-completion in higher education are categorically merged into four key variables for ease of analysis[1], i.e., domestic/familial/parental related reasons, financial constraints, and institution/academic related reasons and reasons related to the participation in economic activity.[2] Compared to the reasons associated with the family of the student, the financial, institutional/academic related reasons and reasons associated with participation in economic activity are found to positively and significantly influence student non-completion in higher education. A student who has financial constraints is less likely to complete their programme of study and the magnitude of effect is around 14.8 per cent compared to 79.8 per cent and 5.9 per cent for institutional/academic reasons and reasons associated with student participation in economic activity. In other words, while financial, institutional/academic and participation in economic activity related reasons influence students not to complete_higher education, the magnitude of effect of the institutional/academic related problems highly and significantly (compare to all other problems) contribute to students' withdrawal from higher education. Thus, in a way a large part of student droppingout behaviour is explained by the problems connected with or derived from the educational institutions themselves. It is towards understanding educational institutions in a more in-depth manner, that we have undertaken analysis of primary data collected at university level.

A student from lower rung of monthly per capita household consumption expenditure [MPCE] of his/her family is more likely to discontinue higher education compared to a student with higher MPCE of family. For instance, keeping other things constant a student whose family's MPCE is below Rs 4000 and Rs 6000 in both rural and urban areas respectively, his/her probability of not completing a higher education degree increases by six per cent for a student in rural area and five per cent in urban area compared to a student from higher MPCE quartile in both locations. A linear relationship is in that it is revealed that the probability of not completing higher education is significantly more with a student who is at lower rung of their family's MPCE and *vice-versa*.

The probability of not completing higher education for a student belonging to lower occupational status of the household, i.e., 'agricultural labour' and 'other labour' is high compared to a student belonging to a household engaged in self-employed or non-agriculture activity in rural India. The magnitude of effect of not completing HE is higher for the student belonging to agricultural labour household 9.1 per cent compared to a student belonging to a household engaged in other labour 7.7 per cent. In urban India, a student belonging to both causal labour and self-employed household has higher probability of not completing higher education vis-a-vis a student from regular wage and salaried household. The magnitude of effect of household occupation on students not completing higher education is higher in case of a student from causal labour household which is 9.6 per cent and then self-employed households by one per cent both in compare to regular wage/salaried households in urban India.

Table 7.3: Determinants of Students of Age 5-29 Years who were Ever Enrolled but Currently are not Attending (Completed) Higher Education (Rural India)

Dependent variable	*Whether Completed! (Yes/No)*		
Variables	*Odds Ratio*	*Standard Error*	*M.E. (dy/dx)**
Column (1)	*Column (2)*	*Column (3)*	*Column (4)*
Sex	0.939	0.137	-.008
Type of Institution last attended	0.963	0.133	-.004
Never Married	Reference Category		
Currently married	1.083	0.143	.010
Widowed/Separated/Divorced	3.643	4.522	.244
Hinduism	Reference category		
Islam	1.612**	0.398	.072
All Other (Religion)	0.836	0.215	-.022
ST	0.853	0.228	-.019
SC	1.184	0.254	.023
OBC	1.479***	0.216	.053
All Others	Reference category		
Land < 0.005	1.213	0.317	.026
Land 0.005 to 0.01	0.442***	0.124	-.085
Land 0.02 to 0.40	0.858	0.167	-.019
Land 0.41 to 1.00	0.853	0.156	-.020
Land 1.01 to 8.00	Reference category		
Types of Education-General	Reference Category		
Types of Education-Professional	0.928	0.287	-.009
Types of Education-Vocational	2.726*	1.649	.178
Parents not interested in studies	2.923***	1.029	.192
College/University is far off	19.540***	9.679	.626
To work for wage/salary	1.676**	0.390	.078
For participating in other economic activity	2.375***	0.517	.143
Look after younger siblings	2.741	1.895	.179
To attend other domestic chores	3.557***	0.977	.235
Financial Constraints	Reference category		
Timings of education institution not suitable	13.838*	19.861	.562
For helping in household enterprises	4.906***	1.302	.312
Student not interested in studies	13.524***	3.318	.550
Unable to cope up or failure in studies	232.17***	100.16	.850
Expenditure Quartile (Below 20 per cent)	1.636**	0.359	.073

(Contd.)

(Contd. Table 7.3)

Dependent Variable	*Whether Completed! (Yes/No)*		
Variables	*Odds Ratio*	*Standard Error*	*M.E. (dy/dx)**
Column (1)	*Column (2)*	*Column (3)*	*Column (4)*
Expenditure Quartile (20 per cent-40 per cent)	1.857***	0.392	.094
Expenditure Quartile (40 per cent – 60 per cent)	1.419*	0.267	.049
Expenditure Quartile (60 per cent – 80 per cent)	0.936	0.168	-.008
Expenditure Quartile (80 per cent – 100 per cent)	Reference Category		
HHT- Self-employed in non-agriculture	Reference Category		
HHT- Agricultural Labour	1.799**	0.463	.091
HHT- Other Labour	1.658*	0.479	.077
HHT- Self-employed in Agriculture	0.966	0.164	-.004
CONSTANT	-2.53***	.259	
Log Likelihood	855.13		
Pseudo R2	0.277		
No. of Observations	2401		
Predicted probability of whether completed			.155

Note: ****p*<.01 (2-tailed), ***p*<.05 (2-tailed), **p*<.10 (2-tailed).*

Table 7.4: Determinants of Students of Age 5-29 Years who were Ever Enrolled but Currently are not Attending [Completed] Higher Education [Urban India]

Dependent variable	*Whether Completed! (Yes/No)*		
Variables	*Odds Ratio*	*Standard Error*	*Marginal Effect (dy/dx)*
Sex	1.099	0.129	.006
Type of Institution last attended	0.794**	0.089	-.017
Currently Married	1.678***	0.187	.038
Widowed/Separated	6.260***	4.468	.267
Islam	1.283	0.230	.019
All Others (Religion)	0.864	0.168	-.010
ST	2.505***	0.558	.092
SC	1.995***	0.362	.063
OBC	1.320**	0.164	.021
Land 0.005 to 0.01	1.259*	0.166	.017
Land 0.02 to 0.40	1.352**	0.193	.023

(Contd.)

(Contd. Table 7.4)

Dependent variable	*Whether Completed! (Yes/No)*		
Variables	*Odds Ratio*	*Standard Error*	*Marginal Effect (dy/dx)*
Land 0.41 to 1.00	0.730	0.257	-.019
Land 1.01 to 8.00	1.451	0.349	.030
Types of Education- Professional	0.049***	0.094	-.049
Types of Education- Vocational	0.818	0.620	-.013
Financial constraints	3.627***	0.610	.148
Institutional/academic reasons	87.264***	23.853	.798
Participation in Economic Activity	1.988***	0.265	.059
Expenditure Quartile (Below 20 per cent)	1.043	0.279	.003
Expenditure Quartile (20 per cent-40 per cent)	1.906***	0.482	.060
Expenditure Quartile (40 per cent – 60 per cent)	1.999	0.210	.013
Expenditure Quartile (60 per cent – 80 per cent)	1.109	0.145	.007
Self-employed	1.158	0.129	.010
Casual Labour	2.700***	0.693	.106
CONSTANT	-3.303***	0.175	
Log Likelihood	-1341.40		
Pseudo R2	0.181		
No. of Observations	4904		
Predicted probability of whether completed			.078

*Note: ***p<.01 (2-tailed), **p<.05 (2-tailed), *p<.10 (2-tailed).*

SECTION-C

Findings, Discussion and Conclusion

Socio-economic Characteristics

Despite years of policies and programmes for better access, participation and completion of weaker sections in higher education, the probability of completing a higher education degree remains dim for SCs, STs and OBCs compared to non-SC/ST/OBC others both in rural and urban India. The magnitude of deprivation is higher for SCs compared to STs and OBCs in both rural and urban regions of India. Students from these three categories do not face similar problems in higher education. While caste-related factors are significant for SCs, geographical-cultural isolation/distance is the outcome of STs under-development. On the other hand, many believe OBCs as a group is a political outcome at some period of Indian political history that substantially shifted policy attention on weaker sections to a more well-off section. Moreover, these groups are not homogeneous and graded diversities exist in their objective situations. These differences and diversities are importance explanations of why SCs, STs and OBCs differently perform in different contexts with regard to their participation in higher education.

The religious identity of a student holds significant with regard to the probability of continuing and completing a higher education degree in rural areas. Students belonging to the Muslim minority community are more likely to discontinue their higher education compared to Hindu community students. On the other hand, the probability of completing a higher education degree is higher for non-Hindu/Muslim other religious minority communities. Alarmingly the low completion rate of Muslim minority students in rural areas suggests that the pattern and expectations and belief system of Muslims have not substantially changed as is seen in the case of the urban Muslim community. Young generations from this minority community prefer to work and earn in unorganised sectors; [e.g., mostly in small-scale industries, factories, garages etc.] rather than the continuing or complete higher education. Though the majority of the Muslims stay in urban and semi-urban areas, the problems of participation in higher education in rural areas do need critical policy attention that matches with their religious and cultural expectations.

Across the two parameters, i.e., family consumption expenditure [64th round NSS] and family income [student survey in two universities], students belonging to the lower rung of both expenditure as well as income are more likely to dropout from higher education compared to students belonging to higher rung of income and expenditure of their household. This conveys the fact that poor among the marginalised as well as non-marginalised sections do face problems in sending their son/daughter to higher education. Again, if they are able to send than they are less likely to persist in the system without supportive financial mechanisms. Expenditure is largely a function of household income and less the expenditure more the likelihood that a poor student from that household will face problems of retention and persistence. Lower expenditure or income of the household suggests lower economic/financial potentials which have significant bearings on whether or not a student from that household would persist in the system of higher education.

Parental Education and Occupation

Both in rural as well as urban India the probability of completing a higher education degree lean towards students whose parents are highly/salaried and are employed in non-agriculture. For instance, findings from 64th round NSS reveal that the likelihood of not completing a degree is higher for students belonging to agricultural household and the same for urban students is casual labour and/or self-employed households. This suggest the fact that students from lower educational [i.e., low educational attainment level] and occupational [i.e., agricultural household, casual labour etc.] status of their parents have to go through several difficulties inside the institution as well as in their own families. It also indicates the conditions framing the student's pre-university studies: the education, occupation and income of parents are strong determinants of their children's educational opportunities. For example, patterns and traditions of family structure mean that in rural villages, and even urban areas, it is likely that the students were managing their studies and helping their parents in agricultural production and this would have necessarily impacted upon their opportunities to study effectively. Importantly, familial circumstances also frame the students' understanding of what it is reasonable to value and to expect (Bourdieu and Passeron, 1977; Bourdieu, 1997).

Marital Status

Compare to a student who is not married, probability of completing a higher education degree is reduced by 3.8 per cent points and 26.7 per cent points respectively, if we add one student from each marital category of 'currently married' and 'widowed/divorced' from urban India into the sample. The findings here is closely associated with the assumptions of existing theories on sociology and gender studies on marriage who claim that due to various commitments connected with marriage [the extent of commitments differ for both newly married and widowed/divorced], it is less likely that a married person/couple and divorced/separated would complete higher education compare to an unmarried student.

Dropping out behaviour of students are found to be statistically and significantly associated with the types of education being pursued by the students. The probability of completing a higher education degree is much higher for students pursuing professional education degree compare to general education degree both in rural and urban India. On the other hand, completing a vocational degree finds it difficult in rural India compare to urban India. The emerging patterns of course type and droppingout behaviour of students may imply that a professional degree course is well-planned by the student and his/her family with practical considerations on private expenditures and the likelihood of market efficiency of the course in getting a job after completion. On the other hand, both a general education and vocational education degree is generally considered as courses chosen as last option or more practically having very little or no marketability. Even when one considers marketability of vocational courses, [for instance, vocational training is intended to provide hands-on experiences for short term employment in workplaces and industries] the short-term, fragile nature of such jobs may be one reason that explains why students pursuing these courses are less likely to complete their degree.

Reasons for Droppingout

Against the much expected and generally perceived reasons that hinder students to complete higher education, factors connected with the institution are potentially responsible for student dropout. Researches previously had revealed that lack of income of the family or not providing financial assistance to the student is one of the substantial reasons why student leave their education half-way. However, the results now indicate a divergent trend in that the educational institution itself responsible for predominant share of dropout decision made by the students. Institutions with their processes of teaching, learning, assessment, peer and teacher interactions etc create conditions that hinder marginalised students to cope with and/or failure in their studies. For instance, results from 64th round of NSS data reveal that a student who is not able to cope with the institution/academic expectations is significantly and more likely to dropout compare to a student who has financial problem. While inability to cope with the dominant academic culture suggest a lack of cultural code specifically require to participate in higher education which in turn suggest lack of socio-cultural capital on the part of student. On the other hand, there can be the case that marginalised students are specifically targeted may be because they belong to identically an inferior social community and because that they receive benefits of affirmative action. There are many instances of discrimination and neglect in the universities specifically done to weaker sections by expecting them to behave in a particular way or secure/debate up to never-reach-expectations of teacher. In the process, these expectations are placed in such a manner in curricular processes that these students find it beyond their scope and ability to meet them and the end result is that they leave the system.

Quite a large number of students decide to dropout because they personally are not interested in studies. Yet others decide to dropout because they find their parents are not interested in their studies. In both cases, the decision to dropout suggest lower socio-economic development of the family, lack of expectations of parents on student education and lack of confidence on the part of student herself to excel in higher education. This is pertinent to note that lack of interest in higher education is not a problem by itself or an independent problem, rather it is the outcome of lack of facilities and opportunities that the student require to participate in education effectively. Lack of interest for higher education on the part of parents and students do reveal a complex and unequal structure of familial and social demand and expectations for and out of higher education. For example, a rural remote agricultural parent might find it reasonable to be disinterested in their children's education if the poverty level of the family is so intense and that demand the student to work for wage and livelihood. Yet in many other cases, the prospects of a student to continue and complete higher education is jeopardised by the conservative baggage being carried on by parents on the possible role that higher education can play to solve various socio-economic issues they meet in their daily life. In other words, many parents stop sending their children to higher education may be because they doubt the potential that higher education can offer in solving problems of the poor.

Yet other reasons for which students dropout from higher education are connected to a whole set of economic/income/wage related activities. There are large numbers of students who help their parents in their own household enterprises and others do leave their studies they have to earn soon for their family.

Notes

1. Reasons for droppingout are; parents not interested in studies, college/ university is far off, to work for wage/salary, for participating in other economic activity, look after younger siblings, to attend other domestic chores, financial constraints, timings of education institution not suitable, for helping in household enterprises, student not interested in studies.

2. *Domestic/familial/personal reasons include*; parents not interested in studies, to look after younger siblings, to attend other domestic chores, student not interested in studies. (2) *Institutional factors*; institution is far off, timings of educational institution is not suitable, language and medium of instruction not familiar, unable to cope up or failure in studies and unfriendly atmosphere in institution. (3) *Financial factor*; financial constraints. (4) *Reasons connected to the participation in economic activity*; to work for wage and salary, for participating in other domestic activity, for helping in household enterprises.

References

———— (1965), '*The Problem of Teaching, Conference of Australian Universities'*, The Australian University, 3, 3.

—— (1969), The Educational and Vocational Development of College Students, Washington: American Council on Education.

—— (1972), College dropout: A National Profile, ACE Research Reports, Washington DC. : American Council on Education.

———— (1977) , Preventing student from droppingout, San Francisco; Josrey-Bass Publishers.

———— (1981), '*A long Way to go: Report on a Survey of Scheduled Caste High School and College Students in fifteen States of India*, Allied Publishers, New Delhi.

———— (1987), Leaving College: Rethinking the Causes and Cures of Student Attrition. Chicago: University of Chicago Press.

————(1988), Stages of student departure: reflections on the longitudinal character of student leaving. J. Higher education, 59, 438-455.

————(1997), Classrooms as communities: exploring the educational character of student persistence. J. Higher Educ., 68, 599-623.

Ahuja, G. C. (1980), Educational Wastage and Stagnation among Tribal Children, *Journal of Indian Education*, 6 (1), 58-70.

Aitken D. Norman (1982), '*College Student Performance, Satisfaction and Retention: Specification and Estimation of A Structural Model' The Journal of Higher Education,* 53, 1, 32-50.

Astin, A.W. (1964), Personal and Environmental Factors associated with college dropouts among high aptitude students, Journal of Educational Psychology, 55 (4), 219-227.

Bayer, A. (1968), '*The College Dropout: Factors Affecting Senior College Completion*', *Sociology of Education*, 41, 305-16.

Bean, J.P. (1979), Dropouts and Turnover: The Synthesis of a Causal Model of Student Attrition, *Dissertation Abstract International*, 39 (8), 4750-A.

Blanchfield, W.C. (1971), College Dropout Identification: A Case Study, *The Journal Of Experimental Education*, 40 (2), 1-4.

Bourdieu, P. (1997), The Forms of Capital. In A.H. Halsey, H. Lauder, P. Brown, and A. Stuart Wells (Eds) *Education: Culture, Economy, Society*, Oxford, Oxford University Press.

Bourdieu, P. and Passeron, J. C. (1977), *Reproduction in Education, Society and Culture* (London and Beverly Hills, Sage Publications).

Bragg, Emma W. (1956), '*A Study of Student Withdrawal at 'W. U.*', *Journal of Educational Psychology*, Vol. 47 (4), 199-202.

Chapman, D. W., and Hutcheson, S. M. (1982), '*Attrition from Teaching Careers: A Discriminant Analysis*', *American Educational Research Journal,* 19: 93-105.

Chitnis S. (1972), '*Education for Equality: Case for Scheduled Castes in Higher Education*',

Cliff, M. (1962), An Investigation of Factors Associated with Dropout and Transfer by Scholarship Applicants, *Journal of Educational Psychology*, 55 (4) 219.

Donovan R. (1984), '*Path Analysis of a Theoretical Model of Persistence in Higher Education among Low-Income Black Youth*', *Research in Higher Education*, 21, 3, 243-59.

Economic and Political Weekly, 7, 31-33, 1675-81.

Edelbrock, G.R. (1975), '*Personality Characteristics of Selected Community College Dropouts*', *Dissertation Abstracts International*, 36, (7-8), 4900-A.

Forster, M. (1959), *An Audit of Academic Performance*, Queens University, Belfast.

Grace, H.A. (1957) ,'Personality Factors and College Attrition', Journal of Peabody Education, 35, 36-40, In *Journal of Educational Psychology*, 1964, 55 (4), 219.

Hammond, S.B. (1957), '*Draft Report of First Year Student Survey, 1955-56*', Mimeo, University of Melbourne.

Holmes, C.H. (1964), '*Why They Left College and University*', *Journal of Educational Psychology*, 55 (4), 220.

Jackson, C.M. (1978), '*A Follow-Up Study of Educational Opportunity Fund Students: Graduates and Dropouts*', *Dissertation Abstracts International*, 39 (3), 1369-A.

Kamat, A. R. and Deshmukh, A. G. (1963), *Wastage in College Education*, Poona: Asia Publishing House.

Karandikar, S. P. (1975), '*Problems and Conditions of Students in the Poona University Area*', Ph.D. Thesis, in M.B. Buch, Second Survey of Research in Education, Faculty of Education and Psychology, Baroda, 1972-78, 521.

Khan, M.Z. and Singh, D. R. (1978) ,'*College Youth and their Course of Study and their View of Society*', *Journal of Higher Education*, 4 (1), 57-66.

Kohen, A. I., Nestel, G., and Karmas, C. (1978), '*Factors Affecting Individual Persistence Rates in Undergraduate College Programs*', *American Educational Research Journal,* 15: 233-252.

Kumar, E. R. (1980), '*Dropouts, 'Dilemma*', The *Illustrated Weekly of India*, 23 (3), 29.

Loeb, J. and Duff, F. (1974), '*Graduate Student Cohort Data for Individual Advising and Resource Allocation*', *Research in Higher Education,* 2: 325-340.

Lunneborg, C. E., and Lunneborg, P. W. (1973), 'Doctoral Study Attrition in Psychology', *Research In Higher Education*, 1: 379-387.

Malik, Y. (1984), 'A Study of the Attitude of Students of Jawaharlal Nehru University Towards Higher Education', *Unpublished M.Phil. Dissertation, JNU, New Delhi.*

Mary Ott et al. (1984), '*Logit Analysis of Graduate Student*', *Research in Higher Education*, 21, 4, 439-460.

Mathews, T.H. (1957), *Academic Failures: Canada's Crisis in Higher Education*, University of Toronto Press.

Maxwell, M.J. (1960), '*An Analysis of the California Psychological Inventory and the American Council of Education Psychological Test as Predictors of Success in Different College Curricula*', *Journal of Educational Psychology*, 55 (4), 219.

McCloy, C. H. (1980), '*A Study to Determine the Factors that Cause Students to become Dropouts at Chattanooga State Technical Community College*', *Dissertation Abstracts International,* 40 A (9), 4864-A.

Munro, B. H. (1981), '*Dropouts from Higher Education: Path Analysis of A National Sample*', *American Educational Research Journal*, 18: 133-141.

Naylor, P. D., and Sanford, T. R. (1982), '*Intra-Institutional Analysis of Student Retention Across Student Levels*', *College and University,* 57: 143-159.

Peng, S. S., and Fetters, W. B. (1978), '*Variables Involved in Withdrawal During the First Two Years of College: Preliminary Findings from The National Longitudinal*

Study of the High School Class of 1972', *American Educational Research Journal,* 15: 361-372.

Phadke, J.K and Shukla, R.C. (1980), Educational Waste— A Study in Dropouts among Scheduled Tribe College Students in Vyara, Vyara Institution of Tribal and Rural Development and Research.

Rawat, P. L. (1970), *History of Indian Education*, Agra, Ram Prasad & Sons.

Reddy, Y.M. (1971), '*A Study of Adjustment Problems of Adolescents in Relation to Their Fathers' Occupation*', Research Bulletin of the Department of Psychology, 6, 34-41.

Rong Chen (2008), '*Financial Aids and Student Dropout in Higher Education: A Heterogeneous Research Approach*', in J.C. Smart (Eds.) *Higher Education: Handbook of Theory and Research,* XXIII, 209-40, The Netherlands: Springer.

Rumberger, R. W. (1983), 'Dropping Out of High School: The Influence of Race, Sex, and Family Background', *American Educational Research Journal,* 20: 199-220.

Schonell, F. J. (1962), *Promise and Performance: A Study of Student Progress at University Level,* University of Queensland and University of London Press.

Sewell H. Williams and Shah P. Vimal (1967), '*Socioeconomic Status, Intelligence, and the Attainment of Higher Education*', *Sociology of Education*, 40, 1, 1-23.

Sharma, S. (1972), '*Sex and Caste Affiliation, a Source of Variation in School Achievement of Adolescents*', *New Trends in Education*, 3 (2), 28-32.

Singh, A. and Sharma, G.D. (1981), *University and College Finances*, New Delhi; Association of Indian Universities.

Slocum, W.L. (1964) ,'Social Factor in Academic Mortality', College and University, 1956, 32, 53-64, In *Journal of Educational Psychology*, 55 (4), 220.

Smith P. Jeremy and Nayar A. Robin (2001), 'Droppingout of University: A Statistical Analysis of the Probability of Withdrawal for UK University Students', *Journal of The Royal Statistical Society Series A (Statistics In Society),* 164, 2, 389-405.

Stork, D., and Berger, P. D. (1978), 'Attrition in The Liberal Arts College of a Major Metropolitan University' *Research in Higher Education,* 9: 281-289.

Terenzini, P. T. And Pascarella, E. T. (1977), 'Voluntary Freshman Attrition and Patterns of Social and Academic Integration in A University: A Test of a Conceptual Model', *Research in Higher Education,* 6: 25-43.

Terenzini, P. T. and Pascarella, E. T. (1978), 'The Relation of Students' Precollege Characteristics and Freshman Year Experience to Voluntary Attrition', *Research in Higher Education,* 9: 347-366.

Thomas L. (2002), '*Student Retention in Higher Education: The Role of Institutional Habitus*', *Journal of Education Policy*, 17, 4, 423-42.

Tinto, V. (1975), Dropout from Higher Education: A Theoretical Synthesis of Recent Research. Rev. Educ. Res., 45, 89-125.

Turkel B. Susan and Abramson T. (1986), '*Peer Tutoring and Mentoring as a Drop-Out Prevention Strategy*', *The Clearing House*, 60, 2, 68-71.

UNESCO (1965), *Access to Higher Education: The International Study of University Admission,* Vol. 11, National Studies, Paris, International Association of Universities.

Yoshino, I.R. (1964), 'College Dropout at the end tf the Freshman Year', in *Journal of Educational Psychology*, 55 (4), 219.

8

Education Status of Scheduled Tribes in Andhra Pradesh: A Case Study of Lambada Tribe

Bikku

Abstract

Education is the process of instruction aimed at an all-round development of individuals, it provides the necessary tools and knowledge to understand and practice in day to day life. For many, education is understood to be a means of overcoming handicaps, achieving greater equality and acquiring wealth and status. It helps every individual to develop fullest potential (Sargent, 1994). The formal education among the tribal in India is low. The dropout rates are very high in the primary and secondary schools level, especially girls are higher compared to boys though various policies and programmes have been implementing by the government and other Non-governmental Organisations (NGOs) and others. The literacy rate of Scheduled Tribe (ST) in India is 47.1 per cent according to census 2001.

The Lambada Tribe are semi-nomadic residing in the various states of India, having different names like, Banjaras, Brinjaris, Lamans, Lambanis, Sugalis (Thurston, 1909), in the south India they are the more populated especially they constituted majority among all tribal community in Andhra Pradesh. The present study is carried out from fieldwork among the Lambadas of Zaheerabad Mandal of Medak district in Andhra Pradesh. The paper is an attempt to discuss about the education status and dropouts which linked to a set of relationships in the social, cultural and economic aspects, through anthropological perspective.

Key Words: *Education, Status, Scheduled Tribe, Literacy, Lambada, Andhra Pradesh.*

Introduction

The education is an important parameter to measure any society or community development, that is how much that society got educated and has literacy rate? Education cannot be the only literacy but it is in much broader sense much more than the literacy. Man thinking and behaviour has always been influenced by the education, the process of man evolutions him-self occurs through the process of education, in this process and the education shape the man and society. It enriches the knowledge in human being through which mans present and future will be decided. Education is important and one of the most powerful means of bringing about socio-economic development in the society. Education is the process of instruction aimed at an all round development of individuals, providing the necessary tools and knowledge to understand and participate in day to day activities. Education is the only wealth which cannot be stolen. It builds character, provides strength of mind and increases knowledge. Education sustains the human values which contribute individual and collective well-being. It forms the basis for life-long learning and inspires confidence to face challenges. It provides the skills to become more self-reliant and creates awareness of opportunities and rights.

As John Dewey (1921), said that in his book Democracy and Education: An *Introduction to the Philosophy of Education* "Education, in its broadest sense, is the means of this social continuity of life"

According to a philosopher of education George F. Kneller (1941), education "in its broad sense, education refers to any act or experience that has formative effect on the mind, character, or physical ability of an individual ... In its technical sense, education is the process by which society, through schools, colleges, universities, and other institutions, deliberately transmits its cultural heritage at its accumulated knowledge, values, and skills from one generation to another".

Moreover, Emile Durkheim, a prominent figure in the area of sociology of education in his book titled *Education and Sociology* wrote in 1956 defined education as "Education is the influence exercised by adult generations on those that are not yet ready for social life. Its object is to arouse and to develop in the child a certain number of physical, intellectual and moral states which are demanded of him by both the political society as a whole and the special milieu for which he is specifically destined".

In socialisation process the education play vital role, so individual and communities live dignified life with education. As India is diverse country in which there are more than 550 tribal communities, as these tribal communities are backward in terms of economically and politically. Then there is need to stress on, how the education playing role in this tribal communities overall their development? Another question on which this paper will focus is why there is lack of education among the tribal communities?

Universal primary education is a constitutional directive. Article 45 of the Directive Principles urges all states to provide 'free and compulsory education for all children until they complete the age of fourteen years' within a period of ten years from the commencement of the constitution. The right to education is recognised as fundamental in the 83rd constitutional amendment, but the goal of universal education has remained a distant dream to these tribal communities.

The term Scheduled Tribes first appeared in the Constitution of India. Article 366 (25) defines Scheduled Tribes as such tribes or tribal communities or parts of or groups within such tribes or tribal communities as are deemed under Article 342 to be Scheduled Tribes for the purposes of this Constitution Article 342 prescribes the procedure to be followed in the matter of specification of Scheduled Tribes.

The NPE, 1986 and the Programme of Action (POA), 1992, recognised the heterogeneity and diversity of the tribal areas while underlining the importance of instruction through the mother tongue and the need for preparing teaching/ learning materials in the tribal languages. A working group on Elementary and Adult Education for the Tenth Five Year Plan (2002-07) emphasised the need to improve the quality of education of tribal children and to ensure equity as well as further improving access. In general, the tribes that remain geographically isolated are able to retain their traditional cultures and religions longer. On the other hand communities that are either nomadic or live in the periphery of civilised life are prone for drastic changes (Manjunatha B.R. and Annapurna M. 2012). Fifty-four years after Independence on November 28, 2001 the Government enacted the 93rd Amendment to the Constitution making the Right to Education a Fundamental Right. It puts the onus of sending children to school on parents rather than the State. It is not enough to talk of fundamental rights and fundamental duties of the citizens. It is equally necessary to dwell on the fundamental duties of the government. The extent to which this enactment will be increasingly backed by resource allocation will be the test of the seriousness of purpose of the government to implement the law.

Objectives

1. To study the educational status among the Lambada tribe.
2. To understand the dropouts related to socio-cultural and economic aspects.

Methodology

This paper is based on the both primary and secondary data source. Primary data has been collected from the fieldwork. The field work techniques were included unstructured interviews (including with school teachers), observation, group discussions; these are the conventional random samplings. The secondary data includes books, journal articles, news papers and government records and census, etc. The primary data collected from four

Lambada Thandas namely Hothi (K) Thanda, Vittu Nayak Thanda, Govindpur Thanda and Jamgar Baudi Thanda in Zaheerabad Mandal of Medak district of Andhra Pradesh.

Tribal Education in Indian Contest

There are nearly 600 tribal communities in India which consists of 8.2 per cent of total population in India. However, traditional tribal societies are undergoing a rapid change with the mainstreaming policy of the Indian government. For the tribal communities the process of becoming a part of the mainstream has meant a declining control on their resources and erosion of their cultural heritage. The major issue affecting the tribals in India is displacement: not merely displacement by large projects but resource displacement, thus violating the basic survival rights of tribal communities. Tribal areas reveal a high degree of land alienation. Non-tribals have invaded tribal protected areas. Deforestation, mainly due to exploitation of forests for industrial purposes, is another manifestation of resource displacement. This has resulted in decreasing access to forest resources by tribal communities. With increasing globalisation and privatisation, the land rights of tribal areas is under even greater threat since these are regions, which have a high natural resource base and has tremendous potential to meet multiple market demands. Added to resource displacement is project displacement where development projects have threatened the livelihood needs of tribal communities. More than 40 per cent of displaced persons of all large development projects are tribals. There is proper rehabilitation and resettlement of displaced people led them more dropouts.

More importantly displacement has been accompanied by erosion of the identity of tribal communities, which is being subsumed within the dominant culture. There is a breakdown in their own community institutions, which hitherto safeguarded their resources, traditional practices and values. In the process the richness and wealth of their knowledge systems, identity and survival with integrity is being destroyed.

The Educational Context in the Tribal Areas of Andhra Pradesh

In Andhra Pradesh there are nearly 35 different tribal communities living, According to 2001 census the total tribal population in Andhra Pradesh 50,24,104 (male 2548295 and female 2475809) against total population 7,62,10,007 which consists of 6.59 per cent. The highest population of district is Khammam which consists of 26.47 per cent (6,82,617) and least populated district is Hyderabad which consist 0.90 per cent.

Lambada Tribal Education Status in Andhra Pradesh

The Lambadas are a scheduled tribe inhabiting throughout Andhra Pradesh. They are also known as Sugalis or Banjara. They are the largest tribe in Andhra Pradesh. They Lambadas also inhabited in several states in India such as Karnataka named by Lambani, Maharashtra, Lambani, Banjara, Gujarat Banjara, Rajasthan Banjara, Gouar. But they called themselves Goar Banjara or Goar Mati. Lambadas are dependent on agriculture. The Lambada tribal population consists about 20,77, 94 (40 per cent above) (10,71,589 of males and 10,06,358 of females) against 50,24,104 of all tribal communities in Andhra Pradesh. They live in exclusive settlements of their own called Thandas, usually away from the main village, tenaciously maintaining their cultural and ethnic identity. Tribal literacy rate is about 5, 81,334 which consists of 35.74 per cent (4,10,888 (50.57 per cent) of males and 1, 70,446 (12.19 per cent) of females.

In Medak district the according to 2001 census the literacy rate 28.08 per cent (41.06 of male and 14.26 per cent female). In the case of Zaheerabad Mandal the tribal literacy rate is 32.31 per cent (47.52 of male and 15.96 per cent of female.

There are 42 villages and nearly 40 Lambada tribal Thandas are located in Zaheerabad Mandal in Medal district of A.P. In this mandal majority of population are Lambadas and others are Yerukula tribes and few of koyas. The total tribal population is 10, 574 (5, 458 males and 5,116 females) and the literacy rate is 32.31 per cent (47.52 per cent of male and 15.96 per cent of female) as per 2001 census. There are 25 private high schools and 14 government high schools, and there are more than 90 primary schools in this mandal.

Lambada tribes in the four Thanda are all homogeneous communities. The Hothi (K) Thanda total population consists of 383 out of 54 households and literacy rate 44 per cent. Govindpur Thanda has 89 households the total population is around 650 and literacy rate 42 per cent. Vittunayak Thanda has nearly 320 household's population around 3000 and the literacy rate 32 per cent. Jamgar Baudi Thanda has nearly 55 households and total population in this village is nearly 450 and the literacy rate is 32 per cent.

Schools and Colleges in Zaheerabad Mandal

Table 8.1

	Primary Schools	*High schools*	*Junior Colleges*	*Degree and PG College*
Govt.	40	14	1	1
Private	3	25	6	3
	Primary Schools	High schools	Junior Colleges	Degree and PG College
Govt.	40	14	1	1
Private	3	25	6	3

Education

There is one school in the Hothi (K) Thanda that teaches up to 5th standard. It is a Government school; medium of education is Telugu. There are two teachers in this School. Out of the total population of 283, only 126 males and females have attended school. There are 92 educated males (32.5 per cent of the men) and 34 educated women (12 per cent of the female population) in the Thanda. When they settled in this Thanda, educated people were rare. Among educated persons 49 are educated upto primary only. Banjaras of this Thanda send their girls to school to pursue education till primary and upper primary levels. After that most of girls get engaged in house work, cattle raring and helping their parents in the agriculture work, financial difficulties, and general apathy of parents towards formal educations. In this Thanda only two girls are studying higher education, one girl is doing B.Ed (bachelor of education) and another girl is studying in a nursing school.

Education Level in the Hothi (K) Thanda

Table 8.2

Education Level	*Male*	*Percentage of male*	*Female*	*Percentages of female*	*Total of male and female*	*Percentages of total male and female*
Primary	31	10.95	18	6.36	49	17.31
Upper Primary	13	4.59	9	3.18	22	7.77
High-School	24	8.48	5	1.76	29	10.25
Inter(10+2)	15	5.30	0	0.00	15	5.30
Degree	7	2.47	0	0.00	7	2.47
Masters	1(MCA)	0.35	0	0.00	1	0.35
Others	1(IT Diploma)	0.35	2(1 B. Ed, 1 Nurse)	0.70	3	1.06
Total	**92**	**32.50**	**34**	**12.00**	**126**	**44.50**

The Banjaras of Hothi (K) Thanda have a positive view towards urban culture for education. Traditionally Banjaras are illiterates. After the independence, the Central and State Governments; provided free education to them. Zaheerabad is a town (now a growing urban area) about four kilometers away from Hothi (K) Thanda. In the urban area they get education facilities from primary school to degree colleges and some private colleges also boys till matriculation. There is one school in this Thanda up to 5th class. It is government school. Medium of education is Telugu. There are two teachers teaching in this School. Out of the total population of 283 there are 126 males and females who attended school. There are 92 educated males in percentage of 32.50 and 34 women are educated. The percentage of educated women is only 12 per cent in the Thanda. Among the men and women, 49 people are educated till primary level.

Andhra Pradesh Tribal Educational Dropouts

On November 20, 1989, the United Nations (UN) General Assembly adopted the Convention on the Rights of the Child (CRC), a historic document for

Table 8.3

Sl. No.	*District*	*I - V (6-10 Years)*			*VI - VII (11-12 Years)*			*VIII - X(13-15 Years)*		
		Boys	*Girls*	*Total*	*Boys*	*Girls*	*Total*	*Boys*	*Girls*	*Total*
1.	Srikakulam	122.34	115.16	118.77	103.39	82.75	93.00	69.21	50.42	**59.77**
2.	Vizianagaram	251.41	233.52	242.55	137.13	101.03	118.99	79.12	64.02	**71.55**
3.	Visakhapatnam	348.04	341.79	344.98	226.45	166.67	196.76	128.85	88.82	**109.01**
4.	East Godavari	85.33	86.11	85.71	70.34	68.14	69.24	37.50	37.80	**37.65**
5.	West Godavari	58.07	61.55	59.83	37.02	35.66	36.34	24.06	23.87	**23.97**
6.	Krishna	67.54	68.52	68.02	35.84	30.38	33.14	25.92	17.11	**21.57**
7.	Guntur	114.17	112.81	113.51	53.76	36.56	45.22	31.90	18.75	**25.39**
8.	Prakasam	114.09	107.63	110.95	40.48	29.61	35.12	21.58	14.15	**17.93**
9.	Nellore	204.93	201.49	203.24	77.88	67.67	72.81	43.03	34.06	**38.59**
10.	Kurnool	57.05	56.53	56.80	36.80	36.62	36.71	25.68	22.81	**24.27**
11.	Anantapur	74.45	74.43	74.44	61.99	56.05	59.08	47.91	36.85	**42.51**

(Contd.)

(Contd. Table 8.3)

Sl. No.	*District*	*I - V (6-10 Years)*			*VI - VII (11-12 Years)*			*VIII - X(13-15 Years)*		
		Boys	*Girls*	*Total*	*Boys*	*Girls*	*Total*	*Boys*	*Girls*	*Total*
12.	YSR Kadapa	70.79	65.60	68.27	43.31	34.09	38.76	25.17	18.89	**22.08**
13.	Chittoor	81.96	80.91	81.45	60.96	49.74	55.39	32.48	26.23	**29.39**
14.	Ranga Reddy	175.57	170.09	172.95	109.97	76.90	93.91	59.69	37.11	**48.74**
15.	Hyderabad	40.60	39.46	40.06	24.93	21.67	23.36	15.09	12.92	**14.05**
16.	Nizamabad	205.54	191.20	198.41	131.97	76.20	103.84	69.06	30.35	**49.57**
17.	Medak	183.30	173.19	178.38	86.88	46.27	66.83	45.56	17.94	**31.95**
18.	Mahabubnagar	255.85	223.66	240.20	138.85	65.29	102.58	68.04	26.54	**47.62**
19.	Nalgonda	293.14	261.30	277.70	182.25	118.89	151.10	102.86	54.77	**79.26**
20.	Warangal	395.22	405.36	400.15	250.35	188.28	219.72	138.36	93.30	**116.16**
21.	Khammam	579.12	593.40	586.08	506.09	456.44	481.56	280.49	212.11	**246.77**
22.	Karimnagar	95.13	92.21	93.69	58.20	45.68	51.94	32.71	23.10	**27.92**
23.	Adilabad	513.80	504.34	509.16	327.74	266.74	297.39	135.69	103.19	**119.55**
Andhra Pradesh		**176.91**	**172.23**	**174.63**	**112.61**	**86.73**	**99.80**	**62.40**	**43.34**	**52.99**

Source: Directorate of Economics and Statistics, Hyderabad.

children all over the world. By providing a legal framework to the 'rights of a child' it holds the governments accountable for enforcing these. In the Indian

Table 8.4: Dropout Rates of Scheduled Tribes (2005-06)

Sl. No.	*District*	*Class I – V*			*Class I – VII*		
		Boys	*Girls*	*Total*	*Boys*	*Girls*	*Total*
1.	Srikakulam	27.80	32.90	30.34	63.80	68.73	**66.20**
2.	Vizianagaram	15.13	24.05	19.52	58.20	68.83	**63.46**
3.	Visakhapatnam	46.90	52.88	49.82	59.99	70.07	**64.98**
4.	East Godavari	27.95	26.44	27.22	57.01	56.55	**56.78**
5.	West Godavari	34.12	28.27	31.20	59.10	58.10	**58.61**
6.	Krishna	33.21	39.83	36.49	62.71	70.98	**66.89**
7.	Guntur	50.22	53.85	52.00	69.89	81.11	**75.40**
8.	Prakasam	46.84	51.18	48.97	79.96	85.62	**82.66**
9.	Nellore	41.89	38.52	40.27	78.03	79.69	**78.82**
10.	Kurnool	32.07	33.54	32.77	58.68	57.77	**58.25**
11.	Anantapur	17.80	20.74	19.25	46.78	50.10	**48.37**
12.	YSR Kadapa	24.50	26.89	25.64	53.64	61.17	**57.17**
13.	Chittoor	13.42	15.72	14.55	51.40	58.14	**54.65**
14.	Ranga Reddy	53.15	60.00	56.48	75.88	81.21	**78.31**
15.	Hyderabad	23.02	48.50	35.95	35.46	48.11	**41.93**
16.	Nizamabad	58.91	62.69	60.71	80.23	87.23	**83.41**
17.	Medak	66.37	73.10	69.48	80.19	86.73	83.00
18.	Mahabubnagar	63.54	71.07	67.04	82.84	90.99	**86.45**
19.	Nalgonda	58.37	68.13	63.06	77.89	84.19	**80.74**
20.	Warangal	62.80	65.75	64.28	81.04	85.24	**83.09**
21.	Khammam	32.86	35.27	34.05	61.62	66.60	**64.09**
22.	Karimnagar	46.21	51.35	48.69	70.52	73.67	**71.99**
23.	Adilabad	39.02	45.14	42.10	77.78	83.01	**80.38**
Andhra Pradesh		**47.46**	**52.13**	**49.73**	**72.16**	**77.50**	**74.71**

Source: Directorate of Economics and Statistics, Hyderabad.

context, the Convention has come under criticism because of its distance from the actual situation of children along with there being very little awareness about the rights of the child among children, social activists working for the rights of children and even those responsible for making child rights a reality offer science subjects at master level. Hostel accommodations are provided to girls and in India, the problems faced by children, especially in the rural areas and more so by the girl child, are manifold and most of the times situation specific. Children are involved in various kinds of activities ranging from working in fields or cottage industries (carpets, matches, firecrackers, bidis, bangles, traditional handicrafts, etc.) alongside their parents, on tea plantations, tend cattle, fetch water and wood, as domestic servants, rag pickers, helpers on construction sites, in tea stalls, as apprentices, in stone quarries, and many others. Most of these activities go unreported as they are not in lieu of wages and thus do not get covered under the official definition of work. Most of these children also get left out of the education system as the schools that they would need to go to, would have to be flexible and suited to their work schedules. (Usha, 2001)

Dropouts Levels among the Tribal in Andhara Pradesh

In Andhra Pradesh the percentage of dropouts among the STs are more at high school levels, According 2005-06 report there 49.73 per cent (47.46 per cent of boys and 52.13 per cent of girls) dropouts at primary educational level. In the case of high schools level dropouts is 74.71 per cent (72.16 per cent boys and 77.50 per cent of girls). In Medak district there are nearly 18 tribal groups which consists 1,34,533 populations are living, the Lambada tribe is majority which consists 1,18,642 population. The dropout rate is 83 per cent (86.73 per cent girls and 80.19 per cent are girls) in I-VIII the class in the Medak district.

The Reasons for Dropout

(A) Economical Aspects

1. One of the main reasons for dropout of children from Lambada community is due to prevalence of wide spread poverty.
2. Many children are enrolled as unemployed for MGNREGS, (Mahatma Gandhi National Rural Employment Guarantee Scheme) to work for this scheme to earn money they are skipping the school.
3. Their agriculture is depending on rainy season, if there is low or high rainy rain then their crops will get spoil, so they will migrate to cities like Hyderabad, Mumbai, Pune, etc., for work. When they migrate to cities they will take their children with them, this also one of the main reasons for dropout.
4. The crop failure also impact on agriculture labourers, this lead to agricultural labours migrate to the cities.
5. There is stigma that government school are not good, so as they cannot send their children to the private school due to high fee and costly education,

so they think that sending them to government school in no use. This reason for more dropouts from government school.

6. Some of the families are sending their children to the private school till fifth or six class, but after that they cannot offer fees of school.

7. Children are going as wage labour for their family burdens.

8. During the agriculture or crop season, due to scarcity of labour children are going for work to help parents, and those who are poor they think that this is the season to earn the money, so they will take their children for work.

9. Especially among the Lambada community there is prevalence of seasonal migration to other regions and cities, e.g., paddy harvesting, sugar cutting.

10. Money lender is the main reason because they lent money with high interest, and government is not proving the loans, so due to high interest they have to work. Thus it leads to bounded labour and migration, this also leading to the child labours.

(B) Socio-cultural Aspect

1. One of the social reasons for dropout is early marriage to the children or child marriage.

2. Due to the family burden children are living the school.

3. Now there exist wrong belief among the people is that though you study high, you will not get jobs, so they are starting work in the early stage only.

4. One of the main reasons for dropout is due to the language problem, as they speak Lambada language, so they are getting communication problem.

Conclusion

There is need to bring awareness among the tribal communities about the education and its fruits. In order to do this state must plays active role to provide education as well. There is need to provide informal education and training to uplift to the tribal communities. It is not only the state but responsibility lies on all of us to bring awareness among tribal communities that they can realise that with education they can live with dignity.

References

1. Bakshi, P.M (2010), "*The Constitution of India,*" Delhi: Universal Law Publishing Co. Pvt. Ltd.

2. Bikku (2010), "*Urban Impact, Cultural Adaptation and Persistence of Traditional Values and Customs among the Banjara of Hothi (K) Thanda of Andhra Pradesh*" M.Phil dissertation submitted in University of Hyderabad, Hyderabad, India.

3. Dewey, John (1921): "*Democracy and Education: An Introduction to the Philosophy of Education*", New York: The Macmillan Company. p. 3.

4. Educational Statistics of Andhra Pradesh (2011 – 2012), *"Commissioner and Director of School Education State Project Director RVM (SSA)"*, Hyderabad: AP Government Publication.

5. George F. Kneller (1941), "*The Educational Philosophy of National Socialism"*, London: Oxford University Press.

6. Government of India (1992), "*National Policy on Education 1986" (Programme of Action 1992),* New Delhi: Ministry of Human Resource Development.

7. Jayachandran, Usha (2001): "*Taking Schools to Children 'Bhonga Shalas'*", *Economic and Political Weekly,* September 1, pp. 3347-50.

8. Manjunatha B.R. and Annapurna M. (2012): "*An Investigative Study on School Dropouts in Tribal Settings: A Case of Three Selected Tribes in South Karnataka*", *Antrocom Online Journal of Anthropology*, Vol. 8. No. (2), pp. 421-427.

9. Nambissan, Geetha B (1994), "*Language and Schooling of Tribal Children: Issues Related to Medium of Instruction*" *Economic and Political Weekly,* October 15.

10. Ramachandran, Vimala (2004), "*Is Schooling for the Poor on the Government Agenda?*", *Economic and Political Weekly*, July 24.

11. Rao. Vasanta Sriniva (2009), "*Lack of Community Participation in the Sarva Shiksha Abhiyan: A Case Study*" *Economic and Political Weekly*, Vol. XLIV, No.8. February 2.

12. Sargent, M. (1994), "*The New Sociology for Australians",* Melbourne: Longman Cheshire.

13. Thurston, Edgar (1909), "*The Caste and Tribes of South India*", A-B. Madras: Government Press.

9

Development and Displacement–A Question of Human Right: A Case Study of POSCO Project in Odisha

Chitta Ranjan Mishra

Introduction

After the independence with an objective to achieve to speed economic growth many developmental projects have taken in our country for our nation building. These projects placed in second five year plan in our country. These projects include construction of megadams, powerplant, largescale industries, and mining.Though these developmental projects have provided irrigation to thirsty lands, energy for the growing industries, and brought about the economic prosperity for the country but in another side these projects leads towards the displacement of large number of people in our country. Among the people displaced by various developmental projects a large number of people from schedule tribe, schedule caste or other indigenous people. Mostly developmental projects were took place in tribal areas and they suffer more in this model of development. In the name of development the poor people often pay a very heavy price which not only involves the simple loss and destruction of goods and property, but people's lives and ultimate source of substance. Development does not benefit to all people, it is only for small number of people in our country. But such consequences in the path of nation's development are often deliberately ignored and authorities continue to remain tight-lipped, trying to camouflage vices under the lofty banner of national growth and development (Dutta, 2007). Various studies conducted by scholars show that as many 75 per cent of displaced people have not been rehabilited

(Fernades,1991). In the absence of proper resettlement and rehabilitation pushed them in to impoverishment, marginalisation and more backwardness. Michael M. Cerenea (1995) has rightly pointed out that development induced involuntary displacement leads to eight impoverishment risk, i.e., Landlessness, joblessness, homelessness, marginalisation, food insecurity, increased morbidity and mortality loss of access to common property and social disarticulation of the displaced population. With the following the old colonial rules of Land acquisition policy government now acquire the Tribal land in the name of "Public interest". When people resist against this in human activities government use brutal force to depress their voice which leads towards the violation of the democratic or human rights of the tribal or indigenous people in our country. This paper mainly studies the industrialisation with reference to POSCO project in Odisha. This paper mainly studies the discourse of development and displacement and aspect of human rights of indigenous people in our country with relate to Odisha.

Overview of Development and Displacement in India and Odisha

The process of socio-economic development stated soon after the independence of India under the successive five year plan. Government established many developmental projects which lead towards the large displacement in our country. Industrialisation is one of the strategies for development. So both Central and State governments established many industries after the independence for economic development. But it displaced many people from their native home, from their livelihood and their also their lives. Tribals or indigenous people were affected more through this projects. Industrialisation proved good for the nation but disastrous for the Tribal. A conservative estimate of the number of people displaced from 1950-1991 was about the 2,13,00,000 (Fernades,1991). As per the government records at least 75 per cent of those displaced are still not resettled. Historical evidence suggests that in first half of the 19th century a major wave of development displacement took place between 1830 and 1842. British government passed Land Acquisition act in 1894 which taken as a legal instrument of economic control over the people of India. By using the concept of "public domain" the British were able to theorise and legitimise their control over land. After the above the 60 years of the independence India following the same shame full policy for land acquisition which leads towards problem for the poor indigenous tribal people in our country. It maintains social in justice till today. Odisha is identified as the natural resources based state in our country which invited various companies to invest this place. There is an estimate that around 10 lakhs people have been physically displaced and 60 lakhs people have been disposed from their land. Displaced tribals who constitute more than 40 per cent of the total displaced population in Odisha are worst suffer. In Odisha project based development began in late 40s but gain momentum in the 50s after the implementation of the five year plan. The major developmental projects undertaken in the 50s were the Rourkela steel plant and Hirakud Dam project. During the 70s several multipurpose Dam likes Rengali, Upper Kolab, Upper Indrâvati and Subarnarekha were stated in the state. The Thermal Power Station (ITPS), Talcher Super Thermal Power project (TSTP) and the National Aluminium Company (NALCO) came up in the eighties. These projects were established in the resource rich highland districts of Odisha, which are predominantly inhabited by Tribals and other indigenous people in the state. These large projects left a massive effect towards the inhabitants in that place. In order to economic development the government of Odisha has launched a massive programme for industrialisation in post economic reform phase. In this phase Odisha has attracted investment of 41 lakhs crores (The Economic Times, 2007). In 2005 alone the state government has signed as many as 43 MoUs with various corporate bodies for setting up their industrial units at an investment of Rs 1,60,000 crore (Mishra and Maitra, 2007), POSCO was among them which was signed MoU with state government in 2005 to establish Steel plant in Jagatsinghpur. Odisha like other developing economics has however faced peoples protest during its industrial process. In last few years it has faced a number of protests against setting up of industries like Vedanta Alumina limited in Langigarh, Tata Steel at Kalinganagar and now POSCO in jagatstinhapur. The Kalinganagar incident is part of serious resistance of the people threatened with displacement by mega project.

Development, Displacement and Discourse

Development means making a better life for everyone. In common parlance the term development implies some shorts of advancement in positive direction (Martinussen, 1997). Views of development are inevitably linked to some idea of progress, which involves change from one state to another (Harrison, 1989). But after some days it changes its connotation.With the rise of capitalism and industrial system in western countries the concept of development changes and only one way of development is developing of GNP or per capital income. The meaning of development gained momentum in 1950s after the independence of third world countries from the British rule. Many third world countries follow the one way of development that is modernisation and western path of development to strengthen their economy.The third world became the favoured recipient large shift of foreign from the western countries and western technology and follow the industrialisation as their development strategies. So development became strong economy related after the independence of third world countries and it became strong as to synonymous with economic development. The development defined in terms of economic growth was the core development thinking in the 1950s. Unlike other third world countries India also followed the same model of economic development. At that time there were two version of economic development, one was Gandhi's village economy model and other was Neheruvians western model. Gandhi was against the industrialisation and western model of development and he clearly put it on his most popular book "*Hind Swaraj*". But in another side Nehru was against the Gandhi's views on economic model of development and advocated that it leads towards the slow growth of country's economy and western model of industrialisation leads towards the high growth of economy in the country. So Nehru in second five year plan placed industrialisation as his model of development. Development was inclusively defined in terms of growth of GNP. But this development was not for all. Though it helps India to become an economic healthy country but it leads towards the inequality and huge displacement of large section of society, among them mostly Tribal or Indigenous people. It leads towards the violation of human rights. They became poorer after displacement of their native place. This development model raises question that development for whom in our society? The indigenous or tribals deprived from their own land. During the current time around five lakhs people displacing in every year in the name of development (Medha Patkar, 2000). The issue of development and displacement now became question of national importance.

Scheduled Tribes and Human Rights

The great gift of classical and contemporary human thought to culture and civilisation is the notion of Human Rights. Human rights include, right to life, right to an adequate standard of living, freedom from all type of torture and other ill-treatment. Human rights in general are those minimum rights which every individual being a member of human family must possess consideration of other enjoy. To protect the Human rights of tribal or indigenous people United Nation announced different declaration like Universal Declaration of Human Rights in 1948.This declaration provides that right to live, right to liberty and security. Article one of the Universal Declaration of human rights provides right to equality. In 1966, United Nation Declaration on the Right to Development adopted by the General Assembly on 4th December, 1986 which deals with that development should participatory. International Labour Organisation (ILO) has also defended the social and economic rights of indigenous people (J. K. Das, 2001). United Nation has commemorated the year 1993 as the International Year for the World's Indigenous people. Another positive step towards the promotion of the rights of indigenous peoples is that the UN General Assembly in its resolution 48/163 of 21st December, 1993 proclaimed the UN International Decade of World's Indigenous people (1995-2004) which commenced on 10th December, 2004. Indian Constitution also provides many rules to protect the interest of the Tribals in our country. Fifth and sixth schedule of our constitution deals with the schedule tribe and schedule caste in our constitution. Currently India passed law regarding the Scheduled Tribes and other Traditional Forest Dwellers (Recognition of Forest

Rights) Act 2006 to reserve or protect the forest for the Tribals. It empowered the Gram Sabha which represents the Tribal people.

POSCO Project and People's Protest

South Korean Pohang Iron and Steel Company Limited which known as POSCO India has signed a MoU with the state government of Odisha to establish Steel plant, an Iron-Ore mine and a port in Jagatsinghpur district, which will be the largest investment 12 billion dollars) foreign company in our country (The Times of India, 2007). It requires 12,000 acres land. Government agreed to provide land in three packages like, 25 acres of land in Bhubaneswar, 4,000 acres in Jagatsinghpur for plant and 2000 acres for township, port and also remaining for other purposes (The Sambad, 2008). It will displace around the 613 families in plant areas which is matter of concern. In the purposed areas people farming the betel vine and other vegetables for their occupation which will be destroyed after the establishment of company.

People's Protest

People's agitation is continuing against this project because, it will deprived them from their native place, livelihood. There are some fact that they earn 14,000 to 20,000 as their earnings from betel and also other people earning the healthy money from the fishing. Among them some are Tribals and Indigenous people. More than 8,000 people depending on this livelihood. So they are agitating against this project or land acquisition. Women, children and social activist are participating in this protest. POSCO Pratirodha Sangrama Samiti (PPSS) leads this protest with the leadership of Abhaya Sahoo. People claim that government acquires land with the brutal force. It is also violating the Forest Right Act, 2006, because purposed areas are included in forest reserve areas according the act. Though company promised to give compensation to affected people but it will not sufficient for the people. Centre also made different committee on this. Saxena Committee suggest Central government for withdrawing the support from that are, because it violates the Forest Right Act and without concerning the Gram Sabha government acquires lands from the people violates their rights but Meena Gupta Committee was for the project.

Government now able to acquires land for its first phase production. Agitation now only exists in Dhinkia.

Conclusion

New development paradigm leads towards the large problems for the people, mainly the indigenous Tribal people. They are getting nothing but only losing everything in the name of development. This development not for the all section of the society. It is only for the some section of the society. Due to the weak policy of government larger section suffer more and they protest. But the government depresses them with using brutal force which leads towards the violation of the human rights of the poor, indigenous and Tribal people in our country. Government should follow the proper policy for this and should follow proper rehabilitation policy.

References

Barnett, Tony (1988), *Sociology and Development*, London: Htchinson Press.

Chakravorty, Sanjoy (2013), *The Price of Land: Acquisition, Conflict, and Consequences*, New Delhi: Oxford University Press.

Das, J.K. (2011), *Human Rights and Indigenous Peoples*, New Delhi: APH Publication.

Dewet, Chris (2001), "*Economic Development and Population Displacement: Can Everybody Win*?" *Economics Political Weekly*, Vol. 36(50), 15th March.

Dhagamwar, V. and Verma, N. (2003*), Industrialisation Development and Displacement: The People of Korba,* New Delhi: Saga Publication.

Dutta, Ashirbani (2007), *Development-Induced Displacement and Human Rights*, New Delhi: Deep and Deep Publications.

Kannongo, Sanghamitra (2011), *Tribal and Human Rights*, Delhi: Swastik Publication.

Madangopal, Dakshyayani (2010), *Marginal Zones: Development–Induced Displacement in Mumbai*, Bangalore: Books for Change Press.

Mishra, Banikanta (2011), "Paan or POSCO?", *Economics Political Weekly*, Vol. xlvi(27), 25th June.

Mishra, Sudarsan (2008), "POSCO Project in Orissa", *The Times of India*, Bhubaneswar, 8th March.

Mohanty, Biswaranjan (2001), "Displacement and Rehabilitation of Tribals", *Economics Political Weekly*, 40 (13), 26th March.

Parida, Jayanta (2006), *Tribals: Development, Displacement and Rehabilitation*, New Delhi: Classical Publishing Company.

Patekar, Medha and Bhaduri, Amit (2009), "Industrialisation for the people by the people, of the people", *Economic s Political Weekly*, 40(12), 13th January.

Pati, Sikta (2012), *Industrialisation and Displacement: An Economic Impact*, New Delhi: Concept Publication.

Peet, Richard and Hartwick, Elaine (2009), *Theories of Development: Contentions, Arguments, Alternatives*, New York: The Guilford Press.

Sachan, A.K. and Jaiswal, B. (2005), *Development Induced Displacement and Rehabilitation,* New Delhi: Alpha Publication.

10

Development Induced Displacement of Tribals in Odisha: Issues and Concerns

Dasarathi Bhuiyan

Development, through industrialisation, science and technology, has become a major concern *vis-à-vis* livelihood of the people. Today in many parts of the country, there is a strong opposition against dams, industries and other such development related projects. This understanding of development is being questioned at the grassroots level by various struggles from the standpoint of tradition and culture. It is in this context, that this paper discusses the anti-industrial movement in Odisha and attempts to understand the various debates emerging from the movement. The key questions examined here are as follows: First, on what basis is the movement opposing the industrial project? Second, if the movement is opposing modernisation and industrialisation, then is it free of modernisation? And, how does the movement look at such developmental projects: as a blend of "development and resistance" and "tradition and modernisation", or something else? Accordingly, the information collected about the movement during the field visit and through secondary sources is analysed within the framework of Development and Resistance: Encounter between the State and Communities. [1]

Development and Displacement in Odisha

Odisha is one of the backward States of the country. It however possesses vast deposits of various valuable minerals and other resources, which remained unutilised and underutilised due to various reasons. The State saw the setting up of large development projects like multipurpose river valley projects- Hirakud Dam, Rengali, Upper Kolab, Indravati, Subarnarekha etc. Large industries — Rourkela Steel Plant, NALCO, HAL, POSCO and the like. Besides several private sector projects have either set up or signed MoUs with the State Government to start their units which include industrial giants Tata, Jindal, Birla, POSCO and others. But what is painful is the large-scale involuntary displacement of weaker sections, particularly the tribals. Statistical data indicates that a large portion of the project affected families belong to the tribal group. Since the tribal belt is invariably rich in mineral deposits, they are affected much by the ongoing power, mining and industrial projects. Therefore, these weaker section communities are opposing the ongoing projects. As a result, there emerges an encounter between the State and affected Communities.[2]

Objectives of the Study

Keeping the aforesaid objectives in view and the tribals in particular an empirical study was undertaken to find out the status of Development and Resistance between the the displaced tribal families and government. However, the broad objectives with which the empirical study was undertaken are the following: Assess the status of the displaced tribals: (i) Find out the extent of livelihood restoration of those affected (ii) Identify the factors responsible for resistance against development (iii) Recommend on the basis of research findings specific critical areas that need to be looked in to by the policy makers and implementing agencies for more effective resettlement and rehabilitation measures for the displaced persons in general and tribal displaced persons in particular in development projects.

Geographical Coverage of the Study and the Sample

The study on the basis of which the present report is based has been undertaken on the sample displaced tribal families in various projects located in the tribal Pocket of Odisha.

Methodology

For collecting empirical data a number of sociological and anthropological research tools were used. Some of the major research tools used for the study are:

(i) Interview schedule
(ii) Focus Group Discussion
(iii) Participatory Rural Appraisal
(iv) Case Study

Possible Areas for Exploration

The larger political and economic forces isolate, bypass the local governance during the process of establishment of any proposed projects. Weather it is Tata, Jindal, POSCO, Birla or the State Government authority almost all the forces have neglected the local governance while establishing their major establishments in the weaker sections habited regions.

Even the tribal regions which fall under PESA, both the government and the industry have collaborated to negotiate directly with people without engaging village panchayats in the tribal areas. Therefore, it is an important area of research relating to exclusion of panchayat institutions in situations of political conflict or economic contestation. Research needs to address this field to generate insights on what happens to inclusion when local governance institutions themselves get excluded from the processes of development and governance.[3]

Case Studies

In this context this study explores two case studies. To a greater extent the Tribals of Odisha are driven by traditional way of life. Though Odisha has been subject to many new projects, dams or minings they are opposing the mega projects and tribals are the active supporter of this movement. Some Tribals have been actively engaged in the operational setup of the Naxal movement in Odisha which involves it damaging the property of multinational companies those are working in the tribal areas for their development.[4]

Conflict over the mining of bauxite in the Kashipur region of Rayagada district in southern Odisha had taken a violent turn with the killing of three innocent tribal people. On December 16, 2001 two platoons of armed police entered Maikanch village in Kashipur block and opened fire at the residents. Abhilas Jhodia (25), Raghu Jhodia (18) and Jamudhar Jhodia (43) died and eight others sustained serious injuries.[5]

Ever since the entry of multinational companies for bauxite mining and processing in 1993, the tribal people of Kashipur and Laxmipur blocks of Rayagada district, Dasmantpur block of Koraput district and Thuamulrampur of Kalahandi district have been apprehensive of displacement and loss of livelihood.[6]

Odisha is known for its rich mineral deposits. The assessed reserves of chromium and nickle ores and bauxite in the state constitute a substantial proportion of the total deposits of them in the country. Taking advantage of the process of liberalisation and the opening up of the economy, private companies set their sights on the Kashipur region, which has considerable concentration of bauxite. In the region, the Baphilimali hill is estimated to have a deposit of 1,957. 3 lakh tonnes of bauxite, Kadingamali 914 lakh tonnes, and the Sasubohumali hill 860 lakh tonnes. The Katuramali hill in nearby Thuamularmpur block has a deposit of 400 lakh tonnes. Utkal Alumina, a consortium of Indian Aluminium Company (INDAL) (now owned by HINDALCO, part of the Aditya Birla group), the Tatas (they pulled out in 1998), Hydro Aluminum of Norway (or Norsk Hydro) and ALCAN (Aluminum Canada), are in the forefront of the mining-related activities. The Odisha Mining Corporation, the state government organisation, has been sidelined in the process. In the case of Utkal Alumina, it is estimated that, 1,750 hectares of land will be required for mining, the plant site, a township and dumping spots. Apart from this, a stretch of land approximately 20 km long and 50 meters wide will be required for conveyer and corridor maintenance. The entire project is 100 per cent export-oriented.[7]

Unaware of Government rules, most of the tribal people do not register their land rights. In these areas land is broadly divided into two categories – forest and unsurveyed upland (Dongar). Upland constitutes about 60 per cent of the total land in tribal-dominated areas such as Rayagada, Koraput and Kondhamal. Such upland is considered unsuitable for cultivation and a record of right is not allowed in its case. Although the tribal people in the lowland areas own land, their rights are either not recorded or are recorded in the names of others. Illegal transactions of land are common and the tribal people are often at the receiving end.

Since the finalisation of the proposal, the Odisha government has actively tried to hand over the land to the companies. Government officials now say that the transfer of land has been made and that the tribal people have to vacate. Encouraged by the support from the State government and the local authorities, corporate houses claim that they are the real owners of the land.[8]

Displacement of populations, loss of livelihood and damage to the environment and ecology of the region, which have been the consequences of mining and industrial activities, were kept hidden from the outside world or presented in a misleading manner.

Concerned over the prospect of having to leave their hearth and home, people started organising themselves. Road blockades, demonstrations and dharnas were organised in front of government offices at Kashipur and Rayagada. Survey teams of the companies were denied access to the area. Day and night vigil was maintained to prevent the entry of the government and company officials.[9]

The responses of the tribal people were co-ordinated by organisations such as the Prakrutik Sampada Surkhya Parishad, the Baphilimali Surkhya Samiti and the Anchalika Surakhya Samiti. Every village had a resistance body.

The Administration visited Kashipur, Maikanch, Kucheipadar, Tikir, Rayagada town and other places and met a number of people. Meanwhile, under the direct patronisation of the companies, a pro-project group had also been formed. Those who fight for the rights of livelihood and against displacement were branded as people who oppose industrialisation and development. The pro-project group propagated the idea that the mining of bauxite was the only means for the area to cross the boundaries of backwardness. The tribal people were advised to sacrifice their "petty" rights in the "interest of the nation."[10]

The pro-mining group, which included professionals, traders, contractors and others, feel that the tribal people would have gained enormously with the implementation of the projects. The government machinery, which is supposed to protect the interests of the people, were not perceived as such but were identified with the strident moves of these groups, which were not affected by the projects.

The state machinery in Odisha appears to have capitulated to the designs of the companies. All the major political parties, the local administration and the police apparently act in concert to help them. "All-party committees" have been floated, with parties such as the Biju Janata Dal (BJD), the Bharatiya Janata Party (BJP) and the Congress (I) on them. Political leaders, police and administration officials visit the tribal areas; the tribal people alleged that they create panic among the residents.[11]

The December 16 incident was preceded by certain actions of an 'all-party committee", which the tribal people looked at with suspicion. On December 15, under the leadership of N. Bhaskar Rao, Rayagada district president of the BJD, and Krishna Mohapatro, a former block chairman of Kashipur, a group of people reached Maikanch and allegedly tried to disrupt a gathering of tribal people who were to discuss a "road blockade" (Chakajam) programme at Rafkana junction, 30 km away from Kashipur, scheduled for December 20. The Paribesh Sampad Surkhya Parishad planned the programme. The companies and the State administration obviously wanted to foil it.[12]

The people resisted the efforts to disrupt the meeting. On December 16, armed with a First Information Report (FIR) filed at the Kashipur police station, two platoons of armed policemen led by Circle Inspector Subash Swain and Kashipur Block Development officer (BDO) Golak Mohanty reached Maikanch. The policemen allegedly beat up the women and asked for the whereabouts of the men, who were hiding in the nearby hills, Hearing the commotion, the men returned from the hills. It was alleged that as soon as the policemen noticed the men, they opened fire.[13]

The version of the police and the administration was that the police party went to Maikanch to investigate the "attack" on Bhaskar Rao on December 15. Residents of the village attacked the police party by means of bows and arrows and threw stones at them, and this forced the police to open fire, it says. Several political parties, such as the BJD, the BJP and the Congress (I) and the State administration allege that a non-governmental organisation, Agragamee, which has been working among the tribal people of Kashipur, for about 20 years, and its director Achyut Das are inciting the tribal people to resort to violence and refuse to vacate the area. It is alleged that Agragamee planned the attack on BJD leaders. The BJD organised rallied and meetings at Rayagada demanding the arrest of Achyut Das and a ban on Agragamee. It is a fact that Agragamee played a role in raising the consciousness of the people, uniting them and making them aware of their rights.[14]

A three-member delegation of Left parties, comprising Ali Kishore Patnaik, member of the Odisha State secretariat of the Communist Party of India (Marxist), Pradipta Panda, CPI(M) Member of Legislative Assembly (MLA) and Biswanath Sahoo, former Communist Party of India (CPI) MLA, visited the area on December 19 and 20. It also met the Collector and District Magistrate at Rayagada.

On December 21, at a press conference convened in Bhubaneswar, the team members described the police firing as "pre-designed murder" to crush the movement against displacement. It was "murder" because all the three people who died received the bullets above the chest, they said. It cannot be disputed that the police opened fire as soon as they saw people coming down from the nearby hills because three cows and one buffalo that were grazing on the hillock also died. Naveen Patnaik government ordered an inquiry into the firing, which was conducted by a senior civil servant, Sanjeev Kumar Hota. Several organisations had protested against the killings and supported the tribal residents right to livelihood. At Berhampur, a daylong dharna was organised in front of the office of the Revenue Divisional Commissioner (Southern Division) by the Adivasi Dalit Vikas Manch on December 23. At Bhubaneswar similar protests were held by various NGOs. The resistance to the alumina project and the police firing had important implications.[15]

Ever since the entry of multinational companies, the tribal people of Odisha have been apprehensive of displacement and loss of livelihood. It has been a surprise for many that Odisha, which is so well situated and blessed with mineral riches, should be one of the poorest states in the country. In terms of industrialisation, it ranks below many of its smaller and less endowed neighbours. Odisha is the richest mineral state in the country. Therefore, Odisha is surely getting attention from big industries. Mineral rich Odisha has been demanding a second steel plant in Odisha after the Rourkela Steel Plant, which was set up in the fifties.

Since the finalisation of the Mega projects, the Odisha government has actively tried to handover the land to the companies. Encouraged by the support from the state government and the local authorities, corporate houses claim that they are the real owners of the land. Displacement of tribal populations, loss of livelihood and damage to the environment and ecology of the region, which have been the consequences of mining and industrial activities, were kept hidden from the outside world or presented in a misleading manner. Concerned over the prospect of having to leave their hearth and home, the tribal people started the organising road blockades, demonstrations and dharnas. On December 16, 2000, two platoons of armed police entered Maikanch village. In Kasipur block and open fired at the tribal. As a result, three innocent tribals died and others sustained serious injuries. Conflict over the displacement of the tribals in Kalinga Nagar region of Jajpur district in Odisha had taken a violent turn with the killings 12 tribals in January 2006. At the centre of controversy is a mega steel plant project, which is being persuaded by TATA steel.[16]

However, tribals of Odisha who stand to lose their homesteads, think differently. Livelihoods are closely tied with land in this region. Compensation could conceivably be awarded for homesteads that are lost at the projects. But these schemes are rather skewed in their application. Private land can be compensated for, but common and forest lands are not deemed to warrant material orders. Odisha also has a curious law, which holds that land situated on a gradient would not be eligible for compensation. But in order to ensure sustained development through a participatory and transparent process, Government of Odisha has framed a comprehensive resettlement and rehabilitation policy in 2006 after the Kalinga Nagar incident.

In the Kalinga Nagar incidence more than 11 tribals were killed opposing to industrialisation by the Tata group of companies. Also, it is natural that a closer contact with the masses would help the Maoists to engineer the economy of the area.

The land of tribals, for instance, in Odisha is owned through customary right. Ownership documents exist mainly for the plain lands and only customary rights are there for the land in the hill slopes, which means they do not have 'legally' defined ownership. Thus, even in the wake of proper compensatory measures, many of the tribal people would be left out from the compensation, as they do not have 'legal' ownership. On the other hand, land is seen as inalienable resource for the livelihoods of the tribal people. Apart from providing them with sustainable livelihood, the land also provides them with freedom to work independently according to their needs. This dependence on land and forest produce has relatively isolated the tribal people from the mainstream economy. In other words the absence of modern legal system denotes the weak penetration of modernisation in this region. In recognition of this tradition, the Indian state provides statutory guarantees under V Schedule of the Constitution; where in tribal land cannot be sold or bought by a non-tribal. However, in UAIL case the rule was bent to suit the needs of industrialisation and development.[17]

The tribal people generally cultivate both plain and hill lands to enable them to different crops. Land forms a very important and crucial aspect of tribal life – land is the basis for the formation of their culture, economy, society and their polity. To quote:

"Our life, culture, and employment everything revolves around the soil. In the month of Asadha (signifying the rainy season) we have Kulimaruparba, we get the root of the crop home and worship it. In the month of Bhoda (the following month) we worship maize. From making the plough to agriculture work, we do everything together. So there is peace in our village. But once industrialisation starts, our festivals will vanish and our region will be destroyed.... We will get jobs, but who will do the cultivation? People will eat money or what? We cultivate; therefore we eat." (Buka Miniaka, a tribal of Kashipur says,)[18]

The tribal people believe that they can be free and independent as long as they own the land. Dangar is the widely practised mode of cultivation.[19] They grow different varieties of paddy, maize, and various types of pulses and oil seeds like, *kandul, masur, mung, chana, alsi, castor, mustard*, etc. As most of the villages are surrounded by perennial springs on all the four sides, water is available throughout the year. Their food habits are in tune with the crops that they cultivate. In the morning, generally, they have *mandia paej* (gruel prepared out of *ragi*), which is also their staple food. Rice with some cereal forms is another major part of their food. However, since the last one decade, there is also increase in the cultivation of various vegetables. As a result something or the other is available around the year. Apart from this, they also grow various roots and tubers in their kitchen gardens, which also form their staple food. Whatever is available through agriculture activity is not accumulated in the modern sense, but exchanged in return for other goods.[20]

Whose Development...?

The state in India looks at the development process, particularly, as a part of modernisation.[21] Hasan (2000) argues that the Indian state pursued twin goals through the process of development: unifying the nation and social transformation. These two objectives were crucial as the Indian state was formed on modern premise with a traditional society as base. On the other hand, the movement by way of questioning the process of development appears to be also questioning the basis of modernisation itself. But the question remains whether the movement is articulating tradition against modernisation or is it just struggling for alternative notion of development that is inclusive of tribal identity and culture within it.[22]

"We have seen big projects in our Odisha like Indravati project and NALCO project. We have heard about Hirakud and Upper Kolab hydro projects. We have seen deprivation and sorrow of local people caused by these development projects. In our view development means that all should live peacefully and happily. But that some should die for development – we do not require this kind of development." This is the opinion of Bhagaban Majhi: a tribal of Kashipur.[23] Thus, any meaningful development needs to recognise the rights of the tribal people over land, forest, and other resources that are related directly and indirectly to their livelihood. To sum up, in the words of one tribal woman: What is development? Whose development? Does development imply cars and vehicles for everyone? The Chief Minister and others may need cars but why does everybody need it? Is it possible to give cars and vehicles to everyone? We don't need cars and motors. We are people of the soil and our lives revolve around the soil (Bulka Miniaka).[24] Thus for the tribal people development is something that has livelihood, land, water, forests, culture, identity, history, community, freedom, as the key ingredients.[25]

Why Encounter between the State and Tribal Communities?

PESA Act 1996 (Panchayat Extension to Scheduled Areas Act) extends Panchayats to the tribal areas of eight states of India namely, Andhra Pradesh, Bihar, Gujarat, Himachal Pradesh, Maharashtra, Madhya Pradesh, Odisha and

Rajasthan with the intention to enable tribal society to assume control over their own destiny to preserve and conserve their traditional rights over natural resources.

However, most states have been indifferent to the Act as well as corresponding transfer of powers the tribal population (to access and utilise natural resources for consumption and livelihood). Women, dalit and tribal have suffered social and economic marginalisation for a long time and therefore are considered for affirmative action. Particularly in the rural setting, the socio-economic hierarchies are inter-related. Hence, the groups who occupy low position in social hierarchy such as dalit, women, and tribal also invariably occupy low position in economic hierarchy.

The larger macro political and economic context in which local governments operate:

How local governments can or cannot promote inclusion in the contexts of (a) violent conflicts and political unrest, and (b) neo-liberal economic growth, globalisation and commoditisation of commons such as land, water and forests.

(a) Despite India being a stable democracy, political conflicts have festered in specific regional contexts. Two types of conflicts have been most visible and have escalated in the recent times—the armed conflict in the North Eastern region which has taken the shape of separatist movements; and conflicts between the state and the Maoist groups (popularly known as Naxalites) in Chhatisgarh, Jharkhand, Odisha and Andhra Pradesh where the Maoist groups claiming to be supporters of the poor have launched violent assault against the government. It is imperative to explore how political contexts as described above affect the functioning of local governments and implications of this for the resource poor communities and those considered being most vulnerable to unrest such as poor and women.

(b) Economic conflicts between those whose resources are threatened by rapid economic growth agenda of neo-liberalism and globalisation, and those who are actively pursuing these have intensified in recent times.

In pursuing economic growth panchayats as local decision-making institutions are either bypassed or co-opted by the economically powerful forces in executing their agenda. In many parts of India this has resulted in contestations spearheaded by those who are threatened with loosing the resources on which their survival depends. Examples include Singur and Nandigram in West Bengal and Kalinga Nagar in Odisha where the Special Economic Zones are contested by people; in tribal areas of Odisha mining operations by multinationals have faced opposition from local people. In other parts of India, it is not entirely unknown for financial incentives in the short run inducing a peaceful cooption of the panchayats in the neo-liberal agenda of the state but in the long run carrying with the possibility of the communities losing control over their natural resources.[26]

Impact of Development Projects on Displaced Tribals

On the basis of the empirical study conducted on the displaced families, the following are some of the important impacts that have been revealed from the analysis of data by the researcher:

1. *Decline in Joint Family System:* The pre-displacement level of nuclear and joint families was changed in both tribal and non-tribal families showing the same trend of breaking down of joint family to nuclear families. This is a general feature noticed in most of the development projects.

2. *Landlessness:* India being a farm dominated society with agriculture as the main occupation, displacement from land, removes the main foundation on which people's productive systems, commercial activities and livelihood are based. Unless this foundation is reconstructed elsewhere or replaced by steady income-generating employment, landlessness sets in and the affected families are impoverished. In most of the cases/ projects, land for land, norm could not be followed. But cash compensation is inadequate to make up for the loss of land. This impact has serious implication in the current project under study and therefore needs special consideration by the project implementing agencies in general and the policy makers formulating strategies for the impacted people of development projects at government level.

3. *Joblessness and increase in the proportion of workers:* When people were displaced from their habitat, they lose their means of livelihood. Creation of new jobs or alternative sources of income for them becomes very difficult since the oustees do not possess any skill to learn new methods of earning their livelihood. Hence those who were owners of the means of production before displacement have now become daily wage earners. In these projects, taken up for the study, though the project authorities followed the policy of providing a job to each displaced family, the other members of the displaced families remained jobless. The policy also discriminated against the landless labourers, artisans, share croppers and petty businessmen among others.

4. *Homelessness:* Loss of house and shelter may be only temporary during the transition period for most of the displaced. But for some, homelessness remains a permanent feature. The project authorities only provided homestead plots while the displaced persons have themselves built their houses. Again when a split occurs in the family, those who leave the family become homeless.

5. *Food insecurity:* Forced displacement increases the risk of chronic food insecurity. In India, crops are grown to provide food to the family while vegetables are grown in the kitchen gardens that take care of the food needs of the family. Surplus is also sold in the market. But forced displacements deprive the oustees from their former resource of livelihood rendering them landless. Even when homestead land was provided, the oustees could not properly reclaim and level the hilly area. In the LB Valley project, the displaced families have to buy everything including food items from the market.

6. *Loss of access to common property:* For the poor people, particularly, the landless and otherwise asset less people, loss of access to common property (forest lands, water bodies, grazing land, etc.) leads to a major deterioration in their income and livelihood levels. Such lost resources are rarely compensated by the Government in the relocation sites. There are also frequent conflicts between the host population and new settlers over the use of forest land and other government land. As a result, the resettler do not get fuel wood and other minor forest produce, which they used to collect from the forests in their old habitat.

7. *Social Disintegration:* Forced displacement tears apart the social fabric of the oustees. Production systems are dismantled, kinship groups and family systems are often scattered and cultural identity of the people is under threat. Social and community networks that help people to cope with poverty through exchange of food and clothing, mutual help with farming, building houses and caring children are disrupted. Social disintegration has been a major impoverishment risk in all the projects undertaken. In the LB Valley project, the mutual help arrangement and other socio-economic relationships have been totally disrupted.

8. *Increased Morbidity and Mortality:* Loss of ancestral and homestead land, less no access to health care facilities, the psychological trauma caused thereby and the food insecurity together often leads to serious diseases. There is also the danger of parasitic and vector born diseases in the relocated sites because of unsafe water, poor sewerage etc. In fact, lack of food, unhygienic living and environmental degradation in the new place were found in the project area to have a serious impact on the health of the oustees. In these projects, pollution caused by coal dust and frequent blasting has caused skin diseases, eye irritation, gastric disorders, diarrhoea and other ailments. Though medical centers have been opened in the resettlement colony they are dysfunctional in the absence of the doctors. The findings of empirical study in the project resettlement areas and the analysis of the empirical data gathered from the study reveals that the following situation prevails in the resettlement area and to the displaced people in general and the tribal displaced families in particular (as majority of the sample households were tribals): [27]

- The general socio-economic condition of the oustees has deteriorated significantly.
- Socio-economic inequalities have widened.
- The cropping pattern has changed drastically.
- Dependence on trees and livestock has reduced substantially.
- Increase in the proportion of agricultural labourers.
- Increasing trend towards nuclear family.
- Poor dwelling conditions of the oustees.
- Improper use of compensation money.
- Rise in the incidence of indebtedness.

- Drastic reduction in the socio-economic condition of women in the PAFs.

Conclusion

In view of these after effects of displacement, especially on the tribals it is necessary not only to identify, avoid and mitigate risks in each development project that entails displacement, but also to focus on benefits over and above compensation and rehabilitation for damages as well as benefit sharing arrangement. A prudent approach demands long term commitments, financial and institutional guarantees and the use of professional approach in dealing with the issues of social development of indigenous people. Constant monitoring by technically competent independent observers can go a long way in ensuring more effective resettlement and rehabilitation arrangements in case of the displaced families which can end up in not only restoring the pre-displaced living condition of the millions of displaced families but also in substantially bringing in improvement in their socio-economic condition in the post-project period.

Notes

1. Rajashree Mahanty. "Impact of development project on displaced tribal: A case study of a development project in Eastern India". Odisha review, Sep-Oct 2011, pp. 67-68.
2. Alcan, (2006), "Backgrounder: The Utkal Project", http://www.business-humanrights.org downloaded on 07-05-07.
3. Syed S. Kazi, "Displacement and Rehabilitation", in civil services chronicle, (English monthly), Vol. XVI, No.12, New Delhi, Jun. 2006, p. 26.
4. Adivasi, Journal of the Scheduled Castes and Scheduled Tribes Research and Training Institute, Bhubaneswar, Vol. 46, No. 2, December 2006, Editorial page.
5. Nair, Suresh, "AV Birla group begins work on Utkal project", Economic Times, April 14, 2004. Norwatch Newsletter, 1-96 at www.norwatch.no
6. Bulliyya, G. J. K. Nayak and G. Mallick, (2005), "Forest Habitat and Tribal Subsistence Economy Rights in Scheduled Tribal-Domain State of Odisha", Man in India, 85, (3 and 4), pp. 125-139.
7. Das, Achyut and Vidya Das, "Chronicle of a Struggle – the Kashipur Anti-Mining Movement", <http://www.sanctuaryasia.com> downloaded on 07-05-07.
8. Prafulla Das, "Odisha the fight continues" the Hindu Survey of the Environment (Annual Issue 2006), New Delhi, p. 100.
9. Manoranjan Mahanty, "KBK to Kalinga Nagar a Dangerous Drift for Odisha and India", in main-stream (English Weekly), New Delhi, Vol. XLIV, No. 43, October 13-19, 2006, p. 25.
10. Dr Snehalata Panda, "Socio-economic profile and Development of tribals in Odisha", in Kurukshetra, (English monthly). Vol. 55, No. New Delhi, August 2007, p. 32.

11. Prafulla Das, "Odisha the fight continues" the Hindu Survey of the Environment (Annual Issue 2006), New Delhi, p. 100.

12. Trilochan Sahoo, "Industrialisation and Displacement in Odisha", Adivasi, *op. cti.*, pp. 133-134.

13. Mahapatra, L.K. (1991). "Development for Whom? Depriving the Dispossessed Tribals's." Social Action, 41(3): July-Sept, pp. 271-288.

14. Ramesh, K.S (1998). "Resettlement and Rehabilitation of Family Displaced by Development Projects: Corporate Social Responsibility." ASCI Journal of Management, 28(1): pp. 29-36.

15. R.C. Pandit, "Development vs. Displacement of Tribals people in india and problems and prospects". New Delhi, 2009. p. 179.

16. Fernandes, Walter (1996). "Land Reforms Ownership Pattern and Alienation of Tribals Livelihood." Social Action, 46(4): Oct-Dec.

17. Rajashree Mahanty. "Impact of Development Project in Eastern India. Sep-Oct 2011 (Odisha Review), p. 68.

18. Buka Miniaka, a tribal of Kashipur says Dangar is slash and burn cultivation. Each village has a traditionally demarcated area for dangar use of the people of that particular village. If the possessor of the land does not use it for consecutively for two years, then the village community will decide about its redistribution.

19. Syed. S. Kazi, "Displacement and Rehabilitation," in civil services chronicle, (English monthly), Vol. xvi, No. 12, New Delhi. June 2006, p. 26.

20. Hasan, Zoya, ed., (2000), Politics and the State in India: Readings in Indian Government and Politics-3, New Delhi: Sage Publications.

21. Hasan, Zoya, ed., (2000), Politics and the State in India: Readings in Indian Government and Politics-3, New Delhi: Sage Publications.

22. Bhagaban Majhi: a tribal of Kashipur.

23. Bulka Miniaka: a tribal of Kashipur says.

24. Samal, K.C. (1998). Poverty Alleviation after liberalisation: Study of a Tribals Block in Odisha. EPW, Vol. XXXIII, No. 28, July 11, pp. 1947.

25. Indian People's Tribunal Report on Environment and Human Rights, (2006), Kashipur: An Enquiry into Mining and Human Rights Violations in Kashipur, Odisha, IPT, Mumbai.

26. Mishra, Banikanta (2006), "People's Movement at Kalinganagars; An epitaph or an Epitome?" Economic and Political weekly, Vol. XLI. No. 7, Feb 18, pp. 551-554.

27. Pathy, Jaganath, (1992), "Articulation of Capitalism and Destitution of the Scheduled Tribes of India", in Buddhadeb Chaudhuri, ed., Tribal Transformation in India: Economy and Agrarian Issues, Vol-I, inter-India Publications, New Delhi, pp. 488-495.

11

Ramoshi the Denotified Tribe in India: Understanding their Struggle and Politics of Exclusion

Dattatary Bhandalkar

Abstract

This paper is a sincere attempt to bring to the forefront the voices and experiences of the Ramoshi tribes in Maharashtra about being "Denotified" in society. The 'Ex-criminal Tribes' of India, now referred as 'Denotified' tribes, comprise a significant population who were once declared as 'Criminals' by the British with the enactment of Criminal Tribes Act, 1871. They continue to remain stigmatised and discriminated by dominant sections, deprived of access and excluded of opportunities to exercise the basic human rights. Caste as a character of societal structure played a significant role. The interplay of caste and power relations in society affected the community in context of livelihood, access to common resources in villages, employment opportunities, ownership of land, participation and representation in village panchayat.

The paper interestingly shows how ancestral labelling gradually affects their lives in context of acceptance, being viewed as 'Others' in society and follows with occupational crisis, under representation in local self-governance, resulting into poverty and marginalisation of the population. The paper is a reflection of the field reality of the Denotified tribes and explains their situation through their lenses. The paper emerged out of an empirical research, with a qualitative approach, exploratory research design, undertaken with the Ramoshi tribes in Maharashtra. It highlights the politics of exclusion experienced by the tribes from treatment by dominant others in society to participation in village, experiences of land alienation, displacement and migration over years to ill-treatment by police officials. The paper exemplifies the existence of power relations and interplay of caste politics with the reality of being treated unfairly and indifferently in society. It reflects on the historical background of the tribe and how it is still affecting the community eventually leading to construction of labeling and exclusion of the tribe.

The Denotified Tribes in India– A History of Exclusion

The tribal of our nation are known for their diverse and rich culture and practices. However, the reality of the tribes in our country has gradually changed over the years. Among many tribal communities in India a significant population of marginalised tribal communities were once classified and declared as 'Criminal Tribes' with the declaration of Criminal Tribes Act in 1871. With the enactment of the Act, these tribesmen were registered and notified as 'Criminals' in society. Their movements and actions were restricted by the British government; elaborate arrangements were made for their supervision and settlements were made in different corners of the country to separate them from other sections of society. A majority of this tribe still exhibit their primitive and ethnic traits. Many of them still live in tribal groups, wander from one place to another in search of livelihood and they do not have any permanent home of their own. They have specific rituals, beliefs, religious practices of their own and those are unique to themselves. Neither globalisation, liberalisation nor any social advancement could improve their conditions to a significant extent. Although the government of independent India officially 'Denotified' these tribes in 1952, it made no provisions for improving their situations. The CTA gave the police arbitrary powers to even kill members of the declared 'criminal' tribes. Although the notified criminal tribes were 'denotified' the communities are not categorised under the constitutional schedules like the scheduled caste and scheduled tribes. Some de-notified and nomadic communities have been included in the respective state lists of SCs and STs. However, there is no uniformity in the status of these tribes across the country. The human rights violations against the DNTs are not covered by legislation such as the Scheduled Castes and Scheduled Tribes (Prevention of Atrocities) Act (1989) that protects the SCs and STs. The DNTs do not possess traditional land rights or house titles. The tribal population being majorly nomadic in nature yet; is not included in the census of the country. They remain denied of citizenship rights including voting rights. They are mostly engaged in informal means of livelihood. Presently, there are 198 denotified tribes in India, with 14 such communities in Maharashtra (Rathod, 2000). These groups of communities are scattered in nature and mostly situated in the drought prone areas. These tribesmen are not just a neglected section of our society but a complex one as well. Their problems are not only grounded in contemporary reality, but also deeply rooted in history. They have suffered injustices at the hands of both polity and society; their issues have not been sufficiently redressed as well. They are still being treated as criminals by birth and subjected to harassment and persecution at the hands of the police and the state machinery. In the backdrop of prolonged conflict in context of caste system in India, a significant population group has been oppressed; they are subject to stigma, discrimination and their social, economic and political rights have been violated strikingly. There is an immense need to explore and understand the issues of the de-notified population in India and address them to ensure justice to these ethnic groups.

The *Ramoshis* of Maharashtra

The *Ramoshi* tribe is one among many tribal communities who were declared as "criminal tribes" in Maharashtra and further classified as 'Denotified tribes' in post independence era. The *Ramoshis* were known as 'warrior tribes' and were majorly a wandering population with their traditional occupation being hunters, gatherers and guardsmen. These tribes primarily belonged to Karnataka, Madhya Pradesh, Andhra Pradesh and Maharashtra. The *Ramoshis* in Karnataka and Andhra Pradesh were referred as *Berad* and *Boya*. The *Ramoshis* in Maharashtra are majorly concentrated in areas of Satara, Solapur, Sangli and Purander Taluka in Pune. With the declaration of the Criminal Tribes Act, 1871, the *Ramoshis* along with many other tribal communities were notified as criminals in society. Although post-independence, the tribes were decriminalised, they were further classified and notified as 'Habitual Offenders' with the declaration of the Habitual Offenders Act, 1959 and later notified further as 'Denotified tribes'. The process of labeling and notifying the *Ramoshis* continued even after decriminalisation. The tribe remains identified as 'Criminal tribes' even today and face stigma and exclusion both in the hands of polity and society.

The *Ramoshis* were warrior tribes and were associated with many empires and majorly used to work as warriors fighting battles, as hunters, protecting watchmen and guards for properties of emperors. They were often referred as '*Bedar*' meaning fearless. The *Ramoshis*, once included in the Criminal Tribe category of Bombay Presidency, were involved in uprisings against the British. The tribe primarily used to reside in the forests, away from the villages. They were known for their valor during the Maratha Empire. The changes of the British National Forest Policy during the early nineteenth century created conflicts over forest use. The *Ramoshis* with their traditional occupation on force of arms and with poor skills to earn livelihood were forced into criminal livelihoods. The tribe organised themselves and revolted against the British. The rising protest and fight against the British alarmed them and eventually the Criminal Tribes Act, 1871 was declared. As per the Census of 1901, their population was 60,555 of which 31,444 were males and 29,111 were females

(Singh, 2004). The *Ramoshis* were the first among many other de-notified tribes in Maharashtra, who started settling down in villages post independence era. Some of them continued staying in the settlements, while others started migrating to other places in Maharashtra in search of their livelihood. They were majorly an unsettled population then, without lands and without any means to earn their livelihood. However, although over the years the tribe gradually settled in the villages, the stigma of criminality attached to the community continues and the tribe continue facing stigma and exclusion in the hands of the polity and society.

The Unheard Voices

The Denotified tribes are indigenous population and are distinguished in relation to their ancestry, their livelihood patterns, their nomadic nature and many other distinct features. The tribes before the colonial era were distinguished by such features, but during the colonisation period with the declaration of Criminal Tribes Act (CTA), 1871, the tribes were classified and tagged as 'Criminal' in society. The tribes were majorly engaged in hunting before the British colonisation, but with the changes of the British National Forest Policy, their livelihood was compromised. The tribes lacked any other skills for earning their livelihood. Their revolt against the British led to declaration of the CTA to get control over movements and actions of these tribes and settlements were built to capture them and keep in isolation, segregated from rest of society. This was the turning point which affected not only the existing population at that point of time but continues to influence the tribal population even today. The act of declaration and tagging a large group of tribal population resulted into restriction in movement and freedom of the tribes, people started perceiving them differently in society. The tribe began to be seen as 'Others' in society.

Interplay of Caste and Power

The Caste System in India is unique to our country which classifies individuals before their birth. This classification started with the Varna system which classified people based on their occupations and tagged them as 'lower' and upper' castes. The occupation based caste system in India had fixed job for all in society based on the caste they are born with. The denotified tribes majorly wandering in nature had hunting as their primary occupation. An elderly village member who belonged from outside the tribal community added that—

According to *Balutedari* (*Jajmani* system) there were fixed jobs for each community but not for the *Ramoshis*. So they started stealing for upper caste communities, providing them security, guard them from other powerful people in society and others. In British era the *Ramoshis* used to work for *sahukar*, rich people of the village. They used to plunder rich travelers, rich people of other villages and they used to offer the entire wealth to the *sahukar*. The *sahukars* in return used to give grains and other groceries for their family.

The participant's response reflects the struggle of the tribe for basic necessities like grains, groceries for their families and how for earning the basic necessity the tribe indulges into criminal activities. Livelihood crisis at a large level leads to poverty which in turn compels their involvement in many other illegal activities like production of illegal liquor, smuggling of river sands etc. With great despair one of the participants reflect —

"Each family has three or four children, how would they feed them? Now here in these villages if you see, our community is majorly engaged in illegal liquor business".

The tribe remains in the circle of poverty and marginalisation due to several social, economic and political factors playing in the situation. A majority of the respondents shared experiences that how their family has been affected due to nomadic nature and historical background of the tribes. The tribesmen in recent days are also involved in illegal ways of liquor production in villages. They are quite often arrested by policemen. In such cases their wife and children continue the business. Due to nomadic lifestyle and criminalisation of the community, children also face discrimination in schools. This affects their education. Some of the respondents said that due to high consumption of alcohol among youth, death at an early age is also common. The wives are left alone at a very early age with children. Hence the historical background of the community, recent business involvement in liquor production, habits of alcohol consumption affects the family system of the *Ramoshis*.

An old man belonging to *Ramoshi* community remarked with great annoyance about the condition of the tribe and how Caste as a dominant factor interplayed in the situation of the Denotified tribes.

We were not criminals. For earning our livelihood we used to work for upper caste. At times due to extreme livelihood crisis we used to get involved in crime. The upper caste people took this opportunity and forced us for all kinds of illegal activities, theft, plundering, crime etc. But we have to change and society should accept us as we are. Police played the biggest role in the criminalisation of *Ramoshis*. Still our people go for petty work at their home; we have to come out of this '*gulami*'. They also took our land from us but still we are working for them.

The response shows his annoyance. He emphasises by saying that they are not criminals and the livelihood crisis compelled their involvement in crime. He clearly mentions about how the dominant upper castes interplayed into the situation leading to increased involvement in crime. The power dynamics existing in the village affected the *Ramoshi* population not only in terms of their livelihood but also access to common resources in villages, employment opportunities, ownership of land, participation and representation in village Panchayats. The responses of the participants show that the tribe also experienced land alienation and hence had no opportunity of cultivation to earn their livelihood. In many cases the participants reported of their land being taken away by the dominant sections in the village and the tribe continued working as wage labourers in their lands in exchange of grains for their families. Some of the participants also reported of being displaced of their own land and they were forced to stay outside the main territory of the village. The researcher also observed that the location of houses of the *Ramoshi* community were outside the village territory, separate from all other houses in the village. The oppression was not only from the dominant castes of the village but also the police personnel. Other responses of the participants indicate that the treatment of police personnel towards the tribes were also to dominate, marginalise and stigmatise them rather being just to their concerns. Many times the tribesmen are arrested only on basis of suspicion by virtue of being labeled in history as 'Criminal Tribes'.

Perception as 'Others' in Society

The treatment of police personnel and other dominant castes resulted into building up of a negative image of the tribe in society. The tribe was perceived as different from others; others who have a criminal involvement and hence they have been identified as 'Criminals' in society. The demonstration of this image is visible in everyday acts of their lives like the location of their houses being outside the village territory, no involvement in village activities, no participation in Village Panchayat, no participation in village meetings and other decision making processes. These actions due to dominance of upper castes and ill-treatment of police personnel create also a perception of 'them' among the tribes. The tribesmen start perceiving themselves as 'others' different from the rest in society. It leads to formation of a self-concept and they construct an identity of themselves as deviant in society. With a deep sigh, the participants respond that their being deviant in society earns their livelihood, gets those grains from the upper caste.

Struggle for Constitutional Status

The several versions of the Criminal Tribes Act never recommended any provision for the betterment of the tribe, rather continued classifying and re-classifying them. No efforts have also been taken over years to develop a means to protect these tribes form atrocities. No special constitutional remedies have been suggested so far for the 'Denotified' tribes as a special group. In some state they are included in scheduled caste, some in scheduled tribes, majorly in other backward classes. In Maharashtra, a special group has been created as 'Denotified and Nomadic' (DNT) community classified as '*Vimukta Jati*'. Due to the wandering nature of the community and hunter and gatherers being primarily their traditional occupation over years, the tribe is not house listed and in most cases do not have any proof of identification losing their voting rights. As responded by one of the participants, they are treated as 'un-registered citizens' who have no access to exercise their basic rights.

For years many non-governmental organisations along with several commissions set up by government have been trying to put forth the major concerns of the tribal population with recommendations to make special provision for the Denotified population. With special constitutional remedies, safeguards the core issues of the tribe could be addressed; their issues of stigma, discrimination, ill treatment by police personnel, domination of other castes, livelihood crisis, problems of unemployment, poor skills, low income etc., could be holistically addressed. The atrocities with the de-notified tribes is also very high, however no safeguards in forms of laws are available to the tribe. Their cases are not registered, rather they are often arrested on cases not proven guilty based only on suspicion of the police by virtue of belonging to the tribes.

Living with Exclusion

The responses about the historical background of the community across the case studies suggest that the Criminal Tribes Act 1871 played a significant role in the lives of the *Ramoshis*. It was a turning point in history of *Ramoshis* since they were declared legally as criminals in society by the British. This action imposed the Label of criminal upon *Ramoshis*. This labelling began in history with the declaration of the Act which continued over the years.

The voices of the participants reflect interestingly the *emergence of themes* like History of the community, involvement in crime, occupational crisis, treatment of Police officials, stigma and discrimination leading to formation of perception among others and them and under representation in local self-governance. The reflections from the field elaborate the cycle of life of the *Ramoshis* beginning from criminalisation due to ancestral labeling, leading to stigma and discrimination in society, following with occupation crisis and involvement in crime, with poor participation and no representation in village decision-making leading to exclusion of the population from the society. Exclusion is a complex and multi-dimensional concept associated with several other structural problems in society like poverty, inequality, discrimination and marginalisation, etc., power is an important aspect which interplays between groups leading to exclusion. The process of exclusion involved two groups – the one who holds the power to exclude and the other who is excluded. This process works through systematic way through the agencies of society like state, police, courts etc. This further leads to cumulative form of exclusion.

The responses of the participants about the background of the community emphasised that due to wandering nature of the tribes and occupation based caste system adhered to the tribe, they were majorly involved in occupations like watchmen and guards post independence. They used to work for the upper dominant castes in guarding their properties etc. During the struggle for freedom with the British, the tribe was involved in the uprising against the British in the leadership of *Umaji Naik.* They also worked as brave warriors in the Maratha leadership. However post independence, after the repeal of the Criminal Tribes Act and enactment of the Habitual Offenders Act, the tribesmen were distributed with lands, decriminalising them but further classifying them into 'De-notified' tribes. The lands given were majorly in hilly areas and not fertile enough for cultivation to earn their livelihood. They continued remaining stigmatised and were often compelled by the dominant sections to work for their personal advantages.

The history of the community eventually led to entanglement in criminalisation of the tribe and their occupational patterns were compromised. The occupation based caste system played a significant role in shaping the occupational pattern of the *Ramoshis.* Regarding the present occupation status of the *Ramoshis*, the responses of the participants highlight that some of the Ramoshis work as cheap agricultural labors in the fields of other dominant castes in the villages, some of them run illegal liquor business and are themselves victims of substance abuse. The participants report of experiences of land alienation and how they are forced to live outside the village territory. Being forced to stay outside the village territory, they are also excluded from involvement and participation in village activities, meetings etc and have no voice in the village Panchayat. The participants report that the *Ramoshi* tribe was majorly nomadic in nature and post-declaration they were imprisoned in settlements where they had hardly any freedom. The tribe soon ran away from the settlements. They did not have any specific skill and according to the Jajmani (Balutedari) system prevalent during that period, all castes had specific jobs to earn their livelihood. Once labeled, it was difficult for them to get employment and they started working for upper caste communities, who used them for personal purposes. The *Ramoshis* involved in criminal activities like theft, plundering, kidnapping, blackmailing etc. The Policemen and other dominant sections in the villages continued oppressing them. They used to offer food grains and crops in exchange of criminal activities. The *Ramoshis* in order to feed their family continued their involvement in crime.

The location of houses of *Ramoshis* in villages was majorly outside the village, away from the main village. The responses of the participants emphasised that this was majorly due to low acceptance of the community in the village. Being located outside the village also restricted involvement of the *Ramoshis* in village activities. Thus the occupational pattern, oppression by upper castes, the general perception of people from other communities contributed significantly in stigmatising the community. They continue being subject to discrimination even today. Some of the participants expressed that sometimes even though the *Ramoshis* are not involved in agricultural theft, they were observed suspiciously by other communities. Even policemen arrest them without any formal procedure but on prior assumptions based on their historical background.

The involvement in village activities and representation in panchayat meetings or bodies were merely there. They were not included in any village meetings and hence had no voices in decision making process of the village. There was no representation of the tribe at the Panchayat level. Their voices remain unheard even today. Under representation in Panchayat levels as well as in village meetings prevents their issues to be brought up and discussed in society at large. Although days have passed, times has changed, the label of criminal is still attached to the community affecting their everyday lives. The reality of being 'un-registered' as citizens due to lack of proof of identification makes them vulnerable in the hands of the police and other state machinery. They have no voice in democracy due to no or poor representation in the political system. They are majorly scattered population and move around from one village to the other in search of livelihood. There is a need to mobilise them as groups to represent their population and voice their opinions. However being less mobilised and scattered in nature, their participation in democracy is lost. Their voices still remain unheard.

Conclusion

The Denotified tribes in India, although have been decriminalised post-independence with the repeal of the CTA, 1871, the population continues to live with stigma and exclusion even today. The population got deeply affected due to the history attached to the community during the British colonisation period. The changing law and order during the British period affected not only the livelihoods of the population then, but continues to affect the present generation of denotified tribes in terms of their education, employment, livelihood, acceptance in society and denies their basic rights. Although the population was decriminalised post-independence, no efforts were taken to improve the situation of the tribes with any amendments in the constitution providing safeguards considering them as separate groups. The process of ancestral labeling began with declaration of the CTA and the process continued affecting the population over generations. The responses of the participants elaborate on the ill-treatment of the local police officials and other dominant castes in the village towards these tribes. However no provision has been made so far for protecting the population from the atrocities. The population being wandering in nature traditionally continues to move from one to the other even today. Those who have gradually settled down in villages majorly reside in hilly or drought prone areas. The responses of the participants also report of land alienation and hence either they work as cheap labourers in their own lands or keep wandering for earning their livelihoods. They are not house listed and remain excluded from the census. They lose their voting rights and their voices are hardly reflected in the democracy. Representation of the population even at Panchayat levels is very poor. They live in temporary huts or sheds outside the villages and not much involved in the village activities or Panchayat meetings. They under-representation in governance even at village levels restrain their opinions being considered in democracy. The population continues to struggle for earning their basic livelihoods and entitlement of the rights of the de-notified population is still a far achieved dream.

References

Abraham, Susan (1999), Steal or I'll call you a thief 'criminal' Tribes of India, economic and political weekly.

Bates Crispin, (1995) '*Race, Caste and Tribe in Central India: the Early Origins of Indian Anthropometry*', International Standard Book Number.

Bharal, G.P. Denotified Communities and their Problems of Rehabilitation, Indian Journal of Social Work, Vol. 28 (4), 1968, pp. 353-362.

Bokil, Milind (2002), De-Notified and Nomadic Tribes: A Perspective, Economic and Political Weekly, Vol. 37, No. 2 (Jan. 12-18), pp. 148-154.

Dandekar Ajay, (2009), '*Disenfranchised by History: The Tribes and their Narratives*'. Publisher: Muukt-Saad.

D'souza, Dilip. (2001), Branded by Law, Penguin Books India, New Delhi.

Draxe, P. B. (2005), Afailed Revolt against the Raj: the Rebellion of the Berad, A Criminal Tribe, under the Leadership of Umaji Naik. Sage Publication.

Criminal Tribes Act, 1871: Act XXVII. British Library, Oriental and India Office Collections, Shelfmark V/8/42.

Jha, Arvind Kumar, (2010), Formal Education and Pardhi Tribe's Culture in Mulshingi of Kolhapur, Maharashtra, Afro Asian Journal of Anthropology and Social Policy Vol. 1, No. 2, July- December, 161-165.

Mackintosh, Captain Alexander, (1833), '*An Account of the Origin and Present Condition of the Tribe of Ramoossies*'. American Mission Press, 1883.

Mehta, B. H. Ex-Criminal Groups in India, Indian Journal of Social Work,Vol. 16 (1), 1955, pp. 10-18.

Radhakrishna, Meena (2006), Criminal Tribes and the Debates on Criminal Law Criminal Tribes Act, 1871: The Construction of an Indian Criminal, working paper of social sciences.

Ratthod, Motiraj (2000), Denotified and Nomadic Tribes in Maharashtra, The Denotified and Nomatic Tribes Rights Action Group Newsletter Published by DNT Rights Action Group.

Simhadri, Y. C. Differential Association and Denotified Tribes, Indian Journal of Social Work, Vol. 39 (2), 1978, pp. 161-174.

Simhadri, Y. C. Caste and denotified Tribes, Indian Journal of Social Work, Vol. 37 (4), 1977, pp. 373-383.

Simhadri, Y. C. Ex-criminal Tribes and Criminological Theories, Indian Journal of Social Work, Vol. 34 (2), 1973, pp. 107-112.

Simhadri, Y.C. (1991), Denotified Tribes, Classical Publishing Company, New Delhi

Singh, K.S. Bhanu, B.V. (2004), '*Anthropological Survey of India, People of India: Maharashtra'*, Vol. 3. Popular Prakashan.

12

Social Exclusion and Marginal Communities: Some Reflection on Development Induced Displacement in India

Niharranjan Mishra, Dinabandhu Sahoo

Abstract

The uprooting of millions of people to new unknown places is a matter that is now becoming increasingly a continuous issue. Forced displacement results from the need to build infrastructure have raised major issues of social justice and equity. With the onset of economic reform in 1990s the State led development seems to have negotiated with corporate at the cost of natives. The resource-centric development approaches being sponsored by State and Central Government has changed the physical ecosystem and has destroyed the age-old livelihood source of marginal communities especially the tribal communities who lives in resource reach areas. As it is reflected in most of the literatures that the reasons for displacement vary, in a large majority of the cases the rehabilitation and resettlement has only left bitterness for the displaced populations. There are hardly any cases to cite as successful rehabilitation programme. The State which is worried about development has ignored the rights of marginal communities and has thrown them in cross road with lots of promises. The displaced communities are looking for the ways to come out from the clutch of exploitation. They are in dilemma where to go-be happy with the compensation given; join hand with activists to fight for their right; support what their political leader says; leave everything and search for a new life; or give an end to their life. In view of this, taking some literatures into account the present paper has made an attempt to answer following questions.

Can development provide justice to the marginal communities? Can State bring the so-called development ignoring the voice of poor? Why always marginal communities are being affected due to the State-led development initiation? Can we bring a solution to all these problems? Can a Government bring an inclusive growth for these displaced people who have sacrificed a lot for the cause of country's economic development? Can we really restore the livelihood of marginal communities who are displaced?

Introduction

Development-induced displacement is not a new and recent phenomenon. The evidence of land acquisition for the development of towns is found in ancient period between 7th and 4th century B.C, in the Mauryan period (321-181 B.C) and its state control over economy and other aspects, in the Gupta age (3rd- 6th century A.D), Khalsa lands (lands reserved for the state) in Medieval Muslim rule. It seems to be extended under Mughal rule. Another example, in 18th century the Jai Samand Tank near Udaipur in Rajasthan displaced many people (Ganguly Thukral and Singh 1995). The process got intensified in the colonial age in early 19th century when coal mining began in Raniganj and extensive irrigation started in North India, coffee plantation in Mysore, tea gardens in Assam, reconstruction of Grand Trunk Road, Major Irrigation Works in South India, construction of railway lines, irrigation system in Bari Doab, beginning of Scientific Forestry, establishment of Iron and steel plant in Jamshedpur and beginning of countless such Projects (Mankodi 1989:141-143). However, in those days displacement was not a problem because of adequate availability of land and low density of population. But recently displacement has been a concern especially for developing countries because of neo-liberalism and its policy of 'accumulation through encroachment'.

In the last decade, the magnitude on which displacement of peasant communities has occurred in Africa, Latin America, Central Asia, South Asia including India and China is really unbelievable (Cotula *et al.* 2009 and Pearce 2012). One of a recent report put "the number of reported deals concluded worldwide between 2000 and 2011 at around 2000 covering 203 million hectares. Africa accounted for 948 acquisitions covering 134 million hectares—an area larger than France, Germany and the UK combined" (Africa Progress Panel 2012:40). In India alone in the last sixty years following independence the development projects have displaced roughly sixty million people and among them 75 per cent are adivasis and 25 per cent are Dalits (Fernandes 2008). Now the local communities finding no alternative way are either resisting or involuntarily accepting the development projects. In view of this, taking some literatures into account the present paper has made an attempt to answer following questions. Can development provide justice to the marginal communities? Can State bring the so called development ignoring the voice of poor? Why always marginal communities are being affected due to the State led development initiation? Can we bring a solution to all these problems? Can a Government bring an inclusive growth for these displaced people who have sacrificed a lot for the cause of country's economic development? Can we really restore the livelihood of marginal communities who are displaced?

Development-induced Displacement the Number Involved

Sainath (1996) on the number of displaced people from 1951 to 1990 said that over 21.6 million people are displaced by dams and canals alone, 2.1 million people are dispossessed by mining, 2.4 million people are dislocated by industries, thermal plants, sanctuaries and defence installations. Thus, around 26 million Indians have been displaced between 1951 to 1990. He calculated displaced people in terms of direct displacement, i.e., those lose their land only. His estimate leaves out many groups who are affected but do not own land. Further he states that it is not even possible to arrive at a rough figure of people displaced for the country as a whole.

The Indian Institute of Public Administration (IIPA), study estimates that one dam on an average displaces 44,182 people. Hence, in India 3300 dams would displace 44,182 times 3300 or 145 million.[1]

Countering the IIPA estimates of 145 million people as too large, Arundhati Roy (1999) puts the number of dam displaced as 50 million. Similarly, an unofficial figure pointed out by N.C. Saxena, secretary to the Planning Commission as a total of 50 million, out of which 40 million are displaced by dams.

Another estimate of World Bank (1996), if applied to India's 3300 dams, then on an average 4189 people per dam the maximum number of displaced people can be about 14 million.

The International Rivers Networks, an anti-dam organisation states that there are about 40,000 big dams in World and they displaced people between 30 to 60 million.[2] If 45 million is considered as a representative figure, then one dam on an average displaces 1125 people and India's total 3300 big dams displace 3.7 million people.

The Central Water Commission (CWC), data states that a big dam whose height is 15 m or above displaces an average of 19,425 people while a dam whose height is 25 m or above displaces an average of 22,349 people.[3]

Bhalla and Mookerjee (2001), estimated by a particular economic method put the number of big dam displaced people between 3.4 to 3.7 million or three to four million.

Fernandes (2011), criticises both Ray and Bhalla's estimate on the ground that both have taken CWC definition of all dams above 15 metres as large. They then calculated the average number of displaced people for each dam and multiplied it by the number of large dams. However, all the dams in India are not large dams, there are minor, medium and large dams. All the dams also differ in submergence, height and capacity.

Fernandes and other scholars have undertaken studies of all displacement after Independence. They combining all completed studies and partial data from some other states pointed an all India figure of 60 million DPs/PAPs till 2004 from 25 million hectares, including seven million hectares of forests and six million hectares of common property resources (2008).

From the above estimates it is concluded that there are different estimates, some are too low while some are too high. The country even after six decades following Independence does not have an accurate official database on the number of those have paid the price of development. The official data many a times have been underestimates. The country need to undertake official studies to determine the total number of displaced or affected people. Walter Fernandes and his associates studies have definitely advantages which need to be completed and extended to all states those have partial data. It also be extended from the period 2004 to the present. Besides the coming development projects require accurate calculation of DPs and PAPs by displacement specialists.

Development-induced Displacement–its Human Costs

Deprived of livelihood and income, they face penury. As their families split up and spread out, their community bonds crumble. Cut off from their most vital resources, those uprooted are then robbed of their history, traditions and culture. May be even forced to adopt an alien diet. Higher rates of disease and mortality pursue the dispossessed. So do lower rates of earnings and education. Also, growing joblessness, discrimination and inferior social status. Oddly, it all happens in the name of development. And the victims are described as beneficiaries.

—(*Sainath* 1996)

The above paragraph is a quotation from one of India's leading journalist, who over his long term journalistic career observes the costs of development India has offered to its millions of people for the greater common good.

For the last two decades, development projects have caused displacement of about 15 million people world-wide per year (Cernea 1996b). According to Francis Deng, the former representative of the UNs Secretary General on Internally Displaced persons, among the 20-25 million internally displaced people in the world, 50 per cent of them are forced migrants within African continents. The present representative of the UN Secretary General on IDPs, Walter Kalin remarked Africa's displaced persons are among the world's most vulnerable. Downing said that in India out of the 20 million people displaced since Independence, it is estimated that 75 per cent of them have been impoverished due to development projects. Walter Fernandes who is conducting an all India survey on the nature and extent of displacement and resettlement said that the number of Displaced Persons (DPs) or those affected by projects without relocation, called 'Project Affected Persons' (PAPs) has increased enormously after two decades of globalisation, but no official database exist on their total number or type. The reliable data-based studies have been completed only in 13 states that give a total of 20.42 million DPs-PAPs. Studies have not been done in the high displacement states like Madhya Pradesh, Maharashtra and Chhattisgarh. In Odisha, Andhra Pradesh, Assam, West Bengal and Tripura only around 80 per cent of the data could be accessed and in Mizoram, Jharkhand, Kerala, Meghalaya and Sikkim it was around 60 per cent. Many studies done were for 1951-1995 are being updated to 1947-2010. Extrapolation based on this research and on new case studies brings one to 60 million DPs-PAPs between 1947-2000 (Fernandes et al. 2012:17).

The discipline of 'development studies' has witnessed new development today. In the new decades of globalisation and its flows and networks, there are emerging currents that are attempting to deterritorialise development. The Welfare State is no longer the leading saviour and is seeking new partners in multilateral agencies, non-government organisations (NGOs) and local social movements as it is being confronted with a network of non-state actors like diasporic communities and transnational coalitions. Amidst these shifting transnational dynamics, development projects by the state and international agencies are being forced to factor in regard for its environmental and social costs by transnational coalitions and networks (Khagram 2004). Joseph Stiglitz (2002) views that the 'the new development paradigm' as a real societal transformation. Besides, minimalist, residualist and welfarist approaches of dealing with displaced populations are gradually giving way to the Realisation that Resettlement and Rehabilitation (R&R) process needs to be seen as a development project in its own right (Mathur and Marsden 1998). But what needs more attention today is 'managing resettlement' rightly and efficiently (Mathur 2006).

The most widespread consequences of DIDR is impoverishment risks of a large segment of population (Cernea 1996, 2000; Mahapatra 1999b; Mathur and Marsden 1998). The concept 'Risk' refers to the possibility that some course of action will trigger future injurious effects-losses and destruction (Giddens 1990). Luhman (1993) says that risk postulates as a counter-concept to security. John Adams (1998) says that the higher the risks, the lower the security of the displaced populations. Risks are often directly perceptible and can be measured through science as they have objective reality. The term 'Impoverishment' refers to a situation in which people's welfare and livelihood worsen as a result of specific intervention. The concept impoverishment in many sense is related to the concepts like 'absolute poverty' 'relative poverty' 'the ultra-poor' and 'the assetless'.

The chief identifiable impoverishment risks that displaced population many a time suffers are: 1. landlessness, 2. joblessness, 3. homelessness, 4. marginalisation, 5. food insecurity, 6. increased morbidity and mortality, 7. loss of access to common property resources and 8. Community disarticulation.

Bondage Labour

Displacement and resettlement sometimes turn many DPs into bondage labour. Some 30,000 out of the 150,000 construction workers of the Asiad facilities in 1982 were slave labourers from Odisha and Chhattisgarh, brought by labour contractors with promise of job in Baghdad. They were the oustees of Hirakud dam and other projects. Today such people form a large proportion of construction and brick kiln workers (Fernandes *et al.* 2001).

Impact on Children

Displacement sometimes results child labour, when parents do not have access to work, they are forced to push their children into labour. The 56 per cent of all displaced families in Assam and 49 per cent in West Bengal were forced to pull their children out of school and turn them into child labourers in order to earn an income for the family (Fernandes, 2008). Many a time due to lack of school facility or long distance to school, children deprive of their school education.

Impact on Social Structure

Felix Padel and Samarendra Das (2011), highlighted that the social structure of a village is radically altered and dismantled as a result of displacement. The economy is completely transformed when people who have essentially been cultivators are uprooted from their land and pushed into the industrial labour. Food security disappears and money takes a greater importance in defining relations between people.

The material culture of the village is changed beyond recognition. From making most of their own food, tools and houses, villagers have to depend on factory made goods. The influx of cars, buses and trucks into their area makes life more dangerous and pollutes the atmosphere, as do the industries that become the centre of the local power structure.

People's identity is radically altered. From being largely self-sufficient for their basic food wants and material needs, they become dependent on a hierarchy outside their control for jobs and every aspects of life. Their lands and houses that were made by their parents or forefathers, so losing their land and ancestral village creates a traumatic break with previous generations.

People's religious life is also transformed. The outsider tear apart the natural surroundings, engage in blasting rock formations and cutting down trees to make profit, undermines people's sense of sacredness in nature, which lies at the heart of traditional tribal religion. A women in Vedanta's refinery project in Lanjigarh said '*Amoro deveta bi nasht kole*' that means "they even ruined our deities" referring to the *Darni Vali* (Earth goddess stones). Similarly, the Hirakud and Indravati reservoir displaced say that their 'deities were drowned'.

Cultural Genocide, Felix Padel and Samarendra Das opined is another phenomenon which is often least recognised, but perhaps most painful aspect of displacement due to the drastic drop in the quality of life of people and the disruption and dismantling of a culture.

Impact on Women

Forced displacement is more severe for women than men, because of difference in caste, class, religion or region. Everywhere women bear the brunt of the forced move a lot more than the male counterparts of their families. Resettlement marginalises women in various ways (Mehta 2009). Displacement forces the women into a double bind in two ways. First, the widespread nature of male biases in Indian society perpetuates gender inequality in terms of unequal resources allocation and distribution and also legitimises the silencing of women's interests. Second, biases within state institutions, structures and policies help perpetuate the societal inequalities. This is the double bind that displaced women often face due to displacement and resettlement (*ibid*).[4] The gender bias is evident in law and is also present in displacement policies. Project authorities rarely consult women on their problems and needs while designing resettlement plans. Under the land acquisition law, it is men as owner of land who get the compensation amount, not women (Basu, 2006).

Women's position is also badly affected, even where education, health centres and self-help groups (SHGs) are provided for oustees. The reason for this is that in a village, women often retain a large degree of control over their own labour, working essentially for themselves and their families, at times of their own choice. Even when they do coolie labour, this tends to supplement work on their own land as they see fit. Losing their land, they become more dependent on their husbands and often bear the brunt of men's frustration, in a situation where work ceases to be on their own terms. Tribal women who retain their land go to market to sell their own produce. The dignity from this self-sufficiency is destroyed by displacement. Many studies show that prostitution grows enormously after displacement, because men do not have work and so also women, they view their body as a resource for the present.

Development-induced Displacement and Marginal Community

While there is absence of official data on the magnitude of displacement, some non-official studies have estimated displaced persons since Independence at about 60 million till 2004, of which 40 per cent are tribals (Fernandes 2006 and 2011). Another official report by the Expert Group on Prevention of Alienation of Tribal Land and Restoration puts the number at 47 per cent (MoRD 2004). Of the total tribal victims of displacement around 75 per cent have not been rehabilitated (Fernandes 1991 and 1998; Planning Commission 2003).

Tribals are victimised as a result of development because of multiple causes. The tribals suffer displacement due to their powerlessness and having no voice in the decision-making process, for example the transfer of army firing range from Bihar to Jharkhand (Fernandes, 2008).[5] Besides politics often mediated in the process of site selection (Balagopal 2007). The tribals suffer extensive displacement due to a factor which termed as the process of sequential exhaustion in the context of forests (Gadgil 1989). Due to this process, the contractors expliote the forests which constitute the lifeline of tribals living in the vicinity for commercial and industrial use. These agencies exhaust forest resources near tribal villages and then in the interior forests and replacing with commercial plantations. A similar process is observed in the case of dam construction, which in early phase acquires the non-tribal dominated developed agricultural lands and exhausting these sites the focus shifted to hilly areas inhabited by tribes (Fernandes, 1991).

In the tribal areas the lands held by tribals is not transferable due to legal restrictions on its alienation. The market value of land in tribal areas in comparison to non-tribal areas is too low. So the cost of acquiring in terms of compensation is low. The obligatory criteria to rehabilitate the tribals are also low. This is the reason why much more land is acquired than is actually necessary and later lavishly utilised by project authorities for township, housing, infrastructure and other institutional needs unrelated to the project. For example, Arcellor Mittal Steel Limited applied 7750 acres of land to Odisha government for its steel project in Patna Tahasil in Keonjhar district, while it does not applied any land for its R and R colony establishment. Similarly Tata Steel in Kalinga Nagar has acquired 3500 acres. The amount of land applied shows much larger amount than is actually needed. However, the former has cancelled its project due to varieties of reasons. This is not part of present discussion.

The literacy and level of awareness among the tribal people are considerable low. The tribals have been politically marginalised and there is lack of empathy for their suffering in the larger society. There is no sustained protest for land acquisition due to these reasons and their protests are easily subdued by the local officials with the use of force.

The effect of multiple displacements is another phenomenon for tribal marginalisation. Once a tribal area is declared for industrialisation, numerous industries follow. Some are ancillary industries while others are attracted by infrastructure boom resulting from the setting up of industry. As a result additional lands need acquisition, which further displaces the tribals and huge influx of manpower takes place in the area for supply of labour and services which pushes the magnitude of displacement far beyond the level caused by the formal land acquisition. The tribals become the easy victims of these developments due to their social fragility against the dominant groups and political marginalisation (Saxena, 2012).

Provision of Justice

The Constitution of India has given social justice and special provisions to the tribes and their habitations. Besides provisions relating to the fundamental rights and the Directives of Principles of state policy which provide entitlements to all citizens, Articles 244, 244A, 275(A), 342, 338(A) and 339 deal exclusively with the tribals. These include, among others, reservation of seats in legislature, public services and educational institutions

Special provisions are given to 'Fifth' and 'Sixth' schedule areas. In case of Fifth schedule areas, the governor of the state, who has special responsibility in respect of these areas, has powers to stop, amend or modify the operation of any central or state law. The governor is required to send a report regarding this schedule area every year to the president. Besides Article 238(2) authorises him to make regulations for peace and good governance of the scheduled areas. This power can be used to restrict transfer of land by or among the members of the scheduled tribes, regulate allotment of land and money lending. There is a provision for constitution of a Tribal Advisory Council in the Fifth schedule areas which the governor is required to consult in discharge of his responsibility for the welfare of the tribes. Similarly, the Sixth schedule contains provisions for the administration of tribal areas relating to the specified states including in it. The laws enacted by the state governments to prevent alienation of the tribal land to the non-tribals continue to operate (Saxena 2012).

PESA Act (Panchayat Extension to Scheduled Areas Act 1996) has extended to Panchayati Raj Institutions to scheduled areas under which *Gram Sabha* has been granted special powers relating to the land acquisition, grant of prospecting license and mining lease, minor forest produce and protection against alienation of land. This law recognises village community's competence to manage natural resources in schedule areas and consultation of *Gram Sabha* mandatory relating to these subjects. The Supreme Court in a land mark judgement, *Samatha Vrs* the state of Andhra Pradesh, has prohibited transfer of leasing of tribal land to the non-tribals or private industries in scheduled areas (Balagopal 2007). Reservation of seats for the tribals in panchayats and chair persons of panchayats has also been mandated.

The Denying Justice

It is true that the Constitution of India has given a lot of social justice measures for the protection, survival of tribal people. But the question arises "whether the constitution or any respective states are abiding these rules?" or "Are they violating these in favour of development?" Some Fundamental Rights are being violated and compromised in case of development-induced displacement. For instance, the right to reside and settle in any part of the territory guaranteed under Article 19(1-C) of the constitution is ignored when people are involuntarily shifted from their existing habitat. The right to live with dignity in terms of Article-21 gets violated by the forced deprivation of the means of livelihood and life supporting resources to these displaced.

Right to equality and equal protection is denied since development projects lead to unequal distribution of benefits and suffering. The Directive Principle of State policy particularly enshrined in Article 39(b) and (c) are sidetracked. The special protection given to 'Fifth' and 'Sixth' schedule areas in the Constitution are infringed as development projects lead to eviction of the affected tribes from these areas (Saxena 2008). The adverse consequences unleashed by development projects force the tribal people to migrate to other areas where they face hostility and face further marginalisation as a community and lose their identity and benefits as schedules tribes. The PESA Act 1996 is violated and its provision of *Gram Sabha* is formally held or manipulated in favour of the corporation. The *Samtha* judgement no longer comes to practice when huge lands being transferred to private corporate industries.

The ILO Convention 107 (1957), dealing with indigenous people in which India is a party is also not observed when displacement occurs (Mahapatra, 1999). Article II of this convention prescribes the recognition of collective ownership of land and 12.2 and 12.3 about provision of land to oustees, both of which have been ignored in the process of resettlement (Saxena, 2008). Displacement therefore denies justice to the marginal communities and fundamental rights and forces them to exclude from the mainstream of the community.

Conclusion

The foregoing discussion makes it clear that there is no respite for the tribal communities the burden of displacement. Today the marginal communities are facing more complex problems emanating from various issues like globalisation, apathy of state apparatus, inactive civil society and the defective policy formulation. The tribals have been victimised against the ideology of development and for the national interest for inclusive development, which is based on new liberal policy of 'accumulation through encroachment'. The new policy paradigm on the other hand brings on its fold displacement, human suffering, human rights violation, misery and social exclusion. The tribals have no power in politics or mediation which can reduce the magnitude, scale and pace of displacement. They have little support from the mainstream society and political establishment to provide them proper rehabilitation and resettlement. The grand provisions for their protection and the vibrant democracy with a lot promises and assurance by the ruling political elites provide no comfort to them in the coming future.

Notes

1. Bhalla, S. Surajit and Arindam Mookerjee. 2001. "Big Dam Development: Facts, Figures and Pending Issues"
2. Taylor and Francis Ltd. 17(1) 89-98. doi: 10.1080/713672558.
3. *Ibid.*
4. *Ibid.*
5. This was spoken in an address by Walter Fernandes at the release of Social Development Report 2008 at the Council for Social Development, New Delhi on 18th September, 2008.

References

Adams, John. 1998. *Risks in a Hyper-Mobile World.* London: Geography Department, University College, Africa Progress Panel 2010

Balagopal, K. 2007. "*Impact of Grants to Industries.*" *Economic and Political Weekly* 42 (39).

Balagopal, K.2007. "*Illegal Acquisition in Tribal Areas.*" *Economic and Political Weekly* 42 October.

Basu, Malika. 2006. "*Gender Focus in Resettlement Planning.*" *In Managing Resettlement in India: Approaches, issues, experiences,* edited by Hari Mohan Mathur. New Delhi: Oxford University Press.

Cernea, M.M. 1996b. "*Public Policy Responses to Development-induced Population Displacement*" *Economic and Political Weekly* 31, 1515-1523.

Cernea, M.M. 2000. "*Risks, Safeguards and Reconstruction: A Model for Population Displacement and Resettlement*" *Economic and Political Weekly* 35(41): 3659-3678.

Fernandes, Walter. 1991. "*Power and Powerlessness: Development Projects and Displacement of Tribals.*" *Social Action* 41(3): 243-270.

Fernandes, Walter. 1998. "*Development-induced Displacement in Eastern India.*" pp. 217-300 in *Antiquity to Modernity in Tribal India Volume 1*, edited by S.C. Dube. New Delhi: Inter- India Publications.

Fernandes, Walter. 2006. "*Liberalisation and Development-induced Displacement*" *Social Change* 36 March.

Fernandes. Walter 2008. "*Sixty years of Development-induced Displacement in India: Impacts and the Search for Alternatives.*" in *India Social Development Report 2008: Development and Displacement,* edited by H.M. Mathur. New Delhi: Council for Social Development and Oxford University.

Fernandes, Walter, Nafisa Goga D'Souza, Arundhati Roy Choudhury and Mohammed Asif. 2001. *Development-induced Displacement in Andhra Pradesh 1951-1995: A Quantitative Study of Its Extent and Nature.* New Delhi and Guwahati: North Eastern Social Research Centre.

Fernandes, Walter.2011. "*Development-induced Displacement in the era of Privatisation.*" pp. 301-316 in *Resettling Displaced People: Policy and Practice in India*, edited by Hari Mohan Mathur. New Delhi: Routledge Taylor and Francis Group and Council for Social Development.

Fernandes, Walter, Shanti Chhetri, Sherry Joseph and Satyen Lama. 2012. *Progress: At* Whose Cost? Development-induced Displacement and Deprivation in West Bengal 1947 2000. Guwahati; North Eastern Social Research Centre.

Gadgil, Madhab.1989. "*Forest Management, Deforestation and Peoples' Impoverishment.*" *Social Action* 39 (4).

Giddens, Anthony.1990. *The Consequences of Modernity*. Stanford: Stanford U.P.

Khagram, S. 2004. *Transnational Struggles for Water and Power*. Ithaca: Cornell University Press.

Kothari, S. 1996. "Whose Nation: The Displaced as Victims of Development." *Economic and Political Weekly* 31(24): 1476-1485.

Luhman, Niklas.1993. *Risks: A Sociological Theory*. New York: Aldin de Gruyter.

Mahapatra, L.K. 1999a. *Resettlement, Impoverishment and Reconstruction in India*. New Delhi: Vikas Publishing House.

Mahapatra, L.K. 1999b. *Resettlement, Impoverishment and Reconstruction in India: Development for the Deprived*, New Delhi: Vikas Publishing House.

Mathur, H.M, ed. 2006. *Managing Resettlement in India*. New Delhi: Oxford University Press.

Mathur, H.M. and David Marsden, eds. 1998. *Development Projects and Impoverishment Risks: Resettling Project Affected People in India*. New Delhi: Oxford University Press.

Mehta, Lyla. 2009. "Introduction." *In Displaced by Development: Confronting Marginalisation and Gender Injustice,* edited by Lyla Mehta. New Delhi: Sage Publications.

Ministry of Rural Development (MoRD). 2004. *Report of Expert Group on Prevention of Alienation of Tribal Land and its Restoration*, New Delhi: Government of India.

Padel, Felix and Samarendra Das. 2011. "Resettlement realities: the gulf between policy and practice" in *Resettling Displaced People: Policy and Practice in India*, edited by Hari Mohan Mathur. New Delhi: Routledge, Taylor and Francis Group and Council for Social Development.

Saxena, K.B. 2008. *Development, Displacement and Resistance: The Law and the Policy on Land Acquisition*. New Delhi: Council for Social Development.

Saxena, K. B. 2012. "Development is War; Underdevelopment is Benign: Political Economy of Tribal Displacement in India." pp. 26-79 in *The Other Side of Development: The Tribal Story,* edited by A. K. Ghosh and R. D. Munda. New Delhi: Konark Publishers Pvt Ltd.

Stiglitz, J.E. 2002. *Globalisation and its Discontents*. U.K: Allan Lane, The Penguin Press.

World Commission on Dams (WCD). 2000. *Dams and Development: A new framework for decision-making*. London: Earth scan Publications Ltd.

13

Status of Schedule Tribes in Andhra Pradesh: With Special Reference to Educational, Economical, Socio and Political Contexts-A Brief Review

C. Rama Mohan Reddy, T. Sasikanth Reddy

The Constitution of India does not define Scheduled Tribes as such; Article 366(25) refers to scheduled tribes as those communities who are scheduled in accordance with Article 342 of the Constitution. According to Article 342 of the Constitution, the Scheduled Tribes are the tribes or tribal communities or part of or groups within these tribes and tribal communities which have been declared as such by the President through a public notification. The Constitution of India incorporates several special provisions for the promotion of educational and economic interest of Scheduled Tribes and their protection from social injustice and all forms of exploitation. These objectives are sought to be achieved through a strategy known as the Tribal sub-plan strategy, which was adopted at the beginning of the Fifth Five Year Plan. The strategy seeks to ensure adequate flow of funds for tribal development form the State Plan allocations, schemes/programmes of Central Ministries/ Departments, Financial and Developmental Institutions. Schedule Tribes (ST's) are Indian population groups that are explicitly recognised by the Constitution of India order 1950. The order lists 744 tribes across 22 states in its first schedule. In Andhra Pradesh 35 types of Schedule Tribes are living in eight districts. ST's are 6.6 per cent are in total population of Andhra Pradesh.

Historical Facts

From the 1850 ST community is referred to as the depressed class. During British period the Minto-Marley report, Montague-Chelmsford reforms report,

Simon Commission, etc., proposed the issue of reservation of seats for depressed class (SC & ST's) in provincial and central legislations. In 1935, British passed the Government of India Act 1935 in which reservation of seats for depressed class was incorporated into the Act. After independence the constitution assembly continued the prevailing definition of Schedule Tribes and gave the president of India and governance of states responsibility to compile a full listing of tribes and also the power to edit it later as required. The actual complete listing of tribes was made with the Constitution (Schedule Tribes) Order 1950. Article 366(25) of the Constitution of India refer the Schedule Tribes as those communities, who are scheduled in accordance with Article 342 of the Constitution. The essential characteristics of Schedule Tribes are identified by the Locur Committee. Indications of primitive tribes, distinctive culture, shyness of contact with the community at large, geographical isolation and backwardness are most identified features of ST's community. There is 7.5 per cent reservation facility for employment opportunities and they are experiencing political reservations also at present based on their population.

Tribes in Andhra Pradesh

As per 2001 in India the population of tribes is 8.2 per cent. In Andhra Pradesh 6.6 per cent tribes population exists. In the state, Tribes are of two groups. One group is at presently across the hilly tract of the Deccan Plateau and by the rivers Godavari and Krishna. The second group is present along the extended areas between the river Krishna and Godavari. According to ST order Act 1976 there are 33 types of Tribes in eight districts and other 50 lakh nomads are surviving. In overall of the state, in Coastal Andhra 5.96, in Rayalaseema 2.86 and in Telangana 8.87 Tribal population exist. The prominent tribes are *Khonds, Kholamis, Nayakpods, Koyas, Konda doras, Valmikis, Bhagats, Savaras, Jatayus, Godabas, Yanadis* and *Chenchus*. 76 per cent of Tribes are covered by Sugali (4.4 per cent), Koya (11.3. per cent), Yanadi (9.2 per cent), Yerukula (8.7 per cent), Gonda (5 per cent) and remaining 24 per cent of population belongs to small tribes. Nomadic tribal are—*Pichukaguntulu, Balasanta, Saradakandru, Veeramustivaru, Bhavaneelu, Birannalavaru, Golla Suddulu, Pasaralu, Jangamulu* and *Kommuvaru,* etc., are other tribes surviving in Andhra Pradesh. They don't have scripts for their language. They follow their customs and traditions strictly. 92.5 per cent population is living in rural areas. Their livelihood based on the occupations like making of toys, baskets, mats, cosmetics and collection of leaves, honey etc. The life style of tribes has been changing gradually after initiation by the government contribution. Reservation in education, employment and in legislative assemblies and local bodies are changing the life style of the tribals.

Constitutional Safeguards

The Constitution of India mentioned development of schedule tribe in Directive Principles. The Constitution (Schedule Tribes) Order 1950 identified schedule tribes' population-based some peculiar characteristics. Those communities are in accordance with Article 342 of the constitution. Some other safe guards are there in the constitution of India. Articles 23 and 24 mentioned social safe guards. Articles 244 and 275(1) referred special economic safe guards. Education and cultural safeguards are referred by Articles 15(4), 29(1) and 350(a). Political safe guards are mentioned in accordance with 164 (1), 330, 332, 334, 243(0), 371(A), 371 B, 371 C, 371 F etc. Service safe guards are mentioned by articles 16(4), 16(4A), 16 (4B), 335, 320(4) etc. Article 335 puts limitations for reservations, Article 338 emphasis appointment of special officer whenever necessary regarding tribe matters. Article 339(1) refers establishment of commission on tribal issues by President of India. But it is the responsibility of state to look after the benefits which are available from these articles.

Educational Status

In Andhra Pradesh literacy rate is 60.4 per cent. But, the literacy of schedule Tribe is 37.04. After 30 years also illiteracy rate is 63 per cent. In rural areas the illiteracy rate of ST's is 70 per cent. For the improvement of literacy the Andhra Pradesh Government has started hostels for boys and girls. Residential schools, vocational training centers etc. National Policy of Education (1986 and revised Policy in 1992) suggested the following programmes for education of tribal people.

1. Opening primary schools in Tribal Areas
2. Need to develop curricula of their language
3. Promoting schedule tribes youth to work as teachers
4. Ashram schools, Residential schools should be established in large scale in Tribal areas.
5. Incentives to encourage their life style through education.

Problems

To promote education in schedule tribes two types of problems are there. Internal problems like school system, content, curricula, medium, pedagogy, academic supervision, etc., and external problems like education policy, planning, implementation and administration, etc., are influencing education in tribal areas.

Economic Status

In the state, agriculture labour of ST's is 10.3 per cent. In the state 115.31 lakh land holdings are there. Among them ST's have only 7.5 per cent of holdings. In total land of Andhra Pradesh ST's have only 8.2 per cent of land. So there is need for distribution of land for tribes. In total employees, STs are representing 4.9 per cent. As literacy rate is 37 per cent the work participation rate (WPR) is 53.9. Male work participation is 55.7 per cent and female work participation is 52. A report in 2000 said that 45 per cent of Rural ST population is below poverty line and in urban areas 35.6 per cent is under below poverty line. According to National Sample Survey Organisation 61st round estimates, in India monthly per capita expenditure of tribes is Rs 426.19. In Andhra Pradesh monthly per capita expenditure is Rs 420.01. Less population is able to use schemes of government for their opportunities. Majority population survive on their traditional occupations like making of toys, baskets, mats, cosmetics and collection of leaves, honey, shifting, agriculture etc. The main obstacles to Economic Development of Schedule Tribes are destruction of forests, illiteracy, indebtedness lack of awareness about the schemes for them, strict follow of traditions and customs, in effective implementation of schemes etc. Though there is an improvement of conditions of Schedule Tribes, it is not at desired level. So, much more measures to be taken by the governments.

Social and Political Status

The article 338A relates the population ST's. Before and after Independence ST's as vulnerable section were given reservation to enter into Parliament and legislative assemblies, but this facility is not applicable to Rajya Sabha at present. After 2002, separate National commission for schedule Tribes was started and came to effect from 19th February 2004 due to 89th amendment. Priority was given to protect the culture, traditions and customs by the constitutions. To protect their rights and to avoid suppression from other communities. Prevention of Atrocities Act was formed in 1989. The ministry of tribal affairs was constituted in October 1999 with the objective of development of Schedule Tribes in a coordinated and planned manner. This is also a significant step to lift the tribal communities. In Andhra Pradesh fourteen MLA's three MP's belongs to ST communities. The implantation of political reservations should be reviewed and revision as per their population. The health policy 1983 emphasis improving tribal health especially through detection and treatment of endemic and other diseases specific to tribes.

Schemes for the Prosperity of the Scheduled Tribes

For the development of Schedule Tribes Special Central Assistance grant has been released under 275(11) Article of Indian Constitution. Investment share, price support, village, train, bank scheme, etc., are introduced. Besides this National Schedule Tribe Financial and Development Corporation was established with 500 crore authorised capital. Integrated area development and modified area development were introduced. The following are important land marks in Tribal development:

1. Programmes were designed with as special fusion ST's (1951).
2. Adoption of Panchsheel principles for process of tribal development (1956).
3. Opinions of multi-purpose tribal development blocks for intensified development of ST's 1961.
4. Introduction to strategies of TSP and SCA for tribal development (1974).

5. Expansion of infrastructure facilities for poverty alleviation in 1985.

6. Setting up of tribal co-operative marketing development federation 1987 and Finance Development Corporation in 1989.

7. 73 and 74 amendments and Panchayat extension to Scheduled Areas Act.

8. Sections up on separate ministry of Tribals 1999 and National Schedule Tribes Finance and Development Corporation 2001.

The Following are Recent Measures taken by the Government

1. Recognition of forest Act 2006 will be administered by the Ministry of Tribal affair to protect interest of the Tribals in forests.

2. The scheme of vocational Training Centers has been revised as vocational training in Tribal areas with effect from 01-04-09.

3. During 2009-10 the ministry has founded 14 education complexes under the scheme of strengthening education among schedule tribe girls in low literacy districts.

4. Under the scheme of grant-in-aid to voluntary organisation durings 2009-10. The ministry funded about 237 projects covering schools, hostels, libraries etc.

5. Under the scheme of development of particularly vulnerable Tribal groups, the ministry released Rs 40.43 crore for six states.

6. Under the scheme of Market development of Tribal products/produce ministry released Rs 9.68 crores. But states have to take responsibility to give fruits of the schemes.

Measures to be Taken for Prosperity of Scheduled Tribes

Many programmes helped tribal to improve their conditions. The following are important for further improvement.

1. Strict implementation of reservation of seats in public sector employment.

2. Proper looking into reservation of seats in institutions of higher learning.

3. Formulation of proper welfare schemes for prosperity of Tribals based on fact data.

4. In private sector also these should be reservations for schedule tribes.

5. The present 7.5 per cent of reservation for government services should be increased whenever necessary.

6. Destroy of their habitations should be reduced because, major projects, SEZs and other projects are causing for migration of ST's.

7. Their habilitation (Thandas) should be converted into gram panchayats.

8. Development of forest villages is needed for Tribal prosperity.

9. Empowering Tribals in governance is the most needed one.

10. During every plan review and revision is must to alter policies.

11. Stopping of corruption and ineffective work progress in the implementation of schemes belonging to Schedule Tribes.

The directive principles of Indian constitution referred the development of Schedule Tribes in the society. Though policies are vast implementation is not proper so both state and Central government have to take proper steps. Since 1951 governments are implementing number of programmes and schemes for the development of Schedule Tribes. But the implementation is not effective. Besides this, lack of awareness about the programmes is also strong factor due to illiteracy among tribes. Therefore, there is need for extension of contribution from government side and other voluntary organisations and likeminded NGOs for effective implementation of programmes and bringing awareness among Tribes. Then only the future of the Schedule Tribes will be in good prosperity.

References

1. K. Sunitha Rani (2006), *Struggle for Survival - Tribal of Andhra Pradesh* Fifty Years of Andhra Pradesh CDRC: p. 469.
2. K. Sujatha (1992), *Study of tribal teachers working in tribal areas*: Journal of educational planner and administrator: Vol. 6, No. 4.
3. N.K. Acharya (2006), *Reservation for SC, ST's, OBC's*, Fifty Years of Andhra Pradesh CDRC: p. 461.
4. Sachchidananda and R. R. Prasad (1998), *Encyclopaedic Profile of Indian Tribes with Maps and Photographs*: Discovery Publishing House, New Delhi.
5. www.planning commission.nic.in.
6. www.nhrc.nic.in.
7. www.tribal.gov.in, Annual Report 2009-10 of Ministry of Tribal Department.

14

Policies against Tribals: A Study of Displacement through Development Projects

Johani Xaxa

The process of change and development in India has not only been technological and economic, but also has been a political struggle, related with the changes in the power relations and decision-making process within the system. Since independence, India was engaged in nation-building or modernisation process and fast development of infrastructure and economic conditions of the people, and the country as a whole. But the question arises whether development should mean profit for capitalists or protection of the rights of the people (Indigeneous) and the prosperity or greater good far the larger numbers? However, the pursuit of development adversely affected the marginalised sections causing deprivation, displacement and devastation and invariably led to the 'disempowerment of the tribes' (Xaxa, 2001:206). Further, question arises for development, for what and at what social cost (Baboo, 2002:195). When the nation developed it was at the cost of the marginals. When the majority developed in the country, the marginals excluded systematically. The development projects are meant for the development of the country, and ultimately of the people as a whole, but it is resulted in displacement of lakhs of people and forced them to leave their home and land to struggle for livelihood.

There are two faces of the "temple of modern India", one, the glorification of development, the other fact that like monuments of the past. These present-day temples too are built on the blood and sweat of million of people, whilst slaves and prisoners built the former, today's farmers and others who live off the land, forests and other resources are being impoverished in the name of 'development' (Fernandes). Nations are thus not only oppressive to others but can be brutal to its own people. In this way the whole issue of displacement takes place as a result of development projects where the majority of the development-displaced are tribals and landless dalits. Odisha's tribals are also not excluded from it. This paper intended to focus on the problems of displaced poor, down trodden tribal's tragedy in the state of Odisha.

The State of Odisha occupies a unique place amongst the undeveloped States of India, because of it's large concentration of tribal population in one hand, and on the other, the people are poor but their land is rich in resources. The Scheduled Tribe constitutes nearly 22.5 per cent of the total population of Odisha. (Indian Census Report 2011) 62 tribal communities has been designated as Scheduled Tribe of which 13 recognised as Primitive Tribal Group (PTG). Nearly half of the State's area (45 per cent) is under 5th Scheduled of the Indian Constitution. Odisha is one of the poorest States in India, with an estimate of 47 per cent of its population living less than a dollar a day (Haans & Dubey, 2003). In 1999-2000, 37 per cent of the Scheduled Tribes in Odisha were Below Poverty Line as compared to 55 per cent and 33 per cent respectively for Scheduled Castes and General Castes (Haans & Dubey, 2003). The populations in the Scheduled areas are comparatively much poorer than the population in non-Scheduled areas. In South Odisha the situation is even worse with 87 per cent of the Scheduled Tribes below the poverty line.

Tribals are agriculturists by their occupation; hence land is the main source of their livelihood. But in the Scheduled areas of Odisha, an average 74 per cent of the land is categorised as State land (forest land and non-forest land). Thus, three-fourth of all land in the tribal dominated districts belong to the State. However, most of the tribals in these areas are either landless or marginal landowners. They own only 4.8 per cent (in standard acres) of agricultural landholdings with an average holding of only 0.44 standard acres. Thus, more than 50 per cent of all Scheduled Tribe landowners in Odisha are marginal landholders and another 20 per cent at least are landless.

In context of landownership, the communal landownership and swidden/shifting cultivation was never settled with respective tribal communities. These lands were, if settled then, settled either as forest land or as government revenue land. In practice much of the customary owned land is still under cultivation of tribals and is treated as encroachments. As all customary tribal lands are government land, the state government found it very easy to divert customary tribal lands for development projects and forcibly ousted them from their land and inhabitat, carries with it the risk of becoming poorer than before displacement. Michael Cernea, a sociologists has identified eight interlinked potential risks intrinsic to displacement such as; Landlessness, Joblessness, Homelessness, Marginalisation, Food insecurity, Increased morbidity and morality, loss of access to common property, and Social Disintegration (Cernea, 1999).

Odisha is extremely rich in minerals, most of which lies in the tribal districts. The hilly terrain and availability of water also makes them suitable for reservoirs and dams. The major dams taken up in Scheduled areas are the Machhkund, Salandi, Balimela, Upper Kolab, Indrawati and Mandira etc. The major industrial projects taken up in Scheduled areas have been the Rourkela Steel Plant, NALCO's Alumina Refinery at Damanjodi, Hindustan Aronetic Limited (HAL), Sunabeda. Large numbers of industrial projects are under implementation as proposed in Scheduled areas including the alumina refineries of UAIL (Utklal Alumina India Ltd.) in Kashipur, Vedanta at Lanjigarh, Tata Steel Plant at Kalinganagar in Jajpur, POSCO Steel Plant at Paradeep in Jagatisinghpur. The richness of forests and wildlife has also led to increasing number of protected areas (Wild life Sanctuaries and National Parks) in the Scheduled areas of Orissa. Such protected areas have created a major problem as the rights of the inhabitants in and around these areas in the forest and forest land is being extinguished, affecting their livelihoods and sometimes leading to displacements.

Most of the minerals are deposited in Scheduled areas. The most important mining zones within Scheduled areas are iron ore and manganese mining in Sundargarh and Keonjhar districts, coal in Sundargarh district, bauxite in Kalahandi, Koraput and Rayagada districts. Apart from displacement, mining and industries lead to large scale influx of non-tribals, this often leads to Social and Political marginalisation of the tribals. The environmental impacts are drastic and affect much larger number of people than directly displaced.

The liberalisation of mining and industrial policies which allowed for direct foreign investments, facilitated number of mining and industrial projects located in Scheduled areas. Some of these propose mining areas are inhabited by Primitive Tribal Groups, such as Paudi Bhuiyans in Keonjhar and Sundargarh districts. Almost all the iron ore mines deposits in Odisha are located in the Scheduled areas of Keonjhar and Sundargarh districts. The life of the inhabitants (tribals) are already disturbed with massive mining, leading to displacement of tribals, destruction of their livelihood, support system including forests and water resources, large scale air and water pollution and cultural genocide through massive influx of outsiders, and also entry of giant factories as POSCO, Jindals, Tata Steels etc. The mining areas were originally inhabited by Scheduled Tribes, especially PTGs and whose livelihoods have been destroyed completely. Bauxite are also located in Scheduled areas in Kalahandi, Rayagada and Koraput districts with the major mining being done by NALCO in Koraput district. These has been a major source of controversy with the local tribals opposing proposed mining projects tooth and nail, and the state government using all possible strategies, including coercion and repression to make these deposits available to mining multinationals. The resistance of Kashipur tribals against UAIL's mining project and alumina refinery has been going for over 10 years now. Similarly, flashpoints building up near proposed bauxite mining on

Niyamagiri by Vedanta, Sunger by L & T, Kodingamali by Aditya Aluminum and Maliparbat by Hindalco. The bauxite deposits are all located on top of the highest mountains in South Odisha which are called Malis and are sacred to tribals as they are often the only source of water of drinking and irrigation of fields in summer season, and sustain local agricultural economy. This reality of tribals has created massive resistance against bauxite mining amongst tribals.

In Kashipur and Lanjigarh the tribals organised continuous resistance against displacement from mining and the environmental impacts of mining. Similar situation is now emerging in all tribal areas where industrial projects are being planned. Part of the reason for the strong resistance is bitter experience of the tribals of Koraput and Rayagada with the earlier projercts such as Upper Kolab, Indrawati, HAL, NALCO, etc., which has led to destitution of a large number of tribals and destruction of their livelihoods base and their culture. Another important reason is that inspite of most of the land in the area proposed to be acquired being categorised as Government, are under cultivation by the tribals. Thus, in Lanjigarh, while acquiring land for Vedanta, the local tribals cultivating government land were simply evicted without compensation, destroying their livelihoods. In Lanjigarh, for instance almost 64 landless Kondh households (Scheduled Tribes) had been cultivating Revenue Land for the last 30-40 years. When the Revenue Department, filed the case against those people, the notice showed, the physical possession of lands for at least seven to eight years. However, the tribals claimed that even their forefathers were cultivating the land. Both as per the principle of adverse possession and as per the section 7(a) of Orissa Prevention of Land Encroachment Act, 1972, such land should have been settled with the landless persons to the extent of one standard acre (equivalent to 4.5 acres to uplands), when the tribals tried to get the land regularised in their name prior to this issue, they were asked to pay bribes up to Rs 5000 per acre, which they could not afford. In 2003, instead of settling this land with the tribal cultivators cultivating the lands, the district administration evicted these 64 families by force without compensation, there by taking away their main livelihoods. By law, this action of administration violated the protection provided to the Scheduled Tribes in Scheduled V of the Constitution, and the Section 3 (iii) of the OSATIP Regulations (1956) by turning Scheduled Tribes effectively landless. Therefore, it is correct to comment that "industrialisation is necessary evil". As for the development, industrialisation is necessary, but at the same time industries requires the minerals and both mining and industrialisation caused displacement of millions of poor tribals.

As a consequence of development projects, the tribal people in Odisha have become poorer than before. Partly this is due to a process of alienation of the rights over land, forests, water bodies and other resources. Although these rights guaranteed under 5th Scheduled of the Indian's Constitution, the State Governments including Odisha, are not inclined to recognise them and, are in fact, looking for an escape route. Odisha government has also not considered the rights of the tribal people to be consulted on matters concerning the acquisition of land for project purposes, which the Panchayats (Extension to Scheduled Areas) Act, 1996 (PESA) has specifically conferred on them.

The displaced poor tribals have scarified more than the benefits they got from the development projects. The development projects become curse to them, as it has convert them to homeless and landless and place them to zero stage. It is evident from the Government's development programs that, Government's policies are against tribals life. The problems they facing are:

- First of all, they lost their home and community villages with which they were emotionally attached. Though poor, they usually have 2/3 living rooms of mud walls and home-made tile roof, sufficient area for garden, cow-shed, goat-shed, pig-shed, etc., when they displaced it is very difficult to build a new set of house in a new place. The displacement reversed their life to years back to improve.
- When they moved to government's resettlement and rehabilitated colonies, which allotted with small houses like Indira Awas. It is very difficult for them to adjust there.
- From several study it has been revealed that in most cases the government failed in giving sufficient compensation to displaced tribals. They also do not know how to utilise the money properly.
- Most of the times, the government instead of giving compensation, evict them forcefully, as they do not have legal documents (Legal land patta). Because, most of their lands are unauthorised occupation. Hence they get no compensation and become landless and marginal labourers.
- When they have been given compensation of land for land, the lands more often the barren lands in lieu of their fertile land, which take them back to some more years to develop (thus it is right to say, government's development policies led to disempowerment of tribals).
- The displaced families have been thrown out at resettlement colonies without basic amenities of life. Some time places are arid and hilly regions, Roads and Communications, Schools and Colleges, Markets, Hospitals, Wells and Tanks and drinking waters, etc., have not been provided to resettlement and rehabilitated colonies.
- The displacement not only disturbed their economy but also social, cultural and educational rights. Socially, they preferred to live together in their community. Through their social and religious customs and traditions, they protect and maintain their tribal Culture and Identity. For the matrimonial relations, they need their own community. Thus displacements have shattered their Culture and Identity.
- Educationally, too, their children suffered a lot because they have to go to school for four to five kilometers. In some places they have to go through jungles, have fear of wild animals. Therefore, their children do not go to School in due time, and starts school in late age, or drop out from school.

• In the resettlement colonies hardly they can get electricity. Those who sacrificed their every comfort to illuminate the urban towns, live in darkness.

• Medical facilities are not provided to them. They have to depend on herbal medicines. Due to lack of medical facilities, they died without medical aid or because of rough communications; the critical patients die before reaching hospital.

• The PESA Act is openly violated by the state government. In the scheduled Area, the State government has to consult the Gram Sabha or the Panchayats at the appropriate level, before acquisition of land for development projects. But the State never consults the Panchayats and, thus violating the right to decide their own priorities as a part of right to development as an inalienable human rights.

The development projects as adopted by Odisha Government with a desire to bring national development has not only worsened the life of the tribal population but also denied their basic rights to livelihood and substance, culture, land, common property resources employment and participation. A State's prime duty is the welfare and protection of its all citizens, but it has turning the tribals life into refuges and foreigners in their own country. The acquisition of tribal land in the name of development has evicted them from their home state and deprived them of a decent living, which is marked by widespread poverty, hunger and starvation death, migration to neighbouring States in search of a minimum livelihood. Thus, development policies of the Government directing against tribal's development.

Suggestions

• The Central Government as well as the State Government should stop alienation of land inhabited by the tribal people. It must correct the loopholes in existing lows and take steps to restore lands transferred from tribals to non-tribals and register land records for tribal land.

• In the Scheduled Areas under Fifth Scheduled, Government should adhere to PESA Acts. According to this Act, it is mandates that Gram Sabha or Panchayats should be consulted before acquiring the land for development projects.

• After the use of land for project purposes, the surplus lands should takeover by the government and return them to landless tribal families and also other landless families. It has been seen that, the Government had sold the surplus lands (acquired from tribals) to non-tribals.

• Before displacement, the government must be developed the resettlement colonies with all amenities required by the tribals as par their original place. The settlement colonies must have educational institutions for tribal children. The road communication must be developed, so that they can easily move from resettlement colonies to nearby cities. The medical facilities must be well developed. The proper water supply and electrification should be provided to each and every house.

• The poor tribals have no knowledge of monitoring the compensation money. Hence, the government, instead of giving lump sump money as compensation, should give them facilities of fixed deposits or else help them to start any kind of business.

• Those who, do not want money as compensation, should be provided with farming land, having equal fertility status and equal gross yield as their own lost land.

• Dam construction for irrigation purpose need not be of great heights, because greater the height of the dam more will be the encroachment of land by the water. For the purpose of Hydro-Electricity, the heights of dams ought to be high but it is not so in case of irrigational dams.

Lastly, the final view is that Development work of the country should not be stopped, it is necessary but not in the cost of tribals.

References

1. Xaxa, Virginius. 2001. *"Empowerment of Tribes"* in Singha Roy, Debal K (ed.) Social Development and the Empowerment of the Marginalised Groups: Perspectives and Strategies, New Delhi: Sage Publication, p. 205.

2. Baboo, Balgovind. 2002. *"Dams, Displacement and Violation of Human Rights: Case of Harked Dam in Orissa"* in Katare, P.M. and B.C. Barik (eds.) Development, Deprivation and Human Rights Violation, New Delhi: Rawat Publication, p. 195.

3. Fernandes, Walter. "*Paying the Price for Someone Else's Displacement*" http:/intochangeindia.org/agenda/migration-a-displallcement/payingf the.

4. Cernea, Michael. 1999. "*When Economic Analysis is Essential to Resettlement: A Sociologist's View*" in Michael Cernea (ed.) The Economics of Involuntary Resettlement: Questions and Challenges, (Washington, D.C., World Bank).

5. Census Report India, 2011.

6. Sharma,, R.N. 2003. "*Involuntary Displacement: A few Encounters*" *Economic and Political Weekly*, March 1.

7. Bandopadhya, D. 2004. "Rayagada Story Retold: Destitutes of Development" *Economic and Political Weekly*, January 31, Vol. XXXIX, No. 15.

8. Das, J.K. 2001. *"Human Rights and Indigenous Peoples"* New Delhi: A.P.H. Publishing House, pp. 58-93.

15

Tribal Land Alienation

Palla Trinadha Rao

This article presents the problem of tribal land alienation in the Scheduled Areas of Andhra Pradesh. The chapter examines the causative factors for tribal land alienation and its varied dimensions. Historically tribals owned the land in their own customary rights. Their entire life process was centered and built upon two major means of production, i.e., the forest and the land. Both land and forest lands are slipping from their control due to multiple interventions. Historical evidences are ample which reveals the uneven structural changes that have taken place from time to time due to the commoditisation of the tribal economy in which land plays a critical and predominant role. This chapter argues that the laws which have been promulgated to protect the tribal land interests are not effectively implemented resulting in external appropriation of tribal lands in the Scheduled Areas.

Introduction

Scheduled Tribes (STs) account for 8.6 per cent of India's population. 35 tribal communities are notified in Andhra Pradesh as STs and their population is about 59.18 lakhs as per the 2011 Census reports. The Tribal Sub-plan area extends over 31,485.34 sq. kms. in the districts of Srikakulam, Vizianagaram, Warangal, Visakhapatnam, East and West Godavari, Khammam, Adilabad and Mahaboobnagar districts constituting the traditional habitat of nearly 30 tribal groups. The tribal groups of Yerukula, Yanadi and Sugali or Lambada live mainly in the plain areas outside the Scheduled Areas.

The question of land tenure has been a pivotal and sensitive political issue in the context of Scheduled Areas of Andhra Pradesh. Agriculture continues to be the main source of livelihood for majority of the tribals.[1] However, large tracts of tribal land are concentrated in the hands of predominantly elite non-tribal sections of society. Consequently, tribals are marginalised and deprived of their traditional land rights. The alien systems of land tenure introduced during colonial times have had far reaching adverse effects depriving tribals of their dignity and their access to land justice.

The 'alienation' of humankind in a fundamental sense refers to the loss of control; its embodiment in an alien force which confronts the individual as a hostile and potentially destructive power. When Marx analysed 'alienation' in his Economic and Philosophic Manuscripts of 1844, he indicated four principal aspects—the alienation of human beings from nature, their own productive space, as a member of the human species and from each other.[2] Alienation, in the Marxist conception of man in the capitalist society, is the process that facilitates the exploitation of many by a few.[3]

Seen from the tribal point of view, tribals may be thought of as an alienated group. They suffer from several forms of alienation since, 'in a system of cumulative inequalities privileges, property and power are combined in the certain individuals and while the socially underprivileged are economically and politically deprived'.[4] Alienation of land itself, however, constitutes just a small component of this entire process of alienation, albeit an essential one. It is therefore, imperative to view this single phenomenon, within the holistic context of tribal existence and tribal cultural ethos.[5]

The 'alienation' of tribals from their traditional habitat is caused due to the policies of the State. The process of induction of non-tribal population into these Scheduled Areas was expected to bring progressive assimilation of the local tribals into the new socio-economic order of the immigrants, while raising their income, productivity and standard of living. 'However, often the outcome has been contrary to the above expectations, reducing the share of tribals in the gross regional product, substituting one institutional exploitation by another, uprooting them from their native land and reducing them to the status of aliens on their own soil.'[6]

In the early years of the 20th century, many tribal communities lived by and large freely, in pre-capitalistic socio-economic formations.[7] This is because the community ownership of land in India was not commoditised prior to the British rule. Tribals in their pre-capitalistic socio-economic formations had not regarded land as a commodity as it was freely available to them for cultivation. Thus, the concept of alienation with regard to the problem of land alienation in tribal areas can be understood in relation to the concept of private property relations, commoditisation of the means of production as land, labour and capital and the very process of penetration of the private sphere by the state capital.

The loss of private holdings by tribals, despite a number of laws being passed by both the pre-colonial as well as post-colonial state to check land alienation, has been a cause of concern. These laws had many shortcomings and were unable to check the transfer of land from tribals to non-tribals.[8] Even where legislation is designed to protect tribal land interests, such as restricting alienation of tribal land or ensuring that tribals receive the benefit of land tenure reforms, the results have been disappointing.[9]

Several legislations have been passed since Independence but 'despite the legislation in force against alienation of land from tribals to non-tribals, a fair proportion of them have either been dispossessed of their land or have parted with their land due to some other reason.'[10]

Tribal Identity and Land Rights

Tribals share a symbiotic relationship with natural resources. Agronomic practices and their relationship with land are based on the nature-man-spirit complex and sustenance of the economy which is unique to tribal cultures in many parts of the country.[11] Traditional communal Land tenure systems continue to exist even where formal land tenure systems emphasise on individual property rights.[12] In the predominantly agricultural societies, the importance of land cannot be over-emphasised. It is a symbol of security, the main source of income and wealth, as well as of social, political and economic power. 'The land tenure system reflects social class structure and class relations, as they represent an array of legal, contractual or customary arrangements whereby people engaged in cultivation gain access to productive opportunities linked with land and thereby income.'[13]

The British legal concept of individual private property destroyed the tradition of collective ownership and sharpened tensions within the Adivasi society while eroding their relationship with nature. These same tendencies are visible today in various developmental policies that are being implemented in the country in the post-independence era. It is the primary cause of conflicts between the tribals and the larger non-tribal society. The entire worldview of Adivasis is situated around their land. They cannot imagine their physical existence apart from it and therefore eviction from their land or encroachments by outsiders has resulted in resistance and even armed struggles in Andhra Pradesh ever since the British era.[14] There have been and continue to be, several rebellions across the country. Prominent among them in Andhra Pradesh are Alluri Seetarama Rao's armed resistance in Visakhapatnam Agency and the Gond Rebellion led by Komram Bheem in Adilabad Agency in Nizam state.[15] The Rampa Rebellion (1922-23) from East Godavari to Vizianagaram under Alluri Seetarama Raju was in protest of the Madras Forest Act of 1882 which placed restrictions on the free movement of tribals in the forest areas and prevented them from engaging in their traditional practice of *Podu* or slash and burn cultivation.

Post–independence, tribal unrest has been primarily on issues relating to restrictions on *podu* cultivation and encroachment of non-tribals in large numbers into Agency areas (tribal areas), posing threat to the existence and identity of tribal society. Special laws to protect the tribals from land alienation have been violated and about 48 per cent of the land in Agency areas is formally owned by non-tribals. Large scale manipulations during the Survey and Settlement period of 1970-76 led to grant of land entitlements of tribal land as settlement *pattas* in the name of non-tribals. According to the Koneru Ranga Rao Land Committee Report, 'Every year more and more land is passing into the hands of non-tribals and if not checked with a very strong executive force, very soon the tribals may not have any land at all.'[16]

The historical and legal perspective is that land in the Scheduled Areas once belonged to tribals. Until and unless the contrary is proved, the land in occupation by non-tribals shall be deemed to have come through a transfer from tribals. So the burden of proof lies on the non-tribals to legally prove that the land in their possession had been with them even prior to the Andhra Pradesh Agency Tracts Land Transfer Act of 1917, which restricts land transfer between the tribals and the non-tribals. The tribals have customary boundaries to the village and land is a community asset rather an individualised economic asset. The object of the Fifth Schedule and the Land Transfer Regulations is to preserve tribal autonomy and their culture, to help in their economic empowerment, to ensure social, economic and political justice for preservation of peace and good governance in the Scheduled Areas. The word 'regulate' in the allotment of land to members of STs in the Scheduled Area must be read as an endeavour to ensure regulation of the land only for and among the members of the STs in the Scheduled Area.[17]

Non-tribals and the State in Scheduled Areas

Land of the tribal communities in this region has been taken away by the non-tribals who have penetrated the region for economic gains. The penetration of non-tribals was aimed at gaining access to forest and land to exploit them as economic resources, mainly for the market, thereby undermining the traditional subsistence economy and society of the tribals.[18] This penetration was engineered by the British to serve their own colonial interest. Otherwise, there was no reason as to why a mass of non-tribal people should suddenly begin encroaching upon tribal land, something they had not done in the past. The newly imposed British land system was radically different from that prevalent among many tribal groups.[19]

The colonial period witnessed a progressive and aggressive monetisation of the economy of the tribal region for revenue generation, making dependence on the forest ever more precarious and thus destroying tribal self-reliance. Moreover, as the forests were taken over by government agencies and commercial interests, the tribals were forced more and more to live by farming the land, where they were progressively pushed into bonded labour by exploitative landlords, moneylenders, government officials and other outsiders. The creation of private property rights over land was an equally disastrous break with tribal tradition in which land was always held by the community even when it was assigned to private use.[20]

The first phase of migration of non-tribal peasants from the plains occurred around 1820 when a number of *zamindaris*, either whole or in part, came into the auction market and the highest bidder got the rights of ownership. This auction process was initiated to raise revenue. But it paved the way for the non-tribals to infiltrate tribal areas. The administration made further steady inroads for the control of the productive resources of the tribals by passing forest laws in 1882 and *abkari* laws in 1864 .These laws were meant to regulate the forest usage and consumption of toddy or alcohol.[21] The Godavari River facilitated the movement of non-tribals from the widely populated plain areas of East and West Godavari to the sparsely populated tribal areas, by country craft, mechanised boats and launches.[22] Towards the end of the nineteenth century, the British began leasing out the rights to extract bamboo and timber from the forests on both sides of the river to the non-tribal merchants of Rajahmundry. When motor boats were introduced in the second decade of this century, a larger number of merchants and their agents moved into these settlements.[23]

The huge influx facilitated further opening up of tribal areas intensifying the demand for land for diverse purposes—housing, infrastructure, business and social utilities which further led to the dispossession of the tribals. For instance, if one travels by road through the long stretch from Bhadrachalam in the Khammam district of Andhra Pradesh to Raipur in Chhattisgarh, a distance of about 550 kms and almost entirely a Fifth Schedule region where tribal land may not be sold or passed on to the non-tribal people, yet, one can see that most of the shops and land along the roadside are owned or occupied by non-tribals. This blatant encroachment upon tribal land is overlooked by a largely non-tribal government that accepts tribal people's displacement as a precondition for development.[24]

Yet, another form of land alienation is when the States promote development projects as hydroelectric power stations and mining and industries. These developmental activities do not confer any benefit on the tribals directly and render them landless.[25] The construction of irrigation dams and industrialisation are the major reasons for massive and irreversible deforestation and subsequent land loss of the tribal communities. In the last sixty years, in the new era of development, tribal communities have been displaced on a large scale. Displacement has taken place as an offshoot of the economic development by the State itself and, in particular, its industrialisation and irrigation policy.[26] For instance, there are eighteen major dams in Andhra Pradesh and six of the large ones alone have been responsible in displacing about half a million people. The proposed Indira Sagar Project (Polavaram) threatens involuntary displacement of 2.37 lakh people from 276 villages in the Scheduled Areas of Andhra Pradesh, 55 per cent of them being tribals. It will result in the submergence of 94,357 acres of land situated in the Scheduled Areas, of which 29,852 acres are *poramboke*. In addition to this, the Polavaram Project will submerge 3,223 hectares of forest.[27]

Tribals suffer from physical displacement in several parts of the country due to development projects initiated by the government.[28] Displacement among the tribals is on a massive scale and often with adverse implications on the communities, mainly due to laws that do not recognise the communal and customary rights of tribal people over their territories. Resettlement literature is replete with case studies on development projects that ignore the customary rights of the tribal people and treat them as illegal occupants of government land. Such an approach invariably leads to the impoverishment of once well settled communities; precisely the opposite of what development promises.[29]

Loss of Tribal Land during Survey and Settlement Operations

After abolition of intermediary land tenure systems, survey and settlement operations work was undertaken in the Scheduled Areas of Srikakulam, Vizianagaram, Visakhapatnam, East Godavari, West Godavari, Nugur and Bhadrachalam taluks of Khammam district of the Andhra region.

The survey and settlement operations are covered by Andhra Pradesh Regulations 1/69, 2/69 and 2/70, to settle the land occupations of both the tribals and non-tribals. Three tenures viz., *malguzari, muttadari* and estates prevailing in these areas were converted into *ryotwari*. The intermediaries *mahaldar, muttadar* and *zamindar* between the government and ryots were abolished.

All the Settlement Regulations referred above in fact dilute the letter and spirit of Land Transfer Regulations 1 of 70 by enabling non-tribals to claim patta over land situated in the Scheduled Areas, in effect negating the presumption that unless and until contrary proved, the land in occupation by non-tribals would be deemed to have come from the tribals through a transfer.

The Expert Group on Prevention of Alienation of Tribal Land and its Restoration, Ministry of Rural Development, Government of India, headed by the Planning Commission Member, B.N. Yugandhar has also cast a serious doubt on the settlement *patta* throughout Schedule Five areas. Similarly, the denial of *pattas* to the tribals is the other side of the coin of Settlement *Pattas*, which calls for a scrutiny of the rejection orders.[30]

As per the 1990 Report of Neerabh K Prasad, an IAS Officer, entitled 'Protection of Tribal Land' in the Settlement Regulations 2/69 and 2/70, it has been stipulated that the non-tribals had to prove eight years of continuous possession of land prior to 1969 and 1970 and an absence of any prohibited transfer as per Land Transfer Regulations, to be eligible for a grant of a *patta*. Further, it states that norms were openly flouted by the non-tribals. False receipts were created by the *mutta* clerks or estates clerks showing payment of taxes. The tribals were driven out by creating terror through organising police raids, thus making it convenient for the non-tribals to get the tribal land measured in their names. In a specific case at Nelakota village of East Godavari District, the village abuts a huge inland tank by the name of Ramavarapu Ava and gets irrigation from the same. The non-tribal residents of the adjacent villages, especially Ramachandrapuram, dubbed the tribals as naxalites (post-1969 Srikakulam Naxalite Movement period) and organised police raids. The tribals had to flee from the hill tops and stayed there for more than a month. This period was used by the non-tribals to get the land surveyed and settled in their favour. Land with rich forest growth was taken as *patta* even though tribals were never in occupation of the land; obviously with an eye to the rich timber. The cases of Jangalthota and Chintalpudi of Y. Ramavaram Mandals of East Godavari are glaring examples of these. The tribal claims were never properly examined and were largely unaware of the settlement operations. By the time the tribals realised that their land was being granted as *pattas* to the non-tribals, it was too late for an appeal. As a result of these dubious measures, the land holdings of the non-tribals jumped from 9,805 hectares before 1969 to 16,789 hectares by 1976 in the Scheduled Area of East Godavari District. [31] The non-tribals in three Agency mandals of West Godavari District hold *pattas* for over 53,719 acres, while tribals have *pattas* for over 37,042 acres only in the Scheduled Area as per the Minutes of the Cabinet Sub-Committee circulated on 24th July 1997:

Just before the abolition of the Estates, the landholders accelerated issuance of *pattas* in several cases even with regard to the waste land in the estates by receiving paltry sums. So the Settlement Officer is directed to reopen all the *pattas* that were granted till now under the provisions of Ryotwari Settlement Regulations 2 of 1970, observed by Justice BSA. Swamy while dealing with a case in relation to land disputes in West Godavari District Agency Areas.[32]

In Bhadrachalam division in Khammam district, 8,297 non-tribals were granted *pattas* for 29,554.16 hectares according to the Report of Secretary to Government (1992). Expressing concern over the grant of *ryotwari* settlement *pattas* to non-tribals in the Scheduled Areas during the survey period, the Secretary to Government, Govindarajan (1992) reports two cases have come to the attention of the Government during the course of verification by special officer for survey of tribal land and assignment to tribals in Khammam district in the month of July 1990. In one case five non-tribals were granted *ryotwari patta* in respect of an extent of 30 acres of land while the tribals are in possession and enjoyment of the said land. In another case, non-tribals have obtained *ryotwari pattas* in respect of an extent of 101 acres where as the tribals are in continuous occupation and enjoyment of the said land.

During 1996-1997 when land disputes erupted in tribal areas of West Godavari District, one of the major contention of the tribals was that they should be given possession of land as per the 1902 Resettlement Register (RSR) and the non-tribals who were occupying land classified as tribal or government in the 1902 Resettlement Register should prove that they had got hold of the land in a legal manner. The Resettlement Register of 1902 is currently not even available with the offices of the Commissioner, Tribal Welfare or the district.[33]

Extent of Tribal Land Dispossession

Dispossession of land for a variety of reasons is evident, including for mines, industries, hydro power, and irrigation projects resulting in both direct and indirect eviction of the tribal communities.[34] The decline in the percentage of cultivators among the ST households from 45 per cent to 35.4 per cent during the period 1994-2005 indicates the loss of land and their increasing dependency on agricultural labour which increased from 37 per cent to 43.7 per cent during the period 1994-2005. The percentage of population depending on agricultural labour increased only in the case of STs, while it has declined for the Scheduled Caste. [35] Even the existing land holdings of the marginalised have been alienated, in spite of score of laws in force for ensuring protection of the land rights of the marginalised, especially the Adivasis.[36]

Had history been otherwise, nearly five lakh tribal families living in the Scheduled villages of Andhra Pradesh would have presently together been the proud owners of 18,48,209.30 acres of land with an average household landholding of 3.69 acres. But instead, presently more than 48 per cent of this land is cultivated by the non-tribals. In some districts as Warangal, Khammam and Adilabad, more than 50 per cent of the land in the Scheduled villages is held by the non-tribals. The pernicious poverty of the tribals has led them to become victims of schemes of non-tribal money lenders, thus resulting in indebtedness and consequent alienation of land. To check the land alienation, several Land Transfer Regulations including 1 of 59 as amended by 1 of 70, were created prohibiting the transfer of land between tribals and non-tribals, and among the non-tribals since 1917. In spite of these restrictions, land alienation is still prevalent amongst the Adivasis. [37]

Implementation of Land Transfer Regulations

In 1917, soon after a two year long hit-and-run tribal insurgency in the Godavari Agency, the British enacted the first Agency Tract Interest and Land Transfer Act, to prohibit land transfers between hill tribes and non-tribals without prior permission from the District Collector. Subsequently, Land Transfer Regulations 1 of 59, as amended by 1 of 70, were made. Despite these being in force for long, 56 per cent of the cultivable land in the Scheduled Areas (about 8.7 lakh acres) is owned by the non-tribals, while the extent of land restored to tribals under these enactments is only nine per cent of this area (about 80,000 acres).[38] And, if anybody can ever manage to estimate the extent of agricultural land that is supposedly owned by tribals but in reality is being held and cultivated by the non-tribals, then these statistics would reveal an even more unequal state of affairs.[39]

There is another important legislation in respect of lands in the Telangana area of the State. The Andhra Pradesh (Telangana Area) Tenancy and

Table 15.1 : Outcome of Cases under LTR at SDC Courts as on 31st January, 2010

Sl. No	*District*	*Cases detected*		*Cases Disposed*		*Cases Decided in favour of STs*		*Cases Decided in favour of Non-STs*		*Land Restored to Tribals*		*Balance cases at the end of the month (col. 3-5 and 4-6)*	
		Nos	*Extent (Acres)*	*Nos*	*Extent (Acres)*	*Nos*	*Extent (Acres)*	*Nos*	*Extent (Acres)*	*Nos*	*Extent (Acres)*	*Nos*	*Extent (Acres)*
	1	2	3	4	5	6	7	8	9	10	11	12	13
1.	Srikakulam	462	1100	453	1024	296	538	157	486	250	522	9	76
2.	Vizianagaram	1364	7544	1343	7501	955	5631	388	1870	850	5498	21	43
3.	Visakhapatnam	5708	22731	5480	22087	4359	17721	1121	4366	3029	13944	228	644
4.	East Godavari	8485	49637	8264	48768	3751	19667	4513	29101	3392	17685	221	869
5.	West Godavari	11611	62121	11477	60820	2584	11082	8893	49738	2451	10081	134	1301
6.	Khammam	33582	126713	33325	125834	15514	52192	17811	73642	12750	41662	257	879
7.	Warangal	7289	15784	7052	15218	4865	8964	2187	6254	4865	8964	237	566
8.	Adilabad	8245	54008	7564	51543	4175	27839	3389	23704	3305	23606	681	2465
9.	Mahbubnagar	16	61	15	57	13	49	2	8	13	49	1	4
	Total	**76762**	**339699**	**74973**	**332852**	**36512**	**143683**	**38461**	**189169**	**30905**	**122011**	**1789**	**6847**

Source: Office of the Commissioner of Tribal Welfare, Hyderabad, Admin. Report, Jan. 2010.

Agricultural Land Act of 1950 classifies all tenants into ordinary and protected tenants. The Act further stipulates that if the tenant personally cultivated the land continuously for a period of six years during a stipulated period, he shall be deemed to be a protected tenant. As a protected tenant he reserves the right to purchase the land from the owner. This Act was also in force in the tribal areas of Telangana region. The non-tribals who gained access to land from tribals through clandestine and dubious methods were protected by the legislation. There was no law strictly prohibiting the transfer of land between tribals and non-tribals till 1963 in the Telangana region barring a revenue division Bhadrachalam in the Kammam district. The land reforms which were introduced by the State of Andhra Pradesh protecting the tenancy was made applicable to tribal areas without taking into cognisance the tribal interest.

The greater part of land alienation occurred after the 1940s. There are several loopholes in the existing Land Transfer Regulations 1 of 70. For instance, the law does not act retrospectively and thus cannot be applied to land transfer deals between the tribals and the non-tribals prior to the enforcement of the Act. Therefore, the exploitative relations in Agency areas still dominate the social structure. Hence, the problem of land alienation becomes part of the bigger problem of the existence of unequal class relations between the tribals and the non-tribals in the present day society.[40]

The suo motu power given to the government to proceed against non-tribals without waiting for a complaint from a tribal seems to be an ideal arrangement, but in the given administrative culture, it has perhaps been more of a boon to the non-tribals than to the tribals. In proceedings taken up suo motu by the government, the non-tribal faces only the government. The government does not take the trouble of finding out who among the local tribals may have a claim to the land. It does not publicise the enquiry in the village. The officer hearing the cases, designated as Special Deputy Collector, merely looks into the documents provided by the non-tribal, and if they appear reliable, he approves the right of the non-tribal over the land.[41]

Of 76,762 cases covering an extent of 3,39,699 acres of land, 74,973 cases covering an extent of 3,32,852 acres were disposed off by the SDC Courts in the State of Andhra Pradesh by the end of January 2010. The courts decided 36,512 cases covering an extent of 1,43,683 acres of land in favour of the tribals. However, the enforcement machinery set up under the regulations could only restore 1,22,011 acres of land pertaining to the 30,905 cases out of a total of 36,512. On the contrary, the non-tribals were able to secure orders in their favour in 38,461 cases and retained 1,89,169 acres of land in their possession.

Table shows that the success rate for land acquisition is 49 per cent in the case of tribals, and 51 per cent in the case of non-tribals. Tribals were able to regain land possession from non-tribals only to the extent of 43 per cent of the total extent of land, covered by cases disposed off, while the non-tribal could retain 57 per cent of the disputed land. Due to the failure of the implementing machinery in implementing the orders passed by the SDC Court in favour of the tribals, only 85 per cent of the total cases were disposed off in favour of the tribals, and only 85 per cent of land extent was physically handed over to them. This shows the failure of the administrative machinery in executing orders passed by the court in the favour of tribals. The non-tribals continued to possess land even when the eviction orders were passed against them.

The Scheduled Areas is to ensure justice to tribals, their survival and livelihood. But as K. Balagopal pointed out:

It is not enough if a disadvantaged class of people are endowed with legal rights. Legal instruments created for the benefit of the socially privileged can be expected to find their way to implementation without anything else. This is not the case with legal rights enacted for the benefit of the disadvantaged.'[42]

Conclusion

The extent of land alienation in the Scheduled Areas is a cause for public concern. The process of land alienation has not stopped even after the promulgation of tribal protective land laws due to weak enforcement of the laws. Tribals have lost their land due to multiple attacks, including the exploitative mechanism compounded by forcible acts of the non-tribal settlers and the interventions of the state in dispossessing their land. The tribal land alienation issue is further complicated by the mainstream political parties due to their tilt towards the non-tribal vote bank policies. The special protection extended for tribal rights through various legislations with the support of main opposition parties are part of the welfare measures of the State, but without the political will to actually convert them into a reality. As a result of land alienation, the tribals have lost livelihood and their cultural linkage with the natural resources. Perhaps, the tribal belt will experience more and more incursions of the non-tribals and industrial interests in future and lose its character despite the Fifth Schedule of the Constitution. The magnitude of the problem is of national importance and needs to be tackled and solved through Parliamentary intervention and effective enforcement of the laws.

Notes

Abkari tax	:	Excise Tax.
Koneru Land Committee	:	Koneru Land Committee headed by the State Minister Koneru Ranga Rao was constituted in 2005 to study the tribal land problems and give recommendations, followed by discussions held between Maoists and State of Andhra Pradesh.
Mukhasa	:	Mukhasa is a village or land assigned to an individual either rent free or at a low rent, on condition of services.
Mutta	:	A village or group of villages held by a Muttadar.
Muttadar	:	A person who holds Mutta under a Sanad granted by the Government subject to payment of a fixed amount of land revenue

		and who assists the Government in maintaining law and order in the Mutta.
Patta	:	Land entitlement deed.
Pattadar	:	The Ryotwari proprietor is usually termed as pattadar.
Poromboke	:	Poromboke is a land belonging to Government which is not *prima* facie available for assignment.
Proprietor	:	Land lord or Land holder of villages held by Estate, Mutta, Mukasa.
SDC court	:	Special Deputy Collector (Tribal Welfare) is a designated enquiry officer under Land Transfer Regulations to conduct enquires for restoration of lands from the possession of non-tribals in the scheduled areas. The court is manned by SDC.

References

1. Ambagudia, Jagannath. Tribal Rights, Dispossession and the State in Orissa, Economic and Political Weekly, 14th August 2010, Vol. xlv, No. 33, 2010.

2. Areas of Srikakulam, Vijayanagaram, Visakhapatnam, East and West Godavari, Kammam, Warangal and Adilabad districts were notified by the President of India under Fifth Schedule to the Constitution of India.

3. Arnold, David. Rebellious Hillmen: The Gudem Rampa Rising 1839-1924 in Ranajit Guha (Ed.), Subaltern Studies I, OUP, Delhi, 1982.

4. Ashokvardhan, C. Tribal Land Rights in India, Centre for Rural Studies, LBS National Academy of Administration, Musoorie, 2006.

5. Balagopal, K. Foreword to book Land Rights of Adivasis by P. Trinadha Rao (2004) Laya Publication, Visakhapatnam.

6. Balagopal, K. Land Unrest in Andhra Pradesh – III – Illegal Acquisition in Tribal Areas, Economic and Political Weekly, 6th October 2007, p. 4031.

7. Balagopal, K. Pitting the Tribals against the Non-tribal Poor, Economic and Political Weekly, 27th May 1989, p. 1151.

8. Beteille, Andre. (1974). Studies in Agrarian Social Structure. Oxford: Oxford University Press.

9. Burman, Roy B.K. Communal Land System of the Tribals and Problems of Institutional Finance in Manipur and Tripura, Delhi, 1986.

10. Draft National Policy on Tribals, Ministry of Tribal Affairs, GoI, New Delhi, 2004.

11. For details see, Patnaik, S.C. and S. Patel. Impact of Modernisation on Tribals: Economic dualism and path of change (A case study of Malkangiri sub-division in Koraput district), paper presented in the Seminar on 'Prospectus of Economic Development of Tribal of Koraput District held in October (Mimeo), 1982, pp. 2-14.

12. For instance Vidyarthi, LP (1963) The Maler: The Nature-Man-Spirit Complex in a Hill Tribe introduces the concept of 'nature-man-spirit' in anthropology and Bharath Bhushan M and Satyamohan PV (1990) study of the tribal scenario in Andhra Pradesh The Koyas - A Study of Nature–Man-Spirit-Complex among the Koyas of Bhadrachalam (mimeograph) explains the inseparable link of land with tribal

life. The ethnographic film in Search of Ethnic Dimension - The Koyas made for the University Grants Commission deals with the nature-man interaction and the associated belief system. It examines the features of the environment in relation to the Koya economic system. Also see http://video.google.com/videoplay?docid= 12041 60986501454199&hl=en#.

13. Girglani Commission. J.M. (2005), Committee Report of Ministry of Rural Development (Government of AP).

14. Godavari district Gazetteer, Government Press, Madras, 1907, p. 101.

15. Heredia, Rudolf C. Tribal History, Living Word or Dead Letter, Economic and Political Weekly, 29th April 2000.

16. Istvan Meszaros (2006), "Marx's theory of Alienation". Aakar Books, New Delhi.

17. Mohan Lal, Morley. Poverty Alleviation: The Indian Experience. Delhi: Himalaya Publishing House, 1988, p. 386.

18. Nath, N, D.K. Behera, and Sarkar, R.M. (Eds.). The So-called Development, Displacement and Dispossession: An Analysis on Land and Forest Rights of the Project Affected People. Land and Forest Rights of the Tribals Today, Serials Publications, Delhi, 2006.

19. Note on Land Problems in Agency Areas of West Godavari, Social Welfare (TW) Department, Government of AP, Hyderabad, 1997.

20. Gangamma P.Vs. Vasudha Misra and another. 1998(2) ALD 35.

21. Philip Viegas (1991), Encroached and Enslaved, Indian Social Institute Publication, Delhi, p. 32.

22. Pinto, Ambrose. Fillip to Land Transfers Land Acquisition Bill, Economic and Political Weekly, 5th December 1988.

23. Ramnath, Madhu. Surviving the Forest Rights Act: Between Scylla and Charybdis, Economic and Political Weekly, 1st March 2008.

24. Ranga Rao, Koneru. The Land Committee Report - 2006, GoAP, Hyderabad, 2006, p. 57.

25. Rao, Trinadha P. Tribal Development in Question, Laya Publication, Visakhapatnam, 2004.

26. Rao, Trinadha P. Nature of Opposition to Polavaram Project, Economic and Political Weekly, 15th April, 2006.

27. Rao, Trinadha P. Persisting Alienation of Tribal Land, A.P. Social Watch Report, Hyderabad, 2007.

28. Rao, B. Janardhana. Land Alienation in Tribal Areas of Andhra Pradesh, Kakatiya University, Warangal, 1987.

29. Rao, B, Janardhana. Adivasis in India – Characterisation of Transition and Development, Adhyayana Publications, Warangal, 2000.

30. Rao, Jayaprakash P. The Struggle for Land: Tribal Revolts in Two Villages, in K. Murali Manohar, P. Ramaiah and C. Sivaramakrishna Rao (Eds.) Political Economy of Tribal Development, Indian Institute of Public Administration, Warangal, 1985.

31. Reddy, Subba N. Sword of Damocles over Tribal People of Andhra Pradesh, Economic and Political Weekly, 1st July 1989, pp. 1442-3.

32. Report of Commissioner for SC and ST (Fifth Report), Ministry of Tribal Affairs, GoI, Delhi, 1982-83, p. 28.

33. Report of Ministry of Rural Development Department of Land Resources, Govt. of India, Delhi, 2000.

34. Report on Human Development, CESS, Begampet, Hyderabad, 2007.

35. Samata Vs. State of Andhra Pradesh AIR 1997, p. 3301.

36. Sastry, VNVK. Between Gonds Rebellion, Udyama Publications, Hyderabad, 1989.

37. Satyanarayana, K. A Study of History and Culture of the Andhras, People's Publishing House, New Delhi, 1975, p. 44.

38. Shah, G. Social Movements in India: A Review of Literature, Sage, New Delhi, 1990.

39. Sharma, T.R (1979), "Karl Marx: From Alienation to Exploitation", Indian Journal of Political Science. Vol. 40, No. 3rd September.

40. The Twenty-Ninth Report of the Commissioner of Scheduled Castes and Tribes (1990) says that even though tribal people form about 7.5 per cent of the population, over 40 per cent of the people displaced till 1990, belonged to these communities. A report of the Official Working Group on Development and Welfare of Scheduled Tribes during the Eighth Five-Year Plan (1990-1995) on the rehabilitation of tribal people, based on a comprehensive study of 110 projects, has concluded that of the 1.694 million people displaced by these projects, almost 50 per cent (814,000) were tribals.

41. Tribal Welfare Department, Government of Andhra Pradesh, Land Reforms and Land Transfers, Report of Tribal Welfare Department, Hyderabad, 1995.

42. Trivedi, H. Tribal Land Systems Land Reform Measures and Development of Tribals, Concept Publications, New Delhi, 1993.

16

Governance in Tribal Areas in Contemporary Time: Tribal Peoples' Voice and Livelihood from Chhattisgarh

Pradip Kumar Parida

Key Words

Ecology vs. Economy, Right to Life with Dignity, 'People's Voice in Development, Tribal Development, Crisis in Governability, Law and Order Problem-It's Socio- Economic Roots.

Abstract

In the name of good governance the Indian state has molded contemporary economic policy in such a way that it creates question mark not only on the environmental issues but also the very existence of certain section of society. The trajectory path of development in India is producing 'forced migration' as well as 'development refugees'. People are becoming refugee in their own land. This is a process of further marginalisation for the already marginalised people and also accelerating the process of 'alienation' among the tribal's of the country. When people protest against these types of activities, it is termed as movement against the state. What about the 'life' and 'livelihood' of a citizen from the point of view of 'human security'. What about the right to life with dignity? What about ecology of the society and the involvement of the community in terms of maintaining their livelihood vs. the economic development of the state and the security of the individuals, i.e., life and liberty. Can the state sacrifice the environment justice in the name of market driven development paradigm?

Introduction

There is a rough consensus among all of us that, the movement towards good governance must include initiatives to strengthen the institutions of government and civil society with the objective of making government more accountable, transparent, open, democratic, participatory as well as promotion of law. The word 'Governance' dates back to origin of civilisation, to the pre-historic period. Since then the growth of civilisation though has undergone a zigzag motion, 'governance' has remained the key to 'state structure' in terms of its relationship with citizens, irrespective of region, religion, social structure, level of economic development as well as the nature of political regime. Etymologically 'governance' means, how to govern oneself—for example, the citizens in a state. In other words, governance is a process and government is an agency of governance where the citizens are the primary stake holders in this larger picture.

As a matter of fact, 'governance' legitimises the actions and duties as well as responsibilities of a 'citizen' in a given 'state structure'. As per the law of the land 'what is the entitlement of a citizen', keeping in background the political history, socio-economic development, resources available with the government at that particular point of time, social structure, cultural factors, level of participation of the people etc. Hence, providing the space for legitimate entitlement of a citizen in a state and creating a conducive atmosphere to realise the best potential within the individual concerned are the two key tasks with the government, as far as governance is concerned. This spreads into all the aspects of society—social, economic, political. This spreads from individual to local to district to regional to national to global level. It also clovers the arena of State, Civil society and Market. All of them influence the decision making process and behaviour of the individual— 'citizen'. It is perceived that 'accountability and transparency' will be at the heart of 'governance'. This is a broader term than 'government' and refers to traditions, norms, institutions, practices, space to the citizens and the procedures by which individuals and groups exercise power in public decision making. It also gives more space to the citizens by making them actively involved in implementation of various programmes. However accountability may not necessarily be considered as accountability from government side to people. It is also other way round, which means people should be accountable to other fellow citizens as well as government, for the day to day actions in a true civic sense, by maintaining the true spirit of democracy.

Contemporary Situation across the Globe

How the citizens participate in the governance process at the local level and more particularly the local bodies' there—be it political, economic, cultural activities, taxation system or decision making process. There is no short cut to it. But it becomes questionable, when there is lack of transparency and accountability from the local bodies/local government in terms of sharing power or resources with the common citizens—which otherwise is the crux of the 'decentralised democracy'- 'empowerment of people'—the basic philosophy and objective behind formation of 'local self government'—'self-ruling institutions'. Millen Development Goal (MDG) of the United Nations categorically mentions about the minimum amount of development standards or parameters a country must achieve in this millennium, so that there will be universal minimum standard of living across the globe. How does one achieve that goal? What are the mechanisms? When we talk about "*Dignity with Development*", how much dignified our public policy in terms of giving the space to citizens. What are the alternatives before us at the present juncture? *As we know the economic development will lead to more and more social opportunities* and will widen the scope of human civilisation in terms of sustenance. How one can come to such a conclusion, giving the background of governance in our country today. These are the questions before us.

As a matter of fact 'Government' is one of the most powerful institutions in our society in any system of governance. But free market, privatisation, structural adjustment, deregulation and decentralisation, the traditional role of 'government', has changed a lot. The actors of governance, Corporate Sectors in 'market economy' and Civil Society in 'development sectors' are playing important role in this scenario. Hence, naturally the question comes to us, is governance becomes 'good' with the minimum role of government in policy matters. The proponents of neo-liberal favours minimalist role of government and prefers market can do everything on the basis of principle of market economy. The most important point is people in a democracy are not merely 'customers' or 'clients', of the government, rather they are also 'subjects', and 'citizens' are also bounded by mutual obligations and are entitled to enjoy public infrastructure provided by the government, such as roads, ports, communications, court of law, monetary system, public sanitation etc.

In this context, it is argued by many that the pure private sector management model cannot cater to the needs of the citizens. As a matter of fact private goods are necessary. But they are worthless without public goods—such as policing and economic policies, meant to protect citizens. For example, media, it must not be fully under government control nor should be it is entirely in private hands. However, the objective of democratic government is to create a conducive environment and protect free people, not free private groups, and institutions supporting them. Hence we can say that attacks on government are attacks on the very fabric of society.

Environmental and Livelihood Issues

'Sustainable development' has become the key word in the contemporary discourse in development. The way natural resources are being exploited for the consumption purposes, that is not only giving a space for indiscriminate use of natural resources, but also creating problems for lives and livelihood of thousands of aboriginal people who are original inhabitants of this country, who are primarily residing in forest, i.e., so called adivasis (tribal's). Forget about future generation, even we are not considering our present generations. Otherwise, we would not have exploited our recourses in that fashion. Above all the natural resources are not infinite in nature. There is certain limit to it. What about the blue print on it. For example, what is the amount of natural resources, where are they located, exact amount, its utility at present and in future, modality of extraction, who will extract—whether private or government, what is the mechanism for that,—all these issues, are they are in public domain.

If we will look into the industrialisation process carried out in contemporary times across the globe, we will find not only natural environment is getting polluted but also the socio-cultural practices, economic issues (livelihood) political factors (people's protest against this), legal issues (who is the original owner—is it the state or people who are enjoying the nature for centuries and generations) are intimately involved in this. Particularly in India, since the new economic policy (NEP) started due to the onslaught of globalisation and opening of the whole market for private players (be it local industrial houses or MNCs), the people's displacement is becoming rampant, without proper rehabilitation policy. Their resettlement is becoming more problematic. People are becoming 'refugees' in their 'own home land'. What type of development is this? If we will examine these issues more minutely, whole social movements in the last two decades across South-Asia including India is primarily concentrating on control over natural resources—*Jal, Jingle* and *Jamin* (water, land, forest). All these are part of the local ecology, where an individual is leading his day to day life on the lap of nature.

On the name of industrialisation where market economy determines everything, who cares about the lives and livelihood issues of innocent tribals? Are the industrial houses getting clearance from the tribal's panchayats (as per PESA Act) genuinely or in fraudulent manner? What is the proper mechanism to get the approval of tribal people? What about the Environment/Social Impact Assesessment? What about placing it in public domain? Who are the gainers and who are the loosers at the end of the day? These are very important issues in this context. When we talk about industrialisation, do we give also equal importance to our fellow citizens' 'right to lead a life with dignity'? Today we found the undercurrent of a strong Maoist movement in the certain states of central India, where the exploitation of natural resources and displacement of tribal's due to it has taken to the maximum extent. This symbolically reflects something very serious.

The Stories from a Tribal Belt of Chhattisgarh

The fundamental question is why this is happening in such a manner today? Though that part of Chhattisgarh is full of natural resources, forests, minerals, the tribal's are at the bottom of everything. Hardly any parameter of the so called 'development' has reached to them, i.e., primary schools, primary health centres, land holding for them who has accepted agriculture as occupation—whatever miniscule it may be, village networking roads, all these are lacking. A tribal is not feeling as a part of the state system. *Their alienation from the State and the larger society is increasing day by day including land alienation.* The massive exploitation by petty contractor, forest mafia, usurping land by big industrialists at a nominal price or free of cost, creating suspicion in the minds of a tribal. What about his expectations from the state? Who is reaping the benefit? For example, though the Bastar region has abundance of mineral resources, i.e. Bailadila mines and large forest tracts and one Railway line—Kirandul exists, has it given any benefits to the tribal's? The iron ore being expropriated from Kirandul has been exported to Japan. No industry has been established there. At present whatever industry is being established, the land is taken without their permission, even if it comes under PESA and so also as far as jobs are concerned tribal's are only given as unskilled labourers.

There is lack of proper implementation of any development programmes, for example, recently enacted NREGA (according to many fact finding reports from the field including the report of Prof. Jean Dreeze). Has it any impact on tribals of Bastar. I think, a well documented and focused research is needed to come out for a conclusion. What about their livelihood pattern in a changing economic scenario? The tribal's who were dependent on forest resources and rivers for centuries, generation after generation are deprived of all these due to increasing state control as well as 'privatisation of water', timber, forest resources. Hence their grievances, frustration is taking another channel, where Naxalism is getting the chance to breed. Nothing new in it. The tribal's found a hope to express their hopes as well as frustration. Hence there is a clear cut vacuum in the governance system of the state, which is now occupied by Naxalites. But to stop it the state is responding in a more fascist way. (As an academician and researcher I am not supporting violence at any cost by any logic. As violence breeds violence). But what is the alternative for tribal's in such a situation.

Fundamental Rights of an Individual in a given State Structure

What are the rights of a 'citizen' in such a situation? As a 'citizen' in a 'democratic state', where is the space for me to ventilate the grievances within the 'state structure' itself? Where is the channel of communication between the government and people? What is the alternative mechanism to address these problems? Is the naxalite movement is simply a 'law and order' problem or it has certain larger socio-political and economic dimensions involved with it? Is it SPO-private militia is the solution to curb the violence by Naxalism. By the way Naxalite were ideologically in favour of militant armed struggle against the state, to abolish the state structure and transfer the state power. How to stop the violence created by them? It has its root in socio-economic issues, underdevelopment, bad governance system etc. Hence it is also a socio-economic problem which has culminated into a political problem having symptoms like law and order problem in the present context. Hence, it has to be tackled at political level, which is totally undermined today. Where is the space for dialogue, discussion, debate with those groups, who are against the state in armed struggle?

Findings from Tribal Belts across the Country

There is a need of changing paradigm of public policy to address these types of challenges. Not only Chhattisgarh, the other tribal belts of the country, i.e., Nagaland, Bodoland, Gorkhaland, Mizoram, Tripura, Jharkhand, some part of Orissa, Andhra Pradesh, Madhya Pradesh is witnessing this problem. Personally I feel, it is global phenomena, where the movement of the global political economy is controlling everything today. Whatever might be the circumstances and causes of problem, ultimately it is the innocent tribals are the worst sufferers. 'Human Security' is affected to a larger extent. The right to life with dignity is undermined at any cost. The aftermath of neo-liberal regime in the context of globalisation is witnessing these types of phenomena all over the world, across the globe. The reason being when market economy determines the state policies, particularly public policies, rights of the citizens, particularly 'human rights' takes a back seat. In this context the most vulnerable sections are – 'the sub-alterns', i.e., dalits, tribals, minorities and other socially marginalised sections. The present scenario of Chhattisgarh is classic example of this. However the commonality among all the movements of aboriginals across the world is who controls the natural resources and why the state is taking decisions in an arbitrary manner rather taking the affected into confidence.

Conclusion

We must have to have a paradigmatic shift from social science perspective to understand this to relate an individual and state in terms of the 'rights' of the tribal's of the country. When the fundamental rights of the people is violated (i.e., right to life with dignity, right to livelihood etc.) which are guaranteed by the constitution, what is the remedy for that. Even if some rights are not guaranteed by the constitution but enjoyed by the human beings because they are part of human civilisation. When these are violated, affected people protest against it. But if it does not stop, they protest it violently. How the solution can be arrived in this case? What about dialogue, debate and discussion in this scenario? Where is the space for democratic process? Government is a product of historical evolution. The basic argument is that government as an instrument of governance is indispensable. The 'state' came into existence due to certain rationality. Hence, the 'state' has certain activities for the citizens that are protection of life, liberty and creating a conducive atmosphere for their development and maintenance of law and order. In that context it can be argued that if the state fails to fulfill its obligation, the tribal people have every right to question the actions of the government, particularly, when their life and livelihood is at stake, they must revolt against the state, otherwise their voice will be unheard.

References

1. Bhaduri Amit and Deepak Nayar, *The Intelligent Persons Guide to Liberalisation*, Penguin, New Delhi, 1996.
2. Soros George, *On Globalisation*, Viva Books Private Limited, New Delhi, 2004.
3. Mathur, Kuldeep, *From Government to Governance*, NBT India, New Delhi, 2008.
4. Bhagwati Jagdish, *India in Transition*, Clarendon Press, Oxford, 1995.
5. Basu, D.D., *Constitution of India*, Prentice Hall India, New Delhi, 1998.
6. Bhaduri Amit, *Dignity with Development*, NBT, New Delhi, 2004.
7. L.P. Vidyarthi and Binay Kumar Rai, *The Tribal Culture of India*, Concept Publishing Company, New Delhi, 1976.
8. Dhebar, U.N.: "*Dhebar Commission Report*".
9. Ghurye, G.S.: "*The Scheduled Tribes*", Popular Book Depot, Mumbai, 1959.
10. Majumdar, D.N.: "*Affairs of a Tribe*", Universal Publishers, Lucknow, 1953.
11. Sachidanand: "*Culture and Change in Tribal Bihar*", Bookland Limited, Calcutta, 1964.
12. Elwin, Verrier: "*Nagaland*", Research Department, Advisor's Secretariat, Shillong, 1961.
13. Srinivas, M.N.: "*Social Change in Modern India*", Allied Publishers, Bombay, 1961.
14. Srivastava, S.K.: "*The Tharus A Study of Culture Dynamics*", Agra University Press, Agra, 1958.
15. Rao, V.K.R.V: "*Social Change and Tribal Society*", Journal of Social Research, Vol. IX, No. 2nd, September 1966.
16. Vidyarthi, L.P.: "*Ghaghra-A Village of Chhotanagpur*", Manager Publications, New Delhi, 1966.
17. Sundar, Nandini. *Subalterns and the Sovereign*.
18. Chakravarty, Sudip. *Traverse in Red Corridor.*
19. Planning Commission Report on Naxalite Affected Areas.
20. Supreme Court, High Court and other tribunal judgments related to the above mentioned issues.

17

Environmental Approach to Tribal Development

Satchidananda Misra

Our so called development projects push the tribals out of their natural habitat. Most often new development experiments result in tribal displacement by new migrants. We presume that tribal population benefit by the general development programme. But the hopes in this regard were belied as the benefits of the development programme did not percolate to the tribals. The task force on development of tribal areas observed that factors for the failure of tribal development programme include non-involvement of tribal people in the process, attitude of planners and decision-makers towards the tribals.

The present scenario demands a revitalising of existing development strategies and new orientation to the perspective of tribal development. Environmental approach to the tribal development can solve a lot many problems of the tribals. The tribal man puts least pressure on nature for his subsistence. He is the—— 'noble savage', the natural and the 'primitive' idealised by many thinkers. An insight into the tribal culture and their way of life can vindicate the environmental dimension of development. Development becomes a myth without tribal upliftment. A development project which creates a lot of deforestation and environmental hazards bring endless miseries for the man in the forest.

All round development of tribes is possible through environmental conservation. The tribe must be allowed to participate in the process of decision making. During last century the erosion of tribal rights in land and forest resources has led to tribal resistance in different parts of the world. Despite a plethora of legislations, special safeguards and other development programmes, tribal right in land and forest resources, large scale displacement, increasing inequalities and poverty, degraded social states causing tribal tensions, identity crisis have emerged as baffling problems. The beauties of the country landscape and virtues of simple tribal life are to be celebrated in contrast to the growing urbanisation. A time has come to extend the benefits of globalised world to him through development projects without jeopardising the pristine nature which alone can assure them a good life. Environmental approach to tribal development can alone achieve this objective.

Environmentalism has given a new perspective to the tribal problems. Environmentalism and tribalism are very closely related. Hills and Forests, the very natural habitat of the tribes are the store house of experiments for the environmentalist. The causes of basic problems of the tribal people like alienation, poverty, starvation, malnutrition, poor health are attributed to environmental hazards.

With the advent of globalisation world is shrinking. The difference between 'we' and 'they', the 'non-tribals' and 'tribals' narrows down. Over the years as a result of culture contact with globalised modern societies, the primitives have been deprimitivised. No longer the tribes reside in pristine serenity. Concept of 'noble savage' is becoming meaningless. Scholars in this area have observed that the people whom we study are no longer hidden, forgotten, lost or cloistered.

Malinowski's Concept of practical anthropology has become very important for the present day planners and policy-makers of a welfare state. They tend to use anthropological knowledge to diagnose the problem and to suggest remedies for the social, economic and cultural problems. The administrators are getting themselves trained in the use of these practical methods to cope with the problems in general and in the field of tribal development in particular. India has the largest concentration of tribal people anywhere in the world except in Africa. 2001 Census keeps the tribal population somewhere around 84 millions. It has identified 698 Scheduled Tribes. 75 out of 698 tribes have been identified as primitive tribal groups.

Hence development policies and process emphasise the need of tribal development. Sachchidananda in one of his articles 'Tribal Development: Challenges in the Nineties' mentioned— "Promotion of the economic interest of the tribals has been one of the basic planks of planned development. It was presumed that the tribal population benefit by the general development programmes in the normal course. Besides this, provision was made through special central assistance to supplement these efforts. This was to speed up the process of development so that they could be brought on par with the rest of the people in the shortest possible time. But the hopes in this regard were belied as the benefits of the general programmes did not percolate to the tribals and the supplementary programmes in fact supplanted them." Singh (1977: 242) rightly said ... "Tribal development is at crossroads. Objectives have been planned and declared. Financial resources have been garnered and earmarked. The planning process, set in motion has proceeded far. If we fail to achieve the objectives, tribal expectations having been aroused, we shall succeed in generating frustrations."

Wherever new development experiments are conducted in tribal areas, the tribal people are losing land and are being pushed back from wherever new opportunities are arising. They are pushed back by new migrant. They lose their land as it is taken by new establishments. The task force on 'Development of Tribal Area' observed that one of the factors for the failure of the development programme is that the Scheduled Tribes and tribal areas have been looked upon as a 'Welfare' problem. Another reason for the failure of development schemes for tribals is that the tribal are not involved in the process. Something like a so-called development is imposed on them. As the problem of the tribals are unique, it is not only essential that they are actively involved in planning as well as implementation of the programme but also create confidence among them in the policies of the Government. Same mechanism must be evolved in order to bring them closer to the mainstream. The process of tribal development should be participatory.

Another important area of study is the tribal rights. During the last century, the erosion of tribal right in land and forest resources has led to movements of tribal resistance in different parts of India and world. The notion of human rights in one of greatest gifts of classical and contemporary human thought to culture and civilisation. These rights to life, right to adequate means of livelihood, freedom from exploitation. The question is to what extent the society has become able to extend these rights to the tribals who live mostly in isolation from mainstream. Despite a plethora of legislations, special safeguards and other development programmes tribal rights in land and forest resource, large scale displacement, increasing inequalities and poverty, degraded social status causing tribal tensions, identity crisis have emerged as baffling problems.

'Development' is not a linear process of creating economic abundance. It is a holistic process. Creative participation of all the members of the society is mandatory in order to bring alround amelioration for all sections of the society. Emphasis on 'Creative participation' of the members and institutions implies minimisation of the entropy or disorderliness in a social system and maximisation of creativity. The problem of distributive justice is also associated with tribal development.[1] Problems like poverty alleviation, land alienation, health and disease, displacement are the consequences of so-called development models for tribals. Most of the tribal development projects have cosmetic approaches rather than the real intentions of providing genuine remedies to the problems of tribes. A report of Planning Commission of India states that a large majority of India's population is denied access to natural resources. These natural resources rather are diverted towards the urban centre to support luxury consumption.[2] The biggest failure of models for development of tribals is that it has disintegrated the symbiotic relationship between man and nature through its overemphasis on econocentrism and consumerism. Hence, the desired goal i.e., enduring and sustainable development for the tribal is defeated.

S.N. Tripathy, a researcher in the field of tribal studies has tried to find out the characteristic features of tribal economy and attempted at evaluating the government policies in connection with tribal development. He has observed that the backwardness of tribal regions widespread poverty of the tribal and problems of integrating them with the mainstream of modern civilisation are great hindrances in the path of tribal development.[3] During the British reign because of the policy of 'leave them alone' tribals were left out of the process of development. Even though this policy of isolation was meant for retention of distinct tribal lifestyle and culture, impoverishment continued. After independence Indian planning aimed at the protective and development aspect of tribal development. The protective aspects aimed at preservation of their unique cultural traits and development aspects aim at bringing about various welfare measures for them. In various five-year Plans due attention was given for tribal development. The objectives of these plans are to (i) give priority to agriculture and rural development with a view to generate adequate productive employment and eradication of poverty, (ii) ensure food and nutritional security for all particularly the vulnerable section of society, (iii) accelerate growth rate of tribal economy with stable prices (iv) provide basic minimum service like safe drinking water, primary health care facilities etc. (v) ensure environmental sustainability of development process (vi) strengthen efforts to build-up self-reliance, etc. The Annual Report of Ministry of Welfare, Government of India (1995-96) exposes the disadvantages and handicaps of the tribes. The strategy for tribal development should be devised in such a way that it can solve perpetual deprivations of the tribes without jeopardising the eco-system.

Viewing the deteriorated socio-economic conditions of the tribal people as a result of their contact with non-tribal cultures one school of thought advocates measures to put a stop to culture contact and to preserve the tribes in their pristine purity. But the second school of thought advocated policy of complete assimilation of tribe with neighbouring non-tribal cultures.[4]

One of the most exciting areas of research today is tribal development. The study of tribes becomes still more interesting with the present day environmental crises in the background. Anthropological studies of aboriginal tribes include areas like tribal rituals, culture, customs, history etc. Tribalism has evoked a lot of debate between the 'isolationists' and 'assimilationist'. One group attempts to protect the tribal interests and rights through a policy of isolationism. It feels that tribes need to be protected from outside interference. The other group wants to protect the tribal culture through the process of assimilation with the mainstream.

The policy followed by the Government for the development of the Scheduled Tribes in independent India bears a strong imprint of the colonial legacy. The immediate task before the Government of free India is to remove the communication gap between tribals and regional community in the framework of national integration, to protect the resource base and to initiate measures to meet the immediate needs of the tribes.

Four phases of the development policies regarding scheduled tribes can be identified in the post-independent period—(a) Provision of immediate relief in terms of amenities and building up the productive infrastructure for future growth (b) emphasis on resources mobilisation and provision of social service infrastructure (c) reduction of disparity and growth with justice and (d) participatory development with focus on self-management harnessing of productive forces for meeting the basic needs as well as to contribute to self-reliant growth.[5]

The tribes live in intimate relationship with forests and their entire existence has been linked with forestry due to historical and environmental factors. The life of the tribes rotate around the forests. Hence forest policies of the state have a direct bearing on tribal development. The National Forest Policy 1952, 1980, Recommendation of Debar Commission, B.K. Ray Burman Committee, National Committee on Development of Backward Areas (1980) are of relevance in context of tribal development. The new forest policy categorically stated that rights and concessions enjoyed by them should be fully protected. Their domestic requirements of fuel wood, fodder, minor forest produces and construction of timber should be allowed to be fulfilled through forest products. But an analysis made by Nadeem Hasnain has exposed the inadequacies of the National Forest Policy of 1988 in catering to the needs of the tribes.[6]

Development involves change in land and water use patterns. Since independence the five-year plans resulted in displacement of many tribals. The more unfortunate event is multiple displacement. The tribal groups are displaced several times due to development projects. If displacement is inevitable, resettlement must include reconstruction of production system, raising standards of living and minimising, the conflict with host community. "The commitment therefore has to be not just for resettlement but for rehabilitation which should be an entitlement and not an act of reluctant generosity." (Smith Kothari, 1995)

Apprehensions are expressed that modern development programme and projects for the tribes may be injurious to their culture. The development perspective has to consider preservation and promotion of the essential components of the cultural heritage of the tribes. Preserving the cultural heritages on the one hand and working out a process of development on the other may be guided by certain principles. (i) The cultural principles without which the oustees will loose their identity and cultural heritage should be identified and their positive and negative impacts on the society as perceived by the people themselves should be critically examined and enumerated. (ii) The changes the oustees welcome after critical assessment of the situation due to resettlement should be examined. Researches should be conducted regarding the identification of the tools of developments and to ascertain how these could be used for the formulation of the programme of tribal development while presenting their cultural milieu.[7]

The strategy of sustainable development can be successful when the development programmes selected and implemented are consistent with the cultural heritage and cultural dynamics. The programme should be based on right type of tools of development, mostly eco-friendly tools identified for the tribal community.

Scholars observe that the programmes of tribal development are so far like 'straight jacket', generic and universal packages which are delivered at the threshold of tribal communities. The programmes like IRDP, ICDS and JRY must be added with an environmental dimension in order to increase their acceptability before the tribal communities. The environmental approach to tribal development emphasises the role of NGOs working in a tribal belt. They work as agents of change for them and act as bridges between the tribes and non-tribes. The success of resettlement and rehabilitation programmes depends largely on these voluntary groups which are the harbingers of tribal movement. Sometimes the tribal development programmes are pursued keeping political goals in view. This will not help much.

The present scenario demands a revitalising of existing development strategies and new-orientation to the perspective of tribal development.

Some suggestions are extended by the scholars working in this field for ensuring development for the tribes.

(a) The complex problems facing the scheduled tribes can be tackled more smoothly if we empathise with them and take a holistic view of life. The tribals can avail of the welfare and development programmes only if the anti-exploitative measures are effectively implemented.

(b) Instead of Tribal sub-plan, a separate plan for tribal areas in each state should be formulated. On the basis of the allocation of funds area specific and people specific tribal plans may be formulated.

(c) Another important job is to assess the state of culture and developmental needs of a group. A thorough survey is to be conducted in order to obtain quantitative data on educational and economic level. More education facilities should be provided which can open up scope to understand the world around.

(d) Awareness drive has to be accelerated in the tribal areas about tribal rights, participatory process.

(e) Forest Conservation Act should be relaxed as to ensure subsistence to tribals in general and 'Primitive' tribal groups in particular.

(f) Priorities are not be set by planners (outsider) but by the tribes as they are the clientele.

(g) Quite a number of the so-called primitive tribes particularly those who depend upon forest resources for their livelihood, have often had their way of life disrupted by a drastic change in the ecology. Sufficient awareness is to be created among the non-tribals about environmental conservation.

(h) This concern for environmental conservation in my view is the most important thing which can go a long way in protection of tribal culture and right. The rest of this article shall throw some light on the link between tribal development and environmental conservation.

The development paradigm which has direct bearing on tribal people's problematique has an anthropocentric tinge and a reductionist perspective of natural world. This has destroyed the ecological resource base and caused inroads in the customary tribal matrix of harmonious equilibrium between nature and man. The doctrine of individualism and statist ideology being crucial of capitalistic and neo-colonialistic development stigmatises and severely impairs the collective identities. The dominant notion of development is gradual triumph of rationality and value-neutrality. Hence, it has cultivated a contempt towards tradition, values. The development projects in a nutshell do not pay any need to the culture and ecological complexities prevailing in tribal areas. The tribal get marginalised in the process. Their customary, holistic and anticipatory conception of nature, generic and corporate character of land, community oriented values and collective identities, self-management systems, cognitive heritage, unique. Socio-cultural-linguistic framework and consensual decision-making process are derecognised and castigated resulting in a silent and subtle form of ethnocide.[8]

The tribal man puts least pressure on nature for its subsistence. Rather it is a glory for him when he identifies himself with nature. A man who stands in the globalised society is the consumer that strains the nature around him. It overuses nature. His attitude is the attitude of domination over nature. His approach is anthropocentric. With the advent of science, technology and globalised market economy he becomes highly competitive. He justifies his action by quoting Francis Bacon—that the conquest of nature is the goal of science, and 'Knowledge is power'. Civilised man interprets that political order is designed primary to protect right to life, liberty and estate. John Locke's writings endorsed individualism, the accumulation of wealth and subjugation of nature. To the so-called leaders of industrial revolution the environment was primarily a source of raw-material, along with rising standard of living came increasing burden on environment. Technological optimism gave rise to environment degradation and the innocent tribe is the first prey.

To other attitudes are 'unity, with nature' and 'stewardship of nature'. To save the tribe, we must save environment. The idea of unity with nature is somewhat opposed to domination over nature' when we will have an insight into the tribal life-style and culture, we may feel that tribal attitude is more or less close to 'unity with nature' attitude. The eastern and western religions, the romantic movement in literature and philosophy, evolutionary biology and ecology put emphasis on this attitude. This view stresses humanity's harmony with nature. For Blake, Wordsworth and Goethe nature is not an impersonal machine but an organic process with which humanity is united. They idealise 'the noble savage' and exalted the 'natural' and 'primitive'. If we view tribalism with this view we can find the natural and the primitive in the tribals. We can advocate for wilderness preservation in the same tone with John Muir. Features like totemism of the tribal trend minus its superstitions dimension can help shaping this attitude that respects nature.

Some of such attitudes have become the attributes of youth counter culture of 1960s which has been disenchanted with technology. Our globalised outlook and preoccupations with efficiency and productivity has alienated the primitive society from nature. Our so-called developed projects pushed the tribal out of their natural habitat. Steps like deforestation have brought endless miseries for the man in the forest, since forest constitute the only source of livelihood for them.

Development is a myth without tribal uplift. A holistic perception will help us in this regard. The twentieth century science of ecology implies the ecosystem concept emphasising the interdependence of all form of life. Some authors have found more specific, ethical guidance in ecology. Rachel Carson's early writings combined scientific knowledge with a sense of spiritual unity with nature. In her book *Silent Spring* (1962) the call for an ecological conscience was tied up to scientific studies of the effects of pesticide on bird population.

An insight into tribal culture and way of life can vindicate the utility of ecological development in bringing about all round amelioration of the tribal communities. The development programmes all over the world and in the third world countries in particular were monopolised by economist and politicians. Now cultural anthropology dominates. The understanding of the culture and social relationship that prevail in the underprivileged weaker society like the tribal society is of utmost importance in designing development policies. It is clear that culture impinges on development in all its aspects. Since ultimate values belong to the realm of culture, questions like what is development? Change in what direction is to be regarded as development? or what are the objectives of development are people-related.

The real development for the tribes can be achieved with ensuring quality of life for them. Sometimes the tribal habits smack of ignorance or too much of innocence and barbarism. That drag them to a state of superstitions. An ecological model of development shall put emphasis on the training of the tribes for wise use of nature. Gifford Pinchot has thought of scientific management of natural resources or stewardship of nature. The biologist Rene Dubos extends a philosophy of respectful use of nature and creative intervention. The practices of '*Podu*' and 'Jhum' cultivation can be given a new touch to devoid them of the destructive impacts on nature. We know the tribals have more intimate relation with the nature and animal world. This relationship can be harassed to yield positive results that in the long run can help improving tribal life.

Another dimension of tribal development is participation of tribal people in the process of development. Environmental Conservation fosters the concept of sustainable development. Sustainable growth itself is complete only when people for whom the development is meant are taken into confidence and involved in the process of decision-making. Strategies and concerted action are best implemented if the affected people are allowed to see their own interests. The focus should be on strengthening local capacities for planning and implementing development activities. In case of tribal development, this experiment of course is difficult. To sensitise the innocent, native tribes in the process of development is extremely difficult as they most often view the non-tribal would with suspicion. The government official and NGOs implementing tribal development schemes must exercise caution and work with patience. In some tribal pockets these activities may be slightly easier, where some tribal organisation easier, where some tribal organisation, customs and rituals thrive on community participation. Some studies have been conducted on this front in the context of Chipko movement (in hills of UP), the Gonds of Adilabad (Andhra Pradesh), Jharkhand. Chipko movement particularly extends a platform where dwellers of hill forests were united under the banner of environmental conservation. Even the tribal awakening at the foothills of Kerandimal of South Orissa provides an interesting case-study for scholars in this field.

The environmentalists have distanced themselves from the political movement in Adilabad and Jharkhand. But they have identified overwhelmingly with the Chipko movement. Chipko movement particularly has become a symbol for the world—an environmental icon. Today few environmentalists remember that the villagers were just not against tree-felling. They also fought for greater control over forest resources. In 1973 the Chipko movement spelt out six-point charter in a meeting in Garud of Chamoli district. The points are:

(1) Abolition of the auction/contractor system and the formation of forest labour co-operatives.

(2) People's participation in forest management.

(3) Establishment of local, small-scale forest based industries to generate employment.

(4) A new forest settlement to determine the people's right to forest produce.

(5) Assistance to village efforts for afforestation.

(6) Ban on felling green trees in areas critical for the protection of water sources and prevention of landslides.

In November 1986, the Chipko charter was reiterated by Chandi Prasad Bhatt at a meeting of national and International environmental activists at Suraj Kund. The principles are—

1. To understand what the forest itself wants and to analyse the socio-economic conditions of the people in order to establish the type of forestry required.

2. To identify and reserve areas affected by landslides and erosion or crucial for the conservation of water-resources.

3. To establish the minimum needs of the people living next to forests and an administration such that these rights may be easily exercised.

4. Complete stoppage of the contractor system and instead the people to be organised to undertake conservation, development works.

5. Trees of use to villagers to be planted near the village so that people need not enter reserve forests.

6. Village industries based on minor forest produce to be set up to prevent migration.

Two leaders of Chipko movement Bahuguna and C.P. Bhatt hold two different stands of environmental activism. Bahuguna finds the outside elements like forest official and contractors responsible for the degradation of Himalayan eco-system whereas C.P. Bhatt does not deny the native's role in deforestation but holds that his has been a result of separating the local population from management of forest wealth. Further Bhatt argues, both forest officials and commercial forestry are merely agents of development process, biased in favour of the urban-industrial complex and against local needs. He is also sharply critical of the growing separation between the state and the people, as clearly manifest in the framing of development schemes by urban-centered technocrats that have little relevance to the realities of tribal rural India". (Unquiet Woods - R.C. Guha).

It is not suprising that tribals in many pockets of the country indulge themselves in some act like tree felling, Podu cultivation etc. which causes environment hazards. But it is more due to ignorance. And they do it for subsistence not for luxury.

The ethos, modern science and technology holds is different from the value systems of so-called primitive tribal societies. They view the eco-system in its totality, thereby ensuring a rational and sustainable use of resources. What helps more the tribal natives is appropriate rural technology than modern technology that alienates itself from the local needs. Appropriate technology is eco-friendly and it promotes self-reliance (both in terms of invoking mass participation and using local resources). It reduces inequality and builds itself upon the traditional skills of the native. Thus native skills are reinforced (not neglected.)

Tribal indigenous knowledge of nature has something which can strengthen the sense of environmentalism of the non-tribal world. There is a need to document these knowledge and make it available for future use. Environmental consciousness of the society can again be fed back to the tribal world for their sustainable development. Like the non-tribal world the tribes are confronted with the conflicting values (a) the material values like survival, health, and material welfare and employment (b) social values like distributive justice, participatory freedom, inter personal community, personal fulfillment and (c) environmental values like resource sustainability, eco-system integrity, environmental preservation etc. But the thing is that the innocent tribal man is not aware of these conflicting values. For him the material values like food, shelter and health are the immediate concerns. But environmental values add quality to the life they live.

The so-called development process has marginalised the tribal people. The tribal people are losing their land and being pushed back from where new opportunities and avenues are arising. In spite of so much of programmes of tribal development, the tribal people still remain at the bottom. Environmental ethics can go a long way in solving tribal problems. Development process inspired by environmental values can alone take cognisance of tribal values and interests. Since the causes of environmental exploitation and tribal exploitation are the same tribal development in the true sense of the term is possible through environmental conservation measures.

Any development policies and programmes for the tribal population all over the world must possess an environmental dimension if they really mean development for the tribes. With globalisation we are urbanised. But the pastoral motif must continue. The beauties of country landscape and the virtues of simple tribal life are to be celebrated in contrast to the growing urbanisation. A tribal man standing in the midst of uncorrupt nature is the greatest ecologist. A time has came to extend the benefits of globalised world to him and allow his spirit to guide our actions in pursuit of material happiness in the modern world. Environmentally sensitive development projects for the tribes are the only answer. The development programmes can be effective only when based on tribal values inculcated by the tribes in the wilderness which is a 'sacred space'. In this wilderness we rediscover our primeval intuitive capacities long suppressed by calculative rationality.

References

1. Anand Kashyap, Parameters of Tribal Development: Some Key Conceptual Issues, Tribal Situation in India, p. 29, Rawat Publication, New Delhi, 1998.

2. Pandey Deep Narayan (1995), The 'Problem' Seminar, No. 426, p. 13.

3. S.N. Tripathy, Dynamics of Tribal Migration, Sonali Publication, New Delhi, 2006, p. 127 (Chapt. V)

4. S.H.M. Rizvi and Shibani Roy, Scheduled Tribes, B.R. Publication (Delhi) 1998, pp. 18-19.

5. A. Kumar, Tribal Development in India, Sarup and Sons, New Delhi, 2002, p. 226.

6. Nadeem Hasnin, Tribal India, Palaka Prakashan, Delhi, 2005, p. 220.

7. W.S.K. Phillips; Perspective in the development of the tribals affected by the Sardar Sarovar project, Tribal situation in India, Rawat Publication, New Delhi, 1998, p. 246.

8. Jaganath Pathy, Impact of Development Project on Tribals, Tribal Situation in India, p. 282.

18

Adivasis from Public Policy Perspective in India

Satyam Sunkari

Abstract

Public policy is whatever governments choose to do or not to do (Thomas R, Dye, 1972:3). David Easton defines public policy as "the authoritative allocation of values for society" (1953:48). In contemporary democratic and political arrangements of India, policies obviously are being made by political system. In such political spheres, policies for the Adivasis are governed by the state's power elements rather than people's needs though the Constitution of India has clearly laid down the principles in its document for the just society with special arrangements. My paper argues based on empirical studies that policies have been formulated and operationalised since long back but outreach of its objectives have not been perpetrated in terms of financial allocation and distribution, reaching targeted people and finally changing their socio-economic conditions which were essentially suppose to be brought changes.

Adivasis – Socio-economic and Political Set Up

Inequality among Adivasis remains an important aspect of social sciences' research in Indian academics. Societal and political issues like denial of equality, accessing developmental and welfare measurements—education, employment, livelihoods, natural resources (land, water and forest resources) political participation, and political leadership are still rampant. Adivasis communities are characterised by geographical isolation, lack of socialisation at larger social context, and socio-economic backwardness in political context. They have their own and unique lifestyle, having an inherent set of cultural and religious beliefs. India has about 8.2 per cent of the Scheduled Tribes of the total population (Census, 2011). Most of Adivasis have close association with natural resources like land, water and forests for their livelihoods. Of the total, more than 93 per cent of Adivasis are settled in rural areas and only six per cent are living in urban areas. Demographically, Adivasis are largely distributed in the states of Madhya Pradesh, Maharashtra and Orissa and in some extent of populated states are Andhra Pradesh, Assam, Bihar, Gujarat, Kerala, Madhya Pradesh, Orissa, Rajasthan, Uttar Pradesh and West Bengal. Sparsely, with an about ten per cent people, belonging to this community distributed in states like Karnataka, Maharashtra and Tamil Nadu. While some of the states—Haryana, Punjab, Chandigarh and Union Territories like Delhi and Pondicherry have not accounted a single Scheduled Tribe (Census, 2011).

Geographically, central India consists of Madhya Pradesh, Maharashtra, Andhra Pradesh, Orissa, Chhattisgarh and Jharkhand is unique in terms of homelands for majority of Adivasis. There are about 100 districts of all central Indian states with around 55 million Adivasis which are accounted for more than 70 per cent of India's tribal population. The region is home to one of the largest concentrations of rural poverty in the world even though the area is with the rich vegetation and good rainfall. Notwithstanding favourable resource conditions, Adivasis regions have been neglected in terms of infrastructure, agriculture, education, health, housing, food security and almost all human development indicators (International Water Management Institute, 2007). A large number of Adivasis in rural areas are still dependent on forests for their livelihood. In the forest based Adivasis economy provisions for basic necessities like food, fuel, housing material, etc., is made from the forest produce (ftp://ftp.fao.org, *2011)*.

Concerning Adivasis social and economic development, recent Human Development Report of UNDP stated that majority of Adivasis are multidimensionally poor (UNDP Human Development Report, 2010). Human Development Report further elaborated multidimensionally poor in terms of "poverty go far beyond inadequate income—to poor health and nutrition, low education and skills, inadequate livelihoods, bad housing conditions, social exclusion and lack of participation. A household is multidimensionally poor if it is deprived in at least two to six indicators involving cooking fuel, toilet, water, electricity, floor and assets, nutrition, child mortality, children enrolled in school and years of schooling" (UNDP Human Development Report, 2010).

As regards the availability of amenities such as percentage living in pucca houses, percentage having toilet facilities and percentage using PDS, access to protected water and electronic connections, STs are relatively disadvantaged when compared to other general populous (ftp://ftp.fao.org, 2011). Further, some of the Scheduled Tribes are categorised into 'Primitive Tribal Groups' (PTGs) by the Government of India in 1975 based on more backwardness among the tribal population groups. So far seventy-five tribal communities have been identified as 'primitive tribal groups' in different States of India. The special development packages for PTGs have been provided to the Indian States and Union Territories since fifth five year plan period (1974-1979) apart from Special Central Assistance (SCA) to Tribal Sub-Plan (TSP).

Keeping in view of disgusting situations of Adivasis, Government of India has initiated 'Affirmative Actions'. Generally, affirmative action is understood as a mechanism to do away with socio-economic, political and cultural inequalities as quoted by Leaber (1991). "The aim of affirmative action is to protect or promote the welfare of a person or a group who/which was previously marginalised, suppressed or discriminated" (Leaber, 1991 quoted by Uddhab Pd Pyakurel, 2011). As pointed out by Thorat, S.S. *et al* (2005) "Bhimrao Ambedkar suggested four or more remedies to be employed in combination to ensure equal opportunity as well as fair access and participation of the marginalised sections in the social, political and economic process in the society. These included equal rights, legal safeguards against violation of rights in terms of punitive measures, measures to ensure equal access and participation through reservation policy in civil, political and economic spheres, and a definite strategy by the state for the development and empowerment of marginalised to compensate for exclusion in the past" (Thorat et, 2005 quoted by Uddhab Pd Pyakurel, 2011). Such ideological, philosophical foundations and situational social and political complexities have led to formulate welfare and developmental policies for integrated development of Adivasis by the Government of India.

Objective

In this context, the paper intended to explore policy based outcomes, and issues and challenges in reaching objectives of welfare and developmental policies to targeted communities (Adivasis) based on empirical studies from the selected areas. The following sections elucidates policy's objectives, outreach and grass-root issues critically keeping in the minds of targeted goals.

Methodology and Area of the Research Study

According to Thomas R, Dye (1972), policies can be evaluated and studied in different forms like hearings and discussions on the programmes within administrative circles, programme measures by government agencies on policy output, comparison with professional standards by guessing ideal levels of benefits and services, evaluation of citizen complaints, before versus after comparisons, projected trend-line versus post programme comparisons, comparisons between jurisdictions with and without programmes and comparisons between control and experimental groups before and after program implementation (Thomas R, Dye, 1972). The present study followed the policy form of evaluation of citizen complaints in which issues and critics were brought into limelight. But, it sometimes fails to bring what actual changes are there in society rather convey what are the issuès are in ongoing programmes. In present study, I have brought mostly representation of public views and their opinion.

As regards to the methodology of the paper, I have selectively done fieldwork which I have conducted in different areas and periods on different policies. For instance, policy based study on drinking water and sanitation, primary education, empirical study was done in eight villages – Shettihadpanur, SC Guda, Patel Guda, Pataguda, Kallur Guda, Rajula Guda, Bimangutta and Shivaguda — of Narnoor mandal, on Mahatma Gandhi National Rural Employment Guarantee Programme (MNREGP) and Agricultural Inputs, Subsidy and Farmers' Debt Relief Scheme, selected villages were Chenchupalugu, Rangapur, Bolketpali, Bonala and Billakal villages of Achampet mandal of Mahabubnagar district. Further recent forest and landbased policies like Forest Rights Act (FRA) and Forest Development Agency (FDA) were conducted in four Adivasis habitations—Lokonda, Kittalapadu, Mamidijola and Jagannathapuram (Heeramandalam mandal), of Srikakulam district. The main criteria for selection of different habitations for different policies are to gain more and in-depth understandings on respective policies in this study.

Since this paper confined to target oriented concerning individual's social welfare and changes of the community, policies like PESA and other rights based issues were not covered in this study. The period of this paper was June 2010 to December 2011. During this period, extensive field visits were done in exclusively in Adivasis habitations for the research and other developmental activities purposes and specific issues relating to welfare and developmental policies of Adivasis were captured and analysed in systematic way so as to meet the present research paper's objectives.

Limitations of the Study

Since the study focussed on major policy interventions of Adivasis, I have selected different study locations to assess welfare and development-oriented policy initiatives from the people's point of view and uniform field selections were not followed to avoid narrow or uniform views. That was the reason I have tried to understand and evaluate each programme from different locations to absorb diversified views on the presently implementing welfare and development policies. Further, qualitative arguments were only documented and presented and quantitative analysis was maximally minimised in this paper. It was also essential to note that the study had not focused on the Panchayats (Extension to the Scheduled Areas) Act, 1996 (PESA) since it was exclusively initiated to enable Adivasis to assume control of its own destiny to preserve and conserve the traditional rights over resources, due to its broad area and targets, i.e., community based intervention, so the paper confined only to the programmes which were targeted to enhance living standards of Adivasis.

Policy Based Explorations

According to David Easton, a political system works through three types of elements— demands, support and outputs. In such system, demands emerge from the open environment (society), supports comes from within the system through organised institutions or political originations and outputs of the political system framed by authority in terms of decisions and policies. Finally, in political system, political decisions or policies have materialises to adjust the system (society) (David Easton, 1953). Thus, David Easton defines public policy as "the authoritative allocation of values for society" (David Easton, 1953 quoted by Maheshwari, S.R. 2006:48). In terms of Thomas R, Dye, public policy is whatever governments choose to do or not do and further he asserted that "policy analysis encourages scholars and students to attack critical policy issues with the tools of systematic enquiry. He asserted that policy analysis is 'thinking man's response' to demands that social science become more 'relevant' to the problems of society" (Thomas R, Dye, 1972: 7). In contemporary democratic and political arrangements of India, policies obviously being made by political system in which different forces try to influence policies. Here in this paper, an attempt was made to understand the causes and consequences of public policy and drawn the research findings based on empirical explanations.

The significant policies of Adivasis are—Community Development Projects (including Adivasis and other rural communities and it was initiated during First Five Year Plan), Special Multi-purpose Tribal Blocks (SMPT–was given special focus in areas with prominent tribal population [Second Five Year plan (1956-1961), Tribal Development Blocks (SMPT was renamed as TDBs), Tribal Development Agencies (TDA's were established on similar pattern of Small Farmers Development Agency [SFDA] to address the problems of the tribal people), Tribal Sub-plan [TSP] (it was adopted during the Fifth Five Year Plan and it aimed at to provide mechanism for integrating the developmental activities of the government and the semi-government organisations by financing through the Integrated Tribal Development Projects [ITDP]) and Integrated Area Development Plan (this focused on was on the specific problems of the area and the tribal people in each ITDP) (Mehta P.C. 2000 and Planning Commission reports [First Five Year Plan to 11th Five Year Plan]). During the Fifth Five Year Plan, Special Central Assistance (SCA) to Tribal Sub Plan (TSP) and Grant-in-Aid under Article 275(1) of the Constitution were adopted to provide additional funds flow to TSPs for income generating activities, infrastructure development and administrative reinforcement (Planning Commission, 2012, http://tribal.nic.in, 2012).

Importance was given to community-based economic activities in the Sixth Five Year Plan (1980-85). A 'Modified Area Development Approach' (MADA) was adopted for Adivasis concentrated pockets of 10,000 populations with at least half of them being STs. Primitive Tribal Groups (PTGs) were also given emphasis for their overall development. Supportive financial institutions at national like Tribal Cooperative Marketing Development Federation (TRIFED) as an apex body for State Tribal Development Cooperative Corporations and

National Scheduled Castes and Scheduled Tribes Finance and Development Corporation (NSFDC) were set up to provide remunerative price for the Forest and Agriculture Produce, credit support for employment generation and skill development of Adivasis during the Seventh Five Year Plan (1985-90).

The Ninth Five Year Plan (1997-2002) approach envisaged advancement of STs through a process of (i) Social Empowerment, (ii) Economic Empowerment and (iii) Social Justice for socio-economic development. An exclusive Ministry of Tribal Affairs was set-up in 1999 for a focused approach to the development and welfare of the Adivasis in the country. Centrally sponsored schemes supported by the Ministry of Tribal Affairs and other Central Ministries and Departments were continued in the 10th Five Year Plan (2002-07). The 11th Five Year Plan was given much focus on educational, economic and social development. One of the highlights of the plan was the proposal made to set up a Commission on Land Reforms to specifically look into issues of land. Another important pro-active policy is the Scheduled Tribes and Other Traditional Forest Dwellers (Recognition of Forest Rights) Act, 2006 (henceforth FRA) which has been in operation since 2008 to recognise and regularise the land entitlement to Adivasis. Apart from specific targeted policies, major rural poverty alleviation programmes classified into three major categories—first one is wage employment programmes, second category is area development programmes and third one is social assistance programmes.[1] After Community Development Programme (CDP 1952), specifically focused programmes were initiated along with specific programmes of Adivasis. Accordingly, empirically observed outcomes and issues of policies concerning Adivasis are presented in the following sections.

Drinking Water, Sanitation, Health and Primary Education

As keeping in mind that safe drinking water is a birth right of every individual, water supply and sanitation were given due priority in the national agenda during the first five-year planning period (1951-1956), consequently increasing investments have been made in subsequent plans. Since the issue of sanitation and providing drinking water was aired as politically debatable and academically interpretative with social policy perspective, it is indispensable to note down on. Keeping in view of issues on drinking water and sanitation, programmes like Accelerated Rural Water Supply Programme (ARWSP 1972-73), National Drinking Water Mission (NDWM 1986) Central Rural Sanitation Programme (CRSP 1986), Rajiv Gandhi National Drinking Water Mission (NDWM was renamed as RGNDWM in 1991) and National Water Policy (2002) were initiated to improve the standards of sanitation and dignity to women including Adivasis' populated areas (Department of Drinking Water Supply—Ministry of Rural Development, 2002:1, Planning Commission, 2002).

It is observed in the policy notes that preference was given to the Scheduled Castes and Scheduled Tribes. I have analysed existing and available drinking water facilities keeping in the mind that whether water policies reached to the Adivasis habitations or not based on empirical investigation in these specific study locations. In this state of policy affairs, I would like to present a case study analysis from Adivasis habitations of the mandals of Utnoor, Narnoor which was done during the summer season of 2010. Water and Sanitation issues were analysed based on the empirical study done in Sirpur-U Mandal and health and education issues were drawn from Sedwai, Admiyan, Gadiguda and Rampur villages of Narnoor mandal.

Empirical Investigation on Water and Sanitation

The present analysis is completely based on empirical investigation. In fact, in the summer season (April) of 2011, I have extensively visited tribal habitations which were presented in the Table 18.1 of Sirpur-U mandal of Adilabad district to understand the severity of drinking water scarcity, irrigation and livelihoods of respective local people. Simultaneously, I have also documented all the social and economic issues including drinking water sources.

Drinking Water

Table 18.1: Revenue Village - Shettihadpanur

S.No.	*Name of Habitation*	*Water Resources*	*Total Households*
1.	Shettihadpanur	• Well – 1 and Hand pump - 1	36
2.	SC Guda	• Well – 1 and Hand pump - 1	43
3.	Patel Guda	Well – 1 and Hand pump – 1 (not working) Submersible pump set (only works in rainy season)	87
4.	Pataguda	• Well – 1 (Kunta)	23
5.	Kallur guda	• Well – 1 and Hand pump – 1 (not working)	36
6.	Rajula guda	• Well – 1 and Hand pump – 1 (not working)	187
7.	Bimangutta	• Well – 1 and Hand pump – 2	210
8.	Shivaguda	• Hand pump-1	N/A

Source: Information is based on Field Visits, as on April 2011.

The field studies has been carried out in Shettihadpanur revenue village of Sirpur –U Mandal. Shettihadpanur revenue village has seven other villages and views and data collected from these habitations to substantiate my argument in this regard. The data of Table reveals that all habitations have dependent still on traditional wells along with hand pumps. It can be also observed in the Table 18.1 that of the total eight hand pumps, four were physically verified and indicated that they were not in proper working conditions and reasons are lack of technical personnels. Habitation named Pataguda is still depending on traditional well (or pit) but not it exactly well, it's local name is a kunta (pit) and it has highly chances to contamination of drinking water. If we look at household wise drinking water resources, in Shettihadpanur habitation, there are 36 households and only one hand pump and one traditional well for their regular water consumption and in the same way, in SC Guda, 43 households are there but drinking water sources only one hand pump and well. And it can be seen similar situation in all habitations. The same conditions were evident in other field studied locations.

Responses on severity of water scarcity was drawn from 16 respondents from eight selected villages and data shows that 81.25 per cent respondents said "there is severe problems in accessing minimum water for drinking, 18.75 per cent replied "need urgently drinking water facilities". The responses clearly indicated to respond positively to address the problem from existing water policies. If we observe the present situational analysis on this part we would come to know what actually has been going. Being policy oriented analysis, it would be essential to present down to earth aspects of the connected issues. Hence, rapid action is required. It is obvious based on the field data many of the schools located in these mandals have poor hygienic conditions or do not have water, sanitation and hand washing facilities at all. Along with physical observation, I have also interviewed community members, local leaders and elected representatives including sarpanch. The elected sarpanch of Grama Panchayat is woman named Parwati Bai, elected from habitation of Bimangutta. She said that the officials of concerning departments like Panchayati Raj, Irrigation and Rural Water Supply cannot respond immediately to solve the problems. Further she said that "they, generally, says reasons for delay that shortage of adequate technical and other administrative staff, and very pressure from other villages".

Again she suggested some measures to deal with the problems, in her opinion, "there should be efficient mechanism to handle problems aroused in our habitations because we have just dependent on hand pumps, that too, our habitations are located in different distances. In addition, in our mandal, setting of all habitations is similar. So we need exclusively one technical persons to handle and solve repairable problems of our hand pumps because we completely dependent on them. But, in every summer season, we bring drinking water from natural stream. We also know that many human and animal improper disposals of wastes including feces contaminate water sources. Many ignorant people improperly dispose of urine, feces, and kitchen wastes close to our streams. Even then, we have to use such water because we do not have any alternative". Another woman, named, Rupa Bai, aged 26, shared her regular experiences with relation to water need in her home. She said that she does wake up early morning 4 am to bring water for drinking and cooking purposes far away from at least 200 meters and again at 6 am she goes for water for the purposes of bathing and washing. Thus, she has to do regularly and has to, again, involve in labour works after completion of all such domestic works. Though the policy of *drinking water supply under the programme of* National Rural Drinking Water (NRDWP) which was initiated in 2008 and it is targeted to ensure availability of potable drinking water on sustainable basis in SCs/STs dominant habitations has exclusive focus on tribal habitations and also allotted substantial financial resources. But it is lacking with committed bureaucratic personals at grass-root and intermediary level.

Sanitation

Case study analysis on sanitation was also done in Shettihadpanur revenue village of Narnur mandal. The seven villages of Shettihadpanur revenue village–Shettihadpanur, SC Guda, Patel Guda, Pataguda, Kallur guda, Rajula guda, Bimangutta and Shivaguda. The responses shows that 34.8 per cent of the respondents accepted that sanitation is essential for better health by facilitating proper bathrooms, latrines and proper water supply, 51.4 per cent have raised their voice on insufficient water and strongly responded as water is essential for maintenance of sanitation but unsurprisingly, 13.8 per cent gave answers that 'what is sanitation and is it essential to construct bathrooms and latrines, we have been following our own practices with our existing knowledge'. A case study presented here to make clear the existing experience.

A woman named, Rukma, aged 42, from the same habitation, expressed her problems with regard to Sanitation (bathroom and latrine) and water for household needs. In her words, "We have been thinking to construct a bathroom with the help of government's scheme, but there is no any option to get water connectivity. Even in midnights also we (women) go for nature calls to far away from my house. My daughter also got some health problem of urinal infection due to lack of space for proper bathroom and toilets. So if we get individual taps we will construct the bathroom and our long awaited problems may be solved". This is her opinion and expression which says severity of water and sanitation needs for household consumption. It is obvious that sanitation and drinking water scenarios are yet to be developed in more holistic approach so as to change present situations at habitations of Adivasis and need to improve habit of the importance of sanitation and hygienic conditions at their surroundings.

Health Issues

The Government of India has launched the National Rural Health Mission (NRHM) in 2005 to provide accessible, affordable and accountable primary healthcare services to poor households of rural India in 2005 (Gill Kaveri, 2009). One of the major important aspects of this policy is the creation of female health activists (ASHAs) and involvement of grass-root committees like village health and sanitation committees (VHSCs) and convergence with PRIs to reach promptly the desired objectives. But, it is obvious from the field areas that the functioning of ASHA was not evident, according to the women belongs to the villages of Shettihadpanur, SC Guda, Patel Guda, Pataguda, Kallur guda, Rajula guda, Bimangutta and Shivaguda and the responses emerged that 92 per cent viewed that "they are not actively working with proper facilities. They contact us only for the sake of name" and remaining were not replied positively regarding health and sanitation committees which are important to campaign health issues among the members and community. They have experienced distinctive health problems in last rainy season governed by their habitat, difficult terrains and ecological conditions. It is understood that the utilisation of government provided healthcare services at grass-root level is relatively low. Primary Health Centers have not yet opened.

Primary Education

Regarding primary school, observatory statement and people's opinion was documented. The primary school was located in the village of SC Guda. The school, at the time of my interview with community, was occupied with two bullocks. I immediately asked the people who were there at that point of time with me that why were there bullocks in the school? "School was not running and teacher comes periodically, not regular and local assistant prepare meals and arrange for the students" replied 92 per cent of the people (there were 25 people at that point of time) and remaining said that "teacher comes occasionally, especially at the time of supervision by higher officials". Here, I would like to raise a question that why rigorous and thorough supervision has been neglecting and why mass campaign to enhance the student's enrollment in schools was not taken comprehensively. The questions need to be seriously looked in. The proper function of primary schools at grassroots level is essential to promote equitable social development and bring justifiable society. Since the upgrading the class of the student from lower level to further levels is perfectly connected with the school which has proper function system. But, in the Residential School's system, the system of school education in some extent is acceptable in terms of regular functioning, teacher attendance, meals, supply of books and supervision. Issues like irregular teachers and students and proper maintenance of the school premises were observed in other non-residential (primary and upper primary levels) schools like Shettihadpanur, Patel Guda, Pataguda, Kallur guda, Rajula guda, Bimangutta and Shivaguda.

Rural Housing

Empirical study was conducted in the habitations of Hemayikuntan (Indravelli mandal), Rampur (Narnnor mandal), Bimangutta (Sirpur -U Mandal) to evaluate the housing scheme (Indiramma housing scheme) and PDS. It was seen that most of the houses were still in semi-completed condition and most of houses were stopped at basement stages. Surprisingly, opinions on housing scheme and its implementation process was collected from recent beneficiaries and leaders each four respondents from Hemayikuntan, Rampur and Bimangutta and thus total twelve responses collected on the process of housing scheme. Data shows that 84 per cent aware about middlemen involvement and reluctance of officials in proper implementation was viewed by remaining sixteen per cent. It was clearly mentioned by respondents that benefits of the houses were taken by the middlemen those who were engaged in sanctioning house and very less amount was given to house beneficiaries for their signatures on the loan amount papers. Unfortunately, the overall process of housing loans and its sanctioning process were still not understood by the community members. Their unawareness and lack of information properly, procedures were helped middlemen and officials to interrupt implementation process.

Public Distribution System (PDS)

Views on appropriateness of PDS and needs of Adivasis' families were collected from (Hemayikuntan (Indravelli mandal), Rampur (Narnnor mandal), Bimangutta [Sirpur-U Mandal]) the selected 30 women respondents while focusing on the issues like adequate food grains, irregular distribution and malpractice. It is clear from three habitations that all the households have white ration cards and availing the benefits of PDS. But contrast views were emerged on accuracy of implementation process. Majority respondents (73 per cent) were opined that regularly inadequate and irregular supply of food grain is caused to really hunger of their children because "we engage mostly in labour works and we cultivate cotton and cultivation of paddy crop is very less" replied by local women members. 27 per cent accepted with a view of malpractice in PDS in terms of diverting food grains and illegal selling of rice and sugar. It is understood that adequate food grains supply with proper distribution system is essential to achieve desired results of PDS.

Views on Social Assistance Programmes

Observations on the National Social Assistance Programmes (NSAP) were drawn from Hemayikunta of Indravelli mandal, Rampur of Narnnor mandal and Bimangutta of Sirpur-U Mandal.[2] It was clear by women of these habitations that the objectives of the programmes are good and really helps us if regularity maintains in implementation. A pregnant woman from Bimangutta said that "still corruption by local officials is continuing, whenever we go to them we have to pay and process is very long. In maternity cases the amount is very low but in case of Family Benefit Scheme, they asks large amount to sanction the loan". "Recognition and application of Old Age Pension is taking long time and we have to visit the offices of concerned very frequently" replied by woman from Rampoor. According to study's field data, 26.32 per cent (of the total 30 respondents) felt that awareness on the programmes is not communicated to us (women of these habitations) and nearly 53.33 per cent of the VSSs agreed with the view that delay in process and identification of the beneficiaries even though higher officials ordered to identify and distribute the benefits. Remaining was not responded to these responses.

Mahatma Gandhi National Rural Employment Guarantee Programme (MNREGP)

Opinions, activities and livelihood promotions through Mahatma Gandhi National Rural Employment Guarantee Programme (MNREGP) were collected from the selected members (one woman and one man from each habitation) of five Adivasis's habitations—Chenchupalugu, Rangapur, Bolketpali, Bonala and Billakal villages of Achampet mandal of Mahabubnagar district. Thus, total 10 members were interviewed in this specific issue.

Table: 18.2

S.No.	*Statement of Response*	*Percentage of Responses of members of VSS*
1.	Soil and Moisture Conservation	44 (88)
2.	Plantation	3 (6)
3.	Nurseries/regeneration	3 (6)
4.	No works	0 (00)
Total		**50 (100)**

Source: Field Study Interviews.

The types of activities taken up under MGNREGA were presented in Table 18.2 based on the field based interviews. The data shows that 88 per cent of respondents replied that the activities like soil moisture and other environmental related works taken up and 12 per cent viewed 'plantation and regeneration works' were taken for the livelihood creation in selected five habitations. Further, I have evaluated on whether MGNREGA was promoted or increased livelihoods or any change was taken place.

Table: 18.3

S.No.	*Statement of Response*	*Percentage of Responses of Members of VSS*
1.	Livelihoods improved	13 (26)
2.	Reduced Work days	0 (00)
3.	No Change	8 (16)
4.	Reduced Migration	29 (58)
Total		**50 (100)**

Source: Field Survey in five Habitations.

The perceptions on changes in livelihoods were presented in Table 18.3. Only 26.31 per cent of the respondents have agreed with a view that the works under MGNREGA have improved livelihoods and 16 per cent opined 'no change' was seen through this programme. Most importantly, responses emerged to substantiate with a view that the programme has reduced migrations in these specific habitations during the period of implementation.

Agricultural Inputs, Subsidy and Farmers' Debt Relief Scheme

The study on Agricultural Inputs, Subsidy and Farmers' Debt Relief Scheme was conducted in Chenchupalugu, Rangapur, Bolketpali, Bonala and Billakal villages of Achampet mandal of Mahabubnagar district from the state of Andhra Pradesh based on high dependency on agriculture comparatively with other Adivasis habitations. These villages are called as forest fringe villages according to Forest Department since they have located nearby forest. From each village, two farmers with the size of two-three acres were selected and thus, ten members interviewed on the issues like subsidised fertilisers, availability of crop loans, and distributional pattern of seeds and beneficial pattern under the scheme of Farmers' Debt Relief Scheme. In this connection, the question was asked "have you received subsidised fertilizers?" Responses emerged from farmers, as many as, 90 per cent of the respondents gave as 'not received' and remaining ten per cent did not answer either way. Respondents felt that subsidised products are available at mandal headquarter. Some farmers said "soon after we reach to the office of fertilizers stock, nothing left there. Then, we go for private shops to buy fertilizers".

An attempt was made to know the opinion on crop loans. In this regard, it was asked "have you received crop loan for your agricultural purpose?" The answers show that 80 per cent replied 'no' and only 20 per cent farmers have availed crop loans. The reason is that lack of proper titles of the lands. The study also tried to find out whether 'Farmers' Debt Relief Scheme' was reached or were they utilised this scheme? As regards to this question, 60 per cent of the respondents replied that "the scheme was helped to those who were taken loans and who were not paid for long, but, we used to pay loans regularly, some of us were not into that scheme". Very few (40 per cent) have said that "the scheme was really helped in overcoming our burden of debt in bank". The responses on availability of subsidised seeds show that only 30 per cent (not in regular seasons) have got such assistance and remaining (70 per cent) were not received from that initiation. Adivasis farmers detailed their experience that "the officials concerning subsidised seeds waste so much of time in the process of distribution of seeds" and very few people get subsidised seeds. Sometimes, it was understood that farmers had failed to get subsidised seeds due to heavy rush at the counters. It was also observed that, most of the times; stocks of seeds were inadequate and moreover unreasonably distributed, experiences of farmers disclosed.

Forest Rights Act (FRA)[3]

FRA has aimed at to ensure, recognise and regularise Adivasis rights over land by granting legal entitlement to those millions of families who are today seen as encroachers and thus empower and improve livelihood chances of a historically marginalised people. The Act has taken an initiative to correct the historical injustice of Adivasis. In this backdrop, the study examines the challenges and problems of tribal people with relation to implementation of FRA. The study tried to bring the issues in implementation of FRA based on empirical investigation. For this purpose, an empirical study was conducted in the study was done in four Adivasis habitations – Lokonda, Kittalapadu, Mamidijola and Jagannathapuram (Heeramandalam mandal), of Srikakulam district. From each habitation, four eligible claimants and sixteen respondents were interviewed and interaction was also held with Chief Functionary of an NGO-Samyogitha, which is located at in these field locations. In this study, policy process was evaluated based on the implementation process in connection with the eligible claimants (beneficiaries). Awareness, Formation of Forest Rights Committee (FRC), The Process of Verification, Composition of FRC, FRC—Preparation of record of claims and evidence, problems with Forest Department Officials and Sub-Divisional Level Committee (SDLC).

It is observed in the forest fringe villages of that most of the respondents (87.5 per cent) have had not aware about the Act. The objective of the Act is to ensure livelihood and food security of Adivasis, but only 12.5 per cent of community leaders were aware about the Act and its implementation process. The Forest Rights Committee (FRC) was, according to the local people, influenced by Forest Officers in formation process along with the Gram Sabha where it has to be formed by Grama Sabha.[4] Since Grama Sabha is organising at Grama Panchayat, actual voice of the Adivasis was not reflected because Grama Sabha consists of all sections of village. They demanded Grama Sabha should be organised in their habitations as a unit. This was also accepted by local NGO functionary (Samyogitha).

In the process of verification by Forest Rights Committee, it was found that in some hamlets the verification is not properly conducting and some areas, verification is taking place in nominal way; effective participation of people in verification is not there in the study areas. In practice, the members of FRC are not intimated about the verification. No intimation to members of FRC on meeting is found, sometimes informally giving, there is no evidences of issuing notices of the meetings. It has to intimate the members while specifying the purpose of the meeting, date, time and place. Other issues like proper preparation of consolidation of claims list, submitted claim forms, Village Map, Forest map to help in identifying the forestland or status of land applied by claimants was not observed and respondents were said that such information is only available at the Tahasil (Mandal Revenue) Office and the Divisional Forest Office (DFO). This observation indicates that thorough awareness programmes and interface with other developmental departments and programmes are essential to achieve desired outcomes of the Act.

Some important issues were also emerged from these habitations that there is lack of data on claims (facilitate and submitted), status reports at FRC, no registers and authentic seals at FRC level, conflict between the forest department and community on forest and agricultural land issues, delays in distribution of individual titles even after of sanctions, discouragement by forest officials (especially forest guards) in submitting claims, overriding bribes by forest department, unnecessary deadlines by government to submit the claims (even today, people are not even able to understand the process of implementation) and most importantly the land distributed under this Act were not recognised by the local banks to support or sanction crop loans.

Forest Based Afforestation Scheme under Forest Development Agency (FDA)

National Afforestation Scheme is aimed at to develop the forest resources with people's participation, with focus on improvement in livelihoods of the forest-fringe communities, especially the poor.[5] The scheme is targeted to support and accelerate the ongoing process of devolving forest protection, management and development functions to decentralised institutions of Joint Forest Management Committee (JFMC) at the village level, and Forest Development Agency (FDA) at the forest division level. The components under the scheme are Aided Natural Regeneration, Artificial Regeneration, Bamboo Plantation, Cane Plantation, Mixed Plantation of trees having MFP and medicinal value, Regeneration of perennial herbs and shrubs of medicine value, Pasture Development/ Silvipasture, Soil and Moisture Conservation and Entry Point Activity for village development and Fencing, Monitoring and Evaluation, Training, Awareness raising in JFMCs. The study was done in similar villages of study on FRA. In this study, open discussion was held with chairpersons, vice-chairpersons and presented members of committees from these villages. The issues like awareness, people's participation and pattern of funds flow were discussed.

It was observed that awareness levels on institutional framework and it's functioning like regular meetings, trainings, activities suppose to be taken, whether trainings were held or not, whether there is relation between Gram Panchayats and FDA, and election process. It is obvious from these habitations that training activities were communicated only to the members who have regular connections with concerned officials, which in turn objectives of trainings were, in large extent, not reached. Trainings on forest regeneration activities were not produced desired and expected outcomes. "Relation between the FDA's and Gram Panchayats was not clear. In addition, guidelines were not issued or some times, guidelines were kept with the officials only and this led to gap between the targets and outcomes of the FDA" responded by members of these habitations. Some of the respondents (members) replied that meetings supposed to be held at Grama Panchayat level but these were taken at Forest Offices only with few people and signatures were collected through respective chairpersons.

Moreover, "members of these committees felt that activities under FDAs are not at all a source of regular incomes, but, if the government officials, especially concerned Forest Department's officials seriously focus on the proper functioning of JFMCs, definitely there would be better chances to earn better incomes" expressed by one chairperson who was, in some extent, in support of community members. It was observed based on the financial transactions by the Bank Account that there was evidence of funds flow for livelihood activities. Contrarily, "funds were used only by few members and misuse of funds was proved in general body meetings, but, this issue was managed by some concerned officials. There was always skepticism about financial transactions. There should be appropriate and accurate mechanisms with trained personalities at grass-root level. Another important issue in this policy context which needs to be discussed was representation of women in the committees. Though there is policy level measures to encourage women participation and representation, inadequate representation of women in General Body (GB) meetings and Executive Committees (EC), was quite visible. The reasons were varied as women of Adivasis were greatly involved in diversified activities like farming, labour, domestic and other non-farms.

Conclusion

The present analysis brought some issues based on empirical investigation. Though policies targeted to ensure availability of potable drinking water on sustainable basis in SCs/STs dominant habitations, the study found issues like lack of committed bureaucratic personnels to achieve desired policy outcomes at grassroots level. It was clear on sanitation and drinking water issues that there should substantial policies to focus on community health, sanitation, drinking water, education and housing. In case of PDS, still malpractices like diverting food grains and to open markets were evident. Some of the issues like corruption of local officials and regularity in reaching assistance were missing though social assistance programmes were targeted to reach desires of the people. Some of the programmes like Mahatma Gandhi National Rural Employment Guarantee Programme (MGNREGP) and Agricultural Inputs, Subsidy and Farmers' Debt Relief Scheme were yet to reach targeted communities and delay in process and low outreach in implementation led to inequality of benefits sharing.

Concerning on FRA, data on claims, status reports, conflict between the forest department and community on forest and agricultural land issues, delays in distribution of land holding claims, discouragement by forest officials (especially forest guards), overriding (invisible) bribes and non-recognition of distributed land for crop loans under FRA were mostly seen in the study. And National Afforestation Scheme is being implemented to develop the forest resources with people's participation, with focus on improving livelihoods of poor, low level of awareness, irregular meetings, improper training calendar, and deficient institutional relations between FDA's (village level committee) and Grama Panchayats were for the most part playing in derailing expected outcomes. And important aspect like creation of sustainable livelihoods through natural resource regeneration process is in some extent neglected by the concerned officials. In views of Adivasis, inadequate and irregular incomes, scrawny standards of health and nutrition, low level of educational standards, and inadequate livelihoods, improper housing conditions, lack of participation were clearly visible. According to UNDP's Human Development Report (2010), Adivasis are still in multidimensional poverty based on the indicators stipulated by it.

Notes

1. Wage employment programmes - Integrated Rural Development Programme, Training of Rural Youth for Self Employment (TRYSEM), Development of Women and Children in Rural Areas (DWCRA), Supply of Improved Tool Kits to Rural Artisans (SITRA) and Ganga Kalyan Yojana (GKY) were introduced as sub-programmes of IRDP, Swarnajayanti Gram Swarojgar Yojana (SGSY), National Rural Livelihood Mission (NRLM), The Food for Work Programme (FWP 1977), National Rural Employment Programme (NREP, 1977), Rural Landless Employment Guarantee Programme (RLEGP), The Million Wells Scheme (MWS), Jawahar Rozgar Yojana (1989), The Employment Assurance Scheme (EAS), The Jawahar Gram Samridhi Yojana (JGSY, 1999), The Sampoorna Grameen Rojgar Yojana (SGRY, 2001), National Food for Work Programme (NFWP 2004), Mahatma Gandhi National Rural Employment Guarantee Act (MGNREGA 2005).

II. Area Development Programmes - Intensive Agricultural District Programme, Drought Prone Area Programmes (DPAP), Desert Development Programmes (DDP), Hilly Area Development Programmes and Tribal Area Development Programmes), Special-Group Development Programmes (Small Farmers Development Agency (SFDA) and Marginal Farmers and Agricultural Labourers Agency [MFALA]), Minimum Needs Programme (MNP), Watershed Development Programmes (1990), National Watershed Development Projects for Rain fed Areas (NWDPRA), Integrated Wastelands Development Programme (IWDP 1989-90), and

III. Social Assistance Programmes - Public Distribution System (PDS), Rural Housing (Indira Awaas Yojana), Pradhan Mantri Gramodaya Yojana (2000-01), Pradhan Mantri Gram Sadak Yojana (2000) and National Social Assistance Programmes (NSAPs) like National Old Age Pension Scheme (NOAPS), The National Family Benefit categories – first one is wage employment programmes, second category is area development programmes and third one is social assistance programmes. After Community Development Programme (CDP 1952), specifically focused programmes were initiated along with specific programmes of Adivasis. Accordingly, empirically observed outcomes and issues of policies concerning Adivasis are presented in the following sections.

Scheme (NFBS), The National Maternity Benefit Scheme (NMBS), Antyodaya Anna Yojana, The Annapurna, Farmers' Debt Relief Scheme,

Pradhan Manthri Adarsh Gram Yojana and National Rural Health Mission (NRHM 2005).

2. The National Social Assistance Programme (NSAP) "comprised National Old Age Pension Scheme (NOAPS), National Family Benefit Scheme (NFBS) and National Maternity Benefit Scheme (NMBS). These programmes were aimed to provide social assistance benefit to the aged, the BPL households in the case of death of the primary breadwinner and for maternity" (Ministry of Rural Development [http://rural.nic.in/sites/programmes-schemes-NSAP.asp], 2012).

3. The Scheduled Tribes and Other Traditional Forest Dwellers (Recognition of Forest Rights) Act, 2006 (in brief - FRA) has been in operation since 2008 to recognise and regularise ground reality by granting legal entitlement to those millions of families who are today seen as encroachers and thus empower and improve livelihood chances of a historically marginalised people. Further, it is claimed that the Act will reduce social conflict. The Act also ensured the tribal people to involve meaningfully in the protection and management of forests and wildlife. In addition to all, the Act has taken an initiative to correct the historical injustice of the tribal people.

4. Forest Rights Committee (FRC) is required to initiate the process of verification of claims on individual and community forest rights mentioned in Section 3 of the Scheduled Tribes and Other Traditional forest dwellers (Recognition of Forest Rights) Act, 2006. The FRC, constituted by Gram Sabha, is responsible for initiating the process of verification of claims on behalf of Gram Sabha after due intimation to the concerned claimants and the Forest Department.

5. Ministry of Environment and Forests was operating four centrally sponsored afforestation schemes during the 9th Plan, i.e., Integrated Afforestation and Eco-development Project Scheme (IAEPS), Area Oriented Fuelwood and Fodder Project Scheme (AOFFPS), Conservation of Non-Timber Forest Produce including Medicinal Plants (NTFPS), and Association of ST and Rural Poor in Regeneration of Degraded Forests (ASTRPS). The Mid-Term Evaluation of the projects under these Schemes recommended a decentralised approach and speedy fund transfer mechanism. Taking cue from these recommendations, a Pilot Scheme, Samnavit Gram Vanikaran Samridhi Yojana (SGVSY) was launched in 2000-01 utilising the delivery mechanism of Forest Development Agency (FDA) and Joint Forest Management Committee (JFMC). As per Tenth Five Year Plan document of Planning Commission (the Forests and Environment sector), the National Afforestation Programme (NAP) Scheme was initiated by scaling-up the SGVSY project experience and converging all afforestation schemes of the Ninth Five Year Plan period to avoid duplicity or redundancy, and at the same time keeping in focus the decentralisation agenda of the government. NAP is being operated as a 100 per cent Central Sector Scheme".

References

The Hindu Editorial, Where There is a Will, 5th December 2012, p.10. http://www.hindu.com/2010/10/20/stories/2010102050560300.htm, viewed on 5th December 2012.

Government of India, Ministry of Environment and Forests, National Forest Policy (1988), http://envfor.nic.in/divisions/fp/nfp.pdf, viewed on 5th December 2012. www.aptribes.gov.in/html/guidelines/13-1-FP-1%20to%206.pdf, 11/3/2011).

Department of Environment, Forests and Wildlife, Circular No. 13-1/90-FP of Government of India, Ministry of Environment and Forests, dated 18.9.90, http://tribal.gov.in/index1.asp?linkid=360&langid=1, viewed on 27/11/2012.

Sarkar, R.M. 2006, Land and Forest Rights of the Tribals Today, Eastern Book Corporation, Delhi, p. 275.

Vidyarthi L.P. and Binay Kumar Rai, (2000) Tribal Culture of India, New Delhi: Concept Publishing Company.

Office of the Registrar General and Census Commissioner (Ministry of Home Affairs, Government of India), Census Report 2011, http://censusindia.gov.in/2011-prov-results/prov_results_paper1_india.html, viewed on 11/6/2012.

Kunharnan, M. (1997) Tribal Development in India - Retrospect and Prospect, Budgeting for whom. Update quarterly, No. 1, April-June.

Kulkarni, P.D. (1964) "Tribal Welfare Some Problems of Implementation", Published in Souvenir: National Seminar on Welfare of Tribes and Denotified Communities with Reference to Fourth Plan, Bhopal, 1964, p. 122.

Prakash, C.M. (2000) *Tribal Development in 20th century,* Udaipur: Siva Publishers.

Planning Commission, Government of India, First Five Year Plan, (1951-1956) New Delhi, pp. 636-640.

Bhownick, P.K. (1981) "Reports of Scheduled Tribes an Appraisal" in Vidyarthi, L.P. (ed.) *Tribal Development and its Administration,* New Delhi: Concept Publishing Company.

Planning Commission, Government of India, Approach Paper for Ninth Five Year Plan (1997-2002).

Thakur, R.N. (1997) "Tribal Development Need for a Fresh Perspective", *Kurukshethra,* March-April.

Uddhab Pd Pyakurel, (2012) "A Debate on Dalits and Affirmative Action in Nepal", *Economic and Political Weekly*, October 1, 2012, Vol. XLVI (40), pp.71-78.

Deb, Kaushik, (2004), *Reforms in Drinking Water and Sanitation*, New Delhi: Teri Press.

Climate Institute, Water, http://www.climate.org/topics/water.html, viewed on: 14/10/2011.

Grail Research, (2009) Water - The India Story, http://grailresearch.com/pdf/ContenPodsPdf/Water-The_India_Story.pdf, viewed on: 10/10/2011.

Indira Khurana, Romit Sen, (2008) Drinking water quality in rural India: Issues and approaches, www.wateraid.org, viewed on: 1/10/2011.

Ministry of Planning and Programme Implementation (Department of Statistics), 1997 Compendium of Environment Statistics. New Delhi: Government of India.

Ministry of Rural Development (Department of Drinking Water Supply), 2010 Rajiv Gandhi National Drinking Water Mission, National Rural Drinking Water Programme - Movement towards Ensuring People's Drinking Water Security in Rural India: Framework for Implementation, New Delhi: Government of India. http://www.ddws.gov.in/sites/upload_files/ddws/files/pdf/RuralDrinkingWater_2ndApril_0.pdf, viewed on: 15/09/2011.

Muralidharan, D., R. Rangarajan and GBK. Shankar, 2011 "Scientific Correspondence- Vicious cycle of fluoride in semi-arid India – a health concern", *Current Science*, Vol. 100, No. 5, pp. 638-640.

Hedstrom Peter, Richard Swedberg and Lars Udehn (1998) "Poppers's Situational Analysis and Contemporary Sociology" Online Journal of *Philosophy of the Social Sciences*, 28 (3): 339-364.

Planning Commission (Government of India), (2002) India Assessment, *planningcommission.nic.in/reports/genrep/wtrsani.pdf,* viewed on: 4/9/2011.

Panda, R.C. (2003) "Drinking Water Mission - Drinking Water Quality and Related Health Impact in Rural India" presented in the 3rd World Water Forum, Kyoto. www.cerna.ensmp.fr/Documents/cerna_globalisation/maria-delhi.pdf, viewed on: 9/9/2011.

Easton, David (1953), *The Political Systems: An Enquiry into the State of Political Science*, Calcutta: Scientific Book Agency.

Dye, Thomas R. (1972), *Understating Public Policy*, Englewood Cliffs, N.J.: Prentice Hall, Inc.

Prakash C.M. (2000), *Tribal Development in 20th Century*, Udaipur: Siva Publishers.

Planning Commission (Government of India), First Five Year Plan, (1951 - 1956) New Delhi, pp. 636-640.

Planning Commission (Government of India, 1997-2002), Approach Paper for Ninth Five Year Plan.

International Water Management Institute (2007) Rethinking Tribal Development: water management strategies for revitalising tribal agriculture in central India, *Water Policy Briefing*, http://www.iwmi.cgiar.org/publications/Water_Policy_Briefs/PDF/WPB27.pdf, viewed on: 9/9/2011.

May 2007 – A policy briefing based on research presented in the book titled "Mainstreaming the Margins: water centric livelihood strategies for revitalising tribal agriculture in Central India, 2005 and a paper titled.

Phansalkar, S.J., Shilp Verma, (2004) Improved Water Control as Strategy for Enhancing Tribal Livelihoods, *Economic and Political Weekly*, 31st July, pp. 3469-3476.

Planning Commission (Government of India) (2010), Mid-term Appraisal Report of the 11th Five Year Plan, http://planningcommission.nic.in/plans/mta/11th_mta/MTA.html, viewed on: 5/9/2011.

Gill Kaveri, (2009), A Primary Evaluation of Service Delivery under the National Rural Health Mission (NRHM): Findings from a Study in Andhra Pradesh, Uttar Pradesh, Bihar and Rajasthan, Working Paper 1/2009 – PEO, New Delhi: Planning Commission of India, May, http://planningcommission.nic.in/reports/wrkpapers/wrkp_1_09.pdf, viewed on: 5/9/2011.

Gopalakrishnan Shankar, (2010) India: Social Development Report 2010 – The Land Question and the Marginalised (Council of Social Development), New Delhi: Oxford University Press.

Maa Adavi (Vanasamakhya [in Telugu]), Atavi Hakkula Chattam Sakramanga Amalu Ayenduku Injadri Krushi, Vol.19, March 2010, p. 4.

19

Awareness of Human Rights among Tribal and Non-tribal Higher Secondary Students – A Comparative Study

KV Sridevi, Asha BN

Introduction

Human rights—the rights related to life, liberty, equality and dignity of the individual–are the very essence of rule of law. They comprise civil, political, social, economic and cultural values. It is the peculiarity of the Indian situation that the issue of human rights has come into public focus rather in a negative way. Human rights have become a matter of public concern in the view of:

(i) increasing incidents of arbitrary arrest and custodial violence.

(ii) Other abuses of power resorted to by the law enforcement agencies especially in states affected by terrorism and insurgency.

The entry of Human Right issue into public consciousness coincides with the growth of terrorists and separatist movement in Punjab and Jammu and Kashmir in mid 80s and early 90s. The issue has also acquired importance due to the attempts of the US and western powers to link the international aid to the developing nations with their Human Rights Record on the ground that Human Rights situation in any country in today's world is not a domestic matter but the legitimate concerns of the international community. The proliferation of Human Rights NGO's and other groups especially in the areas affected by militancy in the recent years has also added to the popularity of the subject.

The important dimensions of human rights that are usually considered for evaluating the awareness of the same are–law and administration of justice, equality of opportunity, history, civil and social rights and responsibility, consumer rights, violence and identity.

Human Right Education in India

In 1964 the first commission of SC and ST, Government of India traced the progress of Education in tribal areas after independence and pointed out that the state of education among the tribes is not seen satisfactory in different parts of India.

Kothari commission (1966) in its report devoted high attention for tribal education. It made thirteen recommendations on various aspects such as wastage and stagnation, hostels, scholarship and shortage of teachers, etc.

The National Policy of Education, 1986 laid down for the first time in the history of Indian Education, a national curriculum framework as the basis for building national system of education. Most of the core elements identified in the policy are related to one or the other dimensions of Human Rights Education: The history of India's freedom movement, constitutional obligations, and other content to nurture national identity. It has been laid down that "these elements will cut cross subject areas and will be designed to promote values such as India's Cultural heritage, Egalitarianism, Democracy, Secularism, Equality of sexes, protection of Environment, Removal of social barriers, Observance of small family norms and inculcation of the scientific temper". NPE also recommended that Human Rights Education should be promoted by:

- Identifying and culminating from the school system all that is prejudicial to human rights.
- Bringing to Human Rights Education a greater conceptual clarity and sharper focus and
- Articulating general guidelines to translate conceptual clarity and focus on each stage and for various subjects.

Objectives of the Human Rights Education

- To advocate and promote availability of all physical and cultural inputs needed for healthy children such as minimum caloric requirements, education toys, play grounds to all children of preschool age free or subsidised.
- To promote the goal of equal educational opportunities.
- To promote the realisation of goal of free and compulsory education up to the age of 14 especially by allocating funds and facilities for disadvantaged and backward groups.
- Advocate the affirmative action for weak social sectors including relaxation in admissions.
- Promote education to all levels and humanistic education ideas and models conducive to the inculcation of the values of freedom, equality and dignity at all.
- To wipe out class discrimination and class disparities especially in rural areas.

Human Rights Education at Higher Secondary Stage

NCERT has recommended a core course in general studies compulsory to all students. This includes the study of Human Rights in historial perspective, universal declaration of Human Rights, Human Rights Conventions, the states of Human Rights, racism and apartheid and struggle against them; unequal international economic relations and world economic development, social structure and social justice, social and economic equality, economic exploitation and atrocities against the weak, child labour, status of women and dynamics of the quest for equality, national unity, communalism, revivalism, castism and various kind of the chauvinism and respect for diversity. The course also recommends placing local problems within the broad framework of those themes.

The Common Wealth Study on school-based understanding on Human Rights in four countries India, Botswana, Zimbabwe and Northern Ireland has been published as an educational research paper no. 22. The result of the study on young people are acquiring basic concepts in different dimensions of Human Rights indicated that in India students have got solid understanding about all these aspects. The study conducted by READ (Rehabilitation Education and Development) in 30 villages of Karnataka also inferred that the general public is not much aware of human rights; even it is true in the case of tribal people.

Tribes are indigenous people; it is indeed a shameful fact that their education and living are still in poor condition even after decades of the independence. One cannot expect them to be aware of Human Rights since they are educationally and culturally backward. In Kerala literacy rate of tribes is about 30 per cent. The tribes in the State constitute 1.03 per cent of the total population. Wayanad is one of the districts of Kerala which is considered as an educationally backward area. In this area the tribal students constitute a major part of the student community.

Article 46 of Constitution of India states that "the State shall provide special care, the educational and economic interest of the weaker section of the people".

One of the guiding principles of the Constitution of India is that 'rights and duties' of citizens co-exist. Higher secondary schools are the workshops where the molding of new generations—*who determines the future of the nation*—is being done. In order to meet the ends, it is very much essential to have awareness about human rights at the right time. It is in this context the investigators made an attempt to study the awareness of higher secondary students' awareness of Human Rights among tribal and non-tribal higher secondary students of educationally backward district Wayanad of Kerala. In this area a major part of the students constitute tribal students who live in deep forest and high hills without being greatly disturbed by the overwhelming changes in the outer world. Human right violations are usually occurring in every field of this district. The dropout rate is very high as both the parents and students are not interested in education.

It should be noted that the higher secondary students have to cast their votes just after one year of completion of their course. They are inevitable part of the largest democracy of world. So their awareness towards constitutional and society issues has got a great significance.

There were many studies carried out to find out the educational level or academic achievement (Aruna, 1981; Varma, 1985; Amarjan and Thimmappa, 1986; Srikanthan Nair, 1987); socio-psychological variables like intelligence, self concept, achievement motivation, emotional adjustment, perception of environment etc. (Anita, 2000; Dutt, 1983; Kaul, 1983; Chand, 1983; Fatmi, 1986; Sing,1981; Gator, 1992, Rosily, 1994). Very few studies were conducted on human rights awareness among tribal population especially people and higher secondary students of Wayanad District, Kerala. Hence this study was taken up.

Objectives of Study

1. To compare Human Rights awareness between tribal and non-tribal higher secondary students.
2. To study the difference in Human Rights awareness between tribal and non-tribal higher secondary students with respect to their
   - Gender
   - Stream selected

Hypotheses of the Study

1. There is no significant difference in the Human Rights awareness between tribal and non-tribal higher secondary students.
2. There is no significant difference in Human Rights awareness between tribal and non-tribal higher secondary students with respect to their
   - Gender
   - Stream selected

Methods

It is a descriptive study and survey method is used to collect data.

Sampling Procedure

The population for the present study was higher secondary school students at Wayanad District in Kerala. Cluster random sampling technique is followed for the selection of tribal students and non-tribal students.

Sample of the Study

The total sample was selected from both tribal and non-tribal higher secondary schools in Wayanad district, Kerala. A total number of 240 sample were chosen, 120 each from tribal and non-tribal. Due care was taken to have equal gender representations as well as from stream selection (Science and Humanities).

Instrumentation

Human Rights Awareness Test: A test developed by Chandran A G in 2002 is used in the present study. The test comprises 40 objective type questions. The split half reliability for the test is 0.93.

Personal information Blank: This has been developed to collect the data regarding background variables of the students.

Statistical Treatment of Data

After the collection of data, all the response sheets were scored with the help of scoring key. Each correct answer was assigned one mark and each wrong answer fetched zero. Thus, obtained raw data was set for analysis using statistical techniques such as "t" test. The results of the analysis are tabulated in the following table:

Table 19.1: Statistics for the Whole Data

Variable	*Groups*	*N*	*Mean*	*SD*	*'tvalue'*
Overall	Tribal	120	21.92	4.71	2.33*
	Non-tribal	120	23.33	4.67	
Gender	Girls	107	22.49	4.67	0.48*
	Boys	133	22.21	4.26	
Stream Chosen	Science	120	22.33	4.95	3.71*
	Humanities	120	25.17	6.72	

*Significant at 0.05 level.

From the Table 19.1 it is clear that the mean score on human rights awareness test of non-tribal students (23.33) is more than the tribal students (21.92). The t-value obtained (2.33) is found to significant at 0.05 level. In other words non-tribal students have better awareness on Human Rights when compared to tribal higher secondary students.

Table 19.2:'t' Values of Human Right Awareness between Various Groups

Variable	*Groups*	*N*	*Mean*	*SD*	*'t-value'*
Tribal (Gender)	Boys	85	22.0	4.90	0.43*
	Girls	35	21.6	4.56	
Stream opted	Science	60	21.35	5.00	0.08
	Humanities	60	21.42	4.83	
Non-tribal (Gender)	Boys	48	27.69	4.64	5.03*
	Girls	72	23.0	4.68	
Stream opted	Science	60	22.25	4.90	2.66*
	Humanities	60	24.41	3.96	

*Significant at 0.05 level.

The Table 19.2 even indicates that girls have better awareness towards human rights when compared to the boys in general (t-value 0.480 is found significant). The students with Humanities background were found to possess better awareness than their counterparts from science background (as the t-value 3.70 is significant).

From the Table 19.2 it is clear that the mean score on human rights awareness test of tribal boys (22) is more than the tribal girls (21.6). The t-value obtained (0.43) is found to significant at 0.05 level. In other words tribal boys have better awareness on Human Rights when compared to tribal girls.

The Table 19.2 even indicates that there is no significant difference in the awareness of higher secondary students on Human Rights between with respect to the stream selected.

Whereas it is also evident that non-tribal girls have better awareness on human rights than the non-tribal boys. In case of non-tribal students the students who opted for science were found to possess better awareness when compared to the students who selected Humanities stream (as the t-value (2.66) is significant).

Major Findings of the Study

The following are the major findings of the present study:

1. Human Rights Awareness among the non-tribal students is found to be more when compared with tribal students.
2. Human Rights Awareness among the girls is found to be more when compared to boys.
3. Human Rights Awareness among the humanities students is found to be more when compared to science students.
4. Tribal boys have better awareness on Human Rights when compared to tribal girls. Whereas non-tribal girls have better awareness on human rights than the non-tribal boys.
5. There is no significant difference in the awareness of higher secondary students on Human Rights between with respect to the stream.
6. Non-tribal students who opted for science were found to possess better awareness when compared to the students who selected Humanities stream.

Educational Implications of the Study

1. From the present study the investigators found that there is a significant difference between tribal and non-tribal students in human rights awareness. This clearly shows that the government initiatives (with all the noise it made) in this regard, has not been successful enough.
2. The government initiatives have to be evaluated thoroughly and should see that the awareness level of tribal students is raised on human rights.

3. The study indicates that students of humanities were found to have better awareness than science students as they study in their curriculum, schools have to conduct some seminars, guest talks regarding the human rights and it is not enough having it as a compulsory subject at high school and higher secondary level.

4. To identify the relevant and significant objectives of Human Rights Education that is to be accomplished at various levels of school education as well as higher education level is the need of the hour. This is because the criteria for selecting contents of Human Rights Education are determined by these objectives. To transact the syllabus of Human Rights Education, the following steps have to be taken by the government:

- Teachers have to be specially trained to this context as a separate subject for all higher secondary students.
- Special classes are to be provided for its transaction using innovative methods of teaching at school level.
- Special education to women for awareness of elimination of discrimination against women to be provided.
- Non-formal education can be media to promote Human Rights Education to contribute to their promotion of awareness to right to education and health and an adequate livelihood including food, water and housing to just a favourable condition of work security and freedom from violence.

References

Bini Borgahan (1999). Human Rights: Social and Political Challenge, New Delhi: Kanishka Publishers.

Anita (2000). Study of achievement motivation among tribal and non-tribal secondary school pupils in Wayanad District. Unpublished M.Ed. Dissertation, University of Calicut.

Sam A Chelladurai (1999). Human rights education in India, The READ experience, HURIGHT-OSAIKA.

Rosily, NP (1994). A Study of attainment of biological concept in relation to attitude towards science and achievement motivation of tribal and non-tribal pupils of Standard VIII. Unpublished M.Ed. Dissertation, University of Calicut.

Singh (1981). Achievement of tribal students in relation to their intelligence, motivation and personality, Doctoral Dissertation, University of Bihar.

Fatmi, J M D (1986). A study of achievement related motivation among tribal and non-tribal high school students. Unpublished Doctoral Dissertation, Magadha University.

20

Working of Civil Society Organisations for Development of Tribals: A Study

BK Mahakul

In recent times, in most developed and developing countries, a Third Sector has emerged as a viable institutional framework to serve as a catalyst for development. This is in distinction to the role played by the governmental organisation as the first sector more accustomed to maintain law and order and the private commercial enterprises as the Second Sector known to exist more for profit making than for affecting the process of development. Despite the innumerable difficulties and obstacles which this intermediate zone non-governmental, non-profit organisations often classed under the collective form third sector have a surmount, it has become a major approach to encourage participation, social change and democratisation to the theory of development and to the dispersal of power is the civil society. In its various forms, the third sector is supposed to ease the burden on government expenditure by mobilising resources through other organisations in society, bringing about greater cost efficiency, higher flexibility and improved relations with beneficiaries. Due to changing role of the modern state there is no doubt that governance for the 21st century must overcome bureaucratic unresponsiveness. A modern state in our present understanding is supposed not only to protect the individual's freedom and liberty but also to guarantee social security, increasing affluence and social progress. Thus, the range of public duties has grown up over the years, which is now exceedingly wide. In order to fulfill these duties, the modern state has been encouraging the new sector, i.e., Civil Society Sector.

The tribal people have remained exploited and socio-economically backward through generation. Hence, the urgent need is to lift them up, and to bring them to the mainstream of national life through the performance of required and effective roles by both the Governmental and Civil Society Organisations.

In this benign venture, however, the role of the Government alone seems to be inadequate because participatory democracy requires active participation of citizens and Civil Society Organisations in bringing about holistic development of entire population including the socio-economically backward Scheduled Tribes as the special target groups. The scheduled tribes requires assistance of a very specialised nature, which can help them to terms with their environment and overcome their social, physical, situational handicaps and enable them to fulfill their promise and reach their full potential. The government is aware that in the area of tribal development, the support and cooperation of Civil Society Organisations is very much necessary. Since tribal development is one of the important aspects of a State's overall development the study of the phenomenon of Civil Society Organisations in tribal development have become imperative.

The present research work is intended to study the Working of Civil Society Organisations for Development of Tribals with reference to Orissa. In this research work an endeavour has been undertaken to identify the Civil Society Organisations engaged in tribal development, to enquire into the development programmes undertaken for the tribals and their perception towards the working of Civil Society Organisations.

The present research work attempts to ascertain the development programmes undertaken by Civil Society Organisations and attitudinal pattern of tribals towards tribal development. Therefore, an empirical method of study has been adopted for enquiry and analysis of the impact of development programmes and attitudinal pattern of the tribals. Both the Primary and Secondary sources were used to collect data and information relating to study. For the purpose of primary data, all these 5600 tribal beneficiaries have been interviewed on the basis of a structured interview schedule and their responses have been examined for delineating the socio-economic profile and the pattern of their attitude towards the development programmes undertaken by the Civil Society Organisations. As regards the secondary data, specifically for preparing the concepts like, tribes, development, civil society etc., a number of authoritative works as well as reports and documents have been consulted. On the whole, the method of study adopted for the purpose of this work is empirical as the study is based on facts and data collected from the respondents of the sample through personal interview.

The paper has been divided into two parts. Part-I discusses the concepts like tribes, development, Civil Society etc. from theoretical perspective. Part-II analyses the findings like socio-economic background of the beneficiaries, impact of the development programmes and perception of the tribal beneficiaries and suggestions.

PART–I

Concepts

Tribes: The term 'tribe' has no statutory definition and as such it has a wide variety of meanings. The word tribe is derived from the Latin word '*Tribus*'.

It originally meant a community of persons claiming descent from a common ancestor, definite territory and common cultural pattern. Gradually it stood for aboriginals, native and rascist stereotypes and related to the people of Africa and Asia, as also of North America and even of Australia.[1] In Indian context they are categorised as the Scheduled Tribes. The Imperial Gazetteer of India says, "a tribe is a collection of families bearing a common name, speaking a common dialect, occupying or professing to occupy a common territory and is not usually endogamous, though originally it might have been so".[2]

The constitution of India does not define the word tribe but declares that the Scheduled Tribes are "the tribes or tribal community", which the President may specify by notification. The Constitution of India empowers the President to declare any community as tribe. President of India, may with respect to any State or Union Territory, after consulting the Governor thereof, by public notification, specify the tribes or tribal communities which shall for the purpose of the constitution be deemed to be Scheduled Tribes in relation to the State or Union Territory, as per Article 342(1) of the constitution. After the lists have been promulgated any inclusion therein or exclusion there from may be made only by Parliament as per Article 342 (2). The tribals, in the context of modern Indian society, signify a group of primitive people living in the hills and forests having their own language and culture.[3]

Development: Development refers to growth, evolution advance, blossoming, elaboration, furtherance, progress, progression, unfolding, expansion, enlargement, extension, spreads, increased, improvement, maturity, flourishing, prosperity, promotion, refinement.[4] Dictionary definitions of the verb 'to develop' suggest that it means to change gradually, progressing through a number of states towards some sort of expansion, improvement, or completeness or a state in which the subject's true identity is revealed.[5] In the economic literature of the early; Post Second World War period, development was defined as "a rapid and sustained rise in real output per head and attendant shifts in the technological, economic, and demographic characteristics of a society.[6] Development, still in the sense of economic growth, came to seen as part of a much wider process of social change described as modernisation. According to Lerner "Modernisations, the process of social change in which development is the economic component".[7] The emphasis in development as modernisation is thus on how to inculcate wealth oriented behaviour and values in individuals. By the end of the 1960s, development came to be seen not simply as raising per capita income but more important, of reducing the poverty level among the masses or, as it was more picturesquely put satisfying their 'basic' needs.

Development has three important implications—first, it emphasises that development is essentially a human issue, a concern with the capacity of individuals to realise their inherent potential and effectively to cope with the changing circumstances of their live or as Cairnecross puts it, 'the key to development lies in men's mind, in the institution in which their thinking finds expression and in the play of opportunity on ideas and institutions.[8] Second, development involves the total and full mobilisation of a society. The task of changing the "institutions in which the thinking of individuals finds expression" cannot be undertaken in an ad hoc, piecemeal fashion. It has to be comprehensive and to involve total political commitment. Hence, Myrdal's definition of development as "the movement of the whole social system upwards".[9] Third, development represents a redefinition of a country's inter-nation relation. It involves a shift from an outward oriented, dependent status to a self-centered and self-reliant position with regard not only to the processes of decision-making, but more importantly the pattern and style of production and consumption. Development is a widely participatory process of directed social change in a society, intended to bring about both social and material advancement (including greater equality, freedom and other valued qualities) for the majority of the people through their gaining control over their environment.

The above analysis on development indicate the following:

- Development as a concept is much broader than economic growth or economic development.
- It is just not to increase national income; it is also for improving the quality of life for each and every member of the society.
- It is also not just social growth or change but also is a process of bringing about, social, economic and political transformation in the life of the marginalised sections of the population.

Civil Society: The term Civil Society has been defined in a variety of ways. Originally, it meant a political community, a society governed by law, under the authority of a state. More commonly, it is distinguished from the state and the term is used to describe institutions that are private ın that they are independent from government and organised by individuals in pursuit of their own ends. Civil Society therefore refers to a realm of autonomous groups and associations, business, interest groups, clubs, families and so on. Hegal defines, Civil Society is a collective body, whose members are conceived as "Self-subsistent persons".[10] In the Hegelian understanding of Civil Society, it is only an intermediary, which will ultimately lead to the formation of democratic state.

According to Michael Walzer Civil Society is the "Setting of Settings"; where people associate with each other on various grounds, but notably for the sake of realising their natures as social beings. He argues that, the picture here is a man freely associating and communicating with one another, forming and reforming groups of all sorts, not for the sake of any particular formation-family, tribe, nation, religion, commune, brotherhood or sisterhood, interest group or ideological movement— but for the sake of sociability itself for 'we are by nature social, before we are political or economic beings'.[11]

Civil Society is a collection of individual and collective for the 'Common Public Good'. In this definition, Civil Society is as linked to a public arena where the promotion of broadly defined public good is the purpose of Civil Society action. This 'Public Good' could include promotion of education, health care or sanitation; it could include prevention or pollution and deforestation, it could include protection of human rights or maintenance of peace and harmony; it could also include expression of dissent.[12]

According to conventional notions in the social science 'Civil Society' refers to that space which (1) exists between the family, on the one hand and the state on the other, (2) makes interconnections between individuals or families possible, and (3) is independent of the state. The concept of Civil Society has been viewed by different scholars in different perspective while some scholars favour a strong, vibrant and assertive Civil Society.[13] Some others favour a strong state to create Civil Society and assume that the state and civil society are intertwined concepts.[14] There are others relate civil society with the process of democratisation and for understanding the process of political change.[15] Others relate Civil Society with associations.[16]

Development Planning is essentially a mechanism to achieve improvement in the quality of life of the people. It is an umbrella concept. It has different connotation such as social development, economic development, political development and so on. Better health, education, income, information etc., can improve these aspects and thereby lead to development. These pre-conditions, aspiration and motivation of the people. Therefore, Civil Society Organisations are emerging gradually and participating actively in the process of social and economic transformation of tribals.

PART-II

Findings: The socio-economic development seems to be significantly influenced by the socio-economic characteristic of the individual, so an endeavour has been undertaken to enquire in to the socio-economic background of the tribal beneficiaries. This has been enquired into in respect of the variables of age, gender, education, income and occupation. Their attitudinal profile have been studied and analysed.

The term beneficiary applies to those respondents who are directly benefited from the services of the organisations under study.

Age: In terms of the variable of Age, the beneficiaries have been grouped under three Age Groups such as Young (who are 35 years or below), those who are between 36 years to 55 years have been grouped under Middle Age Group and those who are above 56 years of age have been grouped under the Old Age Group.

On analysing it is found that 74.85 per cent (4191) of the beneficiaries belong to Young Age Group, 9.23 per cent (517) belong to Middle Age Group, and 15.92 per cent (892) belong to Old Age Group.

Gender Groupings: In terms of the variable of gender, the beneficiaries have been grouped as Males and Females. It is found that female beneficiaries constitute 52.55 per cent (2942) and male beneficiaries constitute 47.45 per cent (2657). The reason for outnumber of female beneficiaries, the government has been giving much more emphasis on Women development/empowerment.

Education: It is found that 30.57 per cent (1711) have studied upto middle level, 22.29 per cent (1249) upto Primary level, 18.15 per cent (1017) Secondary/ Higher Secondary level, 18.47 (1024) are illiterate. 4.14 per cent (231) have studied upto graduation level, 1.60 per cent (90) upto Post-graduation level and 4.78 per cent (681) could not say about their education.

The sample is found to have been dominated by the beneficiaries attained middle educational level.

Income Groupings: On the basis of average annual income approximately, from all sources, beneficiaries have been grouped under four income range. The groups are, below Rs 3000.00 between Rs 3001.00 to Rs 5000.00, Rs 5001.00 to Rs 8000.00 and Rs 8001.00 to Rs 10,000.00

It is found that 39.50 per cent (2212) of the beneficiaries income range of Rs 5001 to Rs 8000, 22.92 per cent (1283) beneficiaries income range of Rs 3001 to Rs 5000, 22.29 per cent (1248) beneficiaries income range of Rs 8001 to Rs 10,000 and 15.30 per cent (857) income upto Rs 3000.00. It is found that maximum no. of beneficiaries belong to the income range between Rs 5001 to Rs 8000.

Occupation: In terms of the variable of occupation of the beneficiaries, from which they earn their livelihood, have been distributed occupations-wise.

It is revealed that as many as 32.48 per cent (1819) beneficiaries are unemployed and has no occupation of their own. It is followed by 28.02 per cent (15.70) reported cultivation as their principal occupation. There are 25.80 per cent (1444) beneficiaries engaged in labour followed by 13.70 per cent (767) beneficiaries reported have petty shop as their principal occupation.

The sample of beneficiaries is dominated by the dependent having no principal occupations. Hence, they intended to get benefits from the developmental schemes through voluntary organisations.

The socio-economic background of the beneficiaries has, thus been enquired in respect of the variables of age, gender, education, income and occupation. It is found that the sample, in terms of the variables of age has been dominated by the Young Age Group, in terms of the variables of education, Middle level Educated Group, female beneficiaries in terms of the variable of gender and no occupation/unemployed in terms of occupation.

Impact of the Schemes and Perception of Beneficiaries

The immense impact of the services rendered by the concerned Civil Society Organisations to the respective beneficiaries can be observed by enquiring their satisfaction. Impact can not be measured only in economic indicators, as welfare service has multi-dimensional aspects which cover material, non-material, economic and non-economic benefits. All these are inter-related and an appraisal of social welfare services involves in their collective use and application. The ultimate aim of effect of these services is satisfaction of beneficiaries. Thus, to know the impact of the services the researcher has obtained information from the beneficiaries implying economic and non-economic changes in their lives.

Classification of Beneficiaries According to Benefits

The researcher has classified the beneficiaries according to the benefits received by them.

Variable	*Groups*	*N*	*Mean*	*SD*	*'t-value'*
Tribal (Gender)	Boys	85	22.0	4.90	0.43*
	Girls	35	21.6	4.56	
Stream opted	Science	60	21.35	5.00	0.08
	Humanities	60	21.42	4.83	
Non-tribal (Gender)	Boys	48	27.69	4.64	5.03*
	Girls	72	23.0	4.68	
Stream opted	Science	60	22.25	4.90	2.66*
	Humanities	60	24.41	3.96	

- There are 28.36 per cent (1588) beneficiaries received benefits under Vocational Education and training scheme which includes computer, cutting and tailoring, embroidery, typing, stenography, craft, vegetable processing etc.
- It is followed by 20.71 per cent (1160) beneficiaries who got financial and material Assistance. Financial assistances are covered under schemes such as scholarship, pension and assistance to poor, relief, prizes and petty shops. The material assistance includes supply of uniforms, blankets, sewing machines, appliances to handicapped.
- 14.03 per cent (786) beneficiaries received health and medical benefits. They are served mainly through nature-cure, physiotherapy, eye-operation camps, ambulance services, free medical check-up and referred services.
- There are 11.45 per cent (641) beneficiaries who received services pertaining to counselling, advice and general awareness. The general awareness covered social problems, health and nutrition, communal harmony, environmental awareness human rights, right to information and need felt political guidance. Under the counselling disputes are settled and legal advice given.
- 8.59 per cent (481) beneficiaries are assisted under the scheme of education. In these cases the civil society organisations managed NCLP School, nursery, Primary education for tribal children.
- 4.14 per cent (232) beneficiaries have got the benefit of guidance in farming know-how.

• 2.86 per cent (160) beneficiaries got employment through civil society organisation in the educational institutions, small business and sale of daily products.

This analysis shows that several services, benefits assistance are arranged by the civil society organisations.

The researcher have enquired into the benefits received by the beneficiaries according to their preference with developmental schemes, in terms of variables of age, gender, education, occupation and income.

On analysing the responses of the beneficiaries in terms of age-groups, it is found that 24.69 per cent (1035) of the Young age-group has been benefited from Vocational Education and Training. 23.82 per cent (998) have been benefited from Financial and Material Assistance. Whereas 16.18 per cent (678), 10.63 per cent (445), 9.37 per cent (393), 8.49 per cent (356), 4.27 per cent (171) and 2.55 per cent (107) of the Young-age group have been benefited from health and medical assistance, education, counseling, advice and general awareness, farming guidance and employment respectively.

The Middle Age Group, it is found that 44.87 per cent (232) of the beneficiaries benefited from Vocational Education and Training followed by 13.73 per cent (71), 10.25 per cent (53), 6.96 per cent (36), 6.96 per cent (36) and 3.48 per cent (18) of the beneficiaries have been benefited from financial and material assistance, counselling, advice and general awareness, employment, health and medical services, education and farming guidance respectively.

From Old Age Group, it is found that 35.98 per cent (321) of the beneficiaries have been benefited from Vocational Education and Training, 26 per cent, 10.26 per cent, 8.07 per cent, 5.94 per cent, 3.92 per cent and 1.90 per cent of the beneficiaries have been benefited from counselling, advice, and general awareness, financial and material assistance, health and medical services, education, farming guidance and employment respectively.

Thus, it is found that in terms of age groups the beneficiaries of all age-groups have been benefited mostly from Vocational Education and Training. It would help them to be economically independent.

On analysing the responses of the beneficiaries in terms of the variables of gender, it is found that 36.89 per cent (980) male beneficiaries have been benefited from Vocational Education and Training, followed by 19.49 per cent, 11.37 per cent, 10.9 per cent, 7.38 per cent, 7.38 per cent, 3.98 per cent and three per cent of the financial and material assistance, counselling, advice and general assistance, health and medical services, education, farming guidance and employment respectively.

On analysing the responses of the female beneficiaries, it is found that 21.81 per cent (642) female beneficiaries have been benefited from Financial and Material Assistance followed by 20.65 per cent, 9.70 per cent, 4.29 per cent and 2.34 per cent of the female beneficiaries have been benefited from vocational education and training, health and medical services, counselling, advice and general assistance, education, farming guidance and employment respectively.

Thus, it is found that the male beneficiaries mostly preferred and benefited from vocational education and training programme, followed by financial and material assistance. While the female beneficiaries mostly preferred and benefited from financial and material assistance followed by vocational education and training.

On analysing the responses of the beneficiaries in terms of education, it is found that 25.91 per cent (268) illiterate beneficiaries have been benefited from Vocational Education and Training, followed by 17.21 per cent of them benefited from Financial and Material Assistance and other 17.21 per cent of have been benefited from Health and Medical Services. While 13.82 per cent, 13.82 per cent, 6.87 per cent and 5.12 per cent illiterate beneficiaries have been benefited from counseling, advice and general awareness, education and farming guidance respectively.

On analysing the responses of the beneficiaries having primary education, it is found that 25.71 per cent of them have been benefited from Vocational Education and Training, followed by 20 per cent benefited from Financial and Material Assistance. While 12.85 per cent, 10 per cent and 5.71 per cent have been benefited from health and medical services, counseling, advice and general awareness, education and farming guidance respectively.

On analysing the responses of the beneficiaries having Middle Education, it is found that 36.46 per cent have been benefited from Vocational Education and Training, followed by 27.08 per cent, 8.30 per cent, 8.30 per cent, 6.25 per cent and 4.16 per cent beneficiaries have been benefited from residential facilities, education, health and medical services, counselling, advice and general awareness and farming guidance respectively.

On analysing the responses of the beneficiaries having Secondary/Higher Secondary Education, it is found that 21.04 per cent have been benefited form Vocational Education and Training, Financial and Material Assistance, followed by 17.60 per cent, 6.99 per cent, 6.99 per cent, 3.53 per centand 1.77 per cent have been benefited from counselling, advice and general awareness, employment, education and farming guidance respectively.

On analysing the responses of the beneficiaries having Graduation level of education, it is found that 38.52 per cent have been benefited from Vocational Education and Training. While 15.59 per cent, 15.59 per cent and 7.36 per cent of the beneficiaries have been benefited from employment, financial and material assistance respectively.

On analysing the responses of the beneficiaries having Post-graduation level, it is found that 36 per cent of them have been benefited from Vocational Education and Training, while 20 per cent each have been benefited from three Developmental Programmes, i.e., financial and material assistance, health and medical services and residential facilities.

On analysing the responses of the beneficiaries having Informal Education it is found that 26.87 per cent, 26.87 per cent, 19.40 per cent, 13.43 per cent, 13.43

per cent have been benefited from vocational education and training, education, counseling, advice and general awareness, health and medical services respectively.

Thus, it is found that the illiterate beneficiaries have been benefited more from financial and material assistance, health and medical services. while primary, middle, secondary/higher secondary, graduate, post-graduate and Informal educated beneficiaries have been largely benefited from Vocational Education and Training Programme of the developmental schemes through Civil Society Organisations.

On analysing the responses of the beneficiaries in terms of Cultivation, it is found that 38.60 per cent (606) have been benefited from financial and material assistance followed by 33 per cent, 15.92 per cent, 3.38 per cent of the beneficiaries have been benefited from vocational education and training, farming guidance, counseling, advice and general awareness respectively.

On analysing the responses of the beneficiaries in terms of Occupation of Labour, it is found that 37.04 per cent (535) have been benefited from Vocational Education and Training Programme followed by 24.70 per cent, 12.40 per cent, 9.83 per cent, 7.40 per cent, 4.91 per centand 3.68 per cent have been benefited from financial and material assistance, education, counseling, advice and general awareness, employment, health and medical services respectively.

On analysing the responses of the beneficiaries who are dependent/ unemployed, it is found that 29.36 per cent (534) have been benefited from Health and Medical Services. While 21.67 per cent, 13.74 per cent, 11.70 per cent, 9.84 per cent, 7.87 per cent, 2.91 per cent and 2.91 per cent have been benefited from vocational education and training, education, financial and material assistance, counseling, advice and general awareness, employment and farming guidance respectively.

On analysing the responses of the beneficiaries in terms of Occupation of Petty shop, it is found that 25.26 per cent (199) have been benefited from health and Medical Services followed by 23.20 per cent, 18.39 per cent, 13.82 per cent, 11.60 per cent, 4.70 per cent and 2.34 per cent have been benefited from Residential facilities, Vocational Education and Training, Counseling, Advice and General Awareness, Education, Financial and Material Assistance respectively.

Thus, it is found that, in terms of Occupation of Cultivation more numbers of beneficiaries have been benefited from Financial and Material Assistance, while in terms of occupation of dependent and Petty shop, beneficiaries have been benefited from Health and Medical Services. While in terms of Occupation of Labour, beneficiaries have been benefited from Vocational Education and Training Programme.

On analysing the responses of the beneficiaries in terms of income, it is found that 50 per cent (428) whose income is below Rs 3000.00, have been benefited from Vocational Education and Training Programme. It is followed by 20.83 per cent, 14.58 per cent, 4.16 per cent, 4.16 per cent and 2.08 per cent have been benefited from financial and material assistance, residential facilities, health and medical services, education, counseling, advice and general awareness and farming guidance respectively.

On analysing the respondents of the beneficiaries in terms of income in range between Rs 3001 to Rs 5000, it is found that 30.56 per cent (392) have been benefited from Vocational Education and Training, followed by 25.01 per cent, 15.28 per cent, 12.48 per cent, 6.94 per cent, 4.13 per cent, 2.80 per cent and 2.80 per cent have been benefited from financial and material assistance, counseling, advice and general awareness, health and medical services, residential facilities, education, farming guidance and employment respectively.

On analysing the responses of the beneficiaries in terms of income in range between Rs 5001 to Rs 8000, it is found that 22.60 per cent (500) have been benefited from Vocational Education and Training, whereas 19.40 per cent, 13.70 per cent, 12.88 per cent, 12.07 per cent, 11.20 per cent, 5.65 per cent and 2.40 per cent have been benefited from financial and material assistance, health and medical services, education, residential facilities, counselling, advice and general awareness, farming guidance and employment respectively.

On analysing the responses of the beneficiaries in terms of income in range between Rs 8001 to Rs 10,000.00 it is found that 22.99 per cent (287) have been benefited from Health and Medical Services, followed by 21.48 per cent, 18.59 per cent, 12.74 per cent, 8.58 per cent, 5.69 per cent and 4.24 per cent have been benefited from vocational education and training, financial and material assistance, counselling, advice and general awareness, education, employment and farming guidance respectively.

Thus, it is found that beneficiaries have been benefited more from Vocational Education and Training Programme followed by Financial and Material Assistance Programme.

Income Before and After Taking Assistance

On analysing the information received from the beneficiaries, it is found that 22.29 per cent (1248) had annual income in range of Rs 8001 to Rs10,000, before taking benefits from the Civil Society Organisations, while 39.50 per cent (2212) had annual income in range of Rs 5001 to Rs 8000.00, 22.92 per cent (1288) had Rs 3001 to Rs 5000 and 15.30 per cent (857) had upto Rs 3000.00.

On the whole, most of the beneficiaries assisted by the Civil Society Organisations were in the low income group before taking benefits.

Inter-incomer Class Shifting

To measure the impact of the schemes of the voluntary organisations on beneficiaries, the shift ability of the beneficiaries from one income class to another have been examined. The classification of beneficiaries has been presented in income group, viz., below Rs 3000, Rs 3001 to Rs 5000, Rs 5001 to Rs 8000 and Rs 8001 to Rs 10, 000.

It is found that 91.40 per cent (5119), beneficiaries shifted to higher income group after taking assistance. This shift is comparatively higher in the income group of Rs 5001 to Rs 8000 followed by income group of Rs 8001 to Rs 10, 000.00. This percentage of beneficiaries is 83.32 per cent and 87.86 per cent of those who shifted to higher income groups from income range of Rs 3001 to Rs 5000 and unto Rs 3000 respectively.

On the whole 91.40 per cent (5119) shifted to higher income group after taking assistance through Civil Society Organisations. From this analysis it can be inferred that there is a positive impact of assistance arranged by the civil society organisations.

Increase in Income

Responses from the beneficiaries are sought to form an opinion, whether or not they feel that their income increased or no change after getting assistance through the Civil Society Organisations.

On analysing the responses, it is found that 91.40 per cent (5119) beneficiaries reported that the schemes helped them in increasing their annual income. Rest 8.60 per cent (481) felt that there is no change in their income. Those who felt that their income could not change after taking assistance mis-utilised the assistance given through the Civil Society Organisations.

Thus, it is revealed that shift in income of 91.40 per cent of beneficiaries, is an important indicator of improvement of their economic conditions.

Satisfaction with Services/ Assistance

If the beneficiaries would be found satisfied with the services rendered or assistance given by the Civil Society Organisations, it would indicate positive impact of the latter.

In this context, it is found that on overwhelming majority, that is 91.40 per cent (5119) of the beneficiaries have been responded in affirmative and are satisfied with the role of the Civil Society Organisations.

Thus, it is found that the beneficiaries are by and large, satisfied with the services rendered/assistance given by the Civil Society Organisations.

Impact on Different Aspects of Life

78.35 per cent (4388) of beneficiaries said that their income has increased, standard of living improved and socio-economic status have enhanced.

From the analysis pertaining to the nature of impact, it can be inferred that the services and assistance arranged by the Civil Society Organisations not only helped in improving their socio-economic conditions but also have strong effect on certain other aspects such as removal of physical hardships, raising confidence, moulding the attitude, raising the educational level and formation of awareness.

Thus it is found that, the developmental schemes through Civil Society Organisations have positive impact on different aspects of their life.

Perception of Beneficiaries about the Civil Society Organisations from which they Received Benefits.

The analysis of the responses of the beneficiaries show that, 46.50 per cent (2604) perceived the Civil Society Organisations role as highly commendable and valuable followed by 35.03 per cent (1962) consider it as enough to meet their development requirements. 14.65 per cent (820) reported their role in social welfare arena as good.

It is inferred from the responses that on the whole the working of Civil Society Organisations is considered by the beneficiaries as commendable and valuable, in the context of over-all tribal development.

Suggestions for Greater Tribal Development by the Civil Society Organisations

At present Civil Society Organisations are inevitable in the context of democracy. It is supposed that it is meant for educating tribal people so that they may become politically and socio-economically conscious as well as dutiful towards nation-building.

Suggestions

- Greater involvement of Civil Society Organisations in tribal development programme should be encouraged.
- Media should be to focus the achievement of Civil Society Organisations.
- More funds should be provided by the government to the Civil Society Organisations to meet the needs and aspirations of the tribal people.
- The government should have a positive stand to support the Civil Society Organisations and to boost up their moral, on recognising their achievements and contributions toward tribal development.

References

1. R.B. Jain and R.K. Nayak (1988): in K.P. Singh (ed.), *Tribal Development in India*. New Delhi, Uppal Publishing House, p. 329.

2. D.N. Majumdar (1961): *Races and Culture of India, Bombay*, Asia Publishing House, p. 367.

3. D. Thakur and D.N. Thakur (1995), *Tribal Law and Administration*, New Delhi, Deep and Deep Publications, p. 25.

4. Martin H. Manser (ed.) (2000), *Chambers English Thesaurus*. Allied Chambers Ltd., p. 202.

5. K.P. Jameson and C.K.Wilber (ed.) (1979): *Directions in Economic Development*. Notre Dame, University of Notre Dame Press, p. 5.

6. Richard A. Easterlin (1968), *Overview on Economic Growth in D.L. Sills (ed). International Encyclopaedia of the Social Sciences*, New York, Vol. 4, p. 395.

7. Daniel Learner (1968): "*Social Aspects of Modernisation*" in International Encyclopaedia of the Social Sciences, New York, Vol. 10, p. 387.

8. A.K. Cairnecross (1961), "*International Trade and Economic Development, Economia*, Vol. 28, No.106, 1st February, p. 250.

9. Gunnar Myrdal (1968), *Asian drama: An Inquiry into the Poverty of Nations*. New York, Vol. 3, p.1868.

10. G.W.F. Hegel (1953), *Philosophy of Rights*, Oxford Clarendon, p.148.

11. Michael Walzer (1998), *The Concept of Civil Society*, Oxford: Berghahn Books, pp.7-28.

12. Rajesh Tandon (2003), "*The Civil Society- Governance Interface,* An India Perspective", in Rajesh Tandon and Ranjita Mohanty (eds.), Does Civil Society Make Governance in Contemporary India?, New Delhi: Sage Publications.

13. G.E. Gellner (1994), *Civil Society in Historical Context. International Social Science Journal*, No.129: 495-510.

14. Neera Chandhoke (198), *State and Civil Society-Exploration in Political Theory*, New Delhi, Sage Publications.

15. John-Hall (1995), *"Civil Society: Theory, History, Comparison,"* Cambridge, U.K. Polity Press.

16. Gurpreet Mahajan (1999), "*Civil Society and its Avtars*: What happened to Freedom and Democracy? Economic and Political Weekly, Vol. 34, No. 20, p. 1189.

21

Empowerment of Tribal's in Assam: Role of Autonomous District Councils

Girija Brahma

Introduction

The constituent assembly felt that the unique cultural and traditional governance practices of various tribes residing in the hills of north-eastern part of the country are good enough for the effective functioning of their existing system. They believed that, the sudden disruption of village customs and ways by sudden exposure to the modern ways of administrations that is majorly based on British administrative legacy would prove to be detrimental.

This however does not negate that the other regions of the country did not have unique practices culture, traditions and governance practices. On contrary, the situation in the north-eastern region was completely different. The north-eastern India was never exposed to the British administrative apparatus as much as the other part of the country. Moreover, prior to the coming of the British, the rest of India the disputes were resolved according to principles laid down in Smriti and Dharmasutra before the coming of the Islamic invaders. After the advent of the Islamic rule certain Shariat law coexisted along with the existing Smriti and Dharmasutra.

Interestingly, all these civil codes did not make way to the hills and valley on a serious note as they were cut off from the rest of the world because of hostile climate and terrains. British policy also helped in preserving the prevailing image of uncharted territory as they did not foray into the region. The passing of Inner Line Regulation in 1873 to prohibit entry of all Britisher subjects or any class of British subjects in the area within the inner line without proper pass-issued by the competent authority was one such attempt. This was followed by the Scheduled District Act of 1874. When Simon Commission Toured India i.e., (The Indian Statutory Commission) they toured the entire British India and almost all the Hill District submitted their various demands. In 1930, Simon Commission recommended for preservation of ancestral customary rights of the tribes. Thus, the Government of India Act, 1935, section 92 enacted provisions that no act Provincial and Central legislatures can be applied to the hills areas. Thus, these hills areas were designated as backward tracts known as the excluded or partially excluded areas.

Later the Cabinet Mission under the Chairman of Sir Stafford Cripps suggested the formation of Advisory Committee on the Rights of Citizens, Minorities and tribal areas. Thus, when Constituent Assembly was set up as per the proposals of the cabinet mission, an advisory committee on tribal areas under the chairmanship of Sardar Vallabhbhai Patel to consider the problem of Assam and the tribal areas. The advisory Committee formed a sub committee under the chairmanship of Gopinath Bordoloi. He toured the entire hill region and interacted with the leaders from the various tribes, the Bordoloi committee was sensitive to the need of the growing aspirations of the tribal people. This committee was responsible for making all the possible arrangement so that the provision of Sixth Schedule that various hill tribes enjoys today could be enshrined in the Constitution.

The Idea of Sixth Schedule Area

For many, the idea of separate provision of Sixth Schedule was sown by the British rule. During the colonial Assam, the Hills district was once administered under special provision for the so called excluded areas and partially excluded areas under the Government of India Act, 1935. With Independence, the Sixth Schedule of the Constitution established autonomous district councils in the same areas, based on the premises that it would help them to maintain their distinctiveness and provide a platform for their survival.

The reason for asking autonomy is highly based on complex web of identity, ethnicity and sub nationalism. Prior to the colonial demarcation of the North-East region, there were many groups of people inhabiting specific areas with political control over a limited territory and controlled over the land and its resources that would not be termed as a nation in any modern sense. For several centuries the valleys and hills of north eastern India had witnessed waves of invasion and migration. In a true sense none of these so called ethnic groups, due to their long journey of migration, can claim racial purity. Speculation about their migrations have been widely made and widely contradicted.

Elements of Sixth Scheduled

As per the provision in the Sixth Scheduled in the Areas of north-east India. "No act of the state legislatures in respect of tribal affairs shall apply to any autonomous district unless the district councils so direct. On the other hand, these areas were given full share in the State Legislatures and State

Cabinet. The Sixth Schedule gives tribal communities residing in the hills a considerable autonomy. The role of the Governor and the State are subject to significant limitations, with greater powers devolved locally. The District Council and the Regional Council under the Sixth Schedule have real power to make laws, possibility on the various legislative subjects, receiving grants-in-aids from the Consolidated Fund of India to meet the costs of schemes for development, healthcare, education, roads and regulatory powers to state control. The mandate towards devolution, de-concentration and divestment determines the protection of their customs, better economic development and most importantly ethnic security.

Limitations Constraints

The relevance of the Sixth Schedule in the present context needs a serious review. The Schedule was specifically created to ensure the protection of the tribes from the threat of marginalisation, domination and homogenisation by the non-tribal populations and their culture in jurisdictional area of the Autonomous District Councils (ADCs). The Schedule succeeded to a great extent to preserve the distinct identity and autonomy of tribal population, yet the same provision has become subject to controversies. It has been alleged time and again that the district councils have failed to fulfil the aspirations of the people because of the lack of funds, lack of administrative and legislative powers. State government continues to pull all the strings. The funds allocated for the District Councils by the Central government are often allegedly diverted elsewhere or not released in time.

More than that, the frequent occurrence of ethic conflict in the schedule areas need a closer scrutiny. The various ethnic conflict with epicentres in these autonomous council have time and again made one ponder about the existence of an inherent ethnic polarisation and sub-nationalism and the air of mutual distrust in the air. For example, the later part of 2005, saw the Dimasa and Karbis at war. It saw the displacement of 44,016 ethnic Karbis, Dimasa and along with other tribal and non-tribal populations. Mid 2012 saw riots in BTAD, the ethic-Bodos who have political control over the area was at war against the illegal immigrants. It saw nearly four lakhs displacement within a short period of 10 days. Asian Centre for Human Rights in its study highlights the fact that in this ethnic war there was a failure on the part of administration to stop killings and arson even after one month of continuous violence. The centre also highlights the bitter reality in its study that the State government do not use the security options available at its disposal. Only after the death toll raises armies are called to aid the civilian has been the order of the day. The state which has withheld the police power and takes the responsibility to protect the lives of the citizens and people in the schedule areas have failed time and again. This results in the feeling that they are not safe and the apprehension of losing their land and identity escalates if they still become a part of Assam. The resultant is that only a separate state for them would give them fullfledged protection. Moreover the earlier move of granting of separate statehood to many of its district council those once were a part of erstwhile excluded and partially excluded areas has given them the hope that they too can get a separate state status. Well some have seen this as attempt to alter the demographic picture of the proposed homeland.

The activities of insurgent group have not been fully controlled by the State. This has proved to be a great hurdle in its peaceful existence of autonomous district council. Whether surrendered or not, whether in ceasefire or not the militants organisation has been detrimental to the achievement of schedule six areas.They all have been busy in the extortion business from the tribals as well as non-tribals that has instilled fears among the masses and have thickened the air of distrust. Various reports say that the Dimasa and Karbi conflict escalated due to the active participation of Militant Groups like Dima Halam Daoga and United Peoples Democratic Solidarity. Similarly, reports suggested the role of NDFB both talk and anti talk faction and the disbanded BLT hands in eruption of riots.

This all shows that the sixth schedule areas have proved to be incompetent time and again as it has failed to empower the tribal's with what it requires the most i.e., peace for safeguarding its distinct identity, law tradition and practices.

Moreover, the Councils are only visible to be functioning at the district level. There is no decentralisation of powers and administration to the grass root level. All it has is the all in all district council, which elects few people and they enjoy unbridled power. But democracy demands that power should not be concentrated in a few hands. Moreover unlike the Panchayati Raj Institutions and Urban Local Bodies they do not have any reservation for women and their representation in all the three district council is also meagre. In the absence of village panchayats, here a body nominated by the Council who carry out the administration at village level. As they are nominated, its defeats the very idea of democratic decentralisation. As the VCDC is nominated by the council, it is always the party member who are members of the ruling party gets a change to serve in the VCDC. The District Council is unreachable for the common masses as there have been no elections.

The Karbi Anglong experiences of autonomy under the sixth schedule tells about the lack of autonomy since its inception. However, to curtain the separatist demands Bodoland territorial council took birth and walked the same route that prevailing in Karbi Anglong long time back. It's worth pondering that the institutions those are supposed to guarantee autonomy that makes them obsolete and ineffective in one context and are sold to others as a means of conflict resolution.

I would like to conclude by saying the problems of encroachment and infiltration will be easier to handle with closer monitoring at local level, this would lessen the so called threat and local masses has to be involved in the day to day functioning of the councils and this can happen only when VCDC member is elected by the villagers by timely elections. Then only the true empowerment of tribal's will began. Moreover the right and healthy programme and policy measures by the State government is only the solution for a healthy functioning of autonomous district councils so that they can bloom to the fullest. Or else the separatist tendency to carve out a separate state in its bid to safeguard its life and property among other interest would prevail in the region. This would see bandhs and violence that would have serious economic consequences. So, to be a prosperous state, the State of Assam should not neglect the autonomous district council or else the state will sooner or later ceased not to exist because the bifurcation of the state will be the only solution left.

22

Politics of SCs and STs Conflict in Kandhamal: Failure of Indian Secularism

Himanshu Sekhar Mishra

This paper elaborates the genesis of 'Kandhas' (SCs)–'Panas' (SCs) in Kandhamal, their relation from cooperative to conflict, the politics played by Sangha Parivar in their conflict to serve their ideology and how Indian secularism becomes crony without understanding inter-religious domination and intra-religious domination simultaneously and giving scope to this kind of force to grow.[1]

In Kandhamal, on 23rd August, 2008, Sri Lakshmananda Saraswati - a leader of the Vishwa Hindu Parishad (VHP) – was murdered by unidentified gunmen under mysterious circumstances. Maoist rebels were initially blamed by the police and some Hindu organisations suspected collusion of Christian missionaries amongst the *Pana* caste. This led to large scale riots between the indigenous *Kandha* tribe (largely Hindu) and the Christian minority amongst the *Pana* caste. The underlying causes are complex and cross political, religious and ethnic boundaries. Justice SC Mohapatra said in his interim report on the violence in Kandhamal that "The violence in Kandhamal was the result of concentrated discontentment prevailing among the people since long. They relate to conversion, re-conversion; land-grabbing and non-maintenance of land records; and fake certificate issues".[2] He, however, does not elaborate on the conversion and re-conversion issues but says that "in spite of the Orissa Freedom of Religion Act, illegal conversions were taking place which created discontentment". To him, suspicion among the Scheduled Tribe and Scheduled Caste inhabitants of Kandhamal is the main cause of riots with the tribal suspecting that 'Pana' dalits are capturing their land through fraudulent means. Besides the issues of land and conversion and re-conversion, Justice Mohapatra says fake certificate is another major factor that creates discontent among 'Kandha' tribals who constitute 52 per cent of Kandhamal's population.[3] The 28 page long report says that land is being grabbed by the 'Pana'. It is a fact that a section of the 'Pana' has encroached upon the vast stretches of land which originally belong to the 'Kandhas'. As per the Land Regulation Law of Orissa, nontribal can neither buy nor take possession of land from tribal owners. Along with these lines, the report says that many 'Pana' Christians who have lost their SC tag after conversion to Christianity has managed to secure a false certificate. Some of the 'Pana' Christians also submit their fake tribal certificate for the government jobs and to grab land and reap quota benefits in education. Though in every issue, SCs and STs Conflict is manifest, but in reality it is a conflict between fundamentalist force (Hindutva forces) and secular forces which has made Indian secularism crony. This paper has three sections. First section deals with *Kandhas* and *Panas* of Kandhamal. Second section deals with the relation between *Kandhas* and *Panas* and its manipulation by the Sangha Parivar. Third section deals with crony secularism where it is elaborated how fundamentalist force strengthens itself because of the failure of secularism.

I

The present Kandhamal district has been carved out of the erstwhile Boudh-Phulbani district, consisting of two Sub-division Kandhamal and Baliguda. This District lies between 19 degree 34 minutes and 20 degree 50 minutes north latitude and in between 80 degrees 30 minutes and 84 degrees 48 minutes east longitude. It is located in the Northern extremity of the Eastern Ghats bounded by Boudh district in the north, Rayagada district in the south, Ganjam District and Nayagarh district in the east and Kalahandi district in the west. The name of the district 'Kandhamal' is derived from the name of its major inhabitants Kandhas, having total populations 6,48,201 according to the census of 2001. Out of which scheduled tribes are 3,36,809 and schedule caste are 1,09,506 and rest belong to other communities. Above all this district is predominated by the tribals. Numerically, the Kandhas constitute the largest tribe among all other tribes nearly 90 per cent of total STs and Panas are nearly 80 per cent of total SCs in Kandhamal District. Besides these SCs and STs, there are different castes such as Brahmins, Kshyatriyas, Sundhi, Karan, Kulta, Gauda, Mali, Teli, Sunari etc. From religious point of view, Hindus (incidentally the STs included despite the animistic religion followed by them) constitute 5,27,757 (82 per cent) and Christians are 1,17,950 (18 per cent) so far as census of 2001 is concerned. Besides these two major religions, there is Islam as well as Buddhist religion also.

Being Dravidians, *Kandhas* were in this hilly tract of the country before the advent of the Aryans. They have been classified under the ancient Gondid race of the Proto-Australoid group, which according to scholars like Risley, preceded the Aryans by many thousand years.[4] After the fall of Harappan culture, the ancestors of *Kandhas* with other inhabitants moved towards Gangetic valley and started their settlement at the feet of Himalayas. In due course after division they migrated to the different parts of the country. Having segregated one section of the tribe used to settle in the soil of Odisha through Vindhya Mountain. In this connection there is a folk song like "*Himalaya ra andh, binja giri ra Kandha, Athe jelen Kandhen, Basalya kalasur mandh*".[5] It is believed that the *Kandhas* migrated from Madhya Pradesh and entered into the district of Kalahandi and divided into two divisions. The branch which took southeast direction might have proceeded to Belghar region, the south-west of Kandhamal district.[6] The *Kandhas* for the first time settled their foot hold Sapangada of Tamudibandh block. There after they established their settlement at Adanga Pata and Sujunga Pata. With increase of their population, the *Kandha* classified among themselves into several sections such as *Kutia Kandha, Dangaria Kandha, Desia Kandha, Bura Kandha, Sita Kandha, Pengo Kandha, Nagala Kandha, Buda Kandha* and *Raja Kandha*.[7] The *Kutia, Dangaria* and *Desia Kandhas* play a major role in the community. The ensuing *Kandha* legend tells that prior to the settlement in this district; it was preoccupied by the 'Kurumas' who belongs to peace loving community. They were domiciled in Paberi, Ghodapathar, Linepada, Purangada, Kainjhar of Khajuripada, Chakapad and Tikabali blocks. After a little skirmish with *Kandhas*, the Kurumas were forced to oust from this land and subsequently they migrated to the neighbouring districts Ganjam and Daspalla of present Nayagarh district. Thereafter, Kandhamal became the stronghold of the *Kandhas*. Out of many *Kandhas*, *Desia Kandhas* are popularly known as Hinduised section of the *Kandha* community who are living throughout of this district.

To analyse the word *Kandha* is a difficult task. The origin of the name of *Kandha* is still not clear. Different scholars have given their different views about this. In the opinion of Krishna Sharma, "the name 'Kandha' has its origin in the root 'Koi' or 'Ku' which signifies only mountain. The Telgu 'Kodu' corresponds to the Sanskrit 'Konda' though 'Konda' in Telgu signifies only mountain and not mountaineer".[8] Another celebrated scholar P.C Ratha opines "the *Kandha*'s of natural Odisha called themselves 'Koi' or 'Koitur'. This means hill man or burn of mountain. Again some of them call themselves *Kuiloka Kuienju*".[9] To the District Gazetteer of the Boudh Kandhamal, the term *Kandha* is derived from Odia word *Kanda*, an arrow.[10] Scholar Raghunath Rath also expresses his view on the derivation of the word *Kandha*. Kangoda mandal, existed between Kalinga and Odra and bounded by the river Mahanadi on the north and Rushikulya in the south and was roughly covered the parts of modern Puri, Ganjam, Kandhamal and Boudh districts, where there were *Kandha* concentration and till now the said piece of land is the homeland of *Kandha*. Hence as the people were called by the plains people as *Kangodia, Kangoda, Kanda, Kandha* and the name *Kandh* distinguished as the name of the tribe in the later ages.[11] Scholar Sarat Chandra Mohanty opines that the hill dwellers that live on roots and tubers after collecting from hills and jungles are known as *Kanda*. Mr. Mohanty also quoted the version of famous British Linguist G.A. Grierson that, "the tribe is commonly known under the name of 'Khond', the Oriyas call them 'Kandhas' and the Telgu people 'Gonds' or 'Kods'. The name which they use themselves is 'Ku' and their language should accordingly be dominated as Kui".[12] With the march of time, though the tribes' men have accepted the name *Kond, Khond, Kondh, Kandha* as conferred upon them by non-tribals. However, the *Kandhas* identified themselves as 'Kui, Kuinga', 'Ku Enju', 'Kui Loku' or 'Koilok'.

On the other side, *Panas* are the majority community among non-tribal communities of this district. The origin of the name *Pana* is difficult to analyse. It is common belief that this caste derives its name from 'Pundrika'.[13] With the march of time the name 'Pundrika' is changed into *Topaunika, Panika, Pan and Pana*. To speak on the other words, it has been derived from Sanskrit word 'Panabika' which means drummer.[14] B.B. Mohanty in order to trace out origin and history of *Pana* quoted the opinions of Russel and Hiralal that the word *Pana* is derived from term of 'Panka', a Dravidian caste of weaver and labourers. [15]*Panas* are classified into five subcastes such as *Odia Pana, Buna Pana, Betara Pana* or *Raj Pana, Pana Baisnab* and *Patradia*. The *Panas* of this district belongs to fourteen clans such as Mahananda, Bhoina, Tandia, Dip Dohara, Bibhara, Bagha, Khura, Rana, Puda, etc., the members of the community of different clans use several surnames suffixed to their name such as Digal, Sethi, Shahani, Behera and Naik.[16]

Panas in this district are migrated from Ganjam during the time of Bhanja administration. They are very common in the district. First they acted as serfs (Agricultural labourers) of the *Kandhas*. But with laps of time, cordial relationship was established between two communities. The *Kandhas* think themselves as king and *Panas* consider as their ministers. Panas can speak Kandha language (Kui) fluently. They acted as intermediary between Kandhas and outsiders.

II

In Kandhamal, originaly the lands of *Kandhas*, the *Panas* were first brought by the Hindu king as well as *Kandha* king for rendering service to their community. Historically, *Kandhas* have control over the total land of Kandhamal and hence, they were considering themselves as *Rajas* (king) and *Panas* as their *prajas* (subjects). The *Panas* initially, worked as wage labourers on *Kandha*'s lands and provide important links between them and the outside world, as said before. They helped the *Kandhas* from tilling the lands, clearing forests for cultivation, to stealing children for human sacrifice (Bali) for which they got a very bad name as 'criminal caste' from the British Police as well as from the Hindus from the neighbouring village. British Gazettee for such records also says, in few cases, the *Panas* were forced to give their children for Bali if they fail to supply. Now, tribes after giving up this inhuman practice call this caste people as 'criminal caste' too.

However, this social solidarity between these two worlds in Kandhamal collapsed, may be due to conversions during post-1947 period or due divide and rule policy of British while capturing *Panas* to clear forests and roads, buildings, railway works or paper industries by enticing them with higher wages, or due to introducing new land relations and depriving the *Kandhas* of their traditional rights over the forest land or due to the British policy of setting up a Shiva temple in 1855 which denied entry to the *Panas*, or due to the formation of the *Babudom* (peons or clerks) among the *Panas*. In retrospect, all of these factors cumulatively contributed to the weakening relationship between *Kandhas* and *Panas*. Along with it, the flurry activities by the elements of Christian Missionaries during 1960s and the later by the Sangh Parivar in the 1970s led by the Hindu leader, Mr. Laxmananda Saraswati, their 'solidarity' began to crumble.[17]

Though there was solidarity between *Kandhas* and *Panas* once upon a time, yet, the natural rift between the two is nothing new. The *Kandhas* have the history of vociferous resistance to religious conversion by evangelists. On the other hand, over the years, a majority of *Pana* have embraced Christianity, leading to an increase in the Christian population in the district from a mere 19,128 in 1951 to 1,17,950 in 2001.[18] Though, there is a process called migration due to the expansion of modernisation, yet Migration process alone cannot explain the rise of Christian population. Conversion could have played a big role in the rise of Christian population during 1951-2001. However, the district has seen growth of church organisation run by the Catholics, Protestants (Church of North India) and Pentecostals (Baptist Church). Apart from voluntary conversion of individual families, there could be also mass conversion, so that there is such an unusual growth of Christians among *Panas*. When both *Kandhas* and the Sangha Parivar denied the *Panas* an entry to the temples as late as in 1994, *Panas* would have realised that Christianity in the district did not practice untouchability at least in the church entry issue. As a result, they might have followed mass conversion. It has played a negative role in 'Hinduisation of Dalits'. Ironically, the Parivar's policy of *Suddhi* (reconversion) does not offer a sacred thread to a *Panas* (SCs) but offers the same to a *Kandhas* (STs), thus showing an example of blatant discrimination against *Panas*. Consequently, the Sangha Parivar loses its moral right to raise any banner against mass conversion.

Bishnu Mahapatra and D Bhattacharya argue that the *Kandhas* felt threatened once the *Panas* started interacting more in market economy following British rule. After independence, they got government jobs and become money lenders with surplus money earned from jobs and business, whereas *Kandhas* decided to stay away from interaction with the British Administration over most part of 19th century.[19] However, by 2008, 20 per cent *Panas* become land owner with an average holding size of half acre of land. After independence, the money lending developed among the *Panas*. They started petty business in trading, in selling cow, hens, buffaloes, etc., to *Kandhas*. Due to the depletion of forest resources, animals have also vanished from the forests and *Kandhas* started to depend on the *Panas* for a regular supply of these sacrificial animals to satisfy their father gods and mother gods. A few *Panas* have taken advantage of money lending and got the *Kandhas* lands mortgaged and thus tribals (Kandhas) lost their land to a few *Panas*.[20] The *Kandhas* felt that the *Panas* who were their dependent minister in one time, could even become land owner. Thus, for the *Kandhas*, the *Panas* became exploiters and land snatchers. But it is not absolutely true that *Panas* has become land owner by exploiting *Kandhas*. It is also a fact that some of them are land owner due to the gifts they received from their *Kandha* king long back for rendering their service to them and helping them human sacrifice and animal sacrifice. This is true that the *Panas*, with the help of the state as well as the church, have been cornering the maximum benefits of constitutional reservation due to their educational and economic advantage. The *Kandhas,* however, allege that the *Panas* hide their Christian identity and even claim to be Scheduled Tribes (ST) or Hindu Scheduled Castes (SC) by producing forged certificates. The *Panas*, they fear, are out to dominate them economically, politically and culturally. Using this situational advantage, Parivar by generating the threat of insecurities among *Kandhas*, had entrenched itself in the district. By using the constitutional provisions for the SCs and STs and by playing with the fear of the STs in the district, the Parivar managed to draw a popular support of *Kandhas*, the late modernisers, now aspiring for modern jobs in the state sector when its space has already shrunk in the area of privatisation. However, the emergence of the *Panas* as an assertive community has become an eyesore to the upper caste Hindus, not only in Kandhamal but also in other parts of Orissa. Thus, stereotypes of the *Pana* as 'betrayer', 'cunning', 'deceitful', 'exploiter', has entered into the caste discourses in Orissa, which was skillfully used by an organised group like Sangha Parivar, to give such a negative image of *Panas* in Kandhamal.

For not depending on *Panas* for animal (meant for Bali), *Kandhas* are taught by Parivar to convince their god and goddess to follow a vegetarian strategy. For not depending on *Panas* for monetary matter, Parivar co-opted the entire road side trader, especially from outside. They were instructed by the Parivar to extend monetary help to the dependent tribe only if they give up animal sacrifice. As in some village, Christian-run NGOs concentrated services among Dalits (SCs), thus leaving out of Kandhas (STs) and OBCs; the Parivar finds this atmosphere very congenial to take *Kandhas* within its umbrella and away from the Panas and Christians in order to manipulate this Hinduised tribe as their 'foot soldier' in their battle against *Pana* Christians for the purpose of satisfying their ideology.

III

The discourses of Hindu fundamentalist and the state government on the other hand primarily discuss Kandhamal riots as ethnic conflict between the

Kandhas (ST) and *Panas* (SC). But actually, it is conflict between fundamentalist forces and secular forces. On one hand, the Hindutva forces are accused of following 'majoritarianism' which in turn has forced the religious majority and minority to resort to terrorism to make their voice felt. On the other hand, Indian secularism has been terribly confused and tries to maintain a distance from this aggressive current. But it is also accused of being complicit with 'minorityism'. There are ideologues in both the political camps who do not see eye to eye with each other.[21] Does Indian secularism have enough courage, conviction, temperance and honesty to face the religious sectarianisms and dialogue with all of them, instead of building a wall of separation? We must critically examine secularism because the weaknesses of secularism have been used opportunistically by fundamentalist forces. Constitutional orders (SC) for Act, 1950 can be taken as beginning of crony secularism in India, which provides for reservation for the Hindu SCs only, thus alluring the Hindu SCs to stay with the Hinduism. This provision got a Hindutva touch later in 1958 and 1990, when it was amended to extend reservation facility to all SCs from among the Hindus, Sikhs, Buddhists and Jains, thus refusing to recognise the existence of SC Muslim and SC Christians. This new provision reinforces a typical Hindutva agenda that claims the other two religious communities have no casteism. In Kandhamal, Sangha Parivar, by using this constitutional provision effectively, tries to convince *Kandhas* that 'Christian Panas' are no more eligible to get reservations facilities and that is why they are trying for duplicate ST certificate in order to get these facilities. In doing so, Parivar is trying to generate two feelings among *Kandha* first, hatred feeling on Christian Panas and second, a trust on itself. These activities of Sangha Parivar are generating communalism by capturing the social imaginaries especially of *Kandhas*. At the first sight, this is in fact not a success of fundamentalist force, rather the failure of secularism from the very beginning (Constitutional orders (SC) for Act, 1950). In this way, crony secularism strengthens the fundamentalist forces in capturing the social imaginaries. In Kandhamal, crony secularism in passive complicit with the Hindu fundamentalism has pushed a few Christian youth to take the shelter in the red terror camps in 2007 and 2008 which is known for retributive justice. This means more such killings are likely to follow. In Kandhamal Maoists have intervened only once in 2008. As they are weakened in Andhra, they are now trying to create a social base in Odisha. And the Sangh Parivar has offered a fertile ground for Maoism to operate in Odisha. In this way, crony secularism thus has produced varieties of terrorism from Kashmir to Kandhamal.

As most of our secular writings concentrate on the operation of fundamentalism, thereby deflating our attention from an internal criticism of secularism, we must concentrate on the serious weakness in secularism. The serious weakness of Indian secular state is its compromise with inter religious domination or intra religious domination by way of patronising elites from among all religious communities. This is how giving a scope to fundamentalist forces to entrench on either side of religious divides. In order to protect itself from cronyism, India's secularism must understand the intra-religious domination (caste and gender inequalities) among Muslim and Christians. Secondly, it must understand various forms of inter religious domination such as temple-mosque controversy or conversion-reconversion controversy. If it will understand at least these two dominations in recent future, then neither Sangha Parivar nor Christian Missionaries will find any scope in Kandhamal to divert such an ethnic conflict towards communal riots. In fact, Kandhamal needs non-intervention of fundamentalist forces and intervention of secular forces.

References

1. This term has been used by Prof Arun Kumar Patnaik in his paper called 'Choosing between Crony Secularism and Hindu Fundamentalism in Orissa: The case of Kandhamal', which had been presented by him in the workshop on "Actually Existing Secularism in India", Centre for the Study of Developing Societies, New Delhi, 10th -12th April, 2009. In this paper crony secularism has been defined is defined as a stage where state extends political, administrative and judicial support to the elites in the religious communities on cultural issues and thereby aiding the fundamentalist forces get entrenched on either side of the religious divide.

2. "Kandhamal lies nailed" Pioneer, 22nd July 2009.

3. *Ibid.*

4. "Kandhamal District" *Orissa Review*, December 2010: 131.

5. Raghunath Ratha, (1993), *Kandha Sanskrutira Analochita Adhyaya.* Koraput: Satta Sahitya Sansad. p. 2.

6. *Ibid.* p. 3.

7. STs and SCs of Orissa (2006), *Data hand book.* Complied statistical cell, Bhubaneswar: SCST RTI. p. 1.

8. Krishna Sharma (1979), *The Konds of Orissa.* New Delhi-05: Concept Publishing Company, H-13. p. 16.

9. P.C. Ratha (2008), *Foot Prints of Forgotton Genus.* Balangir. p. 293.

10. Nilamani, Senapati and D. Kunar (1983). Orissa District Gazetter, Boudha Kandhamal, Cuttack, p. 69.

11. Raghunath Ratha (2010), *The Kandhas and Kandhamal.* Bhubaneswar: Amedeus Press, pp. 23-24.

12. Sarat Chandra Mohanty (2008), Adivasi. Bhubaneswar: SCST RTI. 48(1). p. 63.

13. Nilamani, Senapati and D. Kunar (1983), *Orissa District Gazetter*, Bouda Kandhamal, Cuttack, pp. 61-67.

14. Nilamani Senapati and Durga Charan Kunar (1977), *Orissa District Gazetter*, Bouda Kandhamal, Cuttack, p. 133.

15. Nilamani Senapati and Durga Charan Kunar (1980), *Orissa District Gazetter*, Bouda Kandhamal, Cuttack, pp. 87.

16. Nrusingha Charan Behuria (1995), *Orissa District Gazetter*, Ganjam, Cuttack. p. 185.

17. Pralay Kanungo (2003), *Hindutva's Entry into a Hindu Province*: Early years of RSS in Orissa. *EPW.* 38(1): pp. 3293-3303.

18. "Kandhamal lies nailed" *Pioneer*, 22nd July 2009.

19. Bishnu Mahapatra and D. Bhattacharya (1996), *Tibal-Dalit Conflict: Electoral Politics in Phulbani.* EPW. 31(2/3), pp. 160-64.

20. See, "The Ugly face of Sangh Parivar", *http://www.humanrightsforum.org/*

21. Arun Patnaik 'Choosing between Crony Secularism and Hindu Fundamentalism in Orissa: The case of Kandhamal' (draft copy).

Bibliography

Ambedkar, B. R. (2004), *Conversion as Emancipation,* Critical quest, New Delhi.

Ambedkar, B. R. (2010), *Philosophy of Hinduism,* Critical quest, New Delhi.

Arun Patnaik, '*Choosing between Crony Secularism and Hindu Fundamentalism in Orissa:* The case of Kandhamal' (draft copy).

Behuria, Nrusingha Charan (1995), *Orissa District Gazetter,* Ganjam. Cuttack.

Bhagwati, Jagdish (2009). 'Secularism in India, why is it imperiled' in T.N. Srinivasan, ed., *The Future of Secularism*. Oxford University Press, New Delhi.

Bhargava, Rajeev (2009), 'The Distinctiveness of Indian Secularism' in T.N. Srinivasan, ed., *The Future of Secularism*. Oxford University Press, New Delhi.

Chatterjee, Partha (1998), '*Secularism and Tolerance' in Rajeev Bhargava* ed., *Secularism and Its Critics*. Oxford University Press, Delhi.

Dhyani, S.N. (1996), *Secularism: socio-legal issue*. Rawat, Jaipur.

Ferrandes, Walter (1999), 'Attacks on minorities and a National debate on conversion', *EPW*, Vol. 34, No. 03.

Galanter, Mark (1998), '*Secularism, East and West*' in Rajeev Bhargava, ed., *Secularism and Its Critics*. Oxford University Press, Delhi.

Heredia, Rudolf C. (2007), *Changing Gods: Rethinking Conversion in India*. Penguin Books, New Delhi.

India. Constituent Assembly, India. Parliament. Lok Sabha. Secretariate (1999). *Constituent assembly debate (official report), Vol-7,* Lok Sabha Secretariate, New Delhi.

Jha, Shefali (2002), '*Secularism in the Constituent Assembly Debates*, 1946-1950' *EPW*, Vol. 37, No. 30.

"Kandhamal District" *Orissa Review*, December 2010.

"Kandhamal lies nailed" Pioneer, 22nd July 2009. Kanungo, Pralay (2003). Hindutva's Entry into a Hindu Province: Early years of RSS in Orissa. *EPW.* Vol. 38, No. 1.

Kim, C.H. (2003), "*In Search of Identity: Debates on Religious Conversion in India*". Oxford University Press, New Delhi.

Mahapatra, Bishnu and D. Bhattacharya (1996), *Tibal-Dalit Conflict*: Electoral Politics in Phulbani. *EPW*, Vol. 31, No. 2/3.

Massey, James (2003), *Minorities and Religious Freedom in a Democracy*. Manohar, New Delhi.

Menon, Kalyani Devaki (2003), "Converted Innocents and Their Trickster Heroes: The Politics of Proselytising in India", in Andrew Buckser and Stephen D. Glazier (eds.) *The Anthropology of Religious Conversion,* Lanham, Boulder, New York, Toronto, Oxford: Rowman & Littlefield Publishers.

Menon, Nivedita (2004), "*The Right to Conversion*", *The Telegraph*, Kolkata, 7 May.

Mohanty, Sarat Chandra (2008), Adivasi. *SCST RTI*. Vol. 48, No. 1.

Pannikar, K.N. (1997), *Communal threat and Secular challenge*. Earthworm Books, Madras.

Pati, Biswamoy (2001), 'Identity, Hegemony, Resistance, Conversion in Orissa, 1800-2000', *EPW*, Vol. 36, No. 44.

Ratha, Raghunath (1993), *Kandha Sanskrutira Analochita Adhyaya*. Satta Sahitya Sansad, Koraput.

Ratha, Raghunath (2010), *The Kandhas and Kandhamal*. Amedeus Press, Bhubaneswar.

Sarkar, Sumit (2007), 'Christian conversion, Hindutva and Secularism' in Anuradha Dingwaney Needham and Rajeswari Sunder Rajan, ed., *The crises of secularism in India*, Permanent Black, Delhi.

Senapati, Nilamani, Durga Charan Kunar (1977), Orissa District Gazetter, Bouda Kandhamal, Cuttack.

Senapati, Nilamani, Durga Charan Kunar (1980), Orissa District Gazetter, Bouda Kandhamal, Cuttack.

Senapati, Nilamani, D. Kunar (1983), Orissa District Gazetter, Boudha Kandhamal, Cuttack.

Sharma, Krishna (1979), The Konds of Orissa. Concept Publishing Company, New Delhi, H-13.

Ratha, P.C. (2008), Foot Prints of Forgotton Genus. Balangir.

STs and SCs of Orissa (2006), Data handbook. Complied statistical cell, Bhubaneswar: SCST RTI.

23

Role of NYKS on Tribal Youth Development: A Case Study of Koraput District, Odisha

Janmejay Sahu, Ashok Behera

Abstract

Nehru Yuva Kendra Sangathan (NYKS) is a largest grassroots apolitical youth organisation under the Ministry of Youth Affairs and Sport, Government of India, working with Indian rural youth through the grassroots institutions such as Youth Clubs, Mahila Mandals and Social/Cultural Association headed by the youth. It aims to utilise the huge youth potential of the country engaging them in nation building. Today's youth is seen as 'Demographic Dividend' who has a significant role in the nation's development however the need is to shape the youth energy and mold them into the positive contribution to the society. The tribal people in India are deprived of the mainstream; particularly the tribal youth are directionless due to lack of proper education, training and employment opportunities however NYKS has been undertaking various programmes for the development of tribal youth giving them rigorous trainings, capacity building programme, field-based youth work and youth exchange programmes. Therefore, the paper tries to understand the functioning of NYKS, Koraput district of Odisha and aims to critically examine the contributions of the NYKS in Koraput district towards tribal development. Also, it attempts to study how the tribal youth of Koraput benefits from NYKS participating in various rural tribal development programmes and activities.

Introduction

In the broad sphere of Indian society, the tribal communities represent an important social category of Indian social structure. They are considered as the original inhabitants of India, who carry forward a legacy of rich and distinct cultural traits for many decades. Tribal society displays a fascinating profile of ethnic diversity. The tribal belong to different racial stocks, speak language of different families and show considerable variations in basic economy. The variation in physical and biological environment of their habitat is equally amazing. This bewildering variety in race, language, habitat and economy is fully reflected in their culture, which like a mosaic evokes the admiration of social scientists to study the dynamics of their society.

Koraput district popularly known as 'Kashmir' of Odisha, it bounds in the imprints of Odisha's glorious past. Temples monasteries and other historical monuments from the medieval period, breathtaking in their beauty and of incalculable historical importance, the art, craft and culture of the Tribals, stands as footprints of time telling the story of the years bygone. The Koraput, considered as 'Hub of Tribals' is one of the southern districts of Odisha located bordering Chhattisgarh and Andhra Pradesh. Out of total population of the district more than 50 per cent belongs to Scheduled Tribes and about 13 per cent are Scheduled Castes. They constitute 50 per cent of the total population with a sex ratio 1031 female against 1000 male.

In the recent past, this district of Koraput has gone through one of its toughest time as there have been enormous incidents of Maoist violence taken place in areas bordered with Andhra Pradesh, disrupting the normalcy, overall mood of the population, especially the younger generation. Currently, a part of the 'Red Corridor', the extreme geographic conditions, lack of health and educational infrastructure facilities makes the development of youth of Koraput more and more challengeable. Amongst the major players of youth development in the district like CAPART, NABARD, Government administration and International NGOs like Action-Aid, UNDP, Nehru Yuva Kendra Sangathan have invariably been playing a key role towards the overall development of the tribal youth of Koraput, ever since its inception. In this backdrop, a case study of Koraput has been taken where NYKS has been working with and for youth and an attempt is made to understand the broad objective of both the quantitative and qualitative aspects of NYKS achievements in the tribal youth development.

Youth and Youth Development

Youth are economic cornerstones and potential assets for the over-reaching goals of economic and social development and generally exhibit greater receptivity to new ideas and are more often innovative. Youth perspective adds value and promotes diversity of membership and representation within a decision-making. In case of tribal youth they have everything which is hidden in them therefore they need to be trained to make them capable for the nation building process. Vered Amit (1995) acknowledges that the nature of youth varies significantly according to the social context, and particularly in relation to factors such as class, gender, and ethnicity. Indeed, social historians have argued that "youth" is a relatively modern invention, which has resulted from the extension of the period of transition that lasts from the end of compulsory schooling to entry into waged labour; and this is clearly something that varies significantly between different social groups and between different cultural settings.

The United Nations (UN) broadly defines youth as those persons between the ages of 15 and 24 years. The UN proposes two categories of youth: "young people between ages 13-19 who are classified as teenagers, whilst those in the 20-24 age groups are characterised as young adults" and in promoting this definition, the UN concedes that the concept of youth hinges on "specific socio-cultural, institutional, economic and political factors" in different contexts (Word Youth Report-2006). Also, the World Bank adopts the UN definition by classifying persons in the 15-24 age groups as youth (World Bank) whereas the definition of Youth in India is cleared described in the National Youth Policy as 'the people coming under the age between 13 to 35 years old are youth'.

The American Youth Policy Forum (1995: 1) identified two premises that, they said, need to act as a foundation and guide for youth development practice: Youth development is an ongoing process in which young people are engaged and invested. Throughout this process, young people seek ways to meet their basic physical and social needs and to build the competencies and connections they need for survival and success. All youth are engaged in the process of development. Youth development is marked by the acquisition of a broad range of competencies and the demonstration of a full complement of connections to self, others, and the larger community. Confidence, compassion, commitment and character are terms commonly used to express the attitudes and behaviours that determine whether and how learned competencies will be used. Nixon (1997), too, defines youth development as a process in which all youths engage over time in order to meet their needs and build competencies. A youth-development paradigm has received worldwide recognition for its potential to transform the lives of youth. The United Nations has advocated youth development as an effective strategy for achieving both youth and community potential (World Sources Online 1999). The term youth development is enjoying greater use in practice involving youth in the United States (Networks for Youth Development 1998a). Moreover, the young people's work that focuses on individual learning and development, rather than on changing their surrounding, is not real participation-participation should not only give young people more control over their own lives and experiences but should also grant them real influence over issues that are crucial to the quality of life and justice in their communities Roman Mullahey (1999).

Nehru Yuva Kendra, Koraput

The Scheme of Nehru Yuva Kendra Sangathan was launched in the year 1972 with a vision to empower the rural youth of India by making them productive citizens, through awareness generation and capacity building programmes, NYKS become autonomous in 1987 under the independent ministry of Youth Affairs and Sports, Govt. of India. Today, it covers all the 623 districts of the country. With the amazing strength of 2.5 lakh voluntary village level youth organisations covering about 10 million youth between the age group of 15-35, NYKS stands as the largest non-political youth organisation in the Asia-Pacific region. Known as one of the oldest district branches of the country, the undivided NYK-Koraput was established in the 1973. Now, as the old district was fragmented to four i.e., Koraput, Raygada, Malkangiri and Nawarangpur, NYK-Koraput has its separate office in the district headquarter to operate with the strength of around ten thousand young people enrolled in the 265 village level Youth Organisations affiliated to NYKS, in a more confined and focused area having two sub-divisions, fourteen Blocks, around two thousand villages under 220 Gram Panchayats, covering a population of about fourteen lakhs, out of which half of the population are youth between the age group of 15-35.

Objectives and Methodology

The study was conducted with the broad objective to learn and assess the various programmes and activities of Nehru Yuva Kendra, Koraput, related to youth development in the last five years i.e., between 2008-09 to 2012-13 and to understand how NYKS creates a space for youth development among the tribal youths of Koraput district in Odisha. The methodology for this study is descriptive in nature. The collection of data was made from both the primary and secondary sources. A survey method was followed with a structured questionnaire among 100 tribal youth respondents of various stakeholders such as the Youth beneficiaries of NYK programmes/activities, student and non-student tribal youths, National Youth Crop youth volunteers of NYK, Koraput, Self employed tribal youths and Tribal opinion leaders of the Koraput districts in Odisha. Also, indepth interviews were conducted among NYK officials as well as the district level government officials to understand about the tribal development initiatives and its status. The limitation of this study is time constraint and as a small study it may not be generalised.

Koraput NYK Programmes and Activities

In the last five years, there has been a range of programmes organised by NYK-Koraput with the objective of youth development in the district, out of which the majority of beneficiaries are from Scheduled Tribes and Scheduled Castes. Following Table 23.1 shows the quantitative data of youth beneficiaries of major NYK-programmes/activities for the period 2008-09 to 2012-13.

Table 23.1: Tribal Youth Participants/Beneficiaries of NYK Programmes/Activities

Broad Category of the Programme	*Type of Activity*	*No. of Programmes*	*No. of Total Beneficiaries*	*No. of Tribal Youth Beneficiaries*		
				Male	*Female*	*Total*
Skill-Development Training Programme for Youth	Long-term and short-training on trades like Tailoring and Knitting, Embroidery, DTP, Screen Printing, Beautician course, Mushroom Cultivation, TV Repairing, Electrical and Refrigeration, Motor-cycle repairing, etc.	50	1500	150	950	1100
Youth Leadership Training Programme	In-house training and orientation for the rural youth on various skills, knowledge and applicability of various development programmes and schemes available for the rural youth.	15	600	260	100	360
Awareness Generation Campaign	Rally, meetings, workshops, seminars to sensitise the youth about their role and contribution towards the development of society, addressing core social issues and problems in their respective areas.	20	2000	1250	250	1500
Sports and Culture	Organisation of drama, folk art, dance and music, various traditional rural sports, athletics, etc.	20	10000	6000	500	6500
Youth Club Development Programme	Under this banner, a range of activities are undertaken to empower the village level youth clubs with the prime objective of making them self-sustaining units.	80	4000	2000	800	2800

(Contd.)

(Contd. Table 7.3)

Broad Category of the Programme	*Type of Activity*	*No.of Programmes*	*No. of Total Beneficiaries*	*No. of Tribal Youth Beneficiaries*		
				Male	*Female*	*Total*
National Service Volunteers/ National Youth Corps Scheme	Young people under the age 25 are given the opportunity to serve the nation under this programme to develop their skill and expertise in the areas of leadership and youth development. Rs 2500 Honorarium is given on monthly basis to the volunteers, deployed for one year in their concerned blocks.	5	150	60	30	90
Work Camps	Community assets were created by the youth through dignity of labour and volunteerism.	16	640	385	30	405
Promotion of National Integration and Communal Harmony	Various days/weeks and occasions like National Integration Camps, Youth Club Exchange Programmes were observed/organised to instill the sense of patriotism and nation building amongst the youth.	2	400	40	25	65
Incentive and Awards to Individuals and Youth Clubs	Outstanding Youth Clubs/Individuals are awarded at district level with cash incentive of Rs 10000 @ one each year	5				3

Source: Annual Progress Report, NYK–Koraput (2008-09 to 2012-13).

Evidence from the Ground

It was clearly visible from the study that the majority of the tribal youth (52 per cent) wants to contribute voluntarily towards the development of the society and stated their willingness to participate in NYK programmes and activities. Although female youth (18 per cent) is a bit shy to come to the forefront in comparison to their male (75 per cent) counterparts, the overall scenario throws a positive signal towards the NYK programmes in the district towards the youth development. Most of the government programmes are made on top-down approach, even though the need assessment survey is done on paper only. While asking whether the need and choices of the tribal youth is addressed while planning the NYK Programmes and activities, the response could reiterate the old trend i.e. the youth were unclear or confused. Only 40 per cent of the youth say that the needs like skill upgradation training and awareness on different development programmes and schemes are addressed in NYK programmes. But the tribal youth needs like income generation, employment, and entrepreneurship is still neglected in NYK Planning of programmes/activities.

Moreover, it is quite encouraging to learn that the majority of the youth (60 per cent) agreed that their lives have been improved after participating in a NYK programme. Asking the areas of improvement most of the respondents pointed out on their skill development such as communication skills, vocational skills and knowledge about government programmes and schemes have been improved through NYK programmes and activities to a considerable extent. Another remarkable improvement is visible in case of male youth (85 per cent) to improve the feeling of national integration and communal harmony through NYK programmes/activities. Responding to the question whether NYK is the right organisation to address various core social issues that affects the tribal the youth has stated a very confirmative view (65 per cent). Further, the youth (90 per cent) including both male (95 per cent) and female (83 per cent) gave an overwhelming response to skill development programmes of NYKS as it offers the scopes and avenues of employment, self-employment and income generation. 70 per cent of the youth voted for leadership and personality development training as the second most effective programme as it ensures employability among them. Other programmes like work camp, sports and cultural programmes and youth club development programmes were also highly appreciated by the tribal youth.

Through in-depth interviews with NYK and district level government officials, it is understood that set of programmes is very less in a district unit like NYK-Koraput having 14 Blocks and around 200 GPs. Even the programmes do not reach to the youth clubs who are affiliated under NYK-Koraput. The officials like District Youth Coordinator, Accountant and paid NYC Volunteers of the district too agreed upon with the statement that budget is a big concern. Moreover, it reveals that the lack of adequate staff in NYK creates a lot of constraints to organise programmes and focusses on youth development in the district. It was understandable that all officials are posted at NYK-Koraput on additional charges to undertake duties at the rate of two days only in a week. The youth too complained that it is very difficult to approach the NYK Officials due to their non-availability in the NYK branch office. Interestingly, this study indicates that the Annual Action Plan of the NYK-Koraput is not based on the need of tribal youth nor they are involved in framing it. The lack of proper coordination and linkage between the NYK-Koraput and other line departments/agencies working at district/block level is seen. It also shows that the programmes allotted by NYK-Koraput to the villages in the remote vicinity and naxal affected are insufficient to cater the needs of the tribal youth. It is revealed from the study that the attendance of the male youth in NYK programmes has been declining due to factors like migration, involvement of the youth in naxal conflict and violence, etc., however, female youth shows a positive approach towards the development programmes.

Specific Suggestions

The role and contribution of NYK-Koraput towards the tribal youth development is quite significant as the organisations stands for the youth of Koraput as a better alternative choice to the youth development. Keeping the findings of the study in the eye, the following suggestions are made may be useful for the better functioning of Nehru Yuva Kendra Sangathan such as:

- The content and approach of the NYK programmes needs to be prepared keeping in view the local needs and aspiration of the youth.
- The set of programmes is to be increased to at least cover all the 14 blocks of Koraput district with more focus on the south and west part as the border areas are much closer to the red corridor and prone to conflict and violence where the youth segment is largely drawn. Programmes like Skill upgradation training and capacity building should be organised in ample manner so that more and more tribal youth can be self-dependent.
- The NYKS should come out with Policy specific and programme specific plans for the tribal youth development.
- Adequate man-power should be given to NYK-Koraput to operate the branch in proper manner with accessibility for the youth with necessary arrangements.
- A coordination and Convergence Plan needs to be prepared by NYK and be approved by the District Committee under the approval of the Collector with responsibility-mapping and devolution. Financial institutions like Banks and DIC needs to be officially sensitised to lend money to micro-level tribal young entrepreneurs.
- The initiatives to be made for proper Monitoring and Evaluation of NYKS programmes and activities and the transparency and accountability should be ensured at all levels.

• The success stories of NYK programmes and activities in the district should be highlighted with timely its publicity through various mediums of media for mass awareness about NYKS works.

Conclusion

It was clearly established from the study that NYKS has been working with its mandate of youth development to a large extent in Koraput. Although there so many bottlenecks, the study finds NYKS has a very good relationship of the youth, particularly tribal youth of the district. The tribal youth, with their strong physique, innocence and rich cultural heritage are nothing less than human treasure for the whole nation that needs to be properly ornamented with much care and emphasis. Nehru Yuva Kendra Sangathan, being the largest youth organisation of the country should be empowered with more qualified personnel and financial strength so that it can enlarge its reach to the remote areas. However, a more comprehensive and unified approach is required to be applied in the planning, implementation, monitoring and evaluation of NYK programmes and activities. It is needless to say that organisations like NYKS should not just only be regarded as mere schemes of the Government but to be viewed as one of the most viable alternative model to counter naxal movements in the red corridor of India harnessing the youth in the manifold of the society.

References

Books and Journals

American Youth Policy Forum (AYPF). 1995. "*Contract with America's Youth: towards a National Youth Development Agenda.*" Washington, D.C.: AYPF.

Networks for Youth Development (NYD). 1998a. "*The Handbook of Positive Youth Outcomes*", New York: NYD.

Nixon, R. 1997. "*What is positive youth development?*" Child Welfare 76:571–575.

Roman Mullahey, Yve Susskind, and Barry Checkoway (1999) *Youth Participation in Community Planning*, America Planning Association, Chicago.

Vered Amit-Talai and Helena Wuff, (1995) eds. *Youth Culture: A Cross-Cultural Perspective,* Routledge, London.

World Sources Online. 1999. "*Challenges facing youth development: National and Global Perspectives*". Independent, November 19, EB 19991119460000029 10:18.

Government Reports

Draft National Youth Policy, 2012

NYKS-Odisha Zone, Annual Progress Report (2008-09 to 2012-13)

World Youth Report, 2006.

Internet Sources

http://go.worldbank.org/F6GNXM7JU0 accessed on 10th July, 2013.

http://www.un.org/esa/socdev/unyin/qanda.htm accessed on 10th July, 2013.

www. odisha.nic.in accessed on 11th July, 2013.

www.nyks.org. accessed on 12th July, 2013.

24

Political Economy of Tribal Development in Madhya Pradesh: The Case of Korku Tribe

Janmejaya Mishra

The Korku tribe

Korku is a scheduled tribe community predominantly found in East Nimar (presently Khandwa and Burhanpur districts), Betul district of Madhya Pradesh and adjoining areas in Melghat region of Amravati district in Maharashtra. The Korkus are found in highest concentration in the highland of Central India, especially in the regions surrounding the Mahadeo hill, a centrally situated peak in the Satpura mountains (Fuchs 1988). The Korkus are a branch of the great Munda tribes and are placed in the vicinity of the great tribe – the Gonds (Deogaonkar et al 1990). Korkus have derived their name from the combination of the word *'koru'* meaning man and *'ku'* which makes it plural meaning tribal men (Russell et al 1916). Korkus are believed to be a hunting gathering community dwelling in the forests of Satpura ranges on either sides of the Tapti river. They were dependent on forest-based resources and practising shifting cultivation on large scale for their livelihoods in earlier times. Eventually, they started settled agriculture. Their late introduction to settled agriculture made them less skilful in comparison to their neighbouring tribesmen of Bhil and Barela tribal communities. Besides deforestation, degradation of land and water resources was also rampant in the area. Massive soil erosion made the land unsuitable for cultivation. Further, scanty and erratic rainfall made the situation more worsen leading many water bodies to dry off. As a result of the direct consequences of degradation of land and water resources, agriculture productivity has been declined substantially over the years thus affecting livelihoods of the Korku tribe and other peasant communities. Chronic poverty, food insecurity, acute under/malnutrition and distress seasonal labour migration are the primary issues that the Korku tribe faces today.

Poverty among the Korkus

The cash flow analysis of Korku tribal households in the Khalwa block reveals many surprising features. Agriculture and manual labour work are the only sources of income for most of the households. Based on household survey data of 2008-09, average annual income of a household is estimated to be Rs 20460 (approx.), wherein the contribution of income from agriculture and labour work is estimated to be nearly Rs 14000 (70 per cent) and Rs 6300 (30 per cent) respectively. Likewise, average annual expenditure of a household is estimated to be Rs 26634 (approx). Thus, there is a net deficit of Rs 6174 per household per annum. To meet this deficit, the tribal families borrow money from informal sources i.e., local money lenders and traders at a very high rate of interest. To pay off the debt and for meeting other household expenditure, a major portion of the workforce migrates to better off areas in neighbouring state of Maharashtra and parts of Madhya Pradesh during lean seasons. Mostly engaged in agricultural labour works, they earn their livelihoods. Saving of money is found very little among the Korku families. On the other hand, expenses on social obligations like marriages, rituals and festivals are very high. Formal financial institutions like banks and credit cooperatives do not easily extend credit to them, leaving these families to depend on the mercy of money lenders and traders to fulfil their credit needs.

Average landholding size of a Korku household is 2.5 to 3 acres. Most of the farmers fall under the marginal/small holder category. Nearly, 85 per cent of the households have land and about 15 per cent are landless. Only, 12 per cent of the land owning households has access to irrigation sources mainly dug wells. Soybean, cotton, sorghum and pigeon pea are the major crops cultivated during kharif season. Wheat and gram are the major rabi crops cultivated only by those farmers who have access to irrigation. The average annual income of the households ranges from Rs 15,000 to Rs 25,000.

Debt, Exploitation and Migration

Significant changes have taken place in the cropping patterns in recent years. Cultivation of cash crops has been widely adopted by the tribal farmers in the region. Korku tribal farmers prefer to cultivate cash crops—soybean and cotton in particular on large scale basis and give less preference for cultivation of food crops such as sorghum, maize, pigeon pea and minor millets. The tribal farmers in the region have been historically exploited by local money lenders and traders. They depend on the private traders and local money lenders—mostly the upper castes for purchasing agriculture inputs such as seeds, fertilizers and pesticides required for the cultivation. However, due to lack of cash during agriculture season, the tribal farmers are compelled to take credits from the money lenders and purchase inputs from them who are also the traders running input supply shops in the name of krisi seva kendras in the local markets. The inputs purchased on credit from the traders and money lenders are very low in quality for which they are charged high price and exorbitant rate of interest. Further, most of the tribal farmers are also get into informal agreements with the traders that they would sell the agriculture produces to them during post-harvest season. As an obligation to repay the credit, the tribal farmers are further compelled to sell their agriculture produces to these traders at much lower price than the prevailing market price from whom they have taken credit during monsoon season. Thus, their continued dependency on the traders and money lenders make them prone to harsh economic exploitations and thus, the Korku tribal farmers are trapped in cyclic indebtedness year after year. Consequently, low crop productivity and negative income from rainfed agriculture and cumbersome debt force them to resort on distress seasonal labour migration. A significant portion of the Korku tribal population migrates to relatively better off areas like Akola, Jalgoan, Akot, Bhusawal, Nasik and Nagpur in neighbouring Maharashtra state and Harda, Hosangabad, Pithampur and Indore in Madhya Pradesh during off-seasons along with their entire family members. The family members of most of the rainfed farmers migrate out for 5-6 months in a year. Among the landless households, duration of migration ranges from 6-9 months. Mainly engaged in agriculture wage labour work in private farms, labour work in cotton, dal mills and construction sites they survive with bare minimum needs.

Mosse *et. al.*, also reported similar features of seasonal labour migration among the adivasis in the western Madhya Pradesh and mentioned that seasonal labour migration has become an irreversible part of the livelihoods of rural adivasi communities in western India. Labour migration is not just a means to cope with below subsistence agriculture and debt have become the only means by which valued agrarian lifestyles can be reproduced. For a few, migration is a route of upward social and economic mobility; but for the vast majority migration not only perpetuates debt and dependence, but exposes the poorest to extreme hardship and cruel exploitation (Mosse *et. al.*, 2005).

Food Insecurity

Sorghum (jowar) is the major staple food of the Korku tribal community. It meets consumption needs and is grown in nearly 20 per cent of the total area. Few farmers grow jowar in large farm lands which is confined to them only. It was also found jowar grows well in the region and gives good yield. However, the amount of jowar grown by the farmers is not enough to meet their consumption needs. Therefore, they rely on the market for purchasing jowar to meet their needs. Pigeon pea (tuar) is another important food crop grown by the tribal farmers which is grown in 14 per cent of land of the study area. It is the only food crop which gives cash income as well as kept for consumption. Tuar is cultivated with cotton as a mixed crop. The yield is around 300 to 500 kg per acre. However, it is prone to frequent pest attacks. The tribal farmers keep some amount of tuar for consumption and sell out the rest in the local markets. Cultivation of wheat is very limited to few farmers. It is cultivated only by irrigated farmers as a rabi crop. Only 10-15 per cent of the total land is under wheat cultivation. The yield from one acre of wheat is around 738 kg. Discussions with the farmers revealed that the cultivation of wheat is very recent in the region. Farmers who have access to irrigation mainly through dug wells are the ones who cultivate wheat. It was also found that those families which are cultivating wheat have shifted their food habit from jowar to wheat. Nearly, 55 per cent of the total produce is sold in the market and the rest is kept for consumption. Those families growing wheat do not face any problem of food scarcity. Seasonality is a major factor which affects the availability of food grains of the households. Discussions with the community members revealed that food grain availability gradually decreases during the period of monsoon (July-August). The stored food grains get finished and farmers have to depend on market for their consumption needs. Forty per cent of the respondents mentioned that they faced problem of food shortage during the month of monsoon. Besides these food crops, traditional minor millets like Kodo, Kutki and Sawariya are also grown in the region. These crops serve as an important source of nutrition especially for the kids and lactating women. However, the area under cultivation the minor millets have drastically decreased over the years. The tribal farmers do not prefer to grow these crops any more.

The functioning of Public Distribution System (PDS) in the study villages was found to be very poor. It was found that families having good landholding have BPL cards whereas those who deserve it most are excluded. Thirty Eight per cent of the ration card holders are BPL and the rest belong to the APL category. Nearly, 18 per cent of the households which indeed deserve ration cards do not have. Black marketing of wheat, sugar and kerosene by PDS dealers came out during discussions with the villagers. Wheat and kerosene are supplied regularly to the households while sugar, rice, salt and pulses are not. Dependency on PDS for food grain was high among the poorest families. Nearly, 32 per cent of the families are completely depended on the PDS for consumption of wheat. Further, though the Integrated Child Development Services (ICDS) is running in most of the villages, only 15 per cent of the parents prefer to send their children to the anganwadi centres. A large majority, 85 per cent of the parents do not send their children to these centres. The major reasons for not enrolling the children in the anganwadi centres are frequent migration by parents to different places in search of labour works, location of anganwadi centres from their home and poor quality of food served at the centres.

Acute under/malnutrition

Malnutrition among the children and under-nutrition among the adult members mostly women are very high in the area. Most of the children are born with underweight. Malnutrition related disease like Kwashiorkor is seen in among the children in all the villages. Nearly, 60 per cent of the children have reddish colour hair which is due to protein deficiency. Also, 15 per cent of the children suffer from skin disease which is due to the prevailing unhygienic conditions. Night blindness caused due to deficiency of vitamin A is found among 15 per cent of the children. Nearly, 10 per cent of children suffer from polio and rickets and Kwashiorkor taken together. Further, diseases like measles and diarrhea are found to be common to most of the children. Nearly, 70 per cent of the women have expressed conditions matching to anaemia. It is not only found among women but also among the adolescent girls. Anaemia is associated with deficiency of Iron in blood. Moreover, exposure to smoke while cooking also is a known risk factor of Anaemia. About, 65 per cent of the respondents perceived that anaemia is the most prevalent disease among adolescent girls. Other common ailments are fever, vomiting and skin disease. These findings were also validated through an interview with the health workers.

Nearly, 60 per cent of the women reported that they prefer to consult traditional birth attendants rather going for institutional deliveries. The remaining 40 per cent have opted for hospitals/private doctors. It was found that the incidence of infant mortality is very high primarily owing to dependency on unqualified traditional birth attendants. Further, 50 per cent of the tribal women responded that they got married at the age between 12 to 14 years, 30 per cent of women getting married at the age of 14-16 years and 20 per cent get married at the age of 16-20 years of age. In 85 per cent of pregnancy cases, the gap between two consecutive deliveries is only one year. Because of early marriages and low gap between subsequent deliveries, the growth of both children and mothers is severely affected.

AKRSP(I)'s Intervention

Aga Khan Rural Support Programme (India) – which was working in Gujarat nearly for 19 years decided to extend its work of rural development in the Nimar region of Madhya Pradesh. It started developmental interventions in the remote and poor districts of Khandwa, Burhanpur, Khargone and Barwani in south-western Madhya Pradesh after a systematic appraisal of the area in 2004-05. At present, it is working with more than 16,000 households of Korku, Bhil, Bhilala, Barela and Gond tribal communities over 120 villages in Khalwa and Pandhana blocks of Khandwa, Khaknar block of Burhanpur, Zirniya block of Khargone and Niwali block of Barwani districts in order to sustain their livelihoods through promotion of community-based institutions which are being capacitated to manage natural resources and address the core issues of poverty through improved agriculture productivity and with locally suitable off-farm activities to improving the economic conditions of poorest tribal households. The key areas of interventions are watershed development, participatory irrigation management, saving and credit services through self help groups, alternate livelihood promotion through animal husbandry, skill development and placements of rural youth.

This author directly worked in the region for three and half a years in the capacity of monitoring and evaluation specialist with AKRSP(I) being based at its regional office in Khandwa from July 2008 to December 2011. Afterwards, he was moved to its central office at Ahmedabad, Gujarat in January 2012, from where he continues to work till date.

AKRSP (I) started its interventions in Khalwa block of Khandwa district in July 2006. Participatory irrigation management, watershed development, Self Help Groups promotion and providing agriculture extension services including agriculture input supply were the major areas of its intervention in Khalwa block. As of now, more than 3000 households of Korku tribal communities in 30 villages of the block have been directly benefitted through these interventions. Broadly speaking, these 30 villages have been covered in three phases. From 2006 to 2009, 17 villages were covered under the European Commission (EC) funded SCALE project. Under this project, AKRSP (I) major thrust was reviving the old irrigation tanks and canals in eight villages which were build by govt's water resources department in 1980s. Remaining villages were covered through watershed development intervention. However, promotion of self help groups (SHGs) and providing agriculture extension services including agriculture input supply were the activities done across the 17 villages.

In the second phase, twelve villages including two old villages were selected for the Integrated Micro-plan Project (IMP) in 2010. The IMP was a newly conceived project by the State MGNREGA Council of the Govt of Madhya Pradesh under MGNREGS. The State MGNREGA Council, GoMP selected AKRSP(I) as its implementing partner for the newly launched IMP project in Khalwa block of Khandwa district and Khaknar block of Burhanpur district. It must be noted that concentration of the Korku tribe is very high in both the blocks of these two districts. AKRSP(I) followed necessary guidelines provided by the State MGNREGA Council and Jila Panchayats of respective districts to implement the projects. While implementation of the IMP project in Khaknar block of Burhanpur district went on smoothly, however, it was not to be so in Khalwa block of Khandwa district. The underlying reasons for this are discussed in detail in the following section.

Politics of Tribal Development in Khalwa Block

AKRSP(I) strictly adhered to the norms and necessary guidelines prescribed by the State MGNREGA Council and Jila Panchayat, Khandwa to implement the IMP project in Khalwa block. As the first step, it started following the set of activities for preparation of detailed project report (DPR) of the project villages. Round of meetings, discussions, PRAs, transact walks and job card verifications were held in the villages by the mid-2011. Thus, DPRs were prepared and approved by the Gram Sabhas held in the villages. All the DPRs approved by Gram Sabhas of respective villages were submitted to Jila Panchayat, Khandwa by the mid-2011. With this all the official formalities were completed by AKRSP(I) for sanctioning of the project and its subsequent implementation at village level and the villagers were promised of the project. However, AKRSP(I) has made several queries to concerned officials at Jila Panchayat, Khandwa for updates on sanctioning of the project since then. But, no clear responses were given to it. The concerned officials have just said that it will take time to move the files for sanctioning of the project which they are trying. Meanwhile, the IMP project in Khaknar block of Burhanpur district for which AKRSP(I) was also the implementing partner was sanctioned and its implementation was in full swing in 14 villages. However, in Khalwa, expectation of villagers of the 12 IMP project villages was on raise and whenever any field staff of AKRSP(I) was visiting the villages, they were increasingly finding it difficult to talk on the status of the project. Instead of waiting for sanctioning of the IMP project, AKRSP(I) started mobilising resources from other sources and implemented agriculture related intervention alongside promotion of self help groups (SHGs) in these villages. On the other hand, it continued to seek updates on sanctioning of the project to concerned authorities at Jila Panchayat, Khandwa. It was in early 2012, the Jila Panchayat officials informed that they have forwarded the files to concerned officials at Bhopal and now nothing is in their hands and the fate of the project lies with the higher authorities at Bhopal. During the same time, another project submitted to National Bank for Agriculture and Rural Development (NABARD) for horticulture promotion in Khalwa and Pandhana blocks of Khandwa district got sanctioned giving much relief to the organisation. By March 2012, the concerned authorities at Bhopal informed AKRSP(I) that now it can talk to the secretariat of the dept. of rural development on status of the project. Soon, AKRSP(I) made contacts with the secretariat of the dept. of rural development. To its surprise, concerned officials at the secretariat informed that now AKRSP(I) should forget about sanctioning of the project because, the minister of tribal development who hails from the same Khalwa region does not want this project to be sanctioned at all and he wants to meet senior officials of AKRSP(I) at his residence in Khandwa. As a follow up to this, two senior level officials of AKRSP(I) met the minister of tribal development at his residence in Khandwa. During the meeting, the minister was very calm and appreciated the organisation's interventions among the Korku tribe in Khalwa block and stated that he has nothing personal against the organisation's working in Khalwa block; that is also his constituency of state legislative assembly which he is holding for past 15 years. He further suggested that AKRSP(I) should now forget the IMP project in Khalwa and if wants can have similar projects elsewhere but not in Khalwa for which the minister can help whatever possible. The two senior staff went to meet the minister returned back in empty hands. It is now understood that why the sanctioning of the project was taking so much time which was almost 1.5 years in this case. After few days of this meeting, the district collector called on the two senior level staff of AKRSP(I) along with the district development manager (DDM) of NABARD, Khandwa to have discussion on the recent sanctioning of the horticulture project by NABARD in Khandwa district. Unlike the minister in the previous meeting, he was rude in his behaviour and asked them who gave permission to AKRSP(I) and the DDM to sanction the horticulture project in Khalwa and Pandhana blocks which was of worth Rs. 7.5 crore and told them categorically that such a situation should not be repeated in future without the permission of the district collector. Later on, it was learnt that he was told by the minister to do so. At present, AKRSP(I) mobilises funding from private sources and is implanting watershed based intervention in Khalwa block.

The minister of tribal development in Madhya Pradesh belongs to Khalwa block. He is being elected to the state assembly consecutively since past 15 years. He himself belongs to the scheduled tribe community of the Gonds. His forefathers were rulers of the erstwhile princely state which was covering Khalwa block before the independence. However, now he rules the region being a democratically elected representative of the people. He has a very good support of the masses at village level and enjoys unconditional support of the people especially the Korkus and other castes in Khalwa block. He offers occasional feasts to the community members and party workers each year and captures the votes of masses by offering populist measures before elections. He has also a stronghold among the other castes especially the Yadavs who are money lenders and traders in the region from whom the Korkus take credits and agriculture inputs during monsoon season at a very high rate of interest and sell their produces at low price and sometime sell in advance. The minister knows very well that if organisations like AKRSP(I) and others are allowed in the region, it would pose threats to his legacy of ruling the region by developing and empowering the Korku tribal community in long run. Hence, they get eliminated on the way in such manner.

Concluding Remarks

Khalwa block in East Nimar – Khandwa district of Madhya Pradesh has been in contemporary debate over development not only in the state but also in national level for many reasons and there is no irony over the fact that Khalwa has its place in the list of most backward blocks in the country. Wide spread poverty, food insecurity, malnutrition, mass scale exploitations by money lenders, traders and political leaders and gross violation of human rights in the region are the main woes to the marginalised Korku tribe of recent times. This paper only provides a firsthand glimpse of these situations. It seems that the future of the Korku tribe lies in their own hands. The sooner they understand the realities the better it is for them, which cannot happen on its own. Therefore, the role of organisations like AKRSP(I) should be making the community aware and empowering them socio-economically. Only then can there be an end to these grim situations prevailing in the region at present.

References

Deogaonkar, S G and S S Deogaonkar (1990): *The Korku Tribals.* Concept Publishing Company: New Delhi.

Fuchs, Stephen (1988): *The Korkus of the Vindhya Hills.* Inter-India Publications: New Delhi.

Mishra, Janmejaya and Raj Kumar Gupta (2010): *"Food Insecurity among the Tribals of Madhya Pradesh: Causes and Consequences",* paper presented at Fifth Annual International Conference on Public Policy and Management held at Indian Institute of Management (IIM), Bangalore on 9th August, 2010.

Mosse, David, Sanjeev Gupta and Vidya Shah (2005): 'On the Margins in the City: Adivasi Seasonal Labour Migration in Western India' in *Economic and Political Weekly*, July 9th, pp. 3025-38.

Russel, R V and Hiralal (1916): *Tribes and Castes of the Central Provinces of India,* Vol. III, London.

Sahoo, Bijaya Laxmi (2009): "*Mapping the Nutritional Status of Tribal Communities in Khandwa and Burhanpur Districts of Madhya Pradesh"*, AKRSP(I): Khandwa.

Acknowledgements

K M Sinha, Ashok Minz, Pradeep Tiwari, Kamal Bhalray, R K Mahajan, Naveen Patidar, Devram Yadav, Gurprit Bhatiya, Chandrarekha Malviya, Sanjiv Tiwari, Sunayana Ingle, Kamlesh Panchole, Raj Kumar Gupta, Kiran Patel, Bijay Laxmi Sahoo, Bisram Patil and Ramkishan Goutam.

25

Land Alienation of Tribals in Andhra Pradesh

Justin Jos

Introduction

Land has always been a prized possession of indigenous people from time immemorial. They worship it, cultivate it, maintain it and also safeguard it but howsoever the post-colonial India has failed to adequately address the issues pertaining to the land belonging to the tribals. This has not only led to widespread alienation of acreage but has also resulted into massive displacement of indigenous people from their original inhabitation to unchartered territories resulting in disruption of their natural way of life. State intervention through constitutional means has also not afforded sufficient remedies to tribals along with unsatisfactory rehabilitation schemes and methods. Other socio-economic factors such as poverty, caste-issues, illiteracy and indebtedness etc., have been belligerent towards achieving equal status for tribals in backward regions. As a consequence of this, the overall development of a certain segment of the society in terms of social, economic, political and upward growth has been militated against. Any exclusion of indigenous people from the societal or political framework amounts to deprivation of "development"of the section as a whole and subsequent denial of equal rights of opportunity towards all aspects of human activity. The problems subsisting in tribal areas has been of utmost grievance and in the political circles however policy-makers, anthropologists and administration have deliberated that land alienation is one of the core problems prevalent in this strata of society.

The tribals present in the State of Andhra Pradesh have suffered extreme economic and collective exclusion on account of absence of social, political and fiscal mobility across the community. The Scheduled Castes and other

Backward Castes who witnessed certain degrees of progress because of protective discrimination policies of the government, the Scheduled Tribes remain abysmally backward and socially excluded, still living in harsh environs.[1] Land has been one of the sources to secure their unstable livelihood in terms of legal entitlements and property but an onslaught by governmental agencies along with other factors has pushed the indigenous into the pit of poverty and deep economic vulnerability. The present paper "Land Alienation of Tribals in Andhra Pradesh" will delineate the fundamental causes of pervasive alienation of land from tribals in Andhra Pradesh and ensuing displacement of tribals under the garb of development by State authorities. The legal framework and constitutional protections guaranteed will be discussed and a viable solution as suggestions will be incorporated towards the end of the paper.

Understanding the Theme

To fully understand the problems with respect to land alienation of tribals in Andhra Pradesh we have to first evolve an analytical step by step approach. The socio-cultural aspects will be subsequently made clear on our better comprehension towards the concepts of alienation, outlining as to qualify as tribals and the geographical regions of the State involved in maximum land alienation. All these questions might seem of trivial importance at the first glance but it is to be mentioned that all the root causes of tribal underdevelopment vis-à-vis land alienation emanate out of these vital areas.

Concept of Alienation

The concept of alienation is a problem which strikes discord with the existing socio-economic order of the tribal society and this concept is based on the central idea that land is the greatest asset belonging to the tribals without it their survival in the state of nature is not only difficult but excruciating. Alienation is inherent in exploitative relations of production and its nature varies with that of exploitation.[2] Therefore the inference drawn is that causes of alienation vary in different systems and the problems of land alienation may be different from another in a different state. Land has always been a major source of living for people from all walks of life in the pre-historic era however in the modern economy-oriented society the model of private property has resulted in huge tracts of natural land being acquired by few. This land holding pattern violates equality on all counts and has become a major source of exploitation through creation of fake paucity of land. As John Locke had stated "The measure of property nature has well set by the extent of men's labour and the conveniences of life: no man's labour could subdue, or appropriate all; nor could his enjoyment consume more than a small part; so that it was impossible for any man, this way, to entrench upon the right of another, or acquire to himself a property, to the prejudice of his neighbour, who would still have room for as good, and as large a possession (after the other had taken out his) as before it was appropriated."[3] Land inequalities has occasioned a grave structuralist problem depriving equal right to land to all especially tribals and power to procure lands in hands of few who are powered through monetary, political and muscular means. The indigenous people have been vulnerable victim of these influential agencies and as a consequence, alienation of their land which qualifies as their dwellings have been forcibly occupied or put into industrial use.

Alienation was defined by Hegel and was used by Marx to describe and criticise a social condition in which man far from being the active initiation of the social world seemed more a passive object of determinate external processes.[4] Alienation's manifestations also differ among societies based on slavery, serfdom and capitalism etc.[5] The process of land alienation has revealed itself mainly in large-scale migration of tribal communities from fertile plain areas to the neighbouring forests.[6] Developments of only a certain section of society has resulted the tribals to forcibly live in places unsuitable for comfortable living. Some examples of this kind of development can be extensive construction of railways and roadways, sale and purchase of fertile land, expansion of cities and towns on account of huge capital influx, indiscriminate land holding patterns etc., and as a consequence of this kind of development peasant struggles in various states has also been witnessed. Land alienation is not only caused due to the above said factors but certain sociological issues such as poverty, indebtedness, illiteracy also result in alienation of tribal land. The history of alienation of tribal land is a result of forced evacuation of tribals in the wake of industrial growth in the 17th and 18th century.[7] There has been declining land holdings and increasing landless labourers for the scheduled tribes in nearly all parts of the country. The Agricultural Census, 1980-81, 1985-86 and 1990-91 has clearly delineated that the large holdings of both SC's and ST's has been on a consistent downfall from 1980-81 to 1990-91 i.e., from 0.9 per cent to 0.6 per cent and 3.4 per cent to 2.1 per cent respectively and the condition is even worse off for those possessing marginal size holdings which have increased from 39.8 per cent to 43.4 per cent for ST's and 68.9 per cent to 72.2 per cent for the SC's.[8] The clear inference which can be drawn from this data is that the majority population of tribal areas possess marginal size holdings which has continually collapsed by the wake of this millennium and it is a bitter truth that this has also led to another deeper problem that the rate of ST agricultural labourers has also been on the rise than that of non ST's implying that the landlessness among them has increased. Apart from the above causes other reasons such as incessant acts of atrocities against the tribals, migration of non-tribal community in search of alternative lands in light of an artificial co-existence of industries in their original inhabitation has also been a major factor of land alienation.

Who are Tribals?

Article 1(1) (b) of the ILO Convention No. 107 defined 'indigenous' as: "members of tribal or semi-tribal populations in independent countries which are regarded as indigenous on account of their descent from the populations which inhabited the country, or a geographical region to which the country belongs, at the time of conquest or colonisation and which, irrespective of their legal status, live more in conformity with the social, economic and cultural institutions of that time than with the institutions of the nation to which they belong." Tribals have always been the first inhabitants of any modern civilisation and over the passage of time they have been neglected in the developmental process by the state as well as by the society. It is to be observed that India's population includes nearly one hundred million tribal populations.[9] These Adivasis are mostly found in North Eastern regions of India, Orissa, Madhya Pradesh, Chhattisgarh, Rajasthan, Gujarat, Maharashtra, Andhra Pradesh, Bihar, Jharkhand, West Bengal, Mizoram and parts of Andaman and Nicobar islands.[10] Tribe has been defined as a social group of a simple kind, the members of which speaks a common dialect, have a single government and act together for achieving common purposes such as warfare.[11] However, any concrete definition of tribals has not been laid down in the Constitution of India. The essential characteristics of these communities that are considered while making such enlistments are:[12]

1. Primitive Traits,
2. Geographical isolation,
3. Distinct culture,
4. Shy of contact with community at large, and
5. Economically backward.

Profiling the Tribal Community in Andhra Pradesh

The total population of Andhra Pradesh is 76210007 out of which the tribal population reaches up to 5024104 therefore per cent of STs in the State to Total State Population amounting up to 6.60 per cent.[13] Twelve tribes, namely, Bodo Gadaba, Gutob Gadaba, Bondo Poraja, Khond Poroja, Parangiperja, Chenchu, Dongaria Khonds, Kuttiya Khonds, Kolam, Kondareddis, Konda Savaras and Thoti have been recognised as Primitive Tribal Groups (PTGs).[14] These tribes are mostly found in adjoining tracts that have been designated as Scheduled Areas overseen by the Integrated Tribal Development Agencies (ITDAs). In conformity with the national Tribal Sub-Plan (TSP) strategy, Andhra Pradesh tribal population is divided into four categories: (i) those living in tribal concentration areas in the scheduled villages and adjoining areas, i.e., the TSP areas administered by ITDAs. (ii) Primitive Tribal Groups (PTGs), i.e., communities who live in near isolation in inaccessible habitats in and outside the Scheduled Areas who are at the pre-agricultural stage of the economy; (iii) those living in small pockets outside the scheduled areas, i.e., Modified Area Development Agency (MADA) areas and tribal clusters; and (iv) Dispersed Tribal Groups, i.e., those dispersed throughout the state.[15]

Table 25.1: List of Scheduled Tribes of Andhra Pradesh[16]

Sl. No.	*Schedule Tribe*
1.	Andh, Sadhu Andh
2.	Bagata
3.	Bhil
4.	Chenchu
5.	Gadabas, Bodo Gadaba, Gutob Gadabad, Kallayi Gadaba, Parangi Gadaba, Kathera Gadaba, Kapu Gadaba
6.	Gond, Naikpod, Rajgond, Koitur
7.	Goude (in the agency tracts)
8.	Hill Reddis
9.	Jatapus
10.	Kammara
11.	Kattunayakan
12.	Kolam, Kolawar
13.	Konda Doras, Kubi
14.	Konda Kapus
15.	Konda Reddis
16.	Kondhs, Kodi, Kodhu, Desaya Kondhs, Dongria Kondhs, Kuttiya Kondhs, Tikiria Kondhs, Yenity Kondhs, Kuvinga
17.	Kotia, Bentho Oriya, Bartika, Dulia, Holva, Sanrona, Sidhopaiko
18.	Koya, Doli Koya, Gutta Koya, Kammara Koya, Musara Koya, Oddi Koya, Pattidi Koya, Rajah, Rasha Koya, Lingadhari Koya (Ordinary), Kottu Koya, Bhine Koya, Raj Koya
19.	Kulia
20.	Malis (excluding Adilabad, Hyderabad, Karimnagar, Khammam, Mahabubnagar, Medak, Nalgonda, Nizamabad and Warangal districts)
21.	Manna Dhora
22.	Mukha Dhora, Nooka Dhora
23.	Nayaks (in the agency tracts)
24.	Pardhan
25.	Porja, Parangiperja
26.	Reddi Dhoras
27.	Rona, Rena
28.	Savaras, Kapu Savaras, Maliya Savaras, Khutto Savaras
29.	Sugalis, Lambadis, Banjara
30.	Thoti (in Adilabad, Hyderabad, Karimnagar, Khammam, Mahabubnagar, Medak, Nalgonda, Nizamabad and Warangal districts)
31.	Valmiki (in the Scheduled Areas of Visakhapatnam, Srikakulam, Vizianagaram, East Godavari and West Godavari districts)
32.	Yenadis, Chella Yenadi, Kappala Yenadi, Manchi Yenadi, Reddi Yenadi
33.	Yerukulas, Koracha, Dabba Yerukula, Kunchapuri Yerukula, Uppu Yerukula
34.	Nakkala, Kurvikaran
35.	Dhulia, Paiko, Putiya (in the districts of Visakhapatnam and Vizianagaram)
36.	Porja, Parangiperja

Table 25.2: Basic Information about Scheduled Tribes in the State[17]

Andhra Pradesh population (2001 Census)	762 lakh
ST population	50.24 lakh (6.59 per cent); Male - 25.48 lakh, Female - 24.76 lakh
ST population in tribal areas	30.47 lakh
ST population in plain areas	19.77 lakh
Tribal groups	35 tribal groups
Primitive Tribal Groups (PTGs)	8
Integrated Tribal Development Agencies (ITDA)	10 --- Seethampeta, Parvathipuram, Paderu, R.C.Varam, K.R.Puram, Bhadrachalam, Eturunagaram, Utnoor, Srisailam and Nellore
ITDA area	31, 485, 34sq.kms.
Modified Area Development Approach (MADA) pockets	41
Clusters	17
Scheduled villages	5938
Non-scheduled villages	809
No. of habitations in ITDA areas	11855
Total No. of SHGs in tribal areas	495646
Total No. of ST members enrolled	1046371

Chronological List of Tribal Laws Implemented in Andhra Pradesh.[18]

1. Ganjam and Vizagapatnam Act, 1939 (Act No. XXIV) of 1839.
2. Scheduled Districts Act 1874 (Act XIV of 1874).
3. Agency Tracts Interest and Land Transfer Act, 1917.
4. The Andhra Pradesh Agency Rules, 1924.
5. Government of India Act, 1935 – Excluded and Partially Excluded Areas.
6. Andhra Pradesh (Andhra Scheduled Areas) Village Courts Regulation, 1940.
7. Andhra Pradesh (Andhra Scheduled Areas) (Estates Land Repealing) Regulation, 1943.
8. The Andhra Pradesh Scheduled Areas Land Transfer Regulation, 1959.
9. AP Scheduled area Land Transfer Regulation (APSALT) Rules.
10. Andhra Pradesh (Andhra Scheduled Areas) Estates (Abolition and Conversion into Ryotwari) Regulation, 1951.
11. Andhra Pradesh Mahals (Abolition and Conversation into Ryotwari) Regulation, 1969.
12. Andhra Pradesh Schedule Areas Ryotwari Settlement Regulation, 1969.
13. Andhra Pradesh Scheduled Area Land Transfer (Amendment) Regulation, 1970.
14. Madras Scheduled Areas Estates (Abolition and Conversion into Ryotwari) Andhra Pradesh Amendment Regulation, 1960.

15. The Andhra Pradesh Scheduled Areas Laws (Extension and Amendment) Regulation, 1963.

16. Nugur and Bhadrachalam Scheduled Areas (Validation of Transfer to Khammam District) Regulation, 1963.

17. Andhra Pradesh (Scheduled Areas Ryotwari Settlement) Regulation, 1970.

18. Andhra Pradesh Scheduled Area Land Transfer (Amendment) Regulation, 1971.

19. Money lending regulation for the relief of the tribals from indebtedness:
    (a) Andhra Pradesh (Scheduled Area) Money Lender Regulation, 1960
    (b) Andhra Pradesh (Scheduled Area) Money Lender Rules
    (c) Andhra Pradesh (Scheduled Tribes) Debt Relief Regulation, 1960
    (d) Andhra Pradesh (Scheduled Tribes) Debt Relief Rules, 1960
    (e) Andhra Pradesh (Scheduled Tribes) Debt Relief Regulation, 1970

20. The Andhra (Telangana Tribal Areas) Regulation, 1359-F.

21. The Hyderabad Tribal Areas Regulation, (Regulation No. III of 1359F).

22. Notified Tribal Areas Rules, 1359-F.

What are Scheduled Areas?

To understand the problem of land alienation, we have to deal with the laws pertaining to administration of scheduled areas. The indigenous people of any community are found in a particular area and these along with adjoining contiguous areas form the basis of their natural habitat. These areas are termed as "scheduled areas" but howsoever, no rigid definition is found in the constitution.

During the pre-independence era, the British enacted several land laws which alienated the tribal people from their rightly owned lands. After independence, all these scheduled areas which were identified by the government were brought under the fifth schedule of the constitution of India and special laws as enunciated in the constitution remained in force in these areas. Part C of the Fifth Schedule of the Constitution, under Article 244 (1), defines Scheduled Areas as such areas as the President may by order declare to be Scheduled Areas. The President has a power to declare any area as scheduled areas through power granted to it under this schedule vide a Presidential Order subject to clauses (a), (b) and (c) of Article 244 (2). The rationale behind implementation of Article 244(1) and 244(2) is to enable the government to enact a separate set of laws with respect to these scheduled areas for better administration and governance.

The executive power of the Union can give instructions to the state for better administration of the areas which are defined as "Scheduled Areas", more over the governor shall submit a report to the president with reference to the administration of these areas and this is provided for in Part A Para 2 and Para 3 of the Fifth Schedule respectively. Establishment of a Tribes Advisory

Council has been provided for in Part B of the Fifth Schedule which is another significant feature for welfare and advancement of tribals. Paragraph five of the Fifth Schedule of the Constitution lays down the laws applicable to these Scheduled Areas. It is given that the governor can exempt these areas or may make regulations necessary for peace and good governance in scheduled areas. Paragraph six of the Fifth Schedule of the Constitution prescribes following route for scheduling, rescindment and alteration of Scheduled Areas.

The scheduled areas in Andhra Pradesh include Visakhapatnam, East Godavari, West Godavari, Adilabad, Srikakulam, Vizianagaram, Mahboobnagar, Prakasam (only some mandals are scheduled mandals).[19]

Tribal Land Alienation: Causes and Ramifications

Land has always been the major source of livelihood for tribals and the reasons for land alienation are many. Howsoever, this has resulted into lack of tribal development and social exclusion of this particular ethnic group. Land alienation in a predominantly agrarian economy characterised by highly skewed distribution of land and adverse land-man ratio aggravates the inequalities in terms of income and wealth.[20] Tribal lands are rich in hydrologic, mineral, oil, gas, forest, and other resources, and this easily makes them the most attractive sites to locate development projects of various kinds.[21] Thus, many development projects in India are located in areas that are densely inhabited by tribal people.[22] The development projects by the state in Andhra Pradesh reflect that massive industrialisation and privatisation has led to incursion of non-tribals into tribal territories. The economic advancement of the country is the argument forwarded by the governmental authorities which cannot be justified on any grounds. Due to poor economic conditions and illiteracy the tribes have not been able to understand the vicious circle thrown by their non-tribal exploiters.[23] This has resulted into tribals turning into landless labourers and long term impoverishment as a consequence. In a tribal economy land comprised the major source of income for the indigenous people. Any deprivation of tribals from their rightly owned land does not only hamper the inclusion of tribals into mainstream society but also alienates them from availing any further legal recourse as the authorities favour the government. In a number of areas new industrial and mining complexes, many major irrigation projects were located in the tribal areas resulting in the submergence of extensive lands belonging to the tribals.[24] This flawed idea of development amounts to a systematic violation of the land laws placed in the state by the state being an accomplice in such a crime. Various studies have pointed out that the lack of political and administrative will continues to be the cause for perpetuation of the problem of land alienation amongst the tribals as reflected in the reluctance to amend legal provisions and plug the existing loopholes and swift administrative action to identify alienated land, and restoring it to the tribals with delivery of possession.[25] Displacement takes place mainly on account of development projects, which include – large irrigation dams, hydro-electric projects, open-cast and underground coal mines, super-thermal power plants and mineral-based industrial units.[26] The trauma of resettlement is exacerbated for tribal people because of their close spiritual ties to their home-land and their apprehension that once they move, their way of life will be lost forever.[27] In large mining projects, tribals lose their land not only to the project authorities, but even to non-tribal outsiders who converge into these areas and corner both land and the new economic opportunities in commerce and petty industry.[28] The solution, as provided by the State, of such land alienation on account of displacement is inadequate compensation through rehabilitation processes. Often the tribals are cornered into barren lands rendering majority of tribal income deficient. Moreover, the impoverishment that tribal people encounter soon after displacement mainly arises from delayed payment of compensation and the exclusion from compensation calculations of the common property resources on which they largely subsist.[29]

Another major cause of land alienation particularly in areas of Srikakulam, Vishakhapatnam, and East and West Godavari districts is lending meager amounts of money to tribals with the ulterior motive of land grabbing. Usually the tribals are unable to re-pay the debt resulting in the landlessness.The rates of interests charged on such sums of money were exorbitant and ridiculous ranging between 25-50 per cent, and sometimes the interest charged on the sums advanced were a whopping 100 per cent.[30] The sahukars of landlords cultivate their lands through Benami transfers and whenever a question arises, the poor tribals are made to state that the lands are in their possession and they are only cultivating their lands.[31] Any form of legal recourse is also a distant dream because these land owners threaten them with dire consequences thereby illegally depriving them of their lands. The reasons for resorting to such money lenders can be narrowed down to inadequate institutional rural credit among the tribal population as one of the important reasons for this state of exploitation coupled with lack of education.[32] The literacy rate of the tribals in Andhra Pradesh is just eight per cent as against the state average of 30 per cent.[33] The condition of the tribals in the state is pathetic and they are being continuously exploited and neglected by the non-tribals and the government.[34] However, the legal measures to curb the activities of money-lenders and traders have failed to have much impact on the severity of the problem due to the ineffective enforcement machinery and lack of alternative sources of credit for meeting the tribals' consumption and productive needs.[35]

Apart from the above, there are various incidental reasons such as a non-tribal marrying a tribal woman and thereby procuring tribal land through such marital relations. The tribal women are kept as concubines or second wives and even there offsprings are treated as tribals furthering non-tribal intrusion into indigenous lands. This gives leeway to non-tribals to prevent legal hurdles and occupy more and more land subsequently. Land alienation through polygamy has been found in Visakhapatnam (Koyyuru Panchayat Area), East Godavari and West Godavari districts.[36]

In Srikakulam and Vizianagaram, tribal areas have preserved a bond of friendship called NESTAM and it has different names in different regions. The tribal groups enter into specific relations with each other by means of exchanging gifts. The aim of this bond is to provide for welfare of each other in times of hardship but the shrewd non-tribals have used this as a means of exploitation for procuring lands from tribals in the garb of affability thereby resulting in landlessness. Another means employed by non-tribal communities to occupy tribal land was to procure false scheduled tribe certificates.[37] Such cases included Plain Kapus being regarded as Konda Kapus, Plain Kammaras as Konda Kammaras, and Plain Reddys as Konda Reddys.[38] The problems of the densely populated plains and urban areas are potentially a much greater threat to the continuing control of the ruling class than those of the peripheral, politically less vocal tribal areas.[39] Therefore the most expedient course of action for any government - state or national - is not to use scarce resources developing the tribal peoples, but rather to exploit the tribal areas for timber, minerals and cheap labour and to invest the surplus created in the potentially explosive non-tribal plains and urban areas.[40]

Judicial Decision Supporting Tribal Rights

In *Samatha vs. State of Andhra Pradesh* the apex court held the mining activity in tribal areas can go on as long as it is undertaken by the government, or instrumentality of state or a cooperative society in favour of the tribals.[41,42] It was also stated that all lands leased by the government or its agencies to private mining companies apart from its instrumentalities in the scheduled areas are null and void. In addition it also held that transfer of land to the government or its instrumentalities is entrustment of public property as the aim of public corporations is in public interest and hence such transfers stand upheld. Transfer of land in Scheduled Area by way of lease to non-tribals, corporation aggregate, etc. stands prohibited to prevent their exploitation in any form.[43] Transfer of mining lease to non-tribals, company, corporation aggregate or partnership firm, etc. is unconstitutional, void and inoperative.[44] State instrumentalities were held to be under the exception and institutions such as APMDC were included in it.

Constitutional Safeguards for Tribals

The Indian constitution has afforded protection to tribals through implementation of both directive principles of state policies and fundamental rights. Tribals possess a unique and different set of culture which is typical to them but including them in the mainstream society cannot be overlooked by the government as it is an obligation under the constitution to promote welfare of all the citizens on an equal basis. For the betterment of these downtrodden societies the framers of the constitution had incorporated various provisions. Article 46 epitomising this policy calls upon the state (Central and State government) to promote with special care the educational and economic interests of Scheduled Castes and Scheduled Tribes and protect them from social injustice and all forms of exploitation.[45] A brief overview of the relevant provisions is made on account of in the following:

Administration: Article 244(1) the administration and control of all the scheduled areas are subject to the fifth schedule.

Tribal Development: Article 275(1) provides for Grant-in-Aid from the consolidated fund of India for a state to meet with the expenses involved in implementation of welfare activities for Schedule Tribes.

Political Safeguards: Reservation of seats for Scheduled Caste and Schedules Tribe communities has been provided for on the basis of population in the House of the People as per Article 330 and in the LegislativeAssemblies of the states as per Article 332 for a certain length of time in the hope that in course of that time its need would disappear.[46]

Employment: Article 16(4) of the constitution expressly empowers the state to promulgate "any provision for the reservation of appointments or posts in favour of any backward class of citizens (including STs) if not represented adequately in the services under the state".

Promotion of Education: Article 15(4) along with subsequent amendments empowers the state to make any special provision for the advancement of any socially and educationally backward classes including STs and also enables the state to reserve seats for them in educational institutions.[47]

Policy Regulations

It is already observed that the Andhra Pradesh government had passed many laws to regulate the administration of tribal lands. We will discuss a selected few legislations which deeply pervaded the rights of the tribals and this will be comprehended thoroughly only after we understand as to the rationale behind enforcing separate laws. It is evident in the contemporary society that the tribals have been excluded and lived in geographical isolation from the non-tribals. The tribals are proven to be culturally backward and that their social and other customs are different from the rest of India.[48] The common trait which is visible in every tribal group is that they are self-contained and homogenous; any intermingling from the outside world is virtually absent. Because of their extreme ostracisation from the non-tribals an inevitable gap has pervaded between the two which is visible. The conventional, and largely accepted, solution is to balance the dichotomy between assimilation of tribal peoples and their independent identity, and delineate the contours of a national policy that would allow them to preserve their way of life without compromising development.[49] The tribals have been a victim of incessant migration of non-tribals into their lands on account of expansion of cities and gestating industrial developmental activities. Apart, from this their ethnic identity is in grave danger owing to pervasion caused by the non-tribals into their daily affairs. Post-independence, the question asked was whether the tribals are competent enough to regulate their administrations on their own? The answer was in the negative on account of excessive disparity between the tribals and non-tribals in parameters of social justice, economic viability and political recourse. This made it imperative on the State to enforce laws which can be read along the lines of tribal improvement and understand their position.

Two Major Protective Regulations

The Agency Tracts Interest and Land Transfer Act, 1917

This was the first ever comprehensive protective legislation that was brought out to check and regulate the rates of interest and also the transfer of land in the Agency Tracts of Ganjam, Vishakhapatnam and Godavari districts.[50] It was enacted primarily to safeguard the interest of the hill tribes in the area over which it extended and to protect them from exploitation by non-tribals and moneylenders. [51] It permitted transfer of land only among tribals and lay down that the interest accrued over the debts borrowed by the tribals shall not exceed the principal amount.[52]

The Andhra Pradesh Scheduled Areas Land Transfer Regulation, 1959

It extends the provisions of the Agency Tracts Interest and Land Transfer Act, 1917. Land has been the major source of livelihood for the tribals taking advantage of ignorance of the latter however; many non-tribal immigrants in the Scheduled Areas have fraudulently alienated large areas of fertile land of tribals.[53] This Regulation was enacted to regulate the transfers of land in the Scheduled Areas in the Districts of East Godavari, West Godavari, Visakhapatnam, Srikakulam, Adilabad, Warangal, Khammam and Mehaboobnagar in Andhra Pradesh. According to Section 3(1) A of the Regulation, "any transfer of immovable property situated in the Agency Tracts by a person, whether or not such person is a member of Scheduled Tribe, shall be absolutely null and void, unless such transfer is made in favour of person, who is a member of ST or a society registered or deemed to be registered under the AP Cooperative Societies Act 1964 which is composed solely of members of Scheduled Tribes." The term "Transfer" as defined in sub-section G of Section two of Regulation 1959 means a Mortgage with or without possession, lease, sale, gift, exchange or any other dealing with immovable property, not being a testamentary disposition and includes a charge on such property or a contract relating to such property in respect of such; Mortgage lease, sale, gift exchange or other dealing. Further as per sub-section (4) of Section 3 of the A.P.S.A.L.T.R, the expression transfer includes a sale in execution of Decree and also a Transfer made by a member of a ST in favour of any other members of ST, Benami for the benefit of a person who is not a member of ST: but does not include a partition or a devolution by succession.[54] Hence even Benami transfers are prohibited under the Regulation. This legislation has prospective effect.

Other Landmark Legislations

(I) The Andhra Pradesh (Andhra Scheduled Areas) Estate (Abolition and Conversion into Ryotwari) Act 1948.

(II) The Andhra Pradesh Mahals (Abolition and Conversion into Ryotwari) Regulation, 1969.

(III) The Andhra Pradesh Mutta (Abolition and Conversion into Ryotwari) Regulation, 1969.

These are revolutionary laws which facilitated state proprietorship of private lands in the Scheduled Areas and made the path clear for tribal sovereignty. Prior to these enactments, private ownership largely regulated the day to day affairs of tribal lands. Mahals were private estates in certain parts of the present Khammam District. These mahals were leased out for cultivation to private estates thereby depriving right of ownership over their inherited land. In the Scheduled Areas of Visakhapatnam and East Godavari districts, the then rulers allowed "Muttarights" to individuals who rendered assistance for revenue duties. Since these were basically grants, the tribals did not have absolute rights over these properties. Through abolition of Estates, Mahals and Muttarights and their conversion into Ryotwari Pattas the issues were settled in favour of the tribals who tilled these lands.

Conclusions and Suggestions

Today the tribal is under severe pressure and their life is being seriously threatened by the massive in roads made into their territories, the rape of their lands by companies and the mining mafia, the decimation of their forests by the forest and land mafia.[55] Along with this is the fact that no real 'development' has been implemented and the last factor to complete their hopelessness and despair is the fact that they have never received any hearing or any form of redressed of their problems.[56] It is observed through the above academic discourse that tribal lands have been alienated to a great extent and this is on the rise because of various factors such as legal loopholes, non-retrospective land regulations, powerful outsiders and a continuing lack of political commitment to protecting tribal rights.[57] The non-tribals have invaded into the private sphere of tribals which has resulted in forced migration of tribals into unchartered territories. Oppression faced by the tribals because of massive corruption and political intervention has also acted as reinforcement into tribal land alienation. Divisive tactics such as establishing friendship and subsequent usurpation of land has resulted in the tribal landlessness. Land alienation due to displacement of tribals for various development projects, and encroachment/ possession of tribals' lands by the non-tribals has rendered a considerable number of tribal families landless and this has further added to their poverty.[58]

In Andhra Pradesh, the tribal areas are used to attract private capital for exploiting mineral resources; the tribals are forced to pay a far higher price in the case of irrigation projects as the lion's share of expected benefits would accrue to non-tribals.[59] According to 2001 Census, the percentage of literate persons (those who can read and write with understanding), aged seven years and above, among ST population of Andhra Pradesh is 37 per cent, which is lower than 60.5 per cent reported for state population as a whole. This clearly points to the fact that the tribal population in the state is unaware of its legal rights and therefore the existence of safeguards in the constitution and state laws do not yield any positive results. Hence, there is an imminent need to provide for legal literacy within the tribal populations which might reduce the rampant land alienation. The illusion of development in the garb of land usurpation is violative of fundamental rights of the tribal who are equal citizens in the eyes of law. Development should positively benefit the tribals and this can be achieved only when tribals are rehabilitated in consonance with sociological factors concurrent to their culture. Such dubious development plans by government are to be detested by the state authorities and only after greater consideration of the harmless indigenous people any project is to be approved.

Active participation by the tribals along with co-operation of the forest officials should be the objective to resist deprivation of property rights of tribals. Granting of arbitrary powers to local authorities has been the root cause of land alienation throughout the country. This coupled with forced eviction will lead not only to economic loss but also loss of a great multitude of tribal life and consequent extinction of tribal culture from the state. Special incentive and training should be provided to forest officers so that they may stick to their duty as guar.

References

1. M. Gopinath Reddy and K. Anil Kumar, Political Economy of Tribal Development: A Case Study of Andhra Pradesh, Working Paper No. 85, February (2010), p. 6.
2. Ramdas Rupavath, Tribal Land Alienation and Political Movements: Socio-economic Patterns from South India, Cambridge Scholars Publishing, (2009), p. 14.
3. John Locke, two treatises on government, Section 36, (1690).
4. Shyama Prasad Rout, Land Alienation and Tribal People's Rights: A Case Study of Mayurbhanj District in Orissa, 1990.
5. *Ibid.*
6. *Supra* Note
7. Samantha Benerjee, In the wake of Naxalbari, Sourna Rekha Publications, Calcutta, 1980, pp. 32-33.
8. Chapter 7 of report of National Commission on Backward Areas of Development available at http://lawmin.nic.in/ncrwc/finalreport/v2b1-2ch9.htm#_ftn9.

9. Hari Priya, Tribal Laws in Andhra Pradesh, available at: http://works.bepress.com/hari_priya/3.

10. *Ibid.,* p. 5.

11. *Anjan Kumar* v. *Union of India,* 2006 AIR 1177.

12. "Basic Statistics on Schedule Tribes of Andhra Pradesh", Tribal Cultural Research and Training Institute, Tribal Welfare Department, Government of Andhra Pradesh, Hyderabad, January 2008 p. 11.

13. Census of India 2001.

14. *Supra* Note 1 p. 9.

15. *Ibid.*

16. Annual Report - 2006-07, Ministry of Tribal Affairs, Government of India available at http://goo.gl/ylbc2.

17. *Supra* Note 1.

18. *Supra* Note 9 p. 45.

19. Issues of Social Justice: Scheduled Castes, Scheduled Tribes and Other Backward Classes–An Unfinished National Agenda, National Commission to Review the Working of the Constitution, p. 11.

20. T. Prabhakar Reddy, Tribal Land Alienation in Andhra Pradesh, Economic and Political Weekly, Vol. 24, No. 28 (July 15, 1989), pp. 1571-1573 available at http://www.jstor.org/stable/4395073.

21. Priya Pillai, Vinuta Gopal, Kanchi Kohli(Greenpeace), Singrauli: A Coal Curse: A Fact Finding Report On The Impact Of Coal Mining, available at http://goo.gl/00DRj.

22. *Ibid.*

23. *Supra* Note 4.

24. Report: National Commission on Backward-Areas Development (1980).

25. Schedule Tribes, Tenth Five Year Plan by Planning Commission, available at http://goo.gl/ZehOR.

26. *Ibid.*

27. Hari Mohan Mathur, *Tribal Land Issues in India: Communal Management, Rights, and Displacement,* Asian Development Bank, 2009.

28. *Ibid.*

29. *Ibid.* p. 182.

30. G.B. Reddy, Land Laws in Andhra Pradesh, Gogia Law Agency, p. 157.

31. BN Bordoloi, Alienation of Tribal Land and Indebtedness, (1986).

32. *Supra* Note 20.

33. *Ibid.*

34. *Ibid.*

35. *Supra* Note 25 p. 17

36. *Supra* Note 31 p. 14.

37. *Supra* Note 9 p. 85.

38. *Ibid.*

39. Steve Jones, Tribal Underdevelopment in India, Development and Change ISAGE, London and Beverly Hills), Vol. 9 (1978) 1, 41-70.

40. *Ibid.*
41. 8 SCC 191 (1997).
42. Issues of India available at http://socialissuesindia.wordpress.com/2012/09/06/the-samatha-judgment-and-the-fifth-schedule-of-the-constitution/.
43. The Fifth Schedule of the Constitution and the Samatha Judgment Available At http://goo.gl/8xzVY.
44. *Ibid.*
45. Dr R.P. Rai, Constitutional Safeguards For Tribals In India And Tribal Administration: Behavioural Aspects, Central India Law Quarterly available at http://indiankanoon.org/doc/1163757/.
46. *Ibid.*
47. *Supra* Note 1.
48. Constitutional Assembly Debates (CAD), Vol. VII. Apps. C and D, p. 157.
49. Shubhankar Dam, Legal Systems As Cultural Rights: A Rights Based Approach To Traditional Legal Systems Under The Indian Constitution, Ind. Intl & Comp. L., Rev. 295, (2006).
50. *Supra* Note 9 , p. 47.
51. *Supra* Note 1, p. 37.
52. *Ibid.*
53. Tribal Welfare Department Departmental Manual available at http://www.aptribes.gov.in/.
54. *Supra* Note 9, p. 51.
55. Shachi Chakrabarty, Rights of the Indigenous People over Forest in India: Rhetorics and Reality, Indigenous People and Human Rights: the Quest for Justice, Kolkata : R. Cambray & Co., (2009).
56. Srilatha Swaminatahan, Tribes and Human Rights, Speech given at Seminar of International Institute of Human Rights Society on 28th August, 2007 at New Delhi.
57. *Supra* Note 9, p. 51.
58. *Ibid.*
59. *Ibid.*

26

Contesting Inclusive Development: Exclusion and Marginality among Scheduled Tribes in North Coastal Andhra Pradesh

KR Rama Mohan

Scheduled Tribes in Visakhapatnam district are experiencing social exclusion and rendered vulnerabilities to various forms of exploitations. The paper explores the different dimensions of power relations which constitute the marginalisation process. The political limitations and social experience of marginality are mainly focussed in the context of their undeclared scheduled areas in the Ravitamakam Mandal in Visakhapatnam district of Andhra Pradesh. The paper contest the notion of 'Inclusive Development' in the light of plights suffering by the scheduled tribes as their villages are denied the status 'Scheduled Areas' according the Fifth Schedule of Indian Constitution. The paper further explains about resource politics and the role of NGO towards fighting for their rights and privileges of the scheduled tribes in this region. Few suggestions are made towards making these scheduled tribes as partners in the 'Inclusive Development' process.

Introduction

Until recently, the concept of 'Social Exclusion' has become a contested concept. The plethora of definitions on social exclusion ranges on different categories, various social, economic, political, religious processes experienced at both individual and collective level reflects the nature and magnitude of the issues that confronts especially the marginalised sections of the society. The inadequacy of a single definition that can be applied to all the socially excluded categories across time is noted to be both an obstacle and a benefit to its meaningful application. (deHaan, 1998, Silver,1994)

In its original conception, idea of social exclusion sought to replace many labels, categories, and issues such as social problems, debates on poverty, caste discrimination, alienation of religious minorities, and any other aspect which affects individuals well being. However, in the case of Scheduled Tribes of Visakhapatnam and Scheduled Tribes of other districts elsewhere, whose villages are not included and undeclared as scheduled areas are caught in a disadvantaged position due to historical and political process.

Madanipour, *et al.*, (2000) takes on the relational view of social exclusion, emphasises structural or social process affecting society in such a way that some groups experience social boundaries as barriers preventing their full participation in the economic, political and cultural life of the society within which they live, is clearly manifested in the villages of whose habitats come under non-scheduled (plain) areas, thus PESA is not applicable for these scheduled tribes.

The paper is an empirical study to call into question the popular and largely uncontested ideas of inclusive development, to unravel the social realities of the scheduled tribes non-inclusion of scheduled areas by the Government of India in many parts of Andhra Pradesh.

Taking a processual approach as its base, the paper seeks to understand how the scheduled tribes are being marginalised in the context of modern politics. The hegemonic and minority dominant non-scheduled caste communities operate and exploit the vulnerable tribal communities are becoming victims in everyday life. Attempt is made to record the social experiences and social responses to the predicament of marginality of these scheduled tribes. Few suggestions are given for the policy-makers to alleviate the suffering and marginality of the scheduled tribes of Ravitavakam mandal of Visakhapatnam district.

What are the Scheduled Areas

'Scheduled Areas' has been defined in the Indian Constitution as "such areas as the President may order /declare to be Scheduled Areas". Paragraph six of the Fifth Schedule of the Constitution prescribes following procedure for scheduling, descheduling and alteration of Scheduled Areas.

The criteria followed for declaring an area as Scheduled Area are preponderance of tribal population; compactness and reasonable size of the area; under-developed nature of the area; and marked disparity in economic standard of the people.

These criteria are not spelt out in the Constitution of India but have become well established. They embody principles followed in declaring "Excluded" and 'Partially-Excluded Areas' under the Government of India Act 1935, Schedule 'B' of recommendations of the Excluded and Partially Excluded Areas

Sub Committee of Constituent Assembly and the Scheduled Areas and Scheduled Tribes Commission 1961.

At the time of devising and adopting the strategy of Tribal Sub Plan (TSP) for socio-economic development of Scheduled Tribes during Fifth Five Year Plan (1974-79), certain areas besides Scheduled Areas, were also found having preponderance of tribal population.

A review of protective measures available to the tribals of these newly identified areas vis-a-vis Scheduled Areas was made and it was observed that a systematic use of protective measures and other powers available to the executive under Fifth Schedule will help in effective implementation of the development programmes in Sub-Plan Areas.

Therefore, in August 1976 it was decided to make the boundaries of the Scheduled Areas co-terminus with the Tribal Sub-Plan areas. Accordingly, Clause (2) of the paragraph 6 of the Fifth Schedule was amended vide the Constitution (Amendment) Act, 1976 to empower the President to increase the area of any Scheduled Areas in any State.

Andhra Pradesh Scenario

- The 1950 'Scheduled Area Order' by the President of India, declared nine districts in Andhra Pradesh.
- Adilabad, Mahaboobnagar, Khammam, Warangal, East Godavari, West Godavari, Visakhapatnam, Vizianagaram and Srikakulam.
- A total of 5,400 Tribal villages were declared as 'Scheduled Areas' in the Fifth Schedule.
- In 1976, the GOI has given consent to modify the 1950 Scheduled Area Act.
- Madhya Pradesh, Bihar, Orissa, Rajasthan, Gujarat, Maharashtra, Himachal Pradesh, Tribal Villages were identified and added to the list.
- During that time, the GOI has requested to send the list of villages with Tribal population.
- The A.P. State Govt. has identified 753 villages with predominant tribal population.

In 1980, the AP Govt has sent the list to GOI

In 1980, the Government of Andhra Pradesh enumerated 805 Girijana (adivasi) villages to incorporate into the 5th Schedule of the Constitution.

Tribal villages of Maharashtra, Rajasthan, and Bihar, who submitted lists at the same time, have been incorporated in the 5th Schedule.

Yet, Tribes of the 805 villages in AP have been waiting for the government to implement this measure!

The State of Andhra Pradesh, where the Tribal sub-plan areas are not coterminous with Scheduled Areas, has also furnished a proposal to this effect which is under examination.

- Andhra Pradesh Govt has identified the following villages as 'Villages with Tribal Population'
- Srikakulam District : 240 villages
- Vizianagaram District : 170
- Visakhapatnam : 55
- East Godavari District : 40
- West Godavari District : 1
- Khammam : 3
- Warangal : 77
- Adilabad : 164
- Mahaboobnagar : 3
- Total : 805 Villages

* *Source:* Tribal Welfare Department Andhra Pradesh Government.

Andhra Pradesh State Government Initiatives

- 1976 Andhra Pradesh State Cabinet Resolution
- Ordered a Fresh Cabinet Resolution to declare the Scheduled Areas
- Koneru Ranga Rao Committee : To study the agricultural Land issues
- 50 per cent or more tribes can be declared as Scheduled Area
- State Government Agreed, could not implement – Central Government consent is required
- 1/70 act : Tribal Areas lands need to be protected from Non–Tribes
- (This is not applicable to Non- Scheduled Areas) though lands belong to Tribes
- East and West Godavari Districts Villages of Andhra Pradesh: Do not register Tribes lands to Non-tribes (Pending)
- The ITDA Project Officer has written a letter to MRO of Ravitakam Mandal MRO soliciting Population List of Tribes/ Non-Tribes, Land particulars - What for ?

Ravitamakam Mandal Scenario:

Cheemalapadu Panchayat

The sixteen habitations: 1. Cheemalapadu 2. Mulakalapalli 3. Kalyanpulova 4. Bangarubanda 5. Kadapeda 6. Jogumpeta 7. Gangampeta 8. Rochupakalu 9.Thatiparti 10. Dokulampadu 11. Kunjarti 12. Valasapalem 13. Ajaypuram 14. Venkatapuram 15.Tamakampeta 16. Jogaripeta Valmiki, Konda Dora and Manne Dora Tribe certificates are issued by the RDO, while Bagata, Khond and Gadaba Tribe certificates are issued by the MRO.

All the scheduled tribes practice settled cultivation, along with minor forest produce collection from the surrounding denuded forests. While there are some economic disparities between Bagata Valmiki, Konda Dora, Manne Dora and the most vulnerable tribes Khond and Gadaba. These two tribal communities are the victims to the non-tribal population compared to the other tribal groups, due to illiteracy and low negotiation skills.

Loss of Autonomy and Non-political Representation

Though there is 90 per cent of tribal population in all the habitations and more than thirteen habitations are 100 per cent tribal population, there is no political representation from the tribes. Few non-tribes are representing the whole Cheemalapadu panchayat of Ravitavakam mandal

PESA is not implemented in these tribal hamlets, as MPTC and ZPTC elected members are from the Non-Tribal members, due to the fact that these villages come under Non Scheduled Areas. In the context of the present Panchayat Raj elections, tribes have no control of governance and are being represented by the Non Tribal members.

Agricultural Land, Land Transfers and Unused Government Lands in Cheemalapdu Panchayat.

The agricultural and non-agricultural lands (houses) can be purchased by the non-tribals in these villages, which is against to the 1/70 Act.

Even a thumb impression of the tribal who own the land is enough to purchase.

All the land disputes are settled in Civil Court Jurisdiction, against Revenue Courts in the Scheduled Areas.

Due to open land deals and any one can purchase lands belonging to Tribals, there is growing number of Touts in these villages who negotiate tribal lands for a cheaper price.

In Scheduled Areas, any government unused land can be given to the tribes either for housing purposes or any commercial development. Videh (2003) reports that despite the categorical legal imperative, land alienation of the tribes in scheduled areas persist, and in large areas of the country it is now endemic. Behura (2006) points out that the Article 19(5) of Indian Constitution safeguards tribal interest in property. While the rights of free movement and residence throughout the territory of India and of acquisition and disposition of property are guaranteed to every citizen, special restrictions may be imposed by the state for protection of the interests of the members of the scheduled tribes under Article 19(5). Unfortunately this constitutional provision is not practiced in these villages.

Non-locals from Z. Bennavaram (8 Kms to Cheemalapadu) encroaching land in Cheemalapadu area by influencing the local non-tribals. There is no mechanism to stop these encroachments.

Position of Jobs in Government Organisations

Government of Andhra Pradesh has a Special Order: In Scheduled Areas, in every Department, some jobs must be given to the Scheduled Tribes.

Educated Youth are denied Jobs in neighbouring scheduled areas.

Unemployment- Frustration – Vulnerability towards joining with extremist groups.

Loan Facilities: Institutional and Non-institutional

In Scheduled Tribal areas, Non-institutional loan arrangements by the private money lenders are guarded from high interest rates and grabbing the agricultural/houses if there is no repayment. Additionally, all the money lenders must register with the MRO.

This is not happening in these Non Scheduled tribal areas, thus tribes who have taken loans from the money lenders are paying high interest rates and are vulnerable to give away their lands.

Loss of Tribal Identity

Due to the presence of non-tribal population and are being influenced by the caste Hindus, tribal customs, norms, mores are being eroded and are being replaced by the mainstream Hindu cultural ethos.

Changes are manifested in marriage system as the Bride Price is replaced by Dowry, Construction of Rama Temple and Unnecessary spending on family functions which are not part of Tribal culture of these tribes.

Additional Issues

These Tribes could not get the jobs assigned to them in the eleven Mandals of Visakhapatnam.

Education facilities are less compared to those of the Scheduled Areas: Tribal Ashram Schools, MPP schools, Government Elementary Schools, Tribal Girls Ashram Schools.

Marriage Alliances are not taking place due to demarcation of Scheduled Areas and Non Scheduled Areas.

Livelihoods are also problem in these areas.

'Rajiv Yuva Kiranalu' jobs in the private sector are given, could not cope with the skills and demands of the private organisations, lag behind and dropped out.

The continuance of the issues in these villages is a grim reminder of the fact that the government functionaries spell out only the symptoms of the issue, but not the underlying socio-political aspects that has crippled the development in these villages.

Alternatives for Inclusive Development of the Scheduled Tribes

Guidelines must be framed to stop land purchase and land grabbing from the non-tribes in these villages with immediate effect.

A separate Cell should be formed within the ITDA to look after the welfare of these tribes in the non scheduled areas.

Ten per cent of fund should be allocated to the tribes of these non scheduled areas within the total budget sanctioned to the ITDA.

Tribal Welfare administration must not only confine to the scheduled tribes in the scheduled areas, they must ensure welfare to the tribes in the non scheduled areas.

Administrative changes are necessary to see the welfare of the scheduled tribes in the non scheduled areas.

Government functionaries must be sensitised about tribal culture, needs and aspirations of the scheduled tribes.

A Committee should look into the various land related issues of the tribes in these villages.

Separate Tribal Girls Hostel should be initiated to encourage tribal girls' education in these villages.

Employability training should be given to the needy youth for these tribes.

Initiatives to curb Malaria and provide adequate healthcare facilities to the scheduled tribes in these villages.

References

Behura, N.K. and Nilakantha Panigrahi (eds) 2006, Tribals and the Indian Constitution, Rawat Publications, Jaipur.

deHaan (1998), 'Social Exclusion' An Alternative Concept for the study Deprivation? IDS Bulletin, 29(1), 10-19.

Madanipour, A., Cars, G., and Allen, J. (Eds.). (2000), Social exclusion in European cities: Processes, experiences, and responses. London: The Stationery Office.

Ministry of Tribal Welfare, Government of India, Report on Scheduled Tribes.

Silver, H. (1994), Social exclusion and social solidarity: Three paradigms. International sLabour Review, 133(5-6), 531-578.

Struggle of Non-Scheduled Adivasis, Association of India's Development, 2013. Retrieved on 28-5-13.

Upadhyay, Videh (2003), Their Lands and Our Laws, India Together Org. Retrieved on 30-5-13.

www.aptribes.gov.in retrieved on 29-5-13.

27

Trends in the Cropping Pattern and It's Impact on the Tribal Households in the Scheduled Areas: A Case Study of Three Scheduled Area Villages from West Godavari District of AP

B Nageswara Rao

Introduction

The inventions of non-tribal population into the tribal areas, the non-tribal lifestyle, production methods, and marketing mechanisms have influenced significantly and the self-sufficient based socio-economic conditions of tribal people have transformed into surplus and market oriented characters, and influenced the cropping pattern in the tribal areas. (Catalyst Management Services Pvt Ltd, 2000; pp.).[1] It leads to more deprivation of the communities and more dependence on non-tribal communities and the State. The changes in the cropping pattern lead to the land alienation in the tribal economy. The dis-economies created due to the changes in the cropping pattern are concerned with more technical which could not understand by the innocent tribal people.

The temporal changes (per cent) in the area share of main crops and crop groups at all India level during 1966-67 to 1996-97 shows that there is tremendous changes in the cropping pattern. The area under cereals (coarse cereals and milets) or under dry cultivation has drastically replaced by the Rice cultivation or wet cultivation (C.R. Hazra, 2000).[2] These trends show that there is continuous surge of diversification in agriculture in terms crops, primarily on economic considerations during post Green Revolution period in India. The changes in the cropping pattern are the outcome of the interactive effect of many factors.

Resource related factors like irrigation, rainfall, soil fertility; technology related factors like seed, fertilizer and water, marketing, storage and processing; household related factors like fodder, self-sufficiency requirements and investment capabilities; price related factors like input and output prices and institutional and infrastructural related factors like farm size, nature and arrangement of tenancy and Government policies etc. (C.R. Hazra, 2000).

But there is another serious problem of food in-security and un-employment has raised in the tribal areas due to chronic declining rate of area under the cultivation of Coarse Cereals, and diversification of Dry cultivation into Wet cultivation, using new technology and HYV seeds became problem in the tribal economy without proper knowledge, training, inputs and infrastructural facilities among tribal farmers in the tribal villages (Mruthyumjaya and Praduman Kumar, 1989 and M.V. Nadakarni, 1986).[3,4] Hence, this study examines the problems and consequences of the changes in the cropping pattern in the tribal economy. This study focuses the changes in terms number of working days, wages and food security among the tribal households of the selected villages. It is a historical study of three villages of Scheduled Area from West Godavari district of Andhra Pradesh.

Three villages are selected for this study from the Scheduled area of West Godavari District of AP. 1. Reddy Ganapavaram from Buttayagudem Mandal (Plain Village), 2. Darbhagudem from Jeelugumilli Mandal (Forest based village) and Reddy Nagampalem (Hill based village) for this study. The sample households are selected randomly through Stratified Sampling method. From Ganapavaram village 78 (16.74 per cent) landholding households are selected out of 466, from Darbhagudem village 34 (25.19 per cent) landholding households are selected out of 135, from Nagampalem 25 (20.16 per cent) landholding households are selected out of 124 randomly in 2005. Total 137 (18.89 per cent) landholding households have selected out of 725 in the three villages. In the West Godavari district Jeelugumilli, Buttayagudem and Polavaram are scheduled mandals. Jeelugumilli and Butyagudem mandals come under excluded area and Polavaram mandal comes under partially excluded area (Tribal Welfare Department, 2002).[5] The situation and existed major occupations among the tribal households in the selected villages in 1932-33.

The changes in the cropping pattern of an economy determine by the nature of the soil and access to water and the nature, attitudes of the economic agents, production methods, and instruments uses by the farming community within the economy. The trends in the cropping pattern in the tribal economy are different from the non-tribal economy. The tribal households collect forest produce for their daily life and material needed for their home and infrastructure. The methods of collection of forest produce and cultivation of food items are traditional and casual but scientific. They are very much attached with the forest and environment. They are self-sufficient but not surplus and market orientated. They maintain barter and share the work, but not wage paid and monetised.

Reddyganapavaram is a semi-forest and plain village, cultivation is the main occupation among the tribal households. They get food grains from cultivation and performing agricultural works provide by the non-tribal farmers in the village. The remaining food and material for shelter collect from the nearby forests. In the case of agricultural labour households the dependency was more on non-tribal farmers for work and they depend on forest for edible roots and fire wood. In the case of Darbhagudem, the situation and nature of the economy is different. Majority of the households were depended on forest resource and they were interested to perform their traditional occupations. They have collected forest produce like Gumkondagogu, Myrabolans, Nuxvomica, Tamarind fruits, Tamarind leaves, Tamarind seed, Pungum seed, Cleaning nuts, Rock bee honey, Marking nuts, Wild brooms, and Amla and other items. They have collected fruits like Jack fruit, Mango, Banana, Papaya, Pine-apple, Water melon, Custard-apple from the forests. Hunting was one of the major occupations among them. Majority of them have collected food and other material and they have used for the self-consumption. Major share of the collected bamboo and fuel wood they used for self-consumption and with reaming bamboo they make baskets, and other agricultural implements to store the produce, to carry seeds, other inputs which uses for agricultural operations. Majority of the forest produce collecting households are depended on basket making and its marketing. Majority of the tribal households they use to take sweet toddy as a main food item in the summer which is un-season for cultivation. They usually practices to collect the forest produce during the months from July to February months. From March to June they depend on sweet toddy and hunting birds and small wild animals of the forest. 95.00 per cent of the households have bamboo baskets which uses to collect the forest produce even today. It shows the level dependency of tribal households on forest produce. 30.00 per cent of the households have arrows which uses for hunting, it shows that hunting is the second occupation among them. Land holding households were less among them.

In the case of Reddynagampalem, the entire structure of the economy is different from other two villages. Ganapavaram and Darbhagudems are revenue villages, whereas Reddynagampalem was a Zamindari village under the control of Hukumpet Zamindar during the pre-independence period. Kondareddi and Koya communities were living together in the village. Among these two communities Kondareddis feel as Kings and superior to other tribal communities. They also feel as superior to Hindu castes people. Basically they prefer hunting, collect forest produce and cultivation. Majority of the households were landholders and but not efficient farmers. They don't prefer to work as labourers in the other non-tribal fields like Koya tribes, and they use the non-tribal labourers in their own fields for cultivation. All the landless households have been practiced hunting Goats, Sheep, Wild boar, Birds, Deers and some of them have practiced fishing. Hunting is two types: 1. Individual hunting and

2. Community or group hunting. Any one or more than one members of the family may perform the activity in the individual hunting which they make for family needs and they hunt birds and small wild animals from the forest. They can claim individual right on such kind of collected or hunted food items. But in the case of community needs like festivals, rituals and traditions, they have to be needed to collect more amount of food and they are needed hunt big animals by a group of experts with the arrows, nets and other materials and they distribute among them equally. Sometimes the share of food also given to the absentee's member of the team or group. They don't claim individual rights for such kind of collected item of food. Majority of the households have been maintaining the arrows and nets which uses for hunting till today in Darbhagudem and Nagampalem. They preferred hunting, fishing and they have used non-tribal labourers for cultivation and household works in Nagampalem. They participate in the non-tribal markets for household's material like cloth, chapels, ornaments, pots, other and agricultural implements.

The Methods of Cultivation among Tribal Farmers in the Selected Villages during Pre-1930s

In Darbhagudem village panchayat hold three Koya tribal gudems namely, Panduvarigudem, Cheemalavarigudem and Thapasivarigudem. Majority of tribal households live in Panduvarigudem. In the Ganapavaram the non-tribal lands are situated very close to the tribal cultivating lands and tribal houses also situated very close to the non-tribal houses in the village. In the Nagampalem, the tribal cultivating lands are situated around the Hill foot and far from the non-tribal lands. In the three villages, the tribal households have cultivated only small millets like Cholam or Korram, Bajra, Ragulu, Varugulu. Mixed crop system they have practiced in Ganapavaram, whereas in Darbhagudem and Nagampalem, they have practiced mono-crop system. In the three villages, they have practiced dry cultivation during pre-1930s. The animal grazing has existed predominantly in Ganapavaram and Nagampalem compared to Darbhagudem. Podu cultivation is two types 1. Individual and 2. Community. In ganapavaram the individual or family type of podu cultivation has practiced by the tribal households, whereas in the Darbhagudem and Nagampalem, the community *podu* cultivation has practiced. In the family or individual cultivation, generally the family members participate in the cultivation and individual or rights may claim for such kind of land and produce which comes from that. It is prevailed in the Ganapavaram where the tribes are very close to non-tribes and they depended on non-tribes.

In the Community or group 'Podu cultivation', a group of people generally male they clean the bushes and trees and they burn the dead trees and plants after falling and cleaning. They till the land with the help of wood tiller and buffalos or axes. The female sow the seeds before when the rain comes, the level of growing germ or sprout depends on the rainfall. The heavy or insufficient rains losses the seeds. They lower level of rainfall helps to fertile the soil and growing the plants healthy in the primitive stage. After 25 to 30 days from the day of seed sowing, the both male and female labourers weed-out once and provide the water to the plants. The ash which comes from the burning of the trees and plants used as best pesticide to protect the growing plants. They use animal dung as best fertiliser to the crop. Generally they cultivate each plot of land or area for 15 to 20 years. After 20 years they go for cleaning another plot for cultivation either it may be individual plot or community plot.

The average size of the holding under Podu cultivation was noted higher in Hill based and forest based villages like Nagampalem and Darbhagudem, whereas it was lower in Ganapavaram where they have practiced mono-crop system. The extent of area under podu cultivation is noted as low in the plain village like Ganapavaram, where they practiced individual podu cultivation with mixed crop system during pre-1930s. The duration of shifting gap from one plot to another is also varying by cropping pattern and access to irrigation. The duration between old plot and new plot was more as 20 years in the case of mixed crop system, whereas it was less as 10-15 years in the case of mono-crop system. Due to this, the extent of area under podu cultivation has noticed more in the forest based and Hill based villages compared to plain villages during pre-1930s. After many years, they may come back to the old plot which has cultivated before. This process continued to the generations. The gap duration between one plot to another has been declining from 15 years to 10 years during 1930 to 1950. As a result of this, the extent of area under Podu cultivation is noted more in 1950. And this type of cultivation has declined in 1970.

The Status of Food Security and Livelihoods

The status of food security is determined on the basis of access to food or food material and drinking water. The status of food security was very low among tribal households during pre-1930s due to heavy dependency on forest resources. They could not collect food material (fruits and vegetables) from the forest during the time of floods and heavy rains but only small animals, fruits and roots. They have been facing problems from the forest department officials. Both the Revenue officials and Forest officials' collects assessment or taxes and fines from the tribal households who collect the forest produce. The economic advantages were low due to migrating nature and Podu-cultivation among the tribal households.

Development of Irrigation Facilities and Change in Cropping Pattern in Reddyganavaram during 1930-50

The tribal farmers have practiced mono-crop system with the help of Sivudu Cheruvu which was based on the rain-fed but whereas the non-tribes have practiced mixed crop and rotation crop system. In the tribal farming, cereals crop has occupied the extent of 26.20 per cent 43.20 acres (26.20 per cent). Small millets like Cholam, Ragi, Samai, Varugu, Bajra and others were the major among the cereals. Pulses crop was occupied in the extent 25.60 acres (15.50 per cent), Condiments and Spices were occupied in the extent of 26.70 acres (16.20 per cent), Topes were in the extent of 25.80 acres (15.60 per cent), Drugs and Narcotics were in the extent of 30.00 acres (18.20 per cent) and Industrial crops were in the extent of 6.60 acres (4.00 per cent). Cereals, Drugs and Narcotics, Topes, Condiments and Spices were the major crops cultivated by the tribal farmers in 1933. Redgram and Horsegram were the major crops among pulses. Only castor is noted among industrial crops. Plantains were major among vegetables, only fruit trees are noted among Topes, Tobacco is noted among Drugs and Narcotics. Leafy crops are also noted among vegetable in Ganapavaram in1933 (R.S.R., 1933).[6] The cultivation of Black Paddy was very difficult to the tribal famers. This crop has introduced by the non-tribal farmers in the village. The demand for Cholam has declined in the non-tribal market due introduction of the new crop in the village. The tribal famers have also habituated to cultivate the Black Paddy; but the productivity among tribal farmers was low compared to non-tribal farmers, because they are not efficient in cultivation of wet crop. Some of the tribal farmers have preferred to leased-out their land to non-tribes instead of cultivating black paddy. Some of them are leased-out to non-tribal farmers. And the dependency on non-tribal farmers and non-tribal market has increased among the tribal farmers to learn the methods of cultivation and marketing their produce in the village market.

During 1930-50, the demand for tribal land has increased due to increase in the irrigation facilities (widening Jilleti Canal) and the conversion of tribal dry crop cultivation land into wet crop cultivation. The extent of cereals cultivation area has increased from 26.20 per cent in 1933 to 40.90 per cent in 1950 among tribal farmers in Reddyganapavaram. One more trend has noticed that some of the non-tribal holdings were situated around the Sivudu Cheruvu and major share of their holdings were situated at a little more distance from the Sivudu Cheruvu. The non-tribal lands get water after the tribal lands were using only, this situation was very difficult to the non-tribal farmers. The demand for tribal lands has increased by having easy access to water. The non-tribal farmers have purchased the major share of the land during 1930 to 1950.

Change in Cropping Pattern in Darbhagudem during 1930-1950

The number of tribal landholding households is noted as 18 in Darbhagudem village. They owned 20 land holdings with the extent of 170.70 acres in 1933. If observe the cropping pattern among the tribal farmers, Cereals has occupied the extent of area 38.60 per cent (59.20 acres), Topes 15.70 per cent (24.00 acres), Condiments and spices 12.40 per cent (22.30 acres) and Drugs and Narcotics 11.90 per cent (18.20 acres) as major crops to the total operational area (RSR-1933).[7]

Tribal gudems are situated besides the Aswarao peta vagu (canal. Tribes have stated that small canals have dig by their fore-fathers. But most of the non-tribal lands are situated around the canal and Pond in 1933. In the rainy season the Pond gets full of water and would be sufficient for a single crop to the extent of nearly 200.00 acres to the surrounding area. But the tribal farmers are not able to get water. Under these conditions the tribal farmers were cultivating rain-fed crops like Cholam, Ragi for food, Tamarind, Fruits and Castor. But the Aswararo pets Vagu has widen during 1933-50 by the Government, the extent of irrigated area has increased among both tribes and non-tribal farmers in the village. The percentage of area occupied by Cholam, Ragi, Varugu crops have declined and that has replaced by Black Paddy among Cereals in Darbhagudem during 1933-50. But the trend was reverse to what happened in Ganapavaram. The tribal households in Darbhagudem did not attracted towards wet cultivation due to increasing irrigation facilities but they have continued dry cultivation and bended towards collection of MFP again during 1950-70. When the tribal households had alternative opportunities in the form of forest resources, they have diverted to easy crops or dry crops again and they have avoided dependency on non-tribal farmers in Darbhagudem. But some of the tribal farmers, they have leased-out their land to non-tribal farmers. The demand for tribal land has increased due to increasing irrigation and the neighbour non-tribal farmers have purchased and occupied the tribal land during the same period. The tribal famers have been alienated 25.30 acres of land to non-tribals during the same period.

Change in Cropping Pattern in Reddynagampalem during 1930-1950

Among the selected landholding households, they had 11 holdings with the extent of 84.70 acres in 1920. But they have operated 69.90 acres and remaining 23.50 acres were leased-out to the non-tribal farmers (Survey -2005).[8] The percentage of cereals cultivated area is noted as 41.80 per cent (28.90 acres), Condiments and Spices is noted as 27.50 per cent (19.00 acres) and Topes is noted as 19.20 per cent (13.30 acres) to the total operated area in Nagampalem in 1920. Among Cereals, Cholam, Ragi and Varugu have been cultivated and Cholam was the main food crop. Among Condiments and Spices, Turmeric and Tamarind are noted and Tamarind was the major crop. Only fruit trees are noted as major crop among Topes in 1920. Only one Panta Kaluva (Government canal) was situated in the fields of the village and most of the tribal lands are situated at the bank of the canal, which comes from the hills. Among cereals, the cholam and ragi cultivated areas were occupied as major shares, among Condiments and spices tamarind and castor, among topes, tamarind and other fruit trees except mango have drastically decreased and that was replaced by food crops like cholam and ragi have replaced. The extent of ownership land declined from 84.70 acres to the extent of tribal land has alienated 52.40 acres during 1920 to 1950. The operating land also declined from 69.20 acres to 32.80 acres during the same period. The Black Paddy has not introduced in the Nagampalem.

The Kondareddi community used the non-tribal labour force; among them SCs used for agriculture, other OBC communities used for both agricultural labour and household labour services. The Kondareddi landholders did not pay either money or kind as remuneration for their services, but a piece of land as annual payment to all the catgories of non-tribal labourers. Kondareddi tribal landholders have paid in-terms of land of 1.40 acres as annual payment to Barber and Washer man during 1933-50. This was a different situation taken place in Nagampalem. But in the same village the Koya community did not used the services of non-tribal labour for household activities. But they also took the help of SCs for agricultural works. This was the one of the main reason to alienate major share of land, and changes in the cropping pattern by non-tribal farmers in the tribal areas was the second reason.

Changes in the State of Food Security during 1933-50

The tribal households have been performing their traditional occupations like collection of NTFM, Hunting, fishery, animal husbandry, Animal grazing but Podu cultivation also significantly increased during 1930-50. Due to the declaration of productive forests as reserved forests by the British Government of India, the dependency of land and cultivation has increased. The state of food security has improved during the same period. The access to food grains (cholam, ragi and varugulu) has improved and substituted in the place of roots and other forest food. The state of livelihood also improved in terms of no. of working days, collecting and producing of food and others. But the extent of land alienation also increased by the more involvement non-tribal into the affairs of tribal economy. The dependency on non-tribes has also increased particularly in Ganapavaram where the tribes are very closely situated with the non-tribes. The economic advantages were low but better compared to the previous conditions. But state of food security was un-certain due to land alienation during the same period.

Changes in Cropping Pattern in Ganapavaram during 1950-51 to 1970-71

The extent of operated area has declined from 101.30 to 75.30 acres during 1950-70 in Ganapavaram. They have cultivated two crops in a year, cereals have cultivated in kharif season and dry crops like pulses, condiments and Spice, Industrial crops, and Topes have cultivated in rabi season in 1970 among tribal farmers in the village. The percentage of extent of cereals cultivated area has increased from 40.90 per cent (41.45 acres) in 1950 to 74.80 per cent (56.30 acres) in 1970, the percentage of extent of area of remaining all other have declined significantly. Because, the population pressure, non-access to forest produce are one side, the land alienation is another side, they created food insecurity among tribal households, they gave more priority to food crops like cereals. The extents of cultivating area of ragi, varugu have declined significantly, cholam area also declined and replaced by white paddy during the same period. The percentage of pulses cultivated area also decreased from 8.21 per cent (20.81 acres) to 9.70 per cent (7.31 acres) during the same period. The extent of topes, condiments and spices cultivated area declined significantly due to dry land conversion into wet land by increasing irrigation facilities during the same period.

The tribal farmers have borrowed money for cultivation of wet crop like black paddy at higher rate of interest. The cost of cultivation has increased due to habituating using more inputs and instruments and labour, but the returns were noted as low compared to non-tribal farmers. They also borrowed money for purchasing animals like sheep, goats, buffaloes and cows from non-tribes during the same period. In this practice, the ideas of non-tribal farmers have played major role because, the tribal farmers are very close to non-tribes in not only economic activities but also in performing social and religious events and activities in Ganapavaram. With the result of this, they could not repay the debt and lost their land to repay the debt and it has been lead to large scale of land alienation in the village.

Changes Cropping Pattern in Darbhgudem during 1950-51 to 1970-71

Two small canals were constructed. One is from Jeelugummilli and another one from Chinthalapudi mandal during this period. These two canals are rain fed canals and can facilitate the irrigation for 250 acres in rainy season. Aswaraopet vagu and Dirisinam Varikunta are the other irrigational sources. The surrounding tribal lands of Vagu and Kunta have been alienated during 1950-70. Then small canals have become main source for tribes. On the other hand the non-tribes have started using bore-well or motor pump-sets for irrigation for second crop, whereas tribes could not have bore-wells or motor pump-sets. The percentage of extent of Cereals cultivating area has increased from 60.67 per cent to 62.62 per cent during 1950-70 in Darbhagudem. Among cereals, cholam, ragi, varugu and samai crops have declined and replaced by black paddy during 1950-70. The percentage of area under Black Paddy has increased from Zero per cent to 7.79 per cent (2.05 acres) during the same period.

They exchange Tamarind with money or other agricultural implements which are needed for "Podu cultivation". The Podu cultivation was started to transform into settled cultivation among tribes by the interference of and interactions with non-tribes. It is connected with the nature of land rights. The village community property right has transformed into individual property right. The changing cropping pattern was one of the reasons to change the ownership pattern of land among tribes during 1950-51 to 1970-71.

Changes Cropping Pattern in Nagampalem during 1950-51 to 1970-71

The irrigation facilities were same during 1950-70 in Nagampalem. The extent of operating area has declined from 35.60 acres to 28.10 acres during 1950-70. The percentage of cereals cultivating area was almost same, but the percentage of area under pulses has declined from 22.47 per cent to 14.59 per cent, the percentage of area under condiments and Spices has also declined from 11.24 per cent to 7.12 per cent during the same period. But the area under industrial crops has increased from 5.62 per cent to 10.68 per cent. The area under topes also has increased from Zero to 7.12 per cent to the total Operating area during 1950-70 in Nagampalem.

Among cereals, the percentage of extent of area under cholam has declined from 70.23 per cent to 62.35 per cent; the area under varugu has declined from 17.59 per cent to 8.65 per cent to the total cereals cultivating area. But the area under ragi crop has increased slightly. The population has increased in one hand, the land alienation has continued on the other and the average size of the per-capita land has declined.

Changes in the Methods of Cultivation during 1950-51 to 1970-71

During this period many major changes have taken place, the shifting cultivation has transformed into settled cultivation is one of the major event. The identification of land right was very much difficult to the local administrators during the previous period, when the tribal farmers have practiced shifting cultivation, but it was easy during 1950-70. And the imposition of land assessment also became clear on whom to impose by the administrator. The individual rights (family right) on a particular piece of land which is cultivated by a tribal family under Podu cultivation could be recognised by the tribal community but it is difficult to the outside community or non-tribal administrator or outside individuals of the tribal community. These difficulties have been overcome by the habituating settled cultivation among tribal farmers during 1950-70.

One more change has noted the practice of traditional methods of cultivation which were used in the cultivation of millets (cholam, ragi and sajjalu) is adapted to the cultivation of black paddy as well as White Paddy during 1950-70. The practice of eco-friendly methods of pest-control and fertilizers has continued in the cultivation of paddy also. But on the other non-tribal farmers have started using new technology (bio-chemical and mechanical) in the cultivation of paddy.

Changes in the State of Food Security during 1950-51 to 1970-71

The state of food security was moderate during 1950-51 and 1970-71. There was recognition of right of land ownership and improvement of alternative occupations like animal husbandry helped in satisfying the needs of agriculture and as well as household. The practice of grazing animals at will is transformed into occupation and became essential to the tribal community for assistance in terms of work and money, when the bartered economy has transformed into semi-money economy. It is easy to transform the surplus (savings) into non-movable permanent assets in the money economy. And increasing land assets provide food security. The dependency on non-tribal farmers also has increased among tribal farmers. These changes have helped the tribal communities to improve the relations with other communities, but at the same time it has made the hurdles, insecure, exploitation and land alienation in the tribal economy. The range of negative effects was more in the Ganapavaram, where the tribes are very closely situated to non-tribes compared to other villages where the tribal households are situated isolated during 1950-70. The external and internal economies have declined due to transformation of economic landholdings into non-economic holdings due to hereditary transfers and land transfers. The state of food security was better in isolated villages like Nagampalem and Darbhgudem and which has forest base compared to semi-plain village like Ganapavaram.

Changes in the Cropping Pattern in Ganapavaram during 1970-71 to 1990-1991

The extent of ownership land has declined from 80.10 acres in 1970-71 to 72.50 acres in 1990-91; the extent of operating area also has declined from 75.30 acres to 70.60 acres during the same period. The percentage share of cereals cultivating area has increased from 74.80 per cent in 1970-71 to 76.50 per cent to the total operating area. Among cereals, the percentages of extent area under black paddy, cholam and ragi have declined but the percentage or extent of area under white paddy has increased significantly from 4.44 per cent in 1970-71 to 62.43 per cent in 1990-91 to the total operating area under cereals in Ganapavaram. Varugu and Samai crops have disappeared during the same period. Among the food grains, White paddy and blackgram have become major crops in the tribal economy, cholam. varugu, ragi and black paddy have disappeared during 1970-71 and 1990-91 in Ganapavaram.

Changes in the Cropping Pattern in Darbhagudem during 1970-71 to 1990-1991

The extent of owned area has declined from 75.30 acres in 1970-71 to 60.10 acres in 1990-91, but the extent of operating area has increased from 42.00 acres to 45.00 acres during the same period. It shows that the extent of leased-out land has decreased in Darbhagudem. If see the trends in the cropping pattern, the percentage of extent of area under cereals has increased from 62.60 per cent to 69.10 per cent; the area under pulses has increased from 12.40 per cent to 34.40 per cent (rabi season); the area under Industrial crops has also increased from 7.6 per cent to 21.60 per cent in rabi season and 16.00 per cent in rabi season during the same period But the percentage of area under condiments and spice and topes has declined significantly during the same period.

Among the cereals, the percentage of area under cholam has declined from 68.14 per cent in 1970-71 to 6.82 per cent in 1990-91, the area under ragi has increased from 8.89 per cent to 11.09 per cent, the area under varugu has disappeared and replaced by the new crop Maize with the percentage area of 4.60 to the total area under Cereals during the same period in the Darbhagudem. Among the industrial crops, the percentage of area under castor had disappeared and replaced by Sugarcane 45.83 per cent, and other 54.17 per cent to the total area under Industrial crops during 1970-71 to 1990-91 in Darbhagudem.

Changes in the Cropping Pattern in Nagampalem during 1970-71 to 1990-91

The total ownership land has declined from 35.10 acres in 1970-71 to 24.30 acres in 1990-91. The extent of operating area has declined from 29.20 acres to 23.10 acres during the same period. The ownership land has declined due to land alienation and the operated land has declined due to leased-out the land to non-tribal farmers in the Nagamapalem village in 1990-91. The percentage area under cereals has declined from 60.50 per cent to 59.30 per cent the percentage of land under condiments and Spices also has declined from 7.10 per cent to 4.30 per cent, but the percentage of area under pulses has increased from 22.50 per cent to 23.80 per cent, the area under industrial crops has increased from 10.70 per cent to 21.60 per cent, the area under topes also has increased from 7.10 per cent to 10.40 per cent to the total Operating area during 1970-71 to 1990-91 in Nagampalem. Somewhat a new trend has noted in Nagamapalem that is the area under Topes and Industrial crops has increased, whereas in Ganapavaram and Darbhagudem it has declined. The area under Cereals has declined in Nagampalem but in the other two villages it has increased during 1970-71 to 1990-91. Because, the Nagampalem is Hill based village, and less irrigated compared to other two villages. The tribal farmers could not transform themselves as completely wet cultivable and still they have been performing their traditional occupations like hunting and fishing.

Among cereals, the percentage of area under cholam has declined from 62.35 per cent to 15.47 per cent, it has replaced by White Paddy from Zero per cent to 49.64 per cent; the percentage of area under ragi has increased from 13.76 to 24.45 per cent; the varugu crop has disappeared and it is replaced by maize by 10.44 per cent to the total cultivating area under cereals among the tribal farmers during 1970-71 to 1990-91 in Nagampalem. The tribal farmers have been continuing their traditional eco-friendly methods of cultivation during 1970-71 to 1990-91, but the neighbour non-tribal farmers have started using technology and machinery, HYV seeds, chemical fertilizers and pesticides during the same period. The power of chemical pesticides and fertilisers are generally high compared to traditional objects. If a neighbour non-tribal farmer applies the chemical objects for pest-control, the pests shift from that particular holding to neighbour holding which did not have or apply the chemical pesticide. Generally majority of the non-tribal famers are habituated to apply the chemical fertilisers and pesticides within a week or two weeks, the pest automatically shifts to the tribal holdings, which have applied traditional methods of pest-control and fertilisers. It leads to loss of crops among tribal farmers. By this kind of practice, the resistance power of pests has improved and could not control by the traditional objects. The tribal farmers also need to be using the same chemical pesticides and fertilisers. These conditions made the tribe to use chemicals which are new to them and don't know about the name, Brand and function of the Pesticide. It has lead to depend on non-tribal pesticide and fertiliser shopholders and sellers. The tribal farmers also cheated by shop holders through selling duplicate brands and chemicals. This is one of the reasons to increase the cost of cultivation among the tribal farmers in 1990-91 in Ganapavaram and Darbhagudem. This impact was low in Nagampalem.

Changes in the Food Security among Tribal Households during 1970-71 to 1990-91

The state of food security is noted as low, it has declined from state moderate in 1970-71 to state low in 1990-91 in the three villages. It is determined on the basis of access to food grains, access to work for food and other related parameters have taken to compare the state of food security during a period of time. During 1970-71 to 1990-91, the state of food security has come down or worst among tribal households, because the average size of holding has declined from 3.64 acres to 0.55 acre in Ganapavaram, from 3.58 acres to 1.77 acres in Darbhagudem and from 0.92 acre to 0.45 acre in Nagampalem during the same period. Most of the economic holdings have transformed into non-economic holdings by both hereditary transfers and land alienation. The marginal cost of cultivation has increased to highest level among the tribal farmers due to adaptation of technology (bio-chemical). Among the agricultural labour households, some of the labourers have transformed into farm servants (un-secure and lowest wage), and majority of agricultural labourers shifted from usual status to usual subsidiary status during the same period. The per capita production of food grains also noted very low in 1990-91 compared to 1970-71. The per capita household's debt, cost of cultivation and incidence of poverty also increased during the same period. These are the main reasons to decline the state of food security during 1970-71 to 1990-91 in the three villages, the condition was more severe in Nagampalem (lack of land) and Ganapavaram (non-tribal exploitation on tribes). The conditions of tribal households were worsen during this period due to lack of access to forest resources (due to expansion of reserve forests) in one hand and cultivating land on the other (due to land alienation) But by the strong democratic tribal movements during 1990-91 to 2005, the tribal households could be able to restore some of the alienated land and socio-economic conditions have changed positively at significant level.

The Changes in the Cropping Pattern in Ganapavaram during 1990-91 to 2005

The extent of ownership land has increased from 72.50 acres in 1990-91 to 148.20 acres in 2005, and the extent of operating area is noted as same, because they did not leased-out their land to the non-tribal farmers in Ganapavaram during 1990-91 to 2005. The percentage of extent of area under Cereals has declined but the extent of area has increased from 54.00 acres in 1990-91 to 101.50 acres in 2005. The percentage of extent area under pulses has increased from 6.40 per cent to 30.50 per cent; the percentage of extent of area under condiments and Spices increased from 6.40 per cent to 10.50 per cent; the percentage of area under Industrial crops also increased from 13.60 per cent to 15.90 per cent during the same period. The area under major categories of crops has increased during this period due to restoration of alienated land.

Among Cereals, the percentage of area under millets like cholam, ragi, varugu and cereals like black paddy has disappeared, and it is replaced by white paddy during 1990-91 to 2005. The percentage of area under white paddy has increased from 62.43 per cent to 83.98 per cent; Maize area has increased from 2.65 per cent to 10.33 in Kharif and 14.90 per cent to the total area under cereals in rabi seasons during the same period. Among pulses, the percentage of area under blackgram has increased from 4.50 per cent to 25.65 per cent (Rabi); the area under redgram has increased from 3.30 per cent to 10.36 per cent. And area other pulses also increased from 4.50 per cent to 9.19 per cent during the same period in Ganapavaram. Among Industrial crops, the percentage area under cotton and sugarcane has increased significantly, and new crop groundnut has introduced during the same period. But the growth rate of area under Cereals and Pulses is noted more compared to Industrial and other crops area during 1990-91 to 2005 in Ganapavaram.

The Changes in the Cropping Pattern in Darbhagudem during 1990-91 to 2005

The ownership land has increased from 60.10 acres to 210.60 acres and the extent of operating area also has increased at the same extent during 1990-91 to 2005 in Darbhagudem. Here, also tribal landholder did not leased-out to non-tribal farmers during the same period. The percentage of area under cereals has declined from 69.10 per cent to 58.70 per cent; the percentage area under pulses and industrial crops also declined, but the percentage of area under Topes has increased from 5.10 per cent to 19.10 per cent during the same period in Darbhagudem. The extent area under cereals and pulses also significantly increased, but it shows low in percentage in 2005 due to higher base in the base year 1990-91.

Among cereals, the percentage of area under cholam, ragi and varugu has disappeared and it is replaced by white paddy. The area under white paddy has increased from 77.49 per cent in 1990-91 to 86.84 per cent in 2005. The area under maize has increased from 4.60 per cent to 8.90 per cent to the total area under cereals in Darbhagudem. Among Pulses, the extent of are under blackgram, redgram and other pulses also has increased during the same period. But the percentage of area is shows as lower in 2005 due to higher base value of the base year 1990-91. Among Industrial crops, the percentage of area under sugarcane, cotton has declined and extent of area under the same crops could not get much change except the area under other pulses in Darbhagudem during 1990-91 to 2005. Here, a new trend that is the importance to the food crops has increased compared to Industrial crops during this period. The profits and revenue from cultivation of Industrial crops became uncertain, noted heavy cost of cultivation and led to increased debt among tribal farmers due more borrowings at higher rate of interests from the non-institutional sources. The price fluctuations are more for the production of Industrial crops compared to food crops. And the average cost of cultivation is also noted low for food crops during the same period.

The Changes in the Cropping Pattern in Nagampalem during 1990-91 to 2005

The extent of ownership land has increased from 24.30 acres in 1990-91 to 50.00 acres in 2005. The operating area also has increased from 23.10 acres to 50.00 acres during the same period in Nagampalem. The percentage of area under cereals has increased from 59.30 to 78.40; the area under Industrial crops also increased from 15.20 per cent to 30.20 per cent in Rabi season; the percentage of area under Condiments and Spices also increased during the same period. But the percentage of area under Pulses and Topes has declined during the same period.

Among Cereals, Black Paddy, Ragi, Varugu and Cholam crops have moved out and White Paddy is replaced. The percentage of area cultivated under White Paddy has increased from 49.64 per cent to 68.72 per cent to the total area under Cereals during the same period. Among Pulses, the percentage of area under Blackgram has declined from 56.36 per cent to 44.78 per cent to the total area under Pulses; but the percentage of area under Redgram and other pulses has increased during same period. Among the industrial crops, the percentage of area under Sugarcane and other industrial crops has declined, but it is replaced by Groundnut. The percentage of area under Groundnut is noticed as 56.52 per cent to the total area under Industrial crops.

Changes in the Methods of Cultivation in the Selected Villages during 1990-91 to 2005

The alienated land has restored successfully in the Darbhagudem and some of the land in Ganapavaram and Nagampalem during 1990-91 to 2005.

The average size of the operational holding among the tribal farmers. The average size of the operational holding has increased a little due to restoration of alienated land. The average size of the household has increased from 0.60 acre to 0.95 acre in Ganapavaram; from 0.85 acre to 3.10 acres in Dabhagudem; and from 0.49 acre to 0.81 acre in Nagampalem during 1990-91 to 2005. The single crop system has changed into double crops both Kharif and Rabi in a agricultural year. Majority of food crops are cultivated in Kharif season and majority of Industrial crops are cultivated in Rabi season in 2005.

The most important change among all, the cost of cultivation has increased significantly by adopting new technology and using chemical fertlisers and pesticides. The demand for chemicals and machinery instruments has increased in the tribal economy. Tribal farmers are habituated both wet crops and as well as dry crops, even though, they are not efficient in wet cultivation.

Changes in the State of Food Security during 1990-91 to 2005

The state of food security has improved from lower stage to moderate stage during 1990-91 to 2005 in the selected villages. They could be able to restored alienated land through movements and the average size of the holding has improved a little. The extent of cereals and pulses cultivated area has increased more than double in the three villages. The white paddy cultivating area also has increased significantly with the constant returns. Majority of the landless agricultural labourers are access to agricultural works and get minimum earning for the existence of life. They did not leased-out their lands to non-tribes and completely cultivating by themselves. The permanent and annual farm servants have transformed into daily wage labourers, majority of usual subsidiary labourers have transformed into usual daily wage labourers due increase in average number of working days among tribal agricultural labour households in the three villages. It is noted more in Darbhagudem due to restoration of highest extent of alienated land during 1990-91 to 2005. Actually, the state of food security has to be highest among tribal households during the post-restoration period, but it is noted as moderate due to lowest net incomes, highest cost of cultivation, highest debt among tribal farmers and still the Industrial crops are occupied significant extent of area and the growth rate of extent of area is noted highest for Industrial crops during 1990-91 to 2005 in the three villages. Particularly, the majority share of the land is not suitable for wet crop in Darbhagudem and Nagampalem which has restored to tribal farmers. But some of the holdings have bore facility.

Main Findings

- An increase in the irrigation and transport facilities in the scheduled areas led to the increase in demand for tribal lands in the non-tribal land market and it has led to massive land alienation.

• An increase in the irrigation facilities influenced the cropping pattern; the small millets and course cereals have been changed into rice, wheat and other pulses which are unknown to the tribal people.

• The tribal farmers felt uncomfort and difficult in the cultivation of rice and commercial crops and it led increase in the leased-out status among the tribal farmers. Major share of the land has leased-out to non-tribal farmers.

• The status of food security among the tribal households has come down due to changes in the cropping pattern from core cereals to rice and other commercial crops.

• The majority of the tribal farmers borrowed money at higher rate of interest from the non-tribal traders and landlords and it has led to fallen in debt trap and increasing poverty among tribal households.

• Most of the tribal farmers have transformed into farm servants and agricultural labourers in their own field in the process of clearing the debts.

• The tribal economy has forcibly transformed from barter to monetary; self-sufficient to surplus by the pressures of the non-tribal farmers, traders and administrators in the tribal areas or Scheduled areas.

Suggestions

• The tribal villages which are included in or merged with the non-tribal villages and Gram Panchayats in the Scheduled areas should be excluded from them and must be reorganised as tribal gram panchayats.

• The tribal villages should be recognised as gram panchayats to habituate institutional system of governance and leadership among the tribal people.

• The Government should take action against violation of LTR Acts 1959 and 1970. The alienated land should be restored in the tribal villages.

• The government officials should prepare the precautions and guidelines to the local authority to restrict the violation of tribal rights, controlling money lending, exploitation of tribal labourers and exclusion of tribal farmers from the availing service of the government.

• The government should provide training to the tribal people on survey, availing baking, educational and other government services.

• The government officials should give priority in providing their services in the Scheduled area or tribal areas.

• The government also should educate the non-tribals to understand the rights of the tribal people and importance of their participation for the development of society as a whole.

Notes

1. Catalyst Management Services Pvt. Ltd, (2000). Impact Assessment of Agriculture Interventions in Tribal areas in MP–Final report.

2. C.R. Hazra (2000), "Crop Diversification in India, Agriculture Commissioner.

3. Mruthyumjaya and Praduman Kumar (1989), "Economics of cropping pattern," Economic and Political Weekly, Vol. 24, No. 51/52 (Dec. 23-30), pp. A159-A161 and A169-A166.

4. Nadakarni, M.V. (1986), "Backward crops in Indian Agriculture: Economy of Coarse Cereals and Pulses, Economic and Political Weekly, Vol. 21, No. 38/39 (Sep. 20-27), pp. A113-A115 and A117-A118.

5. Tribal Welfare Department (1997-98), Annual Report of the Governor on the Administration of Scheduled Areas in AP.

6. R.S.R. (1932-33), Reddyganapavaram village, Government press, Madras Presidency, Madras.

7. R.S.R. (1933), Darbhagudem Village, Government press, Madras Presidency, Madras.

8. Household data (2005), Land registration details, sub-registrar, Kovvur Taluk and MRO, Polavaram.

References

1. C.R. Hazra (2000), Crop diversification in India, Agriculture Commissioner, Department of Agriculture and Co-operation, Ministry of Agriculture, Krishi Bhavan, New Delhi.

2. Catalyst Management Services Pvt. Ltd., (2000). Impact Assessment of Agriculture Interventions in Tribal areas in MP-Final report.

3. Mruthyumjaya and Praduman Kumar (1989), Economics of cropping pattern.

4. Nadakarni, M.V. (1986), Backward crops in Indian Agriculture: Economy of Coarse Cereals and pulses.

5. Tribal Welfare Department (1997-98), Annual Report of the Governor on the Administration of Scheduled Areas in AP.

Table- 27.1: Trends in the Cropping Pattern in Reddyganapavaram during 1933 and 2005

Name of Crop	2005		1990		1970		1950	1933
	Kharif	*Rabi*	*Kharif*	*Rabi*	*Kharif*	*Rabi*	*Kharif*	*Kharif*
Cereals	101.5	21.3	54		56.3		41.45	43.2
Pulses	11.6	45.2	3.3	4.5	14.7	7.31	20.81	25.6
Condiments and spices	15.1	15.6	3.7	4.5		2	17.38	26.7
Industrial	14.2	23.5	9.6	9.67	4.3	0	8.21	6.6
Vegetables		12.3						7.2
Topes		11.2		3.6		2	13.45	25.8
Drugs and Narcotics	5.8							30
All	148.2	129.1	70.6	22.27	75.3	11.31	101.3	165.1
	Percentage to the total operated area respectively (priod-wise)							
Cereals	68.5	16.5	76.5	0.0	74.8	0.0	40.9	26.2
Pulses	7.8	35.0	4.7	20.2	19.5	64.6	20.5	15.5
Condiments and spices	10.2	12.1	5.2	20.2	0.0	17.7	17.2	16.2
Industrial	9.6	18.2	13.6	43.4	5.7	0.0	8.1	4.0
Vegetables	0.0	9.5	0.0	0.0	0.0	0.0	0.0	4.4
Topes	7.6	8.7	5.1	16.2	0.0	17.7	13.3	15.6
Drugs and Narcotics	3.9	0.0	0.0	0.0	0.0	0.0	0.0	18.2
All	100.0	100.0	100.0	100.0	100.0	100.0	100.0	100.0

Table 27.2: Changes in the Percapita Food Grains (in kgs) in Ganapavaram

	2005	*1990*	*1970*	*1950*	*1933*
Population	486	434.5	255	94.5	42
Black Paddy	0.0	11.4	27.2	9.7	0.0
White Paddy	338.1	112.5	8.8	0.0	0.0
Cholam	0.0	24.8	96.4	160.9	330.3
Ragi	0.0	8.9	15.6	43.9	110.7
Samai	0.0	0.0	10.7	16.3	40.8
Varugu	0.0	0.0	9.4	12.3	44.4
Maize	76.2	3.1	8.2	10.3	31.2
Others	29.6	0.0	7.5	8.1	0.0
Millets	109.7	35.4	143.2	252.6	565.7
All	439.0	137.3	180.8	270.1	565.7

Table 27.3: Trends in the Cropping Pattern in Darbhagudem during 1933

	2005		*1990*		*1970*		*1950*	*1933*
Name of Crop	*Kharif*	*Rabi*	*Kharif*	*Rabi*	*Kharif*	*Rabi*	*Kharif*	*Kharif*
Cereals	123.6		31.1		26.3		45.9	59.2
Pulses		51.3		15.5	5.2	3	10.2	19
Condiments and spices	16	22.45	2		4		4.2	22.3
Industrial	26	30.1	9.6	7.2	3.2	2		6.5
Vegetables		5						4
Topes	40	5.5	2.3		3.3	2	13.4	24
Drugs and Narcotics	5						5.2	18.2
All	210.6	114.35	45	22.7	42	7	78.9	153.2
Percentage to the total operated area respectively (period-wise)								
Cereals	58.7	0.0	69.1	0.0	62.6	0.0	58.2	38.6
Pulses	0.0	24.4	0.0	34.4	12.4	7.1	12.9	12.4
Condiments and spices	7.6	10.7	4.4	0.0	9.5	0.0	5.3	14.6
Industrial	12.3	14.3	21.3	16.0	7.6	4.8	0.0	4.2
Vegetables	0.0	2.4	0.0	0.0	0.0	0.0	0.0	2.6
Topes	19.0	2.6	5.1	0.0	7.9	4.8	17.0	15.7
Drugs and Narcotics	2.4	0.0	0.0	0.0	0.0	0.0	6.6	11.9
All	100.0	54.3	100.0	50.4	100.0	16.7	100.0	100.0

Table 27.4: Changes in the Percapita Food Grains (in kgs) in Darbhagudem

	2005	*1990*	*1970*	*1950*	*1933*
Popua	306	265	182	95	49
Black Paddy	0.0	0.0	6.8	0.0	0.0
White Paddy	408.6	80.4	0.0	0.0	0.0
Cholam	0.0	5.1	59.7	202.1	369.5
Ragi	0.0	6.7	6.9	43.9	183.3
Samai	0.0	0.0	0.0	19.1	42.4
Varugu	0.0	0.0	4.2	14.0	69.9
Maize	36.5	3.1	0.0	0.0	0.0
Others	21.1	0.0	7.5	8.1	79.4
Millets	58.0	15.2	75.1	282.7	758.3
All	598.1	93.3	96.1	343.4	910.0

Table 27.5: Trends in the Cropping Pattern in Reddynagampalem during 1920 and 2005

Name of Crop	*2005*		*1990*		*1970*	*1950*	*1933*
	Kharif	*Rabi*	*Kharif*	*Rabi*	*Kharif*	*Kharif*	*Kharif*
Cereals	39.2		13.7		17	21.6	28.9
Pulses		9.2	1	5.5	4.1	8	4
Condiments and spices		7	1		2	4	19
Industrial	4.6	15.4	5	3.5	3	2	4
Vegetables							
Topes	4.2		2.4		2		13.3
Drugs and Narcotics	2						
All	50	31.6	23.1	9	28.1	35.6	69.2
	Percentage to the total operated area repectively (priod-wise)						
Cereals	78.4	0.0	59.3	0.0	60.5	60.7	41.8
Pulses	0.0	18.4	4.3	23.8	14.6	22.5	5.8
Condiments and spices	0.0	14.0	4.3	0.0	7.1	11.2	27.5
Industrial	9.2	30.8	21.6	15.2	10.7	5.6	5.8
Vegetables	0.0	0.0	0.0	0.0	0.0	0.0	0.0
Topes	8.4	0.0	10.4	0.0	7.1	0.0	19.2
Drugs and Narcotics	4.0	0.0	0.0	0.0	0.0	0.0	0.0
All	100.0	63.2	100.0	39.0	100.0	100.0	100.0

Table 27.6: Changes in the Percapita Food Grains (in kgs) in Nagampalem

	2005	*1990*	*1970*	*1950*	*1933*
Popua	486	434.5	255	94.5	42
Black Paddy	0.0	0.0	0.0	0.0	0.0
White Paddy	102.5	22.7	0.0	0.0	0.0
Cholam	0.0	5.1	35.3	96.3	238.6
Ragi	0.0	6.6	6.9	15.3	64.3
Samai	0.0	0.0	0.0	0.0	0.0
Varugu	0.0	0.0	4.3	21.3	59.1
Maize	0.0	3.0	0.0	0.0	0.0
Others	44.9	0.0	7.6	0.0	0.0
Millets	22.5	14.8	41.3	128.0	348.6
All	121.5	40.8	51.7	128.0	348.6

Table 27.7: The Impact of Changes in the Cropping Pattern on Food Security, Land Alienation, Livelihood and Dependency among Tribal Communities during 1930 to 2005

S.No.	*Period*	*Changes in Cropping Pattern*	*Food Security*	*Land Alienation*	*Dependency on State and Non-tribes*	*Livelihood*	*Economies/ Advantages*	*Non-tribal exploitation*	*Forest dept. exploitation*
1.	pre-1933s	Collecting NTFP, hunting, fishery, animal grazing and others	very low	less	very low	very low	very low	very low	low
2.	1933-1950	shifting cultivation of small millets, NTFP, hunting, animal husbandry, fishery and other	low	moderate	low	low	low	moderate	moderate
3.	1950-70	Settled cultivation of cereals, pulses, condiments and spices, industrial, vegetables, topes, drugs and narcotics, fishery, hunting, animal husbandry	moderate	high	moderate	moderate	low	high	high
4.	1970-90	Cereals, industrial, vegetables, fishery and animal husbandry	low	low	high	moderate	moderate	moderate	moderate
5.	1990-05	Cereal, industrial, vegetables and animal husbandry and others	moderate	very low	moderate	high	moderate	low	low

Source: Field survey and study documents of SAKTI (NGO).

28

Rural Employment Act and Tribal Women in North East

Kapil Sikka and ***Vijender Singh Beniwal***

Abstract

The National Rural Employment Guarantee Act, 2005 (NREGA) notified on 7th September 2005 and came into effect on February 2, 2006 in 200 of India's most backward districts. However, from April 1, 2008 the Act covers all of rural India. Vide an amendment in the NREG Act, on 2nd October, 2009, the name of the act has been changed to Mahatma Gandhi National Rural Employment Guarantee Act.

MGNREGA is a unique employment opportunity for rural women who really get a chance to earn through their own income.[1] Women earn same as men on MGNERGA, in a survey it is mentioned that majority of women workers collect their own wages (79 per cent) and also keep them (68 per cent).[2] MGNREGA has significant achievements with regard to mobilisation of women wage workers, gender parity of wages and increased control over women's earnings from MGNREGA. There has been acceptability from large sections of society that MGNREGA has provided better working conditions, exploitation free work culture and of course better wages for women. Though not conceived on the gender lines, it incidentally impacted the empowerment of women at the rural level as it certainly provided the mobility to women at village level, which is one of the essential factors of empowerment. The statistics from the 2006 to the year 2010 show that the participation of the women at national level had increased from 42 per cent to 48.8 per cent which is clearly determining how the scheme has roped in the women at the village and made them the catalyst of rural growth.[3]

Schedule II of the paragraph six of the acts emphasis on the word, priority, which is itself evident of gender mainstreaming, as the text denotes that *"Priority"* should be given to women in the allocation of work in such a way that *"at least one-third of the beneficiaries shall be women"*.[4]

This paper will focus upon how the national rural employment scheme is contributing in the development of the rural women, which in turn are contributing to the development of North East. The increase in per capita income of women is directly influencing the indicators of growth like education for rural children, medical services for elder women, repayment of debts. Over to all, the national level migration rate has come down to 59 per cent, which in turn is a sign of developed society and hence MGNREGA is doing a lot in terms of development of North East.[5]

MGNREGA: The Legislation

The National Rural Employment Guarantee Act, 2005 (NREGA) notified on 7th September 2005 and came into effect on February 2, 2006 in 200 of India's most backward districts. However, from April 1, 2008 the Act covers all of rural India. Vide an amendment in the NREG Act, on 2nd October 2009, the name of the Act has been changed to Mahatma Gandhi National Rural Employment Guarantee Act.

The preface of the Act clearly mentions the reason behind the implementation "An Act to provide for the enhancement of livelihood security of the households in rural areas of the country by providing at least one hundred days of guaranteed wage employment in every financial year to every household whose adult members volunteer to do unskilled manual work and for matters connected therewith or incidental thereto."[6]

MGNREGA is a unique employment opportunity for rural population who really get a chance to earn their livelihood within their own villages. Moreover it is a right based programme, the rights of MGNREGA workers include employment on demand, minimum wages, payment within 15 days and basic worksite facilities, among others.[7] MGNREGA have been a lifeline for rural poor as it had lowered the rural migration level (59 per cent); moreover it had economically benefitted the rural poor by giving an employment guarantee which ensures that they have basic education for their wards, money to get treated for illness, measure for repayment of debts and the non-hazardous quality of work.[8]

Salient Features of Act

1. The Act made supplementary livelihood in rural areas through unskilled manual work a legal right.
2. The Act permits certain categories of work like water conservation, drought proofing, irrigation, land development, rejuvenation of traditional water bodies, flood control and drainage work, rural connectivity and work on the

land of SC/ST/BPL/IAY beneficiaries/land reform beneficiaries/ individual small and marginal farmers to be taken up for providing employment to the job seeking rural households.

3. Crèche, drinking water, first aid at worksites.
4. Grievance redressal mechanisms for workers.

The Act had become an important towards realisation of right to work and right of dignified work. It had been an influential in "arresting out-migration of rural households in search of employment simultaneously enhancing people's livelihood on a sustained basis, by developing the economic and social infrastructure in rural areas." The works under the Act seeks to address. MNREGA works are capable of addressing the causes of chronic poverty such as drought, deforestation and soil erosion. If effectively implemented, the employment guaranteed under the Act has the potential of transforming the geography of poverty.[9]

MGNREGA is a response to sudden economic crises and manmade disasters. The author focuses on the term "livelihood security" enshrined in the preamble of the Act. The rural unemployment remains the genesis of the birth of this Act.[10] The Act had the minimum wage rate for the casual workers which had impacted the wages of the workers in the open market as well. The author tagged the scheme as "bottom up, demand driven". This paper further examines the performance of MNREGA in various states through NSSO data 2009-10. The various stake holders like SC's, ST's and women were also studied to analyse the demand for work vis-à-vis unemployment. Moreover, a comparison had been drawn among the various states based on the "Demand Effect" of poverty.[11]

Gender Status in Informal Labour Markets

Gender equality is both a core concern and an essential part of human development. All too often, women are discriminated against in health, education and the labour market, which restricts their freedoms.[12] The extent of discrimination can be measured through the Gender Inequality Index (GII), which captures the loss of achievement due to gender inequality in three dimensions: reproductive health, empowerment and labour market participation, the higher the GII value, the greater the discrimination, based on 2012 data for 148 countries, India ranks 132.[13]

Women's employment in the informal sector had risen due to various reasons. With the adoption of the structural adjustment programme women tend to loose ground in the formal sectors of the economy. The growth of ancillarisation and industrial employment through sub-contracting appears to be gaining importance. Stagnating and falling incomes of households due to poor performance of the economy also leads to increased entry of women into the labour market. The process of globalisation, export-oriented industrialisation and relocation of industries from the developed to the developing countries also lead to the increase in the employment in the informal sector. Women's employment is often favoured in many of these industries.[14] It has been argued that the growing flexibility in the labour market, or increasing informalisation, had led to feminisation of the labour force (Standing, 1999). Feminisation implies that more women find themselves in jobs traditionally taken by men. Or certain jobs could have changed to have characteristics associated with traditional women's work. Such as informal contracts, lower remuneration, less security provided and lower skills. This process was actually leading to a convergence of male and female patterns of labour force participation. However, it has been argued that this process of narrowing of gender differentials in paid work should in fact be described as "masculinisation" (Elson, 1999). It is part of a process where a large part of women's work becomes directly subject to market force, as was the characteristics of men's work. International evidence has shown a tendency for the female share of non-agricultural employment to rise (Standing, 1999), though the share remains small, in most countries in Africa, Latin America and Asia.[15] Much of women's work remains unrecognised and unvalued. This has an impact on the status of women in society, their opportunities in public life and the gender-blindness of development policy.

Engendering MGNREGA

The preface of the act clearly mentions the reason behind the implementation "An Act to provide for the enhancement of livelihood security of the households in rural areas of the country by providing at least one hundred days of guaranteed wage employment in every financial year to every household whose adult members volunteer to do unskilled manual work and for matters connected therewith or incidental thereto".[16]

The statistics from the 2006 to the year 2010 show that the participation of the women at national level had increased from 42 per cent to 48.8 per cent which is clearly determining how the scheme has roped in the women at the village and made them the catalyst of rural growth.[17] Schedule II of the paragraph six of the acts emphasis on the word, priority, which is itself evident of gender mainstreaming, as the text denotes that *"Priority"* should be given to women in the allocation of work in such a way that *"at least one-third of the beneficiaries shall be women"*.[18] The famous slogan "*Har Haath Ko Kaam Do, Kaam Ko Poora Daam Do*" determines the equality concept amongst the NREGA workers. NREGA provides women an opportunity to earn a minimum wage, and lessens their largely unrecognised role in providing for and sustaining their families. The recognition of the problems they face in accessing the Employment Guarantee and some creative thinking about how to deal with these would go a long way in extending the benefits of the Act to this fundamental section of society.[19]

The NSSO 66th Round indicates that MGNREGA has reduced the traditional wage discrimination in public works. As per the data, average wage for labour in MGNREGA was Rs 90.9 per day for men, and for women it was Rs 87 per day. The difference was larger for labour in other public works; Rs 98.3 per day for men and Rs 86.1 per day for women. Other studies also suggest an upward movement of unskilled wages for women post-MGNREGA. For instance, in Kerala, the wages for women in agriculture and forest work rose from Rs 70–80 in 2007 to Rs 110–25 in 2009. In fact, real wages increased more rapidly for female workers than for male workers. In a survey of 75 villages across four states—Bihar, Gujarat, Kerala and Rajasthan—it was found that the ratio of male-female wage rates, on an average, declined from 1.40 in 2007–08 to 1.30 in 2009–10.[20]

Review of Literature

There is large number of studies related with the impact of MGNREGA on women's participation which generally shows positive impact; some of them are as follows:

1. Jandu (2008) carried out a research in four states namely, Chhattisgarh, Madhya Pradesh, Orissa and Tamil Naidu Survey data shown that women workers are more confident about their roles as contributors to family expenditure and their work decisions and it gives them space in public sphere. Most of the respondent felt that the act is very important for them. The study found positive impact of the MGNREGA on migration patterns.

2. Hazarika (2009) examined the impact of MGNREGA on gender empowerment in Morigaon and Bongaigaon district of Assam. This study showed that almost 70 to 80 per cent of sample workers had meaningful income other than unpaid family work during the pre-NREGA. Majority of the worker felt that they are now in better position to fulfill their own requirement without looking at others. Nearly 65 to 70 per cent women workers attended gram sabha meeting held in connection with NREGA. In Bongaigaon District, a large number of job card holders were found who have become Panchayat representatives.

3. Ramesh and Kumar (2009) in their study also found that MGNREGA hold the powerful prospect of bringing major changes in the lives of women. MGNREGA is playing a substantial role in empowering women economically and laying the basis for greater independence and self-esteem. It has become a beacon of light in the empowerment of the rural women, and contributed substantially for the increased living and economic conditions by creating equal wages to male and female workers and increasing the minimum wages. Their study was conducted in 2009-10 by selecting 500 women beneficiaries. Out of the 670 workers, 74.62 per cent are women and the rest are men. The beneficiaries expressed that this programme helped in easing out the debt burden to some extent.

4. Khera and Nayak (2009), through their sample survey in six Hindi speaking states of North India focuses on impact of NREGA in the lives of women

workers. This study reveals that there is significant benefits reported by women include increased food security and better ability to avoid hazardous work. They pointed out that as per survey data, NREGA works increases average wage rate comparing to private labour market. Besides this in NREGA, the working hours are limited to 7-8 hours in a day and therefore it is helpful to prevent harassment of women workers. By using random sampling they found that NREGA work has allowed women to spend money on their own needs, while earlier they might not have been at the liberty to do so. Some women reported that work with private landlords and contractors are often replete with an underlying threat of possibility of sexual abuse and exploitation. NREGA has brought mental satisfaction.

5. Panda, B. Dutta, A.K. (2009), through their study found that this Act empowered rural tribal women in Sikkim and Meghalaya by enhancing their confidence level and by ensuring some degree of financial independence. They mentioned that in the traditional institution like Durbars women are not allowed to have political representation. But mandatory involvement of women in PRI institution has given boon to women empowerment in the state. Around 94 per cent of women workers in Sikkim and 38 per cent in Meghalaya felt that they have been able to access health facilities better after working in NREGA.

6. Sudarshan (2009) reviews the place of MGNREGA within the border of social protection and gender concern. As examined by him, social protection was applicable mostly in organised sector until 1990s. Since the early 1990 public policy and public works in India tried to include women as a percentage of beneficiaries and have not paid much attention to gender sensitive design. But MGNREGA in its design has attempted some gender sensitivity. In Kerala there has been some shift out of agriculture into MGNREGA, mainly with respect to female workers. The minimum wages paid under the MGNREGA is far greater than agriculture wages. The good performance of MGNREGA in Kerala is possible because of state government commitment and the managerial role of the Kudumbashree and area development supervisors. This study reveals that MGNREGA not only stimulate local development but also overcome the women's weak position in labour market.

7. Pankaj and Tankha (2010) examines the empowerment effects of MGNREGA through field survey in Bihar, Jharkhand, Rajasthan and Himachal Pradesh. The study shown that a women worker's earning from MGNREGA constituted 14 per cent of the total annual income of the household on average across the four sample districts in 2008-09. Majority of women workers collect and retain their wages. Before NREGA 44 per cent women said that they were able to meet their personal needs through their own earning where after NREGA it is 71 per cent. This study shows an increased participation of women in gram sabha meetings. Besides this 73 per cent of women which had attended the gram sabha spoke in the meeting.

Gender Inclusion in North East

National Rural Employment Guarantee Act (NREGA) was originally implemented in 16 districts of eight North-Eastern States, namely Arunachal Pradesh, Assam, Manipur, Meghalaya, Mizoram, Nagaland, and Tripura, but from April 1, 2008, it was extended to all seven states.

Measuring the inclusion of women in MGNREGA in the seven states of North East in past three years gives a very contradicting scenario, as we can see vide Table 28.1, that Meghalaya and Tripura had registered more than 33 per cent women participation in NREGA work in all three years, whereas Arunachal Pradesh had registered a sudden dip in women participation in the year 2012-13. On the other hand, Assam, Mizoram and Nagaland are still to benefit women in essence, as it can be noticed, that in all three financial years, the average rate of participation had remained around 25 per cent. Whereas Manipur, except in the financial year 2010-11, had achieved the 33 per cent benchmark of women reservation.

Table 28.1: Participation Rate of Women in North-eastern States in India

State	*Women's participation Rate (Per cent) 2010-11*	*Women's participation Rate (Per cent) 2011-12*	*Women's participation Rate (Per cent) 2012-13*
Assam	21.22	24.91	25.71
Manipur	29.87	33.58	35.82
Meghalaya	36.54	41.59	41.94
Mizoram	20.45	23.61	23.52
Nagaland	25.12	27.05	25.16
Tripura	37.67	38.64	41.09
Arunachal Pradesh	35.44	40.33	29.39
INDIA	**46.41**	**48.81**	**52.44**

Source: www.nrega.nic.in

Table 28.2: Notified Wages (2012-13)

State	*Wages in Rs*
Assam	136
Manipur	144
Meghalaya	128
Mizoram	136
Nagaland	126
Tripura	124
Arunachal Pradesh	124

Source: www.nrega.nic.in

Participation of Women under MGNREGA in North East:

There have been many positive aspects of the Rural Employment Act in North East:

Increase in average wage

Statistics had shown that average wage in post MGNREGA period had increased many folds. The economic empowerment of female had led to the enhancement in decision making in household matters.

Household Income

- Moreover females now have alternate employment opportunities, which has enhanced women's contribution in household income.

Income-earning Opportunity

- MGNREGA creates opportunity for women to be economically independent. It allows them to fulfill their needs without depending on others. It can be witnessed from the above mentioned statistics that women participation under MGNREGA is very moderate, ranging from lowest in Assam to highest in Tripura and Meghalaya.

Areas of Concern:

Non-availability Crèche Facilities

- According to the act when there are more than five children under the age of six, a female worker is to be appointed to take care of them. Due to non-availability of crèche facilities women either leave the toddlers at home or prefer not to work under this scheme.

Nature of Work under MGNREGA

- As majority of work under this is the unskilled one which requires rigorous labour, which remains another factor of women skipping it.

Inadequate Facilities at Worksite

- Moreover lack of facilities such as drinking water, first aid, shade at worksite etc is a problem for the workers. Because of non-availability of shade for resting, pregnant and aged-women find difficulties to participate in MGNREGA.

Delay in Payments of Wages

- Delay in payment of wages in another area of concern as it is a harassment for women workers to inquire for wages on daily basis.

Conclusion

Nevertheless, the NREGA had been an effective wage earning opportunity for the poor women who use to migrate to nearby villages and towns in search of wage employment along with their children. NREGA has also proved to be a boon for SHGs as many were not able to repay back loans borrowed from the bank because few members use to default as they didn't had much earning opportunities. The act has also brought in improvement in the health status of the women workers. It has further ensured a strong social safety net for the vulnerable rural women, women empowerment happens to be the most visible impact during NREGA. The provision of equal wages for men and women in the Act, the opportunity to share information during the course of work in NREGA work site the opportunity and necessity of interacting with the bank/ post office/government officials have all in a fundamental way empowered the rural tribal women by enhancing their confidence level and by ensuring some degree of financial independence.[21]

References

1. Mahatma Gandhi National Rural Employment Guarantee Act, 2005.

2. Khera, Ritika (2011), The Battle for Employment Guarantee, p. 54, Oxford University Press.

3. Mahatma Gandhi NREGA National Reports 2006-10, MoRD (http://nrega.nic.in/netnrega/home.aspx).

4. Mahatma Gandhi NREGA, Schedule II, Section 6.

5. Dreze, Jean, Ritika Khera (2011),The Battle for Employment Guarantee, p. 51, Oxford University Press.

6. Preface, NREGA, 2005.

7. Dreze, Jean, Ritika Khera (2011), *The Battle for Employment Guarantee*, p. 49, Oxford University Press.

8. Dreze, Jean, Ritika Khera (2011), *The Battle for Employment Guarantee*, p. 51, Oxford University Press.

9. All-India Report on Evaluation of NREGA: A Survey of Twenty Districts (2008). Institute of Manpower Research, Narela.

10. Krishnamurthy, J., 2006. Employment Guarantee and Crisis Response. *Economic and Political Weekly*, Vol. 41(9), pp. 789-790.

11. Dutta, Pooja, Murgai, Rinku and Others, 2012. *Does India's Employment Guarantee Scheme Guarantee Employment?* Policy Research Working Paper, The World Bank.[Online]Availableat:http://www.wds.worldbank.org/servlet/WDSContentServer/WDSP/IB/2012/03/21/000158349_20120321082953/Rendered/PDF/WPS6003.pdf[Accessed 12 November, 2012].

12. Human Development Report (1995), UNDP.

13. Human Development Report (2013), UNDP.

14. Unni, Jeemol, Rani Uma (2000). *Women In Informal Employment In India{Private}* Available at [http://previous.wiego.org/papers/unnirani.pdf].

15. *Ibid.*

16. Preface, NREGA, 2005.

17. Mahatma Gandhi NREGA National Reports 2006-10 , MoRD (http://nrega.nic.in/netnrega/home.aspx).

18. Mahatma Gandhi NREGA, Schedule II, Section 6.

19. Raja, Annie, 2007. Ensuring the Right to Work for Women: A Review of the NREGA from the Gender Perspective. *Gender and Governance – A Review of the*

Women's Agenda in the National Common Minimum Programme, Wada Na Todo Abhiyan, New Delhi-16.[Online] Available at http://www.wadanatodo.net/images/160407/GenderNCMP_Eng.pdf [Accessed 15 November 2012].

20. Ministry of Rural Development, Government of India, *MGNREGA Sameeksha, An Anthology of Research Studies on the Mahatma Gandhi National Rural Employment Guarantee Act, 2005, 2006–2012*, edited and compiled by Mihir Shah, Neelakshi Mann and Varad Pande, New Delhi: Orient Black Swan, 2012.

21. IIM Shillong, 2009; *Appraisal of NREGA in the states of Meghalaya and Sikkim*, A Project report by B. Panda, A.K. Dutta and S. Prusty.

29

Livelihood Security through Land Distribution: An Empirical Study on Chenchus of Andhra Pradesh

L Reddeppa

Abstract

The fulfillment of the country's development objectives depends on the improvement of income and livelihood of the people living under poverty. The stark reality is that the proportion of such people is relatively high in the case of SCs and STs than that of the other social groups in the country. This is more so in the case of Primitive Tribal Groups (PTGs). There is one such PTG, Chenchu a food gather tribe living in Andhra Pradesh. Their livelihood is under threat after the declaration of their areas as tiger reserve forest and the inroads of modern development. To compensate their loss meted out due to policies and the dwindling natural resources in their areas for livelihood, several welfare schemes have been implemented, particularly after establishment of Integrated Tribal Development Agency (ITDA) in the late eighties. Market based Land distribution is the most prominent scheme that the financial assistance under the scheme is higher than that of other schemes for the exclusive benefit of individual landless households. Apart from the land, provisions were also made for promotion of agriculture in order to improve their livelihood. In this context, several questions are raised for greater understanding of their livelihood security. How far the land and other support measures contributing to the family income? What are the other livelihood options available to generate threshold income for crossing poverty line? The study is an attempt to understand the livelihood security from land achieved and suggest appropriate policy. It is observed from the study that the LPS is made effective in improvement of livelihood and crossing poverty line for about 10 per cent of the families and an additional income for about another 20 per cent of the families. However, a large majority of them could not translate their land into income due to various socio-economic and cultural barriers. Half of them not even cultivated their land due to purchase of land with poor quality from private party for lack of adequate budget; pending partisan land to individual beneficiaries; delay or pending energisation bore wells, and lack of small investment and plough bullocks for cultivation. Thus, the ITDA has to provide better land of at least two acres with irrigation facility and timely supply of all inputs needed on subsidy including access to institutional credit for each family, particularly first generation cultivators.

Introduction

The fulfillment of the country's development objectives depends on the well being of the poorest of the poor 'or' the people living under poverty. They have a right to benefit from the growth and development efforts of the Government. But, the high level of poverty that persists in some sections of the people reflects the denial of such right. The stark reality is that the proportion of such people is relatively high in the case of SCs and STs than that of the other social groups in the country. This is more so in the case of Primitive Tribal Groups (PTGs). There is one such PTG, Chenchu a food gather tribe living in Andhra Pradesh. However, after the declaration of their areas as tiger reserve forest, drain of natural resources in their areas, and the inroads modern development with public private partnership, their livelihood is under threat. For them, the Government has distributed lands under Land Purchase Scheme (LPS) and implemented other schemes for promotion of agriculture and allied activities in order to improve their livelihood. Thus, the intension of the Government for intervention is to improve their livelihood and income through settled cultivation.

The sustainable agriculture in the context of individual farmers depends on access to economical size of land holding with irrigation facility. The First Five Year Plan itself suggested the concept of an economically viable land holding size, which was about two acres of irrigated land for self-cultivation. The Maharashtra law defined the economically viable holding as four permanently irrigated acres. However, majority of the states have not defined the economically viable land holding size due to variation in the quality of the soil and irrigation facility, seasonal and climate conditions that are required for the cropping pattern. In recent years, many states have concentrated more on distribution of vacant lands after exhausting the land distribution under land ceiling Laws due to disposal of such land is with the Government. This has significant contribution in Andhra Pradesh. A disquieting feature of land use has been a declined pastures and grazing lands in the country due to distribution of such lands to the landless particularly to the weaker sections of the society. But, the lands are not producing any surplus to the families for their sustenance.

A study carried out by the NSSO (2003) reveals that nearly 40 per cent of the farmer households disliked farming and wanted to give up the profession due to its unprofitable nature.

A significant proportion of the rural poor are living in backward areas that are challenged by difficult agro-climatic conditions, and inadequate infrastructure and support services. At the household level. It is likely to be harder to escape poverty, if the household lives in persistently poor district; is a member of scheduled tribe; relies on casual labour for a significant portion of its livelihood, possibly involving migration from a remote, especially forest area, and is illiterate and lacks kinship and other networks, and is large". Thus, majority of Chenchus are manifested with several such factors and are vulnerable to poverty. In this context, several questions are raised for greater understanding of their livelihood security. How far the land and other support measures helpful in improvement of livelihood in terms of income? What are the other livelihood options available to generate threshold income for crossing poverty line? The present study is an attempt to understand the livelihood security achieved from land in terms of income to suggest appropriate policy.

The study is mainly based on the primary data collected from 322 sample families (proposed one third, but it is 35 per cent) out of 928 families received lands and other inputs for the promotion of agriculture during the period 2000 – 2005. The data was collected from all the villages where the LPS implemented. One third households were chosen from each study village on simple random sampling method. The land use pattern, household data and income has been collected for the cross-section year 2006-07. Apart from this, secondary data had also been collected from the Integrated Tribal Development Agency (ITDA) with regard to the expenditure on various schemes implemented for development of Chenchus, and village wise data on LPS. The study is broadly divided into five sections after brief introduction to the study – (1) Approaches and Schemes implemented for Livelihood improvement of Chenchus; (2) Distribution of Land under LPS and its utilisation; (3) Contribution of Livelihood from land and other Options; (4) Level of poverty and shifting of families from below to above; and (5) Conclusions.

1. Approaches and Schemes for Livelihood Improvement of Chenchus

The Chenchu tribe was declared as a Primitive Tribal Group (PTG) in the year 1975. A separate ITDA was established in the late eighties to look into the all-round development of the Chenchus. The total population of the Chenchus is 41,787 as per the records of ITDA Srisailam. The profile of Chenchus indicates that they are living in 338 gudems (villages) which are close to and within the forest boundaries. They live in 36 mandals all over the six districts. Their population in Prakasam District is substantially high at 13,321; followed by Mahabubnagar (10,406), Kurnool (7,915), Guntur (6,376), Ranga Reddy (2,700), and Nalgonda (1,069) districts. On the whole, their population is more than

3,001 in five mandals; 1001 to 3000 in nine mandals; 501 to 1000 in four mandals; 301 to 500 in six mandals and less than 300 in the remaining 12 mandals. The size of the family among the Chenchus is very small and mostly three to four members. The total population of the 322 sample families consists of 1,121 members, of which 537 are male and 574 are female.

The livelihood patterns of the Chenchus have interwoven with forest resources for centuries.

They consume the fruits, roots and tubers, etc, besides animal meat available in the forests, and also engage in the collection of minor forest products. "The Chenchus do not care much for money or material wealth. They have hardly developed any technique for preserving food. Their care for the future is marginal as they are used to living on a day-to-day basis. Though the tribal work as forest labour at times, they mostly prefer to fall back on their native skills to hunt and gather food". After the inroads of modern development, allotment of vast stretches of tribal lands for mining activity, construction of irrigation projects and declaration of their area as a tiger reserve, imposition of Wild Life Protection Act, the tribals have lost their self-reliance.

Agriculture has been the secondary source of livelihood for them even after many years of Independence. It is observed that the proportion of Chenchu families depending on own cultivation are only 12 per cent, which is far below the level of people in general (27.74 per cent) and STs as a whole (41.19 per cent) in Andhra Pradesh, according to the 1991 Census. The tribals living in forest areas in general are better accessed to the land than that of other social groups. But, it is entirely different in the case of Chenchu tribe that large majority are landless. They are sparsely populated in a separate village with close proximity to forests and also to the non-tribals. But they depend on others only on wage employment from agriculture, which is seasonal for a few days. The situation has changed in recent years as the forest resources are dwindling in their areas. The time has now come to find some alternative sources of income on a sustainable basis. Otherwise, their life would be under threat.

Of late, realising their backwardness, a separate Integrated Tribal Development Agency (ITDA) was established in the late eighties to look into the overall development of them. The welfare schemes implemented for the development of the Chenchus can be broadly classified into four categories – (a) educational programmes, (b) creation of basic infrastructure facilities like drinking water, health, housing, road and bus facility, etc., (c) Economic Support Schemes (ESS) (d) other development schemes like supply of daily requirements through Public Distribution System (PDS).These schemes have been implementing with the funds made available to them under the Special Central Assistance, special budget for PTG development, State Tribal sub-plan and mobilisation of institutional finance.

In the case of ESS, the more important schemes are the land based schemes like land purchase, land development, irrigation, supply of plough bullocks, provision of modern agriculture implements and inputs supplies on free/ subsidised rates, promotion of dairy, sheep rearing, etc., besides youth development through self employment in the lines of industry, service and business (ISB) sectors. The ITDA, Srisailam had spent an amount of Rs 100.32 crores in a period of 17 years, i.e., from the year 1990-91 to 2006-07 for the benefit of total population (41787 people) or about 12,000 households. The amount spent on each family on an average is Rs 83,630 over a period of 17 years. In spite of all the schemes, the problem of poverty is more predominant and persistent among them. Realising this, all Chenchu families were issued Antyodaya Anna Yojana (AAY) ration cards. They get 35 kgs of rice per family per month. Apart from these, they also get red gram, cooking oil, kerosene on subsidy and other essentials on whole sale prices from the Daily Requirement Depots DRDs. This would create physical access at least larger extent of their cereals requirement and over and above are to be managed to get economic access. Apart from this, the ITDA has implemented Land Purchase and allied schemes for promotion of agriculture as permanent solution to their food security and livelihood improvement. But how far these objectives are fulfilled under LPS is discussed in the following sections.

2. Land Purchase Scheme Implemented by ITDA, Srisailam

The traditionally held view is that ownership of agriculture land in rural areas has a bearing on the family in various socio-economic spheres of rural setting—the land ownership ensures family with income, food and livelihood security, social status in the village, community and society at large and credit worthiness. In the modern context, it also facilitates to avail other benefit of the Government for creation of irrigation facility and take up other activities like horticulture, animal husbandry and dairy. Thus, Land Purchase Scheme is being implemented by the ITDA, Srisailam, since 2000. About 1,850 acres of land was purchased for the benefit of 1,149 families in the districts of Kurnool, Prakasam, Mahabubnagar, and Guntur during 2000-2007. The total expenditure incurred during the period was 475.766 lakhs. This shows that the beneficiaries have received, on an average, about 1.61 acres each with an average cost of Rs 25,692 per acre. In the process, the Government has spent an amount of Rs 41407 per beneficiary. However, there were no year-wise targets as such for the scheme. It was observed that land was not purchased during 2003-04 and 2004-05. This may be either due to lack of budget for the scheme or non-availability of lands for sale from land owners.

It was also observed from the data that a major portion of the land was purchased by the ITDA, Srisailam under the Andhra Pradesh Participatory Tribal Development Project (APPTDP) programme during 1999-2003. More specifically, half of the total expenditure on the scheme was incurred in one financial year, i.e., 2002-2003. This could be due to the availability of funds for the ITDA in the closing year (2003) of the project APPTDP. For details, see Table 29.1.

Table 29.1: Expenditure and Extent of Land Purchased from 2000-01 to 2006-07

Year	*Beneficiaries*	*Extent of Area in Acres*	*Expenditure (in Rs)*	*Per Acre Land Cost (in Rs)*
2000-01	117	140.63	3743800	26621
2001-02	95	124.53	3309249	26574
2002-03	556	1052.95	23841887	22643
2005-06	251	322.07	9189800	28533
2006-07	130	211.59	7491890	35407
Total	**1149**	**1851.77**	**47576620**	**25692**

Source: ITDA Office, Srisailam.

The data on land prices indicate that the per-acre price of the land was Rs 26621 during 2000-01; this continued more or less even in the next year. However, during 2002-03, it steeply fell to Rs 22643. This could be due to the three-year drought period that ended in 2003. Subsequently, the prices of the lands increased more steeply to Rs 28533 during 2005-06 and to Rs 35407 during 2006-07 due to better monsoon conditions and introduction of new irrigation projects.

Extent of Farming Activity among the Beneficiaries of the Land

The land was distributed mostly in the name of women and their families were mostly (97 per cent) landless prior to distribution of land under LPS. How far the land distribution programme has helped to bring them in fold of self cultivating category is the moot point? It is observed that about 127 beneficiaries out of the 322 (about 39.4 per cent) have taken up own cultivation; about 46.9 per cent have not cultivate; and 13.7 per cent have leased out their land. The utilisation of land is relatively better in Kurnool district where the number of beneficiaries not cultivated is only 9.4 per cent and remaining are at least leased out their land, if not take up own cultivation. The beneficiaries not take up own cultivation quite high (about 60 per cent) in other district. For district wise details, see Table 29.2.

Table 29.2: Number of Beneficiaries Who Have Taken up Own Cultivation

S.No.	*District*	*No. of beneficiaries*			
		Own cultivation	*Not cultivated*	*Leased out*	*Total Sample*
1.	Kurnool	48(56.5)	8(9.4)	29(34.1)	85(100)
2.	Guntur	16(31.4)	32(62.7)	3(5.9)	51(100)
3.	Prakasam	25(28.7)	62(60.9)	9(10.3)	87(100)
4.	Mahabubnagar	38(38.4)	58(58.6)	3(3.0)	99(1000
	Total	127(39.4)	151(46.9)	44(13.7)	322(100)

Source: Field Data.

The quality of the lands distributed to them is more crucial for analysis before the assessment of lands utilised. It was observed from the field as well as discussions with the beneficiaries on the quality of lands distributed under LPS indicate that 21 per cent of the land was not cultivable, of which eight per cent of the land was not even fit for land development. It means the lands are occupied with big boulders, rocks, and contiguous rock structures. Of the remaining, 13 per cent is cultivable, if taken up land development in terms shrimp clearance and take up soil conservation work, which need more investment. Again, the soil is not sure of good quality.

There are instances that the ITDA had provided alternative land after their rejection due to poor quality of soil or not fit for cultivation. Why the ITDA had purchased the land not fit for cultivation without the approval of the farmers? It is observed that the sellers have disposed their lands by adopted lobbying methods with the ITDA officials. Generally, the beneficiaries would expect a good quality of the land with irrigation facility from the ITDA. Such lands could not come up for sale from the land owners. Even if they come for sale, the offered price for the land from the land owners would be high which is beyond the eligibile limit of the ITDA under LPS as expressed by the ITDA officials.. Thus, proper utilisation of land can be expected from the Chenchus, if the soils are good, availability of irrigation, access to crop loans from formal financial institutions and supply of other inputs on subsidised prices. Otherwise, it would be difficult to achieve good results by the Chenchus from the lands.

Utilisation of Lands and Cropping Pattern

It is clearly observed that own cultivation is observed mainly in villages where the soil is good and land has some irrigation facility, and also the farmers

Table 29.3 : District-wise Area and Yield Distribution under Different Crops

S.No.	*Type of crop grown*	*Area*		*Yield (in quintals)*	
		In Acres	*Per cent*	*Total*	*per acre*
1.	Red gram	129.46	44.62	229.00	1.77
2.	Maize	41.00	14.13	151.00	3.68
3.	Sunflower	33.45	11.53	107.00	3.20
4.	Paddy	27.50	9.48	158.00	5.75
5.	Jowar	21.20	7.31	62.00	2.92
6.	Castor	15.00	5.17	31.00	2.07
7.	Cotton	7.00	2.41	15.00	2.14
8.	Mirchi	3.00	1.03	12.00	4.00
9.	Turmeric	1.50	0.52	20.00	13.33
10.	Others	11.00	3.79	12.00	1.09
	Total	**290.11**	**100.00**	**79.70**	**2.75**

Source: Field Data.

have past experience as agriculture labour in their vicinity. The extent of area irrigated out of the total land purchased was 5.4 per cent. It shows that most of the area purchased was not irrigated. Subsequently, the ITDA has drilled the bore wells who ever asked to provide irrigation depending on ground water feasibility. But more than 60 per cent of the lands yet to receive either bore wells or other sources of irrigation. It is interesting to note that the bore wells drilled were also not energised. Majority of them are waiting for power supply for more than three years even after installation of sub-mergible pump-sets. On the whole, the extent of area cultivated by the sample beneficiaries including land leased out is 290.11 acres out of the total land of 582.68 acres, which constitutes about 49.77 per cent of the area purchased to them. For details of area and yield per-acre, see Table 29.3.

The crops grown by the beneficiaries were paddy, maize, turmeric, mirchi, groundnut, cotton, etc., under the source of bore well and tank irrigation. The other crops grown were red gram, jowar, sun flower, castor, horse gram, green gram, etc. as rain-fed crops. The area under each crop indicate that red gram was the predominant crop grown by them in 129.46 acres, followed by maize (41 acres), sunflower (33.95 acres), paddy (29.50 acres), jowar (22.2 acres), castor (15 acres), cotton (7 acres). The remaining area under each crops like mirchi, ragi, groundnut, bajra, green gram, horse gram, turmeric, korra, black gram, etc were cultivated in less than three acres. The average yield per acre is much less in most of the beneficiaries for lack of adequate experience of crop cultivation. Despite this, about ten beneficiaries have been practicing modern methods of cultivation and their yield levels are also relatively better. It is important to note that the beneficiaries who studied up to the upper-primary and high school level are utilising the land relatively better than the illiterate. For instance, in the Mittameedapalle of Guntur District, the leader of the group studied up to high school; she is utilising the land more productively, cultivating commercial crops like *mirchi*. She produced about 10 to 15 quintals of *mirchi* per acre of land. Though the land was neither distributed to the individual beneficiaries nor provided irrigation facility by the ITDA, the beneficiaries informally shared the land among themselves, purchased water from the landlords and cultivated their lands. This is a classic example that education has made them utilise the land more productively, and proves that education, especially of the younger generation, is important for bringing about a change in living patterns and lifestyles.

It is observed that value of the lands greatly increased in recent years in most of the villages, due to the newly planned irrigation projects and canals in their vicinity and various other reasons. In fact, the land prices were doubled in some of the villages, while they increased by up to 75 per cent in many villages, and many times more in a few places. For example lands purchased for up to Rs 20000 per acre increased to Rs 15 lakhs per acre in Amangal Mandal of Mahabubnagar District due to the land is close to *Outer Ring Road* and real estate market boom in Hyderabad. At present, one of the beneficiaries is using the land for brick manufacturing.

Reasons for Non-cultivation and Leasing Practice

It is observed that about 60 per cent of the beneficiaries are not take up own cultivation. The main reasons for non-cultivation of land as expressed by the beneficiaries of the LPS are: Land was not partitioned to the individual beneficiaries after registration; no irrigation facility to the land; no plough bullocks; crop loss in the previous year; no credit facilities; chronic health problems for one of the family members; and dispute among the co-beneficiaries after partisan the land. In most cases, the beneficiaries have expressed multiple reasons for non-cultivation of their land. The reasons for leasing out land are also similar to those of non-cultivation other than the reasons like non-partisan of land to individual beneficiaries and the land is not fit for cultivation. Land can be leased out if there is good demand. Leasing out land to others for cultivation is always better option than leaving the land fallow, provided good tenants are available in their areas. The beneficiary would get some income in the process, even if it is less. The leasing income for land ranged from Rs 400 to Rs 1000 per acre in case of dry lands, which can be used for the cultivation of rain fed crops, where the scope for irrigation is nil. There is other category that land can also be cultivated with irrigated crops depending on the availability of irrigation in their vicinity, if water is provided for a price. Such cases were seen in the case of a few beneficiaries in two to three villages where the annual lease income vary from Rs 2000 to Rs 4000 per acre.

The land was leased out mostly to non-tribals. The tenants mostly utilised the land to cultivate irrigated crops such as paddy, maize, sunflower and groundnut. After observing the benefits their tenants derive through cultivation, the beneficiaries take over the land for own cultivation in few cases. The crops like paddy, turmeric and mirchi cultivation have also been practiced by Chenchus mainly due to demonstration effect, though it is meager area by very few. This shows that they are under transition to take up own cultivation in the near future. Hence it is observed that the tenant builds the capacity of the beneficiaries or owners of the land, and the owner of the land gains experience through the investment of tenant by working as wage labour under him. More importantly, the beneficiaries personally oversee the type of crops grown, extent of yield extracted from the land and the cost involved for each crop. There is no scope for land alienation or selling land to the tenant as the beneficiaries of LPS have no legal right to sell the land to others. Moreover, as the land is registered in the name of the women beneficiaries, who are more concerned about their family, the scope for alienation of land is considerably less.

3. Livelihood from Land and Other Options

The yield from the crop was nil or less than the value of the cost of cultivation in case of 19.0 per cent of the beneficiaries out of the total land cultivated by them. It shows that they have lost their hard earned money due to the cultivation of the crops, which excludes the loss of their own labour. The total loss in terms of the paid-out cost was varied from Rs 500 to Rs 3,000 per beneficiary. The loss incurred to them mainly due to lack of adequate rains and continuation of long dry spell in the rainy season. In some of the cases, the seed was also not germinated and in some cases, the tender crop was withered away. The loss incurred to the few have a negative effect on cultivation of crops in the subsequent years, particularly rainfed crops. They are not affordable to take such risks. They are not aware of the crop insurance schemes. Even if they have awareness, it is difficult to get claims due to cumbersome procedures, which is even difficult for developed and educated farmers. The farmer's suicides can be minimised, if the insurance policy is consumer friendly. The poor Chenchus not ventured into own cultivation based on the previous experiences. Non-cultivation of land by majority of the beneficiaries (56 per cent) itself reflects the risks involved in cultivation of crops. Despite this, 44 per cent of the beneficiaries have generated a little income either from own cultivation or leasing out their land. The farmers with little income from own cultivation are about 32 per cent, they are mostly covering the opportunity cost of their labour and a little surplus from land. The income generated anything more than Rs 5000 is really achievement for them. This would cover at least opportunity cost their labour. Such families constitute about 10 per cent out of the total families cultivated their land. About 11 per cent are generating between Rs 3001 and Rs 5000. The remaining not even generating opportunity cost of their labour.

Other Livelihood Options

The livelihood options prior to Land available for food security and income were agriculture labour, collection of Minor Forest Produce (MFP), non-agriculture labour, own cultivation, migration, firewood selling, coal preparation and selling, cattle rearing, etc. All these activities are continuing by them even after receiving land depending on the need and survival strategy of the family. Prior to land distribution, the extent of average income generated from own agriculture was Rs 4333 per year for three families, while it was Rs 4008 for 103 families and another 44 families have income from lease of land. It shows that while own agriculture was one of the livelihood activities for just one per cent of the families previously, it increased to 46 per cent after the land distribution; the remaining (54 per cent) did not have any income from agriculture.

MFP collection is also one of the important livelihoods for generation of income to 66 per cent of the families. Mostly, they engage on collection of minor forest produce like gum, honey, tendu leaves, mohua flower, soap nuts, tamarind, etc., and sold these items either to the Girijan Cooperative Corporation Limited or in the private market. Similarly, non-agricultural labour is one of the activities for 45 per cent of the families prior to the land increased to 49 per cent of the families after land. It shows that majority of them are depending on multiple activities for their livelihood. Among all the activities, minor forest produce is the main source of income for them that each family was generated on an average income of Rs 6,953 prior to the land, which was declined to Rs 6,773 after the land. It is also important to note that MFP collection is not available for about half of the households.

The income from agriculture labour is next in the order of highest average income generated to them. The extent of average annual income was at Rs 5,302 per family for 89 per cent of the families prior to the land, which was Rs 5,022 per family for 92 per cent of the families after the land. It shows that agriculture labour and MFP collection are the most important sources of income. For details of average income generated by a family under different source, see Table 29.4.

Table 29.4 : Generation of Income from Different Occupations

Sl. No.	*Occupation*	*Before Land*			*After Land*		
		Total income in lakhs	*Per cent*	*Average income in Rs*	*Total income in lakhs*	*Per cent*	*Average income in Rs*
1.	Own agriculture	0.13	0.33	4333	5.17	11.4	4008
2.	Minor Forest Produce	14.88	38.10	6953	14.41	31.9	6773
3.	Agriculture Labour	14.85	38.00	5302	14.92	33.0	5022
4.	Non-agri. Labour	6.04	15.45	4194	6.67	14.76	4245
5.	Parents	0.08	0.20	2666	0.09	0.20	3000
6.	Other sources	3.12	8.00	5026	3.91	8.66	3994
	Total	**39.08**	**100.0**	**12138**	**45.17**	**100.0**	**14028**

Source: Field Data.

It is important to note that the distribution of land has created seriousness and confidence among them to improve their livelihood depending on multiple activities. This can be observed that the families depending on agriculture labour, MFP collection and other activities have increased even after land.

Improvement of Total Family Income after Land

It would be appropriate to analyse the income levels of the beneficiary families before and after land based on the classification of the families into different size of income. The income generated before and after land are comparable, because majority of the beneficiaries were received lands in the year 2003-2004. The change in the prices of food items and living patterns within a period of two to three years is much less. The ITDA has also been implementing various welfare schemes including supply of food items under public distribution system. The income before land was less than Rs 12,000 per year in 55.6 per cent of the families declined to 36 per cent after land.

On the other hand, the annual income was above Rs 12,000 per family in 44.4 per cent of the families before land increased to 64 per cent of the families after land. It shows that 20 per cent of the families improved their level of income from below to above Rs 12,000 per year. It shows that there was no much improvement in the level of income in the case of the other 80 per cent of the families even after land. This may be perhaps due to non-cultivation of land by a majority and the income generated by a few was very limited. For details, see Table 29.5.

Table 29.5 : Improvement of Family Annual Income before and after Land

Level of Family Income (Rs.)	*Before Land*		*After Land*	
	Nos.	*Per cent*	*Nos.*	*Per cent*
Up to 6,000	14	4.3	2	0.6
6001 – 9000	58	18.0	38	11.8
9001 – 12000	107	33.2	76	23.6
12001 – 15000	79	24.5	103	32.0
15001 – 18000	46	14.3	72	22.4
18001 +	18	5.6	31	9.6
Total	**322**	**100.0**	**322**	**100.0**

Source: Field Data.

4. Families Crossed the Poverty Line

The poverty line was defined in the country that a person need an intake of food which is required to generate 2400 calories of energy in rural areas and 2100 calories in urban areas. Apart from the food needs, every family expects a minimum income to meet other basic needs like cloth, shelter, health, education to their children, etc., besides the cost of transport and recreation. If a family is not able to generate income sufficient to meet these basic needs, then the family can be treated as living Below Poverty Line (BPL). The requirement of such income varies from place to place, and family to family depending on their socio-economic background, educational level and living patterns. Expenditure is appropriate method for assessment poverty that families can meet the expenditure from reserves and assets without participation in any income generating activity. The Planning Commission has been defining poverty line periodically for the population in rural and urban areas separately for both the country based on monthly per capita expenditure data collected by National Sample Survey Organisation (NSSO). Similar estimates are prepared for the states based on the subsidies available for food and for other basic needs, cost of living, etc. According to this, a person needs a per capita monthly expenditure of Rs 356 in rural and Rs 538.6 in urban areas in the country for the year 2004-05. Such figures for the state of Andhra Pradesh are Rs 292.95 in rural and Rs 542.89 in urban areas for the year 2004-2005. Thus, if anybody in the family either individually or collectively not able to generate such income according to their number in the family expenditure can be treated as living under absolute poverty. It shows that the required income to cross the poverty line is much less in the state of Andhra Pradesh compared to the country as a whole.

According to this, a family needs a per capita income of Rs 3,515 per year to cross poverty line in the rural areas, which is applicable for tribal areas. If the family is not generated such income can be treated as living under below poverty. It is observed from the study that the per capita income of the family was up to Rs 3,515 in the case of 47.5 per cent of the families before land declined to 36 per cent after land. It shows that 47.5 per cent of the families were lived below poverty line before land declined to 36 per cent after land. It shows that 11.5 per cent of the families crossed poverty line after land and the other 36 per cent of the families are still living under poverty even after land. The remaining families are living above poverty both before and after the land (Table 29.6).

Table 29.6: Families Crossed the Poverty Line after Land

Per capita family income (Rs.)	*Before Land*		*After Land*	
	Nos.	*Per cent*	*Nos.*	*Per cent*
Up to 2,000	30	9.3	11	3.4
2001 – 3515	123	38.2	105	32.6
Sub Total	**153**	**47.5**	**116**	**36.0**
3516 - 4000	53	16.5	54	16.8
4001 - 5000	55	17.1	64	19.9
5001 +	61	18.9	88	27.3
Sub Total	**169**	**52.5**	**206**	**64.0**
Grand Total	**322**	**100.0**	**322**	**100.0**

Source: Computed based on field data.

Type of Families Improved from Below to Above Poverty Line

It is important to analyse the families' movement of income from below to above poverty or above to below poverty or living in the same income status. It was observed from the data that the level of annual per capita income was less than Rs 2,000 in 30 families before land, of which 30 per cent of families were remain in the same income level. Of the remaining, 54 per cent were shifted to the next level of income from 2001 to 3515 and 16 per cent were crossed the poverty line after land. Similarly, 123 families were lived in an income level of 2001 to 3515. Among them, 70 per cent were remaining in the same level of income without any change, 29 per cent were crossed the poverty lines and one family or one per cent declined their income level prior to the land level. The other 169 families were above poverty line prior to the land also. Among them, 53 families were in the per capita income of Rs 3516 to 4000, of which

62 per cent were remain in the same income level, 34 per cent improved their income level and the other three per cent fallen back into the poverty. Similarly, 55 families were in the income range of Rs 4001 to 5000, of which 69 per cent were in the same income level without any change, 27 per cent improved their income to next level and the other four per cent again fallen back into the poverty. The remaining 61 families were in the income level of above 5001 without any change (Table 29.7).

Table 29.7: Shift of Percapita Income Before and After Land among the Families

Per capita income before land	*Per capita income after land (Rs)*					
	Up to 2000	*2001 - 3515*	*3516 - 4000*	*4001 – 5000*	*5001 +*	*Total*
Up to 2000	9(30)	16(54)	1 (3)	3(10)	1 (3)	30(100)
2001 - 3515	1 (1)	86(70)	20(16)	7 (6)	9 (7)	123(100)
3516 – 4000	1 (1)	1 (2)	33(62)	16(30)	2 (4)	53(100)
4001 – 5000	-	2 (4)	-	38(69)	15 (27)	55(100)
5000 +	-	-	-	-	61 (100)	61(100)
Total	**11 (3)**	**105(32)**	**54(17)**	**64(20)**	**88 (27)**	**322(100)**

Source: Computed-based on field data.

On the whole 116 families or 35 per cent of the families are still living under poverty even after land. The remaining (65 per cent) were above poverty line prior to land distribution. Of which, seven per cent slipped to below poverty line due to crop loss. About 31 families or 10 per cent of the families actually crossed the poverty line after land and made them to improve their income in 61 families (20 per cent) out of the total.

Poverty Assessment Based on the Family Consumption

The family expenditure data has been collected from the sample households and per capita family expenditure is computed for purpose to assess the level poverty among the Chenchus. According to this, the per capita annual expenditure of the family was below Rs 3515 in 27 per cent of the families. Thus, the poverty level according to expenditure method is 12 percentage points lower than the income method. It shows that they may be mobilising loans for meeting their basic needs of the family or may be reported an under estimate of the family income. Whatever may be the reason, 27 per cent of the families are still living under absolute poverty even after distribution of the land as per the family expenditure method. The per capita monthly expenditure requirement to cross the poverty line according to the revised estimate of poverty for rural areas (Tendulkar Committee) is Rs 694 and it is Rs 8328 per annum for the year 2009-10. The per capita expenditure is collected for the year 2006-07. Based on the revised estimate, the sample families living PBL are more than 50 per cent at any rate, if it is revised according to the price index for the year 2006-07.

Their proportion in the total population varies from region to region depending on the livelihood options available to them. It is important to note that large majority of the Chenchus are landless. Thus, the Government is providing wage employment under MNREGP for each family at the rate of Rs 2000 per month to protect them from the poverty. Thus, there is need to build assets under MNREGP works for sustainable livelihood.

Conclusions

Majority of the Chenchus are landless though they are living close to forest areas where the demand for land is relatively less. Land Purchase Scheme (LPS) is an alternative to become owners of the land. The results show that LPS is made effective in improvement of livelihood and crossing poverty line for about 10 per cent of the families and an additional income for about another 20 per cent of the families. However, the land has not brought about any significant changes in food, income and livelihood security for majority of the Chenchus that they have not utilised land properly due to their socio-cultural barriers, lack of small investments for land development and irrigation facility. Apart from these, the LPS beset with problems, such as purchase of poor quality land from private party for lack of adequate budget, delay and dispute in partisan to the individual beneficiaries. Energisation is pending for most of the beneficiaries for the bore wells drilled and installed submersible pump sets for more than three years ago. However, there is no alternative other than the land for livelihood improvement of the PTGs due to their living in remote and backward areas with mass illiteracy, thinly spread population with no or little infrastructure and also no or little network of formal financial institutions where the scope for promotion of non-farm sector growth is limited. It is observed from the study that the land is capital asset and its value is increasing even in tribal areas, and it has potential for improvement of livelihood, if provided with a minimum size of two acres and allocation of higher budget. Thus, distribution of good quality land with viable size, irrigation facility and supply other inputs on subsidy is most essential to achieve productive results, particularly to the PTGs and first generation cultivators.

Index

D